Handbook of Early
Literacy Research

Volume 2

Handbook of
Early Literacy
Research

Volume 2

Edited by

David K. Dickinson
Susan B. Neuman

THE GUILFORD PRESS

New York   London

© 2006 The Guilford Press
A Division of Guilford Publications, Inc.
72 Spring Street, New York, NY 10012
www.guilford.com

Printed in the United States of America

This book is printed on acid-free paper.

Last digit is print number: 9   8   7   6   5   4   3   2   1

ISBN 1-59385-184-7

Library of Congress Cataloging-in-Publication Data may be found
in the paperback edition of the *Handbook of Early Literacy Research,
Volume 1* (ISBN 1-57230-895-8).

About the Editors

David K. Dickinson, EdD, is a Professor at the Peabody School of Education at Vanderbilt University. He received his doctoral training at Harvard University's Graduate School of Education after teaching elementary school in the Philadelphia area for 5 years. Since the early 1980s he has studied language and early literacy development among low-income populations, with a focus on the role of oral language in literacy development. Dr. Dickinson has examined the interrelationships among language, print skills, and phonemic awareness and has conducted detailed studies of language use patterns in early childhood classrooms. He helped create tools for describing literacy support in preschool classrooms, and developed and studied approaches to providing professional development for pre-school teachers. Dr. Dickinson has served on numerous advisory boards and recently was on a commission assisting the National Association for the Education of Young Children with revising its accreditation standards. He has written numerous articles and coauthored books, including *Beginning Literacy with Language: Young Children Learning at Home and School* (2001). Recently, in collaboration with Judith Schickedanz, he coauthored a comprehensive preschool curriculum, *Opening the World of Learning*.

Susan B. Neuman, EdD, a Professor in Educational Studies specializing in early literacy development, returned to the University of Michigan in 2004 after a 2-year hiatus, during which she served as the U.S. Assistant Secretary for Elementary and Secondary Education. Her research and teaching interests include early childhood policy, curriculum, and early reading instruction. In her role as Assistant Secretary, she established the Reading First program and the Early Reading First program, and was responsible for all activities in Title I of the Elementary and Secondary Education Act. Dr. Neuman received her doctorate from the University of the Pacific in Stockton, California, in 1977, and her BA from American University. She recently received an honorary doctorate from the California State University–Hayward, where she also conducted her master's work in reading and curriculum. Prior to coming to Michigan, she was a professor at Temple University, the University of Massachusetts–Lowell, and Eastern Connecticut State University. Dr. Neuman is the coauthor, with Catherine Snow, of a curriculum program in early literacy, *Building Language for Literacy* (2000), and of numerous books, including *Access for All: Closing the Book Gap for Children in Early Education* (2001), *Learning to Read and Write: Developmentally Appropriate Practice* (2000), and *Children Achieving: Best Practices in Early Literacy* (1998).

Contributors

Jane Ashby, MA, received her master's degree from Harvard University's Graduate School of Education in 1991. Her study of reading difficulties and intervention techniques continued in the Language Disorders Clinic at Massachusetts General Hospital in Boston. As an educator at Harvard Children's Hospital, she assessed progress in reading, writing, and mathematics. In addition to teaching children and adults with reading difficulties, Ms. Ashby conducted staff development seminars for early childhood and elementary teachers at private and public schools in Ohio. Presently she is completing a doctorate in psychology at the University of Massachusetts–Amherst, supported by a Kirschstein NRSA fellowship from the National Institutes of Health.

Canan Aydogan, MEd, is a PhD candidate in early childhood education in the Department of Teaching and Learning at Peabody College, Vanderbilt University. She has been involved in research that evaluates the effectiveness of alternative preschool curricula for preparing children from low-income families to transition successfully to school. Ms. Aydogan's current research is on the effects of teachers' use of responsive language on preschoolers' vocabulary development.

Heather J. Bachman, PhD, completed her degree in developmental psychology at Loyola University, Chicago, and is currently a Research Associate at the Institute of Policy Research at Northwestern University, Evanston, Illinois. Dr. Bachman's research involves multidisciplinary approaches for studying children's development in low-income families, with particular focus on the intersection of literacy and social development in early childhood.

Isabel L. Beck, PhD, is a Professor of Education at the School of Education and a Senior Scientist at the Learning Research and Development Center, both at the University of Pittsburgh. Her work has focused on research and development in decoding, vocabulary, and comprehension. Dr. Beck has received awards from the National Reading Conference, the International Reading Association, and the American Federation of Teachers. Before starting her university career, she taught kindergarten and first grade in public schools.

Andrew Biemiller, PhD, is a researcher, educational consultant, and an associate editor of the *Journal of Educational Psychology*. He is a graduate of Harvard (BA) and Cornell (PhD) Universities. As a professor for 36 years at the University of Toronto, Dr. Biemiller taught child development and various aspects of classroom teaching and supervised an elementary program for many of those years. He has published extensively on reading, vocabulary, and educational program design. Dr. Biemiller's recent research on teaching vocabulary in the primary grades is discussed in this volume; his current research project, *Words Worth Teaching*, is expected to be completed by 2006.

Elena Bodrova, PhD, is a Senior Researcher at Mid-continent Research for Education and Learning (McREL), Aurora, Colorado, and a Research Fellow at the National Institute for Early Education Research, New Brunswick, New Jersey. Prior to joining McREL, Dr. Bodrova was a Visiting Professor of Educational Psychology at the Metropolitan State College of Denver. Her work on applying Lev Vygotsky's theory to education started in Russia, where she worked at the Institute for Preschool Education and later at the Russian Center for Educational Innovations. Dr. Bodrova is the author of many articles and book chapters on early literacy, self-regulation, play, and assessment. She is a coauthor of *Tools of the Mind: The Vygotskian Approach to Early Childhood Education* (1995), *Basics of Assessment: A Primer for Early Childhood Educators* (2004), and *For the Love of Words: Vocabulary Instruction That Works* (2005).

Pia Rebello Britto, PhD, is a Developmental Psychologist at Yale University's Child Study Center. Her current research interests focus on exploring literacy and language development in low-income and minority populations, evaluating home visitor training, and service delivery. Presently she is working in partnership with several international agencies and nongovernmental organizations in the area of international policy and child development. Dr. Britto has received several academic awards and has authored articles and chapters on young children's early literacy development.

Jeanne Brooks-Gunn, PhD, is the Virginia and Leonard Marx Professor of Child Development and Education at Teachers College and the College of Physicians and Surgeons, Columbia University. She codirects the National Center for Children and Families at Columbia University's Teachers College and the Columbia University Institute for Child and Family Policy. She has served on three National Academy of Sciences panels (Child Abuse and Neglect, Preventing HIV Infection, and Defining Poverty); was a member of the Social Science Research Council Committee on the urban underclass, focusing on neighborhoods, families, and children; and was a member of the Children's Roundtable at the Brookings Institute. Dr. Brooks-Gunn's specialty is policy-oriented research focusing on family and community influences on the development of children and youth. She has authored more than 400 arti-

cles and 17 books and has received numerous academic awards.

Stephen R. Burgess, PhD, is a Professor of Psychology at Southwestern Oklahoma State University. He received his doctorate in experimental psychology, with a concentration in cognitive development, from Florida State University in 1997. Dr. Burgess's research interests include reading skill and comprehension development; the influence of the home literacy environment and culture on literacy development; literacy interest and attitude across the lifespan; the influence of attitudes and prior knowledge on decision making and critical thinking ability; practical applications of cognitive research; training elementary teachers to teach reading; and the factors related to selected teaching strategies.

Carol McDonald Connor, PhD, serves on the faculty of Florida State University's College of Education, and is also a research faculty member at the Florida Center for Reading Research, Tallahassee, Florida. She completed her PhD in education and a 1-year postdoctoral fellowship in psychology at the University of Michigan–Ann Arbor. Dr. Connor's research centers on children's learning in the classroom from preschool through third grade and the complex links between their learning, language, and literacy skills.

Holly K. Craig, PhD, is a Professor in the School of Education, a Research Professor at the Institute for Human Adjustment, and Director of the Center for the Development of Language and Literacy at the University of Michigan–Ann Arbor. Dr. Craig conducts research in the areas of language and literacy and has published and presented extensively on the acquisition of language and literacy skills in typical and atypical learners across the lifespan. Her current research focuses on the relationships between bidialecticalism and reading achievement for African American elementary grade students.

David K. Dickinson (see About the Editors).

Linnea C. Ehri, PhD, earned her doctorate from the University of California–Berkeley and currently teaches educational psychology at the Graduate Center of the City University of New York. Her research examines how children learn to read and spell and why some children have difficulty. She has received awards from the International Reading Association, the American Educational Research Association, and the Society for the Scientific Study of Reading (SSSR). She is a member of the Reading Hall of Fame, a Fellow of the American Psychological Association, and a past president of the SSSR. She has also served on the National Reading Panel, established by the U.S. Congress to review research and identify effective methods for teaching children to read.

Marilyn J. Essex, PhD, is a Senior Scientist at the University of Wisconsin Medical School, Department of Psychiatry, at Madison. Dr. Essex has authored numerous articles on the influence of psychosocial stress on parents and children, and most recently on the influence of early stress exposure on children's stress response systems and socioemotional development. She is the principal investigator of an ongoing longitudinal study of the social, psychological, and biological risk factors for the emergence of childhood mental health problems and impairments, funded by the National Institute of Mental Health and the John D. and Catherine T. MacArthur Research Network on Psychopathology and Development.

Dale C. Farran, PhD, is a Professor in the Department of Teaching and Learning at Peabody College, Vanderbilt University; has been involved in research and intervention for high-risk children and youth for all of her professional career; and has conducted many studies for the Frank Porter Graham Child Development Center in Chapel Hill, North Carolina, and the Kamehameha Schools Early Education Project in Hawaii. Dr. Farran is the editor of two books about risk and poverty, and she has written more than 80 journal articles and book chapters. Her current research focuses on evaluating the effectiveness of alternative preschool curricula for preparing children from low-income families to transition successfully to school.

Stephen J. Frost, PhD, is a Senior Scientist at Yale University's Haskins Laboratories, a private, nonprofit research institute with a primary focus on speech, language, and reading, and their biological basis. Dr. Frost's research focuses primarily on examining brain–behavior relationships using brain imaging technology. His other research interests include exploring the parallels in the processing of spoken and written language and, in turn, the extent to which any parallels indicate that spoken and written language share common phonological, orthographic, and semantic information.

Allison S. Fuligni, PhD, is a Developmental Psychologist at the Center for Improving Child Care Quality at the University of California–Los Angeles Graduate School of Education and Information Studies. She is co-principal investigator of the LA ExCELS (Los Angeles: Exploring Children's Early Learning Settings) study, a large-scale longitudinal study of school readiness among low-income children, funded by the National Institute of Child Health and Human Development and agencies in the U.S. Departments of Education and Health and Human Services. Dr. Fuligni is a member of the Early Head Start Research Consortium and served as a member of the national evaluation team of the Early Head Start Research and Evaluation Project. She has authored several review articles on early education and intervention for economically disadvantaged children and families.

Elsa Cárdenas Hagan, PhD, is a bilingual speech–language pathologist and a certified academic language therapist and is the Director of Valley Speech Language and Learning Center in Brownsville, Texas, which serves students with language and learning disabilities. Dr. Cárdenas Hagan is the author of *Esperanza (HOPE): A Spanish Language Program* and a co-principal investigator of a longitudinal study entitled "Development of Early Language and Literacy Skills in Spanish-Speaking Children," funded by a grant from the National Institute of Child Health and Human Development.

Elfrieda H. Hiebert, PhD, received her doctorate in educational psychology from the University of Wisconsin–Madison and is currently on the faculty at the University of California–Berkeley Graduate School of Education. Dr. Hiebert's research interests lie in the effects of instructional practices, particularly the selection of texts, on the literacy acquisition of low-income children, particularly those who are not native English speakers.

Erika Hoff, PhD, earned her doctorate from the University of Michigan and is currently Professor in the Department of Psychology at Florida Atlantic University, Davie, Florida. Dr. Hoff's research interests include the process of early word learning, bilingual development, the role of input in early language development, and the relation of family socioeconomic status to mother–child interaction and children's language development. She is the author of *Language Development* (2000).

Connie Juel, PhD, has taught at Harvard University, the University of Virginia, and the University of Texas–Austin, and is currently a Professor at Stanford University's School of Education. Prior to embarking on her university career, she worked as an elementary school teacher. Dr. Juel is noted for her longitudinal research on models of literacy acquisition and how classroom instruction influences growth. She has received the National Reading Conference's Oscar Causey Award for reading research and has been elected to the Reading Hall of Fame by the International Reading Association.

Shin Ji Kang, MEd, is currently a doctoral student in the Department of Teaching and Learning at Peabody College, Vanderbilt University. She has worked with prekindergarten teachers serving children from low-income families in Tennessee to help them improve teaching practices. Ms. Kang's research focuses on teachers' sense of efficacy in relation to teaching practices and student outcomes. Before she came to the United States, Ms. Kang was a pre-K teacher and coauthored a book for Korean early childhood educators.

Perri Klass, MD, is Associate Professor of Pediatrics at Boston University Medical Center and Medical Director and President of Reach Out and Read, a national program that makes literacy promotion part of the health care of young children. She has trained doctors and nurses around the United States in how to counsel parents about the importance of looking at books with young children and in how to integrate books and literacy into routine pediatric care. Dr. Klass graduated from Harvard

Medical School and trained in pediatrics at Boston Children's Hospital; she did a fellowship in Pediatric Infectious Diseases at what was then Boston City Hospital. Dr. Klass has published extensively; her most recent book is *Love and Modern Medicine* (2001), a collection of short stories.

Susan H. Landry, PhD, is a Developmental Psychologist at the Center for Improving the Readiness of Children for Learning and Education (CIRCLE) at the University of Texas Health Science Center in Houston. CIRCLE's activities involve conducting research projects and training activities related to the goal of promoting quality learning environments for young children. A large research database on early childhood has been developed from Dr. Landry's research programs, which include longitudinal evaluations of biological and environmental influences of children's development from infancy through adolescence. CIRCLE uses the knowledge gained from years of studying young children to help promote the goals of early childhood literacy initiatives.

Deborah J. Leong, PhD, is a Professor of Psychology at Metropolitan State College of Denver, where she has taught developmental and educational psychology for 30 years. She has also been involved in in-service and preservice teacher training and is a Research Fellow at the National Institute for Early Education. Dr. Leong received her doctorate from Stanford University and her MEd from Harvard University. She has written extensively in the area of self-regulation, play, assessment, and early literacy. Dr. Leong's publications include *Tools of the Mind: The Vygotskian Approach to Early Childhood Education* (1995), *Assessing and Guiding Young Children's Development and Learning* (3rd ed., 2001), and *Basics of Assessment: A Primer for Early Childhood Educators* (2004).

Paul P. M. Leseman, PhD, is a Professor of Special Education in the Department of Special Education of Utrecht University, The Netherlands. His research interests concern biological and cultural influences on language and literacy development and developmental approaches to learning disabilities. Dr. Leseman currently directs an interuniversity research program on the early development of academic language skill in bilingual children. He is also involved in preschool education and home literacy programs, and is advisor to the Dutch and European Union governments and the Organisation of Economic Cooperation and Development on early childhood care and education.

Sylvia Linan-Thompson, PhD, is an Assistant Professor at The University of Texas–Austin. Her research interests include the development of reading interventions for struggling readers who are monolingual English speakers, English language learners, and bilingual students acquiring Spanish literacy. She is co-principal investigator of three longitudinal studies funded by the National Institute of Child Health and Human Development and the Institute of Education Sciences examining the oracy and literacy development in English and Spanish of Spanish-speaking children and the efficacy of a three-tiered model of reading intervention in general education classrooms and in bilingual classrooms. She has authored curricular programs, book chapters, journal articles, and a book on reading instruction.

Mark W. Lipsey, PhD, is the Director of the Institute for Public Policy Studies Center for Evaluation Research and Methodology at Vanderbilt University. His research has focused on risk and intervention for juvenile delinquency, early childhood educational programs, and issues of methodological quality in program evaluation. Dr. Lipsey is a member of the Technical Advisory Group for the U.S. Department of Education's What Works Clearinghouse, the Methods Group of the Campbell Collaboration, and the National Research Council Committee on Law and Justice.

Christopher J. Lonigan, PhD, is a Professor of Psychology and Associate Director of the Florida Center for Reading Research at Florida State University. Dr. Lonigan received his doctorate in clinical psychology in 1991 from the State University of New York at Stony Brook. After completing his PhD, Dr. Lonigan was awarded a 2-year National Institutes of Health Postdoctoral Fellowship at the John F. Kennedy Center at Vanderbilt University. Dr. Lonigan's research activities focus on the development of emergent liter-

acy skills during the preschool period and how these skills influence later reading. He has been involved in the development of assessment instruments that measure the key areas of emergent literacy and evaluations of preschool interventions and curricula designed to prevent reading difficulties for preschool children who are at risk for later academic problems.

Patricia G. Mathes, PhD, is the Texas Instruments Chair of Reading, Professor of Literacy and Language Acquisition, and Director of the Institute for Reading Research at Southern Methodist University in Dallas, Texas. She has served on the faculties of Pediatrics at the University of Texas–Houston Medical School, the College of Education at Florida State University, and Peabody College for Teachers at Vanderbilt University. Since 1991 she has been conducting large-scale classroom-based reading intervention research with funding from the U.S. Department of Education, the National Institute of Child Health and Human Development, and the National Science Foundation, as well as state agencies. She received the Interpretive Scholar Award from the American Educational Research Association in 2002 and the Distinguished Early Career Researcher award from the Council for Exceptional Children in 2001. Dr. Mathes has published extensively on learning and reading disabilities, accommodating academic diversity, and best practices for struggling readers.

Allyssa McCabe, PhD, is Professor of Psychology at the University of Massachusetts–Lowell. She coedits the journal *Narrative Inquiry* and has researched how narrative develops with age, the way parents can encourage narration, cultural differences in narration, and interrelationships between the development of narrative, vocabulary, and phonological awareness. Dr. McCabe's main study focus is on the assessment of children, especially preventing misdiagnosis of cultural differences in language use as deficits. With Lynn Bliss, she most recently published *Patterns of Narrative Discourse: A Multicultural Lifespan Approach* (2002).

Margaret G. McKeown, PhD, is a Senior Scientist at the University of Pittsburgh's Learning Research and Development Center.

Dr. McKeown's work covers the areas of instructional design and teacher professional development in reading comprehension and vocabulary. She developed, in collaboration with Isabel Beck, the Questioning the Author and Text Talk approaches. She has served as Vice President for Division C of the American Educational Research Association and as the editor of the *American Educational Reserach Journal*. Before her career in research, Dr. McKeown taught reading and language arts in elementary school.

Stuart McNaughton, PhD, is Professor of Education at the University of Auckland, where he teaches courses on the development of language and literacy and the processes of education, socialization, and culture. He is Director of the Woolf Fisher Research Centre, which conducts research on teaching, learning, and development in culturally and linguistically diverse communities. Dr. McNaughton's research focuses on enhancing the language and literacy development of culturally and linguistically diverse children and involves research-based interventions with clusters of schools. He is a member of the New Zealand government-appointed Literacy Task Force and chairs the New Zealand Ministry of Education's Literacy Experts Group.

W. Einar Mencl, PhD, is a Senior Scientist at Yale University's Haskins Laboratories. In previous research he has applied functional magnetic resonance imaging to the study of reading, reading disability, and childhood development of the skilled reading system. He plays an integrative role across several additional neuroimaging studies at Haskins and is active in the development of new statistical analysis techniques to identify neural systems from neuroimaging data.

Heidi Anne E. Mesmer, PhD, began her career as a classroom teacher working in Virginia and rural Maryland and is currently a faculty member in the College of Education at Oklahoma State University. Her work to date has centered on the influences of text features on beginning readers and preschoolers. Dr. Mesmer is currently working on three major research projects: a study of book quality in childcare settings, a survey of

K–3 teachers' uses and beliefs about materials, and an examination of first graders. In addition to publishing her research in a number of journals, she has received a National Academy of Education/Spencer Postdoctoral Fellowship and an American Educational Research Association/Institute of Education Sciences Research Grant.

Dina L. Moore, PhD, is an Assistant Professor of Psychology at Southern Connecticut State University and a Research Affiliate at Haskins Laboratories, Yale University. She completed her PhD in developmental psychology at the University of Connecticut and recently completed postdoctoral training at Haskins Laboratories. Her primary research interests are the neurobiology of reading processes and reading disabilities and long-term neuropsychological consequences of childhood trauma specifically related to language functioning.

Frederick J. Morrison, PhD, is a Professor in the Department of Psychology, Center for Human Growth and Development, and Combined Program in Education and Psychology, at the University of Michigan–Ann Arbor. Dr. Morrison's research focuses on the nature and sources of children's cognitive, language, literacy, and social development during the transition to school.

Lesley Mandel Morrow, PhD, is a Professor at Rutgers University's Graduate School of Education, where she coordinates the literacy program. She began her career as a classroom teacher, then became a reading specialist, and later earned her PhD from Fordham University. Dr. Morrow's research focuses on early literacy development and the organization and management of language arts programs. She has authored more than 200 publications that appear as journal articles, book chapters, and monographs. Dr. Morrow has received numerous grants for her research from the federal government and has served as a principal investigator for several research centers. She has received Excellence in Research, Teaching, and Service awards from Rutgers University as well as the International Reading Association's Outstanding Teacher Educator of Reading Award and Fordham University's Alumni Award for Outstanding Achievement.

Robert Needlman, MD, practices developmental and behavioral and general pediatrics at MetroHealth Medical Center in Cleveland, Ohio, and teaches in the Department of Pediatrics at Case Western Reserve University School of Medicine. Dr. Needlman is cofounder of Reach Out and Read, author of *Dr. Spock's Baby Basics* (2003), and coauthor of *Dr. Spock's Baby and Child Care* (8th ed., 2004).

Susan B. Neuman (see About the Editors).

Gene Ouelette, MSc, is currently a PhD candidate in the Department of Psychology at Carleton University, Ottawa, Ontario, Canada. His research focuses on the developmental connections between oral and written language. Before starting his doctoral studies, Mr. Ouelette worked for 13 years as a speech–language pathologist for school-age children.

Beth M. Phillips, PhD, is a postdoctoral fellow at the Florida Center for Reading Research, Tallahassee, Florida, where she is involved in ongoing research on the overlap between preschool children's behavior problems and their emergent literacy skills. Her research interests are in the areas of assessment of and intervention for early literacy skills with preschool children, behavioral regulation, temperament, and childhood anxiety disorders. Dr. Phillips has coauthored several publications in the areas of emergent literacy and childhood anxiety disorders, and she is involved in the development of an emergent literacy-focused curriculum, evaluations of published preschool and elementary school reading-related curricula, and evaluations of emergent literacy and school readiness assessment measures.

Robert C. Pianta, PhD, is a Professor in The Curry School of Education at the University of Virginia and holds the Novartis US Foundation Chair in Education. He is also Director of the Center for Advanced Study in Teaching and Learning at the University of Virginia. A former special education teacher, he is a developmental, school, and clinical child psychologist whose work focuses on how children's experiences at home and in school affect their development. Dr. Pianta is a principal investigator on several major grants, including MyTeachingPartner, the Institute of Education Sciences Interdisciplinary Doctoral Training Program in Risk and Prevention, and the National Institute of Child Health and Human Development Study of Early Child Care and Youth Development, and is the editor of the *Journal of School Psychology*. He has published extensively on early childhood development, transition to school, school readiness, and parent–child and teacher–child relationships.

Sharolyn Pollard-Durodola, EdD, is an Assistant Professor of Special and Bilingual Education in the Department of Educational Psychology at Texas A & M University in College Station, Texas. She earned master's degrees in Spanish education and in developmental and remedial reading from Columbia University Teachers College and the City University of New York, respectively, and completed her doctorate in curriculum and instruction at the University of Houston. Dr. Pollard-Durodola's primary research interests include beginning reading, classroom observation, curriculum development, reading interventions, teacher quality, and vocabulary acquisition.

Kenneth R. Pugh, PhD, is a Research Scientist in Pediatrics at the Yale University School of Medicine and also holds an appointment as a Senior Scientist at Yale's Haskins Laboratories. His primary research interests are in the areas of cognitive neuroscience and psycholinguistics. Dr. Pugh's research program examines language processing for print and speech and employs combined behavioral and functional magnetic resonance imaging measures to study both skilled reading and reading disability. His current research examines the effects of training and remediation on the developing neurocircuitry associated with reading. Dr. Pugh is the Director of the Yale Reading Study, an National Institutes of Health-funded project examining reading development and disability in adolescence.

Craig T. Ramey, PhD, is the Co-director of the Center for Health and Education at Georgetown University's School of Nursing and Health Studies. He specializes in the study of factors affecting young children's development of intelligence, social competence, and academic achievement. Over the past 30 years, he and Sharon Landesman Ramey have conducted research involving 14,000 children and families in 40 states. Dr. Ramey is the author of more than 225 publications, including five books, and he frequently consults with federal and state governments as well as private agencies, foundations, and the news media.

Sharon Landesman Ramey, PhD, is the Codirector of the Center for Health and Education at Georgetown University's School of Nursing and Health Studies. She is a developmental psychologist whose professional interests include the study of the development of intelligence and children's competency, early experience and early intervention, the changing American family, and the transition to school.

Keith Rayner, PhD, received his doctorate from Cornell University and is a Professor in the Department of Psychology at the University of Massachusetts–Amherst. His research on eye movements has received continual funding since 1974; he received a Research Scientist Award from the National Institutes of Health (NIH) (1995–2000) and currently holds an NIH MERIT award. In 1996 he and George McConkie received the first Outstanding Scientist Award from the Society for the Scientific Study of Reading. He was editor of the *Journal of Experimental Psychology: Learning, Memory, and Cognition* from 1995 until 2000 and is currently the editor of *Psychological Review.* He is a charter fellow of the American Psychological Society and a fellow of the American Psychological Association.

Gary Resnick, PhD, is a Senior Researcher in the Child and Family Study Area at Westat, a social science research organization in Rockville, Maryland. He received his doctorate in applied developmental psychology from the Eliot–Pearson Institute of Child Study at Tufts University. Dr. Resnick's work has focused on the intersection between applied developmental psychology and program evaluation, including the design, measurement, and analysis of large-scale national studies of children and families, such as the Head Start Family and Child Experiences Survey, the Head Start Impact Study, and the Early Childhood Longitudinal Studies Birth Cohort.

Theresa Roberts, PhD, earned her doctorate from the University of California–Los Angeles and currently teaches child development at California State University. She has published studies on early literacy development with a focus on children who are learning English as a second language. Her research interests include alphabetic and vocabulary learning and instruction and family literacy practices, and she has collaborated with preschool and elementary teachers to develop instructional programs on these topics. She is a voting member of Society for the Scientific Study of Reading, an ad-hoc reviewer for the *Journal of Educational Psychology,* and a contributing author to California's *Pre-Kindergarten Learning and Development Guidelines* (2000).

Donna Rodney, BA, is a master's student in the Department of Psychology, Carleton University, Ottawa, Ontario, Canada.

Kathleen Roskos, PhD, teaches courses in reading instruction and reading diagnosis at John Carroll University. Formerly an elementary classroom teacher, Dr. Roskos directed the Ohio Literacy Initiative at the Ohio Department of Education for 2 years, providing leadership in pre-K–12 literacy policy and programs. Dr. Roskos studies early literacy development and learning, teacher cognition, and the design of professional education for teachers, and has published research articles on these topics in leading journals. She is currently a member of the e-Learning Committee and the Early Childhood Commission of the International Reading Association.

Terry Salinger, PhD, is a Chief Scientist at the American Institutes for Research in Washington, DC, where she leads research projects that address issues in early and adolescent reading, professional development in literacy, and assessment of students' literacy skills. Dr. Salinger has been a classroom teacher and a university professor, was a researcher at the Educational Testing Service, and served for 4 years as the Director of Research at the International Reading Association. She has published extensively in the area of literacy assessment and policy.

Rebecca Sandak, PhD, is a Senior Scientist at Haskins Laboratories, Yale University. Her research is focused on understanding the cognitive processes underlying skilled and impaired reading, reading acquisition, and successful reading instruction and remediation. In her recent work she has been employing functional magnetic resonance imaging to investigate how learning conditions, reading expertise, and reading strategies influence the cortical areas that are recruited for reading. She is presently directing a research project (in collaboration with the Kennedy–Krieger Institute and the Educational Testing Service) to evaluate the behavioral and neural effects of several research-driven intervention methods for improving the reading abilities of struggling adolescent readers.

Judith A. Schickedanz, PhD, is a Professor of Education in the Department of Curriculum and Teaching at Boston University's School of Education. She is the author of *Much More Than the ABC's* (1999) and coauthor of *Writing in Preschool: Orchestrating Meaning and Marks* (2004), and has written numerous book chapters, including "Engaging Preschoolers in Code Learning: Some Thoughts about Preschool Teachers' Concerns" (in *Literacy and Young Children*, 2003). Dr. Schickedanz serves on the International Reading Association's Commission on Early Childhood and on the editorial board of the *International Journal of Early Childhood Education.*

Monique Sénéchal, PhD, is a Professor in the Department of Psychology at Carleton University, Ottawa, Ontario, Canada. Dr. Sénéchal is a cognitive developmentalist interested in how young children learn from normally occurring activities. Her research focuses on language development and literacy acquisition.

Karen E. Smith, PhD, received her BA in psychology from the University of South Alabama and her MA and PhD in clinical psychology from the University of Alabama–Birmingham. Dr. Smith completed her internship at the Medical University of South Carolina with an emphasis in clinical child/pediatric psychology and is currently a Professor in the Department of Neurology at the University of Texas Medical Branch, Galveston.

Joseph K. Torgesen, PhD, is the Robert M. Gagne Professor of Psychology and Educa-

tion at Florida State University and serves as Director of the Florida Center for Reading Research. His research has focused on individual differences in the development of early reading skills as well as studies of intervention and remedial methods for students with reading disabilities. Dr. Torgesen was recently appointed to serve on the Board of Directors of the Institute of Education Sciences, and he also serves on the professional advisory board of the National Center for Learning Disabilities.

Cathy van Tuijl, PhD, is an Assistant Professor in the Department of Child and Adolescent Studies at Utrecht University, The Netherlands. Her main focus is on early childhood and early childhood intervention. She has evaluated short- and long-term effects of a home-based educational intervention program for ethnic-minority families with preschoolers and is interested in language development in bilingual preschoolers from disadvantaged families and the role of home support. Dr. van Tuijl coordinates courses on parenting and development and cultural diversity in parenting and education.

Sharon Vaughn, PhD, is the H. E. Hartfelder/The Southland Corporation Regents Chair in Human Relations Development at the University of Texas. With David Francis, Diane August, Sylvia Linan-Thompson and other colleagues throughout the United States, she is co-principal investigator on two Institute of Education Sciences research grants evaluating the effectiveness of interventions for young English language learners with reading difficulties and vocabulary and comprehension interventions for older English language learners. Her research has addressed the social and academic outcomes from interventions for students with reading difficulties and reading disabilities. She has served as the Editor in Chief of the *Journal of Learning Disabilities* and *Learning Disabilities Research and Practice.*

Carol Vukelich, PhD, is the L. Sandra and Bruce L. Hammonds Professor in Teacher Education and Director of the Delaware Center for Teacher Education at the University of Delaware. She also is the Co-director of the Delaware Writing Project. Dr. Vukelich has served as President of the Association for Childhood Education International and the International Reading Association's Literacy Development for Young Children Special Interest Group, and she worked as a classroom teacher as well as a university educator. She is coauthor of *Teaching Language and Literacy: Preschool through the Elementary Grades* (2002), *Helping Young Children Learn Language and Literacy* (2001), and *Building a Foundation for Preschool Literacy: Effective Instruction for Children's Reading and Writing Development* (2004), and has written numerous books chapters and articles.

Julie A. Washington, PhD, is a Professor in the Department of Audiology and Speech–Language Pathology at Wayne State University in Detroit, Michigan. Dr. Washington's research focuses on the language and literacy acquisition of preschool-age African American students. She has published numerous articles and presented many scholarly papers at national meetings on language and literacy topics with this population. Her current research focuses on the transitions between home and entry into formal schooling by African American students.

Nicholas Zill, PhD, heads the Child and Family Study Area at Westat, a social science research organization in Rockville, Maryland. He received his doctorate in psychology from Johns Hopkins University. For more than 28 years, Dr. Zill has helped design, analyze, and report on large-scale studies of children and families, including the Head Start National Reporting System, the Head Start Family and Child Experiences Survey, and the National Survey of Children.

Barry Zuckerman, MD, is the Joel and Barbara Alpert Professor of Pediatrics at Boston University School of Medicine, Professor of Public Health at Boston University School of Public Health, and Chief of Pediatrics at Boston Medical Center. Dr. Zuckerman is cofounder of Reach Out and Read and is presently CEO and Chair of its board. He also developed other innovative efforts in pediatrics, including Healthy Steps and the Family Advocacy Program. Dr. Zuckerman has authored more than 180 scientific publications emphasizing the impact of biological, social, health services, and psychological factors on children's health and development. He is an editor of nine books, including *Behavioral and Developmental Pediatrics: Handbook for Primary Care* (1995).

Contents

III. FAMILIES AND RELATIONSHIPS: SOCIOEMOTIONAL AND LINGUISTIC SUPPORTS

IV. CULTURAL AND LINGUISTIC DIVERSITY

V. SUPPORTING LITERACY IN PRESCHOOL CLASSROOMS

VI. PROGRAMMATIC INTERVENTIONS DURING THE PRESCHOOL YEARS

VII. TOWARD EFFECTIVE PRIMARY-GRADE INSTRUCTION

Introduction

DAVID K. DICKINSON
SUSAN B. NEUMAN

This is an exciting time for research in early literacy development. Important new discoveries in research continue to highlight the critical role of early literacy in young children's development, and encouraging new policies and practices reflect concerted efforts of practitioners to translate research into practices that will benefit young children. Today, more than ever before, early childhood literacy is regarded as the single best investment for enabling children to develop skills that will likely benefit them for a lifetime. At the same time, research in early literacy recognizes that these important foundational skills must never take away from the sheer joys, motivation, and fascination with print that define young children's interest in the early years.

As a field, early literacy has been particularly enriched by the energies of researchers from diverse disciplines. This book comes 3 years after the first volume of the *Handbook of Early Literacy Research*, and these disciplines have helped to contribute new information to important topics such as the role of parents and the intersection between social and emotional development, second language development, assessment, and instruction. In addition, this volume extends coverage to include important topics central to the field, such as phonemic awareness, the impact of social demographic factors, early intervention efforts, and social policy. Given the vibrant activity in the field, this volume

and Volume I, represent a critical corpus of research from the most prominent active researchers in the field.

Research reported in this volume provides evidence of increasing depth in theoretical accounts of early literacy and of growing consensus in several key areas. Cognitive-developmental methods continue to be of central importance. Multiple research teams are investigating the origins and development of phonemic awareness and using sophisticated statistical methods to examine pathways through which precursor abilities help shape later literacy competencies. This volume includes a chapter about one of the most long-standing methodologies used to study cognitive processes as people read—the study of eye movements. This work includes research on children of different ages, and review of development patterns provides interesting insight into changes that transpire as children become more proficient readers.

Brain imaging methods offer a new and exciting way to study cognitive activity during reading. Similar to eye-movement work, these studies examine physical manifestations of intellectual activity. It provides an alternative means of understanding the complex activities that we engage in as we read and, in an exciting new development, a means of tracing changes in neural activity associated with interventions that improve reading skills among disabled readers. Remarkable convergence appears in the advice related to early literacy instruction given by researchers examining the development of phonemic awareness, by eye-movement researchers, and by brain imagining scientists. All support early systematic efforts to teach phonemic awareness and letter knowledge and to foster ability to associate sounds with letters.

A major challenge faced by many societies is the gap in achievement between the children of families whose parents are members of the majority racial and linguistic group and the children of immigrant families, children whose families are from racial minority groups, whose parents are poor and have limited education. Several teams with primary interest in these issues employ Vygotskian theory. Researchers who draw on the theories of Vygotsky frequently employ the methods of cognitive-developmental psychology while also considering affective factors such as the emotional support provided by caretakers and parents. For researchers interested in interventions, there is particular appeal in Vygotsky's focus on the importance of children's acquisition of cultural tools during the preschool years.

In this volume the importance of parents and affective factors is highlighted in a manner not seen in Volume 1. In part, this new emphasis simply reflects our ability to include chapters by research teams who have long been interested in issues concerning early support for literacy-related skills. However, in part this emphasis also reflects a shift in the field: Researchers who study parenting and emotional development are beginning to recognize the importance of linking their work to research on early literacy, and those whose primary interest is early literacy are recognizing the need to consider affective factors. Researchers who give attention to cognitive and affective factors tend to adopt a systems approach to considering development, a theoretical framework that often is seen as being consistent with Vygotskian theory.

An important new theme in this volume is the importance of vocabulary and other language skills. Even as phonemic awareness continues to be acknowledged as being of central importance to early reading success, a number of authors stress the key role that vocabulary plays in supporting initial literacy and, more importantly, later comprehension skills. Although vocabulary is the skill most frequently emphasized, several authors stress the importance of more complex language skills and of world knowledge. It may be the case that the oft-cited power of vocabulary to predict later reading comprehension, in part, reflects the impact of world knowledge on reading.

The research reported in this volume reflects the intersection of scholarly basic science and efforts to respond to societal needs to improve the academic opportunities of children. Policy-oriented concerns take many forms, including efforts to identify specific factors and experiences that give rise to the inequities in literacy development. Several chapters report efforts to move beyond naming the demographic factors that are associated with differential success to identifying specific features of communities, homes, and classrooms that affect children's early development. In addition to the long-standing attention to the role of parents and teachers, authors in this volume encourage greater attention to the impact of communities.

Early literacy research has captured the attention of policy makers and educators because of the promise it holds for significantly enhancing the long-term academic success of children. In this volume, authors address many of these issues by looking beyond the preschool years to examine children's transition to the primary grades, in which more formal instruction takes place. Chapters focus on the research base for leveling text and instructional interventions for minority and second-language children who may need additional supports in the primary grades. Other chapters focus on the consequences of standards-based instruction, Early Reading First, and Reading First policies on monitoring progress and measuring outcomes and on how policies become instantiated in school practices.

Encouraging results are reported for efforts that involve parents, preschools, and schools and for studies that review the long-term effects of intensive high-quality interventions. However, optimism about significantly enhancing children's long-term development must be tempered by realization of the magnitude of the challenges we face. The need for caution is reflected in the chapters that review intervention programs and find effects that are either small or nonexistent.

One implication of the array of factors that shape early literacy—communities, parents, schools, as well as neurological and biological factors—is that interventions that target only one set of factors leave other powerful factors unchanged. Awareness of the difficulty of substantially improving children's development is growing, as evidenced by the attention several authors give to key factors such as the intensity, quality, and timing of interventions.

This volume represents the state of the art of early literacy research, policy, and practice. It highlights the exciting vibrancy of the field—its rich new discoveries, its enormous challenges—and invites readers, researchers, practitioners, and policy makers to join us in our continuing endeavor to enable all children to develop the critical knowledge, skills, and dispositions essential for reading success.

Content of the Volume

Chapters are grouped in seven sections of four or five chapters that address similar sets of issues. Of course, these groupings reflect only convergence around certain core issues; many chapters deal with topics found in other sections of the volume. To help you find your way between sections, we have provided cross-references from one chapter to the next. We also briefly review key points of each chapter in this section.

The first part, "Cognitive and Linguistic Building Blocks of Early Literacy Development," explores early literacy from different disciplinary perspectives. The first two chapters build on our own work in the field. In Chapter 1, David K. Dickinson, Alyssa McCabe, and Marilyn J. Essex lay out a broad view of early literacy development, arguing that adequate understanding of the emergence of literacy must integrate children's acquisition of language and print-related skills, in addition to social and emotional development. They draw on research on brain functioning to bolster this argument and to support their premise that the preschool years represent a developmental era during which high-quality support for language may be critical. They conclude by describing efforts being made to meet children's needs but acknowledge that we still have far to go before we fully meet the needs of young children.

In Chapter 2, Susan B. Neuman presents the argument that our society faces a "knowledge gap" between those with economic advantages and those who lack them. She brings into sharp focus the disparities in economic opportunities in our society and demonstrates how the multitude of obstacles faced by children and families with limited incomes translate into limitation in their opportunities to acquire knowledge, resulting in knowledge gaps between children of more and less advantaged families. She concludes by urging preschool educators to provide more intellectually and literacy-rich classrooms and describes such a setting. Neuman's call for greater attention to children's needs for conceptually rich experiences is extended in other chapters that emphasize the importance of vocabulary knowledge.

Andrew Biemiller, in Chapter 3, argues that research on reading development has underestimated the importance of vocabulary to skilled reading because studies have not been carried out for long enough to see the long-term importance of early vocabulary skills. He notes that schools have not done a good job of teaching vocabulary and presents data suggesting that children typically acquire about 860 root words a year in predictable sequences. Schools, he argues, can do far more to support vocabulary learning, and he advances suggestions regarding promising strategies.

Chapter 4, by Jane Ashby and Keith Rayner, provides an overview of several decades' worth of research on studies of eye movements of children as they read. They outline the emergence of the cognitive processes that result in fluent reading behavior, describing the gradual increase in the width of perceptual span of children as they gain automaticity in processing print. They report eye-movement studies that reveal that skilled readers process all of the letters in words and evidence indicating that these letters are translated into phonological representations. Implications for reading instruction include systematic instruction in phonological awareness and letter–sound correspondences.

Whereas Ashby and Rayner report studies that seek to uncover the functioning of the brain by examining eye movements, in Chapter 5, Kenneth R. Pugh, Rebecca Sandak, Stephen J. Frost, Dina Moore, and W. Einar Mencl review research that examines brain functioning using mental imaging methods. Drawing on findings from exciting new methods that trace the activity of the brain when people are engaged in reading and reading-like tasks, they present research demonstrating distinctive patterns of neural activity that are associated with reading disability. Imaging data indicate that, even among disabled readers, pathways associated with fluent reading are in use but are less active than among skilled readers. Most important, studies of children involved in intensive interventions display changes in activity patterns, indicating increased engagement of previously underutilized pathways.

Part II, "Phonemic Awareness and Letter Knowledge," includes chapters that review new research on phonemic awareness and discussions of findings that are increasingly highlighting the interrelationship between phonemic awareness and letter knowledge. In Chapter 6, Christopher J. Lonigan reviews research on phonemic awareness and presents an argument that there is a single underlying ability that manifests itself in developing ability to attend to progressively smaller linguistic units. Lonigan explores the interrelationships among abilities that are directly implicated in early literacy and states that both vocabulary and letter knowledge contribute to the emergence of phonological awareness. In turn, the code-related competencies—phonological awareness and letter knowledge—contribute in a relatively modularized way to early reading. In an interesting departure from the prevailing emphasis on the central importance of vocabulary, Lonigan notes that results of a recent meta-analysis by the Early Literacy Panel highlight the importance of measures of more complex language, such as syntax comprehension.

Stephen R. Burgess, in Chapter 7, also reviews research on the emergence of phonological awareness. Based on results of longitudinal studies with large samples, he concludes that phonological awareness is best conceptualized as the development of a single unitary underlying competence that becomes increasingly more cohesive and stable as children get older. Burgess then explores environmental factors that contribute

to the development of phonological awareness and concludes that active efforts by parents make important contributions to children's phonological awareness, possibly by helping children learn the names of letters and supporting their oral language abilities, two competencies that contribute to emergence of phonological awareness.

In Chapter 8, Beth M. Phillips and Joseph K. Torgesen begin their discussion of phonemic awareness by noting that it reflects both conceptual insight and skill development. They support current recommendations for explicit instruction related to phonemic awareness, especially for struggling readers, explaining the role that it plays in development of reading fluency. Noting that fluency is primarily determined by number of fully specified orthographic representations, they argue that when confronted with unfamiliar words, children with more highly developed phonemic awareness are more able to fully map the sounds to graphemes. As a result, children are able to move from decoding unfamiliar words to learning sight words—that is, they can teach themselves new words.

In Chapter 9, Linnea C. Ehri and Theresa Roberts present data and theoretical arguments regarding the contribution of knowledge of letter names to phonemic awareness and early decoding abilities. Knowledge of letter names typically comes in advance of phonemic awareness, and training studies show that learning letter names contributes to early reading and supports acquisition of phonemic awareness. Ehri and Roberts discuss the complexity of demands placed on children as they begin reading and stress the need to provide strong support in foundational knowledge prior to the rigors of formal instruction. To assist programs in selection of appropriate instruction, they conclude with a review of a variety of commercial phonics programs.

Part III, "Families and Relationships: Socioemotional and Linguistic Supports," includes chapters that examine emotional supports and interactional experiences that enhance language and early literacy in the home, as well as in classrooms. Chapter 10, by Susan Landry and Karen E. Smith presents evidence of the importance of engaged caregivers during the years from birth to age 3. Parental skill in providing rich input and scaffolding for children's attention and engagement in activities is shown to be important to children's language development. They report results from an intervention in which they videotape mothers as they interact with their babies and then view and discuss the tapes with mothers and other family members; they find the technique to be quite effective. Based on their findings, they suggest that similar interventions might be effective in out-of-home settings.

In Chapter 11, Robert C. Pianta argues that literacy emerges as children learn to coordinate multiple cognitive and affective systems and that warm, supportive relationships with caregivers, both parents and teachers, provide the relational context within which children acquire their ability to regulate activity. He advances a model of how adult–child relationships support early literacy, through a focus either on meaning and communication or on more instructional issues related to learning letter–sound correspondences. He suggests that shifting from a meaning focus to the more explicit instructional focus can threaten the nature of the relationship, making it potentially stressful for teachers to shift from a meaning to an instructional focus.

Erika Hoff, in Chapter 12, reviews research on home factors that affect children's language acquisition. She reviews the rich body of research on features of mother–child interaction that foster language learning. Given that social and economic class have often been found to be associated with vocabulary development, Hoff examines data from a study of children approaching their second birthdays. She finds that interactions such as the variety of input and the complexity of maternal language predict children's language growth and that once these behaviors are taken into account, social class no longer predicts language growth.

In Chapter 13, Monique Sénéchal, Gene Ouellette, and Donna Rodney use data about book reading in homes to address fundamental theoretical questions about the nature of early literacy development. They argue that the contribution of book reading to literacy development has been underestimated because the role of vocabulary in phonemic awareness and reading comprehension in the middle elementary grades has not been recognized. To substantiate this position, they report reanalyzed data from longitudinal studies that provide evidence that kindergarten vocabulary makes significant contributions to phonemic awareness at the end of first grade and to reading comprehension in third and fourth grades.

Part IV addresses critical issues related to "Cultural and Linguistic Diversity" and includes topics of second-language learning, alternative dialects, cultural discontinuities, and cultural-responsive approaches to interventions for parents and children. In Chapter 14, Sharon Vaughn, Sylvia Linan-Thompson, Sharolyn Pollard-Durodola, Patricia G. Mathes, and Elsa Cárdenas Hagan review research on interventions designed to support children whose first language is not English. First they review interventions that were delivered in English, in Spanish, or as bilingual programs and conclude that they are effective when they include systematic instruction that gives attention to phonemic awareness and sound–symbol correspondences, as well as opportunities to read text. An interesting finding concerning those interventions delivered in Spanish is that reading comprehension strategies taught transfer to English reading. The authors conclude by reviewing their own intervention, delivered in Spanish, and conclude that it is quite effective, but they caution that transfer to English must be done in a thoughtful manner because of the complexity of sound–symbol correspondence relationships in English.

Chapter 15, by Holly K. Craig and Julie A. Washington, reviews findings from the authors' decade-long effort to describe the language system of African American children at different points in development. They hypothesized that a portion of the persistent achievement gap between African American children and Caucasian children might be due to the African American English (AAE) that they may acquire in the home. Although information is not yet available to address this issue fully, the authors report data collected that describe in detail the features of AAE and discuss points of contrast to Standard American English (SAE). Correlational evidence is discussed showing that children's development of competence using both AAE and SAE—that is, acquisition of bidialectal competence—is associated with increased reading success.

In Chapter 16, Paul P. M. Leseman and Cathy van Tuijl review findings from a longitudinal study of literacy development among low- and high-income Dutch, as well as Turkish Dutch and Surinamese Dutch, families, two low-income immigrant groups that are learning Dutch as a second language. Using data on basic cognitive functions, higher level reading skills, and emotional support in the home, they find minimal cultural differences in basic cognitive skills but significant differences among higher order skills. They also find culturally linked differences in patterns of emotional support in the home. They examine sources of ethnic and social class differences and identify the impact of ecological factors, such as the nature of parents' employment, on home literacy practices and patterns of emotional support and outline a developmental theory of how culture affects reading development.

Chapter 17, by Stuart McNaughton, reports a program of research in New Zealand, a country that is educating children from mainstream New Zealand homes, children from the indigenous Maori culture, and children from Pacific nations. McNaughton begins by explaining that cultural groups are internally heterogeneous with respect to practices related to literacy and that the act of intervening in families is a cultural act that should enhance the "cultural dexterity" of families. He also argues that schools should assume responsibility for bridging the cultural divides between homes and schools. He reviews alternative approaches to supporting families from diverse backgrounds and concludes by reporting encouraging results from an intervention that changed school-based practices and sought to help families increase facility with practices consistent with school culture.

In Part V, "Supporting Literacy in Preschool Classrooms," includes chapters that discuss instruction to support language and literacy development in diverse early childhood settings. Specifically, these chapters emphasize skills in practice and highlight the importance of high-quality teachers in early childhood settings. In Chapter 18, Elena Bodrova and Deborah J. Leong fuse theory and practice in describing Vygotskian perspectives on teaching and learning in early literacy development. They first provide a critical overview of basic principles of his theory for early literacy and then report the results of a Vygotsky-based literacy curriculum for preschoolers. Their research suggests that the greatest gains were reported in classrooms in which teachers supported the development of deliberate, intentional, and self-regulatory behaviors, defined by Vygotsky as higher mental functions.

Chapter 19, by Dale C. Farran, Canan Aydogan, Shin Ji Kang, and Mark Lipsey, describes prekindergarten classrooms as intervention settings for language and literacy development in children from low-income families. Examining the importance of language development for predicting later literacy and school success, they use findings from a large-scale curriculum research project currently under way to examine how environments can be infused with greater resources and materials and the implications of such changes for language-facilitating activities in today's preschool classrooms.

In Chapter 20, Lesley M. Morrow and Judith A. Schickedanz turn to the importance of play in early literacy development. Reviewing key studies in literacy and play, they highlight the impact of teacher interventions and environmental supports on the nature and quality of children's play. Although they find strong relationships between play and literacy, they argue that more research is needed to establish whether or not, or the degree to which, there is a causal connection between play and literacy.

Threaded throughout many chapters in this volume is an attention to vocabulary development. Margaret G. McKeown and Isabel L. Beck, in Chapter 21, address what is known about the research on reading aloud and its facilitative influence on literacy development and on two key aspects of oral language development—the amount of language heard in the home and children's participation in conversational interactions. With a greater understanding of oral language development, they devised an innovative instructional approach that attempts to capture the benefits of reading aloud. Their data indicate exciting new advances in helping low-income children develop new and deeper knowledge of vocabulary through books.

Completing Part V, Kathleen Roskos and Carol Vukelich, in Chapter 22, trace the recent history and influences of early literacy policy, beginning with the standards movement that originated in states around the mid-1980s. They examine the early reading initiatives of the Bush administration, including Good Start, Grow Smart and Early Reading First, reflecting on the lessons learned from K–3 reading policy research. They provide practical, thoughtful recommendations for early literacy policy research.

Part VI, "Programmatic Interventions During the Preschool Years," includes chapters that discuss different types of interventions for our most vulnerable young children during the preschool years. Although there are only three chapters in this section, note that those who are primarily interested in this topic should review a number of chapters located in other sections—particularly chapters 2 (Neuman), 9 (Ehri & Roberts), 10 (Landry & Smith), 17 (McNaughton), 18 (Bodrova & Leong), and 21 (Beck & McKeown).

Chapter 23, by Pia Rebello Britto, Allison S. Fuligni, and Jeanne Brooks-Gunn, opens this section by placing the spotlight on the impact of poverty on families and children. Although several other chapters in this volume discuss the impact of poverty, these authors add important nuances as they note that it is not simply poverty that is important but the depth and duration of poverty. Also, like Neuman (Chapter 2), they stress the importance of community factors on development and argue that we have not fully appreciated their impact. They then turn to a review of programs designed for poor families who have children between infancy and age 3 and conclude that these programs can have beneficial effects when they include components that are directed at children and when the programs deliver services that are of high intensity.

Chapter 24 is a contribution by Robert Needlman, Perri Klass, and Barry Zuckerman from a pediatric perspective. They describe Reach Out and Read, which is a book-reading intervention that has been devised for use by pediatricians. In this approach, volunteers model strategies for reading books with children in pediatric waiting rooms, and pediatricians dispense books and advice about book reading as part of routine well-baby checkups. Research from correlational and experimental studies indicates that this low-cost and low-intensity intervention has significant and enduring effects on children in low-income families.

Chapter 25, by Nicholas Zill and Gary Resnick, continues the discussion of Head Start as they report data from FACES, the large, nationally representative study of Head Start programs and children. Drawing on a large database, they present data describing the performance of children who attend Head Start and analyses of factors that affect children's development. Using sophisticated statistical methods, they present evidence that Head Start has beneficial effects on language but much smaller effects on phonological sensitivity and letter knowledge. Curriculum is found to have an effect on children's progress, along with teacher education, length of time children are in the program, and parental reports of daily reading. Promising findings from kindergarten and first grade are reported, suggesting that longer term effects may be found.

Part VII, "Toward Effective Primary-Grade Instruction," moves beyond the early years of instruction to examine children's transition to more formal instruction in the primary grades, the influence of text features in learning to read, and strategies for assessing children's achievement. The final chapter highlights general principles of quality intervention in the early years and beyond.

In Chapter 26, Frederick J. Morrison, Carol McDonald Connor, and Heather J. Bachman present a fascinating overview of a working model that details many of the factors and sources of children's literacy development from roughly 3 years of age to third grade across the transition to school. This chapter serves as a helpful overview of the processes, skills, and dispositions related to school readiness and early reading skill growth and its implications for research and for improving literacy for all of our children.

Elfrieda H. Hiebert and Heidi Anne Mesmer, in Chapter 27, examine the research base for different strategies to determine text difficulty or leveling, a common practice in primary reading to ensure that texts are at children's instructional level and not their frustrational level. The authors argue forcefully that more comprehensive text difficulty schemes are needed and that these schemes need to consider progression over the entire period of reading acquisition if children are to receive the supportive texts many require to become proficient readers.

Addressing the transition from preschool to primary instruction, Connie Juel, in Chapter 28, concentrates on two key areas in the early school years: vocabulary and word recognition. She argues, like Biemiller, Beck, and McKeown, that of the two, vocabulary is the one that requires *intense* investment in instructional activities from the early years on up to foster it, whereas the second area, specific word recognition, requires a more focused, time-specific undertaking in instruction. Done well, word recognition strategies can lead to wide reading, broadening vocabulary, world knowledge, and thinking.

Terry Salinger, in Chapter 29, returns to key issues of assessment. In her compelling chapter, she discusses issues concerning early literacy assessment, focusing especially on the policy decisions surrounding the topic and the ways in which some of these decisions are being implemented. She dispassionately looks at the assessment criteria inherent in the Reading First program and discusses the consequences of the national attention currently paid to early reading and its assessment.

Ending the volume, Sharon Landesman Ramey and Craig T. Ramey, in Chapter 30, successfully tie together much of the research in early interventions, focusing on a set of well-established research-based principles that are designed to improve children's academic and social preparation for the transition to school.

In sum, we are heartened by the growing sophistication of theories of literacy development, especially by increasing efforts to expand our attention beyond phonemic awareness to consideration of other abilities, such as language, world knowledge, and self-regulation skills. The convergence of research and theoretical energy from disparate disciplines promises to continue deepening our understanding of the cognitive and affective underpinnings of early literacy. Also encouraging is the deepening understanding of cultural and other environmental factors and the ways they shape children's access to literacy-enhancing experiences. We anticipate that our increasingly sophisticated understanding of the complex web of factors that give rise to early literacy and that impede some children's growth will translate into even more sophisticated, intense, and effective interventions. Great energy has gone into devising early childhood interventions, but evaluation data continue to make evident the complex array of forces that must be addressed if we are to enhance significantly the educational opportunities of many children.

I

COGNITIVE AND LINGUISTIC
BUILDING BLOCKS
OF EARLY LITERACY

1

A Window of Opportunity We Must Open to All: The Case for Preschool with High-Quality Support for Language and Literacy

DAVID K. DICKINSON
ALLYSSA McCABE
MARILYN J. ESSEX

Countries seeking to educate citizens equipped with the literacy skills needed for skilled jobs in this technological era must provide children from low-income families with center-based preschools that offer substantially stronger support for language and early literacy skills than what is commonplace today. In this chapter we provide evidence from multiple domains to support this proposition. After documenting the shortcomings of our educational system, we argue that the years between 3 and 5 are especially important for long-term development. We substantiate this claim with developmental research from three broad areas: (1) early literacy, (2) social and emotional development, and (3) brain development. Theory and research findings from these areas are reviewed and interpreted as indicating that linguistic, cognitive, and affective domains are all critical to long-term literacy development. These domains are shown to be interrelated, with synergistic interdependencies appearing in the later preschool years that result in increasingly well-orchestrated systems of interrelated linguistic, cognitive, and affective/

regulatory abilities. Next we briefly review studies conducted in early childhood classrooms and find that they can play an important role in supporting children's language development. Unfortunately, other research that has examined interaction in preschool classrooms reveals serious limitations in the extent to which the average classroom that serves low-income children provides optimal support for language. We conclude by discussing some of the steps we see as necessary if we are to significantly improve the ability of classrooms to nourish children's early development.

Why We Need High-Quality Preschool Classrooms

An extensive literature documents large and predictable gaps between children from more and less advantaged socioeconomic backgrounds in the United States (Bishop & Edmundson, 1987; Dickinson, 1987; Hart & Risley, 1995; Strickland, 2001; Tarullo & Zill, 2002; Whitehurst & Lonigan, 1998,

2001) and other industrialized societies (Leseman & van Tuijl, Chapter 16, and McNaughton, Chapter 17, this volume). Predictable factors place children at risk of entering kindergarten with limitations in literacy-related skills: Their parents have limited education and economic resources, their ethnicity and/or first language is not that of the mainstream community and is not valued by the majority culture, and their family does not engage in the type of discourse that has been found conducive to acquisition of early literacy skills (Hart & Risley, 1995; Hoff, Chapter 12 and Leseman & van Tuijl, Chapter 16, this volume). When these early problems are combined with the problem of elementary schools that are not successfully bolstering children's phonemic awareness (see Biemiller, Chapter 3, Burgess, Chapter 7, Morrison, Connor, & Bachman, Chapter 26, and Lonigan, Chapter 6, this volume), many children are left at significant risk of failing to acquire high-level literacy skills.

Although such factors place children at risk, longitudinal research indicates that high-quality interventions during the preschool years can have enduring effects on a broad range of developmental outcomes (see Barnett, Chapter 25, and Ramey & Ramey, Chapter 31, this volume). Unfortunately, preschool classrooms that serve the population in need of strong early support do not consistently have a major impact on supporting children's development. Head Start, the government's flagship program that seeks to level the playing field for children from low-income homes, has substantially increased its attention to early academic skills, with benefits being seen in children's language and literacy skills (see Zill & Resnick, Chapter 26, this volume). Nonetheless, we are still far from providing the level of care required to substantially enhance the academic opportunities of children who depend on these classrooms for educational nourishment.

The slow pace of improvement is not surprising. The early childhood system employs staff who have limited education, are poorly paid, and work in a low-status profession, often under difficult circumstances. High levels of attrition are but one outcome of this unfortunate convergence of circumstances (Dickinson & Brady, 2005). Added to the problems that flow from financial constraints on the entire early childhood system

are the conceptual changes that are required. Pianta (Chapter 11, this volume) argues that teachers of young children feel a tension between supporting children's emotional growth through warm and supportive relationships and teaching children information and skills. He argues that the act of explicit instruction often is experienced as a threat to their ability to nourish children's emotional growth. The power of such ways of viewing teaching has helped shape how the broader preschool world has viewed classrooms, with support for literacy too often seen as standing in opposition to support for social and emotional development. This either/or trade-off view was reflected even in the landmark review of research on early childhood programs, *Neurons to Neighborhoods* (Shonkoff & Phillips, 2000), which, in its final summary, included a caution against overemphasis on cognitive goals at the expense of social and emotional goals. We must move beyond such thinking to recognition of the need to address all aspects of development effectively.

Literacy Development from a Systems Perspective

Literacy development can best be understood from a systems perspective (Ford & Lerner, 1992; Nelson, 1996) in which language plays a prominent early role in organizing cognitive and other affective–behavioral systems that support literacy-related activity. Extensive research on early literacy now indicates that language skills broadly conceived—vocabulary, syntax, and discourse, as well as phonemic awareness—are central to early and long-term literacy success and that children reap added rewards when they develop these language and literacy-related capacities in tandem so that interconnections among systems can be fashioned into mutually reinforcing systems (Dickinson, McCabe, Anastasopoulos, Peisner-Feinberg, & Poe, 2003). But long-term literacy and associated academic success require more than acquisition of perceptual, linguistic, and cognitive skills that enable one to read and understand. One also needs to acquire the social and affective–behavioral self-regulatory skills needed to relate effectively to teachers and peers, to attend to difficult tasks, and to develop the motivation that enables one to become a self-sustaining learner. Thus a fully satisfactory theory of the development of early literacy must take into account the interrelationships among language and print-related skills (e.g., letter knowledge, knowledge of sound–symbol correspondences) and consider the interactions among social development and self-regulatory and motivation processes (Dionne, Tremblay, Voivin, Laplante, & Perusse, 2003; Pianta, 1999).

The complexity of such an undertaking is staggering, but it is possible to narrow our focus in a manner that makes the task somewhat less daunting. We hypothesize that language plays a powerful role in the organization of all these systems. Between the ages of 3 and 6, the rapid development of language, particularly the emergence of the more advanced language abilities, may play a pivotal role in the initial organization and subsequent functioning of varied linguistic–cognitive–affective systems that underpin literacy, as well as diverse areas of cognition and social development (Dickinson et al., 2003; Nelson, 1996; Pianta, Chapter 11, this volume; Tomasello, 2000). This perspective has been summarized by Katherine Nelson (1996), who reviewed research from multiple domains including theory of mind, memory, conceptual skills, and narrative, and linked these developmental shifts to the language abilities that become available during this period. Nelson stated that between ages 2 and 6 "language and the surrounding culture take over the human mind. It is during these years that biology 'hands over' development to the social world" (p. 325).

This view of development is consistent with Tomasello's (2000) argument that human cognition is largely the by-product of evolutionary factors that led to the development of the ability of people to understand the perspectives of others and the refinement of abilities to communicate knowledge using language. Both Nelson and Tomasello advance positions that are consistent with two key Vygotskian principles outlined by Bodrova and Leong (Chapter 18, this volume): (1) that mental development results from natural development and cultural development and (2) that the formation of higher mental functions is the major development during the early childhood period.

Recently we reviewed the research on early language and literacy development (Dickinson et al., 2003) and stressed the central role of multiple language abilities in early and later literacy. We hypothesized that early language and print-related abilities may emerge as interdependent systems. Considerable evidence demonstrates that literacy draws on a number of levels of the language system, with these abilities encompassing vocabulary (Biemiller, 1999; Bishop & Adams, 1990; Butler, Marsh, Sheppard, & Sheppard, 1985; Hart & Risley, 1995; Scarborough, 1989; Share, Jorm, Maclean, & Matthews, 1984; Storch & Whitehurst, 2002; Walker, Greenwood, Hart, & Carta, 1994), syntax (for reviews, see Biemiller, 1999; Dickinson, 1987), and discourse (Beals, 2001; Bishop & Edmundson, 1987; Fazio, Naremore, & Connell, 1996; Feagans & Applebaum, 1986; Menyuk et al., 1991; Vernon-Feagans, Hammer, Miccio, & Manlove, 2001). Literacy also draws on the ability to attend to and manipulate the sounds of language. The vital role of phonological sensitivity also has been demonstrated through longitudinal observational studies (Bryant, MacLean, & Bradley, 1990; MacLean, Bryant, & Bradley, 1987; Stanovich, 1992; Vellutino & Scanlon, 2001; Wagner & Torgesen, 1987; Wagner et al., 1997; Whitehurst & Lonigan, 1998) and intervention studies (Ball & Blachman, 1991; McGuinness, McGuinness, & Donohue, 1995).

Although research has tended to correlate reading skill with language functioning in distinct areas, there is considerable evidence that, in the developing child, language ability is not rigidly restricted to the categories we use to describe language. Evidence for this point comes from Scarborough (2001), who conducted a meta-analysis of the impact of oral language on subsequent reading abilities and concluded that successful predictors of future reading abilities usually have not been confined to a single linguistic domain. Indeed, Scarborough suggests that, at different points in development, reading problems may be traced to language-related deficiencies that take different forms at different points in development.

Of course, early reading involves processes and knowledge other than those closely linked to language. In particular, skill in recognizing and interpreting print is vital

(Dickinson et al., 2003; Lonigan, Burgess, & Anthony, 2000; Lonigan, Burgess, Anthony, & Barker, 1998; Storch & Whitehurst, 2002; Whitehurst & Lonigan, 1998, 2001), as indicated by the fact that the ability to identify and name letters has long been recognized as being a strong predictor of later reading (Adams, 1990).

Several decades of intensive study of the importance of distinct domains to early literacy have resulted in abundant evidence of the multiplicity of factors that support the emergence of literacy. In the coming decades researchers will need to examine the interconnections among these diverse domains. Analyses we conducted of data from 4-year-olds suggest that phonological sensitivity, vocabulary, and print skills are correlated and, among normally developing children, are fashioned into mutually reinforcing systems of knowledge. Other studies reported in this volume (see especially Leseman & van Tuijl, Chapter 16; McNaughton, Chapter 17; and Sénéchal, Ouelette, & Rodney, Chapter 13) support the proposition that reading success is based on development of multiple skills, with the centrality of different skills varying by the age of the child and the reading demands encountered at a given age.

A hypothesis that flows from a systems view of development is that the opportunity to substantially affect the nature of the system is greatest at the point at which the processes that are involved are initially being fashioned into a stable, interconnected network. Some data from studies of the emergence of phonemic awareness suggest that this dynamic may be present for literacy-related skills. Studies of the emergence of phonological sensitivity in the preschool years (Lonigan, Chapter 6, this volume; see Burgess, Chapter 7, this volume, for a review), indicate that very young children have some capacity to attend to the sounds of language but that these abilities are not organized enough to enable children to demonstrate consistent access to phonological representations of language. The youngest children show variability from one task to the next and from one point in time to the next. However, as children approach age 5, more stability is apparent, suggesting that these abilities are beginning to be organized into stable systems.

Consistent with this speculation is evidence that the preschool years are a time when literacy-specific aspects of development may be particularly responsive to intervention. The National Reading Panel's review of studies seeking to improve phonemic awareness found that the few studies that involved kindergarten-age children, the youngest group included, had the strongest effects of any age period, with an average effect size nearly double those found for interventions carried out with older children (Ehri et al., 2001). Correlational studies have also provided evidence of the impact of preschool classrooms on emerging aspects of children's language skill. Huttenlocher, Vasilyeva, Cymerman, and Levine (2002) examined the growth of low-income 4-year-old children's syntactic skills over the course of 9 months. Taking into account the impact of maternal language use, they found that the syntactic complexity of teachers' language played a substantial role in accounting for children's fall-to-spring syntactic development.

The Home–School Study of Language and Literacy Development (Snow & Dickinson, 1991), a longitudinal study that examined both home and classroom factors that support the language and literacy of children from low-income families, also found clear evidence that teachers' language use can have significant effects on children's emerging language and literacy skills (Dickinson & Tabors, 2001). When children were 4 years old, their classrooms were visited and coded for educational support, and their teachers were interviewed and recorded throughout the course of one day. Regression analyses found that, after controlling for the children's language skill at age 3 (mean length of utterance during a play episode at home) and family demographics (income, education), the nature of extended discourse involving teachers added significant explanatory power to the models. For example, when predicting vocabulary, the control variables accounted for 18% of end-of-kindergarten variance, and, when a composite measure of teachers' extended discourse was added, the amount of variance accounted for jumped to 41%. In a recent reanalysis of these data, we found that these effects could still be detected at the end of fourth grade. Using stepwise hierarchical regression that controlled for home demographic factors (i.e., maternal education and family income) and the child's mean length of utterance (MLU) at age 3, we found that measures of teacher discourse accounted for significant ($p < .01$) variance in end-of-fourth-grade assessments of vocabulary and reading comprehension (Dickinson & Porche, 2005).

Experimental and correlational evidence suggest that language may be particularly malleable during preschool. If true, this is of considerable importance, because longitudinal studies of vocabulary learning have also provided strong evidence of stability in vocabulary growth (Biemiller, 1999; Cunningham & Stanovich, 1997) and evidence that schools are apparently not successfully fostering vocabulary growth (Biemiller, Chapter 3, this volume; Morrison et al., Chapter 26, this volume). Similarly, Storch and Whitehurst (2002) examined development of vocabulary from preschool through third grade, and at each step the vocabulary scores from the previous year accounted for 88% or more of the variance of the subsequent year. Long-term stability also is present, as Tabors, Snow, and Dickinson (2001) found kindergarten-to-seventh-grade correlations in receptive vocabulary of $r = .63$. Analyses of child outcomes between kindergarten and fourth grade using growth modeling found that kindergarten Peabody Picture Vocabulary Test (PPVT) scores and word recognition were strongly predicted by preschool home and classroom variables. Fourth-grade reading comprehension was strongly predicted by kindergarten vocabulatry and reading controlling for kindergarten–grade 4 rate of growth (Tabors, Porche, & Ross, 2003).

Typically, children who enter kindergarten or first grade substantially behind age norms do not make the gains they need in order to leave school with strong academic skills. High correlations have been reported between kindergarten vocabulary skill and seventh-grade reading (Tabors, Snow, & Dickinson, 2001), as well as reading in first and fourth grades (Juel, 1988). High correlations also were reported between reading achievement in first grade and at the end of high school (Cunningham & Stanovich, 1997). The need for early intervention is further indicated by the fact that, after chil-

dren reach third grade, reading difficulties are far less amenable to remediation (Good, Simmons, & Smith, 1998; McGill-Franzen & Allington, 1991).

Thus multiple language abilities are central to the emergence of literacy during the preschool years and continue to play a major role in later reading success. These abilities develop with great speed during the preschool years, and, as children enter school, selected capacities are recruited for reading and writing. There are hopeful indications that development may be particularly malleable during this era; considerable evidence suggests that as children get older it becomes increasingly difficult to substantially alter their chances of long-term academic success.

Self-Regulation, Social Skills, and Language

Extensive research has been done on the emergence of children's social skills and the importance of self-regulation. Work on social and emotional development comes from varied theoretical perspectives, with the socially based perspective of Tomasello (2000) and Nelson (1996) being particularly relevant to our argument because of the central role accorded to language. Tomasello (2000) argues that the ability to identify with the perspectives of others, combined with the ability to use language, enables people to communicate their mental states and intentions, thereby providing a very powerful means to transmit values and knowledge. Other researchers interested in social and emotional development, especially those focused on the role of cognition (e.g., Saarni, 1999), have also recognized the importance of language in children's emotion-related capabilities. When language is viewed in this way, it becomes evident that, as children learn to use language, they acquire a tool that enables them to regulate their own emotions and behaviors, with important consequences for their social and academic functioning.

Self-regulation refers to the ability to initiate, sustain, modulate, or change the intensity or duration of feeling states in order to achieve one's goals (Baumeister & Vohs, 2004). The capacity for self-regulation is increasingly coming to be seen as essential to social development and to the ability to learn in school. Preschoolers with effective regulatory skills are better able to form positive relations with peers and teachers (Miller, Gouley, Seifer, Dickstein, & Shields, 2004). Further, preschoolers with such skills evidence greater social competence in kindergarten (Denham et al., 2003), as well as greater behavioral self-regulation skills and achievement (Howse, Calkins, Anastopoulos, Keane, & Shelton, 2003), suggesting that effective regulatory skills are central to children's mastery of difficult tasks such as those associated with literacy learning.

Although the majority of research on self-regulation focuses on preschoolers and school-age children, there is evidence that the capacity for "effortful control," a temperamentally based ability to inhibit a dominant response and activate a subdominant response (Rothbart, Ellis, Rueda, & Posner, 2003), becomes increasingly coherent and consistent by age 2 (Kochanska, Coy, & Murray, 2001; Kochanska et al., 1996). In young children, effortful control has been shown to be associated with more regulated emotions and stronger restraint (Kochanska, Murray & Harlan, 2000), and poor effortful control with behavior problems (Murray & Kochanska, 2002; Rothbart et al., 2003). This self-regulation system is partially determined by biologically based control mechanisms, but considerable individual variability also is likely linked to cognitive, speech, and representational abilities. It is intriguing that coherence in an individual's ability to exert effortful control begins to be seen at an age when language abilities are blossoming. Two recent studies provide direct evidence for a link between the development of language and this aspect of self-regulation. In a twin study, Dionne et al. (2003) found evidence of heritability effects on toddlers' aggressive behaviors but not on expressive vocabulary and, most important, moderately strong negative effects of acquisition of expressive vocabulary on aggression. And in a longitudinal study of kindergartners, Hooper, Roberts, Zeisel, and Poe (2003) found that expressive and receptive language deficits predicted conduct problems with increasing accuracy as children moved from kindergarten to third grade, particularly for receptive

language. These findings provide evidence of early positive impact of language-related abilities on behavioral self-regulation.

Once children enter school, self-regulation, social, and language skills all play a role in helping to shape their ability to form positive relationships with teachers and peers and to succeed in school. Effective regulatory skills help reduce the incidence of problem behaviors (Cole, Teti, & Zahn-Waxler, 2003; Cole, Zahn-Waxler, Fox, Usher, & Welsh, 1996; Eisenberg et al., 1996; Eisenberg et al., 1995), and are directly associated with positive social and academic functioning. We have shown that poor self-regulatory abilities explain the greater relationship difficulties with peers and teachers experienced by children from low-SES families (Miech, Essex & Goldsmith, 2001). And other studies have shown that children with strong regulatory skills are more capable of managing interactions that are emotionally charged (Fabes et al., 1999). In a series of studies, Ladd and colleagues have shown that kindergartners who relate to others in a positive manner, avoiding negative or aggressive actions, have more positive relationships with their teachers (Birch & Ladd, 1998) and peers, which, in turn, result in more productive engagement in school and higher levels of school achievement (Ladd, Birch, & Buhs, 1999). In another series of studies, Eisenberg and colleagues have shown that self-regulation predicts later peer popularity and socially appropriate behavior and that these associations are stronger for those children high in negative emotionality, for whom regulation is particularly important (Eisenberg, Fabes, Guthrie, & Reiser, 2000). In contrast, when children enter school with poor self-regulatory skills and aggressive behaviors that are maintained through the early school years, they experience early-emerging and sustained difficulties in their relations with both peers and teachers (Ladd et al., 1999).

The early teacher–child relationship has been shown to be especially important for children's social and academic adjustment (Pianta, 1999; Pianta, Steinberg, & Rollins, 1995), especially for children who enter school with poor self-regulatory skills (Meehan, Hughes, & Cavell, 2003). As stated by a group of highly respected developmentalists, "Children grow and thrive in the context of dependable relationships that provide love and nurturance, security, and responsive interaction, and encouragement for exploration" (Shonkoff & Phillips, 2000, p. 7), and such relationships with teachers can be particularly beneficial in forming a child's self-regulation capacities and for supporting the acquisition of knowledge and academic competencies (Birch & Ladd, 1998; Pianta, 1999). Studies have shown that teachers are more favorably disposed toward children who exhibit positive and cooperative behavior (Pallas, Entwisle, & Cadigan, 1987) and appropriate regulation of emotions (Alexander & Entwistle, 1988). Children also are more likely to be responded to favorably by teachers if they are not highly distractible and exhibit only moderate levels of emotional intensity (Keogh, 2003). Thus children who are able to regulate their emotions and attention and are socially competent benefit because they are more likely to form close ties to teachers, and they display better adjustment and more learning in school (Hamre & Pianta, 2001). Importantly, differences in the quality of these early relationships with kindergarten teachers have long-lasting effects, with indirect effects from kindergarten still apparent in eighth grade (Hamre & Pianta, 2001; Pianta, Hamre, & Stuhlman, 2002).

The importance of acquiring the language-use skills linked to social development is also revealed by children who fail to develop needed skills. Children with difficulties in using social language have been found to have problems forming and maintaining healthy peer relations because they tend to have poor social interaction skills and are more likely to be rejected by their peers (Fujiki & Brinton, 1994; Gertner, Rice, & Hadley, 1994). Recent research suggests that self-regulation may be a key factor in this process (Fujiki, Brinton, & Clarke, 2002). Other research has shown that school-age children who are aggressive demonstrate poorer communication clarity and increased disruptive communication during cooperative communication tasks than do their nonaggressive peers (Dumas, Blechman, & Prinz, 1994). And in a longitudinal study, we have recently shown that children who are stably aggressive across the elementary school years

evidenced poorer self-regulatory skills and poorer receptive language abilities as preschoolers (Park et al., in press). More generally, researchers studying child mental health have found that externalizing problems and disorders, which are defined by poor social and self-regulatory skills, both accompany and are predicted by language-related impairments, including speech and language problems (Hinshaw, 2002), reading disability (McGee, Share, Moffitt, Williams, & Silva, 1998), and neurocognitive problems (Moffitt & Caspi, 2001), such as difficulties in language processing (Hinshaw, Carte, Sami, Treuting, & Zupan, 2002).

Evidence from Studies of Brain Development

The interconnected nature of development has been further reinforced by the increasing recognition in the past decade of the plasticity of the brain and the reciprocal influences of neurobiological mechanisms and child development and behavior (Nelson & Bloom, 1997; P. R. Huttenlocher, 2002). Studies in affective neuroscience have shown that the same part of the brain is critical to the neural implementation of emotion and cognition (Davidson, Scherer, & Goldsmith, 2003). And, most relevant to this chapter, the linkage of brain functioning to early school success has been outlined by Blair (2002), who proposed a developmental neurobiological model of children's school readiness that links emotionality to academic and social competence in school settings.

Linking Emotions and Higher Cognitive Functions

Studies of neural functioning have revealed that prefrontal cortical areas of the brain that support higher cognitive functioning such as memory and attention are connected to subcortical areas such as the amygdala that play an important role in emotion. Blair (2002) reviewed studies of behaviorally inhibited children (i.e., shy, very reserved, fearful) that found that they have a low threshold for limbic arousal, which results in negative emotional expression and activation of the sympathetic nervous system. The behavioral expression of these events is behavioral inhibition, or withdrawal from stimulation. The neural systems governing arousal have also been linked to stress exposure, as revealed by increased cortisol levels that indicate activation of the hypothalamic–pituitary–adrenal (HPA) axis. Recently, we have shown that early exposure to family adversities is associated with increased cortisol levels by preschool, making young children more vulnerable to the development of socioemotional problems when facing the cognitive and social challenges of preschool and the early elementary years (Essex, Klein, Cho, & Kalin, 2002; Smider et al., 2002). Other researchers have also found that dysregulation of the HPA axis is associated with socioemotional difficulties during the preschool and early school years (Gunnar et al., 1997; Schmidt, Fox, Rubin, & Sternberg, 1997; Schmidt, Fox, Sternberg, Gold, Smith, & Schulkin, 1999) that may persist through middle childhood (Granger, Stansbury, & Henker, 1994). Further, although such family adversities are risk factors for all children, they are more prevalent in low-income families. Thus children from low-SES families have higher cortisol levels than children from higher SES families (Essex, Klein, et al., 2002; Lupien, King, Meaney, & McEwen, 2000), with more negative consequences not only for socioemotional functioning (Essex, Boyd, et al., 2002) but also for cognitive functioning (Lupien, King, Meaney & McEwen, 2001).

Together, this research suggests that the development of the affective–cognitive–linguistic systems that children draw on as they interact with peers and teachers and engage in tasks that provide opportunities to learn to use print have their roots in a complex matrix of biologically determined sensitivity to and ways of responding to stimuli and to stress-inducing experiences in the home or in classrooms. In the preschool years children first begin to acquire the ability to regulate their emotions and acquire the social skills for interacting with others. The fact that longitudinal studies find early experiences to predict later functioning suggests that preschool-age children are acquiring patterns for coping with their own emotions, integrated in routine ways of responding to life circumstances. Such patterns of response to social circumstances and to their own affective states may have long-lasting implications for children's social functioning and learning. Furthermore, there is also growing evidence that such patterns of responding and engaging in interactions have an impact on brain development.

Neural Development

Considerable effort is now going into understanding the functioning and development of the brain using varied sophisticated methods. Pugh, Sandak, Frost, Moore, and Mencl (Chapter 5, this volume) review one line of research that is beginning to reveal the connections between activation of selected areas of the brain and reading and reading disability. Interestingly, this work is showing the impact of children's activity on the functioning of the brain, as indicated by the fact that an effective reading intervention results both in improved reading performance and in changed patterns of neural activity. Such work is consistent with the emerging consensus that, for higher cognitive functions such as reasoning, planning, remembering, and reading comprehension, the brain has considerable plasticity (reviewed by Blair, 2002; P. R. Huttenlocher, 2002). For example, P. R. Huttenlocher (2002) notes that the left angular gyrus, an area implicated in reading that abuts Wernicke's area (an area involved in comprehending language), may support language processing in the preschool years and then shifts to support reading. He speculates that language, like other neural functions, may initially be relatively diffusely represented and that as language skills are routinized they may become restricted to particular language areas and the angular gyrus recruited to support reading. Such a shift is one example of neural plasticity and the complex interplay between genetically determined pathways of brain development and experiences that shape development of the brain in a multitude of ways (Black, 2003).

One approach to neural development, known as the *selectionist approach* to developing connectivity in the brain, argues that genetically determined development results in an early overproduction of possible synaptic connections and that these connections are pruned, with certain connections preserved and strengthened whereas others are eliminated (reviewed by P. R. Huttenlocher, 2002). Synaptic connections that are active are maintained and strengthened as they consume available resources (glucose, oxygen) and are organized into interconnected sets of synapses. There is a general timetable for this overproduction and subsequent pruning, but P. R. Huttenlocher (2002) argues that there is not a "critical" period during which experience shapes brain development. Instead, there seem to be "windows of opportunity," which are "periods in brain development during which the effects of environmental stimulation on brain structure and function are maximal" (p. 207). It is during these periods that teaching and enrichment programs are likely to have maximal impact. He concludes that it is between late infancy and late childhood that synaptic density reaches a plateau and that this is the point of maximal responsiveness to environmental input (p. 209). This relatively wide window of opportunity suggests that the preschool years occur at a relatively early point of maximal plasticity. Significantly, it is during this period that synaptic density in three areas that support language functioning—Broca's area, Wernicke's area, and Heschl's gyrus—reach their peak levels of synaptic density. Density subsequently declines until about age 10, when it then levels off (P. R. Huttenlocher, 2002, p. 50). Measures of metabolism of glucose, a measure of neural activity, also reach high levels around age 3 and then decline gradually until about age 10 (P. R. Huttenlocher, 2002, p. 70).

A second approach to considering neural development is the *constructivist approach*, which argues for a potentially larger role for experience in the organization and specification of functioning of the brain, particularly of the neocortex, which supports higher cognitive functions (Quartz & Sejnowski, 1997). According to this theory, early in life relatively little of the cerebral cortex is dedicated to specific functions. Subsequent interaction of neural activity that is responsive to experience and neural growth mechanisms affect the representational properties of the cortex and help shape neural organization. According to this view, plasticity is also evident in the processes by which varied areas of the brain are connected. Reviewing studies of electroencephalographic (EEG) activity, Blair (2002) highlighted evidence indicating the establishment of connections between frontal lobes and sensory areas, which provides a neural basis for understanding the emergence of the executive functions that are important for self-regulation and for higher cognitive activity.

Summary of Theoretical Accounts of Development

A full accounting of the emergence of literacy and of long-term literacy ability requires charting the emergence and interrelationships among multiple linguistic–cognitive–affective systems that are recruited to support this complex and socially valued set of abilities. Language skills are central to initial literacy and to long-term literacy development, and evidence is accumulating that language also plays an important role in development of social and emotional competence. Children who are able to control their own attention and engage in school in positive ways are more likely to have interactions with peers and to form positive relationships with teachers. These relationships have a positive impact on subsequent educational success. Converging lines of research in neural development suggest that experience plays an important role in the organization of the brain, including the interconnectivity between areas that support higher cognitive functioning and regions linked to emotionality. Other work suggests that the preschool years may be a time when a "window of opportunity" opens for experience to have a significant impact on neural development. Finally, we posit that language plays a pivotal role in the orchestration of connections that support literacy and regulation of emotions and emergence of social competence.

The Need for High-Quality Language Support in Preschools

Converging research from different areas of development makes evident the importance of language. Studies of the impact of preschool classrooms on language and cognitive development demonstrate the fact that these are settings that can play an important role in fostering language growth (see also Farran, Aydogan, Kang, & Lipsey, Chapter 19, this volume). Development in preschool is best predicted by varied measures of the quality of teacher–child interaction (Dickinson & Tabors, 2001; McCartney, 1984), yet the more carefully we look at preschool discourse the more we see need for improvement. A number of studies of the language environments of preschool classrooms reveal low levels of interaction. Tizard and Hughes (1985) examined British infant schools and found far fewer extended, intellectually engaging conversations between teachers and children in classrooms than between parents and those same children at home. In the early 1990s in the United States, Layzer, Goodson, and Moss (1993) did intensive week-long observations in 119 classrooms and found teachers talking with individuals or small groups only 26% of the time, less time than they spent not talking with any children (28%). For 20% of the classrooms visited for a week, half or more of the children never had individual attention from a teacher. Preschools associated with universities also have been found to be places of limited teacher–child interaction, as one study conducted in laboratory classrooms found that, when teachers were in close proximity to children (3 feet or less), they usually (81% of the time) did not speak to the children to whom they were near (Kontos & Wilcox-Herzog, 1997).

Recently we studied 77 Head Start classrooms, in which we observed teachers during choice time—the period of the day when children select activities on their own—and meal times (Dickinson, McCabe, & Clark-Chiarelli, 2004) and coded them using a time-sampling system that described the kinds of interactions found to be supportive of development (Dickinson & McCabe, 2001; Dickinson & Smith, 1994). We observed teachers for 8 to 12 intervals of 30 seconds each and found that teachers engaged in instructional talk (talk about language, ideas, print, numbers) only 12% of the time. The teachers who were at the high end of the continuum, the 75th percentile, in use of such talk engaged in instructional talk only 18% of the time. Teachers were able to establish and deepen a topic in only 14% of these intervals, and explicit talk about words was almost absent, being found in fewer than 1% of the intervals. No such interactions were observed at all in 89% of the rooms.

For the Home–School Study of Language and Literacy Development (HSSLLD), we audiotaped teachers and children throughout the day and analyzed interactions in detail. We audiotaped 75 4-year-old children during the day for a total of 6,640 minutes and found that, during choice time, children were silent 59% of the time. They interacted with teachers 17% of the time and with other children 18% of the time (Dickinson, 2001a). Given the results reported here, it seems that those occasions on which children did converse with teachers were rich with educational potential. Although variation in quality clearly had significant effects on children, on average the conversations were far from ideal. We recorded, transcribed, and analyzed 15 minutes of free-play conversation between teachers and children. The measure of language use that was the most predictive of later language development was the percentage of total words used that were "rare" words, defined as words not included on a list of 7,881 words identified by Chall and Dale (1995) as common for third-grade children. We found that these 15 minutes of conversational time included 287 different words, only 14 of which were "rare" words; these 14 uses of such words represented only 9 different word types (Dickinson, 2001a; Dickinson & Tabors, 2001). Given that teachers were interacting with children during a variety of activities with the potential for conversation about a host of interesting topics (e.g., *excavating tunnels* in the sand, noting *evaporation* of water from paint or sand, *constructing skyscrapers* in the blocks area), this reflects a very low rate of use of varied words and suggests that shortcomings result from teachers' conversational habits rather than that they have nothing to talk about.

During book reading, another setting found to relate to later vocabulary development (Dickinson & McCabe, 2003; Dickinson & Smith, 1994), we found that the texts of books yielded 10.6 total rare words and 7.1 different types of words, whereas teachers' conversations about books included only 4.7 rare words and 2.8 different words (Dickinson, McCabe, & Anastasopoulos, 2002). The low density of rare words in teachers' discourse clearly reveals that teachers rarely intentionally use or discuss the interesting words found in books. The limitations in the amount and quality of teacher–child discourse, especially the limited use of rare vocabulary, suggest that teachers typically provide children minimal individualized support for development of language and literacy. Such patterns of interaction highlight shortcomings in support for language and literacy and the paucity of content knowledge instruction. They also suggest that teachers provide little intentional support for children's understanding of the complexities of social interaction, because such interactions necessarily would probe issues such as motivations and intentions, topics that typically result in extended, cognitively rich interactions (Tizard & Hughes, 1985). The pervasiveness and consistency of these findings clearly suggest that there are powerful, systematic forces at work that act to constrain patterns of teacher–child interaction.

Providing Classroom Support for Language, Literacy, and Knowledge

A number of avenues may be pursued in order to bring about changes in the patterns of interaction in preschool classrooms that are of sufficient magnitude to result in substantial improvements in children's achievement. Given space constraints, we touch on a few of the most noteworthy approaches, concluding with a brief discussion of the role of curriculum. We highlight ways in which these efforts may support improved patterns of language use, but we realize that each factor discussed can have multiple effects on teachers and classroom functioning.

Structural Initiatives

Two key regulated features of classrooms are teacher–child ratio and teachers' educational levels. Both higher ratios and higher educational attainment have repeatedly been found to result in better outcomes for children (reviewed in Shonkoff & Phillips, 2000). The ratio of teachers to children has repeatedly been found to result in better outcomes for children most likely, in part, because having fewer children increases the opportunities teachers have to converse with individuals. The positive association between teachers' educational levels and child outcomes also may reflect differences in patterns of language use because teachers with more schooling may have language-based advantages over their less well-educated colleagues. In addition to learning pedagogical methods, as teachers complete college courses they are exposed to and likely acquire new vocabulary and associated world knowledge, and they may gain comfort in reading and talking about books.

Professional Development

Considerable effort and large sums are spent on professional development, but few literacy-focused initiatives have been researched. We have carried out one such line of work (Dickinson, Miller, & Anastasopoulos, 2001a; Dickinson, Anastasopoulos, Miller, Caswell, & Peisner-Feinberg, 2002; Dickinson & Brady, 2005). Our approach has been to use inservice credit-bearing courses to deepen teachers' knowledge of early literacy development. The courses involve readings, videotapes that depict effective classroom practices, and assignments that require teachers to implement new strategies and that guide teachers to reflect on children's learning. These courses have been delivered in face-to-face sessions and by using interactive video conferencing. Comparison group studies have found substantial changes in classroom practices, as well as strong evidence of effects on vocabulary and phonological sensitivity (Dickinson et al., 2002; Dickinson, Sprague, Sayer, Miller, & Clark, 2001).

Other research teams have sought to bolster children's learning by striving to improve the quality of conversations during book reading. Whitehurst's groundbreaking dialogic reading demonstrated that a book-focused intervention can translate into enhanced learning when employed by parents and teachers (Arnold & Whitehurst, 1994). Subsequently, other teams have adopted other approaches to improving book reading in classrooms. Beck and McKeown (see Chapter 21, this volume) developed strategies for helping teachers engage in book discussions that draw children into focused and deep conversations about books. Similarly, Wasik and Bond (2001) devised an intensive intervention that includes in-class modeling that alters practices and improves children's learning. However, limited generalization of conversational strategies was found. These efforts to improve teacher–child interaction during book reading highlight the difficulty we face as we attempt to substantially alter how teachers converse with children. Wasik's difficulty in altering practice in multiple settings is particularly sobering because book reading may be the most well-defined context of the typical preschool day, yet it accounts for only a small portion of the day and does not allow for the kind of individually tailored conversations found to have substantial impact on children's language acquisition (Dickinson, 2001b).

Curriculum

Recently there has been growing awareness that curriculum plays an important role in provision of educationally rich classrooms. Head Start now requires that all programs use some curriculum. Data collected on a representative sample of Head Start classrooms indicates that curriculum choice does make a difference in children's learning (see Zill & Resnick, Chapter 26, this volume). Ongoing federally funded studies will soon begin to provide solid empirical data on the relative effectiveness of these and other early childhood curricula.

Recognizing the need of preschool teachers for considerable support in providing intellectually challenging and linguistically rich conversations, Schickedanz and Dickinson (2005) recently developed a curriculum that provides comprehensive full-day programming. It was designed to support all aspects of development, including skills such as self-regulation and social development. Built around a collection of high-quality children's books, teachers develop thematic units that include content-rich hands-on activities. Key vocabulary is identified, and teachers are given guidance in using these words during book reading and throughout the day, and tips for observing and conversing with children are provided in an effort to encourage teachers to engage in effective interactions throughout the day. Game-like activities target phonemic awareness and print knowledge, and group discussions address socioemotional topics.

Results from pilot studies conducted in programs serving low-income families in Washington, D.C., and Springfield, Massachusetts, are encouraging. For example, in Washington, D.C., where the curriculum was employed for a full academic year, PPVT data were collected from 17 children in the fall, winter, and spring. Average gains of 13.5 points were found, reflecting overall improvement from 89.4 to 102.5. For the eight children who entered with lowest fall scores, average gains of 18.6 points were found. In Springfield, a larger initiative, a partial implementation of the curriculum was carried out. Early data were collected with about a 2-month interval between pre- and posttesting. For the 53 children tested at both times, children's performance on the Preschool Language Survey Receptive Language scale improved from 94 to 102, an increase of one-half standard deviation. A parallel qualitative study carried out in Boston examined patterns of book reading before, during, and at the end of the use of two units of the curriculum. Dramatic increases in the amount of talk about the meanings of words and analytic discussion of the stories were found, with these changes reflecting teachers' use of the guidance provided by the curriculum. These hopeful early findings suggest that strong preschool curricula may substantially boost children's achievement, especially when combined with strong professional development.

Policy

A rapid paradigm shift has been occurring at the highest levels of the early childhood world. In the 1980s policies and statements issued by the leading early childhood organization, the National Association for the Education of Young Children (NAEYC), reflected considerable distrust of literacy (Dickinson, 2002), but by the late 1990s NAEYC released a joint position statement with the International Reading Association that drew on the most current research on literacy development (International Reading Association & National Association for the Education of Young Children, 1998). Further, the new accreditation standards call for considerably enhanced quality with respect to literacy and content learning more generally. Such significant changes in policy cannot help but elevate the value accorded instructional practices that support literacy and content instruction.

Concluding Thoughts

Over the past 30 years we have come to clear recognition of the serious gap in educational achievement between the haves and have-nots of society and are increasingly recognizing the early genesis of this gap. Vigorous research has brought increasing insight into complex pathways of different aspects of development; in the coming decades we are likely to arrive at a far better understanding of the complex intertwined nature of development, especially as we investigate the interactions among different domains. When literacy is viewed as the organization of complex interacting systems, it becomes clear that we need research and theories that consider changes in the interdependencies among domains and efforts to understand the malleability of different aspects at different points of development. Given what we now know, it appears that the later preschool years are one period during which the window to the development of language-related competencies is wide open. Biological findings combine with psychological research to provide social policy with abundant evidence about the sensitivity of preschool-age children to intervention. We need to seize the opportunity to intervene in the lives of children from families that are in need of significant assistance from the educational systems in nourishing their children's language and intellectual development.

Unfortunately, powerful forces have created and continue to sustain an early childhood educational system that is falling short of providing the kind of support children from low-income backgrounds require. We briefly sketched some of the efforts being made to turn the tide in favor of children at risk of educational failure. Although it is important to note hopeful directions, we must temper optimism with caution born of recognition of the array of factors that some families must confront. Too many parents are either unemployed or underemployed, with the result being limited income and stress that contributes to depression that can undermine the type of responsive parenting shown to be critical to establishing strong early bonds (see Landry & Smith, Chapter 10, and Pianta, Chapter 11, this volume). Parents in the types of jobs available to adults with limited incomes may lack the kind of job-related stimulation that seems to enrich household interactions (Leseman & van Tuijl, Chapter 16, this volume). Furthermore, families with limited incomes must live in communities in which access to print and support for learning are limited (Neuman, Chapter 2, and Britto, Fuligni, & Brooks-Gunn, Chapter 23, this volume). The community child care that such families find near them is likely to be staffed by teachers drawn from the community who have limited education and a history of limited access to the type of wide-ranging knowledge about the world that the children they serve need (Neuman, Chapter 2, this volume). These programs may be barely managing to make ends meet and, as a result, may have few books and other supplies to support learning, no funds for professional development, and little ability to allow teachers release time to attend workshops or take courses.

The challenges some families face as they seek to prepare their children for success in school are truly daunting. Our society is slowly beginning to recognize the costs it pays for failing to adequately respond to the needs of such families. On our side is the fact that we typically organize preschools and kindergarten in a fashion that allows for the kind of individualized one-to-one and small-group adult–child interactions that have great potential for nourishing language and intellectual development. In such settings, children have the potential to make remarkable progress if they are taught by energetic and sensitive teachers who understand language, as well as cognitive and emotional, development. We are making hopeful advances in our endeavor to enrich the preschool experiences of children, but far more must be done to improve their classrooms and communities if we are to take full advantage of the window of educational opportunity provided us by biology.

References

Adams, M. J. (1990). *Beginning to read*. Cambridge, MA: MIT Press.

Alexander, K. L., & Entwistle, D. R. (1988). Achievement in the first two years of school: Patterns and processes. *Monographs of the Society* for *Research in Child Development, 53* (2, Serial No. 218).

Arnold, D. S., & Whitehurst, G. J. (1994). Accelerating language development through picture book reading: A summary of dialogic reading and its effects. In D. K. Dickinson (Ed.), *Bridges to literacy: Approaches to supporting child and family literacy* (pp. 103–128). Cambridge, MA: Blackwell.

Ball, E. W., & Blachman, B. A. (1991). Does phoneme segmentation in kindergarten make a difference in early word recognition and developmental spelling? *Reading Research Quarterly, 26,* 49–66.

Baumeister, R. F., & Vohs, K. D. (Eds.). (2004). *Handbook of self-regulation: Research, theory, and applications.* New York: Guilford Press.

Beals, D. B. (2001). Eating and reading: Links between family conversations with preschoolers and later language and literacy. In D. K. Dickinson & P. O. Tabors (Eds.), *Beginning literacy with language: Young children learning at home and school* (pp. 75–92). Baltimore: Brookes.

Biemiller, A. (1999). *Language and reading success.* Cambridge, MA: Brookline Books.

Birch, S. H., & Ladd, G. W. (1998). Children's interpersonal behaviors and the teacher–child relationship. *Developmental Psychology, 34,* 934–946.

Bishop, D. V. M., & Adams, C. (1990). A prospective study of the relationship between specific language impairment, phonological disorders and reading retardation. *Journal of Child Psychology and Psychiatry and Allied Disciplines, 31,* 1027–1050.

Bishop, D. V. M., & Edmundson, A. (1987). Language-impaired 4-year-olds: Distinguishing transient from persistent impairment. *Journal of Speech and Hearing Disorders, 52,* 156–173.

Black, J. E. (2003). Environment and development of the nervous system. In M. Gallagher & R. J. Nelson (Eds.), *Handbook of psychology: Vol. 3. Biological psychology* (pp. 655–668). New York: Wiley.

Blair, C. (2002). School readiness: Integrating cognition and emotion in a neurobiological conceptualization of children's functioning at school entry. *American Psychologist, 57,* 111–127.

Bryant, P. E., MacLean, M., & Bradley, L. L. (1990). Rhyme, language, and children's reading. *Applied Psycholinguistics, 11,* 237–252.

Butler, S. R., Marsh, H. W., Sheppard, M. J., & Sheppard, J. L. (1985). Seven-year longitudinal study of early prediction of reading achievement. *Journal of Educational Psychology, 77,* 349–361.

Chall, J., & Dale, P. S. (1995). *Readability revisited: The new Dale–Chall readability formula.* Brookline, MA: Brookline Books.

Cole, P. M., Teti, L. O., & Zahn-Waxler, C. (2003). Mutual emotion regulation and the stability of conduct problems between preschool and early school age. *Developmental Psychopathology, 15,* 1–18.

Cole, P. M., Zahn-Waxler, C., Fox, N. A., Usher, B. A., & Welsh, J. D. (1996). Individual differences in emotion regulation and behavior problems in preschool children. *Journal of Abnormal Psychology, 105,* 518–529.

Cunningham, A. E., & Stanovich, K. E. (1997). Early reading acquisition and its relation to reading experience and ability 10 years later. *Developmental Psychology, 33*(6), 934–945.

Denham, S. A., Blair, K. A., DeMulder, E., Levitas, J., Sawyer, K., Auerback-Major, S. & Queenan, P. (2003). Preschool emotional competence: Pathway to social competence. *Child Development, 74,* 238–256.

Davidson, R. J., Scherer, K. R., & Goldsmith, H. H. (2003). *Handbook of affective sciences.* London: Oxford University Press.

Dickinson, D. K. (1987). Oral language, literacy skills and response to literature. In J. Squire (Ed.), *The dynamics of language learning: Research in the language arts* (pp. 147–183). Urbana, IL: National Council of Teachers in English.

Dickinson, D. K. (2001a). Large-group and free-play times: Conversational settings supporting language and literacy development. In D. K. Dickinson & P. O. Tabors (Eds.), *Beginning literacy with language: Young children learning at home and school* (pp. 223–255). Baltimore: Brookes.

Dickinson, D. K. (2001b). Putting the pieces together: The impact of preschool on children's language and literacy development in kindergarten. In D. K. Dickinson & P. O. Tabors (Eds.), *Beginning literacy with language: Young children learning at home and school* (pp. 257–287). Baltimore: Brookes.

Dickinson, D. K. (2002). Shifting images of developmentally appropriate practice as seen through different lenses. *Educational Researcher, 31*(1), 26–32.

Dickinson, D. K., Anastasopoulos, L., Miller, C. M., Caswell, L., & Peisner-Feinberg, E. (2002, June). *Enhancing preschool children's language, literacy and social development through an in-service professional development approach.* Paper presented at the Annual Conference of the American Education Research Association, New Orleans.

Dickinson, D. K., Miller, C. M., & Anastasopoulos, L. (2001a, April). *The impact of an in-service intervention with Head Start teachers and supervisors on children's language, literacy and social development.* Paper presented at the annual conference of the Society for Research in Child Development, Minneapolis, MN.

Dickinson, D. K., & Brady, J. (in press). Toward effective support for language an dliteracy through professional development: A decade of experiences and data. In M. Zaslow & I. Martinez-Beck (Eds.), *Critical issues in early childhood professional development.* Baltimore: Brookes.

Dickinson, D. K., & McCabe, A. (2001). Bringing it all together: The multiple origins, skills and environmental supports of early literacy. *Learning Disabilities Research and Practice, 16*(4), 186–202.

Dickinson, D. K., & McCabe, A. (2003). A framework for examining book reading in early childhood classrooms. In A. van Kleeck, E. B. Bauer, & S. Stahl (Eds.), *On reading books to children: Parents and teachers* (pp. 95–113). Hillsdale, NJ: Erlbaum.

Dickinson, D. K., McCabe, A., & Anastasopoulos, L. (2002). *A framework for examining book reading in early childhood classrooms* (No. 1-014).

Dickinson, D. K., McCabe, A., Anastasopoulos, L., Peisner-Feinberg, E., & Poe, M. D. (2003). The comprehensive language approach to early literacy: The interrelationships among vocabulary, phonological sensitivity, and print knowledge among preschool-aged children. *Journal of Educational Psychology, 95*(3), 465–481.

Dickinson, D. K., McCabe, A., & Clark-Chiarelli, N. (2004). Preschool-based prevention of reading disability: Realities vs. possibilities. In C. A. Stone, E. R. Silliman, B. J. Ehren, & K. Apel (Eds.), *Handbook of language and literacy: Development and disorders* (pp. 209–227). Hillsdale, NJ: Erlbaum.

Dickinson, D.K. & Porche, M. (2005, April 8). *Long-term effects of preschool classroom interactions on the language and literacy skills of low-income children.* In D. K. Dickinson (Chair) *The Impact of Global and Specific Aspects of Input on Language Learning.* Biannual conference of the Society for Research in Child Development, Atlanta, GA.

Dickinson, D. K., & Brady, J. B. (2005). Toward effective support for language and literacy through professional development: A decade of experiences and data. In M. Zaslow (Ed.), *Professional development challenges in preschool settings.* Baltimore: Brookes.

Dickinson, D. K., & Smith, M. W. (1994). Long-term effects of preschool teachers' book readings on low-income children's vocabulary and story comprehension. *Reading Research Quarterly, 29*(2), 104–122.

Dickinson, D. K., Sprague, K., Sayer, A., Miller, C. M., & Clark, N. (2001, April). *A multilevel analysis of the effects of early home and preschool environments on children's language and early literacy development.* Paper presented at the biannual conference of the Society for Research in Child Development, Minneapolis, MN.

Dickinson, D. K., & Tabors, P. O. (Eds.). (2001). *Beginning literacy with language: Young children learning at home and school.* Baltimore: Brookes.

Dionne, G., Tremblay, R., Boivin, M., Laplante, D., & Perusse, D. (2003). Physical aggression and expressive vocabulary in 19-month-old twins. *Developmental Psychology, 39*(2), 261–273.

Dumas, J. E., Blechman, E. A., & Prinz, R. J. (1994). Aggressive and effective communication. *Aggressive Behavior, 20*(5), 347–358.

Ehri, L. C., Nunes, S. R., Willows, D. M., Schuster, B. V., Yaghoub-Zadeh, Z., & Shanahan, T. (2001). Phonemic awareness instruction helps children learn to read: Evidence from the National Reading Panel's meta-analysis. *Reading Research Quarterly, 36,* 250–287.

Eisenberg, N., Fabes, R. A., Guthrie, I. K., Murphy, B. C., et al. (1996). The relations of regulation and emotionality to problem behavior in elementary school children. *Development and Psychopathology, 8,* 141–162.

Eisenberg, N., Fabes, R. A., Guthrie, I. K., & Reiser, M. (2000). Dispositional emotionality and regulation: Their role in predicting quality of social functioning. *Journal of Personality and Social Psychology, 78,* 136–157.

Eisenberg, N., Fabes, R. A., Murphy, B., Maszk, P., Smith, M., & Karbon, M. (1995). The role of emotionality and regulation in children's social functioning: A longitudinal study. *Child Development, 66,* 1360–1384.

Essex, M. J., Boyce, W. T., Goldstein, L. H., Armstrong, J. M., Kraemer, H. C., & Kupfer, D. J. (2002). The confluence of mental, physical, social and academic difficulties in middle childhood: II. Developing the MacArthur Mental Health and Behavior Questionnaire. *Journal of the American Academy of Child and Adolescent Psychiatry, 41,* 588–603.

Essex, M. J., Klein, M. H., Cho, E., & Kalin, N. H. (2002). Maternal stress beginning in infancy may sensitize children to later stress exposure: Effects on cortisol and behavior. *Biological Psychiatry, 52,* 776–784.

Fabes, R. A., Eisenberg, N., Jones, S., Smith, M., Guthrie, I. K., Poulin, R., et al. (1999). Regulation, emotionality, and preschoolers' socially competent peer interactions. *Child Development, 70,* 432–442.

Fazio, B. B., Naremore, R. C., & Connell, P. J. (1996). Tracking children from poverty at risk for specific language impairment: A 3-year longitudinal study. *Journal of Speech and Hearing Research, 39,* 611–624.

Feagans, L., & Applebaum, M. I. (1986). Validation of language subtypes in learning disabled children. *Journal of Experimental Psychology, 78,* 358–364.

Ford, D. H., & Lerner, R. M. (1992). *Developmental systems theory: An integrative approach.* Newbury Park, CA: Sage.

Fujiki, M., & Brinton, B. (1994). Social competence and language impairment in children. In R. V. Watkins & M. L. Rice (Eds.), *Specific language impairments in children* (pp. 123–144). Baltimore: Brookes.

Fujiki, M., Brinton, B., & Clarke, D. (2002). Emotion regulation in children with specific language impairment. *Language, Speech, & Hearing Services in Schools, 33*, 102–111.

Gertner, B. L., Rice, M. L., & Hadley, P. A. (1994). Influence of communicative competence on peer preferences in a preschool classroom. *Journal of Speech and Hearing Research, 37*(4), 913–923.

Good, R. H., Simmons, D.C., & Smith, S.B. (1998). Effective academic interventions in the United States: Evaluating and enhancing the acquisition of early reading skills. *Educational and Child Psychology, 15*(1), 56–70.

Granger, D. A., Stansbury, K., & Henker, B. (1994). Preschoolers' behavioral and neuroendocrine responses to social challenge. *Meriill-Palmer Quarterly, 40*, 190–211.

Gunnar, M. R., Tout, K., de Haan, M, Pierce, S., et al. (1997). Temperament, social competence, and adrenocortical activity in preschoolers. *Developmental Psychobiology, 31*, 65–85.

Hamre, B. K., & Pianta, R. C. (2001). Early teacher-child relationships and the trajectory of children's school outcomes through eighth grade. *Child Development, 72*, 625–638.

Hart, B., & Risley, T. (1995). *Meaningful differences in the everyday lives of American children*. Baltimore: Brookes.

Hinshaw, S. P. (2002). Preadolescent girls with attention-deficit/hyperactivity disorder: I. Background characteristics, comorbidity, cognitive and social functioning, and parenting practices. *Journal of Consulting and Clinical Psychology, 70*, 1086–1098.

Hinshaw, S. P., Carte, E. T., Sami, N., Treuting, J. J., & Zupan, B. A. (2002). Preadolescent girls with attention-deficit/hyperactivity disorder: II. Neuropsychological performance in relation to subtypes and individual classification. *Journal of Consulting and Clinical Psychology, 70*, 1099–1111.

Hooper, S. R., Roberts, J. E., Zeisel, S. A., & Poe, M. (2003). Core language predictors of behavioral functioning in early elementary school children: Concurrent and longitudinal findings. *Behavioral Disorders, 29*, 10–24.

Howse, R. B., Calkins, S. D., Anastopoulos, A. D., Keane, S. P., & Shelton, T. L. (2003). Regulatory contributors to children's kindergarten achievement. *Early Education and Development, 14*, 101–119.

Huttenlocher, J., Vasilyeva, M., Cymerman, E., & Levine, S. (2002). Language input and child syntax. *Cognitive Psychology, 45*, 337–375.

Huttenlocher, P. R. (2002). *Neural plasticity: The effects of environment on the development of the cerebral cortex*. Cambridge, MA: Harvard University Press.

International Reading Association and National Association for the Education of Young Children. (1998). *Learning to read and write: Develop-mentally appropriate practices for young children. Young Children, 53*, 3–46.

Juel, C. (1988). Learning to read and write: A longitudinal study of 54 children from first through fourth grade. *Journal of Educational Psychology, 80*, 437–447.

Keogh, B. K. (2003). *Temperament in the classrooms: Understanding individual differences*. Baltimore, MD: Brookes.

Kochanska, G., Coy, K. C., & Murray, K. T. (2001). The development of self-regulation in the first four years of life. *Child Development, 72*, 1091–1111.

Kochanska, G., Murray, K. T., & Harlan, E. T. (2000). Effortful control in early childhood: Continuity and change, antecedents, and implications for social development. *Developmental Psychology, 36*, 220–232.

Kochanska, G., Murray, K. T., Jacques, T. Y., Koenig, A. L., et al. (1996). Inhibitory control in young children and its role in emerging internalization. *Child Development, 67*, 490–507.

Kontos, S. J., & Wilcox-Herzog, A. (1997). Influences on children's competence in early childhood classrooms. *Early Childhood Research Quarterly, 12*, 247–262.

Ladd, G. W., Birch, S. H., & Buhs, E. S. (1999). Children's social and scholastic lives in kindergarten: Related spheres of influence? *Child Development, 70*, 1373–1400.

Layzer, J. I., Goodson, B. D., & Moss, M. (1993). *Life in preschool: Vol. 1. Final report to the U.S. Department of Education*. Cambridge, MA: Abt Associates.

Lonigan, C. J., Burgess, S. R., & Anthony, J. L. (2000). Development of emergent literacy and early reading skills in preschool children: Evidence from a latent-variable longitudinal study. *Developmental Psychology, 36*(5), 506–613.

Lonigan, C. J., Burgess, S. R., Anthony, J. L., & Barker, T. A. (1998). Development of phonological sensitivity in 2- to 5-year-old children. *Journal of Educational Psychology, 90*, 294–311.

Lupien, S. J., King, S., Meaney, M. L., & McEwen, B. S. (2000). Child's stress hormone levels correlate with mother's socioeconomic status and depressive state. *Biological Psychiatry, 48*, 976–980.

Lupien, S. J., King, S., Meaney, M. J., & McEwen, B. S. (2001). Can poverty get under your skin? Basal cortisol levels and cognitive function in children from low and high socioeconomic status. *Development and Psychopathology, 13*, 653–676.

MacLean, M., Bryant, D. M., & Bradley, L. L. (1987). Rhymes, nursery rhymes, and reading in early childhood. *Merrill-Palmer Quarterly, 33*, 255–282.

McCartney, K. (1984). Effect of quality day care environment on children's language development. *Developmental Psychology, 20*, 244–260.

McGee, R., Share, D., Moffitt, T. E., Williams, S., &

Silva, P. A. (1998). Reading disability, behavior problems and juvenile delinquency. In D. H. Saklofske & S. B. G. Eysenck (Eds.), *Individual differences in children and adolescents* (pp. 158–172). New Brunswick, NJ: Transaction.

McGill-Franzen, A., & Allington, R. L. (1991). The gridlock of low reading achievement: Perspectives on practice and policy. *Remedial and Special Education, 12*(3), 20–30.

McGuinness, D., McGuinness, C., & Donohue, J. (1995). Phonological training and the alphabet principle: Evidence of reciprocal causality. *Reading Research Quarterly, 30,* 830–852.

Meehan, B. T., Hughes, J. N., & Cavell, T. A. (2003). Teacher–student relationships as compensatory resources for aggressive children. *Child Development, 74,* 1145–1157.

Menyuk, P., Chesnick, J., Liebergott, J. W., Korngold, B., D'Agostino, R., & Belanger, A. (1991). Predicting reading problems in at-risk children. *Journal of Speech and Hearing Research, 34,* 893–903.

Miech, R. A., Essex, M. J., & Goldsmith, H. H. (2001). Socioeconomic status and the adjustment to school: The role of self-regulation during early childhood. *Sociology of Education, 74,* 102–120.

Miller, A. L., Gouley, K. K., Seifer, R. E., Dickstein, S. E., & Shields, A. (2004). Emotions and behaviors in the Head Start classroom: Associations among observed dysregulation, social competence, and preschool adjustment. *Early Education and Development, 15,* 147–165.

Moffitt, T. E., & Caspi, A. (2001). Childhood predictors differentiate life-course persistent and adolescence-limited antisocial pathways among males and females. *Development and Psychopathology, 13,* 355–375.

Murray, K. T., & Kochanska, G. (2002). Effortful control: Factor structure and relation to externalizing and internalizing behaviors. *Journal of Abnormal Child Psychology, 30,* 503–514.

Nelson, C. A., & Bloom, F. E. (1997). Child development and neuroscience. *Child Developoment, 68,* 970–987.

Nelson, K. (1996). *Language in cognitive development: The emergence of the mediated mind.* New York: Cambridge University Press.

Pallas, A. M., Entwisle, D. R., & Cadigan, D. (1987). Children who do exceptionally well in first grade. *Sociology of Education, 60,* 256–271.

Park, J. H., Essex, M. J., Zahn-Waxler, C., Armstrong, J. M., Klein, M. H., & Goldsmith, H. H. (in press). Relational and overt aggression in middle childhood: Early child and family risk factors. *Early Education and Development.*

Pianta, R. (1999). *Enhancing relationships between children and teachers.* Washington, DC: American Psychological Association.

Pianta, R. C., Hamre, B., & Stuhlman, M. (2002). Relationships between teachers and children. In G. E. Miller (Ed.), *Comprehensive handbook of psychology* (Vol. 7). New York: Wiley.

Pianta, R. C., Steinberg, M. S., & Rollins, K. B. (1995). The first two years of school: Teacher-child relationships and deflections in children's classroom adjustment. *Development and Psychopathology, 7,* 295–312.

Quartz, S., & Sejnowski, T. J. (1997). The neural basis of cognitive development: A constructivist manifesto. *Behavioral and Brain Sciences, 20,* 537–596.

Rothbart, M. K., Ellis, L. K., Rueda, M., & Posner, M. I. (2003). Developing mechanisms of temperamental effortful control. *Journal of Personality, 71,* 1113–1143.

Saarni, C. (1999). *The development of emotional competence.* New York: Guilford Press.

Scarborough, H. S. (1989). Prediction of reading dysfunction from familial and individual differences. *Journal of Educational Psychology, 81,* 101–108.

Scarborough, H. S. (2001). Connecting early language and literacy to later reading (dis)abilities. In S. B. Neuman & D. K. Dickinson (Eds.), *Handbook of early literacy research* (pp. 97–110). New York: Guilford Press.

Schickedanz, J. & Dickinson, D. (2005). *Opening the World of Learning: A Comprehensive Early Literacy Program.* Parsippany, NJ: Pearson Early Learning.

Schmidt, L. A., Fox, N. A., Rubin, K. H., & Sternberg, E. M. (1997). Behavioral and neuroendocrine responses in shy children. *Developmental Psychobiology, 30,* 127–140.

Schmidt, L. A., Fox, N. A., Sternberg, E. M., Gold, P. W., Smith, C. C., & Schulkin, J. (1999). Adrenocortical reactivity and social competence in seven year-olds. *Personality and Individual Differences, 26,* 977–985.

Share, D. L., Jorm, A., Maclean, R., & Matthews, R. (1984). Sources of individual differences in reading achievement. *Journal of Educational Psychology, 76,* 1309–1324.

Shonkoff, J. P., & Phillips, D. A. (Eds.). (2000). *From neurons to neighborhoods: The science of early childhood development.* Washington, DC: National Academy Press.

Smider, N. A., Essex, M. J., Klain, N. H., Buss, K. A., et al. (2002). Salivary cortisol as a predictor of socioemotional adjustment during kindergarten: A prospective study. *Child Development, 73,* 75–92.

Snow, C. E., & Dickinson, D. K. (1991). Skills that aren't basic in a new conception of literacy. In A. C. Purves & E. Jennings (Eds.), *Literate systems and individual lives: Perspectives on literacy and school* (pp. 179–192). Albany, NY: State University of New York Press.

Stanovich, K. E. (1992). Speculations on the causes and consequences of individual differences in early reading acquisition. In P. B. Gough, L. C. Ehri, & R. Treiman (Eds.), *Reading acquisition* (pp. 307–342). Hillsdale, NJ: Erlbaum.

Storch, S. A., & Whitehurst, G. J. (2002). Oral language and code-related precursors to reading: Evidence from a longitudinal structural model. *Developmental Psychology, 38,* 934–947.

Strickland, D. S. (2001). Early intervention for African American children considered to be at risk. In S. B. Neuman & D. K. Dickinson (Eds.), *Handbook of early literacy research* (pp. 322–332). New York: Guilford Press.

Tabors, P. O., Porche, M. V., & Ross, S. J. (2003, April). Predicting reading comprehension in a low-income sample: Longitudinal findings from preschool to 7th grade. In K. Cain & J. Oakhill (Chairs), *Longitudinal studies of comprehension skill.* Symposium presented at the biennial meetings of the Society for Research in Child Development, Tampa, FL.

Tabors, P. O., Roach, K. A., & Snow, C. E. (2001). Home language and literacy environment: Final results. In D. K. Dickinson & P. O. Tabors (Eds.), *Beginning literacy with language: Young children learning at home and school* (pp. 111–138). Baltimore: Brookes.

Tabors, P. O., Snow, C. E., & Dickinson, D. K. (2001). Homes and schools together: Supporting language and literacy development. In D. K. Dickinson & P. O. Tabors (Eds.), *Beginning literacy with language: Young children learning at home and school* (pp. 313–334). Baltimore: Brookes.

Tarullo, L. B., & Zill, N. (2002, May). *FACES: An assessment battery to track children's cognitive development in Head Start and early elementary school.* Paper presented at the NICHD Workshop on Cognitive Development Measures for Large-Scale Studies, Washington, DC.

Tizard, B., & Hughes, M. (1985). *Young children learning.* Cambridge, MA: Harvard University Press.

Tomasello, M. (2000). *The cultural origins of human cognition.* Cambridge, MA: Harvard University Press.

Vellutino, F. R., & Scanlon, D. M. (2001). Emergent literacy skills, early instruction, and individual differences as determinants of difficulties in learning to read: The case for early intervention. In S. B. Neuman & D. K. Dickinson (Eds.), *Handbook of early literacy research* (pp. 295–321). New York: Guilford Press.

Vernon-Feagans, L., Hammer, C. S., Miccio, A., & Manlove, E. (2001). Early language and literacy skills in low-income African American and Hispanic children. In S. B. Neuman & D. K. Dickinson (Eds.), *Handbook of early literacy research* (pp. 192–210). New York: Guilford Press.

Wagner, R. K., & Torgesen, J. K. (1987). The nature of phonological processing and its causal role in the acquisition of reading skills. *Psychological Bulletin, 101,* 192–212.

Wagner, R. K., Torgesen, J. K., Rashotte, C. A., Hecht, S. A., Barker, T. A., and Burgess, S. R., et al. (1997). Changing relations between phonological processing abilities and word-level reading as children develop from beginning to skilled readers: A 5-year longitudinal study. *Developmental Psychology, 33,* 468–479.

Walker, D., Greenwood, C., Hart, B., & Carta, J. (1994). Prediction of school outcomes based on early language production and socioeconomic factors. *Child Development, 65,* 606–621.

Wasik, B. A., & Bond, M. A. (2001). Beyond the pages of a book: Interactive book reading and language development in preschool. *Journal of Educational Psychology, 93*(2), 243–250.

Whitehurst, G. J., & Lonigan, C. J. (1998). Child development and emergent literacy. *Child Development, 69*(3), 848–872.

Whitehurst, G. J., & Lonigan, C. J. (2001). Emergent literacy: Development from prereaders to readers. In S. B. Neuman & D. K. Dickinson (Eds.), *Handbook of early literacy research* (pp. 11–29). New York: Guilford Press.

2

The Knowledge Gap:
Implications for Early Education

SUSAN B. NEUMAN

Today, the United States is experiencing an almost unprecedented sharp increase in economic inequality (Browning, 2003). Wealth distribution—the differences between low-income families and middle- and upper-income families, or the so-called haves and have-nots—is greater now than at any other time in our history since 1929 (Gaziano, 1997). And the ramifications of such income differentials are significant and have far-reaching effects, not only for the earliest years of children's literacy development but also throughout their lifetimes.

This chapter examines the impact of economic disparities on children's beginning experiences with print (see also Britto, Fuligni, & Brooks-Gunn, Chapter 23, this volume). It argues that, in addition to skill delays, differences in socioeconomic circumstances lead to knowledge delays, which, if not addressed in the early years, may lead to a growing knowledge gap. Potentially far more detrimental than achievement score differences, this gap has been shown to relate to social mobility limitations, health and safety problems, anomie, and lack of civic participation (Viswanath & Finnegan, 1996). Consequently, in efforts to prepare children to learn to read, it is crucial to recognize the important role of knowledge in early literacy (Neuman, 2001) and to better balance skill development with conceptual knowledge development. To make this argu-

ment, I first review the concomitants of poverty conditions for children's early literacy development, then describe its implications on increasing knowledge differentials between the "information haves" and the "information have-nots." I end with a set of recommendations for enhancing content knowledge in the early years.

The Economic Gap in Cognitive Skills

America's poor children do not fare well in our society. If you are born poor, you are likely to stay poor. In fact, about 70% of Americans stay in the same social class in which they are born. Children of poorly educated parents make up just 2% of the professional and managerial class (Kahlenberg, 2001). And, more often than not, schools tend to perpetuate the status quo rather than change it. As Juel and colleagues' now-classic study (Juel, Griffith, & Gough, 1986) reports, the probability of a poor reader at the end of grade 1 remaining a poor reader at the end of grade 4 is .88.

Poverty takes no prisoners. When families suffer unemployment, especially in the long term, children's cognitive development tends to suffer (Corcoran & Chaudry, 1997). Disadvantaged children have more hearing problems, ear infections, dental problems, lead exposure, poor nutrition, asthma, and poor housing (Rothstein, 2004). These conditions appear to be far more pernicious for children in the early years of development than in the later adolescent years, shaping children's ability and achievement when cognitive connections are forming (Duncan & Brooks-Gunn, 1997).

Familial processes that may account for poverty taking such a toll on children's cognitive processes have been explained through two major pathways (Foster, 2002). One pathway by which poverty affects children is through its impact on the family's ability to invest in resources related to children's development. Income enables families to purchase lessons, summer camps, stimulating learning materials and activities, and better quality early childhood care. Entwisle and colleagues (Entwisle, Alexander, & Olson, 1997) suggest that these out-of-school experiences are key factors that differentiate low-income from middle-income achievement and that contribute significantly to maintaining, rather than reducing, the achievement gap. A second pathway through which poverty shapes development is that it affects parents' emotional resources, their well-being, and their interactions with children, which in turn are related to child outcomes. McLoyd and her colleagues (McLoyd, 1990), for example, have shown the impact of economic hardship on depression, diminishing parents' abilities to interact and provide warmth and responsive parenting. Taken together, with few material and emotional resources, it is hardly surprising that hundreds of studies (Jencks & Phillips, 1998) have now documented the dramatic, linear, negative relationships between poverty and children's cognitive-developmental outcomes.

These relationships translate into large differences in readiness skills between low-income children and their more middle- to upper-class peers. Before even entering kindergarten, differences in cognitive skills between high-status and low-status children, according to a large-scale study of entering kindergartners (Lee & Burkam, 2002) is, on average, 60%. Other studies (Denton, West, & Waltston, 2003; Vellutino et al., 1996), as well, have documented large differences in children's receptive and expressive language skills; in children's ability to identify beginning sounds and letters, colors, and numbers; and in the number of words they have

been exposed to prior to entering kindergarten (Hart & Risley, 2003; see Table 2.1).

But perhaps even more serious than skill deficiencies are knowledge deficiencies that arise for children who have limited access to the informal informational lessons that can be transmitted through day-to-day interactions. Although a significant amount of research has focused on differences in early language learning (McCardle & Chhabra, 2004), in vocabulary, and phonemic awareness and how they might be acquired, there has been relatively little discussion of differences among children in content knowledge and its relationship to achievement. However, as much of the early childhood community has recognized (Bredekamp & Copple, 1997; Neuman, Copple, & Bredekamp, 2000), skill development apart from meaningful content has limited usefulness or staying power for the young child. Further, indications are that limited content knowledge might ultimately account for what appear to be comprehension difficulties (Vellutino et al., 1996) or higher order thinking difficulties in older children. Therefore, if children's developing conceptual knowledge becomes subordinated to a focus on the relatively small number of necessary procedural skills early on, then the gap between socioeconomic status groups may widen with each

TABLE 2.1. Beginning Kindergarten Students' School Readiness Skills by Socioeconomic Status

	Lowest SES	Highest SES
Recognizing letters of alphabet	39%	85%
Identifying beginning sounds of words	10%	51%
Identifying primary colors	69%	90%
Counting to 20	48%	68%
Writing own name	54%	76%
Amount of time read to prior to kindergarten[a]	25 hours	1,000 hours
Accumulated experience with words[b]	13 million words	45 million words

Note. Adapted from Lee and Burkham (2002). Copyright 2002 by Economic Policy Institute. Adapted by permission.
[a]Adams (1990).
[b]Hart and Risley (1995).

successive grade level, building to insurmountable gaps after just a few years of schooling.

The Knowledge Gap and Its Beginnings

The knowledge gap is rooted in the two pathways (Corcoran & Chaudry, 1997) described previously that separate children from poverty and their middle- and upper-income peers. The first is material resources (Duncan & Brooks-Gunn, 1997). Poor families, unlike their more middle-class counterparts, are likely to lack resources associated with knowledge acquisition. The prime resources for learning are books and reading materials such as newspapers and magazines. Studies (Cunningham & Stanovich, 1998; West & Stanovich, 1991) suggest that print is associated with knowledge acquisition, greater variety of vocabulary, and abstract reasoning. Yet poor communities, despite their eagerness for print resources, often lack the disposable income to afford them (Neuman, Celano, Greco, & Shue, 2001). Further, print resources tend to be scarce in poor communities. Our analysis of four neighborhoods (Neuman & Celano, 2001), for example, provided a striking example of the differences in resources for low- and middle-income families. Examining four neighborhoods, two poor and two middle-income, we found stark and triangulated differences in access to materials between poor and middle-income neighborhoods: Whereas children in the middle-income neighborhoods had multiple opportunities to observe, use, and purchase books (estimated at about 13 titles per individual child), few such occasions were available for low-income children (estimated to be about 1 book for every 300 children). Further, other avenues of access were limited or lacking. School libraries in poor communities were closed and sometimes boarded up, unlike school libraries in middle-income neighborhoods, which were thriving, with approximately 12 books available per child. Public libraries were open only for brief hours in low-income neighborhoods, compared with many open hours in middle-income neighborhoods. Child-care arrangements, including family and group care, also provided limited access to books.

In a national survey of over 300 centers (Neuman et al., 2001), we found on average fewer than one to two books available per child; of those books, the majority were of mediocre or poor quality.

With limited access to print materials and to opportunities for learning, the second pathway is significantly curtailed. This pathway relates to the quality of the home environment (Neuman et al., 1998; Neuman & Gallagher, 1994) and mother–child interactions concerning stimulating activities and learning opportunities. Without opportunities to be read to, children have less experience with new, different, and more sophisticated vocabulary outside of their day-to-day encounters; they are less likely to learn about their world and to hear decontextualized language, the beginnings of abstracting information from print. And, as Stanovich (1980), in his now-classic model of the Matthew effect, posits, differences in these early opportunities become magnified over time so that less-skilled children coming to school have fewer interactions with text than their more skilled peers. Such unrewarding experiences in reading multiply, with the consequences being that children attend less to the comprehensibility of reading, and its purposes and potential usefulness.

As research on social class and parenting styles suggests (Lareau, 1989), patterns of mother–child interaction over print, their use of the reading experience to provide stimulating experiences for children, tend to carry over into other activities as well. In her study of social class and parenting styles, for example, Lareau (2002) reported how middle-class parents appeared to conform to a cultural logic of childrearing, defined as concerted cultivation, that viewed their parenting role as transmitting important skills and information to children. When the children were not attending child care, parents engaged them in numerous age-specific activities, all designed to develop their talents and interests. Given their superior levels of education, middle-class parents could converse easily with other professionals, discuss key terms, and describe their meanings with their child. In contrast, poor families, feeling the pressures of economic shortages and the sheer drudgery of low-level work, had limited energies for interaction. Children participated in few organized activities; given more free time, they interacted with relatives rather than acquaintances, creating a language barrier and a thicker divide between families and the outside world. Baumrind (1966, 1968), as well as Hart and Risley (1995), provided ample documentation of the different interactional patterns between low-income parents and their young children. Parents tend to be more authoritarian, and offer fewer explanations and more directives. As a result, they tend to talk less, provide less encouragement to explore, and expose children to fewer new words and concepts.

Child-care arrangements, unfortunately, offer only a limited safety net (Dickinson & McCabe, 2003; Dickinson, McCabe, & Clark-Chiarelli, 2004; see also Farran, Aydogan, Kang, & Lipsey, Chapter 19, this volume). Recent studies (Helburn & Bergmann, 2002; Peisner-Feinberg et al., 1999) indicate dramatic variations in quality of child care, with infant and toddler care being particularly poor and underfunded. Although many children are able to take advantage of good-quality early education in Head Start, rarely do poor children—those who need the very highest quality programs—receive the cognitively stimulating content and curriculum they need. Too often, programs for the poor are, unfortunately, poor programs.

Consequently, striking differences in material resources and in the quality of the home environment, as expressed by parents' interactions, their skills, habits, and styles, begin to define what children are taught, and what is modeled and reinforced in these very early years, just when cognitive connections are forming. And these differences are the key to understanding the beginnings of the social stratification of knowledge, which, if not quickly overcome, grows ever larger with each successive year.

Schemas: The Building Blocks of Knowledge

Children's earliest experiences become organized or structured into schemas, defined by Rumelhart (1980) as the "building blocks of cognition." Schemas provide children with the conceptual apparatus for making sense of the world around them by classifying these incoming bits of information into similar groupings (Duchan, 2004). Stein and Glenn (1979), for example, provide a compelling case for schemas and their usefulness for recalling information about stories. They found that well-read-to children internalized a form of story grammar, which aided in understanding and retelling simple stories. Similarly, schemas have been shown to aid in remembering, recalling, and classifying particular entities into similar groupings (Anderson & Pearson, 1984), building through analogical reasoning a greater repertoire of knowledge.

But what is particularly important in the process of knowledge acquisition is that schemas provide a kind of organizational prosthetic (Constable, 1986) that serves to diminish the information-processing load. Consider, for example, a young child visiting a library for the first time. It is probably a complex and confusing new world. Not only are there new routines to consider but also categories of choices of books, and activities and different locations and roles of individuals. As the child comes to know the routines and the schemas of visiting the library, he or she begins to form a mental representation of certain activities, devoting less mental energy to the structure of the activity than to the content itself. Certain activities, originally confusing, then become understandable, familiar, and easier to access.

By diminishing the information-processing load, children are able to acquire new information more rapidly. Understanding the basic concept of a "library," for example, enables children to quickly make new associations, creating additional schemas that become increasingly differentiated with more knowledge. Children begin to recognize differences in genres and text types and purposes for reading, resulting in greater speed in gathering and remembering information. Knowledge becomes easier to access, producing more knowledge networks. And conversely, limited knowledge increases the difficulty level of accessing new knowledge.

Widening Knowledge Gaps

A vicious cycle begins. Knowledge disparities among social groups grow as a result of these differences in the amount, rate, and speed of gathering information from multiple media and resources. In its original formulation,

Tichenor, Donohue, and Olien (1970), focusing on media consumption, emphasized the diffusion of innovation. They hypothesized that "information haves" read more and engage more in higher level conversations, creating greater existing pools of knowledge and using information for fulfilling specific purposes and needs. Greater use enhances speed of information acquisition and developing schemas, which over time is likely to accelerate a knowledge gap between those who have access and those who do not. Therefore, although the "have-nots" gain knowledge, the "haves" gain it faster. And by gaining it faster, they are able to gain more.

The 1965 television debut of *Sesame Street*, designed specifically to narrow knowledge disparities as part of President Lyndon B. Johnson's Great Society initiative, provides an illustrative example of the difficulties of closing the gap. The first- and second-year evaluations (Ball & Bogatz, 1970; Bogatz & Ball, 1971) of the program showed evidence of actually increasing differences, helping those children who were already somewhat prepared for formal reading instruction far more than the less-ready children, who benefited little. As a result of the program, studies (Cook et al., 1975; Goldsen, 1977) found larger gaps in skills by kindergarten between middle- and lower-income children than before.

Communications scholars (Comtock, 1980; Salomon, 1984), however, have argued that television content is on average at the fourth-grade level; studies (Neuman, 1995; Salomon, 1984) show that learning definitely peaks over the elementary years, due largely to the limitations of the medium. But computer technology knows no bounds. And whether or to what extent this technology may further widen knowledge differentials is potentially concerning. For example, our 6-year study (Neuman & Celano, submitted for publication) examining the influence of "leveling the playing field" by providing equal resources and technology to neighborhood public libraries in low- and middle-income communities found that, rather than closing the gap, allocating equal resources to unequal socioeconomic groups actually appeared to exacerbate the knowledge gap. From the very beginning, preschool children in middle-income neighborhoods were carefully mentored by adults who taught them to use the resources purposefully and who modeled challenging reading for their children; low-income children rarely came with adults and engaged in only short bursts of behaviors. Technology integration in libraries, even after the novelty wore off, only extended the previous patterns, with poor children reading less, and attending less, and middle-income children reading more, and more often. After more than $20 million dollars was spent to equalize resources, middle-income children were reading approximately three times as much content as poor children.

Taken together, regardless of topic, methodological or theoretical variations, study quality, or other variables and conditions, over 90 studies (Gaziano, 1997) have reported similar demonstrations of the knowledge gap. Studies on topics (Vernon-Feagans, 1996; Viswanath & Finnegan, 1996) as varied as water policy, crime prevention, foreign policy, health, local budget deficits, and alcohol-related problems have shown the persistence of knowledge inequality. Further, these differentials tend to be especially severe for those groups during economic downturns and hard times. Given the rapid growth of socioeconomic divisions in the past two decades, therefore, the knowledge gap deserves our greater focus and attention.

Why Have We Overlooked Knowledge in Early Childhood?

Thomas Kuhn's structural theory of scientific revolutions (Kuhn, 1962) hypothesized that consensus in a particular field of inquiry sometimes halts progress and innovative thinking rather than promotes it. In part, the virtual consensus on the skills necessary to learn how to read, instantiated now in policy (see Roskos & Vukelich, Chapter 22, this volume), may be one reason for the limited attention given to the important role of knowledge in early literacy development. Recent reports (McCardle & Chhabra, 2004), for example, contend that children's future success in becoming skilled readers is dependent on their becoming aware that spoken words are composed of smaller elements of speech, grasping the idea that letters represent these sounds, learning the many system correspondences between sounds and spellings, and acquiring a repertoire of highly familiar words that can be recognized on sight. Much of the research (National Reading Panel Report, 2000), in fact, substantiates the importance of these components in learning to read.

However, research that underlies this model is based largely in the field of reading disabilities. In an attempt to untangle the critical features of reading, sampling criteria in this literature typically excludes disadvantaged children, or partials them out, using statistical strategies to try to equate one group with another. In so doing, these studies have necessarily focused on the relatively small store of foundational procedural skills to understand how children decode text.

Yet when we partial out disadvantage, we partial out many related explanations for predicting, explaining, and potentially preventing reading difficulties. As the previous sections in this chapter illustrate, environmental factors, including material resources and the quality of the home environment, play a central role in learning to read. These factors contribute to background knowledge and concepts, vocabulary, familiarity with syntactic and semantic sentences, and verbal reasoning abilities. Consequently, by controlling for poverty, researchers have tended to overlook a most critical predictor of skilled reading—the ability to derive meaning from text. Lacking the conceptual apparatus to understand the words that they are reading, children ultimately become word callers and struggling readers. Comprehension problems (Hirsch, 2003) are related to limitations in prior knowledge.

The second reason for not recognizing the importance of knowledge in early childhood could be definitional. Although the terms *knowledge*, *skills*, and *dispositions* are clearly familiar to most early childhood educators, rarely have we attempted to define them. Some colleagues (Hirsch, 1987), for example, describe *knowledge* as a series of facts considered to be part of the mainstream culture. Others (Glaser, 1984; Neuman, 2001) identify basic conceptual understandings that underlie disciplines of physical and biological science, art, and social systems. Still others (Gardner, 1983; Neuman, 2001) focus on learning processes, such as problem-solving and thinking skills. As a result, there has been a lack of clarity and understanding about the scope and depth of content knowledge in these early years. Recent efforts by

states to develop prekindergarten standards (Neuman & Roskos, in press) may be helpful in developing content guidelines that are appropriate for children in the early childhood years.

And the third reason for overlooking the importance of knowledge in early childhood might be ideological. The field of early childhood still grapples over the balance between learning processes (i.e., thinking skills), *how* children learn, and content, or *what* they learn (Eisner & Vallance, 1974). With resistence to the notion of a canon of knowledge (Hirsch, 1987), developmentally appropriate content curriculum in early childhood is still elusive. More often than not, young children, particularly those in high poverty areas, are subjected to intellectually trivial activities, limited in content and only loosely connected between subjects. Too often, there has been an overemphasis on active, hands-on learning without any foundational knowledge base. Seppanen, Godon, and Metzger (1993) found, for example, that early childhood Title I classrooms did not provide any regular experiences in topics of math, language, and science. Minds atrophy under such conditions.

Yet for early education to work toward helping children attain social and economic equality, we must develop pedagogy that is both sensitive to children's development *and* representative of conceptual knowledge that has sufficient coherence and depth. Recognizing the divide that begins to separate the "information haves" from the "information have-nots" early on, we need to develop learning experiences that work on the edge of children's competencies and understandings. Research has consistently shown the value of early education in helping to equip children with essential skills. But these skills must be used to develop coherent understandings of knowledge and concepts, the very basic foundations for later learning.

What Can We Do to Improve the Knowledge Base in Early Childhood?

Recently I visited several prekindergarten classes specifically targeted for poor children. Throughout the 3-hour visit, I counted 20 minutes of instruction in these classrooms. Rather than instruction, the day was overtaken by transitions (late arrivals, early dismissals, lunch, bathroom washing, getting ready for outdoor play, getting back from outdoor play, going to and coming back from "specials," cleaning up). Even more troubling, however, was the type of instruction I observed in early literacy and mathematics within those precious 20 minutes. Children were asked to memorize lines of print, to say the alphabet letters and numbers about five times, to spell their names, to spell the names of children who were not there, to read along with the teacher in a highly predictable format, and to chime lines they had surely heard again and again. And throughout these individual exercises, not once was there an effort to engage children's minds through stimulating content learning (Neuman, 2003).

In contrast to this approach, content-centered classrooms (Neuman & Roskos, 1997) involve children in learning about print through literacy in practice. Here, the skills and functions of literacy serve to enhance children's learning with newly developing skills that become meaningful by helping children understand their world. This approach builds on a set of research-based principles about how young children learn and develop schemas necessary to begin building basic knowledge frameworks. Specifically, the principles include:

1. *Children's learning benefits through integrated instruction.* Effective teachers use integrated learning (Schickedanz, Pergantis, Kanosky, Blaney, & Ottinger, 1997) to organize large amounts of content into meaningful concepts. Some teachers may use the project approach (Katz & Chard, 1989); others may call it thematic teaching. Both approaches help children to build knowledge networks and provide more time and focus for repeated practice of familiar concepts. Further, children learn and apply skills in various contexts, increasing the likelihood of transfer and extending understanding.

Skillful teachers recognize that thematic instruction must have coherence and depth. Cafeteria-style approaches that teach a little of this and a little of that give only spotty attention to content and only limited connections between subjects. Thematic teaching that works helps children understand a topic well, as opposed to skimming and covering many areas.

2. *Learning requires children's minds (not just their bodies) to be active.* Effective teachers actively engage children in mastering content (Hirsch, 1996), helping them to connect new learning to what they already know and can do. Consequently, they strike a balance in their instructional planning between structure and choice. Sometimes teachers present a concept that is planned and directed to ensure that knowledge is thoroughly understood and not superficially absorbed. At other times, they recognize that children need to explore, manipulate, and use ideas, working in centers of their choosing that have been carefully prepared with teacher guidance. Both are necessary for young children's learning and development.

3. *High levels of teacher interaction optimize children's learning.* Effective teachers hold great influence in helping children to reach their potential. They assist and guide children's learning (Tharp & Gallimore, 1988), involving them in experiences that are slightly more difficult than what they can master on their own. Teachers carefully scaffold children's learning (Wood & Middleton, 1975), with the level and amount of assistance gradually decreasing as the children are able to perform tasks independently. They encourage children to express their ideas through language and raise questions that enable them to develop more complex ideas and concepts. Effective teachers work on the edge of children's current competence (Bredekamp & Copple, 1997), providing learning experiences that are challenging but achievable.

These teachers use a wide range of teaching strategies. Modeling and demonstrating provide standards of practice; explicit instruction, questioning, and ongoing feedback help to challenge and expand children's ideas and skills. All of these strategies are interdependent and make possible the "art and science" of effective teaching.

4. *Play supports children's learning.* Effective teachers recognize that children's exploration and manipulation of objects, make-believe play, and creative games make important contributions to children's literacy development (Neuman & Roskos, 1992, 1993). In play, children express and represent their ideas, learn to interact with others, and practice newly acquired skills and knowledge.

Teachers provide conditions that affect what children choose to play and the materials that will influence how they play. They construct learning and playing environments that involve children in using literacy in practice. At times, teachers take on roles and actively engage children in content-related activities—such as roles associated with a grocery store or a restaurant—that are first imitated, and expanded on and later integrated in children's developing language repertoire. These teachers seek to enhance language and play while leaving children in control of it.

5. *Developing competence enhances motivation and self-esteem.* Effective teachers recognize that learning experiences and practices that help children to become skillful at learning many things are far more effective than those designed just to be highly motivating. Children thrive in classrooms in which they develop new understandings and are in the company of teachers who combine nurturance and support with high but realistic standards and expectations. Self-esteem

grows when children are challenged and begin to develop a history of achievement through reasonable effort.

In summary, instructional principles that engage children in content-rich contexts integrated across subject domains with high levels of teacher support and guidance and in play to extend learning provide opportunities for all children to achieve while ensuring that individual children will receive the extra support they need to progress. Table 2.2 provides an example of a content-rich thematic unit on the physical world. Throughout these activities, literacy is an integral part of learning through practice.

A Day's Activity in a Content-Rich Literacy-in-Practice Classroom

Content-rich classrooms are carefully constructed to be sensitive to what children should know and be able to do. But they are also sensitive to children's development and

TABLE 2.2. Thematic Study on the Physical World

Unit	Major concepts	Materials needed	Prekindergarten guidelines
Magnetism	Magnetic force attracts things made of iron and steel. Magnets have many uses and help us do many things.	Objects to test and sort Books on magnets	The child: • Uses one more sense to observe phenomena. • Analyzes patterns and relationships.
Colors	There are many different colors, and they have different names. Primary colors are red, yellow, and blue.	Books Paint Colored paper Color swatches Food colors	The child: • Uses different colors to create meaning. • Uses new vocabulary in everyday communication.
Sound	We can identify things by their sounds. Sound is created by vibrations of objects. Sounds can be high/low, loud/soft.	Musical instruments Records Kitchen food containers Chutes and marbles Popcorn cooking	The child: • Identifies similarities and differences. • Begins to distinguish among sounds of several instruments.
Weather, climate, and seasons	Seasonal changes affect plants and animals. Animals store food. People adapt to differences in weather.	Books Logs for observing weather Visit to a greenhouse Picture display of animals in winter	The child: • Begins to observe changes in the environment.

their need to explore new ideas on their own. These environments should be challenging, stimulating for young children, and age-appropriate, as shown in the following example. Table 2.2 provides an overview of the teacher's thematic plan, and the major concepts, materials, and guidelines addressed in her lesson plans.

Children arrive for the day between 8:30 and 8:45 A.M. and are greeted at the door by the teacher. They hang their coats and sweaters in individual cubbyholes, carefully labeled with their names and photos, then check in by finding their names on the attendance chart. Some visit the library corner or the dramatic-play center as they wait for others to arrive.

Around 8:45, the teacher sings a song to indicate that the morning meeting will begin. The children gather around the circle area. After a brief greeting, she describes some of the new choices for the upcoming activity time and gives a brief demonstration of how some piece of equipment or tool may be used. The children show their choices of activity by raising their hands before being dismissed. Because more children want to go into an area than can be accommodated, she shows how they might cooperate so that each child may have a turn.

Activities in the centers have been carefully planned for the day. Because this unit is on sound, in one area children will make popcorn and hear the sounds of sizzling, popping, and corn smacking and will hear when these sounds taper off. In the block area, they will play with chutes and marbles; in the science area they will use resonating bells and voice play to hear different pitches. In the listening center, children will listen to a nature tape and draw pictures of what they hear. And in the manipulative area, the teacher will play rhyming word–picture match with a small group of children whom she has discovered need special assistance with this phonological skill.

Once cleanup is over, children gather for group time. They have much to share about their activities. They review the sounds they have heard and talk about how sounds are made, writing the words, along with a picture, on a chart that will be used throughout the unit. Then the teacher introduces some songs with distinctive rhythms and sounds, such as "Oats, Peas, Beans, and Barley Grow,"

and the children take turns clapping out a rhythm. The teacher introduces a slightly more difficult variation and encourages the children to follow her lead. They then sing "Willoughby Walloby Woo" to help sensitize them to similar sounds at the beginning of words. And in the last few minutes, they play the game, "What begins with. ... " This leads to a smooth transition to snack time. She slowly says the names of two children who will help to put out the snacks, emphasizing the beginning sound. The teacher holds up a menu of today's snack of five graham crackers and one cup of juice, printed along with the pictures.

Today's outdoor activity is an environmental sound walk on which children learn to identify objects and actions by their sounds—the sounds of animals, of the wind, of other children on the playground. Upon returning to classroom, children recall some of the sounds they heard, which are written down on a chart. They gather for story time. The teacher reads first from one of her favorite anthologies of poetry and rhyme and then reads the delightful story about tolerance and sound, *Charlene Loves to Make Noise*, by Barbara Bottner and Alexander Stadler (2002), following each with a short discussion. Tomorrow she will review the different sounds they heard today and help the children categorize loud and soft sounds. Children are then dismissed for the day.

Taking a Closer Look

Children's activities were well paced throughout the day to provide sufficient variation and challenge. The schedule allowed for teacher-directed instruction (group time and story time) and for child choice. During activity times, children were given considerable opportunity to choose their activities, although the teacher had provided guidance and direction through the materials she had organized and the interactions that occurred throughout activity time. Arrival time and dismissal were relatively short to allow more time for in-depth learning.

Children were very active throughout the day, both mentally and physically. The activities all focused on the science of sound. Group time and activities were designed to extend their understandings through varied experiments, stories and poems, and learning experiences, which engaged children in manipulating materials and social interactions. All activities emphasized language.

The topic of sound was substantive. It was broad and varied enough to address a number of science guidelines (i.e., both content and process), as well as oral language, print awareness, and phonological awareness. In subsequent days, as they progressed through the unit, children were involved in opportunities to learn more about sound through listening, fine arts activities, and writing.

This example highlights some essential features of an effective content-rich literacy-in-practice day. It ensured that children were exposed to:

- Time, materials, and resources to actively build linguistic and conceptual knowledge in a rich domain.
- A literate environment in which children have access to a wide variety of reading and writing materials.
- Different grouping patterns (large, small, individual) and different levels of guidance (i.e., explicit instruction, assisted instruction) to meet the needs of individual children.
- Opportunities for sustained and in-depth learning.
- A "masterful" orchestration of pacing and management (i.e., activity, behavior, and resources).

Classrooms such as these help children build schemas, serving to enhance foundational knowledge in core subject areas. Teachers use explicit instruction—modeling, telling, showing, explaining, and demonstrating information—so that children with limited prior knowledge receive the same kinds of opportunities that other middle-class children have had. This knowledge, then, acts as a catalyst for children to acquire more knowledge on their own. In these content-rich settings, early literacy skills ultimately serve, not supersede, children's developing thirst for knowledge and greater understanding.

Conclusions

No nation has entirely overcome the highly predictable relationship between low academic performance and socioeconomic status. As this review has established, key material resources and interpersonal experiences that are common in higher income homes are not available and are unlikely to be available for children in poverty settings. And it is these key experiences that children from low-income communities lack—vital background knowledge for developing concepts and schemas—not their ability to learn that puts these children at a great disadvantage, especially when learning to read increasingly builds on prior knowledge when reading to learn. Because the important role of knowledge in the beginning years has been overlooked, early literacy has become associated with a rather small set of skills. Yet, if time is to be spent effectively in the early years, content knowledge essential to higher order skills must not be subordinated to these foundational skills.

Both skill development and conceptual knowledge development need to occur simultaneously. At-risk children cannot afford to attend to one without the other. Although it is probably impossible to close the gap, it can be significantly reduced with high-quality instruction in the early years that integrates knowledge and dispositions for learning with skills. Unless these early knowledge deficits are quickly overcome, the knowledge gap will continue to grow ever wider with each successive grade level.

References

Anderson, R. C., & Pearson, P. D. (1984). A schema-theoretic view of basic processes in reading comprehension. In P. D. Pearson (Ed.), *Handbook of reading research* (pp. 255–291). New York: Longman.

Ball, S., & Bogatz, G. (1970). *The first year of Sesame Street: An evaluation.* Princeton, NJ: Educational Testing Service.

Baumrind, D. (1966). Effects of authoritative parental control on child behavior. *Child Development, 37,* 887–907.

Baumrind, D. (1968). Authoritarian versus authoritative parental control. *Adolescence, 3,* 255–272.

Bogatz, G. A., & Ball, S. (1971). *The second year of Sesame Street: A continuing evaluation.* Princeton, NJ: Educational Testing Service.

Bottner, B., & Stadler, A. (2002). *Charlene loves to make noice.* Philadelphia: Running Press.

Bredekamp, S., & Copple, C. (1997). *Developmentally appropriate practice—Revised.* Washington, DC: National Association for the Education of Young Children.

Browning, L. (2003, September 25). U.S. income gap widening. *The New York Times*, (p. 28).

Comstock, G. (1980). *Television in America*. Beverly Hills, CA: Sage.

Constable, C. (1986). The application of scripts in the organization of language intervention contexts. In K. Nelson (Ed.), *Event knowledge: Structure and function in development* (pp. 205–230). Hillsdale, NJ: Erlbaum.

Cook, T., Appleton, H., Conner, R., Shaffer, A., Tamkin, G., & Weber, S. (1975). *"Sesame Street" revisited*. New York: Russell Sage Foundation.

Corcoran, M., & Chaudry, A. (1997). The dynamics of childhood poverty. *The Future of Children, 7*, 40–54.

Cunningham, A. E., & Stanovich, K. (1998, Spring-Summer). What reading does for the mind. *American Educator, 22*, 8–15.

Denton, K., West, J., & Waltston, J. (2003). *Young children's achievement and classroom experiences: Special Analysis on the Condition of Education*. Washington, DC: National Center for Educational Statistics.

Dickinson, D. K., & McCabe, A. (2003). A framework for examining book reading in early childhood classrooms. In A. van Kleeck, E. B. Bauer, & S. Stahl (Eds.), *On reading books to children: Parents and teachers* (pp. 95–113). Hillsdale, NJ: Erlbaum.

Dickinson, D. K., McCabe, A., & Clark-Chiarelli, N. (2004). Preschool-based prevention of reading disability: Realities vs. possibilities. In C. A. Stone, E. R. Silliman, B. J. Ehren, & K. Apel (Eds.), *Handbook of language and literacy: Development and disorders* (pp. 209–227). New York: Guilford Press.

Duchan, J. (2004). The foundational role of schemas in children's language and literacy learning. In C. A. Stone, E. Silliman, B. Ehren, & K. Apel (Eds.), *Handbook of language and literacy: Development and disorders* (pp. 380–397). New York: Guilford Press.

Duncan, G., & Brooks-Gunn, J. (Eds.). (1997). *Consequences of growing up poor*. New York: Russell Sage Foundation.

Eisner, W. E., & Vallance, E. (Eds.). (1974). *Conflicting conceptions of curriculum*. Berkeley, CA: McCutchan.

Entwisle, D., Alexander, K., & Olson, L. S. (1997). *Children, schools, and inequality*. Boulder, CO: Westview Press.

Foster, E. M. (2002). How economists think about family resources and child development. *Child Development, 73*, 1904–1914.

Gardner, H. (1983). *Frames of mind: The theory of multiple intelligences*. New York: Basic Books.

Gaziano, C. (1997). Forecast 2000: Widening knowledge gaps. *Journalism and Mass Communications Quarterly, 74*, 237–264.

Glaser, R. (1984). Education and thinking: The role of knowledge. *American Psychologist, 39*, 93–104.

Goldsen, R. (1977). *The show and tell machine*. New York: Dial Press.

Hart, B., & Risley, T. (1995). *Meaningful differences*. Baltimore: Brookes.

Hart, B., & Risley, T. (2003). The early catastrophe. *American Educator, 27*, 4, 6–9.

Helburn, S., & Bergmann, B. (2002). *America's child care problem*. Hampshire, UK: Palgrave Macmillan.

Hirsch, E. D. (1987). *Cultural literacy: What every American needs to know*. Boston: Houghton-Mifflin.

Hirsch, E. D. (1996). *The schools we need and why we don't have them*. New York: Doubleday.

Hirsch, E. D. (2003). Reading comprehension requires knowledge of words and the world. *American Educator, 27*, 10, 12-1316-1322,1328-1329, 1348.

Jencks, C., & Phillips, M. (Eds.). (1998). *The black–white test score gap*. Washington, DC: Brookings Institution Press.

Juel, C., Griffith, P. L., & Gough, P. (1986). Acquisition of literacy: A longitudinal study of children in first and second grade. *Journal of Educational Psychology, 78*, 243–255.

Kahlenberg, R. (2001). *All together now*. Washington, DC: Brookings Institution Press.

Katz, L., & Chard, C. (1989). *Engaging children's minds*. Norwood, NJ: Ablex.

Kuhn, T. (1962). *The structure of scientific revolution*. Chicago: University of Chicago Press.

Lareau, A. (1989). *Home advantage: Social class and parental intervention in elementary education*. New York: Falmer Press.

Lareau, A. (2002). Invisible inequality: Social class and childrearing in black families and white families. *American Sociological Review, 67*, 747–776.

Lee, V., & Burkam, D. (2002). *Inequality at the starting gate*. Washington, DC: Economic Policy Institute.

McCardle, P., & Chhabra, V. (Eds.). (2004). *The voice of evidence in reading research*. Baltimore: Brookes.

McLoyd, V. (1990). The impact of economic hardship on black families and children: Psychological distress, parenting, and socioemotional development. *Child Development, 61*, 311–346.

National Reading Panel Report. (2000). *Teaching children to read*. Washington, DC: National Institute of Child Health and Development.

Neuman, S. B. (1995). *Literacy in the television age: The myth of the TV effect* (2nd ed.). Norwood, NJ: Ablex.

Neuman, S. B. (2001). The role of knowledge in early literacy. *Reading Research Quarterly, 36*, 468–475.

Neuman, S. B. (2003). From rhetoric to reality: The case for high-quality compensatory prekindergarten programs. *Kappan, 85*, 286–291.

Neuman, S. B., Caperelli, B. J., & Kee, C. (1998). Literacy learning, a family matter. *The Reading Teacher, 52,* 244–253.

Neuman, S. B., & Celano, D. (2001). Access to print in middle- and low-income communities: An ecological study of four neighborhoods. *Reading Research Quarterly, 36,* 8–26.

Neuman, S. B., & Celano, D. (2004). *The knowledge gap: Implications for low- and middle-income children.* Manuscript submitted for publication.

Neuman, S. B., Celano, D., Greco, A., & Shue, P. (2001). *Access for all: Closing the book gap for children in early education.* Newark, DE: International Reading Association.

Neuman, S. B., Copple, C., & Bredekamp, S. (2000). *Learning to read and write: Developmentally appropriate practice.* Washington, DC: National Association for the Education of Young Children.

Neuman, S. B., & Gallagher, P. (1994). Joining together in literacy learning: Teenage mothers and children. *Reading Research Quarterly, 29,* 382–401.

Neuman, S. B., & Roskos, K. (1992). Literacy objects as cultural tools: Effects on children's literacy behaviors in play. *Reading Research Quarterly, 27,* 202–225.

Neuman, S. B., & Roskos, K. (1997). Literacy knowledge in practice: Contexts of participation for young writers and readers. *Reading Research Quarterly, 32,* 10–32.

Neuman, S. B., & Roskos, K. (in press). The state of state prekindergarten guidelines. *Early Childhood Research Quarterly.*

Peisner-Feinberg, E., Burchinal, M., Clifford, R., Culkin, M., Howes, C., Kagan, S. L., et al. (1999). *The children of the cost, quality, and outcomes study go to school: Executive summary.* Chapel Hill: University of North Carolina at Chapel Hill, Frank Porter Graham Child Development Center.

Rothstein, R. (2004). *Class and schools.* New York: Teachers College Press.

Rumelhart, D. E. (1980). Schemata: The building blocks of cognition. In R.J. Spiro, B. C. Bruce, & W. F. Brewer (Eds.), *Theoretical issues in reading comprehension* (pp. 34–58). Hillsdale, NJ: Erlbaum.

Salomon, G. (1984). Television is "easy" and print is "tough": The differential investment of mental effort as a function of perceptions and attributions. *Journal of Educational Psychology, 76,* 647–658.

Schickedanz, J., Pergantis, M. L., Kanosky, J., Blaney, A., & Ottinger, J. (1997). *Curriculum in early childhood.* Boston: Allyn & Bacon.

Seppanen, P. S., Godon, K., & Metzger, J. (1993). *Observational study of Chapter 1: Funded early childhood programs.* (Final Report, Vol. 2). Washington, DC: U.S. Department of Education.

Stanovich, K. (1980). Toward an interactive-compensatory model of individual differences in the development of reading fluency. *Reading Research Quarterly, 16,* 32–71.

Stein, N., & Glenn, C. (1979). An analysis of story comprehension in elementary school children. In R. O. Freedle (Ed.), *Advances in discourse processing* (Vol. 2, pp. 53–120). Norwood, NJ: Ablex.

Tharp, R., & Gallimore, R. (1988). *Rousing minds to life.* Cambridge, UK: Cambridge University Press.

Tichenor, P. J., Donohue, G., & Olien, C. (1970). Mass media flow and differential growth in knowledge. *Public Opinion Quarterly, 34,* 159–170.

Vellutino, F., Scanlon, D., Sipay, E., Small, S., Pratt, A., Chen, R., et al. (1996). Cognitive profiles of difficult to remediate and readily remediated poor readers: Early intervention as a vehicle for distinguishing between cognitive and experiential deficits as basic causes of specific reading disability. *Journal of Educational Psychology, 88,* 601–638.

Vernon-Feagans, L. (1996). *Children's talk in communities and classrooms.* Oxford, UK: Blackwell.

Viswanath, K., & Finnegan, J. (1996). The knowledge gap hypothesis: Twenty-five years later. In B. R. Burleson (Ed.), *Communication yearbook* (Vol. 19, pp. 187–227). Newbury Park, CA: Sage.

West, R., & Stanovich, K. (1991). The incidental acquisition of information from reading. *Psychological Science, 2,* 325–330.

Wood, D. J., & Middleton, D. J. (1975). A study of assisted problem solving. *British Journal of Psychology, 66,* 181–191.

3

Vocabulary Development and Instruction: A Prerequisite for School Learning

ANDREW BIEMILLER

In the first part of this chapter, I discuss vocabulary development and implications for academic success, including the relationship between early vocabulary and later literacy, the size and sequence of children's developing vocabulary, influences on vocabulary acquisition, and some mechanisms for word meaning acquisition. In the second part of the chapter, I discuss what can be done to build vocabulary in schools and child-care programs, including reported effects of current schooling on vocabulary development, effects of teaching vocabulary to preschool or primary grade children, a possible explanation of word meaning acquisition in context-based instruction, a basis for selecting words for instruction, a recent study of word instruction in classrooms, and practical implications for classroom programs.

Vocabulary Development and Implications for Academic Success

The Vocabulary–Early Literacy Connection

For adequate reading comprehension from grade 3 on, children require *both* fluent word recognition skills *and* an average or above-average vocabulary. The presence of these two accomplishments does not guarantee a high level of reading comprehension, but the absence of *either* word recognition or adequate vocabulary ensures a low level of reading comprehension.

The significance of vocabulary ("oral language") has often been underestimated because it is not a prerequisite for first- or second-grade reading success. It is not until reading texts involve age-normal vocabulary demands that early (kindergarten or prekindergarten) vocabulary becomes a significant predictor of reading comprehension (Becker, 1977; Scarborough, 2001; Storch & Whitehurst , 2002). Typically, age-normal vocabulary demands appear in third- or fourth-grade books (Chall, Jacobs, & Baldwin, 1990; Chall & Conard, 1991). Many other studies are now pointing to this conclusion. Of course, concurrent vocabulary is an even stronger predictor of reading comprehension by third or fourth grade and thereafter. Cunningham and Stanovich (1997) have also shown a substantial relationship between oral receptive vocabulary in first grade and reading comprehension in 11th grade ($r = .55$, or 30% of variance).

In fact, for most children reading problems—word recognition—probably play less of a role in reading comprehension than does knowledge of word meanings. This claim is made because, by the end of third grade, most children can *read* many more words correctly than they *understand* in context (Biemiller, 2005).

Will teaching vocabulary change children's general vocabulary or reading comprehension? A number of vocabulary instruction studies have shown small but significant effects on general vocabulary or reading with upper elementary children and older groups (Stahl & Fairbanks, 1986; Edwards, Font, Baumann, & Boland, 2003). Stahl and Fairbanks (1986) note that studies in which general vocabulary or comprehension effects have been found were mostly conducted for 6 weeks or longer.

However, teaching 10–50 word meanings, as in typical pilot vocabulary instruction studies, is not likely to change comprehension or general vocabulary. Average children acquire many hundreds of word meanings each year during the first 7 years of vocabulary acquisition (Biemiller, 2005). In order for a vocabulary intervention to have a measurable impact on general vocabulary, a child must acquire several hundred word meanings that would not otherwise be acquired. Most published reports of classroom interventions with young children have simply not been carried out for long enough to influence general vocabulary levels.

Many writers emphasize building children's skills for dealing with unfamiliar vocabulary by stressing increased volume of reading rather than by teaching word meanings directly (Dale & O'Rourke, 1986; Nagy & Herman, 1987; Edwards et al., 2003). Such methods have always presupposed literacy (at least, adequate reading mechanics)—that is, that children are in third grade or older. However, major vocabulary problems develop during the *preliterate* period— before children are reading texts with challenging vocabulary.

Biemiller and Slonim's (2001) findings indicate that once children become literate, most children add word meanings at about the same rate across vocabulary levels. Thus from grade 3 through grade 6, children with relatively small vocabularies show year-to-year gains that are similar to gains seen in children who have large vocabularies (cross-sectional data). However, in the preliterate period, children come to differ by several thousand root-word meanings—a gap that is too often not closed in later years. Hence we must find ways of supporting vocabulary acquisition during the preliterate period.

Vocabulary Development: Numbers of Word Meanings and Their Sequence

NUMBERS OF WORD MEANINGS ACQUIRED

Research by Jeremy Anglin (1993), Biemiller and Slonim (2001), and Biemiller (2005) have shown that average children acquire about 860 root-word meanings per year from age 1 to the end of second grade, or about 2.4 root words per day.[1] This results in their acquiring about 6,000 root-word meanings. Unfortunately, at the end of grade 2 the 25% of children with the smallest vocabularies have *averaged* only about 1.6 root words a day, resulting in about 4,000 root-word meanings. Some of these children acquire even fewer root-word meanings by the end of grade 2. Although many writers have argued that the numbers of words learned are much larger (e.g., Nagy & Herman, 1987), Nagy and Scott (2001) have recently agreed with Anglin's and Biemiller's estimates of numbers of root-word meanings acquired.

IS THERE A SEQUENCE OF WORD MEANINGS ACQUIRED?

The main evidence that words are acquired in a similar sequence by children from quite different circumstances is that the correlation between word meaning averages obtained from different samples are very similar. The correlations between word meaning scores for 50 representative words from (1) a normative population of children in grade 2 through grade 5; (2) an advantaged population in the same grades; and (3) a group of children in grade 5 and grade 6 who do not use English at home (English as a second language, or ESL, students) are all above $r = .90$ (Biemiller, 2005). In addition, an analysis of words known by children with different sized vocabularies (irrespective of age) showed that there are words known by all children studied but that as vocabulary increases, words higher in the sequence are also known (Biemiller & Slonim, 2001). In short, there is a rough sequence of words acquired, and this order holds across a range of populations.

WHY THE SEQUENCE?

Although we do not have a clear theory of *why* word meanings are acquired in a sequence, the existence of a robust sequence should not be lightly ignored for instructional purposes. Possible hypotheses affecting this sequence may include:

• Early-developing words may be those prerequisite to understanding words that are learned later in the sequence.

• It is very likely that the frequencies of word meanings affect word meaning acquisition. Certainly words not encountered cannot be learned. However, frequencies of specific word meanings (oral and later printed) are often quite different from simple printed form frequency. Thus there is little correlation between printed word frequency and word meaning knowledge (Biemiller & Slonim, 2001).

• More cognitively complex meanings are usually learned later (e.g., *biology*) (Case, 1985; Slonim, 2001). However, cognitive complexity clearly does not account for sequence in a large majority of word meanings acquired relatively later. Many of these words are nonabstract (i.e., representing touchable, visible things). (See Appendix 3.1 for examples of words known by most, some, or few second-grade children.)

Sources of Vocabulary Acquisition in the Primary and Preschool Years

HOME SUPPORT

Studies of factors affecting word acquisition lead to two major conclusions. The first is that by age 4, the size of a child's vocabulary is to a large extent determined by the number of different words used by the parents and the total number of words spoken by the parents (Hart & Risley, 1995, 1999, 2003; Wells, 1985). Clearly, one cannot acquire words that are not encountered. More adult clarification of words in the course of conversation is associated with later vocabulary size (Beals & Tabors, 1995; Weizman & Snow, 2001). In addition to the number of opportunities the child has to build a large vocabulary, children may vary in how readily they add words to their stock of familiar word forms while mapping them to referents. However, children with small vocabu-

laries *do* acquire new words during instruction about as well as children with larger vocabularies, suggesting that much of the difference is a matter of opportunity rather than ability. Data supporting this conclusion are given in the second part of this chapter.

SCHOOL SUPPORT

Although home factors are clearly associated with children's vocabulary growth, in the primary grades no comparable evidence has been shown for school factors that affect it. In fact, the limited available data suggest that in many classrooms, a year of school experience has no measurable impact on vocabulary growth. Three studies have shown that January-born kindergarten children (oldest in the class) have about the same average vocabulary size as December-born first-grade children (youngest in the class). These are children who differ in age by 1 month but in schooling by 1 year. Similarly, January-born first-grade children have about the same size vocabulary as December-born second-grade children (Cantalini, 1987; Christian, Morrison, Frazier, & Massetti, 2000). In these studies, schooling was found to have a negligible impact on vocabulary size. Thus at present, *home*, not *school*, determines vocabulary size by the end of second grade—the end of the "preliterate" period for most children. (Some children remain preliterate longer.)

How Are Words Acquired?: The Role of Context

Some years ago, Susan Carey introduced the concept of "fast mapping" word acquisition. Specifically, Carey observed that preschool children could very quickly acquire a "conceptual" referent for a new word but took much longer to have a relatively complete understanding of the word (Carey, 1978). By "conceptual" referent, Carey meant the "relevant part of the internal representational system in terms of which the person or animal describes and understands the world and his own actions in it. . . . Take for example, the lexical domain of color words, and the conceptual domain of mental representation of colors" (1978, p. 269). She described fast mapping as occurring when "One, or a very few, experiences with a new word can suffice for the child to enter it into his mental lexicon and to represent some of its syntactic and semantic features" (Carey, 1978, p. 291).

To illustrate fast mapping, Carey described a study in which children quickly mapped the word *dax* to a specific doll handed to the child ("Here is *dax*"); in another condition, the child mapped the word as an object category ("Here is *a dax*"). This direct connection of an object with a word (along with syntactic specification of *dax* as either a *name* or a *doll*) illustrates how readily children can associate a novel word with a recognizable object that is physically presented. Although children's understanding of *dax* would continue to become richer with extended experience, this initial fast mapping is necessary in order to continue to enrich the referent information. A number of studies have recently supported Carey's fast-mapping theory (e.g., Akhtar, Jipson, & Callanan, 2001; Behrend, Scofield, & Kleinknecht, 2001; Hall & Graham, 1999; Sandhofer & Smith, 1999). All of this research has involved children between 2 and 4 years of age.

Some researchers view such transactions as noninstructional and emphasize the child's inference of what a word means. However, the fact is that a word meaning is not learned without the direct pairing of the novel word and a referent. For children under 3, that means a physical object, action, or modifier paired with the word *by a more advanced speaker of the language*.

When children reach about 3 years of age, word meanings are acquired not only in the presence of specific concrete referents but also of verbally created referents. Word meaning acquisition is unlikely to occur in the absence of a fairly specific concrete referent clearly associated with a word. The word must be learned in the context of a physical task or in the verbal context of a task described in a verbal narrative. The word may be novel, or a familiar word may be given a second meaning. For example, a parent might say, "Here is some lean meat—there is no fat on it." Thus both a task (real or verbally described) and the provision of a new word to access the referent in the task appear to be necessary conditions for acquiring (or "mapping") a word meaning.[2]

This body of research suggests to me that the acquisition of root-word meanings re-

quires instruction or explanation in the majority of cases. Meanings of derived words (prefixed or suffixed) and compound words can probably be largely inferred from context *when root word meanings are known*. In some cases, instruction will facilitate using prefixes and suffixes (Baumann, Edwards, Boland, Olejnik, & Kame'enui, 2003; Graves, 2003; White, Power, & White, 1989).

What Can Be Done to Build Vocabulary in Schools and Child-Care Centers?

To summarize this information about vocabulary development:

- Average children acquire approximately 6,000 root-word meanings by the end of second grade. Children in the lowest quartile acquire roughly 4,000 root-word meanings.
- These differences are related to marked variations in home vocabulary opportunities and support.
- At present, there is little evidence for acquisition of word meanings at school in the primary years.
- There is empirical evidence of a word sequence, but we lack a comprehensive list of such words.

Children enter school (or child care) differing widely in vocabulary, just as they differ in knowledge of numbers or awareness of phonemes. Educators have become increasingly aware of the significance of number knowledge or phonemic awareness. This provides an opportunity to compensate for areas of knowledge that may not have been addressed at home. However, at present no similar effort is made to compensate for differences in language experience. In this section I describe the possibility of helping children to acquire needed vocabulary in the primary grades.

Studies of Teaching Vocabulary to Primary or Preschool Children

EFFECTS OF EXTENDED INTERVENTIONS IN PRIMARY CLASSROOMS

I know of only two studies of vocabulary interventions carried out over a year of school.

Both were by Feitelson and her colleagues. Working with kindergarten children who spoke Arabic, Feitelson, Goldstein, Iraqi, and Share (1991) arranged for 12 books to be read over a 5-month period. The books explicitly used a formal version of Arabic (FusHa) commonly used in print but not in colloquial speech. One book was read to the whole class for about 20 minutes at the end of each school day. Each book was read about nine times over the course of 5 months. Prior to each reading session, the teachers explained up to three unfamiliar words. While reading, teachers might also note colloquial equivalents of words used in the text. On a test of listening comprehension (not involving content from the 12 stories), children who had been read to were near the maximum possible score (averaging 6 correct out of 7 items), whereas those who had not been read to regularly (but had had language lessons) averaged 3.7 out of 7 items. Significant gains were also reported on other measures of language performance. Unfortunately, Feitelson et al. (1991) did not report any specific data on vocabulary, neither general vocabulary nor words from the books read. These results underestimate the effect of the program—many of the children in the intervention program could presumably have scored higher if a more advanced test had been used.

Especially noteworthy is the fact that the children were acquiring not only the vocabulary and knowledge of story structure needed to comprehend this material but also the more formal dialect of Arabic used in most written communications. In disadvantaged English-speaking communities, there is also a need to acquire standard forms of the language used in "educated" contexts.

In a first-grade study with Hebrew-speaking children, a teacher read to the whole class for about 20 minutes at the end of the school day over a 6-month period (Feitelson, Kita, & Goldstein, 1986). "Hard words" were clarified as needed. Fifteen books were read from a series about "Kofiko," a mischievous monkey who sounds rather like Curious George. These books were extremely popular with the children, many of whom insisted that their parents get copies of some of the books.

Children in the experimental class were contrasted with children from two control classes. All came from the same neighborhood, but those in the control classes scored significantly higher on a vocabulary test (an Israeli version of the Wechsler Intelligence Scale for Children) prior to the reading intervention. Unfortunately, this vocabulary test was not readministered at the end of the study. Despite this difference, by the end of the study the children who had been read to daily showed higher achievement in comprehension of a reading passage (82% vs. 63% accurate), in oral reading of a "technical" passage (94% vs. 79% accurate), and used longer sentences when asked to tell a story (5.6 vs. 4.5 words per sentence). This study suggests that time invested in listening to stories (with clarifications as needed) is time well spent, even when the time available for instruction is perceived to be very short.[3]

STUDIES OF WORD EXPLANATIONS AS BOOKS ARE READ ORALLY

A limited number of studies of vocabulary instruction have been done with children in grade 2 or lower. Stahl and Fairbanks's (1986) analysis of 52 studies of vocabulary instruction done before 1986 included only two studies with children in grade 2 and none below grade 2. More recently, we have found seven studies of classroom vocabulary instruction or oral story experience with primary or preprimary children (Biemiller & Boote, submitted). The results of these studies are surprisingly similar: When stories were read only once without explanation, on average, children understood 4% more word meanings than they had before the stories were read (Sénéchal, 1997). When stories were read three or four times without word explanation, 10–15% more word meanings were acquired (Biemiller, 2003; Brabham & Lynch-Brown, 2002; Elley, 1989; Penno, Wilkinson, & Moore, 2002; Robbins & Ehri, 1994; Sénéchal, 1997; Sénéchal, Thomas, & Monker, 1995). When words were read with word explanations, word knowledge gains of 14–29% were reported (Biemiller, 2003; Brabham & Lynch-Brown, 2002; Elley, 1989; Penno et al., 2002; Sénéchal, 1997; Sénéchal et al., 1995). Explanations of each word were given during one of the repeated readings. Note that these results refer to the delayed posttest when reported. (Interestingly, delayed posttest results tend to be slightly higher than immediate posttests.)

In these studies, a major determinant of the actual number of words learned was the number of words taught in each study. This ranged from 10 to 40 instructed words, with gains in word meanings learned ranging from 1.0 to 1.9 word meanings per instructional day. The percentages of words learned was similar, so that when more words were taught, more were learned. One could expect that there is an upper limit to the number of words taught per day. In the studies reviewed here, a range of from 3 to 10 words were instructed per day. There was no relationship between the number of words taught daily and the percentage of words learned.

In the case of word explanation studies, similar methods were used. Stories would be read, and teachers would interrupt to explain some words. Here are two examples of word explanations "in context." These examples are from Biemiller (2003). Similar methods are described by Brabham and Lynch-Brown (2002), Elley (1989), and Penno et al. (2002):

> From *Clifford and the Circus*, the text reads: "A smaller sign said the circus needed **help**." Teacher repeats the target sentence and explains "help." "*A sign said the circus needed **help**. Help in this story has a different meaning. 'The circus needed **help**,' means the circus show wants to hire some people to work at the show—to help put on the show.*"
>
> From *Thomas and the Naughty Diesel*, the text reads: "Diesel could feel his **temper rising**." The teacher rereads the sentence, " '*Diesel could feel his **temper rising**.' Temper rising means Diesel was getting angry or mad.*"

Note that words for instruction in these studies were selected on an intuitive basis. "Words unlikely to be known" were chosen for instruction. In the following study, a different method was used for selecting words, which were then given more intensive instruction.

INSTRUCTION OF "TIER TWO" WORDS

Isabel Beck, Margaret McKeown, and Linda Kucan (2002) divide words into Tier One, Tier Two, and Tier Three. For them:

- Tier One consists of the most basic words—*clock, baby, happy*—rarely requiring instruction in school.
- Tier Two are high frequency words for mature language users—*coincidence, absurd, industrious*—and thus instruction in these words can add productively to an individual's language ability.
- Tier Three includes words whose frequency of use is quite low, often being limited to specific domains—*isotope, lathe, peninsula*—and are probably best learned when needed in a content area. (pp. 15–16)

They argue that vocabulary in the primary grades should emphasize Tier Two words that are less likely to be learned at home, especially in disadvantaged homes.

Isabel Beck and Margaret McKeown (2003) recently reported on a study of story-based vocabulary instruction using "Tier Two words." Working with first-grade children, they spent a week with each of seven books, teaching 6 words per week for a total of 42 taught words. (Note that this is a much smaller number of weekly words than seen in the other "word explanation" studies.) This allowed intensive work on each word, including the use of the words in other contexts. Examples of Tier Two words in this study were *rambunctious* and *immense*.

Unfortunately, although the percentage of taught words that children learned increased slightly, a total of just 13 more words were known after the program than previously. This amounted to about one third of a word per day of instruction. These gains are less than seen in other story-plus-word-instruction studies, in which 1.0 to 1.9 word meanings were acquired per day. (However, these studies were not run for more than a few days.) I suspect that the Tier Two words may be too advanced in the sequence of word acquisition to be readily learned in grade 1, even with fairly intensive instruction.

DIALOGIC READING

"Dialogic reading differs substantially from the manner that adults typically read picture books to children. A shift of roles is central: In typical book reading, the adult reads and the child listens, but in dialogic reading, the child learns to become the storyteller. The adult then assumes the role of an active listener, asking questions, adding information, and prompting the child to increase the sophistication of his or her description of the material in the picture book. As the child becomes more skillful in the role of storyteller, the adult is encouraged to ask open-ended questions and avoid yes–no or pointing questions. For example, the adult might say, 'What is Eeyore doing?' or 'You tell me about this page' instead of 'Is Eeyore lying down?' " (Whitehurst et al., 1994, p. 680)

Whitehurst et al. used a day-care setting for disadvantaged children, in which caregivers read to groups of five 4-year-old children at a time. Some groups of children were also read to at home. Both the caregivers and the parents were trained in dialogic reading using the videotapes reported in Arnold et al. (1994). A 6-week interval of daily 10-minute Dialogic Reading sessions led to a gain of only 2.5 words from the material read and gains of about 0.5 months on standardized vocabulary tests compared with control-group children who did not participate in Dialogic Reading. However, if these gains could be sustained over a year, Dialogic Reading could lead to a 6-month vocabulary gain on the Peabody Picture Vocabulary Test compared with no intervention. Note that there was relatively little emphasis on learning specific words and that the words chosen could be considered Tier Two words, in Beck and McKeown's (2003) term.

In a more recent effort to use Dialogic Reading with preschool children (Hargrave & Sénéchal, 2000), repeated reading twice without word explanation was compared with repeated Dialogic Reading twice. A total of 10 books were read during 4 weeks. Eighteen "book words" were tested (e.g., *croquet, llama*). Prior to reading, the children in the Dialogic Reading group knew an average of 2.2 "book words" (measured by showing pictures). After the program, they knew 4.3 of these words. Thus, they acquired about 0.4 words per instruction day. As in Whitehurst's work, this poor vocabulary gain may be due to insufficient focus on word meanings and selection of rare words.

A Recent Study with Increased Word Meaning Acquisition

In a recent investigation of classroom vocabulary instruction with kindergarten, grade 1, and grade 2, Catherine Boote and I undertook to increase the numbers of words learned on a per diem basis (Biemiller & Boote, in press; Biemiller, 2003). This study involved regular classroom teachers instructing whole classes. Assessment of vocabulary involved a context sentence method in which

sentences from the stories were read and meanings of particular words in the sentence requested (Biemiller & Slonim, 2001). For example, to individual kindergarten children we read, "We saw a sign that said the **circus** was in town. What does the word **circus** mean in this sentence?" Note that this method of assessing vocabulary is more demanding than a multiple-choice test.

Our work was done with kindergarten, grade one, and grade two children in a working class neighborhood. The majority of the children did not speak English at home. Two teachers taught children at each grade level.

We undertook to increase both the percentage and the number of words learned. Words were selected partly on judgment ("probably hard for this population"). We omitted all words that turned out to be at Dale and O'Rourke's (1981) "level 2" words (i.e., word meanings reported to be known by more than 80% of grade 4 children). In addition, word meanings which were known by more than 75% of the children in our study at pretest were omitted after the pretest. We continued to introduce explanations similar to those described in this chapter. In other words, we provided one- or two-sentence explanations of word meanings anchored in the context of the story being read. Our collaborating teachers suggested adding reviews of words taught each day. In addition, we added a final review after having read the book four times (on four separate days). During the final review, all 25–30 words taught during a week were presented again, but in new sentences not derived from the storybook used during the week. At the posttest 4 weeks after the second book was taught, using additional new-context sentences, we obtained gains of about 40–45% in word meaning knowledge. This resulted in the acquisition of 8–12 word meanings per week. The effect sizes (pre–post) ranged from 2.09 (grade 1) to 2.67 (kindergarten). These were statistically very significant. Results were the same whether posttest words were assessed with the same context sentence as used at pretest or with a second, new-context sentence not based on the story read. In kindergarten and grade 2, similar rates of word learning were found among those with small or large pretest vocabularies. In grade 1, children with larger vocabularies acquired more words.

Assuming that this rate of word acquisition can be sustained over 40 weeks of instruction, 400–500 word meanings can be learned. Because these gains are in addition to words already known at pretests, they can be seen as additions to words learned by children at home or in other contexts.

How Are Words Learned through Narrative-Based Explanations?

"Explaining" word meanings in conjunction with stories generally involves creating a "verbal referent." Any narrative describes the task or tasks of its characters (often including emotional concomitants). An "unknown" word meaning occurring in the narrative can generally be explained as:

- An agent or object in the story (e.g., nouns).
- A task setting or location in the story (also nouns).
- An action in the story (e.g., verbs).
- A feature of an object or action in the story (e.g., adjective or adverb).
- An emotional state of a character.

Children are often aware of the specific context in which word meanings were first learned (Biemiller, 1999). Similarly, when words are explained in stories, children sometimes refer to such story experiences much as they refer to actual experiences when explaining words. This is true even if the word meaning is assessed using a different context. Thus word explanations probably create what Carey (1978) called "fast mappings." Continued experience with the newly acquired meanings will require some continued experience with these words.

Choices of Words for Instruction

I propose an approach to selecting word meanings for instruction based on the fact that (1) children appear to acquire word meanings in an identifiable sequence, and (2) therefore, the best words to teach to children with restricted vocabularies are the words already known by those with larger vocabularies.

For work with preliterate children (i.e., before grade 3), I suggest using words typically known by average and advanced children by the end of grade 2, but not by children with more limited vocabularies. Statistically, this means omitting both word meanings known by most children by the end of grade 2 and also omitting word meanings known by few children by the end of grade 2. We find that most second-grade children, even children who do not speak English at home, know most of the meanings that Dale and O'Rourke reported as "known by 80% of grade-4 children" (Dale & O'Rourke, 1981). (These are also the words used by Dale and Chall in their Readability Scale; Chall & Dale, 1995.) Words reported to be known at grade 8 or higher are unlikely to be known by grade-2 children. In current research, we are finding that about 45% of grade-4 words (known by 67–80% of grade 4 children) and 35% of grade-6 words are likely to be known by grade-2 children with advanced vocabularies but not by grade-2 children with less advanced vocabularies.[4] Appendix 3.1 provides examples of well-known meanings, teachable meanings, and little-known meanings.

Most of the words identified by statistical procedures are words of relatively less dramatic—for example, *sliver, fresh* (new, not spoiled), or *stock* (provide, supply)—than the Tier Two words recommended by Beck and McKeown (2003). However, the fact is that children with large vocabularies know these words by grade 2, whereas those making slower progress have not yet learned them.

If we are to raise the vocabularies of children with smaller vocabularies during kindergarten to grade 2, we should concentrate on words that fall into this "known by 40–75%" category. I estimate that this includes approximately 4,000 root-word meanings. Success would be for children with small vocabularies to learn about half of these word meanings. The difference between the vocabularies of average children and children in the lowest quartile is 2,000 root-word meanings.[5]

Practical Implications

Used in kindergarten, grade 1, and grade 2, the rate of word acquisition from instruction seen in many of these studies is sufficient to make a serious impact on children's readiness for academic learning in grades 3 and higher. The missing link at this point is identifying words to be taught. At present, the solution would be to apply teachers' or publishers' judgments to the lists of root-word meanings at levels 4 and 6 in Dale and O'Rourke's (1981) Living Word Vocabulary. There are also a few primary-appropriate word meanings even at Dale and O'Rourke's levels 8 and 10.

Teachers should begin seriously attempting to teach significant numbers of words to children. At this point, pick words that are above grade-2 level and use their judgment about which words will be needed to understand stories, as well as to provide good opportunities for learning. We have not experimented with expository texts as bases for vocabulary instruction and really do not know whether they are as good for teaching word meanings. However, I am not sure that expository text—without a narrative thread—will prove to be as effective as narratives for vocabulary instruction in the primary grades.

Teaching words (through stories or any other effective method) takes time. Most of the vocabulary intervention studies involved about half an hour per day. Setting aside half an hour a day in a busy primary classroom may seem a lot—though it is not as much time as is routinely devoted to decoding. As I said at the beginning of this chapter, *reading print* and *understanding words* are the two conditions needed for success in reading "grade-level" books. At present, we spend a lot of time teaching (and assessing!) reading mechanics—the skills needed to read words on pages. But we spend almost no time on systematically building vocabulary. Until we do so, we cannot see significant gains in reading *comprehension* for the majority of disadvantaged children—children whose vocabularies are well below average.

Notes

1. "Root words are monomorphemic lexical entries that consist of single, free morphemes. Examples are . . . *closet, flop, hermit*, and *pep*" Anglin, 1993, p. 18). Words such as *hermits* and *peppy* are multimorphemic, containing both the root meaning and a grammatical inflection.
2. I suspect that function words (articles, prepositions, pronouns, the verb *to be*) and grammatical affixes (e.g., *-ed* [past tense] or *-s* [plural]) may not involve direct explanation. These function words occur vastly more frequently than nonfunction words (see Sakiey & Fry, 1984).
3. This section on Feitelson's work is adapted from Biemiller (1999). Copyright 1999 by Andrew Biemiller. Adapted by permission.

APPENDIX 3.1. Examples of Word Meanings Known by Most, by Some, and by Few at the End of Grade 2[6]

Known by most		Known by some		Known by few	
fish	a water animal	*sliver*	tiny piece of wood	*know*	recognize
spread	to distribute over a surface (e.g., buttering)	*space*	room	*period*	a time in history
		buckle	to fasten	*because*	for the reason that
throat	passage from stomach to mouth	*fresh*	new, not spoiled	*victim*	injured person
		secure	free from fear	*lash*	fasten with rope
near	close	*justice*	fair dealing	*tree*	rack for shoes, hats
café	eating place	*tally*	count	*text*	schoolbook
stab	stick knife into	*through*	from start to end	*guard*	a defense
subtract	take number from another	*blab*	tell secret	*narrow*	lacking a broad view
loop	a circled string	*litter*	disorder	*induct*	to bring in
done	finished doing	*stock*	supply, provide	*curious*	odd, strange
drop	fall	*possum*	animal	*alias*	false name
fuss	cry and scream	*shimmer*	faint gleam	(and many more advanced words)	
math	school subject	*parcel*	package		

4. I am currently conducting research on all grade-4 and grade-6 words to determine which are likely to be useful for primary education.
5. At present, I am engaged in a testing program to identify these words. I expect to have this research completed in about a year.
6. Meanings sampled from the Living Word Vocabulary (Dale & O'Rourke, 1981) with data from Biemiller and Slonim (2001).

References

Akhtar, N., Jipson, J., & Callanan, M. A. (2001). Learning words through overhearing. *Child Development, 72*, 416–430.

Anglin, J. M. (1993). Vocabulary development: A morphological analysis. *Monographs of the Society for Research in Child Development, 58* (10, Serial No. 238), 1–165.

Arnold, D. H., Lonigan, C. J., Whitehurst, G. J., & Epstein, J. N. (1994). Accelerating language development through picture book reading: Replication and extension to a videotape training format. *Journal of Educational Psychology, 86*(2), 235–243.

Baumann, J. F., Edwards, E. C., Boland, E. M., Olejnik, S. & Kame'enui, E. J. (2003). Vocabulary tricks: Effects of instruction on morphology and context on fifth-grade students' ability to derive and infer word meanings. *American Educational Research Journal, 40*(2), 447–494.

Beals, D. E., & Tabors, P. O. (1995). Arboretum, bureaucratic and carbohydrates: Preschoolers' exposure to rare vocabulary at home. *First Language, 18*, 57–76.

Beck, I. L., McKeown, M. G., & Kucan, L. (2002). *Bringing words to life: Robust vocabulary instruction.* New York: Guilford Press.

Beck, I. L., & McKeown, M. G., (2003, May). *Promoting vocabulary development in the early grades.* Paper presented at the annual conference of the International Reading Association, Orlando, FL.

Becker, W. C. (1977). Teaching reading and language to the disadvantaged: What we have learned from field research. *Harvard Educational Review, 47*, 518–543.

Behrend, D. A., Scofield, J., & Kleinknecht, E. E. (2001). Beyond fast mapping: Young children's extensions of novel words and novel facts. *Developmental Psychology, 37*, 698–705.

Biemiller, A. (1999). *Language and reading success.* Cambridge, MA: Brookline Books.

Biemiller, A. (1999, April). *Estimating vocabulary growth for ESL children with and without listening comprehension instruction.* Paper presented at the annual conference of the American Educational Research Association, Montreal, Quebec, Canada.

Biemiller, A. (2003, May). *Using stories to promote vocabulary:* Paper presented at the symposium on Fostering Early Narrative Competency: Innovations in Instruction, International Reading Association, Orlando, FL.

Biemiller, A. (2005). Size and sequence in vocabulary development: Implications for choosing words for primary grade vocabulary instruction. In E. H. Hiebert & M. Kamil (Eds.), *Teaching and learning vocabulary: Bringing research to practice* (pp. 223–245). Mahwah, NJ: Erlbaum.

Biemiller, A., & Boote, C. (in press). An effective method for building vocabulary in primary grades. *Journal of Educational Psychology.*

Biemiller, A., & Slonim, N. (2001). Estimating root word vocabulary growth in normative and advantaged populations: Evidence for a common sequence of vocabulary acquisition. *Journal of Educational Psychology, 93*, 498–520.

Brabham, E. G., & Lynch-Brown, C. (2002). Effects of teachers' reading-aloud styles on vocabulary acquisition and comprehension of students in the early elementary grades. *Journal of Educational Psychology, 94*, 465–473.

Cantalini, M. (1987). *The effects of age and gender on school readiness and school success.* Unpublished doctoral dissertation, Ontario Institute for Studies in Education, Toronto, Ontario, Canada.

Carey, S. (1978). The child as a word learner. In M. Halle, J. Bresnan, & G. A. Miller (Eds.), *Linguistic theory and psychological reality* (pp. 264–293). Cambridge, MA: MIT Press.

Case, R. (1985). *Intellectual development: Birth to adulthood.* New York: Academic Press.

Chall, J. S., & Conard, S. S. (1991). *Should textbooks challenge students?* New York: Teachers College Press.

Chall, J. S., & Dale, E. (1995). *Readability revisited: The new Dale–Chall readability formula.* Cambridge, MA: Brookline Books.

Chall, J. S., Jacobs, V. A., & Baldwin, L. E. (1990). *The reading crisis: Why poor children fall behind.* Cambridge, MA: Harvard University Press.

Christian, K., Morrison, F. J, Frazier, J. A., & Massetti, G. (2000). Specificity in the nature and timing of cognitive growth in kindergarten and first grade. *Journal of Cognition and Development, 1*(4), 429–448.

Cunningham, A. E., & Stanovich, K. E. (1997). Early reading acquisition and its relation to reading experience and ability 10 years later. *Developmental Psychology, 33*, 934–945.

Dale, E., & O'Rourke, J. (1981). *Living word vocabulary,* Chicago: World Book/Childcraft.

Dale, E., & O'Rourke, J. (1986). *Vocabulary building: A process approach.* Columbus, OH: Zener-Bloser.

Edwards, E. C., Font, G., Baumann, J. F., & Boland, E. B. (2004). Unlocking word meanings: Strategies and guidelines for teaching morphemic and contextual analysis. In J. F. Baumann & E. J. Kame'enui (Eds.), *Vocabulary instruction: Research to practice* (pp. 159–178). New York: Guilford Press.

Elley, W. B. (1989). Vocabulary acquisition from listening to stories. *Reading Research Quarterly, 24,* 174–186.

Feitelson, D., Goldstein, Z., Iraqi, J., & Share, D. I. (1991). Effects of listening to story reading on aspects of literacy acquisition in a diglossic situation. *Reading Research Quarterly, 28,* 70–79.

Feitelson, D., Kita, B., & Goldstein, Z. (1986). Effects of listening to series stories on first graders' comprehension and use of language. *Research in the Teaching of English, 20,* 339–356.

Graves, M. F. (2004). Teaching prefixes: As good as it gets? In J. F. Baumann & E. J. Kame'enui (Eds.), *Vocabulary instruction: Research to practice* (pp. 81–99). New York: Guilford Press.

Hall, D. G., & Graham, S. A. (1999). Lexical form class information guides word-to-object mapping in preschoolers. *Child Development, 70,* 78–91.

Hargrave, A. C., & Sénéchal, M. (2000). A book reading intervention with preschool children who have limited vocabularies: The benefits of regular reading and dialogic reading. *Early Childhood Research Quarterly, 15,* 75–90.

Hart, B., & Risley, T. (1995). *Meaningful differences in the everyday experience of young American children.* Baltimore: Brookes.

Hart, B., & Risley, T. (1999). *The social world of children learning to talk.* Baltimore: Brookes.

Hart, B., & Risley, T. R. (2003). The early catastrophe: The 30 million word gap by age 3. *American Educator, 27*(1), 4–9.

Nagy, W., & Herman, P. (1987). Depth and breadth of vocabulary knowledge: Implications for acquisition and instruction. In M. G. McKeown & M. E. Curtis (Eds.), *The nature of vocabulary acquisition* (pp. 19–36). Hillsdale, NJ: Erlbaum.

Nagy, W. E., & Scott, J. A. (2001). Vocabulary processes. In M. L. Kamil, P. B. Mosenthal, P. D. Pearson, & R. Barr (Eds.), *Handbook of reading research* (Vol. 3, pp. 269–284). Mahwah, NJ: Erlbaum.

Penno, J. F., Wilkinson, A. G., & Moore, D. W. (2002). Vocabulary acquisition from teacher explanation and repeated listening to stories: Do they overcome the Matthew effect? *Journal of Educational Psychology, 94,* 23–33.

Robbins, C., & Ehri, L. C. (1994). Reading storybooks to kindergartners helps them learn new vocabulary words. *Journal of Educational Psychology, 86*(1), 139–153.

Sakiey, E., & Fry, E. (1984). *3000 instant words* (rev. ed.). Providence, RI: Jamestown.

Sandhofer, C. M., & Smith, L. B. (1999). Learning color words involves learning a system of mappings. *Developmental Psychology, 35,* 668–679.

Scarbrough, H. (2001). Connecting early language and literacy to later reading (dis)abilities: Evidence, theory, and practice. In S. B. Neuman & D. K. Dickinson (Eds.), *Handbook of Early Literacy Research* (pp. 97–110). New York: Guilford Press.

Sénéchal, M. (1997). The differential effect of storybook reading on preschoolers' acquisition of expressive and receptive vocabulary. *Child Language, 24,* 123–138.

Sénéchal, M., Thomas, E., & Monker, J.-A. (1995). Individual differences in 4-year-old children's acquisition of vocabulary during storybook reading. *Journal of Educational Psychology, 87*(2), 218–229.

Stahl, S. A., & Fairbanks, M. A. (1986). The effects of vocabulary instruction: A model-based meta-analysis. *Review of Educational Research, 56,* 72–110.

Storch, S. A., & Whitehurst, G. J. (2002). Oral language and code-related precursors to reading: Evidence from a longitudinal structural model. *Developmental Psychology, 38,* 934–947.

Weizman, Z. O., & Snow, C. E. (2001). Lexical input as related to children's vocabulary acquisition: Effects of sophisticated exposure and support for meaning. *Developmental Psychology, 17,* 265–279.

Wells, C. G. (1985). *Language development in the preschool years.* New York: Cambridge University Press.

White, T. G., Power, M. A., & White, S. (1989). Morphological analysis: Implications for teaching and understanding vocabulary growth. *Reading Research Quarterly. 24,* 283–304.

Whitehurst, G. J., Arnold, D. S., Epstein, J. N., Angell, A. L., Smith, M., & Fischel, J. E. (1994). A picture book reading intervention in day care and home for children from low-income families. *Developmental Psychology, 30,* 679–689.

4

Literacy Development: Insights from Research on Skilled Reading

JANE ASHBY
KEITH RAYNER

Reading seems like such a natural act. Literate adults find it almost impossible to look at a word and not read it. Once reading becomes an automatic process, it feels effortless. Just as most adults move from place to place without thinking about the muscle movements involved in walking, skilled readers are rarely conscious of coordinating the cognitive processes involved in reading. Instead, readers mainly focus on the *why* and the *what* (the goals and the content) of the reading material. Indeed, that is a central goal of reading instruction: to help children learn how to read effortlessly so they can ignore the reading process and focus on the content.

Understanding how to help children become better readers is a complicated process with many dimensions. As skilled readers, we can attest to the joys of reading and convey these to children at home and at school. Another important dimension of reading education includes understanding what skilled readers do when they read. This chapter discusses how research on the cognitive processes of skilled readers can inform teachers' understanding of reading development. Understanding which cognitive processes operate during skilled reading allows teachers to focus early literacy activities on the essential processes that will eventually contribute to skilled reading.

Research on skilled reading offers some unexpected insights into reading development, even to teachers with considerable professional experience (see Rayner, Foorman, Perfetti, Pesetsky, & Seidenberg, 2001, 2002, for a more complete review of this research). There are several reasons why the processes involved in skilled reading are not obvious. Although teachers accumulate a wealth of case-study information about the reading development of particular children, these experiences do not allow many opportunities to learn about the end point of reading development. Reflecting on one's own skilled reading processes is not very informative, either. Because skilled reading processes are automatized and, therefore, removed from conscious awareness, intuitions about how we read can be misleading. The effortlessness of skilled reading interferes with our ability to understand it through introspection. Fortunately, psychologists have been studying the nature of the cognitive processes involved in skilled reading over the past few decades (Rayner & Pollatsek, 1989; Rayner et al., 2001). Understanding the nature of these processes and how they contribute to skilled reading can help teachers encourage children to develop good reading habits by strengthening the critical processes that support skilled reading.

Before we begin the discussion of skilled reading processes, it may help to clarify some of the terms that we use. In this chapter, reading is considered apart from literacy. To be literate, a child must acquire a range of skills that are embedded in technological and cultural contexts. Reading, on the other hand, is a necessary foundation for literacy. Use of the term *reading*, then, refers to the process of gaining meaning from print. Because the basic unit of meaning is the word, reading words quickly and accurately is a necessary step in becoming a skilled reader. The ability to identify words automatically is termed *word recognition*. This chapter focuses mainly on the word recognition processes of skilled readers. Although other important processes (e.g., comprehension and vocabulary) are involved in skilled reading as well, developing efficient word recognition processes is the major obstacle faced by beginning readers as they learn to convert print to language (Rayner et al., 2001). Words that a reader can recognize belong to that reader's *lexicon*, or mental dictionary. The lexicon stores the meaning and pronunciation of the items (words) it contains. The process of mapping a printed word onto a specific meaning is termed *lexical access*, and this is the centerpiece of early literacy instruction.

A Long-Standing Debate about Lexical Access Processes

Which cognitive processes are engaged in order to achieve lexical access? An ongoing debate concerning this issue has affected educators' concepts of reading instruction for the past 30 years. The debate concerns whether skilled readers use phonological coding or direct access to identify words. Phonological coding refers to the process of assigning speech-based codes to the print we read, whereas direct access refers to the process of accessing meaning directly from the visual word form. Whether skilled readers use direct access or phonological coding has profound implications for the nature of early reading instruction. Before reviewing the experimental evidence pertaining to this debate, let's examine the rationale that underlies the direct-access view in terms of the nature of writing systems and how they operate.

To support the claim that phonological coding is unnecessary for reading, Smith (1999) describes how in the course of daily life we see an object (such as an angry dog) and identify its meaning immediately, without needing to convert that object into spoken words. Smith argues that if we can access the meanings of objects directly, then we should be able to access meaning directly from the visual stimulus of the print. According to this view, writing systems consist of words that, like objects, are units whose meanings can be directly accessed. Although Smith's analogy may seem persuasive at first, it rests on an assumption of similarity between print and physical objects. In one sense they are similar, as print is technically a collection of objects, or marks on paper. Beyond this point, however, written language differs from other physical objects in some important ways. Most obviously, objects are perceptually distinct from each other in texture, shape, and color, whereas the 250,000 or more printed words in English are composed of only 26 letters that are easily confused. Unlike any other set of objects, writing systems are comprehensive and productive archival systems. A writing system can represent any topic that spoken language can communicate, whether that is the adventures of a superhero, despair, art history, or auto mechanics. These ideas can be communicated in novel ways that affect the reader's understanding of the basic message, as in a love poem or political pamphlet. As a writing system records thoughts and actions, it archives this information for the future. In fact, writing systems arose from the need to maintain a record of traded goods. Thousands of years ago, the Phoenicians developed a phonetic alphabet that spread throughout the Mediterranean among their trading partners. The Greeks adopted that alphabet in 1000 B.C. and it served as the foundation for our current Western alphabetic systems (Crystal, 1997).

Reading, then, is much more than an automatic act of object perception. Reading engages a complex set of cognitive processes to use a technology that was developed for a specific purpose (trade) and adapted to a wide range of communicative functions. Given these vast differences between objects and written words, it would be quite surprising if the identical set of cognitive processes were involved in each identification task. Instead, it seems reasonable to consider writing systems as ways of encoding language, and we fundamentally experience language as speech. From this perspective, one might expect that phonological coding plays a role in skilled reading. For skilled readers, phonological coding may be consciously experienced as inner speech, or the voice they hear in their head during reading. Skilled readers notice their inner speech to varying degrees, but many of us have had the experience of reading a letter from our mother and hearing the words pronounced in her voice (Rayner & Pollatsek, 1989). The extent of the role of phonological coding in lexical access has been examined by cognitive psychologists and is discussed further in the next section.

Cognitive Processes Involved in Skilled Reading

The progress scientists have made in understanding reading processes has brought about notable changes in reading theory since the 1970s. At that time, reading was viewed as a hypothesis testing activity (Levin & Kaplan, 1970) or a psycholinguistic guessing game (Goodman, 1970). Skilled reading was thought to proceed in the following fashion: A reader would generate a hypothesis about what an upcoming word would be, move the eyes to that word and quickly confirm the hypothesis, then use the identity of that word (along with other contextual information) to predict what the next word would be, and so on. Since then, a large amount of research on skilled reading has led to a replacement of this view with one in which the word-form information contained in the print is used to identify words rapidly. According to this view, the lexical information needed for reading enters the cognitive system very quickly. Context still plays a role in interpreting the meaning of a sentence, but skilled readers identify words quickly even without the help of context. Surprisingly, it is the less skilled readers who rely on context information to support lexical access (Perfetti, Goldman, & Hogaboam, 1979; Stanovich, 1980; Ashby, Rayner, & Clifton, 2005). This current view of word recognition in reading has been shaped by two influential lines of research: studies of isolated word identification and studies of eye movements during reading.

Word Identification Studies

Research on word identification uses a variety of tasks to measure the relative ease or difficulty of identifying single words under different conditions. These experiments are conducted in order to answer specific questions about how skilled readers identify words. One central question in this research concerns whether words are processed letter by letter or as whole units. More than 100 years ago, Cattell (1886) reported that when words and letters were presented for a fraction of a second, participants were better able to identify a letter presented in a word than a letter presented alone. As the skilled readers in Cattell's experiment seemed to process words as wholes, rather than letter by letter, education policy makers advocated for a transition from phonics-based reading instruction to whole-word teaching methods early in the 20th century. However, when later experiments were conducted using better experimental designs and more modern technology, the findings did not support whole-word instruction (Reicher, 1969; Wheeler, 1970). Reicher (1969) and Wheeler (1970) did replicate Cattell's effect; they found that single letters were identified better when presented in a word than when presented alone or in a nonword. This finding was subsequently called the *word-superiority effect*. The word-superiority effect indicated that words are not processed one letter at a time; otherwise, single letters would have been reported better than letters presented in a group (or word). Instead, skilled readers processed letters in parallel, at least in short words. Reicher (1969) and Wheeler (1970) also tested participants' accuracy for reporting letters at different positions in a word and found that the word-superiority effect held for letters in every position. This finding indicated that readers were processing all of the letters in a word, not just a global impression of the word based on their perception of some of the letters. Skilled readers store very specific representations of words in their lexicon and apply that detailed information when recognizing words.

A second central question in word identification research is how much skilled readers use phonological coding to identify words. As we mentioned earlier, there is a longstanding debate about whether skilled readers access the meaning of words directly from their visual perception of the letters or whether they assign sounds to the letters in the process of accessing the meaning. Direct access (print to meaning) has been argued to be the more efficient process for identifying words (Smith, 1973), as that system avoids the extra step of phonological coding (word to sound to meaning) and can cope with the many irregularly spelled words in English (*pint, have*, etc.). Although skilled readers' ability to access the meanings of irregular words (i.e., words that violate letter–sound correspondence patterns, such as *aisle*) and homophones (e.g., *plane–plain*) clearly indicates that a direct access route exists, there is considerable evidence that phonological information plays an important role in word recognition (see Frost, 1998, for a thorough review). As an example, the categorization studies by Van Orden (1987; Van Orden, Johnston, & Hale, 1988) indicate that skilled readers use phonological information when reading single words. In these studies readers were presented with a question, such as "Is it a flower?", before reading a word (*rose*) and deciding whether it is a member of that category. On the critical trials, the word was a homophone of the actual category member (*rows*). On a significant number of homophone trials, readers incorrectly identified the homophone (*rows*) as being a member of the category (flower). These response errors would not have occurred unless readers were phonologically recoding the words in the process of reading them. In different series of experiments, Perfetti and Zhang (1995) demonstrated that even skilled readers of Chinese used phonological recoding while reading. It appears, then, that phonological recoding is used by skilled readers in identifying isolated words. One might argue that reading single words is fundamentally different from the reading processes adults use daily. Therefore, it is important to study how word recognition processes operate during silent reading when words occur in context and reading is relatively natural.

Eye Movements in Reading

Few people are aware of their eye movements during reading. Even when skilled readers try to be aware of their eye movements, they often experience the illusion of their eyes moving across a page smoothly. Actually, the eyes are moving and stopping several times while reading a line of text. Each rapid movement of the eyes is termed a *saccade*, and saccades move the eyes from place to place in the text. During the fixations between the saccades, the eye is relatively still. It is during these fixations, which typically last about .25 seconds, that people get information from the text. No new information is acquired during saccades because vision is suppressed. Contrary to most people's intuitions about how their eyes process text, visual processing during reading is similar to a slide show, in which the text appears for a quarter of a second, is interrupted briefly by a saccade, then reappears, and so forth. Each time the eyes fixate, a new slide appears, and readers get a glimpse of another part of the text.

The reason that the eyes move so often during reading may not be obvious. It should be possible, in principle, to take in large sections of the text in one fixation. The physiology of the visual system prevents readers from doing so, however. Humans see the most clearly and accurately in the center of their visual field, which is called the *fovea*. Because readers have the best acuity when perceiving letters that are in foveal view, they move their eyes frequently in order to bring different parts of the text into foveal view. With each fixation, several letters in foveal view are being processed in parallel in order to reach lexical access for that word. Outside the fovea, in the parafoveal and peripheral regions, vision receptors are not able to make out the fine details of the letters. The clarity of the visual field, then, is not uniform. If we imagine the visual field as an archery target, the bull's-eye area in the center would have the highest acuity. Between the bull's-eye and the first ring, in the parafovea, letter forms are partially discriminated. Outside of the first ring, in the periphery, only gross shapes are detected (such as word length). This metaphor is somewhat inaccurate, however, because these perceptual regions are not sharply demarcated and are larger to the right than to the left of the center of fixation for readers of English.

Many people are surprised by this description of how the eyes process visual information. It is a striking example of how little conscious awareness we have of the cognitive processes involved in reading. How the eyes operate during reading is one of the major discoveries of psychological research, and understanding this mechanism has led to a greater understanding of how skilled readers process text (Rayner, 1975, 1998). Several classic experiments used a highly sensitive eye tracking system to monitor skilled readers as they read silently from a computer screen. Rayner and colleagues used an eye-contingent display-change technology to investigate questions about how many letters readers could perceive during one fixation (McConkie & Rayner, 1975; Rayner, 1975; Rayner & Bertera, 1979). The eye-contingent display-change technology allowed experimenters to rapidly change the text that readers saw when they were looking at a particular location on the screen. By manipulating what readers saw and measuring their fixation durations, researchers infer how readers are processing text. Display changes that interfered with word recognition processes resulted in longer fixation durations on average, whereas changes in the text that facilitated word recognition resulted in shorter fixations on average. Data from these display-change experiments indicated that replacing letters in a text with x's had variable effects depending on the relationship of the location of the x's to the location at which the reader was looking. When x's appeared in foveal view, reading was slowed dramatically, because readers were prevented from directly fixating on the word and processing its letters. In contrast, reading speed was not affected when x's appeared more than 15 letter spaces to the right of a reader's fixation.

These experiments helped scientists understand the features of the perceptual span in reading (or how many letters readers perceive in any one fixation). Readers' perceptual spans are asymmetrical, extending from 3 to 4 letter spaces to the left of fixation out to 14 or 15 letter spaces to the right of the fixation. Typically, skilled readers use information within only 7 or 8 letter spaces to the right of fixation to support their recognition of upcoming words, and much of that information is parafoveal. Gross information, such as word length, is acquired up to 15 letters out from fixation. The perceptual span also varies depending on the language being read (Rayner, 1998). Cross-language research in Chinese, Japanese, and Hebrew indicates that the experience of reading affects both the length and the asymmetry of the

perceptual span. In writing systems that are written left to right, such as English, the perceptual span in reading extends farther to the right of fixation than to the left. In writing systems that are produced right to left, such as Hebrew, the span extends farther to the left of fixation than to the right (Pollatsek, Bolozsky, Well, & Rayner, 1981). In both cases, the perceptual span is asymmetrical in the direction of the upcoming text. The size of the perceptual span in skilled readers also varies with the semantic density of the writing system. In Chinese, for example, in which two characters can express complex meanings, the perceptual span includes far fewer characters than is the case for English readers (Inhoff & Liu, 1998). It appears, then, that reading practice develops a perceptual span that is useful for fluently reading a specific writing system.

One consequence of the perceptual span is that readers can process some words without fixating directly on them. Skilled readers typically fixate only about two thirds of the words in a text. The words that are not fixated are usually short, function words (*a*, *the*, *for*) and words that are highly predictable from the preceding context. There is evidence, however, that readers process all the words in a text, even those that the eyes skip. Several experiments have observed that readers make longer fixations on a word if they are about to skip the next word than if they are planning to fixate the next word, and this suggests that readers are sometimes processing two words although their eyes may fixate only on one (Rayner, 1998).

Eye-movement experiments have proliferated in cognitive psychology because they offer a direct way of studying reading processes as they occur during silent reading of connected text. Data collected at different labs by a variety of researchers have extended our understanding of the role of eye movements in reading and how they reflect the cognitive processes used by skilled readers. Eye movements are influenced by low level factors, such as word length, and higher level processes, such as lexical access. Skilled readers get most of the information needed to recognize a word after fixating it for about 50 milliseconds (Rayner, Inhoff, Morrison, Slowiaczek, & Bertera, 1981; Rayner, Liversedge, White, & Vergilino-Perez, 2003). Although visual information gets to the brain very quickly, the ease or difficulty of identifying a printed word strongly influences how long it is fixated. Words are typically fixated for about 250 milliseconds (the average time for lexical access), but very familiar words are fixated for less time than that and unfamiliar words receive longer fixations. This suggests that eye movements are closely linked to lexical access processes that operate very efficiently during skilled reading.

Eye-movement experiments have also demonstrated that skilled readers activate phonological information early in a fixation (Pollatsek, Lesch, Morris, & Rayner, 1992; Rayner, Sereno, Lesch, & Pollatsek, 1995; Lesch & Pollatsek, 1998; Lee, Rayner, & Pollatsek, 1999). Collectively, these experiments indicate that phonological coding occurs at the level of the string of phonemes that constitute the word. In addition to phoneme segment information, recent research suggests that more complex phonological information is represented during silent reading. Eye-movement research by Ashby and Rayner (2004) suggests that syllable information is represented parafoveally and used to support word recognition during a fixation. Ashby and Clifton (2005) found that readers represent lexical stress information during silent reading. These eye-movement studies indicate that skilled readers represent complex aspects of a word's phonological form, including syllable and stress information. Paradoxically, much of this information is not explicitly coded in our writing system. Thus, finding that skilled readers routinely represent multiple layers of phonological information also suggests that readers access their stored representations of spoken words.

Rapid phonological coding appears to accompany the visual word recognition processes of skilled readers en route to lexical access. By phonologically recoding the words in a text as they are identified, skilled readers can integrate each word into a working memory representation of the sentence, which then feeds comprehension processes. In this way, skilled readers move their eyes systematically through the text, using a complex set of cognitive processes to identify each word before moving to the next one. The sum of the evidence from word-identification experiments and eye-movement experiments indicates that skilled readers process text thoroughly and automatically from the letter level on up. Modern reading research does not support the claim that skilled readers engage in a psycholinguistic guessing game.

Research Implications for Early Reading Development

In this section, findings from research on skilled reading are linked to the behavior of beginning readers that can be observed in any classroom. Some of these findings help us better understand why children struggle with reading early on, whereas others inform instructional choices by indicating what early skills are essential to continued reading development. Although these insights are useful, we do not mean to imply that the pedagogy of beginning reading instruction should emulate reading instruction in the later grades. In fact, our point contrasts markedly with that idea. We hope that these findings from research with skilled readers will emphasize the developmental nature of reading acquisition and help teachers realize the implications of early reading instruction for reading achievement in adulthood.

Eye Movements and Reading Development

One difference between skilled and beginning readers is the nature of their eye movements (Rayner, 1998). This difference may appear physiological, but actually it reflects differences in cognitive processing during reading. The characteristics of early readers' eye movements both reflect and affect their reading processes. The eye movements of beginning readers primarily reflect the difficulty they have identifying words in the text. Because they are unfamiliar with the written form of most words they encounter, children's fixation times are considerably longer, and they regress much more often than do skilled readers (Rayner, 1986). As readers become more skilled, their fixation durations decrease as words are identified more quickly and accurately. Beginning readers also have a smaller perceptual span, and it is not initially asymmetrical in the direction of reading (Rayner, 1986). They make many more fixations and have shorter saccades than skilled readers, as a shorter perceptual span restricts the number of letters that early readers can hold in foveal view. The combination of children's shorter perceptual spans and the increased font size common in most early books further restricts the number of letters children perceive in one fixation. Unfortunately, having a shorter perceptual span probably contributes to the tendency to limit attention to the initial letters in a word and guess the rest. A guess about an unfamiliar word can often be made quickly, given pictures and other cues, causing only a minor disruption to the flow of language in the sentence. Attending to all the letters in a word, in contrast, might require a child to make additional fixations. Initially, the process of fully inspecting an unknown word might take more time, but when the child identifies it, he or she will be mapping the details of the full letter string onto a word in spoken language. The specificity of that representation supports advances in later reading development, as the word-superiority effect demonstrates that skilled readers process all of the letters when identifying a word. Therefore, reading instruction should encourage children to attend to all of the letters in a word, not just the first and the last (Ehri, 1980; Perfetti, 1992; Venezky & Massaro, 1979). Books with short words allow children to register all of the letters in a word during a single fixation.

Another developmental difference between skilled and beginning readers involves the use of phonological coding during reading. Numerous word-identification and eye-movement studies have demonstrated that phonological information is available to skilled readers early in a fixation and that phonological recoding occurs automatically during skilled reading (Frost, 1998; Rayner, 1998). In contrast, many early readers struggle with phonological coding. Several factors contribute to this struggle, including their limited perceptual span. Another major factor is early reader's limited knowledge of letter–sound correspondences, or the connection between print and spoken language. Given these obstacles, early readers might opt to use other strategies to identify a word. They might attempt to guess the word by using context and picture clues or by visually matching the letter string to a word seen before. This visual matching behavior, when

successful, is an example of using the direct route to access the meaning of a written word.

Pedagogical Influences on Reading Development

Direct-access theories have had a profound impact on early reading instruction, but problems can arise when instruction de-emphasizes phonological coding. Consider what happens when a young reader comes upon an unfamiliar word in the course of reading a story. Because this letter string has not been processed before, there is no association between the word form and its meaning, and the direct-access mechanism cannot operate. At this point, the child can guess what the word is based on its context, but cannot know whether the guess is correct. However, a child who can phonologically recode the letter string by converting it into speech sounds can match it to his or her knowledge of a spoken word. In this way, phonological decoding also serves as a mechanism for generalizing the meaning of spoken words to the meaning of written words and, thus, is a valuable self-teaching tool even for skilled readers (Jorm & Share, 1983). Because such a child can identify words without depending on context cues, he or she is able to enjoy books that use language creatively and contain unpredictable plot lines. As ambiguous language and unusual word choices pervade our most sophisticated literature, using context to identify individual words does not appear to be a promising long-term strategy. Furthermore, because phonological decoding requires that every letter in a word be processed, it helps build high-quality memory representations of word-specific letter strings (Adams, 1990; Ehri, 1980; Perfetti, 1992; Venezky & Massaro, 1979) that are necessary for speedy word recognition. A year or two of practice at phonologically decoding unfamiliar words leads to the accumulation of several thousand lexical entries that are print accessible (Share & Stanovich, 1995). Thus early decoding practice supports the development of the automatized phonological coding processes that characterize skilled reading.

Once word-recognition processes are automatic, the ease of single-word reading permits readers to process text effortlessly and to experience the author's use of language, rather than focusing on the letters that make up the print. The automaticity of basic reading processes also helps skilled readers comprehend text at a level that is comparable to their listening comprehension skills. In contrast, beginning readers generally have stronger listening comprehension skills than reading comprehension skills (Curtis, 1980). As printed-word recognition improves, the correlation between reading comprehension and listening comprehension improves to nearly .90 (Gernsbacher, 1990). This high correlation indicates that developing efficient word-recognition processes is necessary for text comprehension. That makes sense, if one considers that word-recognition skills mediate the first line of contact between reader and text. If the print gets converted to language inaccurately, then higher order comprehension processes operate on the wrong word. If the print-to-language conversion is laborious and inefficient, readers may not be able to allocate sufficient cognitive resources to operate higher order processes (Perfetti, 1985, 1992). Becoming a skilled reader, then, fundamentally involves learning how to convert printed words into spoken words (Bradley & Bryant, 1983; Juel, Griffith, & Gough, 1986).

Instruction that develops a child's ability to read unfamiliar words accurately (and familiar words quickly) will, by definition, build the efficient word-recognition processes that are necessary for text comprehension. The importance of building both the accuracy and the speed of word-recognition processes is easy to overlook, however. Intuitively, it may seem most important to get children reading familiar words quickly and easily. That goal can be achieved by having children visually memorize the most common words, such as those on the Dolch list. Memorizing whole words can lead to rapid progress in early reading, particularly for children with good visual memories. As their sight vocabulary expands, reading becomes much more fluent and pleasurable. In this way, "word wall" activities can boost reading fluency because many of the one-syllable, high-frequency words encountered in early reading (such as *could*, *the*) have an irregular pattern of letter–sound mapping that requires whole-word memorization. On the other hand, the majority of the 100 most common words are spelled using letter–sound correspondences that are regular, predictable, and decodable. These hundred words make up about half of all written material (Fry, Fountioukidis, & Polk, 1985).

Whole word memorization can initially jump start reading development, but relying on this approach may be problematic for long-term reading development. First and most obviously, whole word instruction does not help children learn to read new words independently. Every word must first be pronounced by someone who "knows" the word, and the process of how one becomes a "knower" is often obscured. Second, whole word instruction is time consuming. To increase a child's sight-word vocabulary, teachers must provide frequent opportunities to practice *each word*, as opposed to learning patterns of letter–sound correspondences that can generalize to many words. For example, if a child knows the sounds of three consonants (*p*, *t*, and *s*) and two vowels (*i* and *o*), he or she can independently read and spell nearly two dozen words and learn that -*s* marks the plural form of many nouns. Third, focusing children's efforts on visual memorization implicitly directs attention to the visually salient letters in a word, such as those in the initial and final position, while drawing attention away from interior letters, such as vowels, that are key to the accurate mapping between print and spoken language. As a sight vocabulary expands, it begins to contain several words that differ by only one letter (*bank/band*, *coach/couch*). This visual similarity can cause problems, as children might become prone to misreading and misspelling words. Many such inaccuracies in spelling and reading can be self-corrected if children have learned to decompose words into sounds. Last, the whole word approach can present roadblocks both early and late in reading development. Children who have poor visual memory are stymied early in reading, as they struggle to memorize new words. Conversely, children who have good visual memory are initially successful at learning many words. As they receive plenty of reinforcement, they may continue to rely on visual memorization to learn new words. These children, however, do not know how to read new words independently, and so they tend to guess at or skip over the new words encountered during reading. Such habits can hamper the growth of word-recognition skills later in reading development, as children store inaccurate or incomplete word representations in memory.

Given these potential consequences of whole word instruction, putting a heavy emphasis on the ability to read familiar words quickly may not be advisable in early reading instruction. Children must also learn how to read unfamiliar words accurately in order to store complete representations that can be retrieved quickly (Ehri & Wilce, 1983; Perfetti, 1992). To do this, they need to understand that the letters in a word represent sounds and to be given many opportunities to practice converting print into spoken language (Adams, 1990; Perfetti, 2003). When children have truly learned to read, they can independently convert familiar and unfamiliar written words into spoken language and understand the author's intended meaning. Developing skilled reading necessarily involves perfecting this conversion process until it is accurate, automatic, and effortless. It is the ease of lexical access, the automaticity of word recognition, that ultimately allows a child to enjoy reading for pleasure. The critical role that phonological coding plays in learning to recognize words quickly and accurately provides the primary foundation for reading development across the lifespan.

Conclusions

Over the past 20 years, findings from reading research have converged on the importance of phonological coding in reading development (Rayner et al., 2001, 2002). In every language studied to date, reading involves the phonological recoding of print. Even readers of Chinese show evidence of phonological coding during reading, although the process occurs somewhat later than it does in reading English (Spinks, Lui, Perfetti, & Tan, 2000; Zhang, Perfetti, & Yang, 1999). Perfetti (2003) coined the phrase *universal grammar of reading* to refer to the obligatory nature of phonological processing in reading. The central role of phonological recoding in skilled reading implies that instruction in letter-to-sound

mapping is an essential part of reading instruction. The issue currently under debate, then, is not *whether* phonics should be taught but *how* it should taught. One's position in that debate largely depends on the perceived goals of early literacy education. If the goal is to expose young children to the wonder of books and to get them acting like readers and authors, then a whole language approach is warranted. If the goal is to teach the habits that will actually help as many children as possible become skilled readers and intelligible writers, then phonics instruction is necessary (Rayner et al., 2001; Bruck, Treiman, Caravolas, Genesee, & Cassar, 1998). For decades teachers have been told that the first goal of early literacy education described here renders the second one unnecessary. Research on skilled reading, however, suggests that it may be time to reevaluate that belief.

A brief description of these instructional approaches might help clarify the role of each in helping children become skilled readers. In a whole-language classroom, children are immersed in literature as they listen to their teacher read lavishly illustrated Big Books each day. Letter–sound correspondences are taught incidentally, at the moment when a new word needs to be identified, and are not practiced. Most new words are identified with the help of the teacher. Children spend time every day acting like adult readers as they attempt to read engaging texts silently. During silent reading time, they encounter both simple words (*dog*) and complex ones (*elephant*). They practice the strategies they know for identifying new words (e.g., using picture clues to guess the word and predicting the word based on other words in the text). During this time, the children who know many words gain valuable practice recognizing them automatically. Children who have not memorized as many words practice using context and picture clues to guess the word. Both groups of children are enjoying their books, yet one could argue that these children are only pretending to read, as the inherent magic of reading rests on the reader's independence. Any reader of an alphabetic language can pick up any text and convert it into language, even if that reader has never seen those particular words before. And the reader does not need any help. In whole language classrooms, it seems that the wonder of books has overshadowed the magic of reading. Yet this need not be the case.

Early reading education can help children experience the magic of reading by teaching how spoken language is encoded in print and by providing time to practice those skills. The foundation of successful instruction in the alphabetic principle is awareness of the phonological structure of spoken words. This instruction can begin as early as preschool, with activities such as rhyming games, and should continue through kindergarten and first grade with syllable counting, identifying words with matching initial and final sounds, and forming new words by substituting and deleting sounds (Adams, 1990). Because phonological awareness activities focus on how speech sounds make up spoken words, children need not know letter names and/or the alphabet in order to participate (although this knowledge will probably correlate with their success). While children are learning to write letters, they can begin to master the basic letter–sound correspondences, such as consonant sounds and short vowels, and practice sound blending as part of their writing instruction. Phonics instruction continues systematically with more complex mappings, such as long vowels and vowel teams, until most of the hundred or so letter–sound patterns have been introduced by the end of first grade. As children are developing advanced phonological awareness in spoken language, they learn how to map those speech sounds to written language in their spelling and to use those mappings to decode new words as they practice reading decodable texts. Thus children learning phonics can participate in a coherent educational program that emphasizes the alphabetic principle and its application. As children are learning how to read, teachers continue to emphasize the wonder of books by reading aloud to children each day and engaging them in other literature-based activities. Such a program makes the process of reading explicit, so that all children can understand how it works, without forsaking the pedagogical creativity that is the hallmark of whole language instruction.

Despite the appeal of such a balanced approach to early literacy instruction (Rayner et al., 2001), two main obstacles interfere with efforts to establish this approach in classrooms. The first obstacle is practical: Creating engaging activities that build the phonological knowledge of early readers requires an explicit knowledge of the phonological structure of written English. Teachers, as skilled readers, have automatized their own reading processes to the point of removing that knowledge from conscious awareness. Thus teachers tend to lack specific knowledge about the alphabetic principle and the structure of written language (Moats, 1994). Unfortunately, the omission of such topics from teacher education programs has virtually guaranteed a need for tightly scripted programs for teaching phonics in the classroom. Instead, teachers might develop a working knowledge of the scope and sequence of phonics instruction that will guide, rather than dictate, their classroom activities (Moats, 2000). The second obstacle to adopting a balanced approach is philosophical. Since the birth of the whole-language movement, one of its main tenets has been a resounding denial of the usefulness of direct phonics instruction (Goodman, 1963; Smith & Goodman, 1971; Smith, 1999). It may be time for teachers to reconsider that belief in light of the evidence from decades of reading research. Phonological coding is important for skilled reading, and systematic instruction in phonological awareness and letter–sound correspondences is critical for early reading development (Rayner et al., 2001).

Acknowledgments

Preparation of this chapter was supported by a Kirschstein National Research Service Award (No. HD045056-01) to Jane Ashby and by Grant Nos. HD17246 and HD26765.

References

Adams, M. J. (1990). *Beginning to read: Thinking and learning about print*. Cambridge, MA: MIT Press.

Ashby, J., & Clifton, Jr. (in press). The prosodic property of lexical stress affects eye movements during silent reading. *Cognition*.

Ashby, J., & Rayner, K. (2004). Representing syllable information during silent reading: Evidence from eye movements. *Language and Cognitive Processes*, 19, 391–426.

Ashby, J., Rayner, K., & Clifton, C. E., Jr. (in press).

Eye movements of highly skilled and average readers: Differential effects of frequency and predictability. Quarterly Journal of Experimental Psychology, Section A.

Bradley, L., & Bryant, P. E. (1983). Categorizing sounds and learning to read: A causal connection. *Nature, 301,* 419–421.

Bruck, M., Treiman, R., Caravolas, M., Genesee, F., & Cassar, M. (1998). Spelling skills of children in whole language and phonics classrooms. *Applied Psycholinguistics, 19,* 669–684.

Cattell, J. M. (1886). The time it takes to see and name objects. *Mind, 11,* 63–65.

Crystal, D. (1997). The medium of language: writing and reading. In *The Cambridge encyclopedia of language* (2nd Ed., p. 204). Cambridge, England: Cambridge University Press.

Curtis, M. E. (1980). Development of components of reading skill. *Journal of Educational Psychology, 72,* 656–669.

Ehri, L. C. (1980). The role of orthography in printed word learning. In J. F. Kavanagh & R. L. Venezky (Eds.), *Orthography, reading, and dyslexia* (pp. 155–170). Baltimore: University Park Press.

Ehri, L. C., & Wilce, L. S. (1983). Development of word identification speed in skilled and less skilled beginning readers. *Journal of Educational Psychology, 75,* 3–18.

Frost, R. (1998). Toward a strong phonological theory of visual word recognition: True issues and false trails. *Psychological Bulletin, 123,* 71–99.

Fry, E. B., Fountoukidis, D. L., & Polk, J. K. (1985) *The new reading teacher's book of lists,* (2nd ed.). Englewood Cliffs, NJ: Prentice Hall.

Gernsbacher, M. A. (1990). *Language comprehension as structure building.* Hillsdale, NJ: Erlbaum.

Goodman, K. S. (1963). A communicative theory of the reading curriculum. *Elementary English, 40,* 290–298.

Goodman, K. S. (1970). Reading: A psycholinguistic guessing game. In H. S. R. B. Ruddell (Ed.), *Theoretical models and processes of reading* (pp. 259–272). Newark, DE: International Reading Association.

Inhoff, A. W., & Liu, W. (1998). The perceptual span and oculomotor activity during the reading of Chinese sentences. *Journal of Experimental Psychology: Human Perception and Performance, 24,* 20–34.

Jorm, A. F., & Share, D. L. (1983). Phonological recoding and reading acquisition. *Applied Psycholinguistics, 4,* 103–147.

Juel, C., Griffith, P. L., & Gough, P. B. (1986). Acquisition of literacy: A longitudinal study of children in first and second grade. *Journal of Educational Psychology, 78,* 243–255.

Lee, H.-W., Rayner, K., & Pollatsek, A. (1999). The time course of phonological, semantic, and ortho-graphic coding in reading: Evidence from the fast-priming technique. *Psychonomic Bulletin and Review, 6,* 624–634.

Lesch, M. F., & Pollatsek, A. (1998). Evidence for the use of assembled phonology in accessing the meaning of printed words. *Journal of Experimental Psychology: Learning, Memory, and Cognition, 24,* 573–592.

Levin, H., & Kaplan, E. L. (1970). Grammatical structure in reading. In H. Levin & J. P. Williams (Eds.), *Basic studies on reading* (pp. 119–133). New York: Basic Books.

McConkie, G. W., & Rayner, K. (1975). The span of the effective stimulus during a fixation in reading. *Perception and Psychophysics, 17,* 578–586.

Moats, L. C. (1994). The missing foundation in teacher education: Knowledge of the structure of spoken and written language. *Annals of Dyslexia, 44,* 81–102.

Moats, L. C. (2000). *Speech to print: Language essentials for teachers.* Baltimore: Brookes.

Perfetti, C. A. (1985). *Reading ability.* New York: Oxford University Press.

Perfetti, C. A. (1992). The representation problem in reading acquisition. In P. B. Gough, L. C. Ehri, & R. Treiman (Eds.), *Reading acquisition* (pp. 145–174). Hillsdale, NJ: Erlbaum.

Perfetti, C.A. (2003). The universal grammar of reading. *Scientific Studies of Reading, 7,* 3–24.

Perfetti, C. A., Goldman, S. R., & Hogaboam, T. W. (1979). Reading skill and the identification of words in discourse context. *Memory and Cognition, 7,* 273–282.

Perfetti, C. A., & Zhang, S. (1995). Very early phonological activation in Chinese reading. *Journal of Experimental Psychology: Learning, Memory, and Cognition, 21,* 24–33.

Pollatsek, A., Bolozsky, S., Well, A. D., & Rayner, K. (1981). Asymmetries in the perceptual span for Israeli readers. *Brain and Language, 14,* 174–180.

Pollatsek, A., Lesch, M., Morris, R. K., & Rayner, K. (1992). Phonological codes are used in integrating information across saccades in word identification and reading. *Journal of Experimental Psychology: Human Perception and Performance, 18,* 148–162.

Rayner, K. (1975). The perceptual span and peripheral cues in reading. *Cognitive Psychology, 7,* 65–81.

Rayner, K. (1986). Eye movements and the perceptual span in beginning and skilled readers. *Journal of Experimental Child Psychology, 41,* 211–236.

Rayner, K. (1998). Eye movements in reading and information processing: 20 years of research. *Psychological Bulletin, 124,* 372–422.

Rayner, K., & Bertera, J. H. (1979). Reading without a fovea. *Science, 206,* 468–469.

Rayner, K., Foorman, B. R., Perfetti, C. A., Pesetsky, D., & Seidenberg, M. S. (2001). How psychological science informs the teaching of reading. *Psychological Science in the Public Interest, 2,* 31–74.

Rayner, K., Foorman, B. R., Perfetti, C. A., Pesetsky, D., & Seidenberg, M. S. (2002). How should reading be taught? *Scientific American, 286,* 70–77.

Rayner, K., Inhoff, A. W., Morrison, R., Slowiaczek, M. L., & Bertera, J. H. (1981). Masking of foveal and parafoveal vision during eye fixations in reading. *Journal of Experimental Psychology: Human Perception and Performance, 7,* 167–179.

Rayner, K., Liversedge, S. P., White, S. J., & Vergilino-Perez, D. (2003). Reading disappearing text: Cognitive control of eye movements. *Psychological Science, 14,* 385–388.

Rayner, K., & Pollatsek, A. (1989). *The psychology of reading.* Englewood Cliffs, NJ: Prentice-Hall.

Rayner, K., Sereno, S. C., Lesch, M. F., & Pollatsek, A. (1995). Phonological codes are automatically activated during reading: Evidence from an eye movement paradigm. *Psychological Science, 6,* 26–32.

Reicher, G. M. (1969). Perceptual recognition as a function of meaningfulness of stimulus materials. *Journal of Experimental Psychology, 81,* 275–280.

Share, D. L., & Stanovich, K. E. (1995). Cognitive processes in early reading development: Accommodating individual differences into a model of acquisition. *Issues in Education, 1,* 1–57.

Smith, F. (1973). *Psycholinguistics and reading.* New York: Holt, Rinehart, & Winston.

Smith, F. (1999). Why systematic phonics and phonemic awareness instruction constitute an educational hazard. *Language Arts, 77,* 150–155.

Smith, F., & Goodman, K. S. (1971). Psycholinguistic method of teaching reading. *Elementary School Journal, 71,* 171–182.

Spinks, J. A., Lui, Y., Perfetti, C. A., & Tan, L. (2000). Reading Chinese characters for meaning: The role of phonological information. *Cognition, 76,* B1–B11.

Stanovich, K. E. (1980). Toward an interactive-compensatory model of individual differences in the development of reading fluency. *Reading Research Quarterly, 16,* 32–71.

Van Orden, G. C. (1987). A ROWS is a ROSE: Spelling, sound, and reading. *Memory and Cognition, 15,* 181–198.

Van Orden, G. C., Johnston, J. C., & Hale, B. L. (1988). Word identification in reading proceeds from spelling to sound to meaning. *Journal of Experimental Psychology: Learning, Memory, and Cognition, 14,* 371–386.

Venezky, R. L., & Massaro, D. W. (1979). The role of orthographic regularity in word recognition. In L. B. Resnick & P. A. Weaver (Eds.), *Theories and practice in early reading* (Vol. 1, pp. 85–107). Hillsdale, NJ: Erlbaum.

Wheeler, D. D. (1970). Processes in word recognition. *Cognitive Psychology, 1,* 59–85.

Zhang, S., Perfetti, C. A., & Yang, H. (1999). Whole word, frequency-general phonology in semantic processing of Chinese characters. *Journal of Experimental Psychology: Learning, Memory, and Cognition, 25,* 858–875.

5

Neurobiological Investigations of Skilled and Impaired Reading

KENNETH R. PUGH
REBECCA SANDAK
STEPHEN J. FROST
DINA L. MOORE
W. EINAR MENCL

Identification of the factors that govern the successful acquisition of literacy skills and of the cause(s) of reading failure has long been a high priority for researchers in developmental and educational psychology. More recently these issues have become a major focus for researchers in the emerging field of cognitive neuroscience. Over many years, much progress has been made in identifying important cognitive, linguistic, and perceptual factors associated with reading success or failure. Research aimed at identifying neurobiological factors in reading development and reading disability has benefited in recent years from rapid advances in several neuroimaging technologies (e.g., positron emission tomography [PET]; functional magnetic resonance imaging [fMRI]; magnetoencephology [MEG]). These new tools have been used with increasing frequency to examine the functional brain organization for language and reading in children and adults with and without reading disability (see Papanicolaou, Pugh, Simos, & Mencl, 2004, for a discussion of these various techniques that allow us to measure brain activation during performance of cognitive tasks).

Both in the history of the human species and the development of the individual child,

spoken language capacity develops prior to the secondary, derived language abilities of reading and writing. Although brain organization for spoken language perception and production is, at least to a large degree, a biological specialization (Liberman, 1992), reading, by contrast, is almost certainly not. Indeed, unlike speech communication skills, reading must be explicitly taught. Moreover, although relatively few children will fail to master spoken language communication skills without explicit training, significant numbers of children in whom spoken language communication skills are adequate fail to obtain accurate and fluent reading levels even with intensive training efforts on the part of teachers and parents. When considered from the neurobiological perspective, the acquisition of reading skills requires the integration of visual, language, and associative brain regions, which can eventually permit the rapid translation of the visual forms of words to already well-instantiated linguistic representations (Pugh et al., 2000).

Neuroimaging techniques can help us to chart the neurobiological developmental trajectory of reading acquisition, as well as identify deviations from this trajectory in struggling readers. Moreover, once we have described these trajectories and deviations from typical trajectories, we can determine the role of the child's educational environment and, ultimately, the associations between experience, reading performance, and neurobiological activity. Thus we anticipate that incorporating neuroimaging techniques into broader efforts to study reading development will facilitate a better understanding of why certain instructional methods result in improved performance.

Although studies identifying neurobiological markers of reading disability (RD) have generated a good deal of enthusiasm lately, it should be remembered that functional neuroimaging measures are not intrinsically explanatory of the causes of RD; they simply describe brain organization at a given point in development. Functional imaging can provide a description of how the brain solves the problem of building a reading circuit; however, a more complete understanding of the critical etiological factors in reading disability and how these factors conspire to limit the development of an efficient reading circuit requires the use of multiple research tools at behavioral, neurobiological, and genetic levels of analysis. At minimum, however, for neurobiological findings to become relevant to our understanding of the causes of reading success or failure, we must establish meaningful links between well-studied behavioral/cognitive skills that are required for reading and the development of the neural systems that support these skills (Pugh et al., 2000). It is therefore crucial that neuroimaging research be informed by cognitive theory and research from the outset.

Behavioral Studies of Reading Disability

Reading disability has been characterized as the failure to develop age-appropriate reading skill despite normal intelligence and adequate opportunity for reading instruction. Significant progress has been made in understanding the cognitive and linguistic skills that must be in place to ensure adequate reading development in children (Bruck, 1992; Fletcher et al., 1994; Liberman 1992; Shankweiler et al., 1995; Stanovich & Siegel, 1994). Although it has been argued that the reading difficulties experienced by some children may result from difficulties with processing speed (Wolf & Bowers, 1999), rapid auditory processing (Tallal, 1980), general language deficits (Scarborough & Dobrich, 1990), or visual deficits (Cornelissen & Hansen, 1998), there is good consensus that a core difficulty in reading manifests itself as a deficiency within the language system and, in particular, a deficiency in mastering phonological awareness skills (e.g., Fletcher et al., 1994; Shankweiler et al., 1995; Stanovich & Siegel, 1994).

Phonological awareness, in general, is defined as the metalinguistic understanding that spoken words can be decomposed into phonological primitives, which in turn can be represented by alphabetic characters (Brady & Shankweiler, 1991; Bruck, 1992; Fletcher et al., 1994; Liberman, 1992; Rieben & Perfetti, 1991; Shankweiler et al., 1995; Stanovich & Siegel, 1994). As to why children with RD should have problems developing phonological awareness, there is some support for the notion that the difficulty resides in the phonological component of the larger specialization for language (Liberman, 1992). If the phonological system is compromised, its representations will be less than ideally distinct, and therefore harder to bring to conscious awareness; that in turn will preclude the development of efficient decoding routines required for the assembly of the phonological code from print.

Although the etiological underpinnings of the failure to develop phonological awareness are still actively being investigated, it is clear that deficits in phonological awareness are associated with difficulties in learning to read: Phonological awareness measures predict later reading achievement (Bradley & Bryant, 1985; Stanovich et al., 1984; Torgesen, Morgan, & Davis, 1992); deficits in phonological awareness consistently separate children with RD and nonimpaired (NI) children (Fletcher et al., 1994; Stanovich & Siegel, 1994); phonological deficits persist into adulthood (Bruck, 1992; Felton et al., 1990; Shaywitz et al., 1998); and instruction in phonological awareness promotes the acquisition of reading skills (Ball & Blachman, 1991; Bradley & Bryant, 1985; Foorman et al., 1998; Torgesen et al., 1992). Behaviorally, phonological processing deficits are evident at the level of single-word and pseudoword reading. Many lines of evidence converge on the conclusion that the word and pseudoword reading difficulties found in individuals with reading disabilities, to a large extent, manifestations of more basic deficits at the level of rapidly assembling the phonological code represented by a token letter string (Bradley & Bryant, 1985; Liberman, 1992). For individuals with RD, word and pseudoword reading is both slow and inaccurate relative to NI readers, particularly for pseudowords, which place greater demands on phonological assembly. Again, the failure to develop efficient phonological assembly skill in word and pseudoword reading, in turn, appears to stem from difficulties in attaining fine-grained phonemic awareness. For children with adequate phonological skills, the process of phonological assembly becomes highly automated and efficient and, as a growing body of evidence suggests, continues to serve as an important component in rapid word identification even for mature skilled readers (Frost, 1998; Lukatela & Turvey, 1994).

Given this background, our own functional neuroimaging research program and the studies selected for discussion in this review compare RD and NI reading groups on word and pseudoword reading tasks that tap into phonological processing and decoding. For a discussion of functional neuroimaging studies that have examined sensory-level processing deficits in developmental dyslexia

(e.g., Demb et al., 1998; Eden et al., 1996; Hari et al. 2003), the reader is referred to Eden and Zeffiro (1998) and Habib (2000). For reviews of research examining anatomical/structural brain differences between RD and NI groups the reader is referred to Filipek (1995), Galaburda (1992), and Habib (2000).

The Cortical Reading Systems and Their Roles in Skilled Reading

Recently, functional neuroimaging techniques have been employed in the study of reading development, reading disability, and intervention (see Pugh et al., 2000; Sandak et al., 2004; Sarkari et al., 2002, for reviews). There is converging evidence suggesting that skilled word recognition requires the development of a highly organized cortical system that integrates processing of visual–orthographic, phonological, and lexical–semantic features of words. As illustrated in Figure 5.1, the reading circuitry includes two broad posterior components in the left hemisphere (LH): a ventral (occipitotemporal) system and a temporoparietal system. A third component, anterior to these (centered in the inferior frontal gyrus), also plays a functional role in reading.

The temporoparietal system broadly includes the angular gyrus and supramarginal gyrus in the inferior parietal lobule and the

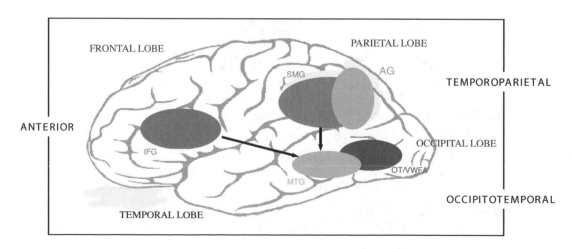

FIGURE 5.1. AG, angular gyrus; IFG, inferior frontal gyrus; MTG, middle temporal gyrus; OT/VWFA, occipitotemporal/Visual word form area; SMG, supramarginal gyrus.

posterior aspect of the superior temporal gyrus (Wernicke's area; see Figure 5.1). Evidence from both lesion and neuroimaging studies suggest that this system is critically involved in mapping visual percepts of print onto the phonological and semantic structures of language (Black & Behrmann, 1994; Price, Wise, & Frackowiak, 1996; Simos et al., 2002; Xu et al., 2001).

The anterior system, especially posterior aspects of the inferior frontal gyrus (IFG; see Figure 5.1), appears to be associated with phonological processing during reading, among other functions. The phonologically relevant components of this system have been found to function in both silent and spoken reading tasks (see Fiez & Petersen, 1998; Indefrey & Levelt, 2004; Poldrack et al., 1999; Pugh et al., 1997). We have speculated that this anterior system operates in close conjunction with the temporoparietal system to decode new words and that these two systems play a crucial in reading development (see Pugh et al., 2000, and Sandak et al., 2004, for a detailed discussion of the evidence supporting these claims).

The ventral system includes a left inferior occipitotemporal/fusiform area and extends into the middle and inferior temporal gyri (see Figure 5.1). Importantly, the functional specificity of this region appears to be late developing in children and is critically related to the acquisition of reading fluency (Booth et al., 2001; Shaywitz et al., 2002). This system, particularly more posterior aspects, is fast-acting in response to linguistic stimuli in skilled readers but not in individuals with reading disabilities (Salmelin, Service, Kiesila, Uutela, & Salonens, 1996; Tarkanien, Cornelissen, & Salmelin, 2003).

During initial reading acquisition, reading tasks appear to predominately activate the temporoparietal and anterior systems in typically developing children, with activation in the ventral system increasing as children develop greater proficiency in word recognition. We observed (Shaywitz et al., 2002) that typically developing children younger than 10.5 years of age showed very limited engagement of the ventral system during reading tasks. In contrast, children older than 10.5 years of age showed robust activation of the ventral system, which in turn is associated with increasingly skilled reading. We employed multiple regression analyses to ex-

amine the relation between reading skill (measured by performance on standard reading tests) and activation level in the ventral system and found that the greater the reading skill level, the stronger the response in the LH ventral system. Several other regions, especially right hemisphere (RH) sites, showed age- and skill-related reductions (see also Turkeltaub, Gareau, Flowers, Zeffron, & Eden, 2003, for evidence of reduced RH activation as reading skill develops). Based on these developmental findings, we concluded that a beginning reader on a successful trajectory employs a widely distributed cortical system for print processing, including temporoparietal, anterior, and RH posterior areas. As reading skill increases, the LH ventral system becomes more active, and presumably more central, to the rapid recognition of printed (word) stimuli (see Booth et al., 2001; McCandliss et al., 2004; Tarkiainen et al., 2003; Turkeltaub et al., 2003, for similar arguments). In sum, it appears from the existing studies that when reading development (at a cognitive level of analysis) is progressing adequately, the anticipated neurobiological signature is the development of a robust and efficient LH ventral reading specialization. Atypical development, by contrast, is associated with a very different trajectory, and we discuss evidence regarding these differences in RD development next.

Altered Circuits in Reading Disability

There are clear functional differences between NI readers and those with RD with regard to activation patterns in temporoparietal, ventral, and anterior systems during reading tasks. Many functional imaging studies with individuals with RD have observed an apparent LH posterior functional disruption (at both temporoparietal and ventral sites) during phonological processing tasks (Brunswick, McCrory, Price, Frith, & Frith, 1999; Paulesu et al., 2001; Pugh et al., 2000; Rumsey et al., 1997; Salmelin et al., 1996; Shaywitz et al, 1998; Shaywitz et al., 2002; Temple et al., 2001). This functional disruption is usually apparent as a relative underengagement of these posterior regions in readers with RD, specifically when processing linguistic stimuli (words and pseudowords) or during tasks that require explicit decoding. This neurobiological signature finding in RD research has been observed consistently in children (Shaywitz et al., 2002) and adults (Salmelin et al., 1996; Shaywitz et al., 1998); reduced activation, especially at the angular gyrus within the temporoparietal region and the ventral occipitotemporal skill zone, is detectable as early as the end of kindergarten in children who have not reached important milestones in learning to read (Simos et al., 2002). Moreover, the failure to activate posterior regions, particularly the ventral components, has been seen as a critical marker of RD across several alphabetic languages, including English, French, Italian, and Finnish (Paulesu et al., 2001; Salmelin et al., 1996).

Neuroimaging studies have tended to focus on identifying specific brain regions where activation patterns discriminate readers with RD from NI readers, and the LH posterior disruption appears to be very diagnostic (e.g., Rumsey et al., 1997; Shaywitz et al., 1998; Simos et al., 2002; Temple et al., 2001). However, in order to achieve a deeper understanding of the neurobiology of RD, we must also consider relations *among* brain regions that function cooperatively as circuits, or networks, to process information during reading; this issue has been referred to as one of functional connectivity (Friston, 1994; McIntosh et al., 1996). Evidence consistent with the notion of a breakdown in functional connectivity within the LH posterior reading systems in readers with RD has been reported by Horwitz, Rumsey, and Donohue (1998). Using activation data from the Rumsey et al. (1997) PET study, Horwitz et al. (1998) examined relations between activation levels in the LH angular gyrus and other brain sites during two reading-aloud tasks (exception-word and pseudoword reading). Activations in the LH angular gyrus and occipital and temporal lobe sites exhibited strong positive correlations in NI readers such that when activation increased in the angular gyrus, activation also increased in the occipital and temporal sites, suggesting that these regions function cooperatively in skilled reading. In contrast, the correlations between these sites were weak in readers with RD. This finding suggests a breakdown in functional connectivity across both the temporoparietal and ventral components of the LH posterior reading systems in RD.

We also examined whether the angular gyrus and other LH posterior regions were functionally connected in an examination of a large sample of adults with RD and NI readers (Pugh et al., 2000). We looked at connectivity between the angular gyrus and occipital and temporal lobe sites on tasks that systematically varied demands on phonological assembly. LH connectivity was weaker in readers with RD during complex phonological tasks (word-category judgment and pseudoword rhyming; thus replicating Horwitz et al., 1998). However, there appeared to be no disruption in functional connectivity when readers performed a simple phonological judgment (a single-letter rhyme task) or complex visual–orthographic coding (a case-judgment task). These results appear to be most consistent with a specific phonological deficit hypothesis: Our data suggest that communication among these areas is disrupted only when orthographic-to-phonological assembly is required. Thus it is not the case that functional connectivity in this system is disrupted across all types of cognitive behaviors relevant to reading, and this in turn suggests that LH posterior systems are weak but not fundamentally dysfunctional. Moreover, we found that on the word and pseudoword reading tasks, right-hemisphere counterparts or "homologues" appear to function in a compensatory manner for readers with RD; correlations among these regions in the right hemisphere were strong and stable for both reading groups, with higher values in readers with RD.

Potentially Compensatory Processing in Reading Disability

Behavioral research has identified a number of markers of reading impairment. Poor readers compensate for their inadequate phonological awareness and knowledge of letter–sound correspondences by overrelying on contextual cues to read individual words; their word-reading errors tend to be visual or semantic rather than phonetic (see Perfetti, 1985, for a review). These behavioral markers of reading impairment may be instantiated cortically by compensatory activation of frontal and RH regions. In our studies

(Shaywitz et al., 1998; Shaywitz et al., 2002), we found that on tasks that made explicit demands on phonological processing (pseudoword- and word-reading tasks), readers with RD showed a disproportionately greater engagement of inferior frontal regions than did NI readers (see also Brunswick et al., 1999; Salmelin et al., 1996, for similar findings). Evidence of a second, potentially compensatory, shift—in this case, to posterior RH regions—comes from several findings. For instance, using MEG, Sarkari et al. (2002) found an increase in the apparent engagement of the RH temporoparietal regions in children with RD. A more detailed examination of this trend, using hemodynamic measures, indicates that hemispheric asymmetries in temporoparietal activation vary significantly among reading groups (Shaywitz et al., 1998): greater RH than LH activation was observed in readers with RD but greater left than right hemisphere activation was seen in NI readers. Rumsey et al. (1999) examined the relationship between RH activation and reading performance in their adult participants with RD and their NI participants and found that RH temporoparietal activation was correlated with standard measures of reading performance only for readers with RD (see also Shaywitz et al., 2002).

We hypothesize that a possible reason that readers with RD tend to strongly engage inferior frontal sites is their increased reliance on covert pronunciation (phonological recoding) in an attempt to cope with their deficient phonological analysis of the printed word. In addition, their heightened activation of the posterior RH regions, paired with their reduced activation of the LH posterior regions, suggests a process of word recognition that relies on less phonologically structured word recognition strategies. These differential patterns, especially the increased activation in frontal regions, might also reflect increased effort during reading; underengagement of LH posterior areas, particularly ventral sites, would not be thought to reflect this increased effort, but rather the failure to engage these areas likely precipitates any change in effort.

In our view, neuroimaging research conducted to date on reading development and reading disability supports the following tentative conclusions:

1. Skilled readers engage a largely LH reading circuitry with three broad component systems (temporoparietal, ventral, and anterior).
2. With regard to reading acquisition, beginning readers (progressing adequately at the behavioral level of analysis) activate a widely distributed set of bihemispheric regions, including temporoparietal and anterior sites; increases in reading skill in typically developing children are associated with an increased specialization for reading in the LH ventral system.
3. Substantial converging evidence suggests that LH posterior reading circuits (both temporoparietal and ventral) are disrupted in RD (evident both by reduced activation and diminished functional connectivity).
4. Two apparently compensatory patterns have been observed in adults and children with RD: increased activation at RH posterior regions, homologous to the disrupted LH sites, and heightened activation of bihemispheric frontal lobe regions.

Neurobiological Effects of Successful Reading Remediation

This evidence on the anticipated neurobiological trajectory for typically developing readers and on deviations from this trajectory in readers with RD, helps us to frame hypotheses regarding neurobiological indices of successful remediation in readers with RD. On the hypothesis that these critical LH reading-related systems are weakened, but not fundamentally disrupted, in children with RD, we might predict that optimal remediation techniques will be associated with a more "normalized" localization of reading processes in the brain (essentially, a normalization in the neurobiological trajectory for reading). Recently, several large-scale intervention studies, using pre- and postintervention neuroimaging protocols, have addressed this issue. In a recent MEG study, eight young children with severe reading difficulties underwent a brief but intensive phonics-based remediation program (Simos et al., 2002). After intervention, the most salient change observed on a case-by-case basis was a robust increase in the engagement of the LH temporoparietal region, accompanied by a moderate reduction in the activation of the RH temporoparietal areas. Similarly, Temple et al. (2003) used fMRI to examine the effects of an intervention (FastForword) on the cortical circuitry of a group of 8- to 12-year-old children with reading difficulties. After intervention, increases in activation of LH temporoparietal and inferior frontal sites were observed. Moreover, the LH increases correlated significantly with increased reading scores. In a recent collaboration with Benita Blachman of Syracuse University, we conducted a longitudinal study examining three groups of young children (average age was 6.5 years at Time 1) with fMRI and behavioral indices (Shaywitz et al., 2004). The three groups consisted of a treatment RD group that received 9 months of an intensive phonics-based intervention (Blachman, Tangel, Ball, Black, & McGraw, 1999) and two control groups—one typically developing and one RD control group. Relative to RD controls, RD treatment participants showed reliable gains on reading measures (particularly on fluency-related measures such as Gray Oral Reading Test rate scores). When RD groups were compared at Time 2 (postintervention), reliably greater activation increases in LH reading-related sites were seen in the treatment group. Moreover, when pre- and postintervention activation profiles were directly contrasted for each group, it was evident that both RD treatment and typically developing controls showed reliable increases in LH reading-related sites, whereas RD controls did not. Prominent differences were seen in the LH inferior frontal gyrus and, importantly, in the LH ventral "skill zone." These changes were quite similar to changes observed in the NI controls as they also learned to read, again suggesting that the phonologically analytic intervention led to patterns of activation associated with typically developing readers. Importantly, 1 year after intervention was concluded, the treatment group showed further increases in LH activation, along with further decreases in RH activation.

Together, these initial neuroimaging treatment studies suggest that a potentially important neurobiological signature of successful intervention, at least in younger children, appears to be increased engagement of the critical LH reading-related circuits and reduced compensatory reliance on RH homologues. This general finding seems to imply that the LH systems that support skilled reading are not fundamentally disrupted (and essentially untrainable) in RD and that given the right sort of environmental experiences, children with RD can develop a coherent reading response in these LH systems. The identification of a neurobiological signature of successful intervention (LH posterior increases; RH decreases) yields a potentially sensitive outcome measure to help discriminate between different approaches that might all produce some transient gains in reading performance. Thus we suspect that approaches to remediation that have a "normalizing" effect of the neurobiological substrate for reading will also have the most stable long-term behavioral outcomes.

Next Steps

In recent years, significant progress has been made in the study of reading and reading disability with the use of functional neuroimaging techniques. A good deal is now known about the distributed neural circuitry for reading in skilled adult readers, about the developmental trajectory toward this mature reading circuitry in typically developing children, about deviations from this trajectory in RD, and about the ways in which intensive training for struggling younger readers alters brain organization for reading. Further advancement in developing an adequate theory of the neurobiology of reading demands considerable progress in a number of domains.

Extending Research on Intervention, Populations, and Skilled Reading

As discussed in the preceding sections, it appears that successful reading interventions in at-risk children result in increased response in critical LH posterior regions, regions that support fluent reading in typically developing cohorts (Shaywitz et al., 2004; Simos et al., 2002; Temple et al., 2003). Each of these studies has utilized training programs that emphasize phonological awareness training to differing degrees. These preliminary studies, although promising, raise many issues that need to be explored using combined brain–behavioral approaches.

Research on adolescent reading, RD, and treatment generally lags behind work on younger cohorts. A critical question to be addressed is whether similar neurobiological markers of successful remediation will be obtained for older populations with persistent reading difficulties. It is not clear whether neurobiological changes in adolescents will resemble those of younger children discussed previously (reduced RH and increased LH ventral activation patterns). The answer likely depends on the plasticity of the adolescent brain. If a large degree of cortical plasticity remains in adolescent learners, then growth in reading skill might very well produce cortical changes similar to those seen in younger children who respond successfully to intervention. Alternatively, if plasticity is greatly reduced, it is conceivable that improvements in reading could be obtained in a different or "compensatory" manner, which might lead to a different pattern of alteration in brain organization. With some work now in place helping to establish brain signatures of successful treatment in younger children, examining parallels or differences in older cohorts can help us to develop a neurobiologically grounded framework for contrasting alternative approaches to training and remediation in this population.

More complex intervention designs are called for as well. The treatment studies conducted to date, although they demonstrate neurobiological changes associated with reading-performance gains, have been, in many ways, quite limited in scope. We have focused primarily on comparing one specific treatment with a nontreatment control group. For each of the treatments explored thus far, the majority of participants will show some reading gains; however, in any study, some percentage of children would be classified as treatment resisters. The existing research provides little insight into why some children are treatment resisters and others are not. To begin to explore this individual difference dimension, important questions need to be explored using combined behavioral and neuroimaging measures: We need to identify the neurocognitive primitives that support reading acquisition (and other cognitive skills), and relate these to their brain bases. We can then ask whether individual differences (at both levels of analysis) prior to treatment predict differential responsiveness to specific interventions. In essence, we need to ask whether there are specific etiological factors that distinguish children who demonstrate only minimal gains with a specific treatment from those who respond to that treatment. If there are, then might alternative instructional approaches be more effective for these children? These are complex issues that demand large-scale studies that compare and contrast several interventions and examine interactions with individual difference or subtype dimensions. Such contrastive research will greatly extend the utility of brain-based developmental research, in our estimation.

There is a pressing need to identify brain–behavior precursors of abnormal reading trajectories in very young (pre-school-age) children; such research might be very helpful in developing appropriate early preventative approaches. Whereas it is known that the development of phonemic awareness is strongly and causally related to the development of reading skill (e.g., Bradley & Bryant, 1985; Wagner & Torgesen, 1987), little is known about the cognitive (and neurobiological) primitives underlying the development of phonemic awareness. Indeed, it is possible that in different children, different etiological factors undermine the development of phonemic awareness. Combined behavioral and neuroimaging approaches focused on prereaders might help to better characterize etiological primitives and how differences in these early factors ultimately relate to differences in responsiveness to contrasting approaches to reading instruction and remediation.

Beyond the issue of reading disability and its remediation, we suggest that the extant literature on the neurobiology of reading can begin to inform research on reading instruction in populations of readers who struggle due to other (noncongenital) factors. For instance, functional neuroimaging might be particularly helpful in assessing the efficacy of different approaches to the teaching of reading in English-language learners (ELLs; Simos et al., 2002). The acquisition of literacy skill is a major cognitive challenge for any child, and in any population significant numbers of children will fail to obtain age-appropriate reading levels. For ELLs, especially those children with limited English proficiency (LEP), the challenge can be all the more acute, and the incidence of reading difficulties in this population is alarmingly high. The National Assessment of Educational Progress (NAEP, 2000) reports that LEP students, especially Hispanic students, lag far behind their white and Asian peers in reading performance. Studies to date have focused on monolingual cohorts, but general lessons have been learned that may apply to bilingual readers as well. These extant studies, discussed previously, converge to indicate that development of the LH posterior reading system constitutes an important neurobiological outcome variable associated with successful instruction and remediation. Thus functional neuroimaging might be used in this manner to help in evaluating the sorts of reading instruction that work best for ELL children (whether at risk for RD or not). Again, in any population of readers at risk for reading failure, the identification of a neurobiological signature of successful intervention/instruction (e.g., LH posterior increases) might give us a particularly sensitive outcome variable in helping to compare and contrast different approaches to remediation and training.

Links to Computational Models of Word Recognition

There is also much work to be done in developing a detailed, neurobiologically grounded theory of reading; in the absence of proper models linking variation in behavior to underlying brain states and generating testable hypotheses, real bridges to clinical and/or education application are difficult to make. In recent years, computational models of reading have furthered our understanding of reading and reading development. Such models (e.g., the interactive "triangle" model; Harm & Seidenberg, 1999; Seidenberg & McClelland, 1989; and dual-route models, Coltheart, Curtis, Atkins, & Haller, 1993) are able to simulate a wide variety of behavioral effects seen in impaired and nonimpaired readers. Contrasting the different architectures and computational principles of these models has led to important questions and insights into the process of word recognition and reading failure (cf. Harm &

Seidenberg, 1999). A critical next step in reading research is to attempt to integrate neurobiological data with these computational models in order to develop neurobiologically plausible theories that in turn can guide us toward establishing meaningful links between individual differences in performance and individual differences in brain organization for language.

Conclusions

In recent years, significant progress has been made in studying the neurobiology of reading development and reading disability with the use of functional neuroimaging techniques. There is substantial converging evidence that skilled word recognition is associated with the development of a highly integrated cortical system that includes left hemisphere temporoparietal, ventral, and anterior subsystems. In this chapter we have focused on some key findings regarding the functional role of these regions during skilled reading, the developmental trajectory toward this mature reading circuitry in normally developing children, deviations from this trajectory in reading disabled populations, and the ways in which successful reading remediation alters the brain organization for reading. Although a number of important brain–behavior relations have been identified to date, much remains to be done in order to progress from largely descriptive toward potentially explanatory accounts.

Acknowledgments

This research was funded by NICHD grants R01-HD40411 to Kenneth R. Pugh, F32-HD42391 to Rebecca Sandak, and P01-HD01994 to Haskins Laboratories.

References

Ball, E. W., & Blachman, B. A. (1991). Does phoneme awareness training in kindergarten make a difference in early word recognition and developmental spelling? *Reading Research Quarterly, 26,* 49–66.

Black, S. E., & Behrmann, M. (1994). Localization in alexia. In A. Kertesz (Ed.), *Localization and neuroimaging in neuropsychology* (pp. 331–376). New York: Academic Press.

Blachman, B. A., Tangel, D. M., Ball, E. W., Black, R., & McGraw, C. K., (1999). Developing phonological awareness and word recognition skills: A two-year intervention with low-income, inner-city children. *Reading & Writing, 11,* 239–273.

Booth, J. R., Burman, D. D., Van Santen, F., Harasaki, Y., Gitelman, D. R., Parrish, T. B., & Mesulam, M. M. (2001). The development of specialized brain systems in reading and oral-language. *Child Neuropsychology, 7,* 119–ì.

Bradley, L., & Bryant, P. (1985). *Rhyme and reason in reading and spelling.* Ann Arbor: University of Michigan Press.

Bruck, M. (1992). Persistence of dyslexics' phonological deficits. *Developmental Psychology, 28,* 874–886.

Brunswick, N., McCrory, E., Price, C., Frith, C. D., & Frith, U. (1999). Explicit and implicit processing of words and pseudowords by adult developmental dyslexics: A search for Wernicke's Wortschatz. *Brain, 122,* 1901–1917.

Coltheart, M., Curtis, B., Atkins, P., & Haller, M. (1993). Models of reading aloud: Dual-route and parallel-distributed-processing approaches. *Psychological Review, 100,* 589–608.

Cornelissen, P. L., & Hansen, P. C. (1998). Motion detection, letter position encoding, and single word reading. *Annals of Dyslexia, 48,* 155–188.

Eden, G. F., & Zeffiro, T. A. (1998). Neural systems affected in developmental dyslexia revealed by functional neuroimaging. *Neuron, 21,* 279–282.

Fiez, J. A., & Peterson, S. E. (1998). Neuroimaging studies of word reading. *Proceedings of the National Academy of Sciences, 95,* 914–921.

Filipek, P. A. (1995). Neurobiologic correlates of developmental dyslexia: How do dyslexics brains' differ from those of normal readers? *Journal of Child Neurology, 10*(Suppl. 1), S62–69.

Fletcher, J. M., Shaywitz, S. E., Shankweiler, D. P., Katz, L., Liberman, I. Y., Stuebing, K. K., et al. (1994). Cognitive profiles of reading disability: Comparisons of discrepancy and low achievement definitions. *Journal of Educational Psychology, 86,* 6–23.

Foorman, B. R., Francis, D., Fletcher, J. K., Schatschneider, C., & Mehta, P. (1998). The role of instruction in learning to read: Preventing reading failure in at-risk children. *Journal of Educational Psychology, 90,* 37–55.

Friston, K. (1994). Functional and effective connectivity: A synthesis. *Human Brain Mapping, 2,* 56–78.

Frost, R. (1998). Toward a strong phonological theory of visual word recognition: True issues and false trails. *Psychological Bulletin, 123,* 71–99.

Frost, S. J., Mencl, W. E., Sandak, R., Moore, D. L., Mason, S. A., Rueckl, J. G., et al. (2004). *Capturing interactions between semantics and phonology in brain.* Manuscript submitted for publication.

Galaburda, A. M. (1992). Neurology of developmental dyslexia. *Current Opinion in Neurology and Neurosurgery, 5*(1), 71–76.

Habib, M. (2000). The neurological basis of developmental dyslexia: An overview and working hypothesis. *Brain, 123,* 2372–2399.

Harm, M. W., & Seidenberg, M. S. (1999). Computing the meanings of words in reading: Cooperative division of labor between visual and phonological processes. *Psychological Review, 106,* 491–528.

Horwitz, B., Rumsey, J. M., & Donohue, B. C. (1998). Functional connectivity of the angular gyrus in normal reading and dyslexia. *Proceedings of the National Academy Sciences, 95,* 8939–8944.

Indefrey, P., & Levelt, W. J. M. (2004). The spatial and temporal signatures of word production components. *Cognition, 92,* 101–144.

Katz, L., Lee, C., Frost, S. J., Mencl, W. E., Rueckl, J., Sandak, R., et al. (2004). *Effects of printed word repetition in lexical decision and naming on behavior and brain activation.* Manuscript submitted for publication.

Liberman, A. M. (1992) The relation of speech to reading and writing. In R. Frost & L. Katz (Eds.), *Orthography, phonology, morphology, and meaning* (pp. 167–178). Amsterdam: Elsevier.

Lukatela, G., & Turvey, M. T. (1994). Visual lexical access is initially phonological: 1. Evidence from associative priming by words, homophones, and pseudohomophones. *Journal of Experimental Psychology: General, 123,* 107–128.

McIntosh, A. R., Bookstein, F. L., Haxby, J. V., & Grady, C. L. (1996). Spatial pattern analysis of functional brain images using partial least squares. *Neuroimage, 3,* 143–157.

National Assessment of Educational Progress (2000). Retrieved from http://nces.ed.gov

Papanicolaou, A. C., Pugh, K. R., Simos, P. G., & Mencl, W. E. (2004). Functional brain imaging: An introduction to concepts and applications. In P. McCardle & V. Chhabra (Eds.), *The voice of evidence in reading research* (pp. 385–416). Baltimore: Brookes.

Paulesu, E., Demonet, J.-F., Fazio, F., McCrory, E., Chanoine, V., Brunswick, N., et al. (2001). Dyslexia: Cultural diversity and biological unity. *Science, 291,* 2165–2167.

Perfetti, C. A. (1985). *Reading ability.* New York: Oxford University Press.

Poldrack, R. A., Wagner, A. D., Prull, M. W., Desmond, J. E., Glover, G. H., & Gabrieli, J. D. (1999). Functional specialization for semantic and phonological processing in the left inferior prefrontal cortex. *Neuroimage, 10,* 15–35.

Price, C. J., Wise, R. J. S., & Frackowiak, R. S. J. (1996). Demonstrating the implicit processing of visually presented words and pseudowords. *Cerebral Cortex, 6,* 62–70.

Pugh, K. R., Mencl, W. E., Jenner, A. R., Katz, L., Frost, S. J., Lee, J. R., et al. (2000). Functional neuroimaging studies of reading and reading disability (developmental dyslexia). *Mental Retardation and Developmental Disabilities Research Reviews, 6,* 207–213.

Pugh, K. R., Shaywitz, B. A., Shaywitz, S. A., Shankweiler, D. P., Katz, L., Fletcher, J. M., et al. (1997). Predicting reading performance from neuroimaging profiles: The cerebral basis of phonological effects in printed word identification. *Journal of Experimental Psychology: Human Perception and Performance, 2,* 1–20.

Rumsey, J. M., Horwitz, B., Donohue, B. C., Nace, K. L., Maisog, J. M., & Andreason, P. A. (1999). Functional lesion in developmental dyslexia: Left angular gyral blood flow predicts severity. *Brain and Language, 70,* 187–204.

Rumsey, J. M., Nace, K., Donohue, B., Wise, D., Maisog, J. M., & Andreason, P. (1997). A positron emission tomographic study of impaired word recognition and phonological processing in dyslexic men. *Archives of Neurology, 54,* 562–573.

Salmelin, R., Service, E., Kiesila, P., Uutela, K., & Salonen, O. (1996). Impaired visual word processing in dyslexia revealed with magnetoencephalography. Annals *of Neurology, 40,* 157–162.

Sandak, R., Mencl, W. E., Frost, S. J., Mason, S. A., Rueckl, J. G., Katz, L., et al. (2004). *The neurobiology of adaptive learning in reading: A contrast of different training conditions.* Manuscript submitted for publication.

Sarkari, S., Simos, P. G., Fletcher, J. M., Castillo, E. M., Breier, J. I., & Papanicolaou, A. C. (2002). The emergence and treatment of developmental reading disability: Contributions of functional brain imaging. *Seminars in Pediatric Neurology, 9,* 227–236.

Scarborough, H., & Dobrich, W. (1990). Development of children with early language delay. *Journal of Speech and Hearing Research, 33,* 70–83.

Shankweiler, D., Crain, S., Katz, L., Fowler, A. E., Liberman, A. M., Brady, S. A., et al. (1995). Cognitive profiles of reading-disabled children: Comparison of language skills in phonology, morphology, and syntax. *Psychological Science, 6,* 149–156.

Shaywitz, B. A., Shaywitz, S. E., Blachman, B. A., Pugh, K. R., Fulbright, R., Skudlarski, et al. (2004). Development of Left Occipito-Temporal Systems for Skilled Reading Following a Phonologically-Based Intervention in Children. *Biological Psychiatry 55,* 926–933.

Shaywitz, B. A., Shaywitz, S. E., Pugh, K., R., Mencl, W. E., Fulbright, R. K., Skudlarski, et al. (2002). Disruption of posterior brain systems for reading in children with developmental dyslexia. *Biological Psychiatry,* 101–110.

Shaywitz, S. E., Shaywitz, B. A., Pugh, K. R., Fulbright, R. K., Constable, R. T., Mencl, W. E., et al. (1998). Functional disruption in the organization of the brain for reading in dyslexia. *Proceedings of the National Academy of Sciences, 95,* 2636–2641.

Simos, P. G., Breier, J. I., Fletcher, J. M., Foorman, B. R., Castillo, E. M., & Papanicolaou, A. C. (2002). Brain mechanisms for reading words and pseudowords: An integrated approach. *Cerebral Cortex, 12,* 297–305.

Stanovich, K. E., & Siegel, L. S. (1994). Phenotypic performance profile of children with reading disabilities: A regression-based test of the phonological-core variable-difference model. *Journal of Educational Psychology, 86,* 24–53.

Tallal, P. (1980). Auditory temporal perception, phonics, and reading disabilities in children. *Brain and Language, 9,* 182–198.

Tarkiainen, A., Cornelissen, P. L., & Salmelin, R. (2003). Dynamics of visual feature analysis and object-level processing in face versus letter-string perception. *Brain, 125,* 1125–1136.

Temple, E., Deutsch, G. K., Poldrack, R. A., Miller, S. L., Tallal, P., Merzenich, M. M., & Gabrieli, J. D. E. (2003). Neural deficits in children with dyslexia ameliorated by behavioral remediation: Evidence from functional MRI. *Proceedings of the National Academy of Sciences, 100,* 2860–2865.

Temple, E., Poldrack, R. A., Salidis, J., Deutsch, G. K., Tallal, P., Merzenich, M. M., & Gabrieli, J. D. (2001). Disrupted neural responses to phonological and orthographic processing in dyslexic children: An fMRI study. *NeuroReport, 12,* 299–307.

Torgesen, J. K., Morgan, S. T., & Davis, C. (1992). Effects of two types of phonological awareness training on word learning in kindergarten children. *Journal of Educational Psychology, 84,* 364–370.

Turkeltaub, P. E., Gareau, L., Flowers, D. L., Zeffiro, T. A., & Eden, G. F. (2003). Development of neural mechanisms for reading. *Nature Neuroscience, 6,* 767–773.

Wagner, R. K., & Torgesen, J. K. (1987). The nature of phonological processing and its causal role in the acquisition of reading skills. *Psychological Bulletin, 101,* 192–212.

Wolf, M., & Bowers, P. (1999). The double-deficit hypothesis for the developmental dyslexias. *Journal of Educational Psychology, 91,* 415–438.

Xu, B., Grafman, J., Gaillard, W. D., Ishii, K., Vega-Bermudez, F., Pietrini, P., et al. (2001). Conjoint and extended neural networks for the computation of speech codes: The neural basis of selective impairment in reading words and pseudowords. *Cerebral Cortex, 11,* 267–277.

II

PHONEMIC AWARENESS
AND LETTER KNOWLEDGE

6

Conceptualizing Phonological Processing Skills in Prereaders

CHRISTOPHER J. LONIGAN

Learning to read is a significant milestone in the development of young children. Whereas many children learn to read without significant difficulty, a sizable percentage of children experience at least some difficulty, and a significant number of children experience substantial difficulties. The most recent results of the National Association of Educational Progress (National Center for Education Statistics, 2003) indicated that among fourth-grade children in the United States, only 31% performed at or above the proficient level in reading. Children who read well read more and, as a result, acquire more knowledge in numerous domains (Cunningham & Stanovich, 1998; Echols, West, Stanovich, & Zehr, 1996; Morrison, Smith, & Dow-Ehrensberger, 1995). Children who experience difficulties learning to read tend to read less. Nagy and Anderson (1984) estimated that the number of words read in a year by a middle-school child who is an avid reader might approach 10,000,000, compared with 100,000 for the least motivated middle-school reader. Such large differences in exposure to print may lead to what Stanovich (1986) termed a "Matthew effect" (i.e., the rich get richer while the poor get poorer), such that those children with poor reading skills fall further and further behind their more literate peers in reading, as well as in other academic areas (Chall, Jacobs,

& Baldwin, 1990), which become increasingly dependent on reading across the school years.

Whereas a number of early theories of reading posited significant involvement of visual–perceptual systems (Monroe, 1935), most recent conceptualizations have focused on linguistic factors. There is now considerable evidence that phonological processing skills play a key role in the acquisition of reading and spelling in alphabetic languages. Phonological processing refers to activities that require sensitivity to, or manipulation of, the sounds in words. Research with a variety of populations and using diverse methods has converged on the finding that there is a link between the normal acquisition of reading and an individual's ability level on tasks designed to measure phonological processing (Adams, 1990; Wagner & Torgesen, 1987).

Prior research has identified three inter-related clusters of phonological processing abilities: phonological awareness, phonological access to lexical store, and phonological memory (Wagner & Torgesen, 1987). These three phonological processes are related strongly to subsequent word decoding abilities, and, in the absence of intervention, they are highly stable individual differences from the late preschool period forward (e.g., see Burgess & Lonigan, 1998; Lonigan, Burgess,

& Anthony, 2000; Wagner, Torgesen, Laughon, Simmons, & Rashotte, 1993; Wagner, Torgesen, & Rashotte, 1994; Wagner et al., 1997).

Phonological Awareness

Phonological awareness refers to the ability to detect or manipulate the sound structure of oral language. Research with a variety of populations and using diverse methods has converged on the finding that phonological awareness plays a key role in the normal acquisition of reading (e.g., Adams, 1990; Byrne & Fielding-Barnsley, 1991; Stanovich, 1992; Wagner & Torgesen, 1987). Children who are better at detecting and manipulating syllables, rhymes, or phonemes are quicker to learn to read, and this relation is present even after variability in reading skill due to factors such as IQ, receptive vocabulary, memory skills, and social class is partialed out (e.g., Bryant, MacLean, Bradley, & Crossland, 1990; Wagner & Torgesen, 1987; Wagner et al., 1994).

Phonological Access to Lexical Store

Phonological access to lexical store ("lexical access") refers to the efficiency of retrieval of phonological codes from permanent memory (Wagner & Torgesen, 1987). In older children, lexical access typically is measured as the rate at which an array of letters, digits, or colors can be named. Lexical access measures are significant predictors of growth in decoding skills in school-age children (Wagner et al., 1994; Wagner et al., 1997) and appear to have an independent effect on growth in decoding above that of phonological sensitivity and phonological memory, consistent with the double-deficit hypothesis (Bowers & Swanson, 1991; Kirby, Parrila, & Pfeiffer, 2003; Manis, Doi, & Bhadha, 2000; Schatschneider, Fletcher, Francis, Carlson, & Foorman, 2004). As a phonological skill, efficiency in lexical access might influence the ease with which a child can retrieve the phonological information associated with letters, word segments, and whole words and increase the likelihood that he or she can use phonological information in decoding.

Phonological Memory

Phonological memory refers to the coding of information in a sound-based representation system for temporary storage (Baddeley, 1986) and is typically measured by immediate recall of verbally presented material (e.g., repetition of nonwords or digits). Efficient phonological memory might enable children to maintain an accurate representation of the phonemes associated with the letters of a word while decoding and, therefore, devote more cognitive resources to decoding and comprehension processes. Results from studies by Wagner and colleagues (1994; Wagner et al., 1997) indicate that phonological memory is a significant correlate of growth in decoding skills but that it does not provide unique predictive variance to growth in decoding beyond that provided by phonological awareness for school-age children.

In terms of understanding reading difficulties in alphabetic languages, the general consensus is that a core phonological deficit (i.e., awareness or access) exists in nearly all poor readers and that deficits exist as well in other reading-related skills (e.g., vocabulary) in some poor readers, depending on the degree to which their level of reading is discrepant with their level of general cognitive and academic functioning (Stanovich, 1988; Stanovich & Siegel, 1994). Some evidence suggests that children with a *double deficit* (i.e., deficits in both phonological awareness and lexical access) tend to be at the very bottom of the distribution of reading ability (Bowers, 1995; Bowers & Wolf, 1993; McBride-Chang & Manis, 1996; Torgesen & Burgess, 1998); however, other research has challenged this position (Pennington, Cardoso-Martins, Green, & Lefly, 2001; Schatschneider, Carlson, Francis, Foorman, & Fletcher, 2002). For instance, Schatschneider et al., (2002), in a study of 362 first- and second-grade children, reported that the greater severity of reading impairment present in children with a double deficit was likely due to a statistical artifact that was caused by grouping children based on their performance on two correlated continuous variables. They found few children in quadrants representing significantly low scores on both phonological awareness and lexical access measures.

In older children, the three ability clusters are relatively distinct, and phonological awareness tends to be the strongest predictor of reading skills (McBride-Chang & Manis, 1996; Wagner et al., 1993; Wagner et al., 1994; Wagner et al., 1997). However, in younger children the three ability clusters may be less distinct (e.g., see Wagner & Torgeson, 1987; Wagner et al., 1993).

Development of Early Literacy Skills in Prereaders

The majority of research to date on the component skills that underlie the acquisition of skilled reading has focused on school-age children. Over the past 15 years, however, researchers have begun to examine the developmental precursors to reading before children enter a formal school environment. This area of study is often referred to as emergent literacy (Sulzby, 1989; Sulzby & Teale, 1991; Teale & Sulzby, 1986; Whitehurst & Lonigan, 1998). Whereas traditional approaches to the study of reading often take as their starting point children's entry to the formal school environment, an emergent-literacy approach conceptualizes the acquisition of literacy as a developmental continuum with its origins early in the life of a child, rather than an all-or-none phenomenon that begins when children start school. The emergent-literacy approach departs from other perspectives on reading acquisition in suggesting that there is no clear demarcation between reading and prereading.

Whitehurst and Lonigan (1998) proposed that emergent and conventional literacy consist of two interdependent sets of skills and processes, *outside-in* and *inside-out*. Outside-in skills represent children's understanding of the context in which the target text occurs (e.g., knowledge of the world, semantic knowledge, and knowledge of the written context in which a particular sentence occurs). Inside-out skills represent children's knowledge of the rules for translating the particular writing they are trying to read into meaningful sounds (e.g., letter knowledge, phonological processing skills, and perhaps vocabulary). Inside-out skills reflect code-related components of reading that are mostly specific to reading, whereas outside-in skills reflect more general abilities, such as language and general knowledge, that support comprehension. Whitehurst and Lonigan (1998) hypothesized that inside-out (code-related) skills would be most important early in the sequence of learning to read, when the primary task is the development of accurate and fluent decoding skills, whereas outside-in (language) skills would become more important later in the sequence of learning to read, when the task shifted to comprehension. Skilled reading is a complex task that requires the coordination and interaction of many skills. Although these processes may be difficult to separate in a mature, skilled reader, it is unlikely that they are well integrated in the early stages of learning to read.

Links between Early Skills and Later Reading

The National Early Literacy Panel (2004) conducted a meta-analysis of published studies (in peer-reviewed English-language journals through 2002) that included data concerning the predictive relation between a skill measured in preschool or kindergarten and reading outcomes for children learning to read in an alphabetic language. A subset of the results of this meta-analysis is shown in Table 6.1. The data reported in the table include the average zero-order correlation for decoding and reading comprehension across all retrieved studies, the number of studies contributing to each average correlation, and the number of children contributing data to the correlation across studies.

What is apparent from the data in Table 6.1 is that both alphabet knowledge and phonological awareness (i.e., measures of detection or manipulation of rhyme, syllables, onset-rime, phonemes) have sizable relations with both decoding and reading comprehension. Other predictor variables, such as lexical access (RAN Graphological [naming letters or digits] and RAN Nongraphological [naming objects or colors] in the table) and oral language, have moderate relations with decoding and comprehension, whereas phonological memory (phonological STM in the table) has a relatively weaker relation to decoding and a moderate relation to comprehension. Whether phonological awareness

TABLE 6.1. Average Correlations between Predictor Variables Measured in Preschool or Kindergarten and Reading Outcome Based on Meta-Analysis of National Early Literacy Panel

| Predictor variable | Reading outcome | | | | | |
| | Decoding | | | Comprehension | | |
	Average r	No. of studies	No. of children	Average r	No. of studies	No. of children
Alphabet Knowledge	.45	26	2,826	.45	6	668
Phonological Awareness	.44	47	4,334	.41	13	1,007
RAN Graphological	.41	8	1,029	—[a]		
Oral Language	.38	12	1,578	.39	10	1,024
RAN Nongraphological	.34	8	861	.37	4	509
Phonological STM	.25	21	2,384	.38	8	1,260

Note. RAN, Rapid Automatized Naming (lexical access).
[a]Fewer than three studies retrieved from search of literature.

was measured in preschool or kindergarten did not influence the size of the correlation. Alphabet knowledge measured in preschool was a stronger predictor of later decoding (though not comprehension) than alphabet knowledge measured in kindergarten, perhaps due to ceiling effects in kindergarten (see Schatschneider et al., 2004, for similar findings). Phonological memory was a stronger predictor of both decoding and comprehension when measured in preschool than when measured in kindergarten. In these studies, lexical access was measured only in kindergarten.

To the extent that it was possible to examine different aspects of oral language and their relations with decoding and comprehension in these studies, the results suggested that more complex aspects of oral language, such as listening comprehension, understanding syntax, and definitional vocabulary, had stronger associations with decoding and comprehension than did expressive or receptive vocabulary. Although the average correlations between oral language and decoding and comprehension were only moderate, the strength of the correlation was similar for decoding and comprehension, a finding not consistent with the distinction between the relative temporal contribution of inside-out and outside-in skills.

A likely explanation for the similarly strong link between oral language skills and both decoding and comprehension concerns the overlap of oral language skills with code-related skills in younger children (see Storch & Whitehurst, 2002, and the discussion of

the link between oral language and phonological awareness, later in this chapter). Multivariate studies in which the longitudinal predictive influence of multiple components of emergent literacy are examined simultaneously provide clarification of the zero-order findings. Lonigan, Burgess, and Anthony (2000) studied the relation between phonological awareness, letter knowledge, and oral language to decoding skills in a group of 97 5-year-old preschool children followed longitudinally for 1 year. Using structural equation modeling, Lonigan and colleagues found that only phonological awareness and letter knowledge contributed unique variance to the prediction of decoding skills. Although oral language was correlated with the code-related skills and decoding, it was not related to reading once phonological awareness and letter knowledge were in the model. Sénéchal and LeFevre (2002) also failed to show an independent relation between oral language and reading in the first and second grades. In one of the most comprehensive studies to date, Storch and Whitehurst (2002) followed 626 children from preschool through fourth grade. They measured code-related skills (i.e., print concepts and phonological awareness) and oral language in preschool and kindergarten, and they measured decoding and reading comprehension in the first through fourth grades. Using structural equation modeling, they found that there was a strong connection between code-related skills and oral language during preschool, that reading skill during the early elementary period was determined primarily by children's code-related skills, and that reading comprehension in later elementary school was significantly influenced by children's oral language skills.

Taken together, these findings, similar to those for older children, indicate that phonological processing skills—at least phonological awareness—and letter knowledge are important determinants of early reading acquisition for children when measured in preschool and kindergarten. Multivariate studies suggest that the code-related skills are relatively modular in their effects on decoding. Shatil and Share (2003) came to the same conclusion in their longitudinal study of 349 Hebrew-speaking 6-year-old kindergarten children. Print-specific measures from late kindergarten uniquely predicted 33% of the variance in decoding skill, whereas general measures (oral language, cognitive ability) explained only 5% of the variance in decoding. In contrast, reading comprehension was substantially predicted by both print-specific measures (51% of variance) and general measures (44% of variance). Early in development, code-related skills and oral language skills are interrelated (Lonigan, Burgess, Anthony, & Barker, 1998; Storch & Whitehurst, 2002). These studies also reveal a striking continuity between the level of skills displayed in preschool and the level of skills displayed in kindergarten (e.g., Lonigan et al., 2000; Storch & Whitehurst, 2002), suggesting that the developmental and environmental antecedents of the skills that underlie the acquisition of reading are found early and prior to the onset of formal schooling.

The Nature of Phonological Awareness: A Developmental Continuum

Relative to the large amount of research that has supported the significance of phonological processing abilities, print knowledge, and oral language for the development of reading in grade-school children (e.g., Metsala & Ehri, 1998; National Early Literacy Panel, 2004; Snow, Burns, & Griffin, 1998), there has been far less systematic research concerning the development and predictive utility of these emergent literacy skills in preschool children. However, as noted previously, a growing body of evidence highlights the presence of phonological processing abilities

and print knowledge during the preschool period (Chaney, 1992; Lonigan et al., 1998) and shows that they are stable individual differences from the late-preschool period forward (Burgess & Lonigan, 1998; Lonigan et al., 2000; Wagner et al., 1997) and are predictive of beginning reading and spelling (Lonigan et al., 2000; MacLean, Bryant, & Bradley, 1987; Storch & Whitehurst, 2002).

Almost all research on phonological processing skills involving preschool children has examined phonological awareness. The question of the role of children's early phonological awareness for later reading is complicated by controversy concerning the structure and significance of preschool phonological awareness. Several authors have argued that various tasks designed to measure phonological awareness tap separate and independent abilities (e.g., Muter, Hulme, Snowling, & Taylor, 1997; Muter & Snowling, 1998; Yopp, 1988). Advocates of this separate phonological-abilities model tend to stress the importance of phoneme manipulation skills (i.e., phonemic awareness) for reading because it is at the level of the phoneme that graphemes correspond to speech sounds and because individual phonemes do not have separable physical reality (e.g., Liberman, Cooper, Shankweiler, & Studdert-Kennedy, 1967; Morais, 1991, 2003; Nation & Hulme, 1997; Tunmer & Rohl, 1991). Significantly, this narrow conceptualization of phonological awareness excludes those skills that involve manipulation of linguistic units larger than a phoneme and those skills that involve detection rather than production or manipulation of phonological information (e.g., Morais, 1991, 2003).

The importance of this debate for the study of emergent literacy is that phonological awareness tasks that involve manipulation of phonemes are too difficult for the majority of preschool children. In contrast, supraphoneme awareness tasks that involve detection or manipulation of larger linguistic units (e.g., syllables, onset–rime) are within the capacities of many preschool children (Lonigan et al., 1998). We have examined the issue of the dimensionality of phonological awareness empirically in a number of studies involving preschool and early-grade-school children (Anthony & Lonigan, 2004; Anthony et al., 2002; see also Stahl & Murray,

1994). In several samples of 2- to 6-year-old children, we used confirmatory factor analysis (CFA) to compare plausible theoretical and atheoretical model variations (e.g., single-factor model, phoneme vs. supraphoneme two-factor model) that could account for children's performance across tasks that required children to detect, blend, or elide words, syllables, onset–rimes, or phonemes. Across these diverse samples of children, a single-factor model provided an adequate characterization of the data. Models with two or more factors generally did not provide a better fitting model. Using CFA and item-response theory (IRT) analyses of responses to 105 phonological-awareness items by 945 kindergarten through second-grade children, Schatschneider, Francis, Foorman, Fletcher, and Mehta (1999) also reported support for a single-ability conceptualization of phonological awareness. Anthony, Lonigan, and Schatschneider (2003) found a similar pattern of results using IRT analyses of phonological-awareness items for a sample of over 1,000 2- to 5-year-old children. The conclusion supported by these analyses is that all of these phonological-awareness tasks—regardless of level of linguistic complexity or operation involved—are indicators of the same underlying ability.

Analyses of the longitudinal relations among phonological-awareness tasks and between different phonological tasks and later reading also support a unitary conceptualization of phonological awareness. For example, Anthony and Lonigan (2004) found 1-year cross-time correlations between an Onset–Rime Awareness factor and a Phoneme Awareness factor of .88 and .89 for kindergarten to first grade and for first grade to second grade, respectively. Other studies have revealed 1-year cross-time correlations among phonological-awareness factors that differ in the phonological awareness skills (e.g., linguistic complexity) used to index the factors ranging from .83 to 1.00 in preschool, kindergarten, and older children (Lonigan et al., 2000; Wagner et al., 1994; Wagner et al., 1997). The results of Lonigan et al. (2000) indicated that the global construct of phonological awareness, defined by variance common to sensitivity to words, syllables, onset–rime, and phonemes, was a significant and strong longitudinal predictor of children's decoding skills. In this study, the phonological-awareness factor that comprised the initial measures of phonological awareness, which were weighted heavily in favor of lower levels of linguistic complexity (i.e., words, syllables, onset–rime), was as predictive of later decoding as was the phonological-awareness factor of the later measures of phonological awareness, which were weighted heavily in favor of higher levels of linguistic complexity (i.e., phonemes).

In a recent study in which they argued for the primacy of phoneme-level tasks over supraphoneme-level tasks, Hulme et al. (2002) directly compared the predictive relations of phoneme and onset–rime tasks measured when children were 5 to 6 years old for decoding measured 7 to 14 months later. Each of four linguistic levels (i.e., onset, rime, initial phoneme, final phoneme) was measured by three tasks (i.e., detection, oddity, deletion). Whereas all 12 tasks were significantly intercorrelated with each other and with concurrent reading, in regression analyses only initial phoneme tasks uniquely predicted concurrent reading skill. In longitudinal analyses, all levels except rime were significantly correlated with time 2 decoding. In regression analyses in which decoding skill at Time 1, time between assessments, and initial receptive vocabulary score were controlled, only final phoneme tasks contributed uniquely to the prediction of decoding. Although Hulme et al. (2002) suggest that their results support the greater predictive validity of phoneme-level tasks, several commentaries (Bowey, 2002; Bryant, 2002; Goswami, 2002) called this conclusion into question. As noted by Anthony et al. (2002), predictive analyses such as these fail to consider that the largest amount of predictive variance is shared between phonological awareness tasks. That a variable at one point in time may be more or less uniquely predictive may reflect measurement artifacts that have little to do with skill being measured (e.g., floor and ceiling effects). Moreover, analyses such as the CFAs reported earlier that fail to establish distinct constructs in tasks measuring nominally different skills do not support an analytic strategy wherein these tasks are used to represent distinct constructs.

Overall, consistent with the views articulated by Adams (1990) and by Goswami and Bryant (1990), most results suggest a developmental conceptualization of phonological awareness in which phonological awareness manifests in increasingly complex ways as children mature. Phonological awareness appears to develop along two dimensions, linguistic complexity and cognitive operations. In terms of linguistic complexity, development follows a progression in which children are sensitive to smaller and smaller units of sound across the preschool and early grade-school period. This stage-like development, which parallels a hierarchical model of word structure, progresses from sensitivity to larger linguistic units that are based on the concrete physical characteristics of an auditory stimulus (i.e., words, syllables) to smaller abstract linguistic units that have only a psychological reality (i.e., phonemes). In terms of cognitive operations, development allows increasingly complex operations and an increasing number of operations on phonological information.

Using data from 947 2- to 5-year-old children from diverse backgrounds who had completed multiple measures of phonological awareness across dimensions of linguistic complexity and cognitive operations analyses, Anthony, Lonigan, Driscoll, Phillips, and Burgess (2003) provided direct support for this developmental conceptualization of phonological awareness. Children were able to perform word-level phonological skills before syllable-level phonological skills, syllable-level phonological skills before onset–rime-level phonological skills, and onset–rime-level phonological skills before phoneme-level phonological skills. Children could detect manipulations of phonological information before they were able to perform manipulations of phonological information, and children learned to blend phonological information before they learned to elide phonological information. The results supported a quasi-parallel development within dimensions of linguistic complexity and task complexity. That is, rather than acquiring these skills in a stage-like fashion in which acquisition occurs in temporally discrete sequential stages (i.e., mastery of one level before development in the next level), children's acquisition of these skills followed a temporally overlapping sequence (i.e., development of multiple levels simultaneously).

Other Aspects of Preschool Phonological Processing Skills

The majority of research to date concerning prereaders' phonological processing skills has examined phonological awareness (see Table 6.1). As noted, there is substantial evidence that phonological awareness, phonological memory, and lexical access can be represented as distinct constructs in older children (Wagner et al., 1993; Wagner et al., 1994; Wagner et al., 1997). Wagner and colleagues (1987; Wagner et al., 1993) reported results of CFAs in which phonological awareness and phonological memory were not distinct factors. In our own data (Lonigan, Anthony, Burgess, & Phillips, 2004), however, CFA yielded distinct phonological awareness, phonological memory, and lexical access factors both in a group of 4- and 5-year-old children and in a group of 2- and 3-year-old children. It is likely that differences in the tasks used in the different studies account for the different results. Additional study of this issue is warranted. If it is the case that phonological awareness and phonological memory represent a common underlying ability in younger children, it may be easier to measure this ability using memory measures (see Wagner et al., 2003).

Issues surrounding measurement of lexical access with younger children are also complex. Rapid-naming tasks that are most predictive of later reading skills are most often those that involve the rapid naming of letters or digits (Schatschneider et al., 2004; see also Table 6.1). However, the majority of young children know few letters and digits. Because scoring of these tasks is based on speeded accuracy, they cannot be used with most preschool children. Preschool children can complete rapid-naming measures in which they name pictures of objects. These tasks tend to produce reliable scores; however, the relation between these preschool scores and later reading are not yet known.

Reciprocal Linkages between Phonological Awareness, Letter Knowledge, and Decoding

Evidence suggests that the development of phonological awareness is both a cause and a consequence of learning to read (e.g., Perfetti, Beck, Bell, & Hughes, 1987; Wagner et al., 1994; Wagner et al., 1997). In addition to its direct role in facilitating decoding, letter knowledge appears to play an influential role in the development of phonological awareness, both prior to and after the initiation of formal reading instruction. Higher levels of letter knowledge are associated with children's abilities to detect and manipulate phonemes (e.g., Bowey, 1994; Johnston, Anderson, & Holligan, 1996; Stahl & Murray, 1994) but not rhyme and syllables (Naslund & Schneider, 1996). Wagner et al. (1994; Wagner et al., 1997) reported the results of a longitudinal study that explicitly tested the influence of letter knowledge on subsequent phonological awareness development. They found that individual differences in kindergarten and first-grade letter knowledge were significantly related to measures of phonological sensitivity 1 and 2 years later.

In a longitudinal study of preschool children, Burgess and Lonigan (1998) found that preschool children's letter knowledge was a unique predictor of growth in phonological awareness across 1 year. Conversely, initial phonological awareness predicted growth in letter knowledge. Share (2004) found a similar effect of phonological awareness on growth in letter knowledge in an experimental study on the effects of teaching children letter names. In this study, children were first taught either letter names corresponding to letter-like symbols or meaningful words corresponding to the letter-like symbols. Following this training, children were taught the "sounds" of these letter-like symbols. Learning letter names conferred an advantage to children in learning the letter sounds; however, the benefit of learning letter names was moderated by the level of phonological awareness exhibited by children prior to training. de Jong and Olson (2004) found that phonological memory and lexical access were both unique predictors of growth in letter knowledge (phonological awareness was not measured in this study). Murray, Stahl, and Ivey (1996) demonstrated that exposure to alphabet books with letter–sound information resulted in more gains in phonological sensitivity than exposure to either alphabet books without letter–sound information or storybooks. Consequently, there is evidence for a reciprocal relationship between phonological processing skills and letter knowledge in preschoolers. Having more letter knowledge promotes the development of higher levels of phonological awareness, and having higher levels of phonological awareness, or phonological processing skills generally, promotes the development of letter knowledge.

Linkage between Oral Language and Phonological Awareness

As noted previously, most multivariate studies do not support a direct role of oral language in the development of decoding. However, phonological awareness and oral language are significantly related during the preschool period (Chaney, 1992; Lonigan et al., 1998; Lonigan et al., 2000; Storch & Whitehurst, 2002), and studies with slightly older children have demonstrated significant concurrent and longitudinal associations between children's vocabulary skills and their phonological awareness (Bowey, 1994; Cooper, Roth, Speece, & Schatschneider, 2002; Wagner et al., 1993; Wagner et al., 1997).

One potential explanation for this linkage is the *lexical restructuring model* (Fowler, 1991; Metsala & Walley; 1998). According to this model, representations of words in the lexicon of very young children are holistic (i.e., represented as whole words) and gradually become more fine-grained and segmented through the preschool and early school-age years. Lexical restructuring is assumed to be a function of vocabulary growth that occurs in response to the learning of individual words within a spectrum of phonological similarity (i.e., neighborhood density). Evidence suggests greater segmental representation for high-frequency words and words from dense phonological neighborhoods (see Walley, Metsala, & Garlock, 2003). Stated simply, as children learn more words, it becomes more efficient to remember and recognize words in terms of their constituent parts rather than as wholes. Children who have small vocabularies may be limited in their phonological awareness because their memory for words has not moved from global to segmented. These findings suggest that vocabulary development may set the stage for the emergence of phonological awareness, which in this view is dependent on access to segmentally represented speech sounds.

Whereas there are data to suggest word-frequency and neighborhood-density effects on segmental representation and data to suggest that vocabulary size is related to phonological awareness skill, at present all research in this area is correlational. This leaves open the question of whether or not vocabulary development really *causes* the development of phonological awareness. In an earlier oral-language intervention study (Lonigan, Anthony, Bloomfield, Dyer, & Samwel, 1999), we found a small but statistically significant effect of the intervention on measures of phonological awareness. However, the design of the study did not allow us to isolate the effect as a result of an effective vocabulary intervention. To partially address this question, a reanalysis of another early literacy intervention study (see Lonigan, 2003) was conducted. In this study, 285 preschool children (mean age = 53.9 months; SD = 5.65) were randomly assigned to one of five conditions. The conditions consisted of partially crossed combinations of oral-language, phonological-awareness, and print-knowledge interventions and a control condition. All children were attending preschools, and the intervention program was administered as a small-group pullout program lasting 15 minutes a day for the majority of a school year. This reanalysis addressed four questions:

1. Did the vocabulary intervention have an impact on children's vocabulary?
2. Did the phonological-awareness intervention have an impact on children's phonological awareness?
3. Did the phonological-awareness intervention have an impact on children's vocabulary?
4. Did the vocabulary intervention have an impact on children's phonological awareness?

As with the earlier analyses of this study, the different interventions had a significant effect in the targeted domains. Significant effects of the oral-language intervention were found on measures of vocabulary ($p < .02$), and significant effects of the phonological-awareness intervention were found on measures of rhyme ($p < .03$) and blending skills ($p < .001$). There was no effect of the phonological-awareness intervention on

children's vocabulary ($p > .05$). However, there were significant effects of the oral-language intervention on measures of rhyme ($p < .05$) and blending ($p < .02$) skills. These findings, representing a partial dissociation effect, indicate that the effects of the oral-language intervention on children's phonological awareness were not simply the result of receiving an intervention (i.e., there was no impact of the phonological-awareness intervention on children's vocabulary skills). The results are supportive of the hypothesis that vocabulary development is causal in the development of phonological awareness. Clearly, more research is needed to confirm this result, perhaps specifically manipulating vocabulary exposure along the dimensions of frequency and phonological-neighborhood density. However, this is one of the first studies of preschool children to identify a potentially causal factor not involving direct training of the skill in the development of phonological awareness.

Summary and Future Directions

The evidence reviewed in this chapter indicates that the developmental origins of learning to read begin prior to the onset of formal reading instruction. Research supports a linkage between phonological processing skills, print knowledge, and oral language in the preschool period and reading in the school period, once formal reading instruction has commenced. These emergent literacy skills are partially interdependent. Phonological processing skills appear to be, in part, a product of the development of vocabulary and the development of print knowledge. Similarly, development of phonological processing skills influences the development of print knowledge. Despite these interdependencies, these early literacy skills are relatively modular with respect to their relation to later reading and spelling. Early reading development (i.e., decoding) is most dependent on code-related skills. Later reading development (i.e., comprehension) is also dependent on oral-language skills.

This conceptualization of the linkages between preliteracy skills and later reading and writing has implications for early identification and intervention. Many of the skills related to later reading are relatively stable individual differences from the late preschool period. Consequently, assessment of the developmental precursors of reading is possible before children begin school and before they experience academic difficulties. For children with demonstrated weaknesses in the developmental precursors of reading, intervention may reduce the risk of later reading failure. In contrast to the significant body of research concerning reading-related intervention for children in kindergarten through third grade (National Institute of Child Health and Development, 2000), there is significantly less research on reading-related intervention for preschool children. As an example, the National Early Literacy Panel's (2004) search of the published evidence for phonological-awareness intervention with preschool and kindergarten children yielded approximately 55 studies. Of these studies, only 6 included primarily preschool children (e.g., Bradley & Bryant, 1983; Byrne & Fielding-Barnsley, 1991, 1993, 1995). This limited number of studies indicates that phonological awareness intervention with preschoolers can have a significant positive effect on later reading skills; however, more research directed at understanding the nature and timing of effective interventions for preschoolers at risk of later reading difficulties is needed. Although there is a more substantial body of research for oral-language intervention with preschool children, evidence suggests that such interventions by themselves do not have a substantial impact on children's reading skills (Whitehurst et al., 1994).

Acknowledgments

Preparation of this work was supported, in part, by grants from the National Institute of Child Health and Human Development (Nos. HD38880 and HD30988), the National Science Foundation (No. REC-0128970), and the Institute of Education Sciences, U.S. Department of Education (No. R305J030093). Views expressed herein are solely those of the author and have not been cleared by the grantors.

References

Adams, M. J. (1990). *Beginning to read: Thinking and learning about print.* Cambridge, MA: MIT Press.

Anthony, J. L., & Lonigan, C. J. (2004). The nature of phonological sensitivity: Converging evidence from four studies of preschool and early-grade school children. *Journal of Educational Psychology, 96,* 43–55.

Anthony, J. L., Lonigan, C. J., Burgess, S. R., Driscoll, K., Phillips, B. M., & Cantor, B. G. (2002). Structure of preschool phonological sensitivity: Overlapping sensitivity to rhyme, words, syllables, and phonemes. *Journal of Experimental Child Psychology, 82,* 65–92.

Anthony, J. L., Lonigan, C. J., Driscoll, K., Phillips, B. M., & Burgess, S. R. (2003). Preschool phonological sensitivity: A quasi-parallel progression of word structure units and cognitive operations. *Reading Research Quarterly, 38,* 470–487.

Anthony, J. L., Lonigan, C. J., & Schatschneider, C. (2003, June). *Investigating the dimensionality of phonological sensitivity: An Item Response Theory approach.* Paper presented at the meeting of the Society for the Scientific Study of Reading, Toronto, Ontario, Canada.

Baddeley, A. (1986). *Working memory.* New York: Oxford University Press.

Bowers, P. G. (1995). Tracing symbol naming speed's unique contributions to reading disabilities over time. *Reading and Writing, 7,* 189–216.

Bowers, P. G., & Swanson, L. B. (1991). Naming speed deficits in reading disability: Multiple measures of a singular process. *Journal of Experimental Child Psychology, 51,* 195–219.

Bowers, P. G., & Wolf, M. (1993). Theoretical links among naming speed, precise timing mechanisms and orthographic skill in dyslexia. *Reading and Writing, 5,* 69–85.

Bowey, J. A. (1994). Phonological sensitivity in novice readers and nonreaders. *Journal of Experimental Child Psychology, 58,* 134–159.

Bowey, J. A. (2002). Reflections on onset–rime and phoneme sensitivity as predictors of beginning word reading. *Journal of Experimental Child Psychology, 82,* 29–40.

Bradley, L., & Bryant, P. E. (1983). Categorizing sounds and learning to read: A causal connection. *Nature, 301,* 419–421.

Bryant, P. (2002). It doesn't matter whether onset and rime predicts reading better than phoneme awareness does, or vice versa. *Journal of Experimental Child Psychology, 82,* 41–46.

Bryant, P. E., MacLean, M., Bradley, L. L., & Crossland, J. (1990). Rhyme and alliteration, phoneme detection, and learning to read. *Developmental Psychology, 26,* 429–438.

Burgess, S. R., & Lonigan, C. J. (1998). Bidirectional relations of phonological sensitivity and prereading abilities: Evidence from a preschool sample. *Journal of Experimental Child Psychology, 70,* 117–141.

Byrne, B., & Fielding-Barnsley, R. F. (1991). Evaluation of a program to teach phonemic awareness to young children. *Journal of Educational Psychology, 82,* 805–812.

Byrne, B., & Fielding-Barnsley, R. F. (1993). Evaluation of a program to teach phonemic awareness to young children: A one-year follow-up. *Journal of Educational Psychology, 85,* 104–111.

Byrne, B., & Fielding-Barnsley, R. (1995). Evaluation of a program to teach phonemic awareness to young children: A 2- and 3-year follow-up and a new preschool trial. *Journal of Educational Psychology, 87,* 488–503.

Chall, J. S., Jacobs, V., & Baldwin, L. (1990). *The reading crisis: Why poor children fall behind.* Cambridge, MA: Harvard University Press.

Chaney, C. (1992). Language development, metalinguistic skills, and print awareness in 3-year-old children. *Applied Psycholinguistics, 13,* 485–514.

Cooper, D. H., Roth, F. P., Speece, D. L., & Schatschneider, C. (2002). The contribution of oral language to the development of phonological awareness. *Applied Psycholinguistics, 23,* 399–416.

Cunningham, A. E., & Stanovich, K. E. (1998). Early reading acquisition and its relation to reading experience and ability 10 years later. *Developmental Psychology, 33,* 934–945.

de Jong, P. F., & Olson, R. K. (2004). Early prediction of letter knowledge. *Journal of Experimental Child Psychology, 88,* 254–273.

Echols, L. D., West, R. F., Stanovich, K. E., & Zehr, K. S. (1996). Using children's literacy activities to predict growth in verbal cognitive skills: A longitudinal investigation. *Journal of Educational Psychology, 88,* 296–304.

Fowler, A. E. (1991). How early phonological development might set the stage for phoneme awareness. In S. A. Brady & D. P. Shankweiler (Eds.), *Phonological processes in literacy* (pp. 97–117). Hillsdale, NJ: Erlbaum.

Goswami, U. (2002). In the beginning was the rhyme? A reflection on Hulme, Hatcher, Nation, Brown, Adams, and Stuart (2002). *Journal of Experimental Child Psychology, 82,* 47–57.

Goswami, U., & Bryant, P. E. (1990). *Phonological skills and learning to read.* Hillsdale, NJ: Erlbaum.

Hulme, C., Hatcher, P. J., Nation, K., Brown, A., Adams, J., & Stuart, G. (2002). Phoneme awareness is a better predictor of early reading skill than onset–rime awareness. *Journal of Experimental Child Psychology, 82,* 2–28.

Johnston, R. S., Anderson, M., & Holligan, C. (1996). Knowledge of the alphabet and explicit awareness of phonemes in prereaders: The nature of the relationship. *Reading and Writing: An Interdisciplinary Journal, 8,* 217–234.

Kirby, J. R., Parrila, R. K., & Pfeiffer, S. L. (2003). Naming speed and phonological awareness as predictors of reading development. *Journal of Educational Psychology, 95,* 453–464.

Liberman, A. M., Cooper, F. S., Shankweiler, D., &

Studdert-Kennedy, M. (1967). Perception of the speech code. *Psychological Review, 74,* 431–461.

Lonigan, C. J. (2003). Development and promotion of emergent literacy skills in preschool children at-risk of reading difficulties. In B. Foorman (Ed.), *Preventing and remediating reading difficulties: Bringing science to scale* (pp. 23–50). Timonium, MD: York Press.

Lonigan, C. J., Anthony, J. L., Bloomfield, B., Dyer, S. M., & Samwel, C. (1999). Effects of two preschool shared reading interventions on the emergent literacy skills of children from low-income families. *Journal of Early Intervention, 22,* 306–322.

Lonigan, C. J., Anthony, J. L., Burgess, S. R., & Phillips, B. M. (2004). Development of phonological processing skills in preschool children. Unpublished raw data.

Lonigan, C. J., Burgess, S. R., & Anthony, J. L. (2000). Development of emergent literacy and early reading skills in preschool children: Evidence from a latent variable longitudinal study. *Developmental Psychology, 36,* 596–613.

Lonigan, C. J., Burgess, S. R., Anthony, J. L., & Barker, T. A. (1998). Development of phonological sensitivity in 2- to 5-year-old children. *Journal of Educational Psychology, 90,* 294–311.

MacLean, M., Bryant, P., & Bradley, L. (1987). Rhymes, nursery rhymes, and reading in early childhood. *Merrill-Palmer Quarterly, 33,* 255–282.

Manis, F. R., Doi, L. M., & Bhadha, B. (2000). Naming speed, phonological awareness, and orthographic knowledge in second graders. *Journal of Learning Disabilities, 33,* 325–333, 374.

McBride-Chang, C., & Manis, F. R. (1996). Structural invariance in the associations of naming speed, phonological awareness, and verbal reasoning in good and poor readers: A test of the double deficit hypothesis. *Reading and Writing, 8,* 323–339.

Metsala, J. L., & Ehri, L. C. (Eds.). (1998). *Word recognition in beginning literacy.* Mahwah, NJ: Erlbaum.

Metsala, J. L., & Walley, A. C. (1998). Spoken vocabulary growth and the segmental restructuring of lexical representations: Precursors to phonemic awareness and early reading ability. In J. L Metsala & L. C. Ehri (Eds.), *Word recognition in beginning literacy* (pp. 89–120). Mahwah, NJ: Erlbaum.

Monroe, M. (1935). *Children who cannot read.* Chicago: University of Chicago Press.

Morais, J. (1991). Constraints on the development of phonological awareness. In S. A. Brady & D. P. Shankweiler (Eds.), *Phonological processes in literacy: A tribute to Isabelle Y. Liberman* (pp. 5–27). Hillsdale, NJ: Erlbaum.

Morais, J. (2003). Levels of phonological representation in skilled reading and in learning to read.

Reading and Writing: An Interdisciplinary Journal, 16, 123–151.

Morrison, F. J., Smith, L., & Dow-Ehrensberger, M. (1995). Education and cognitive development: A natural experiment. *Developmental Psychology, 31,* 789–799.

Murray, B. A., Stahl, S. A., & Ivey, M. G. (1996). Developing phoneme awareness through alphabet books. *Reading and Writing, 8,* 307–322.

Muter, V., Hulme, C., Snowling, M., & Taylor, S. (1997). Segmentation, not rhyming, predicts early progress in learning to read. *Journal of Experimental Child Psychology, 65,* 370–398.

Muter, V., & Snowling, M. (1998). Concurrent and longitudinal predictors of reading: The role of metalinguistic and short-term memory skills. *Reading Research Quarterly, 33,* 320–337.

Nagy, W. E., & Anderson, R. C. (1984). How many words are there in printed school English? *Reading Research Quarterly, 19,* 304–330.

Naslund, J. C., & Schneider, W. (1996). Kindergarten letter knowledge, phonological skills, and memory processes: Relative effects on early literacy. *Journal of Experimental Child Psychology, 62,* 30–59.

Nation, K., & Hulme, C. (1997). Phonemic segmentation, not onset–rime segmentation, predicts early reading and spelling skills. *Reading Research Quarterly, 32,* 154–167.

National Center for Education Statistics. (2003). *The nation's report card: Fourth-grade reading 2003.* Retrieved November 12, 2003, from http://nces.ed.gov/nationsreportcard/reading/results.

National Early Literacy Panel. (2004). *Report on a synthesis of early predictors of reading.* Louisville, KY: Author.

National Institute of Child Health and Development. (2000). *Report of the National Reading Panel: Teaching children to read.* Washington, DC: U.S. Department of Health and Human Services.

Pennington, B. F., Cardoso-Martins, C., Green, P. A., & Lefly, D. L. (2001). Comparing the phonological and double-deficit hypotheses for developmental dyslexia. *Reading and Writing: An Interdisciplinary Journal, 14,* 707–755.

Perfetti, C. A., Beck, I., Bell, L. C., & Hughes, C. (1987). Phonemic knowledge and learning to read are reciprocal: A longitudinal study of first grade children. *Merrill-Palmer Quarterly, 33,* 283–319.

Schatschneider, C., Carlson, C. D., Francis, D. J., Foorman, B. R., & Fletcher, J. M. (2002). Relationship of rapid automatized naming and phonological awareness in early reading development: Implications for the double-deficit hypothesis. *Journal of Learning Disabilities, 35,* 245–256.

Schatschneider, C., Fletcher, J. M., Francis, D. F., Carlson, C. D., & Foorman, B. R. (2004). Kindergarten prediction of reading skills: A longitudinal comparative analysis. *Journal of Educational Psychology, 96,* 265–282.

Schatschneider, C., Francis, D. J., Foorman, B. R., Fletcher, J. M., & Mehta, P. (1999). The dimensionality of phonological awareness: An application of item response theory. *Journal of Educational Psychology, 91,* 439–449.

Sénéchal, M., & LeFevre, J. (2002). Parental involvement in the development of children's reading skill: A five-year longitudinal study. *Child Development, 73,* 445–460.

Share, D. L. (2004). Knowing letter names and learning letter sounds: A causal connection. *Journal of Experimental Child Psychology, 88,* 213–233.

Shatil, E., & Share, D. L. (2003). Cognitive antecedents of early reading ability: A test of the modularity hypothesis. *Journal of Experimental Child Psychology, 86,* 1–31.

Snow, C. E., Burns, M. S., & Griffin, P. (Eds.). (1998). *Preventing reading difficulties in young children.* Washington, DC: National Academy Press.

Stahl, S. A., & Murray, B. A. (1994). Defining phonological awareness and its relationship to early reading. *Journal of Educational Psychology, 86,* 221–234.

Stanovich, K. E. (1986). Matthew effects in reading: Some consequences of individual differences in the acquisition of literacy. *Reading Research Quarterly, 21,* 360–407.

Stanovich, K. E. (1988). Explaining the differences between the dyslexic and the garden-variety poor reader: The phonological-core variable-difference model. *Journal of Learning Disabilities, 21,* 590–612.

Stanovich, K. E. (1992). Speculations on the causes and consequences of individual differences in early reading acquisition. In P. B. Gough, L. C. Ehri, & R. Treiman (Eds.), *Reading acquisition* (pp. 307–342). Hillsdale, NJ: Erlbaum.

Stanovich, K. E., & Siegel, L. S. (1994). Phenotypic performance profile of children with reading disabilities: A regression-based test of the phonological-core variable-difference model. *Journal of Educational Psychology, 86,* 24–53.

Storch, S. A., & Whitehurst, G. J. (2002). Oral language and code-related precursors to reading: Evidence from a longitudinal structural model. *Developmental Psychology, 38,* 934–947.

Sulzby, E. (1989). Assessment of writing and of children's language while writing. In L. Morrow & J. Smith (Eds.), *The role of assessment and measurement in early literacy instruction* (pp. 83–109). Englewood Cliffs, NJ: Prentice-Hall.

Sulzby, E., & Teale, W. (1991). Emergent literacy. In R. Barr, M. Kamil, P. Mosenthal, & P. D. Pearson (Eds.), *Handbook of reading research* (Vol. 2, pp. 727–758). New York: Longman.

Teale, W. H., & Sulzby, E. (Eds.). (1986). *Emergent literacy: Writing and reading.* Norwood, NJ: Ablex.

Torgesen, J. K., & Burgess, S. R. (1998). Consistency of reading-related phonological processes throughout early childhood: Evidence from longitudinal–correlational and instructional studies. In J. L. Metsala & L. C. Ehri (Eds.), *Word recognition in beginning literacy* (pp. 161–188). Mahwah, NJ: Erlbaum.

Tunmer, W. E., & Rohl, M. (1991). Phonological awareness and reading acquisition. In D. Sawyer & B. Fox (Eds.), *Phonological awareness in reading: The evolution of current perspectives* (pp. 1–29). New York: Springer-Verlag.

Wagner, R. K., Muse, A. E., Stein, T. L., Cukrowitz, K. C., Harrell, E. R., Rashotte, C. A., & Samwel, C. S. (2003). How to assess reading-related phonological abilities. In B. Foorman (Ed.), *Preventing and remediating reading difficulties: Bringing science to scale* (pp. 51–70). Timonium, MD: York Press.

Wagner, R. K., & Torgesen, J. K. (1987). The natural of phonological processing and its causal role in the acquisition of reading skills. *Psychological Bulletin, 101,* 192–212.

Wagner, R. K., Torgesen, J. K., Laughon, P., Simmons, K., & Rashotte, C. A. (1993). The development of young readers' phonological processing abilities. *Journal of Educational Psychology, 85,* 1–20.

Wagner, R. K., Torgesen, J. K., & Rashotte, C. A. (1994). Development of reading-related phonological processing abilities: New evidence of bidirectional causality from a latent variable longitudinal study. *Developmental Psychology, 30,* 73–87.

Wagner, R. K., Torgesen, J. K., Rashotte, C. A., Hecht, S. A., Barker, T. A., Burgess, S. R., et al. (1997). Changing relations between phonological processing abilities and word-level reading as children develop from beginning to skilled readers: A 5-year longitudinal study. *Developmental Psychology, 33,* 468–479.

Walley, A. C., Metsala, J. L., & Garlock, V. M. (2003). Spoken vocabulary growth: Its role in the development of phoneme awareness and early reading ability. *Reading and Writing: An Interdisciplinary Journal, 16,* 5–20.

Whitehurst, G. J., Epstein, J. N., Angell, A. C., Payne, A. C., Crone, D. A., & Fischel, J. E. (1994). Outcomes of an emergent literacy intervention in Head Start. *Journal of Educational Psychology, 86,* 542–555.

Whitehurst, G. J., & Lonigan, C. J. (1998). Child development and emergent literacy. *Child Development, 68,* 848–872.

Yopp, H. K. (1988). The validity and reliability of phonemic awareness tests. *Reading Research Quarterly, 23,* 159–177.

7

The Development of Phonological Sensitivity

STEPHEN R. BURGESS

The development of phonological sensitivity and its role in the development of reading is becoming increasingly well understood. Phonological sensitivity is the sensitivity to and the ability to manipulate the sound structure of oral language. It is now recognized to play a causal role in the acquisition of literacy in alphabetic script systems (e.g., Ball & Blachman, 1988; Wagner, Torgesen, & Rashotte, 1994) and to be the core deficit for most children having difficulty learning to read (Stanovich, 1988; Wagner et al., 1994; Wagner et al., 1997). In this chapter, I briefly review research examining the development of phonological sensitivity and describe in more detail work I have participated in that examines some of the factors related to phonological sensitivity development.

Most research has focused on the role of phonological sensitivity in the development of reading in school-age children. Building on the work of Wagner and Torgesen and others, I became interested in questions that explored the development of phonological sensitivity. At the time, phonological sensitivity was primarily seen as a school-age variable driven by reading development or that was bidirectionally related to reading development. Now studies have indicated that preschool-age children are capable of successfully completing phonological sensitivity tasks (e.g., Chaney, 1992; Fox & Routh, 1975; Lonigan, Burgess, & Anthony, 2000; Lonigan, Burgess, Anthony, & Barker, 1998; MacLean, Bryant, & Bradley, 1987;

Puolakanaho, Poikkeus, & Ahonen, 2003). Younger children typically perform better on tasks that deal with words and syllables than with phonemes, but many demonstrate the ability to perform phoneme-level manipulations. Lonigan et al. (1998) tested 238 preschoolers and found that, although their average performance was low, there was evidence that a number of the 2- and 3-year-old children demonstrated phonological sensitivity at all levels of linguistic complexity. MacLean et al. (1987) also found that 3-year-olds demonstrated above chance levels of performance on their measures of rhyme oddity and elision oddity.

Conceptualizing Phonological Sensitivity

Many of the questions surrounding the role of phonological sensitivity in the development of reading stem from the manner in which phonological sensitivity has been conceptualized. Some investigators, primarily those who supported the view that phonological awareness develops as a consequence of reading instruction, confined the use of the term "phonological awareness" to refer to the ability to manipulate words at the level of phonemes (e.g., Morais, Cary, Alegria, & Bertelson, 1979). In contrast, other investigators, primarily those who supported the view that phonological awareness enables or at least facilitates the development of reading, used the term "phonological awareness" to refer to a broader constellation of tasks requiring sensitivity to speech sounds. We are currently much closer to a consensus concerning the terminology to use when referring to the various aspects of phonological awareness and the tasks used in its assessment. The terminology suggested by Stanovich (1992) is useful in delineating this conceptualization. He proposed that the term "phonological sensitivity" be used to refer to the more global set of processing abilities that require sensitivity to speech sounds and "phonological awareness" to the ability to manipulate words at the level of phonemes.

In addition to questions concerning whether preschoolers possess measurable levels of phonological sensitivity and how to conceptualize the construct, a growing body of research has focused on whether phonological sensitivity measured prior to reading instruction is predictive of subsequent phonological sensitivity, whether phonological sensitivity measured prior to reading instruction is predictive of subsequent reading ability, and what kinds of experiences, skills, and abilities predict or facilitate the growth of phonological sensitivity.

The question of whether early phonological sensitivity is predictive of subsequent phonological sensitivity is actually a series of issues. One of the most critical of these issues involves whether phonological sensitivity is a unitary construct. Phonological sensitivity appears to develop gradually in children and is best viewed as a hierarchy of sensitivity or levels of complexity (Adams, 1990; Stanovich, 1992). Higher levels of sensitivity require more explicit awareness and manipulation of smaller-sized sound units (e.g., phonemes), and more rudimentary levels of sensitivity require a more shallow level of awareness and manipulation of larger sound units (e.g., syllables). Evidence for a developmental hierarchy comes from studies that have demonstrated that children achieve syllabic and rhyme sensitivity and sensitivity to onset–rime before they achieve sensitivity to phonemes (e.g., Bowey, 1994; Burgess, 2002; Lonigan et al., 1998; Treiman, 1992).

However, the developmental nature of phonological sensitivity led to some debate over whether phonological sensitivity is a unitary construct. It has commonly been as-

sumed that there is more than one type of phonological sensitivity and that the types may be more or less associated with reading development. For example, because different phonological sensitivity tasks differentially predict reading, it has been suggested that the skill assessed by that task (e.g., phonemic sensitivity) is both different from and more important than other types of phonological sensitivity (e.g., Morais et al., 1979; Muter, Hulme, Snowling, & Taylor, 1997; Nation & Hulme, 1997). Other authors have suggested that different types of phonological sensitivity, such as rhyme detection, may facilitate reading development via a different mechanism than phonemic sensitivity (e.g., Goswami & Bryant, 1990). However, a growing body of evidence clearly indicates that phonological sensitivity is a unitary construct (e.g., Anthony et al., 2002; Anthony, Lonigan, Driscoll, Phillips, & Burgess, 2003; Lonigan et al., 2000; Schatschneider, Francis, Foorman, Fletcher, & Mehta, 1999; Stahl & Murray, 1994; Wagner et al., 1994; Wagner et al., 1997; but see Hoien, Lundberg, Stanovich, & Bjaalid, 1995). Stahl and Murray (1994) assessed 113 kindergarten and first-grade children on four measures of phonological sensitivity varying in linguistic complexity. They found that a single-factor solution explained the majority of the variance in phonological sensitivity tasks. Using confirmatory factor analysis, Anthony et al. (2003) found that a single factor provided the best fit to preschool measures of rhyme, syllable, and phoneme sensitivity. They assessed 947 2- to 5-year-old children using tasks that varied in terms of linguistic complexity (e.g., words, syllables) and task complexity (e.g., blending and elision). They have also added to the body of evidence demonstrating that phonological sensitivity develops as children become sensitive to different linguistic units. Children generally master word-level skills before they master syllable-level skills, syllable-level skills before they master onset–rime-level skills, and onset–rime-level skills before they master phoneme-level skills. These findings were consistent with the idea that children develop various phonological sensitivity skills in overlapping stages rather than discrete temporal stages.

The issue of whether phonological sensitivity is a unitary construct is related to the question of whether early phonological sensitivity predicts subsequent phonological sensitivity. There are highly stable individual differences in phonological sensitivity from the late-preschool period forward (Burgess & Lonigan, 1998; Lonigan et al., 2000; Torgesen & Burgess, 1994; Wagner et al., 1997). Relatively few studies have examined whether preschool measures of phonological sensitivity predict subsequent phonological sensitivity (e.g., Bryant, MacLean, Bradley, & Crossland, 1990; Burgess & Lonigan, 1998; Lonigan et al., 2000). The available evidence does suggest that early measures of preschool phonological sensitivity predict subsequent phonological sensitivity. Bryant et al. (1990) found that phonological sensitivity assessed in 4-year-olds was significantly correlated (average $r = .48$) with phonological sensitivity measured at age 6 years. Burgess and Lonigan (1998) assessed ninety-seven 4- and 5-year-olds and found that a composite measure of phonological sensitivity was significantly correlated with phonological sensitivity measured 12 months later. The Time 1 phonological sensitivity measure explained 22% of the unique variance in the Time 2 phonological sensitivity composite even after accounting for variance due to letter knowledge, oral language, and age. In one of the most extensive studies to date, Lonigan et al. (2000) administered four phonological sensitivity tasks to 193 preschoolers. The older group ($n = 96$, mean age = 60.04 months, range = 48–64 months) at Time 1 demonstrated extremely high stability in phonological sensitivity. The latent variable representing Time 1 phonological sensitivity perfectly predicted Time 2 phonological sensitivity. This finding is consistent with studies using older children (e.g., Wagner et al., 1994).

The younger group ($n = 97$, mean age = 41.02 months, range = 25–61 months) showed less stability in phonological sensitivity. Very early phonological sensitivity was not a strong predictor of phonological sensitivity in the late preschool period. In the younger group, the continuity between Time 1 and Time 2 phonological sensitivity appeared to be mediated by letter knowledge. Therefore, although a number of the young group demonstrated significant levels of performance on the phonological sensitivity tasks, the results indicated that

phonological sensitivity in the late preschool period was only partially a function of early phonological sensitivity. The combination of Time 1 phonological sensitivity and oral language skills accounted for only about 25% of the variance in Time 2 phonological sensitivity. These results were consistent with earlier reports indicating that phonological sensitivity tasks become more reliable with older children. From a developmental perspective, Lonigan et al. (1998) found that estimates of internal consistency and correlations between the tasks indicated that phonological sensitivity becomes more cohesive as a construct as children mature and their level of performance on tasks designed to measure phonological sensitivity increased. Therefore, one would expect that the increasing relative stability of phonological sensitivity tasks as children mature would make predicting phonological sensitivity easier in older children. These findings point to the need for more extensive study of the origin of phonological sensitivity and for refinement in how these skills are assessed in younger children.

Phonological Sensitivity and Its Relation to Reading

An extensive body of evidence has documented the relations between phonological sensitivity and subsequent reading ability (e.g., Wagner et al., 1994; Wagner et al., 1997; Bryant et al., 1990), as well as their bidirectional nature (e.g., Burgess & Lonigan, 1998; Wagner et al., 1997). Most of the research examining this link has utilized school-age children, but a growing number of studies have extended the relations to younger children and to a more diverse range of literacy and literacy-related skills (e.g., Burgess, 2002; Burgess & Lonigan, 1998; Lonigan et al., 2000). Most of the initial work investigating the role of phonological sensitivity focused on formal reading activities (e.g., decoding words). For example, Burgess (2002) found that Time 1 preschool measures of phonological sensitivity predicted subsequent word-decoding skills even after accounting for the variance attributed to letter knowledge, oral language, and age.

However, children develop a wide range of prereading abilities or emergent literacy skills, such as letter knowledge, before actually being able to decode individual words (Whitehurst & Lonigan, 1998). These abilities are predictive of subsequent individual differences in reading ability (e.g., Adams, 1990; Clay, 1979; Whitehurst & Lonigan, 1998). Burgess and Lonigan (1998) tested ninety-seven 4- and 5-year-olds on a variety of phonological sensitivity, oral language, and early reading measures. Time 1 phonological sensitivity predicted significant unique variance in the growth of letter-name and sound knowledge as measured at Time 2 12 months later even when the variance attributable to oral language, age, and Time 1 letter knowledge was accounted for. These results are consistent with the view that phonological sensitivity facilitates the acquisition of letter-name and sound knowledge (e.g. Adams, 1990). The results also indicate that the role of phonological sensitivity begins very early in the development of reading. Interestingly, the effect was found for word- and syllable-level items, indicating that the lower levels of phonological sensitivity, not just phonemic sensitivity, are involved in the facilitative effect. The reason that phonological sensitivity aids the acquisition of letter knowledge is not clear. It is possible that children who are more sensitive to the phonological structure of words may be better able to benefit from the informal exposure to print that many preschoolers receive (Whitehurst & Lonigan, 1998).

Researchers employing preschool-age children have furthered our understanding of phonological sensitivity in the development of reading (e.g., Chaney, 1992; MacLean et al., 1987). Whereas previous studies such as ours (e.g., Burgess, 2002; Burgess & Lonigan, 1998; Lonigan et al., 2000) have demonstrated that phonological sensitivity was predictive of letter-name and letter-sound knowledge and that the relations were bidirectional, recent investigations have explored the role of phonological sensitivity in the development of the alphabetic principle (e.g., Byrne & Fielding-Barnsley, 1993) and other prereading skills in a more direct manner (e.g., Treiman, Tincoff, & Richmond-Welty, 1997; Treiman, Tincoff, Rodriguez, Mouzaki, & Francis, 1998).

Treiman has used the study of the phonological nature of the names of letters to clarify further the role of phonological sensitivity in reading and spelling development. Treiman has developed a large body of research suggesting that phonological sensitivity plays a significant role in a child's ability to benefit from early print experiences by interacting with the phonological information in letter names (e.g., Treiman, 1992; Treiman et al., 1997). Many letter names contain relevant information about letter sounds. Treiman has demonstrated that the learning of letter sounds is influenced by the position and amount of phonological information in the letter name. Children learn letter sounds more quickly when the letter name contains accessible phonological information. Treiman et al. (1998) taught a series of 10 letter-sound correspondences to 5-year-old nonreader children who knew the letter names but not the letter sounds. After three teaching sessions, children demonstrated better learning for letters whose name and sound were more phonologically related, and the effect was greater for letter names having the phonological information at the beginning (e.g., /b/) than at the end of the name (e.g., /f/).

Using Phonological Sensitivity to Benefit from Early Print Exposure

Treiman's studies added additional evidence that young children possess phonological sensitivity abilities and, more important, they also demonstrated that young children are capable of using these abilities to benefit from exposure to print. This assumes that children learn the letter sounds high in phonological information faster than the other letter sounds because of their sensitivity to the phonological information. In order to test this hypothesis, we extended the work of Treiman and colleagues by including measures of phonological sensitivity prior to training in letter names and sounds (Burgess, 2004). In two experiments we trained approximately thirty 4- and 5-year-olds on letter names and sounds that differed in the phonological information contained in the letters. Three categories of letter names were used: (1) phonological information at the beginning of the name (e.g., /d/), (2) phonological information at the end of the name (e.g., /s/), and (3) no phonological information in the name (e.g., /c/). Children were pretested for letter-name and sound knowledge. Children who knew either all the letter names or sounds in a category were excluded. For example, in the letter-name training experiment, children were excluded if they knew all the letter names containing phonological information at the beginning of the letter name. Children were trained on letter sounds of letters for which they knew the name but not the sound. Two letters from each category were selected based on the child's current letter or sound knowledge. Prior to the training the child was shown the six upper-case letters one at a time, told the name of the letter, and asked to name the letter. During the training, which was also an immediate test condition, the child was shown the letter and asked either its name or sound. Corrective feedback was provided if the child gave an incorrect response. The order of letter presentation was randomized across each of up to six trials. Training was stopped if the child named all six letters correctly on consecutive trials. A delayed test was conducted either 24 or 48 hours later. The same procedure was followed during the delayed test.

Tests of group differences found that the children answered correctly more often for letter names and sounds when the letter name contained phonological information at the beginning rather than at the end, with both conditions producing better results than no phonological information in the name. These findings were consistent with Treiman's and extended them to letter names. In order to explore the contribution of phonological sensitivity to the learning of letter names and sounds, multiple regression was used. The combination of phonological sensitivity and initial letter-name knowledge explained approximately 40% of the variance in letter names learned, with only total letter-name knowledge acting as a significant unique predictor. The combination of phonological sensitivity and initial letter-name and sound knowledge explained approximately 60% of the variance in letter sounds learned, with phonological sensitivity and total letter-sound knowledge acting as significant unique predictors. Our goal in this study was to explore the acquisition of letter

knowledge in a direct teaching format. Therefore, we used children who varied in prior letter knowledge. However, because of this, our study did not take into account some of the letter characteristics that Treiman has demonstrated as effecting letter knowledge learning. Additional studies are needed to further explore the role of phonological sensitivity, in terms of both child and letter characteristics, in the development of letter knowledge.

Because children appear to learn letter names that differ in phonological information at different rates when they are directly trained, I decided to explore whether knowledge of letters differing in phonological information provided differential prediction of subsequent growth in phonological sensitivity and subsequent letter knowledge and decoding ability. In a reanalysis of the data set reported in Wagner et al. (1997), I created letter knowledge variables based on the Trieman criteria. There was no evidence that composites representing the letters that differ in phonological information contained in the letter name possessed differential predictive ability or higher concurrent correlations with phonological sensitivity, letter-sound knowledge, or word-decoding skills. However, it is possible that the children were too old to adequately test this premise, that the children were too high in average letter knowledge, or that the manner in which children typically acquire letter knowledge does not take advantage of the phonological information present in the letter name. The present analyses did not find a difference in the ability of the different letter knowledge groupings to predict subsequent phonological sensitivity, letter knowledge, or decoding, but this is an area that requires more detailed and systematic exploration.

Factors in Phonological Sensitivity Development

Although I have been involved in what was needed work on early phonological sensitivity that examined issues dealing with measuring phonological sensitivity and exploring its role in the development of reading, most of my interest has been in the factors that are associated with phonological sensitivity development. These factors can be divided into knowledge and abilities (e.g., letter knowledge, oral language) and environmental experiences and exposure (e.g., shared reading).

Most of the research in this area has examined the effect of learning to read on the development of phonological sensitivity. It is well documented that learning to read facilitates the development of phonological sensitivity, especially higher levels such as phonemic awareness (e.g., Morais et al., 1979; Wagner et al., 1997), and that the effect is bidirectional. As mentioned earlier, more recent studies have documented that phonological sensitivity and letter knowledge also show these relations (e.g., Burgess, 2002; Burgess & Lonigan, 1998; Lonigan et al., 2000). A measurable level of letter knowledge does not appear to be necessary for lower levels of phonological sensitivity (Burgess & Lonigan, 1998), but prior studies have suggested that higher levels of phonological sensitivity, such as phonemic awareness, are dependent on some level of letter knowledge (e.g., Bowey, 1994; Johnston, Anderson, & Holligan, 1996; Stahl & Murray, 1994). Letter knowledge may help direct a child's attention to the components of words and the general idea that they can be represented as smaller units.

Another commonly studied factor is oral language. Researchers have suggested that the development of phonological sensitivity is tied to the development of oral language skills, especially vocabulary growth (e.g., Metsala, 1999; Walley, Metsala, & Garlock, 2003). The lexical restructuring hypothesis proposes that phonological awareness may emerge as a result of the rearrangement of the lexicon that is a normal part of language acquisition (e.g., Metsala, 1999). Lexical restructuring theory is based on the premise that phonological representations become increasingly more segmented and distinctly specified in terms of phonetic features with age. For example, a child would take a word formerly represented at the syllable level and rerepresent it at a more finely grained level, such as the onset–rime. Metsala and Walley (1998) suggested that the process of re-representing individual words is a function of the child's vocabulary size and the rate of expansion of his or her vocabulary. Thus children with large vocabularies who are rapidly acquiring lots of new words would

possess lexicons that are under more pressure to restructure words and to have consequently represented the syllables, onsets, and rimes in more words in their vocabularies. Metsala and Walley (1998) proposed that the degree to which segmental representation has progressed will determine how easily the child will become phonologically aware and be prepared to learn to read and write. This view assumes that segmental representations emerge primarily as a function of spoken vocabulary growth and associated changes in phonological neighborhoods. The extent to which letter knowledge learning is associated with this process has not been extensively explored.

Compared with the number of studies examining ability and knowledge precursors of phonological sensitivity, there has been relatively little exploration of the role of environmental experiences and exposures in the development of phonological sensitivity. However, this is an important area if we are to understand how children are provided access to the exposure to print and oral language that researchers have suggested they require. Both letter knowledge and oral language ability are associated with a variety of home environment variables, including socioeconomic status (SES) and shared reading experiences (e.g., Burgess, Hecht, & Lonigan, 2002; Scarborough & Dobrich, 1994). It has also been consistently demonstrated that SES is significantly related to phonological sensitivity (e.g., Bowey, 1995; Payne, Whitehurst, & Angell, 1994; Hecht, Burgess, Torgesen, Wagner, & Rashotte, 2000). Children from higher SES families tend to have more developed phonological sensitivity skills during the preschool period (e.g., Bowey, 1995; Hecht et al., 2000) and at school entry (e.g., Hecht et al., 2000). These differences have usually been attributed to SES differences in print and oral language exposure (e.g., Bowey, 1995; Burgess, 2002; Payne et al., 1994).

More explicit examinations of the role of the home environment have tended to focus on the role of shared reading and other behaviors directly tied to teaching early literacy skills. Studies have yielded contradictory findings about the relations between shared reading and phonological sensitivity, but most have documented a significant positive correlation between shared reading exposure and phonological sensitivity (e.g., Burgess, 2002; Murray, Stahl, & Ivey, 1996; Sénéchal, Lefevre, Hudson, & Lawson, 1996; Sénéchal, Lefevre, Thomas, & Daley, 1998; but see Evans, Shaw, & Bell, 2000). For example, Sénéchal et al. (1998) found that storybook exposure was significantly associated with oral language skills but not with written language skills such as letter knowledge. They included phonological sensitivity in the oral language composite. Burgess et al. (2002) also found differential relations between different conceptualizations of the home literacy environment and phonological sensitivity. Conceptualizations that emphasized the role of actively exposing the child to literacy (e.g., shared reading, magnetic letters) were more often significantly related to phonological sensitivity than were conceptualizations that utilized more global measures (e.g., SES) or more passive aspects of the home literacy environment (e.g., parental leisure reading). The nature of the relation has been clarified even further by experimental studies indicating that exposure to alphabet books is more effective in developing phonological sensitivity than exposure to picture books (e.g., Murray et al., 1996). Findings such as these support the central role of letter knowledge in phonological sensitivity development. Additional support for the role of phonological sensitivity in benefiting from exposure to print comes from Frijters, Barron, and Brunello (2000). They found evidence that the relationship of home literacy activities to written language was mediated by phonological sensitivity.

Relatively few studies have examined these multiple predictors simultaneously. In a 1-year longitudinal study of ninety-seven 4- and 5-year-olds (Burgess, 2002), I found that early knowledge about print that included letter knowledge, oral language ability, and the home literacy environment (e.g., shared reading activities) at Time 1 were significant unique predictors of Time 2 phonological sensitivity, with the full model explaining approximately 51% of the variance. Speech perception and age were not significant predictors. When the autoregressive effect of Time 1 phonological sensitivity was added in a subsequent model, only Time 1 phonological sensitivity and the home literacy environment were significant unique predictors of the growth in phonological sensitivity

over the time interval examined. The full model explained approximately 67% of the variance in the growth of phonological sensitivity.

Thus a growing body of evidence points to important roles for letter knowledge, oral language ability, and the home literacy environment in the development of phonological sensitivity. Because the home literacy environment should also be important in the development of letter knowledge (e.g., Burgess, 2002) and oral language ability (Sénéchal et al., 1996; Sénéchal et al., 1998), these findings raise issues concerning the home literacy environment that need to be explored. Children enter school with varying levels of letter knowledge. Approximately 24% of 3- to 5-year-old children not enrolled in kindergarten already recognize all the letters of the alphabet, with 15% of 3-year-olds versus 44% of 5-year-olds knowing all the letters (Nord, Lennon, Liu, & Chandler, 1999; Warden & Boettcher, 1990). However, very little is actually known about the letter knowledge experiences and exposure children receive prior to school entry. This involves issues of exposure, as well as the ability to benefit from this exposure.

As Treiman (e.g., Treiman et al., 1998), as well as Burgess (2004), have demonstrated that children as young as 4 years old can utilize their phonological sensitivity ability to benefit from exposure to letters, I wondered about the youngest ages at which this phenomenon could be observed. We collected letter-name and sound knowledge scores on a sample of ninety children under the age of 4 years (Burgess, 2004). There were thirteen children less than 2 years old, twenty-three 2-year-olds, and twenty-four 3-year-olds. We found that children under age 2 had very little letter-name and sound knowledge on average. This made it impossible to examine the phonological information in the letter-name effect for letter names or sounds in this group. The 2 year olds demonstrated considerably more letter knowledge. The average percentage of children knowing letter names with beginning phonological information was 27%; with ending phonological information, 26%; and with phonological information not in the name, 21%. A similar trend was found in the 3-year-olds (53%, 49%, and 44%, respectively). For the 2-year-olds and letter-sound knowledge, the averages were 13%, 11%, and 8% for beginning, ending, and not in name, respectively. The trend became much more pronounced for 3-year-olds (27%, 24%, and 10%). These results indicated that the trend may already be developing for the phonological information in the name effect at 2 years, even though very young children on average possess relatively limited letter knowledge.

Although differences exist across studies and groups (e.g., SES), children seem to show a burst of letter knowledge between the ages of 4 and 5 years (e.g., Burgess, 2004; Warden & Boettcher, 1990). In contrast, knowledge of letter sounds develops at a much slower rate (Burgess, 2004; Burgess & Lonigan, 1998). For example, in the Wagner et al. (1994) sample of 201 kindergartners, approximately half of the participants knew fewer than seven letter sounds. It is possible that these levels of letter knowledge reflect the development of more finely developed phonological sensitivity skills, but it seems more reasonable to attribute the relatively slow rate of development of letter knowledge to a paucity of direct instruction in letter names and sounds. Therefore, assuming that these children are capable of benefiting from exposure to letters, it is likely that most parents are not exposing their children to significant amounts of explicit letter instruction opportunities prior to age 3. It is possible that the children are receiving implicit instruction or exposure during shared reading activities, but based on the children's letter knowledge, they would not be benefiting much from these experiences.

In order to assess this possibility, I surveyed 200 people over age 18. About 25% were parents. They were asked at what age they would start to teach their child letters and how many letters they thought a child should know at kindergarten entry. Approximately 40% said that letter instruction should begin after 3 years, with 39% saying between ages 2 and 3. About 50% expected children to know between 21 and 26 letters at kindergarten entry, and 83% expected children to know at least half of their letters. These results suggest that people have relatively high expectations for children's letter knowledge but that they appear to think that children are not ready to benefit from instructional exposure until the middle to late preschool period. These findings are consistent with parental reports of having letter materials in the home (e.g., magnetic letters) but using them infrequently (e.g., Burgess, 2002, 2004).

Summary and Future Directions

In summary, the available evidence suggests that preschool phonological sensitivity development is linked to abilities such as oral language and letter knowledge and to experiences provided by the home literacy environment. The bidirectional relations between phonological sensitivity and reading appear to begin very early in the development of literacy and to begin at the letter knowledge level. It has been proposed that letter knowledge is very important for phonological sensitivity development and possibly necessary for the development of higher levels of phonological sensitivity (e.g., phonemic sensitivity). However, preliminary evidence reported by Burgess (2004) suggests that parents and other caregivers may underestimate the abilities of preschoolers and delay letter knowledge instruction until age 3 and later.

Reading is a learned behavior, and children in the United States encounter a variety of pedagogical experiences that may lead to letter learning. There is no reason to assume that the order in which letters are taught, either directly or indirectly, will follow a consistent pattern. If letter knowledge is needed for phonological sensitivity development, or at least facilitates its development during the early preschool years, then by not exposing children to letter instruction we may not be taking advantage of the available phonological sensitivity abilities children possess or of activities that may aid the child in gaining an understanding of the alphabetic principle. This paucity of exposure may be associated with a delay in the development of phonological sensitivity. Future research studies are needed to determine whether young preschoolers are able to benefit from print experiences high in letter knowledge content and whether these experiences are associated with subsequent phonological sensitivity levels. For example, do young preschoolers also demonstrate the phonological information in the letter-name effect? As the development of phonological sensitivity also appears to be associated with oral language skill, as suggested by the lexical restructuring hypothesis, it is possible that young preschoolers have not advanced sufficiently in phonological representation to benefit in the same way from letter exposure as older children. For example, does learning letters before age 2 occur via the same mechanism as in 4-year-olds? In order for the phonological information in the name to aid the child, the child would need to possess levels of phonological sensitivity sufficient to benefit from the information in the letter name.

Many of the issues raised in this chapter are theoretical in nature and focus on the early development of phonological sensitivity. It may be difficult to see these issues as directly associated with the current focus on school-based reading instruction and the new guidelines and mandates dictated by No Child Left Behind. However, I propose that it is important to discover the process by which phonological sensitivity develops normally in children, as well as to explore how we could potentially manipulate the home literacy environment to facilitate this process. It is encouraging to suggest that phonological sensitivity development is associated with variables such as oral language and letter knowledge, as these should be manipulatable. In order to accomplish these goals it is important to explore and understand parental expectations for young children and to determine the factors associated with the development and maintenance of the home literacy environment (Burgess et al., 2002; Leseman & de Jong, 1998).

References

Adams, M. J. (1990). *Beginning to read: Thinking and learning about print*. Cambridge, MA: MIT Press.

Anthony, J. L., Lonigan, C. J., Burgess, S. R., Driscoll, B., Phillips, B. M., & Bloomfield, B. G. (2002). Structure of preschool phonological sensitivity: Overlapping sensitivity to rhyme, words, syllables, and phonemes. *Journal of Experimental Child Psychology, 82*, 65–92.

Anthony, J. L., Lonigan, C. J., Driscoll, K., Phillips, B. M., & Burgess, S. R. (2003). Phonological sensitivity: A quasi-parallel progression of word structure units and cognitive operations. *Reading Research Quarterly, 38*, 470–487.

Ball, E., & Blachman, B. (1988). Phonological seg-

mentation training: Effects of reading readiness. *Annals of Dyslexia, 38*, 208–225.

Bowey, J. A. (1994). Phonological sensitivity in novice readers and nonreaders. *Journal of Experimental Child Psychology, 58*, 134–159.

Bowey, J. A. (1995). Socioeconomic status differences in preschool phonological sensitivity and first-grade reading achievement. *Journal of Educational Psychology, 87*, 476–487.

Bryant, P. E., MacLean, M., Bradley, L. L., & Crossland, J. (1990). Rhyme and alliteration, phoneme detection, and learning to read. *Developmental Psychology, 26*, 429–438.

Burgess, S. R. (2002). The influence of speech perception, oral language ability, the home literacy environment, and pre-reading knowledge on the growth of phonological sensitivity: A one-year longitudinal investigation. *Reading and Writing: An Interdisciplinary Journal, 15*, 709–737.

Burgess, S.R. (2004, April). *The role of phonological sensitivity in letter knowledge training with children*. Poster presented at the annual meeting of the Southwestern Psychological Association, San Antonio, TX.

Burgess, S. R., Hecht, S. A., & Lonigan, C. J. (2002). Relations of home literacy environment (HLE) to the development of reading-related abilities: A one-year longitudinal study. *Reading Research Quarterly, 37*, 408–427.

Burgess, S. R., & Lonigan, C. J. (1998). Bidirectional relations between phonological awareness and reading extended to preschool letter knowledge: Evidence from a longitudinal investigation. *Journal of Experimental Child Psychology, 70*, 117–141.

Byrne, B., & Fielding-Barnsley, R. F. (1993). Evaluation of a program to teach phonemic awareness to young children: A one-year follow-up. *Journal of Educational Psychology, 85*, 104–111.

Chaney, C. (1992). Language development, metalinguistic skills, and print awareness in 3-year-old children. *Applied Psycholinguistics, 13*, 485–514.

Clay, M. M. (1979). *The early detection of reading difficulties* (3rd ed.). Portsmouth, NH: Heinemann.

Evans, M. A., Shaw, D., & Bell, M. (2000). Home literacy activities and their influence on early literacy skills. *Canadian Journal of Experimental Psychology, 54*, 65–75.

Fox, B., & Routh, D. K. (1975). Analyzing spoken language into words, syllables, and phonemes. A developmental study. *Journal of Psycholinguistic Research, 4*, 331–342.

Frijters, J. C., Barron, R. W., & Brunello, M. (2000). Direct and mediated influences of home literacy and literacy interest on prereaders' oral vocabulary and early written language skill. *Journal of Educational Psychology, 92*, 466–477.

Goswami, U., & Bryant, P. E. (1990). *Phonological*

skills and learning to read. Hillsdale, NJ: Erlbaum.

Hecht, S. A., Burgess, S. R., Torgesen, J. K., Wagner, R. K., & Rashotte, C. A. (2000). Explaining social class differences in growth of reading skills from beginning kindergarten through fourth grade: The role of phonological awareness, rate of access, and print knowledge. *Reading and Writing, 12,* 99–127.

Hoien, T., Lundberg, I., Stanovich, K. E., & Bjaalid, I. (1995). Components of phonological awareness. *Reading and Writing: An Interdisciplinary Journal, 7,* 171–188.

Johnston, R. S., Anderson, M., & Holligan, C. (1996). Knowledge of the alphabet and explicit awareness in pre-readers: The nature of the relationship. *Reading and Writing: An Interdisciplinary Journal, 8,* 217–234.

Leseman, P. P., & de Jong, P. F. (1998). Home literacy: Opportunity, instruction, cooperation, and social-emotional quality predicting early reading achievement. *Reading Research Quarterly, 33,* 294–319.

Lonigan, C. J., Burgess, S. R., & Anthony, J. L. (2000). Development of emergent literacy and early reading skills in preschool children: Evidence from a latent-variable longitudinal study. *Developmental Psychology, 36,* 596–613.

Lonigan, C. J., Burgess, S. R., Anthony, J. L., & Barker, T. A. (1998). Development of phonological sensitivity in 2- to 5-year-old children. *Journal of Educational Psychology, 90,* 294–311.

McLean, M., Bryant, P., & Bradley, L. (1987). Rhymes, nursery rhymes, and reading in early childhood. *Merrill-Palmer Quarterly, 33,* 255-282.

Metsala, J. L. (1999). Young children's phonological awareness and nonword repetition as a function of vocabulary development. *Journal of Educational Psychology, 91,* 3–19.

Metsala, J. L., & Walley, A. C. (1998). Spoken vocabulary growth and the segmental restructuring of lexical representations: Precursors to phonemic awareness and early reading ability. In J. L. Metsala & L.C. Ehri (Eds.), *Word recognition in beginning literacy* (pp. 89–120). Hillsdale, NJ: Erlbaum.

Morais, J., Cary, L., Alegria, J., & Bertelson, P. (1979). Does awareness of speech as a sequence of phones arise spontaneously? *Cognition, 7,* 323–331.

Murray, B. A., Stahl, S. A., & Ivey, M. G. (1996). Developing phoneme awareness through alphabet books. *Reading and Writing, 8,* 307–322.

Muter, V., Hulme, C., Snowling, M., & Taylor, S. (1997). Segmentation, not rhyming, predicts early progress in learning to read. *Journal of Experimental Child Psychology, 65,* 370–398.

Nation, K., & Hulme, C. (1997). Phonemic segmentation, not onset-rime segmentation, predicts early reading and spelling. *Reading Research Quarterly, 32,* 154–167.

Nord, C. W., Lennon, J., Liu, B., & Chandler, K. (1999). *Home literacy activities and signs of children's emerging literacy: 1993 and 1999* (NCES No. 2000–026). Washington, DC: U.S. Department of Education.

Payne, A. C., Whitehurst, G. J., & Angell, A. L. (1994). The role of the home literacy environment in the development of language ability in preschool children from low-income families. *Early Childhood Research Quarterly, 9,* 427–440.

Puolakanaho, A., Poikkeus, A., & Ahonen, T. (2003). Assessment of three-and-a-half-year-old children's emerging phonological awareness in a computer animation context. *Journal of Learning Disabilities, 36,* 416–423.

Scarborough, H. S., & Dobrich, W. (1994). On the efficacy of reading to preschoolers. *Developmental Review, 14,* 245–302.

Schatschneider, C., Francis, D. J., Foorman, B. R., Fletcher, J. M., & Mehta, P. (1999). The dimensionality of phonological awareness: An application of item response theory. *Journal of Educational Psychology, 91,* 439–449.

Sénéchal, M., LeFevre, J., Hudson, E., & Lawson, E. P. (1996). Knowledge of storybooks as a predictor of young children's vocabulary. *Journal of Educational Psychology, 88,* 520–536.

Sénéchal, M., LeFevre, J., Thomas, E. M., & Daley, K. E. (1998). Differential effects of home literacy experiences on the development of oral and written language. *Reading Research Quarterly, 33,* 96–116.

Stahl, S. A., & Murray, B. A. (1994). Defining phonological awareness and its relationship to early reading. *Journal of Educational Psychology, 86,* 221–234.

Stanovich, K. E. (1988). Exploring the differences between the dyslexic and the garden-variety poor reader: The phonological-core variable-difference model. *Journal of Learning Disabilities, 21,* 590–612.

Stanovich, K. E. (1992). Speculations on the causes and consequences of individual differences in reading acquisition. In P. B. Gough, L. C. Ehri, & R. Treiman (Eds.), *Reading acquisition* (pp. 307–342). Hillsdale, NJ: Erlbaum.

Torgesen, J. K., & Burgess, S. R. (1994). Phonological processing and reading. In V. S. Ramachandran (Ed.), *Encyclopedia of human behavior* (pp. 14-1–14-10). Orlando, FL: Academic Press.

Treiman, R. (1992). The role of intrasyllabic units in learning to read and spell. In P. B. Gough, L. C. Ehri, & R. Treiman (Eds.), *Reading acquisition* (pp. 307–342). Hillsdale, NJ: Erlbaum.

Treiman, R., Tincoff, R., & Richmond-Welty, E. D.

(1997). Beyond zebra: Preschoolers' knowledge about letters. *Applied Psycholinguistics, 18,* 391–409.

Treiman, R., Tincoff, R., Rodriguez, K., Mouzaki, A., & Francis, D. (1998). The foundations of literacy: Learning the sounds of letters. *Child Development, 69,* 1524–1540.

Wagner, R. K., Torgesen, J. K., & Rashotte, C. A. (1994). Development of reading-related phonological processing abilities: New evidence of bidirectional causality from a latent variable longitudinal study. *Developmental Psychology, 30,* 73–87.

Wagner, R. K., Torgesen, J. K., Rashotte, C. A., Hecht, S. A., Barker, T. A., Burgess, S. R., et al. (1997). Changing relations between phonological processing abilities and word-level reading as children develop from beginning to skilled readers: A 5-year longitudinal study. *Developmental Psychology, 33,* 468–479.

Walley, A. C., Metsala, J. L., & Garlock, V. M. (2003). Spoken vocabulary growth: Its role in the development of phoneme awareness and early reading ability. *Reading and Writing: An Interdisciplinary Journal, 16,* 5–20.

Warden, P. E., & Boettcher, W. (1990). Young children's acquisition of alphabet knowledge. *Journal of Reading Behavior, 22,* 277–295.

Whitehurst, G. J., & Lonigan, C. J. (1998). Child development and emergent literacy. *Child Development, 69,* 848–872.

8

Phonemic Awareness and Reading: Beyond the Growth of Initial Reading Accuracy

BETH M. PHILLIPS
JOSEPH K. TORGESEN

The United States is currently conducting the largest initiative ever undertaken to prevent the development of reading difficulties in young children. One of the driving forces behind the Reading First initiative is the belief that recent scientific discoveries about reading and reading instruction, if applied broadly in classrooms across America, can improve reading outcomes for all children. The application of these new discoveries about reading is thought to be particularly important for students who come to school with risk factors (i.e., poverty, minority status) that traditionally have been associated with lower reading performance (Foorman, Francis, Fletcher, Schatschneider, & Mehta, 1998). One of the more prominent of these new findings about reading growth pertains to the role of phonemic awareness in early reading development. It is a requirement of the Reading First initiative that teachers be trained in methods for including explicit and systematic instruction in phonemic awareness during kindergarten and early first grade to assist children in acquiring early reading skills.

All of the comprehensive core reading programs being used to support instruction in Reading First schools include carefully sequenced and explicit instruction in phonemic awareness as an oral language skill in kindergarten. These programs also simultaneously teach children common letter–sound correspondences and then explicitly link phonemic awareness skills to spelling and decoding (Al Otaiba, Grek, & Torgesen, in press). All schools participating in the Reading First initiative are also required to assess the growth of phonemic awareness in kindergarten and first-grade students. The purpose of this assessment is to identify children who may be lagging behind in the development of phonemic awareness so that they can receive more intensive and individualized instruction in this area. Teachers are being taught that early intervention to prevent lags in the development of phonemic awareness can help to ensure that children are not delayed in the development of phonemic decoding skills, which are, in turn, critical to the development of the ability to read text accurately.

The overall focus of this chapter is on the ways that phonemic awareness contributes to the development of reading ability. We consider first the widely accepted idea that phonemic awareness is necessary, but not sufficient, for the development of word reading accuracy, and then we examine evidence that it may play a critical role in the development of reading fluency.

Phonemic Awareness and Reading Accuracy

One issue that needs to be addressed in clarifying the definition of phonemic awareness is whether it should be considered a conceptual understanding about language or whether it should be considered a skill. What do we mean, precisely, when we say that a child's phonemic awareness has increased from the last time we measured it?

Certainly, part of what we mean by phonemic awareness is that it involves an understanding, or awareness, that a single-syllable word such as *cat*, which is experienced by the listener as a single beat of sound, actually can be subdivided into beginning, middle, and ending sounds. It also involves the idea, or understanding, that individual segments of sound at the phonemic level can be combined together to form words. Otherwise, the child would not be able to make sense out of the request to blend the sounds represented by the letters *c - a - t* together to make a word. However, a complete understanding of phonemic awareness must also account for the fact that it behaves like a skill. That is, children seem to acquire an increasing ability to notice, think about, and manipulate the phonemes in words as they attend school from kindergarten through elementary school. By the middle of kindergarten, for example, a child might be able to isolate and pronounce the first sound in a word such as *cat*, but by the end of kindergarten, children can commonly segment all the sounds in three-phoneme words (Good, Wallin, Simmons, Kame'enui, & Kaminski, 2002). Children also show regular improvements during this same period of time in their ability to blend individually presented sounds together to form words (Torgesen & Morgan, 1990). Whereas at the end of kindergarten they may be able to blend three phonemes such as *f-a-n* into complete words, by the end of first grade, most students can blend complex syllables containing both initial and final blends (i.e., *c-l-a-p* or *f-a-s-t*) successfully (Wagner, Torgesen, & Rashotte, 1999).

In order to account for both the conceptual and skill components of the construct, we need a definition of phonemic awareness such as the following: It involves a more or less explicit understanding that words are composed of segments of sound smaller than a syllable, as well as knowledge, or awareness, of the distinctive features of individual phonemes themselves. It is this latter knowledge of the identity of individual phonemes themselves that continues to increase after an initial understanding of the phonemic structure of words is acquired. For example, children must acquire a knowledge of the distinctive features of a phoneme such as /l/ so they can recognize it when it occurs with slightly varied pronunciation at the beginning of a word such as *last*; as the second sound in a consonant blend such as *flat*; in the middle of a word, such as *shelving*; or when it occurs in a final blend, such as in *fault*.

Theoretically, phonemic awareness contributes to the development of reading accuracy primarily through its impact on the development of phonemic decoding skill. *Phonemic decoding* involves the ability to use one's knowledge of the regular relationships between letters and sounds in English, along with phonemic blending skill, to "sound out" unknown words (Torgesen & Morgan, 1990). Early spelling, in contrast, is supported by knowledge of letter–sound correspondences and the ability to identify sequences of phonemes in whole words (DeGraff & Torgesen, in press). Phonemic awareness makes *phonemic decoding* and *phonemic spelling* understandable. In other words, in order to take advantage of the fact that English is an alphabetic language, a child must be aware that words have sound segments that are represented by the letters in print. Without at least emergent levels of phonemic awareness, the rationale for learning individual letter sounds and "sounding out" words is not understandable.

The early development of accurate and fluent phonemic decoding skills (alphabetic reading skills) is critical because learning to read involves *everyday* encounters with words that have never been seen before in print. These words are typically present in the child's oral vocabulary, but their printed form is unfamiliar. The systematic relationships between the phonemes in spoken words and the letters in their printed form is the single most reliable clue to the identity of words when they are encountered for the first time in print (Share & Stanovich, 1995). Children can use a variety of strategies to identify unknown words (Ehri, 2002), but if they do not become skillful at using letter–

sound cues early in development, they almost invariably remain inaccurate readers (Foorman, Francis, Shaywitz, Shaywitz, & Fletcher, 1997).

Given this strong theoretical connection, it should be possible to show that early acquisition of phonemic awareness is *causally* related to the later development of phonemic decoding ability and reading accuracy. In fact, this was the conclusion of the meta-analysis on phonemic awareness included in the National Reading Panel (NRP) report (Ehri et al., 2001; National Reading Panel, 2000). These results strongly and consistently support the theory of a causal relation between phonemic awareness and reading accuracy by showing that experimental manipulations of phonemic awareness through direct training have a positive impact on the subsequent growth of reading accuracy. Although this and the other sections of the report have generated much criticism (e.g., Allington, 2002; Cunningham, 2001; Garan, 2002; Pressley, Dolezal, Roehrig, & Hilden, 2002), as Shanahan (2004) notes, only a small proportion of this criticism relates to the analytic findings themselves. Shanahan's discussion of many of these critiques suggests that most are largely specious arguments.

Further, Camilli, Vargas, and Yurecko (2003) conducted a reanalysis of the studies used in the NRP's phonics meta-analysis. What is most noteworthy about their research is that, despite using a few different studies, data codes, variables, and effect size calculations, their results still demonstrated that systematic phonics has a significantly positive effect on children's reading development. Whereas these findings do not directly bear on the results for phonemic awareness, they do suggest that the findings of this NRP analysis will likely hold up to independent replication. A recent partial reanalysis of the NRP findings concerning phonemic awareness by Burns (2003) supports this idea. Although critical of some aspects of the NRP meta-analysis methods and arguing that phonemic awareness instruction is likely not sufficient to produce fluency and strong comprehension, Burns's results still demonstrated that phonemic awareness was significantly effective in improving single-word and text reading accuracy.

In the most recent critique, Castles and Coltheart (2004) have proposed that the current body of evidence for a causal link between phonemic awareness and reading is insufficient. Their review suggests that no study has appropriately demonstrated causality because none have fully isolated the influence of phonemic awareness on reading from a context in which children may already have acquired rudimentary knowledge of letters (e.g., knowing even a single letter sound). The thrust of their argument is that, without completely removing the potential influence of early orthographic knowledge on both phonemic awareness and reading, causality between phonemic awareness and reading is not demonstrated.

Further, they restrict their assessment of the influence of phonemic awareness to studies that measure and train only full phonemic awareness, eliminating studies of onset–rime, syllable-level manipulations, and other indices of broader phonological awareness on the basis that some head-to-head comparisons of these measures with phonemic tasks have supported the latter as being more strongly related to reading (e.g., Hulme et al., 2002; but see Anthony & Lonigan, 2004).

Castles and Coltheart (2004) base their argument not only on a narrowly defined set of eligibility requirements but also on a very narrowly defined definition of causality. That is, the generally accepted view is that a variable can be considered causal if it can be said to influence the magnitude or rate of growth of a second variable, irrespective of what other variables also might simultaneously or sequentially be influencing these outcomes. Castles and Coltheart's argument is that causality can be attributed only when it is demonstrated that the variable in question is both necessary and sufficient, on its own, to create change in the outcome of interest. Such a definition of causality stands in opposition to the commonly accepted view of multicausality for reading and other developmentally related outcomes.

As exemplified in both the NRP meta-analysis and the Castles and Coltheart (2004) critique of the literature, the strongest support for the causal relation between phonemic awareness and reading comes from experimental studies testing the benefit of providing instruction in phonemic awareness to novice readers. Since the completion of the report by Ehri et al. (2001) on the NRP meta-analyses, quite a few additional intervention studies have been reported (e.g., Castiglioni-Spalten & Ehri, 2003; Gunn, Smolkowski, Biglan, & Black, 2002; Hecht & Close, 2002; Kjeldsen, Niemi, & Olofsson, 2003; Oudeans, 2003).

Building on the foundation provided by Ehri et al. (2001), most of these studies investigated the relative advantages of different methods of training in phonemic awareness and compared them with each other and with controls. Whereas none of these studies alone satisfies the limiting criteria proposed by Castles and Coltheart (2004), collectively they provide an additional layer of evidence supporting the causal association between phonemic awareness and the development of early word-level reading skills. For example, Castiglioni-Spalten and Ehri (2003) tested the relative benefit of a tutoring intervention that taught children to match the phonemes to articulatory gestures represented on small blocks versus tutoring that taught similar skills using only blank blocks; a no-treatment control also was included. All participating children knew some letters but could read no more than 1 of 10 pretest monosyllabic words and had minimal phoneme segmentation skills. After training, both the intervention groups had significantly higher spelling and phonemic awareness skills than the control group. As well, the group that learned articulatory gestures also had significantly better decoding skill than the control-group students.

Similarly, Kjeldsen et al. (2003) investigated the effects of explicit, systematic kindergarten phonemic awareness training of higher and lower intensity and frequency compared with implicit, nonsystematic training, also in high- and low-intensity versions. At initial posttest—and, for most measures, also at a 1-year follow-up—whereas the high-intensity/systematic group significantly outperformed both nonsystematic groups on measures of decoding, phonemic awareness, spelling, and letter knowledge and the low-intensity/systematic group also significantly outperformed the low-intensity/nonsystematic group on all these measures, there were not significant differences between the high- and low-intensity systematic groups. At 2-year follow-up, the systematic versus nonsystematic difference still held for decoding. The authors interpret these findings to suggest that it is the explicit, structured nature

of phonemic awareness training that carries the most impact, more so than how much is received.

Several other recent studies (e.g., Hecht & Close, 2002; Gillon, 2002; Gunn et al., 2002) also provide significant findings of an effect of training in phonemic awareness on reading-related measures. Gillon (2002) reported that at an 11-month follow-up, a group of children with specific language impairments who had previously received 20 hours of training scored significantly higher on measures of phonemic awareness and of real and nonword decoding than a randomized control group. Notably, these results were found despite a substantial number of the control students having participated in Reading Recovery, which is an intervention method that minimizes explicit training in phonemic awareness, during the intervening months.

It seems clear from even this brief consideration of the evidence concerning the relationship between phonemic awareness and the development of phonemic decoding and text reading accuracy that current recommendations to include phonemic awareness as a critical component of reading instruction are warranted. It is obviously true that not every child will require explicit instruction in phonemic awareness in kindergarten in order to learn to read—many children discover phonemes in their initial play with rhymes and letters and seem to require very little direct instruction in this area. However, many other children, particularly those who may have biological weaknesses in the phonological domain (Rayner, Foorman, Perfetti, Pesetsky, & Seidenberg, 2001; Torgesen, 1999) or weakness in preschool language experience (Whitehurst & Lonigan, 1998), appear to profit particularly from explicit instruction in this area (Foorman et al., 1998).

Phonemic Awareness and Reading Fluency

In order to present an adequate account of current theoretical understanding of the role of phonemic awareness in supporting the growth of reading fluency, it is first important to define reading fluency. Meyer and Felton (1999) define reading fluency as the ability to read connected text "rapidly, smoothly, effortlessly, and automatically with little conscious attention to the mechanics of reading, such as decoding" (p. 284). Other definitions of reading fluency go substantially beyond reading rate to include grouping words into meaningful phrases as one reads (Aulls, 1978), prosodic reading (Allington, 1983), or reading with the kind of intonation and stress that maximizes comprehension (Rasinski, 2004). After reviewing a broad range of definitions of fluency, Hudson, Lane, and Pullen (in press) concluded that the richest interpretation of the concept would be to define it as composed of three elements: "*accurate* reading of connected text at a conversational *rate* with appropriate *prosody*" (p. 2).

The latter definition suggests that the concept of fluency can be applied to the entire reading process, from word identification to identification of word meanings to construction of phrase and passage level meaning. Unless one is constructing meaning "on the fly" while reading, it would be impossible to read with proper emphasis, phrasing, and intonation (prosody). We would not argue with this as an ultimate definition of fluent reading. After all, the primary purpose of learning to read is to get meaning from text, and individual differences in speed of all the processes referred to in this more inclusive definition could theoretically influence overall reading fluency. However, for purposes of focusing on the ways in which phonemic awareness might support the development of reading fluency, it is useful to use a somewhat narrower definition of fluency. We borrow the definition of fluency proposed by proponents of curriculum-based assessment, which defines fluency as rate and accuracy in oral reading (Hasbrouk & Tindal, 1992; Shinn, Good, Knutson, Tilly, & Collins, 1992) and has the additional advantage of being the aspect of fluency that is most reliably measured. Further, reliable measures of oral reading rate are highly correlated with more encompassing measures of fluent reading that assess reading comprehension (Good, Simmons, & Kameenui, 2001; Fuchs, Fuchs, Hosp, & Jenkins, 2001).

We have argued elsewhere (Torgesen, Rashotte, & Alexander, 2001) that the single most important factor that limits reading fluency in young children or beginning readers is the proportion of words in the passage

they are reading that they can recognize "by sight" or "at a single glance." If there are too many unknown words in the passage that require the child to apply more analytic (phonemic decoding) or guessing strategies to fill in the blanks, fluency will be impaired. This view of text reading fluency is not new (Adams, 1990), and it has received further support in several recent studies that examined a range of factors that contribute to individual differences in reading fluency in young children (Compton, Appelton, & Hosp, 2004; Jenkins, Fuchs, van den Broek, Espin, & Deno, 2003; Schwanenflugel, Hamilton, Kuhn, Wisenbaker, & Stahl, 2004). The study by Jenkins et al. (2003) indicated that fluency of recognizing individual words contributed relatively more to explaining individual differences in text reading fluency at lower, as opposed to higher, levels of reading skill in fourth-grade children. Both of the other two studies highlighted the importance of fluent recognition of individual words as an important source of individual differences in text reading fluency in second- and third-grade children.

This view of reading fluency is also consistent with what we know about skilled, fluent reading in adults. Two important facts about the nature of word identification processes in skilled readers are relevant here. The first of these facts is that skilled readers fixate, or look directly at, almost every word in text as they read (Rayner & Pollatsek, 1989). Skilled readers are able to process text rapidly not because they only selectively sample words and letters as they construct its meaning but because they read the individual words so rapidly and with so little effort. Skilled readers process words as *orthographic units* (Ehri, 1998). The orthography of a language refers to the way it is represented visually. Hence, when researchers indicate that words are processed as orthographic units, they are implying that they are recognized on the basis of an integrated visual representation.

A key piece of knowledge here, and the second important fact about text processing in skilled readers, is that the mental representations used to identify words as whole units (orthographic representations) include information about all the letters in words (for reviews, see Just & Carpenter, 1987; Patterson & Coltheart, 1987; Rayner et al., 2001). Because many words are differentiated from one another by only one or two letters, a global, or gestalt, image of a word is not sufficient to help recognize it reliably. Instead, the memory image used in reading words by sight must include information about all, or almost all, the letters in a word's spelling. Even when reading very rapidly, the good reader extracts information about all the letters in a word as part of the recognition process.

This understanding of reading processes in skilled readers leads directly to one of the central questions that must be answered by any comprehensive theory of reading growth: How do children acquire the enormous number of *fully specified orthographic representations* (orthographic representations of words that contain information about all their letters) required to read text fluently by second- or third-grade level?

The answer to this question has been the subject of considerable research over the past 20 years. This research has indicated that there are at least two levels of explanation involved in the answer, and both of these levels of explanation identify an important causal role for individual differences in phonemic awareness.

The first part of the answer was most completely explicated in a theoretical article by David Share and Keith Stanovich in 1995 and by Share in other articles (Share, 1995; Share, 1999). We have already established that phonemic awareness is causally related (necessary but not sufficient) for the development of phonemic decoding skills. Share and Stanovich present a compelling case for the role of *phonemic decoding skills* in the development of fully specified orthographic representations of words. Phonemic decoding skills involve using information about letter–sound correspondences to completely or partially "sound out" words in text. In Share's model, as well as in Ehri's (2002) discussions of the growth of orthographic reading skills, emergent skills in phonemic decoding provide the basis for acquiring accurate orthographic representations of words beginning very early in the learning process.

A central tenet of Share and Stanovich's (1995) argument involves the importance of "reading through" each word phonemically as it is first being acquired. If children use phonemic cues to derive an approximate pronunciation for a word in text and combine this approximate pronunciation with contextual cues to identify the fully correct pronunciation, the *prior attention* to individual letters that is involved in phonemic decoding familiarizes the child with the word's spelling. The more complete the phonemic analysis of unfamiliar words, the more fully will the child be aware of *all* the letters in the word's spelling.

Another critical point in the "self-teaching theory of reading acquisition" as outlined by Share and Stanovich (1995) is that, for a word to be added to a child's orthographic reading vocabulary, its *exactly* correct pronunciation must be associated several times with its *exactly* correct spelling. If children encounter the unfamiliar word *sweater* and pronounce it as "sweatshirt," this learning trial will not be as helpful in forming an accurate orthographic representation for *sweater* as would a trial in which the word was pronounced correctly. It is important to note here that children encounter far too many new words in the later stages of elementary school for them all to be directly taught by teachers. For example, Nagy and Herman (1987) report analyses suggesting that the average fifth grader encounters about 10,000 new words during the year! For a word to be added to a child's orthographic reading vocabulary, it must be encountered and pronounced correctly several times (Reitsma, 1983; Share, 1999). Unless a child has the phonemic skills to ensure that word reading is relatively accurate (guessing from context alone produces too many word reading errors; Gough, 1983), it is extremely difficult to acquire enough fully specified orthographic representations to support fluent and accurate reading.

So, one important way that phonemic awareness contributes to reading fluency is through its causal relationships with the early development of phonemic decoding ability, which is critical to the development of early reading accuracy. The early development of reading accuracy is important because children must *accurately* practice the pronunciations of written words several times in order to form a representation of the words' orthography in memory that will allow the words to be recognized "by sight" or "at a single glance."

One important question left unanswered in the "self-teaching theory of reading acquisition" is how children are able to learn so much detail about the spellings of printed words so quickly (after three to seven correct pronunciations). One could imagine that, if spellings were learned by brute force, as we memorize telephone numbers, the process of forming orthographic representations would proceed much more slowly than it does for most children. Ehri (1998, 2002) has suggested that, in order to understand the speed with which children form orthographic representations for previously unknown words, we need a "mnemonically powerful" system. One of the central ideas of her theory of sight word development is that "readers learn sight words by forming connections between letters seen in spellings of words and sounds detected in their *pronunciations already present in memory*" (Ehri, 2002, p. 11; emphasis added). In other words,

> readers learn to process written words as phonemic maps that lay out elements of the pronunciation visually. Beginners become skilled at computing these mapping relations spontaneously when they read new words. This is the critical event for sight word learning. Graphophonemic connections provide a powerful mnemonic system that bonds written words to their pronunciations in memory along with meanings. Once the alphabetic mapping system is known, readers can build a vocabulary of sight words easily. (p. 12)

In order to use a word's phonology as a mnemonic for helping to remember its orthography, children need to be able to apprehend fluently the phonological structure of words as they compute the "mapping relations" between the letters and sounds in words. Thus children with highly fluent and easily applied phonemic segmentation skills (skill in identifying all the individual phonemes in words) should be able to form orthographic representations more easily than children who are less phonemically fluent. This suggests that individual differences in the fluency and accuracy of phonemic segmentation processes should be related to the development of sight word representations and reading fluency.

One level of support for Ehri's (2002) theory comes from studies of beginning readers such as the one reported by Castle, Riach, and Nicholson (1994). These investigators found that children trained in phonemic awareness skills gained significantly more in percentage of correctly represented phonemes in their spellings of real words and nonwords than did children in an untrained control group. They interpreted their results as showing how phonemic awareness enables use of and memory retention of grapheme–phoneme correspondences. In a similar and more recent study, Dixon, Stuart, and Masterson (2002) found that children who could segment both initial and final phonemes, compared with those who could segment either initial phonemes only or neither, learned to read a set of 10 words more rapidly and more accurately. Follow-up assessments also indicated that when shown the target word and seven foils that each differed from the target by a single phoneme, the children with more advanced phonemic awareness skills were sensitive to orthographic errors in multiple positions, in contrast to the children with less phonemic awareness skill who were sensitive only to errors in the initial phoneme position. These results help demonstrate the direct association between phonemic awareness and the development of orthographic representations and also follow the pattern noted by Ehri (e.g., 1998, 2002) that children map the initial phoneme of words prior to mapping the final, medial, and vowel letters in words as they forge full sight word amalgams.

One of the key aspects of the sight word learning model being discussed here is that acquisition occurs as a result of learning trials in which unfamiliar words are pronounced correctly several times during the course of text processing. Share (1999) reported a series of experiments that provide compelling evidence in support of this idea. Consistent with Reitsma's earlier findings (e.g., 1983), Share demonstrated that sight word learning can take only a few exposures, that it requires production of or exposure to the correct pronunciation, and that it is accomplished by activation of the accurate phonological representation occurring simultaneously with the orthographic spelling. Trials on which the complete phonological recode was unavailable or corrupted led to poorer discrimination between the correct, homophonic, and other incorrect spellings of the target words. Consistent with Ehri's (1998, 2002) theory, these results also indicated that the phonological and orthographic forms get linked at the precise phoneme level. As Share pointed out, "letter identity and letter order . . . simply make no

sense unless linked to a specific pronunciation . . . that is fully analyzed at the phonemic level. No other information source
specifies why particular letters appear in a
particular order" (1999, p. 123). A more recent study by Cunningham, Perry, Stanovich,
and Share (2002) also provided empirical
support for the self-teaching hypothesis and
for the critical importance of accurate decoding and orthographic knowledge for this
process.

If the model of sight word development we
have been discussing is correct in its essential features, then individual differences in
phonemic awareness should be significantly
related to differences in reading fluency. This
relationship, however, is not powerfully supported in the current research literature.
For example, a recent longitudinal study by
Schatschneider, Fletcher, Francis, Carlson,
and Foorman (2004) examined the relative
importance of phonemic awareness, rapid
naming of letters, rapid naming of objects,
letter naming, letter-sound knowledge, vocabulary, and visual discrimination measured in kindergarten in predicting reading
accuracy, fluency, and comprehension at the
end of first and second grades. The combination of phonemic awareness, rapid naming
of letters, letter naming, and letter-sound
naming was a strong and significant predictor of all three outcomes at both grades.
However, in this study, as in others (Allor,
2002), rapid naming of letters was a stronger
predictor of fluency than was phonemic
awareness when the variables were considered separately.

A number of studies have directly compared the predictive power of phonemic
awareness and rapid automatic naming
speed, and some have suggested that the importance of individual differences in phonemic awareness may diminish because other
factors become more important in predicting
reading fluency as reading skills develop
(e.g., Allor, Fuchs, & Mathes, 2001; Bowers
& Wolf, 1993; Catts, Gillispie, Leonard,
Kail, & Miller, 2002; Sprugevica & Hoien,
2003; Sunseth & Bowers, 2002). Allor's
(2002) review of 16 studies that included
both phonemic awareness and rapid naming
measures found mixed results as to whether
both contributed uniquely with the other in
the predictive model. Findings varied based
on whether reading was measured as single-

word reading, comprehension, or fluency. In
general, however, rapid automatic naming
tasks were found to be better predictors of
reading fluency than were measures of phonemic awareness.

One unexamined possibility in these longi-
tudinal/predictive studies is that rapid automatic naming tasks may be better predictors
of reading fluency than measures of phonemic awareness because they assess the
fluency of fundamental cognitive processes
required for construction of sight word representations, whereas measures of phonemic
awareness have measured only the accuracy
of these processes. The model of sight word
development considered here would predict
that there should be strong relationships between measures of rapid automatic naming
for letters (assuming that speed of identifying
letter names is highly correlated with speed
of identifying letter sounds) and reading fluency. Rapid computation of mapping relationships between the orthographic and phonological structure of words would require
highly automatic associations between letters and the sounds they typically represent.
However, the model would also predict
strong relationships between individual differences in fluent access to the phonological
structure of words and individual differences
in the speed and ease with which orthographic representations are formed. A more
complete test of this hypothesis must await
the development of reliable and valid measures of fluency of access to the phonological
structure of words.

One final area of research is relevant to the
topic under consideration here. Studies of
children with reading disabilities (dyslexia)
in countries whose language has a more
transparent orthography than English find
that the primary problem for these students
is word reading fluency, not word reading accuracy. Several studies (e.g., Aro &
Wimmer, 2003; Mann & Wimmer, 2002;
Mayringer & Wimmer, 2000; Wimmer,
Mayringer, & Landerl, 2000; Wimmer &
Mayringer, 2002) have indicated that by the
end of first grade, German children (and
other children learning regular orthographies) have substantially better word and/or
nonword reading accuracy scores than their
English-speaking counterparts. Further,
Mann and Wimmer (2002) found this advantage for German students even when the

comparison group of American children had better phonemic awareness and letter knowledge skills in kindergarten. They point to the joint influence of systematic phonics training and a transparent orthography in explaining these results. A longitudinal study with Dutch children (de Jong & van der Leij, 2003) similarly found that whereas sixth-grade dyslexic and normally reading groups were very different on their reading speed or reading level, there was considerable overlap on decoding accuracy. Again, these results are attributed to the benefits of explicit phonics teaching and the transparent orthography.

Notably, despite findings of better decoding accuracy among German children, Landerl, Wimmer, and Frith (1997) found that their sample of German dyslexic students performed equivalently to a sample of American dyslexic students on a difficult measure of phonemic awareness. This finding mirrors that of de Jong and van der Leij (2003), who found that Dutch fourth-grade children with significant reading fluency problems had average decoding skill and performed competently on relatively easy measures of phonemic awareness but were impaired relative to grade-level control students on a more difficult phonemic awareness measure. These authors view these results, considered together with the findings of their longitudinal study, as suggesting that, whereas in regular orthographies phonemic awareness deficits may not influence older students' decoding skill, their effect is still felt on reading fluency.

Wimmer and his colleagues also view their general findings as consistent with Ehri's (2002) developmental model, noting that even the regularity of an orthography cannot completely mitigate the need for phonemic awareness in forming the multiple orthographic–phonemic connections necessary for forming sight word representations (e.g., Landerl et al., 1997). These researchers suggest that dyslexic German children with fluency deficits may repeatedly encounter and decode a word but still not create an orthographic representation in memory for rapid retrieval because of enduring difficulties in using the phonological structure of the word as a mnemonic to remember its printed form. In particular, Mayringer and Wimmer (2000) highlight the idea that across all languages a central problem is impairment in the ability to establish long-term memories for word-specific letter patterns "[that] would allow automatic word recognition in reading and orthographic spelling" (pp. 130–131).

Concluding Comments

Overall, there is compelling empirical support for the role of phonemic awareness as a necessary, but not sufficient, attainment for growth in the development of alphabetic reading skills. Phonemic awareness is obviously not sufficient for the development of full phonemic decoding ability, as that skill also requires fluent and flexible knowledge of letter–sound relationships. However, it is necessary, because phonemic awareness is initially required in order to make sense of the way print is used to represent words from oral language, and phonemic blending and segmenting skills are an integral part of phonemic decoding and phonemic spelling ability. There is also a strong theoretical rationale for the contribution of phonemic awareness to reading fluency, but empirical support in this area is not yet as compelling as in the area of initial reading accuracy. Further research in this area might profit from the development of reliable and valid measures of fluency in the apprehension of the phonological structure of words.

References

Adams, M. J. (1990). *Beginning to read*. Cambridge, MA: MIT Press.

Al Otaiba, S., Grek, M. L., & Torgesen, J. K. (in press). Reviewing core kindergarten and first grade reading programs in light of No Child Left Behind: An exploratory study. *Reading and Writing Quarterly*.

Allington, R. L. (1983). Fluency: The neglected reading goal in reading instruction. *Reading Teacher, 36*, 556–561.

Allington, R. L. (2002). *Big brother and the national reading curriculum: How ideology trumped evidence*. Portsmouth, NH: Heinemann.

Allor, J. (2002). The relationships of phonemic awareness and rapid naming to reading development. *Learning Disabilities Quarterly, 25*, 47–57.

Allor, J., Fuchs, D., & Mathes, P. G. (2001). Do students with and without lexical retrieval weaknesses respond differently to instruction? *Journal of Learning Disabilities, 34,* 261–275.

Anthony, J. L., & Lonigan, C. J. (2004). The nature of phonological awareness: Converging evidence from four studies of preschool and early grade school children. *Journal of Educational Psychology, 96,* 43–55.

Aro, M., & Wimmer, H. (2003). Learning to read: English in comparison to six more regular orthographies. *Applied Psycholinguistics, 24,* 621–635.

Aulls, M.S. (1978). *Developmental and remedial reading in the middle grades.* Boston: Allyn & Bacon.

Bowers, P. G., & Wolf, M. (1993). Theoretical links among naming speed, precise timing mechanisms and orthographic skill in dyslexia. *Reading and Writing, 5,* 69–85.

Burns, M. K. (2003). Reexamining data from the National Reading Panel's meta-analysis: Implications for school psychology. *Psychology in the Schools, 40,* 605–612.

Camilli, G., Vargas, S., & Yurecko, M. (2003). Teaching children to read: The fragile link between science and federal education policy. *Education Policy Analysis Archives, 11*(15). Retrieved June 6, 2004, from http://epaa.asu.edu/epaa/v11n15/

Castiglioni-Spalten, M. L., & Ehri, L. C. (2003). Phonemic awareness instruction: Contribution of articulatory segmentation to novice beginners' reading and spelling. *Scientific Studies of Reading, 7,* 25–52.

Castle, J. M., Riach, J., & Nicholson, T. (1994). Getting off to a better start in reading and spelling: The effects of phonemic awareness instruction within a whole language program. *Journal of Educational Psychology, 86,* 350–359.

Castles, A., & Coltheart, M. (2004). Is there a causal link from phonological awareness to success in learning to read? *Cognition, 91,* 77–111.

Catts, H. W., Gillispie, M., Leonard, L. B., Kail, R. V., & Miller, C. A. (2002). The role of speed of processing, rapid naming, and phonological awareness in reading achievement. *Journal of Learning Disabilities, 35,* 510–525.

Compton, D. L., Appelton, A. C., & Hosp, M. K. (2004). Exploring the relationship between text-leveling systems and reading accuracy and fluency in second-grade students who are average and poor decoders. *Learning Disabilities Research and Practice, 19,* 176–184.

Cunningham, A. E., Perry, K. E., Stanovich, K. E., & Share, D. L. (2002). Orthographic learning during reading: Examining the role of self-teaching. *Journal of Experimental Child Psychology, 82,* 185–199.

Cunningham, J. W. (2001). Review of the National Reading Panel report. *Reading Research Quarterly, 36,* 326–335.

de Jong, P. F., & van der Leij, A. (2003). Developmental changes in the manifestation of a phonological deficit in dyslexic children learning to read a regular orthography. *Journal of Educational Psychology, 95,* 22–40.

DeGraff, A. & Torgesen, J. K. (in press) Invented spelling: A measure of phonemic decoding skills in first-grade children. *Journal of Educational Assessment.*

Dixon, M., Stuart, M., & Masterson, J. (2002). The relationship between phonological awareness and the development of orthographic representations. *Reading and Writing: An Interdisciplinary Journal, 15,* 295–316.

Ehri, L. C. (1998). Grapheme–phoneme knowledge is essential for learning to read words in English. In J. L. Metsala & L. C. Ehri (Eds.), *Word recognition in beginning literacy* (pp. 3–40). Mahwah, NJ: Erlbaum.

Ehri, L. (2002). Phases of acquisition in learning to read words and implications for teaching. In R. Stainthorp & P. Tomlinson (Eds.), *Learning and teaching reading* (British Journal of Educational Psychology Monograph, Series 2, pp. 7–28). London: The British Psychological Society.

Ehri, L. C., Nunes, S. R., Willows, D. M., Schuster, B. V., Yaghoub-Zadeh, Z., & Shanahan, T. (2001). Phonemic awareness instruction helps children learn to read: Evidence from the National Reading Panel's meta-analysis. *Reading Research Quarterly, 36,* 250–287.

Foorman, B. R., Francis, D. J., Fletcher, J. M., Schatschneider, C., & Mehta, P. (1998). The role of instruction in learning to read: Preventing reading failure in at-risk children. *Journal of Educational Psychology, 90,* 37–55.

Foorman, B. R., Francis, D. J., Shaywitz, S. E., Shaywitz, B. A., & Fletcher, J. M. (1997). The case for early intervention. In B. Blachman (Ed.) *Foundations of reading acquisition and dyslexia.* (pp. 243–264). Mahwah, NJ: Erlbaum.

Fuchs, L. S., Fuchs, D., Hosp, M. D., & Jenkins, J. (2001). Oral reading fluency as an indicator of reading competence: A theoretical, empirical, and historical analysis. *Scientific Studies of Reading, 5*(3), 239–259.

Garan, E. (2002). *Resisting reading mandates: How to triumph with the truth.* Portsmouth, NH: Heinemann.

Gillon, G. T. (2002). Follow-up study investigating the benefits of phonological awareness intervention for children with spoken language impairment. *International Journal of Language and Communication Disorders, 37,* 381–400.

Good, R. F., Simmons, D. C., & Kame'enui E. J. (2001). The importance and decision-making utility of a continuum of fluency-based indicators of foundational reading skills for third grade high-stakes outcomes. *Scientific Studies of Reading, 5,* 257–288.

Good, R. H., Wallin, J., Simmons, D. C., Kame'enui, E. J., & Kaminski, R. A. (2002). *System-wide percentile ranks for DIBELS benchmark assessment*

(Technical Report 9). Eugene, OR: University of Oregon.

Gough, P. B. (l983) Context, form and interaction. In K. Raynor (Ed.), *Eye movements in reading.* New York: Academic Press.

Gunn, B., Smolkowski, K., Biglan, A., & Black, C. (2002). Supplemental instruction in decoding skills for Hispanic and non-Hispanic students in early elementary school. *The Journal of Special Education, 36,* 69–79.

Hasbrouk, J. E., & Tindal, G. (1992). Curriculum-based oral reading fluency for students in grades 2 through 5. *Teaching Exceptional Children, 24,* 41–44.

Hecht, S. A., & Close, L. (2002). Emergent literacy skills and training time uniquely predict variability in responses to phonemic awareness training in disadvantaged kindergartners. *Journal of Experimental Child Psychology, 82,* 93–115.

Hudson, R. F., Lane, H. B., & Pullen, P. C. (in press). Reading fluency assessment and instruction: What, why, and how? *Reading Teacher.*

Hulme, C., Hatcher, P. J., Nation, K., Brown, A., Adams, J., & Stuart, G. (2002). Phoneme awareness is a better predictor of early reading skill than onset–rime awareness. *Journal of Experimental Child Psychology, 82,* 2–28.

Jenkins, J. R., Fuchs, L. S., van den Broek, P., Espin, C., & Deno, S. L. (2003). Sources of individual differences in reading comprehension and reading fluency. *Journal of Educational Psychology, 95,* 719–729.

Just, M. A., & Carpenter, P. A. (1987). *The psychology of reading and language comprehension.* Boston: Allyn & Bacon.

Kjeldsen, A. C., Niemi, P., & Olofsson, A. (2003). Training phonological awareness in kindergarten level children: Consistency is more important than quantity. *Learning and Instruction, 13,* 349–365.

Landerl, K., Wimmer, H., & Frith, U. (1997). The impact of orthographic consistency on dyslexia: A German-English comparison. *Cognition, 63,* 315–334.

Mann, V., & Wimmer, H. (2002). Phoneme awareness and pathways into literacy: A comparison of German and American children. *Reading and Writing: An Interdisciplinary Journal, 15,* 653–682.

Mayringer, H., & Wimmer, H. (2000). Pseudoname learning by German-speaking children with dyslexia: Evidence for a phonological learning deficit. *Journal of Experimental Child Psychology, 75,* 116–133.

Meyer, M. S., & Felton, R. H. (1999). Repeated reading to enhance fluency: Old approaches and new directions. *Annals of Dyslexia, 49,* 283–306.

Nagy, W. E., & Herman, P. A. (1987). Breadth and depth of vocabulary knowledge: Implications for acquisition and instruction. In M. McKeown & M. Curtis (Eds.), *The nature of vocabulary acquisition* (pp. 19–35). Hillsdale, NJ: Erlbaum.

National Reading Panel. (2000). *Teaching children to read: An evidence-based assessment of the scientific research literature on reading and its implications for reading instruction.* Washington, DC: National Institute of Child Health and Human Development.

Oudeans, M. K. (2003). Integration of letter-sound correspondences and phonological awareness skills of blending and segmenting: A pilot study examining the effects of instructional sequence on word reading for kindergarten children with low phonological awareness. *Learning Disability Quarterly, 26,* 258–280.

Patterson, K. E., & Coltheart, V. (1987). Phonological processes in reading: A tutorial review. In M. Coltheart (Ed.), *Attention and performance: Vol 12. The psychology of reading* (pp. 421–447). Hillsdale, NJ: Erlbaum.

Pressley, M., Dolezal, S., Roehrig, A. D., & Hilden, K. (2002). Why the National Reading Panel's recommendations are not enough. In R. L. Allington (Ed.), *Big brother and the national reading curriculum: How ideology trumped evidence* (pp. 75–89). Portsmouth, NH: Heinemann.

Rasinski, T. V. (2004). *Assessing reading fluency.* Honolulu, HI: Pacific Reserves for Education and Learning.

Rayner, K., Foorman, B. R., Perfetti, C. A., Pesetsky, D., & Seidenberg, M. S. (2001). How psychological science informs the teaching of reading. *Psychological Science in the Public Interest, 2,* 31–73.

Rayner, K., & Pollatsek, A. (1989). *The psychology of reading.* Englewood Cliffs, NJ: Prentice Hall.

Reitsma, P. (1983). Printed word learning in beginning readers. *Journal of Experimental Child Psychology, 36,* 321–339.

Schatschneider, C., Fletcher, J. M., Francis, D. J., Carlson, C., & Foorman, B. R. (2004). Kindergarten prediction of reading skills: A longitudinal comparative analysis. *Journal of Educational Psychology, 96,* 265–282.

Schwanenflugel, P. J., Hamilton, A. M., Kuhn, M. R., Wisenbaker, J. M., & Stahl, S. A. (2004). Becoming a fluent reader: Reading skill and prosodic features in the oral reading of young readers. *Journal of Educational Psychology, 96,* 119–129.

Shanahan, T. (2004). Critiques of the National Literacy Panel report: Their implications for research, policy, and practice. In P. McCardle & V. Chhabra (Eds.), *The voice of evidence in reading research,* (pp. 235–265), Baltimore: Brookes.

Share, D. L. (1995). Phonological recoding and self-teaching: *Sine qua non* of reading acquisition. *Cognition, 55,* 151–218.

Share, D. L. (1999). Phonological recoding and orthographic learning: A direct test of the self-teaching hypothesis. *Journal of Experimental Child Psychology, 72,* 95–129.

Share, D. L., & Stanovich, K. E. (1995). Cognitive processes in early reading development: A model of acquisition and individual differences. *Issues in*

Education: Contributions from Educational Psychology, 1, 1–57.

Shinn, M. R., Good, R. H., Knutson, N., Tilly, W. D., & Collins, V. L (1992). Curriculum based measurement of oral reading fluency: A confirmatory analysis of its relation to reading. *School Psychology Review, 21,* 459–479.

Sprugevica, I., & Hoien, T. (2003). Early phonological skills as a predictor of reading acquisition: A follow-up study from kindergarten to the middle of grade 2. *Scandinavian Journal of Psychology, 44,* 119–124.

Sunseth, K., & Bowers, P. G. (2002). Rapid naming and phonemic awareness: Contributions to reading, spelling, and orthographic knowledge. *Scientific Studies of Reading, 6,* 401–429.

Torgesen, J. K. (1999). Phonologically based reading disabilities: Toward a coherent theory of one kind of learning disability. In R. J. Sternberg & L. Spear-Swerling (Eds.), *Perspectives on learning disabilities* (pp. 231–262). Boulder, CO: Westview Press.

Torgesen, J. K., & Morgan, S. (1990). Phonological synthesis tasks: A developmental, functional, and componential analysis. In H. L. Swanson & B. Keogh (Eds.), *Learning disabilities: Theoretical and research issues* (pp. 263–276). Hillsdale, NJ: Erlbaum.

Torgesen, J. K., Rashotte, C. A., & Alexander, A. (2001). Principles of fluency instruction in reading: Relationships with established empirical outcomes. In M. Wolf (Ed.), *Dyslexia, fluency, and the brain* (pp. 333–355). Parkton, MD: York Press.

Wagner, R. K., Torgesen, J. K., & Rashotte, C. A. (1999). *Comprehensive Test of Phonological Processes.* Austin, TX: PRO-ED.

Whitehurst, G. J., & Lonigan, C. J. (1998). Child development and emergent literacy. *Child Development, 69,* 335–357.

Wimmer, H., & Mayringer, H. (2002). Dysfluent reading in the absence of spelling difficulties: A specific disability in regular orthographies. *Journal of Educational Psychology, 94,* 272–277.

Wimmer, H., Mayringer, H., & Landerl, K. (2000). The double-deficit hypothesis and difficulties in learning to read a regular orthography. *Journal of Educational Psychology, 92,* 668–680.

9

The Roots of Learning to Read and Write: Acquisition of Letters and Phonemic Awareness

LINNEA C. EHRI
THERESA ROBERTS

In order for beginners to succeed in learning to read in a language such as English, they must acquire knowledge of the alphabetic writing system. The most important acquisitions at the start are phonemic awareness and letter knowledge. These provide the foundation enabling beginners to move into reading and spelling.

Foundational Knowledge and the Writing System

Phonemes are the smallest sounds in speech— for example, *no* consists of two phonemes, /n/ and /o/. (We depict individual phonemes between slashes.) Phonemic awareness (PA) refers to the ability to manipulate phonemes in spoken words. Tasks to assess and teach this ability include isolating the first phoneme (e.g., /s/ in *stop*), recognizing which phonemes in two different words are identical (e.g., /p/ in *stop* and *cup*), segmenting words into phonemes (e.g., *stop* into /s/-/t/-/a/-/p/), blending phonemes to form recognizable words (e.g., /s/-/k/-/u/-/l/ to form *school*) and deleting phonemes to create a new word (e.g., removing /s/ from *smile* makes *mile*). It is important to note that PA applies to spoken language. Although its function is to en-

able beginners to connect speech to print, conceptually it is separate from letters and spellings of words.

Phonemic awareness is different from phonological awareness, which is a more encompassing term referring to various types of awareness—not only PA but also awareness of larger spoken units such as syllables and rhyming words. Tasks assessing phonological awareness might require students to produce rhyming words, or to segment sentences into words, or to segment words into syllables.

Whereas phonemes are the constituents of spoken words, letters are the constituents of written words. Learning letters in English entails becoming familiar with 26 capital and 26 lower-case letter shapes and learning their associations to letter names and to phonemes. If we eliminate duplication from the shapes of 12 capital–lower-case mates that are almost identical (e.g., S and s), there remain 40 distinctive shapes for beginners to learn. Different letters having similar shapes are frequently confused by learners—for example, those in the following sets: b-d-p-q-g, h-n-r, m-w, u-v-y, s-z, i-j, L-I-l-i. Capital letters are learned earlier than lower-case letters, perhaps partly because the shapes of capitals are less confusable (Worden & Boettcher, 1990).

The function of letters, called *graphemes*, is to represent phonemes systematically in the spellings of words. The names of letters are useful for learning grapheme–phoneme associations because most names contain relevant phonemes symbolized by those letters in many words; for example, *tee* contains /t/, and *eff* contains /f/. In fact, relevant phonemes can be found in the names of all but the letter *double-you* (W). Even *wye* (Y) and *aich* (H) contain relevant phonemes, as in *my* and *chip*. Children's knowledge of letter names is typically in advance of their letter-sound knowledge (Worden & Boettcher, 1990). Phonemes that occur at the beginning of letter names are learned more easily than phonemes occurring at the end of names (e.g., *tee*, *kay* vs. *eff*, *em*; Treiman, Tincoff, Rodriguez, Mouzaki, & Francis, 1998). (See Treiman & Kessler, 2003, for a more extensive discussion of letter names.)

Of course, there are additional graphemes whose phonemes are not found in their names, including all the short-vowel phonemes (i.e., vowels in *at*, *Ed*, *it*, *odd*, and *up*) and some consonant phonemes (i.e., Y for /y/ in *yes*, W for /w/ in *we*, H for /h/ in *he*, C for /k/ in *cat*, G for /g/ in *go*). Also, there are graphemes consisting of two letters to represent one phoneme—for example, the consonant digraphs SH, CH, TH, as well as the long-vowel digraphs AI, AY, EE, EA, IE, OA. (For a full description of the major grapheme–phoneme relations, see Venezky, 1970, 1999, or Moats, 2000.)

Whereas the grapheme–phoneme relations in some writing systems, such as Spanish, remain mostly the same across different words, in English the relations are more variable, though still largely systematic. That is, the same grapheme may represent more than one phoneme, and the same phoneme may be represented by more than one grapheme. For example, the letter C may represent the sounds /s/ or /k/; the letter Y may represent the sounds /y/ as in *yes*, /i/ as in *baby*, or /ay/ as in *my*. The vowel spelling system in English is especially variable. English consists of about 15 different vowel sounds. Although the same sound may be spelled in more than one way (e.g., /u/ in *suit* and *move*) and the same vowel letter may represent more than one sound (e.g., *go*, *got*), there is substantial regularity underlying this variability—

for example, the shift in vowel sound signaled by final silent E, as in *mat* versus *mate*, *cut* versus *cute* (Venezky, 1970, 1999).

Regularity in English exists not only at the grapheme–phoneme level but also at the word level. Whereas grapheme–phoneme relations may vary across different words, the spellings of individual words do not. These are prescribed and remain consistent when the same words recur. Spelling regularities within words include grapheme–phoneme relations and also larger spelling patterns. These patterns represent spoken syllabic units such as the onset (i.e., initial consonants) and rime (i.e., vowel and following consonants), as in *str-oke*, and whole syllables, as in *in-ter-est-ing*. These patterns also include morphemes, such as *dis- count -ed* in *discounted*, that are linked to meanings as well as pronunciations. These patterns may be the equivalent of smaller real words—for example, *and* in *sand*, *up* in *supper*. To learn the English writing system, beginners must accumulate knowledge of many regularities as they learn to read. At the outset, they learn grapheme–phoneme relations. This foundation helps them acquire knowledge of the spellings of specific words and spelling patterns that recur across words (Ehri, 1998; Seymour, Aro, & Erskine, 2003).

Predictive studies show that children who enter kindergarten with the ability to segment words into sounds and to identify the names or sounds of letters make faster progress in learning to read during the first 2 years of instruction than children who lack these capabilities (Share, Jorm, MacLean, & Matthews, 1984). Training studies show that children who are taught these capabilities when they first begin learning to read make better progress than children who do not receive this instruction (Ehri, Nunes, Stahl, & Willows, 2001; Ehri, Nunes, Willows, et al., 2001). Studies of children who struggle in learning to read show that these skills are often deficient. These two capabilities are especially central because they enable beginners to unlock and gain access to the alphabetic writing system. Before considering how phonemic awareness and letter knowledge are taught and acquired, we review the processes involved in learning to read to clarify the central role that this foundational knowledge plays.

Overview of Learning to Read

In order for readers to make sense of written language, they must learn to read words. Reading words includes recognizing the correct pronunciations of the words, as well as their meanings and roles in spoken language. There are various ways to read words. Readers may apply one or another of the following strategies to figure out words they have not read before:

1. *Decoding.* Decoding words involves sounding out letters and blending them to form recognizable spoken words. This may be accomplished either by transforming graphemes into a blend of phonemes or by pronouncing and blending larger spelling patterns.
2. *Analogy.* Reading words by analogy involves applying parts of known words to read new words, for example, reading *faint* by analogy to *paint* (Gaskins et al., 1996–97; Goswami, 1986).
3. *Prediction.* Predicting words involves combining cues from the surrounding context and partial letter cues in spellings to anticipate the identity of words (Tunmer & Chapman, 1998).

Whereas readers apply these strategies to figure out unknown words, they read familiar words by accessing them in memory, referred to as reading words by sight (Ehri, 1992). The process of acquiring a sight vocabulary differs from conventional wisdom. It is not a matter of memorizing the shapes or other visual features in words without regard to letter–sound relations. Rather, sight word learning requires readers to form connections between letters in spellings and sounds in pronunciations to retain the words in memory. Knowledge of the alphabetic system enables readers to form these connections. The connections provide the glue that secures specific words in memory for reading and for spelling. When readers encounter an unfamiliar word, they may identify the word by decoding, or analogizing, or predicting, or by asking someone. When the word is seen and pronounced, connections are activated between spelling units and sounds, along with meanings. Reading the word a few times in this way secures it in memory so

that it can be read by sight (Reitsma, 1983; Share, 2004b).

Acquiring reading skill consists of building a very large store of sight words in memory. When skilled readers process print, their eyes land on practically every word (Rayner & Pollatsek, 1989). Words are the stable units that the eyes pick up and process automatically as readers read and comprehend text. When readers can recognize words automatically, they do not need to expend any attention or effort decoding or analogizing or predicting the words (LaBerge & Samuels, 1974). When their eyes land on the words, pronunciations and meanings of the words are activated immediately in their minds (Guttentag & Haith, 1978).

From this description of word reading, it is apparent why letter knowledge and phonemic awareness provide an essential foundation for becoming a skilled reader. Beginners need to know letter shapes and sounds well enough so that this connection-forming material is available for activation when words are read. Beginners need to distinguish phonemes in pronunciations of words and to recognize that these are the same phonemes symbolized by graphemes in the spelling. This makes it possible for the connections to be formed to secure those specific words to their pronunciations and meanings in memory.

Learning to spell is intertwined with learning to read (Ehri, 1997). One reason is that both require letter knowledge and phonemic awareness. In one study, Morris and Perney (1984) found that children's ability to detect and write the sounds in words at the beginning of first grade predicted how well they were reading at the end of first grade. Training studies have shown that teaching beginners to spell words enhances their word reading ability (Ehri & Wilce, 1987; Uhry & Shepherd, 1993). Early spelling requires that beginners know letters and phonemic segmentation so that they can pull apart the sounds in words and represent them with plausible letters (e.g., spelling *watched* as WOCHT).

Beginners may start reading words by sight before they acquire full foundational knowledge of phonemic awareness and the major grapheme–phoneme relations. The course of development in learning to read words has been portrayed as a series of phases (Ehri, 1999, in press). Each phase is labeled to reflect the involvement of alphabetic knowledge in the connection-forming process. Phases are characterized by the *predominant* type of connection that is activated to secure sight words in memory.

The *prealphabetic phase* refers to the earliest period, when children lack much letter knowledge and phonemic awareness and so are unable to form alphabetic connections to read words. By default, they resort to memorizing visual or contextual cues associated with words, such as the eyeballs in *LOOK* or the golden arches rising above McDonald's, but their ability to read words lacking such cues is very limited and unstable (Gough, Juel, & Griffith, 1992; Mason, 1980). They may be able to pretend-read text, but they are unable to fingerpoint the words in the lines they have memorized (Morris, 1993).

The *partial alphabetic phase* emerges when children learn letter names or sounds and some phonemic awareness. They can use this knowledge to remember how to read words by forming partial connections in memory. Beginning and ending letters may be connected to sounds in pronunciations, but not middle letters. For example, they might remember *jump* by connecting the *Jay* to /j/ and the *Pee* to /p/, but ignore *U* and *Em*. This can result in confusions with other words, such as *jeep*. They cannot decode words or analogize, but they can guess words using partial cues and context. They can invent partial spellings that represent some sounds—for example, JP for *jump*—but they have difficulty inventing or remembering correct spellings (Ehri, 1999, in press).

The *full alphabetic phase* emerges when children acquire segmentation and blending skill and learn the major vowel and consonant grapheme–phoneme correspondences. They can use these to connect spellings fully to their pronunciations in memory. For example, they can connect each of the letters in *jump* to its four phonemes. Decoding skill emerges during this phase and helps them read unfamiliar words and retain them in memory (Share, 2004b). They can invent spellings that represent most phonemes in words, and they can begin to remember correct spellings of words.

The *consolidated alphabetic phase* occurs when children form connections out of larger spelling patterns, including syllables and morphemes. These spelling patterns are learned as students acquire a sight vocabulary during the full phase. They learn the spellings of whole words, as well as rime, syllable, and affix spellings that recur in different words. These spellings become consolidated into units that become available for forming connections.

In the remainder of this chapter, we focus on the learning experiences that promote the acquisition of letter knowledge and phonemic awareness during the preschool and kindergarten years, as revealed by findings of research studies. Some of this learning happens informally at home and in preschools. By informal, we mean teaching and learning that arises from circumstance or opportunity as learners interact with caregivers or their environment. More formal, structured learning directed by instructional materials and explicit teaching is typically introduced in kindergarten. Some effective teaching procedures are described. The phases of development most relevant are the prealphabetic and partial alphabetic phases. The goal of teaching is to establish a foundation that enables beginners to move into the full alphabetic phase.

Informal Experiences for Learning Phonemic Awareness

Before children receive formal literacy instruction, their PA is very limited (Liberman, Shankweiler, Fischer, & Carter, 1974). This is not a concept that children discover on their own. One reason is that there are no boundaries in speech to mark phonemes as separate units within words. Speech is continuous and is formed out of phonemes that overlap and are coarticulated (Liberman et al., 1974). For example, when the vocal tract opens to articulate the medial vowel in *jump*, the nasal passage opens at the same time, resulting in a blend of the vowel and the nasal feature of /m/. This overlap makes the phonemic structure of words hard to penetrate and pull apart.

Another factor inhibiting PA is that children's attention is focused on meanings of words rather than sounds. Byrne (1992) showed this in a series of experiments with children in the prealphabetic phase. He taught them to read two words, such as *fat* and *bat*, whose initial letters differed. To find out whether the children had spontaneously induced the relationship between initial letters and sounds in the old words, he pointed to one of the new words containing the same initial letters as the old words—for example, *fun* and *bun*—and asked, "Is this 'fun' or 'bun'?" He found that children responded randomly, indicating that they had paid no attention to letters and sounds when learning *fat* and *bat*.

Byrne (1992) tried many variations of the task, such as using more distinctive geometric shapes rather than letters, but children still did not figure out the relationship. However, when he changed the task from associations involving phonemes to associations involving meanings, children did induce the relationship. For example, if they first learned associations involving "clean chair" and "dirty chair," and then were asked about the shape for "clean" paired with a new shape—"Is this 'clean plate' or 'dirty plate'?"—they were able to transfer their learning. Byrne concludes that prealphabetic children possess a natural tendency to build associations between print and speech at the level of words and meanings, not at the level of phonemes, so this inhibits the process of deducing grapheme–phoneme relations when children are exposed to them in a reading task.

Observational studies also show that prealphabetic children's initial attempts to discover correspondences between the writing system and their language occur at the level of meaning. They may scribble the word *bear* larger than the word *duck*. The word *apple* may be scribbled with a red crayon. They may be puzzled to see that the written word *caterpillar* is longer than the word *bear* because the wormy creature is much smaller (Bialystok, 1991; Levin & Tolchinsky-Landsmann, 1989; Rozin & Gleitman, 1977).

What kinds of informal experiences might draw preschoolers' attention to sounds in words? Learning to recite nursery rhymes has been proposed. Some evidence for the relationship between rhyme awareness and PA has come from longitudinal studies (Bryant, Bradley, MacLean, & Crossland, 1989; MacLean, Bryant, & Bradley, 1987). However, Macmillan (2002) found shortcomings in these studies and suggests that learning about letters rather than rhymes underlies children's informal acquisition of phonemic awareness.

Johnston, Anderson, and Holligan (1996) provided evidence for this. They studied preschoolers ages 4–5 years who had not learned to read and who varied in their ability to write and identify letter names or sounds. In a regression analysis examining factors that explained variance in PA skills, they found that children's ability to produce rhymes explained no unique variance once the effects of vocabulary and letter knowledge were removed. In contrast, letter knowledge explained significant variance in phonemic awareness even after vocabulary knowledge and rhyme production were removed. This suggests that letter knowledge rather than rhyming is the factor enhancing PA in prereaders.

Children may learn about phonemes informally by learning to name letters and recognizing which phoneme in the name is critical. Alphabet books commonly display a letter shape on each page, accompanied by drawings of various animals and objects whose names begin with the critical sound in the letter name—for example, B, named "bee" and surrounded by drawings of a bat, a bear, a basket, a beehive, a bird, and a bicycle. Parents who read alphabet books by emphasizing the initial sounds in all of these words may be teaching their children awareness of initial phonemes, as well as shared phonemes across words. In fact, this is one way that Byrne and Fielding-Barnsley (1991) teach phoneme identity in their program (see the next section).

Children may also learn about phonemes through informal writing activities. The task of having children invent spellings by writing the sounds they detect in words is essentially a phoneme segmentation task. Studies of children given this task show that they use their knowledge of letter names to do this; for example, writing JF for *giraffe*, HN for *chin* (H is selected because its name contains the /ch/ sound) and YF for *wife* (Henderson, 1981; Morris & Perney, 1984; Read, 1971; Treiman, Weatherston, & Berch, 1994). If parents engage children in informal writing activities such as this, children's awareness of phonemes is enhanced.

Instruction to Teach Phonemic Awareness

Because caregivers without special training are not likely to provide much informal instruction in PA, explicit instruction provided in kindergarten is most commonly the way that children learn to focus on and analyze phonemes in words. There are many ways that PA might be taught. As indicated previously, several tasks might be used. Children might be taught to extract and pronounce first or final phonemes in words, to identify the phonemes shared in different words, to segment words into phonemes, to blend phonemes to pronounce a recognizable word, or to delete phonemes from words and say the word that remains. In addition, these tasks might be taught in the oral mode, or tangible markers might be provided to represent the phonemes being manipulated. The markers might be fingers on one's hand, or poker chips, or pictures of the mouth articulating particular phonemes, or alphabet letters representing the phonemes being manipulated.

It is important to note that teaching children PA is a means, not an end. The reason for teaching children to analyze phonemes in words is so that they can connect letters to phonemes when they read or write words. Some words might be segmented in more than one way; for example, segmenting *bowl* into four phonemes /b/-/o/-/w/-/l/ that distinguishes the glide /w/, or into three phonemes /b/-/o/-/l/ that ignores the glide, as would be done in segmenting *toll* into /t/-/o/-/l/. When there are alternatives, segmentation is best guided by the word's spelling, so that learners conceptualize the phonemes in words in terms of their graphemes and the appropriate connections optimizing the match are formed in memory. Ehri and Wilce (1980) found that children's phonemic segmentation was influenced by the spellings of words. Children who knew spellings segmented *pitch* into four phonemes, /p/-/I/-/t/-/ch/, but segmented *rich* into three phonemes, /r/-/I/-/ch/. This inconsistency in phoneme identification makes sense when the graphophonemic, connection-forming function of PA is considered.

PA tasks vary in difficulty. Simpler forms of PA training, such as syllable counting and isolating initial phonemes in words, are appropriate for preschoolers in order to direct their attention to sounds in words. More complex forms are taught as children learn letters and begin reading and writing words. The most important forms of PA involve segmentation and blending. Learning to segment words into phonemes is important for writing all the sounds in words and for forming grapheme–phoneme connections to remember the spellings of words and to read words by sight. Learning to blend phonemes is important for decoding new words.

The National Reading Panel conducted a meta-analysis of controlled experimental studies to evaluate the effectiveness of phonemic awareness instruction (Ehri, Nunes, Willows, et al., 2001). The pool of studies included different types of PA instruction taught to students from preschool through sixth grade. The majority of the studies were conducted with kindergartners. PA instruction was found to be more effective than non-PA forms of instruction for teaching PA and for transfer to reading and spelling. When PA was taught with letters, beginners who knew the letters learned PA better than when it was taught in the oral mode and also performed better on reading and spelling tasks. PA instruction was especially effective when it was taught to small groups rather than to individuals or classrooms of students. Instruction did not need to be lengthy (i.e., more than 20 hours) to be most effective.

A form of PA instruction appropriate for preschoolers without any letter knowledge was studied by Byrne and Fielding-Barnsley (1991). Called "Sound Foundations," the program focused on teaching phoneme identity. Children learned to recognize instances of the same phoneme in initial and final positions across different words. A limited set of sounds received primary attention. Children were shown pictures of a variety of objects, and they selected those having a designated beginning or ending sound, for example, *sea, seal, sailor, sand*. One phoneme in one position was taught in each session. The letter representing the phoneme was introduced as well. The control group engaged in story reading and meaning-based activities using the same pictures. Children were trained in groups for 12 sessions. On posttests, the PA group outperformed controls in a phoneme identity task with unpracticed as well as practiced phonemes. They were also able to identify which of two spoken words matched a written word (e.g., "Does this [*sat*] say "sat" or "mat?"). Some long-range benefits of the program were still evident 3 years later (Byrne & Fielding-Barnsley, 1995).

Making Phonemes Concrete

Phonemes are ephemeral and disappear as soon as they are spoken, so they are hard for learners to hold onto and manipulate. Instruction that provides concrete markers for phonemes has proven helpful in teaching children how to manipulate phonemes in speech.

Elkonin (1973) created one way to materialize speech sounds. He taught Russian children to break words apart into a sequence of phonemes by pronouncing the phonemes as they moved cardboard counters into a row of boxes accompanied by a picture of the word being segmented. (See Figure 9.1.) Children who received this training learned to segment words better than children who were trained with counters but without pictures or boxes and better than children trained without any counters or diagrams. These findings reveal the benefit of making sounds concrete by using counters.

Another way of making sounds concrete that involved mouth pictures was explored by Castiglioni-Spalten and Ehri (2003). Though adapted from the LIPS program (Lindamood & Lindamood, 1998), the present teaching procedure for teaching segmentation with mouth pictures differed somewhat from the approach used by the Lindamoods. Kindergartners were selected who knew the names of most of the letters symbolizing the target sounds to be used. They were taught phonemic segmentation in one of two ways. One group learned to associate eight mouth pictures with specific phonemes—for example, a picture of closed lips saying /m/ or /p/ or /b/, or a picture of the lips slightly parted forming a smile saying /i/ (as in *see*). Figure 9.2 displays the complete set of sounds that were taught using mouth pictures. Children had no trouble learning the associations between pictures and sounds and using the mouth pictures to show sound segments in words. They were taught to segment words into phonemes by monitoring their mouth movements in saying the words and selecting blocks with mouth pictures on them to portray sequentially these mouth movements, for example, the three mouth movements /s/–long o–/p/ in *soap*. Another group was taught to segment sounds rather than mouth movements by using blocks without mouth pictures. A third control group received no treatment.

Findings on the posttest showed that both forms of PA training enabled children to segment better than controls. Also both groups outperformed controls on a spelling task, even though letters were not used during the training. However, only the articulatory instruction enhanced word reading processes. These findings reveal some benefit of materializing sounds by bringing to conscious awareness articulatory gestures involved in producing those sounds. Mouth movements are easier to hold still, analyze, and manipu-

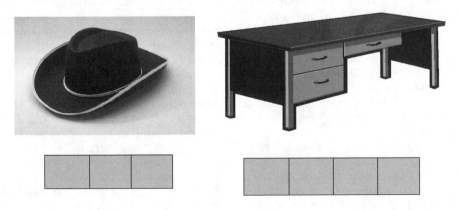

FIGURE 9.1. Elkonin boxes into which children move cardboard counters as they pronounce phonemic segments in *hat* and *desk*.

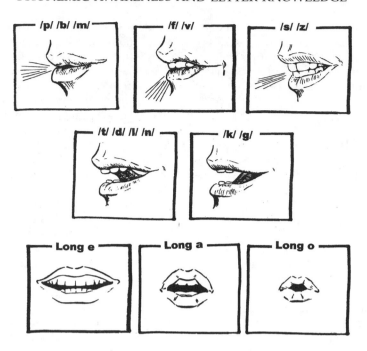

FIGURE 9.2. Mouth pictures depicting 13 consonant and 3 vowel phonemes used to teach children to segment words into a sequence of articulatory gestures. Mouth drawings from C. Lindamood and P. Lindamood (1975). Copyright 1975 by C. & P. Lindamood. Reprinted by permission.

late than the sounds they produce, which are short-lived and fleeting.

Another form of materialization involves teaching PA with letters. Hohn and Ehri (1983) compared two ways of teaching phoneme segmentation, one with blank counters and one with counters displaying letters. The children were kindergartners who knew the names of letters but lacked phoneme segmentation skill and were nonreaders. Results indicated that both PA-trained groups segmented better than a no-treatment control group, indicating that both methods taught the children to segment. However, children who were trained with letters learned to segment better than children who were trained with blank markers. The explanation is that letters provided concrete symbols that helped children focus on and represent phonemes in words.

Blachman, Ball, Black, and Tangel (1994) taught PA using a "say it and move it" procedure. First kindergartners learned to move blank tiles down a page as they segmented and pronounced phonemes in words. After practicing with words containing two and three phonemes, letter–sound correspon-

dences were taught, and children practiced moving tiles displaying letters. Children whose training included this activity along with some other PA activities learned to segment words into phonemes much better than the control group who received traditional kindergarten instruction in letter names and sounds. Moreover, the PA-trained children outperformed controls on reading and spelling tasks.

Teaching students to segment words into phonemes by using letters is actually teaching them to invent spellings of words. In one study, Ehri and Wilce (1987) taught kindergartners to select letter tiles to represent consonant and long-vowel phonemes in words and nonwords containing two to four phonemes; for example, LI (*lie*), KAK (*cake*), NET (*neat*), SLOP (*slope*). Long-vowel letters were topped by a horizontal line. The participants were children who already knew the names of the letters, and all of these names contained the targeted phonemes to be found in the words. The control group practiced matching letters to phonemes pronounced individually. On posttests, the spelling-trained group outperformed controls on tasks assessing phonemic segmentation, sight word learning, and spelling. Thus teaching children to invent spellings of words by using their letter-name knowledge was an effective way to improve their PA, and this learning enhanced their reading and spelling.

Informal Experiences Learning Letters

Whereas phonemic awareness is an unfamiliar concept to parents, alphabet letters are considered an important ingredient in a preschooler's upbringing, at least among many middle-class parents in the United States. Studies indicate that naming and writing letters are the early literacy skills that parents directly teach their children with the greatest frequency. Children who receive parental instruction in letter names know more letter names than other children. Those whose parents teach them about letter–sound correspondences have higher invented spelling scores at age 4.5 years (Crain-Thoreson & Dale, 1992; Hess, Holloway, Price, & Dickson, 1982).

Learning letters is difficult. As mentioned earlier, there are 40 shapes, names, and sounds to be learned. All of this learning involves meaningless bits and arbitrary associations, so much practice and rehearsal are needed to achieve mastery. Various informal experiences may afford an opportunity for children to learn letters: singing the alphabet song, manipulating magnetic letters on refrigerators, watching *Sesame Street*, reading alphabet books and storybooks, learning to write personal names, and reading environmental print.

Reading Books to Children

Adult–child storybook reading has been examined as an activity that may give rise to alphabet knowledge. However, findings indicate that caregivers and children do not talk much about the print during shared reading of narratives. Rather, their attention is focused on meanings, so there is little opportunity to learn about letters (Yaden, Smolkin, & Conlon, 1989). In contrast, shared reading of ABC books directs children's attention to letters. Bus and van IJzendoorn (1988) reported that caregivers and children spent much more time focusing on print while reading ABC books. They found that such a focus was positively correlated with children's ability to name letters.

The success of parental efforts to direct attention to letters is suggested by evidence that middle-class 4-year-olds know on average 54% of the letter names, and 5-year-olds know on average 85% of the letter names (Worden & Boettcher, 1990). In stark contrast, children from low-socioeconomic-status families enter programs such as Head Start knowing on average about four letters. Based on the most recent reports, these children learn on average about five additional letters in Head Start, for a total of 35% of the letter names known at the end of a preschool year. Spanish-speaking children, however, make no gains in letter knowledge (U.S. Department of Health and Human Services, 2003). Although efforts are being made to improve the level of alphabet knowledge of children in such programs, clearly much work remains to be done in order to close the achievement gap between Head Start children and their more economically privileged counterparts (Whitehurst & Massetti, 2004). When intensified efforts are made to implement high-quality programs in Head Start settings, children show good progress in learning the names of letters (Fishel, Storch, Spira, & Stolz, 2003).

Environmental Print

Signs and labels are common sights for young children. However, findings indicate that even though children might be able to read environmental print, this capability does not appear to promote letter learning. Masonheimer, Drum, and Ehri (1984) selected preschoolers who were experts at reading environmental labels and signs accompanied by their logos, for example, PEPSI appearing on its red, white, and blue background. They altered one letter in the label, for example, XEPSI, and showed it to the children. Most failed to recognize the change and continued to read it as "Pepsi" even when they were cautioned that something might be wrong. Clearly the children had not learned to read the signs by paying attention to letters. This is not surprising, as the labels contain more memorable non-alphabetic cues involving colors and eye-catching designs.

In another study, Cardoso-Martins, Rodrigues, and Ehri (2003) worked with illiterate Brazilian adults who already knew many letters but were nonreaders. They read familiar environmental signs printed with single letters replaced, much like the XEPSI example above. Even these adults failed to notice the alterations. This shows that letter identities in environmental signs receive little attention when more salient visual cues dominate, even by those who have sufficient knowledge of letters and extensive exposure to the signs. Thus environmental labels and signs do not afford much opportunity for informal letter learning.

Personal Names

A more promising form of environmental print involves children's personal names printed on cubbies in their preschools. Typically the names appear alone, without other distracting cues, so children are more likely to pay attention to letters. Also, children are especially motivated to read and write their own names and those of their friends, so there may be greater interest in learning letters.

Findings indicate that personal name learning does promote letter learning among preschoolers. In a study of preschoolers and kindergartners, Bloodgood (1999) found that personal name knowledge and letter knowledge were linked. Among 3-year-olds, personal name knowledge occurred in advance of other literacy skills, which were uniformly low. Letters in their own names were the letters known best by the 3-year-olds, confirming that personal names afford a special opportunity for acquiring letter knowledge. Some children could write their own names yet could not name the letters they wrote, showing that only the shapes had been learned. This was evident in one child's description of "t" as "the cross thing."

Treiman and Broderick (1998) also found that prereaders knew names of the initial letters of their own personal names better than other letters. Also, children could write these letters better than other letters. In contrast, they did not know the sounds of these initial letters any better than letters not appearing in their personal names, indicating that letter sounds are not learned informally through personal name learning.

Instruction to Teach Letters

To ensure that children acquire complete knowledge of letters, formal instruction is needed. Formal instruction refers to systematic, planned teaching. Instruction to teach letters should include several ingredients. Children need to learn the shapes of letters not simply through visual recognition but also through handwriting. Some programs prescribe the most efficient ways of forming letters, where to begin, and which strokes to use (Spalding, 1986). Without this, children may devise their own series of strokes, which may be awkward and time-consuming. In addition, children need to associate letter shapes with names and sounds so they can retrieve and produce the items from memory. Practice is needed so that children overlearn and become fast and automatic at processing letters. To facilitate transfer and movement into reading and writing, children need to use the newly acquired knowledge to perform simplified reading and spelling tasks—for example, writing their own names, reading the names of classmates, inventing spellings to label objects in their drawings, writing words by listening for letter names in pronunciations such as "bee" or "ape," and fingerpoint reading familiar text.

Mnemonics

Mnemonics have been examined as a means of reducing the practice time needed to learn letter–sound associations. Marsh and Desberg (1978) compared two types: first-sound mnemonics, involving pictures whose names began with the sound of the letter (e.g., pumpkin for /p/), and action mnemonics, involving pictures depicting an action that produces the sound (e.g., a boy blowing out a candle and saying /p/). Control groups were shown no pictures or irrelevant pictures. Results indicated that children could produce the sounds better than control-group children when the pictures were present, but not when the pictures were removed and only the letters were shown. Very likely, this occurred because the mnemonics did not effectively link the letters to their sounds in memory. That is, the shapes of the letters did not activate routes in memory leading to the mnemonics and their sounds.

An example of a beginning reading program that uses especially engaging action mnemonics to teach letter–sound associations is the Jolly Phonics program (Lloyd, 1998). The actions taught involve hand gestures performed by the children in response to letters—for example, making their fingers crawl up their arm to portray an ant as they chant the initial sound of "ant," /ae/ -/ae/-/ae/, for the letter a. (See Figure 9.3 for more examples.) Although this procedure is focused on sound learning rather than associative learning of sounds and letters, children are given activities that allow them to move in interesting ways that may enhance

their motivation to practice the letter–sound associations. A few of the objects involved in the actions are drawn in the shapes of letters, for example, the bat and ball and the snake in Figure 9.3. Stuart (1999) found that the Jolly Phonics program taught kindergartners to read and write more effectively than Holdaway's (1979) Big Book approach.

Ehri, Deffner, and Wilce (1984) examined a type of mnemonic designed to link letters to sounds in memory. They selected children who did not know the names or sounds of the letters that were taught. Children were assigned randomly to treatment and control groups. The treatment group was taught

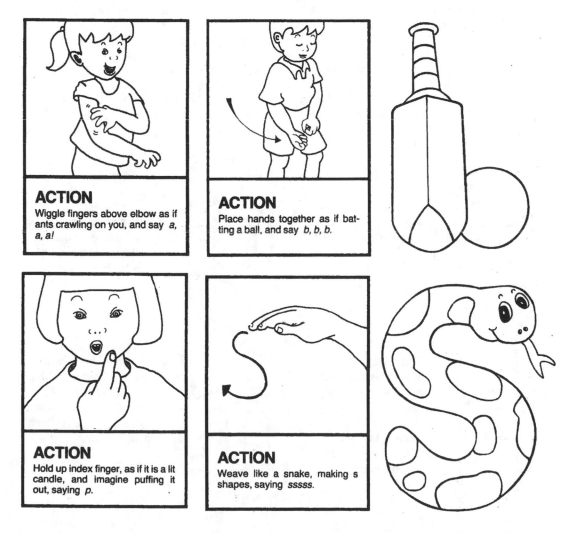

ACTION
Wiggle fingers above elbow as if ants crawling on you, and say *a, a, a!*

ACTION
Place hands together as if batting a ball, and say *b, b, b.*

ACTION
Hold up index finger, as if it is a lit candle, and imagine puffing it out, saying *p.*

ACTION
Weave like a snake, making s shapes, saying *sssss.*

FIGURE 9.3. Action mnemonics to teach the letter sounds for *a, b, p,* and *s.* From Lloyd (1998). Copyright 1998 by Jolly Learning. Reprinted by permission.

five letter–sound associations with integrated picture mnemonics. The letters were drawn to assume the shapes of familiar objects; for example, *s* was drawn as a snake, *h* was drawn as a house with a chimney, *w* was drawn as wings on an insect. Children were taught to look at the letter, remind themselves of the object resembling the letter, and produce the first sound in that object's name (i.e., *s*, "snake," /s/). These mnemonics were thought to be valuable because they provided a nonarbitrary route in memory for retrieving sounds when letters are seen. Without this, the associations would have to be memorized by rote, requiring much practice. Another possible advantage of integrated picture mnemonics is that the associations capitalize on children's interest in meanings.

Two control conditions were included in the study. In one, children were taught the same objects, along with letters and sounds, but the objects were not drawn in the shapes of the letters, so the associative link was not present (i.e., the snake was stretched out rather than wavy). In the other control condition, children learned letters and sounds along with names of the same objects but without any pictures. Results showed that children learned letter–sound associations much better with integrated pictures than with disassociated pictures or no pictures. Findings were replicated in a study teaching Hebrew letters to English-speaking children (Shmidman & Ehri, 2004). This approach has been incorporated into several commercial programs, including Alphafriends (2001) and Letterland (Manson & Wendon, 2003). In these programs, letters are depicted as animate characters with names such as Eddy Elephant, Golden Girl, Harry Hat Man, and Munching Mike (See Figure 9.4).

Of course, if beginners already know the names of letters, then they do not really need to be taught mnemonics in order to learn letter–sound associations present in letter names. Treiman et al. (1998) and Share (2004a) found that children could learn letter sounds much faster if they already knew letter names containing those sounds than if they did not. Many children come to school already knowing at least some letter names. Mnemonics might be most effective

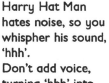

If you ever forget Eddy Elephant's sound just *start* to say his name 'e...'.

Just *start* to say Golden Girl's name and you will find her sound in the back of your throat, 'g...'.

Harry Hat Man hates noise, so you whisper his sound, 'hhh'.
Don't add voice, turning 'hhh' into 'huh'. That would hurt his ears!

Munching Mike is a metal monster and he makes the sound at the start of his name. Just close your mouth and hum, 'mmm'.

FIGURE 9.4. Integrated picture mnemonics to teach the letters sounds for *e, g, h,* and *m.* From Manson and Wendon (2003). Copyright 2003 by L. Wendon. Reprinted by permission.

for teaching children the sounds of letter names that they do not already know, as well as teaching sounds not present in letter names, principally the short vowels and the single consonants (C, G, H, W, Y) and consonant digraphs.

Teaching Letter Names versus Sounds

One issue commonly raised in discussions of letter learning is whether letter names or letter sounds should be taught first. Adams (1990) favors teaching the names first (see Adams, 1990, Chapter 13, for extended discussion of the issue). Several reasons can be identified. Learning letters is a form of concept learning that benefits from having a separate label for each letter category. Letter names provide distinctive labels that help to form the separate concepts in memory. Labels facilitate the process of distinguishing among letters and bonding together all their features and associations in memory, including the visual forms of their upper- and lowercase mates. Moreover, labels allow one to talk about letter referents when using them to read and spell. In contrast to names, sounds of letters make poor labels, particularly because some letters represent more than one sound. For example, do you call C /s/ or /k/? Actually, neither works, because /s/ and /k/ are sounds of other letters. Also sounds are less distinctive and harder to hear than letter names (Treiman & Kessler, 2003).

Another reason favoring letter names is that if children know letter names, then they can learn critical sounds in the names easily (Ehri, 1983; Share, 2004a; Treiman & Broderick, 1998), as reviewed earlier. This means that names and sounds can be taught together, hence precluding the need for a choice about which to teach first. Many children enter kindergarten already knowing many letter names (Worden & Boettcher, 1990), so ensuring that they learn the complete set of names along with sounds makes sense. Teaching letter names and sounds in kindergarten also helps those children without letter knowledge achieve the same footing as more knowledgeable peers before they begin formal reading instruction in first grade. As mentioned previously, however, names are just a beginning. There are many sounds to be learned that are not found in names.

Causal Role of Letter Names

Several years ago, some experimental studies were performed to test the claim that letter-name knowledge helps children learn to read (Jenkins, Bausell, & Jenkins, 1972; Johnson, 1969; Ohnmacht, 1969; Samuels, 1972). Treatment groups receiving letter-name instruction were compared with control groups on posttests to assess whether training transferred to reading. Findings were not supportive. However, Ehri (1983) examined the studies and identified several shortcomings. For example, students already knew many letter names when they entered the study, so the treatment group differed very little from the control group in knowing more letter names following training. Also, the words that students read in the posttests did not contain sounds found in the names of the letters that were taught.

Roberts (2003) performed a study to reexamine this hypothesis. Preschoolers were given 16 weeks of training to teach them the names of the letters from A to P. The control group participated in comprehension instruction involving storybooks. At the end of training, children in the letter condition knew many more letter names than controls.

To assess transfer to reading, Roberts (2003) gave a sight-word learning task. It was patterned after one used by Ehri and Wilce (1985) that distinguished prealphabetic from partial alphabetic phase readers. Children were given practice learning to read two types of words. One type consisted of *visually distinctive* spellings containing no letter–sound relations (e.g., cN for *ball*). The other type consisted of *simplified phonetic* spellings in which the letters symbolized sounds present in the letter names (e.g., BL for *ball*). Roberts created two sets of phonetic spellings—one set from letter names that children had been taught (A–P), and the other set from letter names not taught (Q–Z). There were six words in each set, and children were given several practice trials with feedback to learn to read each set of words.

Ehri and Wilce (1985) had previously found that children without letter knowledge (in the prealphabetic phase) learned visually distinctive spellings better than phonetic spellings, whereas children who knew letter names (in the partial alphabetic phase) learned phonetic spellings better. This is what Roberts (2003) found as well. Children in the letter-name condition learned to read phonetic spellings written with letters they had learned (A–P) better than spellings written with letters they had not learned (Q–Z) and better than visually distinctive spellings, indicating that their letter-name knowledge facilitated their word reading. This letter-name instruction thus enabled them to display word reading characteristic of children in the partial alphabetic phase. In contrast, controls learned to read visually distinct spellings better than both sets of phonetic spellings, indicating that they were using visually salient cues to read words characteristic of the prealphabetic phase. This constitutes strong evidence that letter-name knowledge does function as a cause to enhance word reading skill.

English Language Learners

Participants in the Roberts (2003) and Stuart (1999) studies that were mentioned earlier were English-language learners (ELLs) who were preschoolers or kindergartners. ELL children who are acquiring English as a second language at the same time they are learning to read are thought to have more difficulty than monolingual beginning readers (see Vaughn, Linan-Thompson, Pollard-Durodola, Mathes, & Cárdenas-Hagan, Chapter 14, this volume). A common view supported by correlational evidence is that ELL children need to achieve some proficiency with spoken English before reading instruction begins. However, Roberts's and Stuart's studies, and others, have indicated that young children can learn about the alphabet and how to read in spite of limited oral proficiency in English.

Roberts and Neal (2004) studied 3- and 4-year-olds at a very beginning level in speaking English. The children spoke either Spanish or Hmong as their first language. One group received 16 weeks of high-quality instruction in letter names and rhyming. The control group received instruction in vocabulary and story sequencing. At the end of instruction, the letter-name group named significantly more letters than controls. In fact, the median score was 91% correct. This performance is on a par with middle-class children entering kindergarten. Both Spanish

and Hmong groups showed the same positive outcomes, thus revealing the generalizability of these findings.

For English-language learners, knowledge of the alphabet and phonemic awareness are crucial foundational skills for learning to read, just as they are for English-only (EO) learners (Chiappe, Siegel, & Gottardo, 2002; Geva & Wade-Wooley, 1998; Quiroga et al. 2002). English-language learners and English-only students learn to read in similar ways. When ELLs in preschool, kindergarten, first, and second grades were provided with explicit, high-quality phonics instruction, they were able to acquire word recognition and spelling skills as well as children learning in their first language did (Geva & Siegel, 2000; Lesaux & Siegel, 2002; Roberts & Neal, 2004; Stuart, 1999). Lesaux and Siegel (2002) found no significant difference between ELLs and EO kindergartners on a letter identification task when the children participated in a program that taught the alphabet. Two years later, in second grade, it was found that 7% of the variance in children's reading comprehension was accounted for by their kindergarten letter knowledge. When ELLs and EO children were compared on word identification and spelling measures, the ELLs actually outperformed the EO children. However, the two groups did not differ in their socioeconomic status. These findings indicate that instruction in letter names and letter sounds and the application of this knowledge to word reading are as effective for children learning English as a second language as they are for children learning in their first language.

These findings are not surprising for several reasons. The words and meanings that readers encounter in beginning-level texts are basic and easy to comprehend, so limited knowledge of English vocabulary and syntax should not be a problem. The hardest part is learning letters and the writing system, and these are specialized skills that do not benefit from oral language proficiency but that need to be taught.

Once ELL students learn the writing system, this will actually strengthen their ability to build their English vocabularies. In a recent study, Rosenthal and Ehri (2004) showed that growth in vocabulary was enhanced when second graders saw the printed forms of words as they learned their pronunciations and meanings, more so than when they simply practiced saying the new words. These findings indicate that there is little reason to postpone reading instruction until ELL students gain greater oral English proficiency.

Concluding Comments

To summarize, two accomplishments that provide important foundational knowledge for literacy acquisition received attention in this chapter, letter knowledge and phonemic awareness. We explained what these skills are and how they fit into the larger picture of reading and spelling acquisition. We reviewed how these skills might be learned both informally and formally during the preschool and kindergarten years and the ingredients of effective instruction. We showed that foundational instruction is appropriate and effective even for a special group of young children, English-language learners, who normally might not be taught to read English until later grades. Several points and lines of evidence remain to be offered.

One purpose of writing this chapter was to underscore the importance of children acquiring foundational knowledge before too many demands are placed on them by formal reading instruction. At a minimum, children should be able to name and write all the letters of the alphabet and should be able to isolate initial and final phonemes in words and recognize which words begin with the same phonemes by the end of kindergarten. It is even better if the application of letter knowledge and phonemic awareness is taught and practiced in simple reading and writing tasks. One especially beneficial task is to teach students to invent spellings by detecting sounds in words and selecting plausible letters to write those sounds. Even before kindergarten, children can begin to learn the alphabet and to detect sounds in words. Activities that deepen their knowledge of letter names, that help to make phonemes concrete, and that maintain their interest and active engagement are most effective and beneficial.

Instruction in phoneme isolation, segmentation, and blending may be taught more effectively by integrating it with instruction in letters, developmental spellings, and decoding rather than by teaching it prior to or separately from these processes. Research has indicated that the course of acquisition of PA and reading proceeds reciprocally. That is, teaching PA helps beginners learn to read and write words, and likewise teaching them to read and write words improves their PA (Bentin & Leshem, 1993; Ehri, 1979).

PA instruction can be initiated in the preschool years in the context of teaching the critical sounds present in letter names when alphabet books are read. As caregivers proceed through the pages, each displaying a letter shape plus many objects whose names begin with that letter's sound, children can practice saying the name of each letter, followed by its critical sound (e.g., "bee," /b/), and then the names of the objects along with their initial sounds (e.g., "bear," /b/, "bat," /b/). Integrated picture mnemonics might appear on the pages as well. That is, each letter might form the shape of an animal or object whose name begins with the sound of that letter (e.g., *S* drawn as a snake). Such instruction is a way to link PA instruction to letter-name and letter-sound learning and to help children link the associations between letters and sounds in memory.

In portraying teaching and learning processes, we have suggested that a planned curriculum with a carefully defined sequence of goals related to learning about letters and sounds in words is a critical feature in early literacy instruction. A planned curriculum does not imply rigid, overly controlled instruction in which children passively sit and engage primarily in paper-and-pencil activities. The teaching practices and learner activities used to implement a thoughtfully planned curriculum should ensure children's active participation and enjoyment. A variety of games and contextually embedded learning may be most effective and engaging. For example, in Roberts and Neal (2004), children fed requested letters to a puppet, constructed letter puzzles, found letters in classmates' names, configured their bodies into the shapes of letters, and explored alphabet books with a partner. In the program Sound Foundations used by Byrne and Fielding-Barnsley (1991) to teach phonemic awareness, the children performed activities such as locating and coloring pictures of words that share initial or final sounds, matching pictures of objects that share sounds in a domino game, and playing the card game "Snap" by matching pictures of objects that share sounds. Such games and activities can be used in an organized and thoughtful way to achieve learning. For example, prereaders tend to analyze language in terms of meanings rather than in terms of linguistic units. Not only do they have difficulty analyzing phonemes, as we have discussed, but also they have trouble breaking language into constituent words, particularly context-dependent words that do not have stand-alone meanings; for example, *the*, *and*, *ran*, and *was*.

Ehri (1975) gave children several word awareness tasks. Prereaders had difficulty consciously embedding the words appropriately in spoken statements. For example, when asked to use *the*, one child responded, "A girl went to the zoo and saw a boy saying 'the.' " She remained unaware that she had used *the* twice. After another child heard the word *and* modeled by the experimenter as follows, "The boy *and* his dog walked home," she responded, "The girl is walking home with a cat." She expressed the idea but did not use the target word. When asked to segment sentences into words, prereaders monitored stress points or beats in their speech. This led them to mark syllables rather than words and to overlook low-stress words such as *the*. In contrast, beginning readers showed full awareness of words in these tasks. Ehri (1975) concluded that word awareness emerges when children see and learn to read words in print.

Lack of word awareness was also evident in a fingerpoint reading task. Ehri and Sweet (1991) had 4- to 6-year-old prereaders memorize lines of a story and then point to the words in the story as they recited it. Despite the presence of blank spaces between words, this task gave them great difficulty. In attempting to match stress patterns to the print, they pointed to words but pronounced separate syllables, resulting in a mismatch. Prereaders with some phonemic segmentation and letter knowledge showed more success in the fingerpoint reading task, indicating the contribution of these two skills to helping children perform simplified reading (see Morris, 1993, as well). These findings provide another example of the way an al-phabetic rendering of spoken language clarifies its structure for children moving into reading.

In sum, it is vital to ensure that preschoolers and kindergartners gain control of foundational skills in developmentally appropriate ways. First and second grades are filled with children who lack this foundation and who, as a result, have difficulty trying to build key reading skills as the tasks become increasingly difficult (Juel, 1988). Research conducted since the 1970s has enhanced our understanding about how children learn to read and the forms of instruction that are most effective. These findings need to be incorporated into practice.

References

Adams, M. J. (1990). *Beginning to read: Thinking and learning about print*. Cambridge, MA: MIT Press.

Alphafriends. (2001). *Houghton Mifflin Reading: A legacy of literacy*. Boston: Houghton Mifflin.

Bentin, S., & Leshem, H. (1993). On the interaction between phonological awareness and reading acquisition: It's a two-way street. *Annals of Dyslexia, 43*, 125–148.

Bialystok, E. (1991). Letters, sounds, and symbols: Children's understanding of written language. *Journal of Applied Linguistics, 12*, 75–89.

Blachman, B., Ball, E., Black, R., & Tangel, D. (1994). Kindergarten teachers develop phoneme awareness in low-income, inner-city classrooms: Does it make a difference? *Reading and Writing: An Interdisciplinary Journal, 6*, 1–18.

Bloodgood, J. (1999). What's in a name? Children's name writing and name acquisition. *Reading Research Quarterly, 34*, 342–367.

Bryant, P., Bradley, L., MacLean, M., & Crossland, J. (1989). Nursery rhymes, phonological skills and reading. *Journal of Child Language, 16*, 407–428.

Bus, A. J., & van IJzendoorn, M. H. (1988). Mother–child interactions, attachment and emergent literacy: A cross-sectional study. *Child Development, 59*, 1262–1272.

Byrne, B. (1992). Studies in the acquisition procedure for reading: Rationale, hypotheses and data. In P. Gough, L. Ehri, & R. Treiman (Eds.), *Reading acquisition* (pp. 1–34). Hillsdale, NJ: Erlbaum.

Byrne, B., & Fielding-Barnsley, R. (1991). Evaluation of a program to teach phonemic awareness to young children. *Journal of Educational Psychology, 83*, 451–455.

Byrne, B., & Fielding-Barnsley, R. (1995). Evaluation of a program to teach phonemic awareness to young children: A 2- and 3-year follow-up and a new preschool trial. *Journal of Educational Psychology*, 87, 488–503.

Cardoso-Martins, C., Rodrigues L., & Ehri, L. (2003). Place of environmental print in reading development: Evidence from nonliterate adults. *Scientific Studies of Reading*, 7, 335–355.

Castiglioni-Spalten, M., & Ehri, L. (2003). Phonemic awareness instruction: Contribution of articulatory segmentation to novice beginners' reading and spelling. *Scientific Studies of Reading*, 7, 25–52.

Chiappe, P., Siegel, L. S., & Gottardo, A. (2002). Reading related skills of kindergartners from diverse linguistic backgrounds. *Applied Psycholinguistics*, 23, 95–116.

Crain-Thoreson, C., & Dale, P. S. (1992). Do early talkers become early readers? Linguistic precocity, preschool language and emergent literacy. *Developmental Psychology*, 28, 421–429.

Ehri, L. (1975). Word consciousness in readers and prereaders. *Journal of Educational Psychology*, 67, 204–212.

Ehri, L. (1979). Linguistic insight: Threshold of reading acquisition. In T. G. Waller & G. E. MacKinnon (Eds.), *Reading research: Advances in theory and practice* (Vol. 1, pp. 63–114). New York: Academic Press.

Ehri, L. (1983). Summaries and a critique of five studies related to letter-name knowledge and learning to read. In L. Gentile, M. Kamil, & J. Blanchard (Eds.), *Reading research revisited* (pp. 131–153). Columbus, OH: Merrill.

Ehri, L. (1992). Reconceptualizing the development of sight word reading and its relationship to recoding. In P. Gough, L. Ehri, & R. Treiman (Eds.), *Reading acquisition* (pp. 107–143). Hillsdale, NJ: Erlbaum.

Ehri, L. (1997). Learning to read and learning to spell are one and the same, almost. In C. Perfetti, L. Rieben, & M. Fayol (Eds.), *Learning to spell* (pp. 237–269). Hillsdale, NJ: Erlbaum.

Ehri, L. (1998). Grapheme–phoneme knowledge is essential for learning to read words in English. In J. Metsala & L. Ehri (Eds.), *Word recognition in beginning literacy* (pp. 3–40). Mahwah, NJ: Erlbaum.

Ehri, L. (1999). Phases of development in learning to read words. In J. Oakhill & R. Beard (Eds.), *Reading development and the teaching of reading: A psychological perspective* (pp. 79–108). Oxford, UK: Blackwell.

Ehri, L. (in press) Development of sight word reading: Phases and findings. In M. Snowling & C. Hulme (Eds.), *The science of reading: A handbook*. Oxford, UK: Blackwell.

Ehri, L., Deffner, N., & Wilce, L. (1984). Pictorial mnemonics for phonics. *Journal of Educational Psychology*, 76, 880–893.

Ehri, L., Nunes, S., Stahl, S., & Willows, D. (2001). Systematic phonics instruction helps students learn to read: Evidence from the National Reading Panel's meta-analysis. *Review of Educational Research*, 71, 393–447.

Ehri, L., Nunes, S., Willows, D., Schuster, B., Yaghoub-Zadeh, Z., & Shanahan, T. (2001). Phonemic awareness instruction helps children learn to read: Evidence from the National Reading Panel's meta-analysis. *Reading Research Quarterly*, 36, 250–287.

Ehri, L., & Sweet, J. (1991). Fingerpoint reading of memorized text: What enables beginners to process the print? *Reading Research Quarterly*, 26, 442–462.

Ehri, L., & Wilce, L. (1980). The influence of orthography on readers' conceptualization of the phonemic structure of words. *Applied Psycholinguistics*, 1, 371–385.

Ehri, L. & Wilce, L. S. (1985). Movement into reading: Is the first stage of printed word learning visual or phonetic? *Reading Research Quarterly*, 20, 163–179.

Ehri, L., & Wilce, L. (1987). Does learning to spell help beginners learn to read words? *Reading Research Quarterly*, 22, 47–65.

Elkonin, D. (1973). U.S.S.R. In J. Downing (Ed.), *Comparative reading: Cross-national studies of behavior and processes in reading and writing* (pp. 551–579). New York: Macmillan.

Fishel, J.E., Storch, S.A., Spira, E.G., & Stolz, B.M. (2003, April). *Enhancing emergent literacy skills in Head Start: First year curriculum evaluation results*. Paper presented at the meeting of the Society for Research in Child Development, Tampa, FL.

Gaskins, I., Ehri, L., Cress, C., O'Hara, C., & Donnelly, K. (1996–97). Procedures for word learning: Making discoveries about words. *Reading Teacher*, 50, 312–327.

Geva, E., & Siegel, L. S. (2000). Orthographic and cognitive factors in the concurrent development of basic reading skills in two languages. *Reading and Writing: An Interdisciplinary Journal*, 12, 1–30.

Geva, E., & Wade-Wooley, L. (1998). Component processes in becoming English-Hebrew biliterate. In A. Y. Durgunoğlu & L. Verhoeven (Eds.), *Literacy development in a multilingual context: Cross-cultural perspectives* (pp. 85–110). Mahwah, NJ: Erlbaum.

Goswami, U. (1986). Children's use of analogy in learning to read: A developmental study. *Journal of Experimental Child Psychology*, 42, 73–83.

Gough, P., Juel, C., & Griffith, P. (1992). Reading, spelling and the orthographic cipher. In P. Gough, L. C. Ehri, & R. Treiman (Eds.), *Reading acquisition* (pp. 35–48). Hillsdale, NJ: Erlbaum.

Guttentag, R., & Haith, M. (1978). Automatic processing as a function of age and reading ability. *Child Development, 49,* 707–716.

Henderson, E. (1981). *Learning to read and spell: The child's knowledge of words.* DeKalb, IL: Northern Illinois University Press.

Hess, P. D., Holloway, S., Price, G. G., & Dickson, W.D. (1982). Family environments and acquisition of reading skills: Toward a more precise analysis. In L. M. Laosa & I. Siegel (Eds.), *Families as learning environments for children* (pp. 87–113). New York: Plenum Press.

Hohn, W., & Ehri, L. (1983). Do alphabet letters help prereaders acquire phonemic segmentation skill? *Journal of Educational Psychology, 75,* 752–762.

Holdaway, D. (1979). *The foundations of literacy.* Sydney, Australia: Ashton-Scholastic.

Jenkins, J., Bausell, R., & Jenkins, L. (1972). Comparison of letter name and letter sound training as transfer variables. *American Educational Research Journal, 9,* 75–86.

Johnson, R. (1969). *The effect of training in letter names on success in beginning reading for children of differing abilities.* Unpublished doctoral dissertation, University of Minnesota.

Johnston, R., Anderson, M., & Holligan, C. (1996). Knowledge of the alphabet and explicit awareness of phonemes in pre-readers: The nature of the relationship. *Reading and Writing, 8,* 217–234.

Juel, C. (1988). Learning to read and write: A longitudinal study of fifty-four children from first through fourth grade. *Journal of Educational Psychology, 80,* 437–447.

LaBerge, D., & Samuels, J. (1974). Toward a theory of automatic information processing in reading. *Cognitive Psychology, 6,* 293–323.

Lesaux, N., & Siegel, L. S. (2002). The development of reading in children who speak English as a second language. *Developmental Psychology, 39,* 1005–1019.

Levin, I., & Tolchinsky-Landsmann, L. (1989). Becoming literate: Referential and phonetic strategies in early reading and writing. *International Journal of Behavioral Development, 12,* 369–384.

Liberman, I., Shankweiler, D., Fischer, F., & Carter, B. (1974). Explicit syllable and phoneme segmentation in the young child. *Journal of Experimental Child Psychology, 18,* 201–212.

Lindamood, C., & Lindamood, P. (1975). *The A.D.D. program: Auditory discrimination in depth.* Boston, MA: Teaching Resources Corporation.

Lindamood, P., & Lindamood, P. (1998). *The Lindamood phoneme sequencing program for reading, spelling and speech: The LIPS program.* Austin, TX: Pro-Ed.

Lloyd, S. (1998). *The phonics handbook.* Essex, UK: Jolly Learning.

MacLean, M., Bryant, P., & Bradley, L. (1987). Rhymes, nursery rhymes and reading in early childhood. *Merrill-Palmer Quarterly, 33,* 255–282.

Macmillan, B. (2002). Rhyme and reading: A critical review of the research methodology. *Journal of Research in Reading, 25,* 4–42.

Manson, J., & Wendon, M. (2003). *Letterland early years handbook.* Cambridge, UK: Letterland Ltd.

Marsh, G., & Desberg, P. (1978). Mnemonics for phonics. *Contemporary Educational Psychology, 3,* 57–61.

Mason, J. (1980). When *do* children begin to read: An exploration of four-year-old children's letter and word reading competencies. *Reading Research Quarterly, 15,* 202–227.

Masonheimer, P., Drum, P., & Ehri, L. (1984). Does environmental print identification lead children into word reading? *Journal of Reading Behavior, 16,* 257–272.

Moats, L. (2000). *Speech to print: Language essentials for teachers.* Baltimore: Brookes.

Morris, D. (1993). The relationship between children's concept of word in text and phoneme awareness in learning to read: A longitudinal study. *Research in the Teaching of English, 27,* 133–154.

Morris, D., & Perney, J. (1984). Developmental spelling as a predictor of first grade reading achievement. *Elementary School Journal, 84,* 441–457.

Ohnmacht, D. (1969, April). *The effects of letter knowledge on achievement in reading in the first grade.* Paper presented at the meeting of the American Educational Research Association, Los Angeles, CA.

Quiroga, T., Lemos, K., Britton, Z., Mostofapour, E., Abbott, R. D., & Berninger, V. W. (2002). Phonological awareness and beginning reading in Spanish-speaking ESL first graders: Research into practice. *Journal of School Psychology, 40,* 85–111.

Rayner, K., & Pollatsek, A. (1989). *The psychology of reading.* Englewood Cliffs, NJ: Prentice Hall.

Read, C. (1971). Pre-school children's knowledge of English phonology. *Harvard Educational Review, 41,* 1–34.

Reitsma, P. (1983). Printed word learning in beginning readers. *Journal of Experimental Child Psychology, 75,* 321–339.

Roberts, T. (2003). Effects of alphabet letter instruction on young children's word recognition. *Journal of Educational Psychology, 95,* 41–51.

Roberts, T., & Neal, H. (2004). Relationships among preschool English language learners' oral proficiency in English, instructional experience and literacy development. *Contemporary Educational Psychology, 29,* 283–311.

Rosenthal, J., & Ehri, L. (2004). *Seeing spellings helps children acquire new vocabulary words.* Manuscript in preparation.

Rozin, P., & Gleitman, L. (1977). The structure and acquisition of reading II: The reading process and the acquisition of the alphabetic principle. In A. Reber & D. Scarborough (Eds.), *Toward a psychology of reading* (pp. 55–141). Hillsdale, NJ: Erlbaum.

Samuels, S. (1972). The effect of letter-name knowledge on learning to read. *American Educational Research Journal, 9,* 65–74.

Seymour, P., Aro, M., & Erskine, J. (2003). Foundation literacy acquisition in European orthographies. *British Journal of Psychology, 94,* 143–174.

Share, D. (2004a). Knowing letter names and learning letter sounds: A causal connection. *Journal of Experimental Child Psychology, 88,* 213–233.

Share, D. (2004b). Orthographic learning at a glance: On the time course and developmental onset of self-teaching. *Journal of Experimental Child Psychology, 87,* 267–298.

Share, D., Jorm, A., MacLean, R., & Matthews, R. (1984). Sources of individual differences in reading achievement. *Journal of Educational Psychology, 76,* 1309–1324.

Shmidman, A., & Ehri, L. (2004). *Mnemonics to teach letter-sound correspondences in Hebrew.* Manuscript in preparation.

Spalding, R. (1986). *The writing road to reading* (3rd ed.). New York: Morrow.

Stuart, M. (1999). Getting ready for reading: Early phoneme awareness and phonics teaching improves reading and spelling in inner-city second language learners. *British Journal of Educational Psychology, 69,* 587–605.

Treiman, R., & Broderick, V. (1998). What's in a name: Children's knowledge about the letters in their own names. *Journal of Experimental Child Psychology, 70,* 97–116.

Treiman, R., & Kessler, B. (2003). The role of letter names in the acquisition of literacy. In R. Kail (Ed.), *Advances in child development and behavior* (Vol. 31, pp. 105–135). San Diego, CA: Academic Press.

Treiman, R., Tincoff, R., Rodriguez, K., Mouzaki, A., & Francis, D. (1998). The foundations of literacy: Learning the sounds of letters. *Child Development, 69,* 1524–1540.

Treiman, R., Weatherston, S., & Berch, D. (1994). The role of letter names in children's learning of phoneme–grapheme relations. *Applied Psycholinguistics, 15,* 97–122.

Tunmer, W., & Chapman, J. (1998). Language prediction skill, phonological recoding ability, and beginning reading. In C. Hulme & R. Joshi (Eds.), *Reading and spelling: Development and disorders* (pp. 33–67). Mahwah, NJ: Erlbaum.

Uhry, J., & Shepherd, J. (1993). Segmentation/spelling instruction as a part of a first-grade reading program: Effects on several measures of reading. *Reading Research Quarterly, 28,* 218–233.

U.S. Department of Health and Human Services. (2003). *Strengthening Head Start: What the evidence shows.* Retrieved February 3, 2005, from aspe.hhs.gov/hsp/StrengthenHeadStart03/index.htm

Venezky, R. (1970). *The structure of English orthography.* The Hague: Mouton.

Venezky, R. L. (1999). *The American way of spelling: The structure and origins of American English orthography.* New York: Guilford Press.

Wendon, L. (1992). *First steps in Letterland.* Cambridge, UK: Letterland Ltd.

Whitehurst, G. J., & Massetti, M. (2004). How well does Head Start prepare children to learn to read? In E. Zigler & S. J. Styfco (Eds.), *The Headstart debates (friendly and otherwise).* New Haven, CT: Brooks.

Worden, P., & Boettcher, W. (1990). Young children's acquisition of alphabet knowledge. *Journal of Reading Behavior, 22,* 277–295.

Yaden, D., Smolkin, L., & Conlon, A. (1989). Preschoolers' questions about pictures, print conventions, and story text during reading aloud at home. *Reading Research Quarterly, 24,* 188–214.

III
FAMILIES AND RELATIONSHIPS: SOCIOEMOTIONAL AND LINGUISTIC SUPPORTS

10

The Influence of Parenting on Emerging Literacy Skills

SUSAN H. LANDRY
KAREN E. SMITH

A critically important area for early learning that requires appropriate input and is demonstrated to be affected by young children's interactions with their caregivers is the development of emergent literacy skills. Recent work in the field suggests that the young brain is physiologically predisposed to pay attention to certain aspects of the environment, particularly communications with caregivers (Elman et al., 1996). Environmental factors influence brain development in ways that affect children's learning, behavior, and physical and mental health (Dawson, Klinger, Panagiotides, Hill, & Spieker, 1992; DiPietro, 2000; Elman et al., 1996; Neville et al., 1998). Caregivers support children's development through a variety of processes, including providing emotional support, offering reciprocal communication, supplying cognitive stimulation that scaffolds early learning, and accepting the young child's need for growing independence (Ainsworth, Blehar, Waters, & Wall, 1978; Olson, Bates, & Bayles, 1984; Wertsch, 1979).

Emergent literacy includes such varied components as children's development of language, understanding of the conventions of print, print knowledge, and phonological awareness (Whitehurst & Lonigan, 1998). Language development includes the ability to understand and use vocabulary, to put words together in grammatically appropriate phrases and sentences (i.e., grammar, syntax), to use words together to convey meaning (i.e., semantics), and to use language flexibly to meet the demands of differing social contexts (i.e., pragmatics; Dore, 1979). Conventions of print include a child's ability to understand characteristics of books, such as knowing that writing goes from left to right and top to bottom, grasping the difference between pictures and printed words, and realizing that print carries meaning (Clay, 1979; Tunmer, Herriman, & Nesdale, 1988). Young children are also acquiring knowledge of letters, which directly relates to their later ability to decode words (Mason, 1980; Stevenson & Newman, 1986). A basic aspect of this skill is the awareness that letters have names and are associated with sounds (Tunmer et al., 1988). Another critical predictor of reading success that has its roots in early development is phonological awareness, which includes sensitivity to sounds and the ability to understand that sounds combine to make words and can be segmented in order to make new words (Bradley & Bryant, 1983; Stanovich, Cunningham, & Cramer, 1984).

Parents' interactive strategies, particularly the quality of their language input and shared book reading, show strong relations with children's language development (see

Sénéchal, Ouelette, & Rodney, Chapter 13, this volume), but less is known about relations between the home literacy environment and aspects of children's early literacy skills other than language (Whitehurst & Lonigan, 1998). The few available quantitative research studies examining such influences have shown that the frequency of shared reading (Crain-Thoreson & Dale, 1992) and higher level literacy events in the home (Purcell-Gates, 1996) are associated with children's concepts of print. Children's behavior (e.g., initiative, verbalizations) during shared writing activities with their parents also is related to differences in the level of parental control in the interaction (e.g., Burns & Casbergue, 1992). Other studies have described parent influences on early literacy skills, such as writing, using qualitative techniques (e.g., DeBaryshe, Buell, & Binder, 1996). Studies examining direct links between shared reading and phonological skills have not provided support for a strong home influence (Raz & Bryant, 1990).

Parental Influence on Language Development

Child development research has a long history of understanding the importance of characteristics of parent–child interactions for children's language development, including features of the parents' language input (e.g., word expansion, questioning; Snow, 1986), language input in different social contexts (e.g., book reading, games; Whitehurst & Lonigan, 1998), and parents' speech content (Hart & Risley, 1995; Huttenlocher, Haight, Bryk, Seltzer, & Lyons, 1991; also see Hoff, Chapter 12, this volume). Research findings demonstrate that, in order to develop vocabulary and semantic knowledge, children need to receive rich language input that enables them to understand what objects are called and how they go together or function (Hart & Risley, 1995; Weizman & Snow, 2001). In a seminal longitudinal study examining parents' talk to children among families from varying socioeconomic levels, dramatic differences were found in the richness of words heard by children from lower socioeconomic families compared with those from middle and more affluent levels (Hart & Risley, 1995). For example, in examining

the length of parents' utterances to their children as a representation of complex language, children from lower economic circumstances heard fewer than 100 different vocabulary words in an hour compared with 500 in more affluent families. This represented an astonishing fivefold difference across families in parental input to children that contained what Hart and Risley (1995) refer to as "active listening" features. Other striking differences included a range of just over 200 versus 4,000 total words spoken by parents per hour. Of all the parent measures assessed in this study, one of the most important in understanding differences in children's later cognitive competence was the use of rich and varied vocabulary.

A number of studies have demonstrated the importance of language input for providing children information about natural links between objects and actions and past and current experiences and for noting characteristics of objects. Such input enhances children's growth in vocabulary and builds background knowledge (Bridges, 1979; Smith, Landry, & Swank, 2000). This input often occurs in the context of play-oriented problem-solving activities (e.g., puzzles, block building), but it also is a critically important feature of shared book-reading activities. When it was provided at higher levels during preschool, we found that children's cognitive and memory skills were directly supported (Landry, Miller-Loncar, Smith, & Swank, 2002) and that school-age decoding and later reading comprehension skills were positively influenced (Dieterich, Hebert, Landry, Swank, & Smith, 2004). Parental use of frequent, sophisticated words when assisting their preschool children in play is also important for later literacy skills, as illustrated by the fact that this type of scaffolding accounted for about 40% of the variance in vocabulary skills in kindergarten and second grade (Weizman & Snow, 2001).

Two aspects of children's literacy development that are differentially influenced by home-versus-school experiences are "outside-in" skills (e.g., receptive and expressive language) and "inside-out" skills (e.g., print knowledge, phonological awareness; Whitehurst & Lonigan, 1998). Language skills (outside-in skills), which are strongly influenced by home experiences, are significantly related to the ability to read by the second grade, when demands move from decoding words to reading comprehension. Inside-out skills, whose strongest influences are documented in classroom settings, are more important for reading during the first grade, in which the goal is to learn to decode words. These results highlight the critical role parents play in early literacy development, but they also underscore the importance of early childhood classroom experiences that provide children the necessary experiences with print, the alphabet, and phonological awareness.

When Do Language and Early Literacy Experiences Become Important?

As described in the popular book *The Scientist in the Crib,* by Gopnick, Meltzoff, and Kuhl (1999), the processing of speech sounds begins in early infancy. In a number of experiments, it was demonstrated that the infant quickly becomes a language-specific listener, such that by 4 months attention is paid only to sounds heard in the language to which the infant has been exposed (Kuhl et al., 1997). Prior to this time, infants can distinguish sounds that are not specific to their native language. These findings counter the common perception that children's language learning begins when they say their first words, as does the finding that infants know a number of important features of language from the time they are born. This work, combined with that of others (e.g., Bruner, 1977), highlights the importance of conversations between parents and young children beginning in early infancy.

Conversations with infants have very specific characteristics that appear to support early language development. In a study investigating genetic versus environmental influences on infant communicative competence, two important early direct environmental influences that were not confounded by shared genetic variance were mothers' imitations of their infants' vocalizations and their contingent vocal responsivity (Hardy-Brown & Plomin, 1985). As the first form of infant vocal expression is the infant's cry (Wertheim, 1975), sensitive responsiveness to this early communication signal promotes an awareness that someone attends to the infant in a contingent and sensitive manner

that, in turn, is thought to encourage future signaling and the beginning of parent–infant conversation (Anderson, 1977; Bornstein & Tamis-LeMonda, 1989). Studies also have demonstrated that parents adjust their speech to infants and young children to support language learning. These adjustments include simplification of utterances, redundancy, a higher voice pitch, prosodic contour, and a strikingly high amount of interrogatives, or questions (Snow, 1977). Researchers such as Bruner (1977) highlight the importance of reciprocal characteristics in these early conversations, such that the parent is attempting to communicate specific information to the infant and is receiving information from the infant to shape this input.

Adjustment in parents' language input to match children's capacities to process language continues into the toddler–preschool period (Snow, 1972). Shifts at this later developmental stage include declines in the frequency of imitations and expansions (Slobin, 1968) and increases in descriptions of objects, events, and actions (Nelson, 1973), asking of questions (Moerk, 1975) and discussion of past and future experiences (Moerk, 1975). Some aspects of parents' input in their interactions, such as the degree of directiveness or structure, show varying relations with language and other literacy areas. For example, low levels of structure are related to more initiative and verbal input in shared writing activities between parents and preschoolers (Burns & Casbergue, 1992). The impact of directiveness also can vary across ages, such that in the early toddler period higher degrees can support language skills, but by the preschool period it begins to interfere, particularly considering children's ability to take initiative (Landry, Smith, Swank, & Miller-Loncar, 2000). Other studies have shown that assuring a moderate level of challenge provides strong support for children's literacy gains (Cole & Cole, 1993).

These early literacy experiences occur through games, nursery rhymes, songs, daily conversations, and book-reading activities. Although parents have reported that they engage in such activities as a way to be in close contact and have pleasurable experiences with their children (Newson, 1979), these activities also are promoting skills that are the early foundations for literacy. Bruner (1977) noted the important phenomenon of the reciprocal nature of songs and games, activities in which the parent is using dialogue, rather than monologue. As the child is brought into the activity, efforts are made to support attention and provide opportunities for the child to respond.

Book Reading: An Important Social Context for Parental Influence

A dialogic mode of interaction also is frequently described for book-reading activities between parents and young children. Shared reading is consistently demonstrated to support vocabulary (Elley, 1989; Sénéchal, LeFevre, Thomas, & Daley, 1998; see also Sénéchal et al., Chapter 13, this volume) and general language development (Moerck, 1975). Book reading has been documented as the most frequent activity in which mothers label objects and actions (Ninio & Bruner, 1978). In a study that examined aspects of the home literacy environment for understanding preschool children's language development, characteristics that went into a literacy construct included frequency of shared book reading, earliest age of picture book reading, number of picture books in the home, children's requests for book reading and their play with books, as well as shared trips to the library, and parents own personal reading habits (Payne, Whitehurst, & Angell, 1994). Together these were important in understanding 12–18% of the variability in young children's language skills. Children from lower economic backgrounds are less likely to have these early literacy experiences (Adams, 1990), which may, in part, explain poor language and early literacy competencies for children from families of lower socioeconomic status when they enter school.

Parents from lower socioeconomic backgrounds have been involved in dialogic reading interventions to examine whether teaching parents techniques found beneficial to early literacy skills results in enhanced child outcomes (Whitehurst, Arnold, et al., 1994; Whitehurst, Epstein, et al., 1994). These studies examined the importance of shared reading for language development, as well as other emergent literacy skills such as early writing, print concepts, and identification of sounds and letters. The dialogic-reading method shifts the roles of the parent and child from that of reader and listener, respectively, to the child becoming the storyteller and the adult assuming the role of the listener. Techniques the adult uses include asking *wh-* questions, expanding on the child's utterances, and prompting for more information. With only two training sessions, parents learned to use these techniques with their 3-year-old children. The positive results for the intervention groups documented the efficacy of assisting parents in using techniques that encourage children's more active involvement in shared reading. Moreover, the need for dialogic reading in the home, in addition to exposure in the classroom, is highlighted in this research (Whitehurst, Epstein, et al., 1994). Parents' involvement in these activities with their children provided an added benefit above and beyond that obtained when these experiences were available only in a school environment. The importance of parent–child interactions during the preschool years in fostering increased frequency of reading activities has also been extended to children with developmental delays (Schneider & Frant-Hecht, 1995).

Parental Influence = More Than Rich Language Input

What young children are able to learn about language clearly comes from what they hear. However, this does not suggest that verbal input alone is sufficient to support children's language development most optimally. Because young children have immature attentional systems, self-regulation, and memory capacities, parents' use of strategies that support these immature and developing skills make it more likely that language will be learned most efficiently. Parent's effective support of children's early language skills includes a number of behaviors often referred to as scaffolding techniques, a concept that originated in the sociocultural framework (Bruner, 1972; Vygotsky, 1978). This orientation describes how social and cognitive development occurs in a social context through interactions with responsive, more competent others. Scaffolding of children's immature skills allows them to reach higher levels of learning and self-regulation (e.g., Rogoff, Mistry, Goncu, & Mosier, 1993). From a scaffolding orientation, a highly responsive style limits the work children have to do to coordinate attention and regulate behavior; thus they are more likely to engage and become actively involved (e.g., Bakeman & Adamson, 1984; Landry, Smith, Swank, Assel, & Vellet, 2001; Trevarthen, 1988). Responsive parenting within this framework includes behaviors that encourage joint engagement (e.g., maintaining versus redirecting attentional focus) and reciprocity in dyadic interactions.

Maintaining attention has shown consistent relations with a child's ability to process parents' language input and results in greater competencies in the comprehension and expression of language (Landry, Smith, & Swank, 2002). Parents support a child's ability to maintain attention by noticing the child's focus of attention and by providing sensitive verbal and gestural input. Maintaining attention, a strategy consistent with behaviors deemed effective from a sociocultural framework, is expected to support children's less mature attentional and cognitive capacities by not requiring a shift in their attentional focus. Maintaining children's interest in conversational topics promotes language development as reflected in greater use of one-word utterances as early as 1 year of age (Akhtar, Dunham, & Dunham, 1991). This finding is consistent with research that stresses the influence of caregivers' attending and building on children's interests before labeling objects or actions (Tomasello & Farrar, 1986). This theoretical framework, along with other theories and empirical findings, highlights the importance of matching parental input to the child's capabilities and emphasizes the point that input beyond the child's reach is likely to be ineffective.

A decreased demand on attention, through strategies such as maintaining, allows for greater ability to sustain focus, to understand and build knowledge from the interaction, and to organize a more competent response. In contrast, a maternal behavior referred to as *redirecting attentional foci* is associated with slower rates of growth in language and problem-solving skills (Lan-

dry, Smith, Miller-Loncar, & Swank, 1997). This is thought to occur because redirecting places greater demands on young children's immature cognitive and attentional capacity. When children's ability to respond to maintaining versus redirecting was compared, there was a higher probability that children would show an increase in their level of play with objects with maintaining (Landry, Garner, Swank, & Baldwin, 1996). Maintaining also relates to growth in play, language, and cognitive skills across early childhood (Hebert, Swank, Smith & Landry, 2004; Landry, al., 1997). In early language development, numerous researchers have documented the importance of maintaining children's focus on conversational topics to advancing children's verbal skills (e.g., Akhtar et al., 1991; Tomasello & Farrar, 1986).

Contingency of the parent's response to the child's behavior is another parent strategy that promotes early language (Hardy-Brown & Plomin, 1985; Tamis-LeMonda, Bornstein, & Baumwell, 2001). Most critical to this type of response is parent sensitivity, promptness, and contingency to children's signals. This contingency is expected to provide children with a predictable, positive response that supports their ability to self-regulate through a process of internalization (Maccoby, 1992). This, in turn, promotes a willingness from the child to continue to communicate and cooperate with the caregiver's requests. When children experienced relatively high levels of contingent responsiveness across early childhood, they demonstrated significantly faster rates of growth in social, cognitive, and language skills (Landry et al., 2001; Landry, Smith, & Swank, 2003). This is consistent with research from others (e.g., Bornstein & Tamis-LeMonda, 1989) in which this type of responsiveness was important for understanding early language development, including vocabulary acquisition and milestones such as first words (Tamis-LeMonda et al., 2001). Different aspects of responsiveness, such as responsiveness to children's vocalizations versus their play, differentially predicted milestones such as their ability to combine words and to use language to talk about the past (Tamis-LeMonda et al., 2001).

Parent behaviors such as the use of positive affect, expressions of warmth through physical closeness, sensitive voice tones, and appropriate pacing are often associated with contingent responsiveness and play an important role in supporting children's early literacy skills (Landry et al., 2001; Landry et al., 2002). Behaviors that do not provide this form of emotional support include high levels of restricting behavior, harsh voice tones, physical intrusiveness, and negative statements. Variability in maternal patterns of warm support (e.g., physical nurturance, positive affect) and the absence of negativity (e.g., restrictiveness) across the first few years of life are important in understanding multiple aspects of children's school readiness skills, including language, self-regulation, and social competence (Landry et al., 2000; Landry et al., 2001).

Children's early literacy skills also are influenced by factors beyond direct interactions with the parent. Until more recently, research has not accounted for the larger social and environmental context influencing caregivers' interaction with their children. Caldwell and Bradley have been responsible for studies looking at the influence of factors in the broader home and community context. Using the HOME scale (Bradley, Caldwell, & Rock, 1988), they examined the impact of a broad range of factors in the home environment on children's cognitive (e.g., intelligence, language, reading and math achievement) and social outcomes (e.g., social competence with peers and teachers). Aspects of the home environment that are reported to predict better outcomes include availability of resources that potentially provide cognitive stimulation for the child (e.g., number of books, play materials such as magnetic alphabet letters on the refrigerator, trips to a park or zoo). Interactions with people other than parents (e.g., grandparents, friends) are also important for explaining children's school readiness. Also, although outside the scope of this chapter, research examining parameters of the community, such as access to children's books (Neuman, 1996), the quantity and quality of interactions between the neighborhood schools and parents (Reynolds, 1994), and racial socialization practices within families (Caughey, O'Campo, Randolph, & Nickerson, 2002), can expand our understanding of the complexity of environmental influences on children's cognitive readiness.

Responsive Parent Behaviors Work Together

The influence of parent scaffolding on early literacy is often understood by examining the relation of individual parent behaviors with child skills. However, an enhanced understanding can come from considering the support of these behaviors when they are used in combination, and recent descriptive studies indicate that these behaviors are often used together (Landry et al., 2001; Tamis-LeMonda et al., 2001). Examination of whether parents' use of a contingently responsive style was likely also to include rich verbal input and support for attention skills revealed the strongest effects when behaviors that reflected use of varied strategies were employed together (Landry, Smith, & Swank, 2004). Mothers who cluster on higher levels of consistency in contingent responsiveness also had higher levels of rich language input and were less reliant on restrictiveness. Although research from an attachment framework has clearly demonstrated the importance of responsiveness for social-emotional aspects of development, when social and cognitive skills are examined within the same study, responsiveness is important to both aspects of skill development (Landry et al., 2001; Landry et al., 2003).

Early Childhood: A Sensitive Period for Responsive Parenting

Early parent scaffolding behaviors are expected to be important predictors of early literacy skills because of their specialized support for young children's immature skills (e.g., attention, motor, language). This group of parenting behaviors used with children at older ages might not be expected to be as important. To address this issue, these behaviors, examined in early childhood, were expected to be more predictive of language and cognitive development than their use at later time points would be (Landry et al., 2001). Such a finding would provide support for early childhood being a sensitive period for this form of responsive parenting. Within a large sample of mothers from lower socioeconomic backgrounds, those who demonstrated relatively high levels of responsive parenting across early childhood had children with the fastest rates of language growth and were at average levels by kindergarten. In contrast, mothers who showed inconsistent or low levels of this style had children whose growth rates were much less optimal and developmental levels that often were in delayed ranges. Further evidence that early childhood was a particularly sensitive time for this form of parenting was found when these children and their parents were followed through age 8. Even when controlling for 6- and 8-year responsive parenting, those children with mothers who showed consistently higher levels of responsiveness across early childhood continued to show the most optimal development through 8 years of age (Landry et al., 2003).

Characteristics That Support Parents' Ability to Use Responsive Scaffolding

There is a range of parental personal and social characteristics that provide information on the process by which parenting influences children's development. Personal characteristics of parents, such as beliefs regarding children's developmental needs and the parents' own childrearing history (Fish, Stifter, & Belsky, 1993; Liaw & Brooks-Gunn, 1994; McGroder, 2000), consistently show relations with parent behaviors and, in turn, child outcomes. Mothers who are more likely to believe that children need high levels of restrictiveness and control regarding what is expected (i.e., degree of structure) are less likely to respond to children's needs in ways that provide appropriate nurturance and stimulation (Landry et al., 2001). Additionally, the level of complexity with which parents understand children's development influences a range of parent interactive behaviors and child outcomes (Miller-Loncar, Landry, Smith, & Swank, 2000). Specifically, parents who are flexible in their thinking and use transactional explanations that consider multiple and reciprocal influences for their children's behavior are more likely to react to children in sensitive, responsive ways (Holden & Edwards, 1989; Sameroff & Feil, 1985).

Research also shows a concordance between adults' views of their developmental history and the quality of the relationship they share with their own children (Ainsworth & Eichenberg, 1992; Fonagy, Steele, & Steele, 1991; Main, Kaplan, & Cassidy, 1985). In general, studies reveal that positive relationships with parents in childhood predict a later parenting style that is warm, flexible, and responsive to children's bids for attention. There is somewhat less consistency between negative developmental histories and parenting styles that lack emotional responsivity. Factors such as cultural diversity, life-changing events, and child characteristics are thought to explain exceptional findings (Fonagy et al., 1991). For example, mothers with abusive and hostile child-rearing histories show positive parenting behaviors, but only when their infants are biologically at high risk (Hammond, Landry, Swank, & Smith, 2000). These studies highlight the critical nature of understanding multigenerational influences on children's development.

Another personal characteristic predictive of children's outcomes is parents' psychological well-being (e.g., self-esteem, depression), as the availability of sufficient psychological resources has a positive effect on parenting behavior (e.g., Brody & Flor, 1997; Smith, Landry, Miller-Loncar, & Swank, 1997). Much of this research has examined the effects of parental depression (Assel et al., 2002; Lovejoy, Graczyk, O'Hare, & Neuman, 2000). For example, depressed mothers often report that their depression makes it difficult for them to be nurturant, patient, and involved in the parenting process (Taylor, Roberts, & Jacobson, 1997). This body of research clearly documents the debilitating effects of low self-esteem and high-risk mental health conditions on parents' ability to parent effectively and, ultimately, on children's outcomes.

Social support—including the level, amount, and type of support—is a predictive, external rather than internal, influence associated with more successful parenting (Melson, Ladd, & Hsu, 1993; Simons, Lorenz, Wu, & Conger, 1993). Social networks that provide models for flexibility in interpersonal interactions, respect for others' ideas, and acceptance promote parenting views that consider the child's interest and abilities (Miller-Loncar et al., 2000). Parental warmth, responsiveness, and role satisfaction are related to the extent and amount of support

(Crittenden, 1985). Given that social support is a determinant of children's outcomes (Cochran & Brassard, 1979), targeting change in this area is important, particularly because it may be more open to modification than has been shown for attempts to foster increases in family income or education.

The previously described research outlines a range of factors during early childhood that predict cognitive outcomes. Some of these, such as education and levels of poverty, are assumed to be markers for how parents interact and behave toward their children. Others are more direct indicators of the quality of the parenting environment, such as how parents understand children's needs and parents' internal (e.g., psychological health) and external (e.g., social support in the home and community) resources. These factors are shown to influence children indirectly through a direct influence on parents' behaviors with their children. One avenue by which this research can inform policy and practice decisions is the information it provides on parents who are most at risk. It suggests that interventions that attempt to facilitate change in parents' behaviors may need to consider factors such as parenting beliefs, mental health status, and level of social support in order to maximize effectiveness.

Evidence for the Enhancement of Responsive Parenting

Because of the strong relation between parent behaviors and young children's early literacy and school readiness outcomes, for many years intervention programs have attempted to facilitate parents' use of scaffolding behaviors in hopes of changing children's developmental trajectories (St. Pierre & Layzer, 1998). The results of these programs show mixed impact on parents' increased use of literacy-supportive behaviors that, in turn, promote more optimal child outcomes. Findings from a number of well-designed, randomized home-based parent interventions demonstrate changes in parent attitudes and interactive behaviors, but their impact on child outcomes is not obvious (e.g., Ramey, Yeates, & Short, 1984). Reasons for this lack of success may be that (1) the parental change is too limited, (2) change occurs over

too protracted a time period to have a strong and sustained effect, (3) intensity is insufficient, and/or (4) use of adult learning techniques is insufficient (Bransford, Brown, & Cocking, 2000; Gomby, Culross, & Behrmann, 1999). Many home-based interventions are broad in focus, attempting to change parent style and amount of stimulation. Broad-based parent programs may fail to show sustainable changes in parent behaviors because they lack: (1) a link between intervention goals and techniques and a theoretical orientation that justifies their selection (Drummond, Weir, & Kysela, 2002); (2) a model of change and measurement procedures that account for children's influence on their parents as well as parents' influence on their children (Landry et al., 2004); (3) a direct means of facilitating parents' interactions with their children in ways that are sensitive to cultural and social practices (Hebbeler & Gerlach-Downie, 2002; Howrigan, 1988); and (4) a consideration of the child's larger social context and how to address existing parenting beliefs, knowledge, and/or behaviors for the target population being served in the intervention approach (Olds & Kitzman, 1993). Of critical importance is ensuring that home-visit facilitators understand and accept their role as agents of change (Hebbeler & Gerlach-Downie, 2002; Mahoney, Boyce, Fewell, Spiker, & Wheeden, 1998).

In a recent randomized intervention that incorporated adult learning approaches with the focused goal of enhancing a responsive parenting style for those from low socioeconomic backgrounds, mothers were coached at home to practice the behaviors described in this chapter and to use them in combination to support children's language, cognitive, and social-emotional development (Landry et al., 2004). In addition to using responsive behaviors in everyday activities, an emphasis was placed on using these during toy play and book reading. After viewing tapes of other mothers and practicing the techniques with coaching, mothers were videotaped at the end of each session. Together with their coach, mothers critiqued their own behavior in relation to how their child responded. Other family members were included in the process, thereby allowing mothers to share what they were learning and allowing coaches to evaluate the mothers' progress and other family members to learn some of the techniques (Landry et al., 2004; Guttentag, Pedrosa-Josic, Landry, Smith, & Swank, 2004).

In general, this intervention was effective for mothers across a broad range of ethnic and educational factors. In fact, contrary to expectations, mothers in the intervention versus comparison groups showed increased support for early literacy skills even when they had lower levels of social support and higher levels of depression or hostility (Smith, Landry, & Swank, 2004). The intervention mothers, in contrast to the comparison mothers, showed stronger, positive changes across all scaffolding behaviors, including faster rates of growth. For some behaviors, comparison mothers decreased in their responsive behaviors and increased in negativity, in spite of having a weekly home visitor.

Particularly encouraging was the strong increase in mothers' rich language input found for this group of lower economic families. Mothers across time were demonstrating the ability to use more specific vocabulary, including labeling, as well as explanations and information about conceptual links between objects and actions. Greater increases in the infants' word use were the result of their mothers' greater use of labels and maintaining their attention, behaviors these infants were receiving at the highest levels across 10 to 13 months of age. This is an important period for rich language stimulation, as infants are more capable by the end of the first year of life of benefiting from enhanced verbal input.

The timing and intensity of parent intervention is often a critically important predictor of intervention effectiveness. Additional evidence for this was seen in the need for mothers to receive intervention during the toddler–preschool years in order to show the most optimal increases in rich language input. Other aspects of mothers' behavior, more closely linked to nurturance and responsiveness to signals, required program participation during infancy and the preschool period for the most optimal effects. This is entirely consistent with attachment theory, as it posits the need for a special bond to be established very early in the child's life and for mothers to be consistently nurturing across more challenging developmental periods. The most dramatic evidence for the importance of mothers' participation in the program across infancy and early childhood for early literacy development were children's language outcomes. Language scores grew at faster rates only for children whose mothers demonstrated the most optimal change in their language and responsive input by being in the program in both periods. This study, with random assignment, provides support for the causal inference of positive changes in mothers' language input and other scaffolding strategies on young children's growth in language.

Although parents are a strong influence independent of other factors, the combined influence of quality parent support with a quality classroom experience is optimal (Whitehurst et al., 1994). This finding implies the need for early childhood classroom environments to provide high-quality focused early literacy experiences, in combination with supporting parents who provide such experiences in the home. It also seems beneficial for children's school success to have parents communicating closely with schools about their children's school programs and activities (Reynolds, 1994). There are a number of ways parents can be involved with their children's programs in school, including volunteering to help with school functions, attending meetings about their children's progress, and reading during school hours (Montzicopoulos, 1997). Although it is well documented that the provision of information from schools about how parents can assist their children's academic progress is important, in a large national study, only 37% of parents reported that their child's school provided information on how to help their child at home (National Center for Educational Statistics, 1997).

Summary and Future Directions for Parenting Research

A range of parenting behaviors that cross theoretical orientations appear to establish specialized support for young children's early literacy development. Although these behaviors are unique in the type of support they provide, they are related and, thus, have certain characteristics in common. Together they form an effective style for promoting skills such as language. Early literacy skills are strongly supported by parents' provision of rich language input, which occurs by maintaining the child's focus of attention. However, support for emergent literacy skills goes beyond these two aspects of parent behaviors to include contingent responsiveness, emotional support, and a strong home literacy environment. There is growing evidence that early childhood is a particularly sensitive period for parents' use of these behaviors, in part because they provide specialized support for young children's immature self-regulation and cognitive capacities. Children benefit most if these responsive behaviors adapt to the child's changing developmental needs, such as their need for structure and direction. Because parent intervention programs are often disappointing in their ability to improve children's school readiness, it will be important for interventions to incorporate those aspects of parenting known to influence outcomes, as described herein. Attention also needs to be given to the most optimal timing of parent interventions and the particular behaviors that are most important at different developmental periods. Additionally, as children spend large amounts of time in other caregiving settings (e.g., child care), interventions need to incorporate these multiple settings and research needs to examine effective models for influencing caregiving in home versus center-based care settings.

Acknowledgments

The work described here was supported by Grant Nos. HD24128 and 36099 from the National Institutes of Health. We are grateful to the research staff for their assistance in data collection.

References

Adams, M. J. (1990). *Beginning to read: Thinking and learning about print*. Cambridge, MA: MIT Press.

Ainsworth, M., Blehar, M., Waters, E., & Wall, S. (1978). *Patterns of attachment: A psychological study of the Strange Situation*. Hillsdale, NJ: Erlbaum.

Ainsworth, M. D., & Eichenberg, S. H. (1992). Effects on infant–mother attachment of mother's unresolved loss of an attachment figure or other traumatic experiences. In P. Marris, J. Stevenson-Hinde, & C. Parkes (Eds.), *Attachment across the life cycle* (pp. 160–183). New York: Routledge.

Akhtar, N., Dunham, F., & Dunham, P. J. (1991). Directive interactions and early vocabulary development: The role of joint attention focus. *Journal of Child Language, 18*, 41–49.

Anderson, B. J. (1977). The emergence of conversational behavior. *Journal of Communication, 27*, 85–91.

Assel, M. A., Landry, S. H., Swank, P. R., Steelman, L. M., Miller-Loncar, C. L., & Smith, K. E. (2002). How do mothers' childrearing histories, stress and parenting affect children's behavioral outcomes? *Child: Care, Health, and Development, 28*, 359–368.

Bakeman, R., & Adamson, L. B. (1984). Coordinating attention to people and objects in mother–infant and peer–infant interactions. *Child Development, 55*, 1278–1289.

Bornstein, M., & Tamis-LeMonda, C. S. (1989). Maternal responsiveness and cognitive development in children. In M. H. Bornstein (Ed.), *Maternal responsiveness: Characteristics and consequences* (pp. 49–61). San Francisco: Jossey-Bass.

Bradley, L., & Bryant, P. E. (1983). Categorizing sounds and learning to read: A casual connection. *Nature, 301*, 419–421.

Bradley, R. H., Caldwell, B. M., & Rock, S. L. (1988). Home environment and school performance: A ten-year follow-up and examination of three models of environmental action. *Child Development, 59*, 852–867.

Bransford, J., Brown, A., & Cocking, R. R. (Eds.). (2000). *How people learn: Brain, mind, experience, and school*. Washington, DC: National Academic Press.

Bridges, A. (1979). Directing two-year-olds' attention: Some clues to understanding. *Journal of Child Language, 6*, 211–226.

Brody, G. H., & Flor, D. L. (1997). Maternal psychological functioning, family processes, and child adjustment in rural, single-parent, African-American families. *Developmental Psychology, 33*, 1000–1011.

Bruner, J. (1972). Nature and uses of immaturity. *American Psychologist, 27*, 687–708.

Bruner, J. (1977). Early social interaction and language acquisition. In H.R. Schaffer (Ed.), *Studies in mother–infant interaction* (pp. 271–289). New York: Academic Press.

Burns, M. S., & Casbergue, R. (1992). Parent–child interaction in a letter-writing context. *Journal of Reading Behavior, 24*, 289–312.

Caughey, M., O'Campo, P. J., Randolph, S. M., & Nickerson, K. (2002). The influence of racial socialization practices on the cognitive and behavioral competence of African American preschoolers. *Child Development, 73*, 1611–1625.

Clay, M. M. (1979). *The early detection of reading difficulties* (3rd ed.). Portsmouth, NH: Heinemann.

Cochran, M. M., & Brassard, J. A. (1979). Child development and personal social networks. *Child Development, 50*, 601–616.

Cole, M., & Cole, S. R. (1993). *The development of children* (2nd ed). New York: Scientific American.

Crain-Thoreson, C., & Dale, P. S. (1992). Do early talkers become early readers? Linguistic precocity, preschool language, and emergent literacy. *Developmental Psychology, 28*, 421–429.

Crittendon, P. M. (1985). Social networks, quality of child rearing, and child development. *Child Development, 56*, 1299–1313.

Dawson, G., Klinger, L. F., Panagiotides, H., Hill, D., & Spieker, S. (1992). Frontal lobe activity and affective behavior of infants of mothers with depressive symptoms. *Child Development, 63*, 725–737.

DeBaryshe, B. D., Buell, M. J., & Binder, J. C. (1996). What a parent brings to the table: Young children writing with and without parental assistance. *Journal of Literacy Research, 28*, 71–90.

Dieterich, S. E., Hebert, H. M., Landry, S. H., Swank, P., & Smith, K. E. (2004). Maternal and child characteristics that influence the growth of daily living skills from infancy to school age in preterm and term children. *Early Education and Development, 15*(3), 283–303.

DiPietro, J. A. (2000). Baby and the brain: Advances in child development. *Annual Review of Public Health, 21*, 455–471.

Dore, J. (1979). Conversational acts and the acquisition of language. In E. Ochs & B. B. Schieffelin (Eds.), *Developmental pragmatics* (pp. 339–361). New York: Academic Press.

Drummond, J. E., Weir, A. E., & Kysela, G. M. (2002). Home visitation programs for at-risk young families: A systematic literature review. *Canadian Journal of Public Health, 93*, 153–158.

Elley, W. (1989). Vocabulary acquisition from listening to stories. *Reading Research Quarterly, 24*, 175–187.

Elman, J. L., Bates, E. A., Johnson, M. H., Karmiloff-Smith, A., Parisi, D., & Plunkett, K. (Eds.). (1996). *Rethinking innateness: A connectionist perspective on development.* Cambridge, MA: MIT Press.

Fish, M., Stifter, C., & Belsky, J. (1993). Early patterns of mother–infant dyadic interaction: Infant, mother, and family demographic antecedents. *Infant Behavior and Development, 16*, 1–18.

Fonagy, P., Steele, H., & Steele, M. (1991). Maternal representations of attachment during pregnancy predict the organization of infant–mother attachment at one year of age. *Child Development, 65*, 684–698.

Gomby, D. S., Culross, P. L., & Behrmann, R. E. (1999). Home visiting: Recent program evaluations: Analysis and recommendations. *The Future of Children, 9*, 4–26.

Gopnik, A., Meltzoff, A. N., & Kuhl, P. K. (1999). *The scientist in the crib: What early learning tells us about the mind.* New York: HarperCollins.

Guttentag, C. L., Pedrosa-Josic, C., Landry, S. H., Smith, K. E., & Swank, P. R. (2004). *Changes in responsive parenting profiles in response to an intervention.* Manuscript submitted for publication.

Hammond, M. V., Landry, S. H., Swank, P. R., & Smith, K. E. (2000). The relation of mother's affective developmental history and parenting behavior effects of infant medical risk. *American Journal of Orthopsychiatry 70*(1), 95–103.

Hardy-Brown, K., & Plomin, R. (1985). Infant communicative development: Evidence from adoptive and biological families with genetic and environmental influence on rate differences. *Developmental Psychology, 21*, 378–385.

Hart, B., & Risley, T. R. (1995). *Meaningful differences in the everyday experiences of young American children.* Baltimore: Brookes.

Hebbeler, K. M., & Gerlach-Downie, S. G. (2002). Inside the black box of home visiting: A qualitative analysis of why intended outcomes were not achieved. *Early Childhood Research Quarterly, 17*, 28–51.

Hebert, H. M., Swank, P. R., Smith, K. E., & Landry, S. H. (2004) Maternal support for play and language across early childhood. *Early Education and Development, 15*, 93–113.

Holden, G. W., & Edwards, L. A. (1989). Parental attitudes toward child rearing: Instruments, issues, and implications. *Psychological Bulletin, 106*, 29–58.

Howrigan, G. A. (1988). Evaluating parent–child interaction outcomes of family support and education programs. In H. Weiss & F. Jacobs (Eds.), *Evaluating family programs: Modern applications of social work* (pp. 95–130). Hawthorne, NY: Aldine de Gruyter.

Huttenlocher, J., Haight, W., Bryk, A., Seltzer, M., & Lyons, T. (1991). Early vocabulary growth: Relation to language input and gender. *Developmental Psychology, 27*, 236–248.

Kuhl, P. K., Andruski, J. E., Chistovich, I. A., Chistovich, L. A., Kozhevnikova, E. V., Ryskina, V. L., et al. (1997). Cross-language analysis of phonetic units in language addressed to infants. *Science, 277*, 684–686.

Landry, S. H., Garner, P. W., Swank, P., & Baldwin, C. (1996). Effects of maternal scaffolding during joint toy play with preterm and full-term infants. *Merrill-Palmer Quarterly, 42*, 1–23.

Landry, S. H., Miller-Loncar, C. L., Smith, K. E., &

Swank, P. R. (2002). The role of early parenting in children's development of executive processes. *Developmental Neuropsychology, 21,* 15–41.

Landry, S. H., Smith, K. E., Miller-Loncar, C. L., & Swank, P. R. (1997). Predicting cognitive-linguistic and social growth curves from early maternal behaviors in children at varying degrees of biologic risk. *Developmental Psychology, 33,* 1–14.

Landry, S. L., Smith, K. E., & Swank, P. R. (2002). Environmental effects of language development in normal and high-risk child populations. *Seminars in Pediatric Neurology, 9,* 192–200.

Landry, S. L., Smith, K. E., & Swank, P. R. (2003). The importance of parenting in early childhood for school age development. *Developmental Neuropsychology, 24,* 559–592.

Landry, S. H., Smith, K. E., & Swank, P. R. (2004). *Responsive parenting: The origins of early social, communication, and problem solving skills.* Manuscript submitted for publication.

Landry, S. H., Smith, K. E., Swank, P. R., Assel, M. A., & Vellet, S. (2001). Does early responsive parenting have a special importance for children's development or is consistency across early childhood necessary? *Developmental Psychology, 37,* 387–403.

Landry, S. H., Smith, K. E., Swank, P. R., & Miller-Loncar, C. L. (2000). Early maternal and child influences on children's later independent cognitive and social functioning. *Child Development, 71,* 358–375.

Liaw, F., & Brooks-Gunn, J. (1994). Cumulative familial risks and low-birthweight children's cognitive and behavioral development. *Journal of Clinical Child Psychology, 23,* 360–372.

Lovejoy, M. C., Graczyk, P. A., O'Hare, E., & Neuman, G. (2000). Maternal depression and parenting behavior: A meta-analytic review. *Clinical Psychology Review, 20,* 561–592.

Maccoby, E. E. (1992). The role of parents in the socialization of children: An historical overview. *Developmental Psychology, 28,* 1006–1017.

Mahoney, G., Boyce, G., Fewell, R. R., Spiker, D., & Wheeden, C. A. (1998). The relationship of parent–child interaction to the effectiveness of early intervention services for at-risk children and children with disabilities. *Topics in Early Childhood Special Education, 18,* 5–17.

Main, M., Kaplan, N., & Cassidy, J. (1985). Security in infancy, childhood, and adulthood: A move to the level of representation. *Monographs of the Society for Research in Child Development, 50* (1–2, Serial No. 209).

Mason, J. M. (1980). When children do begin to read: An exploration of four-year-old children's letter and word reading competencies. *Reading Research Quarterly, 15,* 203–227.

McGroder, S. M. (2000). Parenting among low-income African American single mothers with preschool-age children: Patterns, predictors, and developmental correlates. *Child Development, 71,* 752–771.

Melson, G. F., Ladd, G. W., & Hsu, H. (1993). Maternal support networks, maternal cognitions, and young children's social and cognitive development. *Child Development, 64,* 1401–1417.

Miller-Loncar, C. L., Landry, S. H., Smith, K. E., & Swank, P. R. (2000). The influence of complexity of maternal thoughts on sensitive parenting and children's social responsiveness. *Journal of Applied Developmental Psychology, 21,* 335–356.

Moerk, E. L. (1975). Verbal interactions between children and their mothers during the preschool years. *Developmental Psychology, 11,* 788–794.

Montzicopoulos, P. Y. (1997). The relationship of family variables to Head Start children's pre-academic competence. *Early Education and Development, 8,* 357–375.

National Center for Educational Statistics. (1997). *Comparison of estimates in the 1996 National Household Education Survey* (Working Paper no. 97–28). Washington, DC: U.S. Department of Education.

Nelson, K. (1973). Structure and strategy in learning to talk. *Monographs of the Society for Research in Child Development, 38*(1–2, Serial No. 149).

Neuman, S. B. (1996). Children engaging in storybook reading: The influence of access to print resources, opportunity, and parental interaction. *Early Childhood Research Quarterly, 11,* 495–513.

Neville, H. J., Bavelier, D., Corina, D, Rauschecker, J., Karni, A., Lalwani, A., et al. (1998). Cerebral organization for language in deaf and hearing subjects: Biological constraints and effects of experience. *Proceedings of the National Academy of Sciences, 95,* 922–929.

Newson, J. (1979). The growth of shared understandings between infant and caregiver. In M. Bullowa (Ed.), *Before speech: The beginnings of interpersonal communication* (pp. 207–222). Cambridge, UK: Cambridge University Press.

Ninio, A., & Bruner, J.S. (1978). The achievement and antecedents of labeling. *Journal of Child Language, 5,* 1–15.

Olds, D. L., & Kitzman, H. (1993). Review of research on home visiting pregnant women and parents of young children. *The Future of Children, 3,* 53–92.

Olson, S. L., Bates, J. E., & Bayles, K. (1984). Mother–infant interaction and the development of individual differences in children's cognitive competence. *Developmental Psychology, 20,* 166–179.

Payne, A. C., Whitehurst, G. J., & Angell, A. L.

(1994). The role of home literacy environment in the development of language ability in preschool children from low- income families. *Early Childhood Research Quarterly, 9,* 427–440.

Purcell-Gates, V. (1996). Lexical and syntactic knowledge of written narrative held by well-read-to kindergartners and second graders. *Research in the Teaching of English, 22,* 128–160.

Ramey, C. T., Yeates, K. O., & Short, E. J. (1984). The plasticity of intellectual development: Insights from prevention intervention. *Child Development, 55,* 1913–1925.

Raz, I. S., & Bryant, P. (1990). Social background, phonological awareness, and children's reading. *British Journal of Developmental Psychology, 8,* 209–225.

Reynolds, A. J.(1994). Effects of a preschool plus follow-on intervention for children at risk. *Developmental Psychology, 30,* 787–804.

Rogoff, B., Mistry, J., Goncu, A., & Mosier, C. (1993). Guided participation in cultural activities by toddlers and caregivers. *Monograph of the Society for Research in Child Development, 58*(8, Serial No. 236).

Sameroff, A. J., & Feil, L. A. (1985). Parental concepts of development. In I.E. Sigel (Ed.), *Parental belief systems* (pp. 83–105). Hillsdale, NJ: Erlbaum.

Schneider, P., & Frant-Hecht, B. (1995). Interaction between children with developmental delays and their mothers during a book-sharing activity. *International Journal of Disability, Development, and Education, 42,* 41–56.

Sénéchal, M., LeFevre, J., Thomas, E. M., & Daley, K. E. (1998). Differential effects of home literacy experiences on the development of oral and written language. *Reading Research Quarterly, 13,* 96–116.

Simons, R. L., Lorenz, F. O., Wu, C., & Conger, R. D. (1993). Social network and marital support as mediators and moderators of the impact of stress and depression on parental behavior. *Developmental Psychology, 29,* 368–381.

Slobin, D. I. (1968). Imitation and grammatical development in children. In N. S. Endler, L. R. Boulter, & H. Osser (Eds.), *Contemporary issues in developmental psychology* (pp. 437–443). New York: Holt, Rinehart, & Winston.

Smith, K. E., Landry, S. H., Miller-Loncar, C. L., & Swank, P. R. (1997). Characteristics that help mothers maintain their infants' focus of attention. *Journal of Applied Developmental Psychology, 18,* 587–601.

Smith, K. E., Landry, S. H., & Swank, P. R. (2000). The influence of early patterns of positive parenting on children's preschool outcomes. *Early Education and Development, 11,* 147–169.

Smith, K. E., Landry, S. H., & Swank, P. R. (in press). Buffering the negative impact of social risk factors on responsive parenting behaviors through early intervention. *Journal of Consulting and Clinical Psychology.*

Snow, C. E. (1972). Mothers' speech to children learning language. *Child Development, 43,* 549–565.

Snow, C. E. (1977). The development of conversation between mothers and babies. *Journal of Child Language, 4,* 1–22.

Snow, C. E. (1986). Conversations with children. In P. Fletcher & M. Garmen (Eds.), *Language acquisition: Studies in first language development* (pp. 69–89). New York: Cambridge University Press.

St. Pierre, R. G., & Layzer, J. I. (1998). Improving the life chances of children in poverty: Assumptions and what we have learned (Social Policy Report No. 5). Ann Arbor, MI: Society for Research in Child Development.

Stanovich, K. E., Cunningham, A. E., & Cramer, B. B. (1984). Assessing phonological awareness in kindergarten children: Issues of task comparability. *Journal of Experimental Child Psychology, 38,* 175–190.

Stevenson, H. W., & Newman, R. S. (1986). Long-term prediction of achievement and attitudes in mathematics and reading. *Child Development, 57,* 646–659.

Tamis-LeMonda, C. S., Bornstein, M. H., & Baumwell, L. (2001). Maternal responsiveness and children's achievement of language milestones. *Child Development, 72,* 748–767.

Taylor, R. D., Roberts, D., & Jacobson, L. (1997). Stressful life events, psychological well-being, and parenting in African-American mothers. *Journal of Family Psychology, 11,* 436–446.

Tomasello, M., & Farrar, M. (1986). Joint attention and early language. *Child Development, 57,* 1454–1463.

Trevarthen, C. (1988). Universal co-operative motives: How infants begin to know the language and culture of their parents. In G. Jahoda & I. M. Lewis (Eds.), *Acquiring culture: Cross cultural studies in child development* (pp. 37–90). London: Croom Helm.

Tunmer, W. E., Herriman, M. L., & Nesdale, A. R. (1988). Metalinguistic abilities and beginning reading. *Reading Research Quarterly, 23,* 134–158.

Vygotsky, L. S. (1978). *Mind in society: The development of higher psychological processes.* Cambridge, MA: Harvard University Press.

Weizman, Z. O., & Snow, C. E. (2001). Lexical input as related to children's vocabulary acquisition: Effects of sophisticated exposure and support for meaning. *Developmental Psychology, 37,* 265–279.

Wertheim, E. S. (1975). Person–environment interaction: The epigenesis of autonomy and competence. III. *British Journal of Medical Psychology,* *48,* 237–256.

Wertsch, J. V. (1979). From social interaction to higher psychological processes: A clarification and application of Vygotsky's theory. *Human Development, 22,* 1–22.

Whitehurst, G. J., Arnold, D. S., Epstein, J. N., Angell, A. L., Smith, M., & Fischel, J. E. (1994). A picture book reading intervention in day care and home for children from low-income families. *Developmental Psychology, 30,* 679–689.

Whitehurst, G. J., Epstein, J. N., Angell, A. L., Payne, A. C., Crone, D. A., & Fischel, J. E. (1994). Outcomes of an emergent literacy intervention in Head Start. *Journal of Educational Psychology, 86,* 542–555.

Whitehurst, G. C., & Lonigan, C. J. (1998). Child development and emergent literacy. *Child Development, 68,* 848–872.

11

Teacher–Child Relationships and Early Literacy

ROBERT C. PIANTA

A premise of this chapter is that relationships between children and adults are the primary medium through which literacy is acquired. As they grow from birth, children engage in increasingly elaborated and symbolically mediated interactions with caregivers in which emotion, cognition, and communication are intertwined and organized (see Landry & Smith, Chapter 10, this volume, for further discussion). Out of this exceptionally complex, dynamic, multisystem process emerges the capacity, skill, and interest to read, understand, and produce written language (Dickinson & Tabors, 2001; Foorman & Torgesen, 2001; Snow, Burns, & Griffin, 1998). Literacy, which could be viewed as a "behavioral system" in much the way Bowlby (1969) viewed attachment as a behavioral system, recruits and organizes many processes. Among these processes are: interactions at home, in child care, and at school with people who provide foundations for learning and self-regulation; understanding and producing oral language; capacity for short-term memory and attention; and sensitivity to the properties of print and sounds (e.g., Burgess, Hecht, & Lonigan, 2002; Dickinson, Anastasopolous, McCabe, Peisner-Feinberg, & Poe, 2003; Lonigan, Burgess, & Anthony, 2000; Morrison, Bachman, & Connor, 2003; Snow et al., 1998; also see Dickinson, McCabe, & Essex, Chapter 1, this volume). From a develop-

mental perspective, it is within the context of adult–child relationships that these processes are stimulated and become organized as a system of behaviors serving the functional goal of literacy. In fact, literacy is one example of such a progression in which children's capacities and skills emerge from child–adult relationships; it is a precipitate of such interactions (Pianta, 1999; Sroufe, 1996). How relationships serve this function, their role in mechanisms of literacy acquisition, and the consequences of this perspective for research and theory are the focus of the discussion to follow.

With regard to relationships with adults, one of the most common ways in which relationships have been a focus in research on early literacy has been in studies of joint storybook reading by mothers or teachers and children (de Jong & Leseman, 2001; Juel, 1998; Zevenbergen & Whitehurst, 2003; see also Sénéchal, Ouelette, & Rodney, Chapter 13, this volume). However, it is abundantly clear that relationships with adults play a much broader and long-standing role in literacy development than simply as a setting for book reading. Relationships support literacy in terms of providing language stimulation and conversation (see Hoff, Chapter 12, this volume); coregulation of attention, arousal, interest, and emotional experience; direct transmission of phonological information and content; and engagement in the understanding of language that fosters cultural understanding (e.g., Baker, Mackler, Sonnenschein, & Serpell, 2001; Benjamin & Lord, 1996; Dickinson & Tabors, 2001; Hart & Risley, 1992; Morrow, Rand, & Smith, 1995; Whitehurst & Lonigan, 1998). In the context of relationships with adults, experience supporting literacy occurs at multiple levels and across multiple domains, engaging and activating motivational and belief systems that produce interest in printed words that hold meaning and information, as well as cognitive, linguistic, and attentional mechanisms that convey the rules for how phonemes and graphemes map onto one another (e.g., Dickinson et al., 2003).

This chapter examines the intersection(s) of literacy development and the development of adult–child relationships in an effort to derive a theoretical model of the ways in which adult–child relationships support two fundamental components involved in learning to be a successful reader: communication/meaning and print–sound correspondence. There is now ample evidence to indicate that adult–child relationships function as a *support* to the development of basic processes fundamental to literacy, including attention, conceptual development, communication, reasoning, motivation and interest, and help seeking. Relationships provide this support largely through oral language and gestural, nonverbal interactions that provide the communicative and motivational infrastructure for literacy growth. Through these interactions, adult–child relationships enable the child to enjoy attending to an adult teacher, cooperating with that adult, and ensuring the adult's value as a transmitter of meaning and information. The second function served by adult–child relationships is *instructional* (Foorman & Torgesen, 2001) and *intentional* (Pianta, 2003) in that the adult focuses interaction with the child toward a specific skill goal. For literacy development, this function is explicitly teaching grapheme–phoneme code information in all its forms. Through instructional interactions during joint storybook reading, parents offer cues and clues to decoding: They point out letter–sound correspondence, rhyme, and sight words, all of which promote growth in code-breaking skills (Burgess et al., 2002; Foorman & Torgesen, 2001; Juel, 1998; Whitehurst et al., 1994).

This chapter provides the conceptual and

empirical support for this theoretical model of adult–child relationships and literacy and discusses its implications for some of the issues that challenge the field of early education. Toward this end, the chapter's first section presents relevant perspectives from developmental systems theory. In the second section, components of literacy development are integrated into a discussion of adult–child relationship processes starting early in infancy. In the final section, the theoretical model of literacy and adult–child relationships is presented, along with implications for research and for practice.

Background Conceptualization: Literacy, Relationships, and Developmental Systems

Before moving further into discussing the role of teacher–child relationships in the acquisition of literacy competence, two conceptual points require attention. First, this chapter takes a broad view of the role of *teacher*, particularly in relation to acquiring proficiency in literacy. For the most part I discuss teachers' roles using the traditional definition of the teacher as an educational professional who engages development through interactions with children in classrooms and schools; however, I recognize the foundational teaching role that all adult caregivers (parents, child-care providers, relatives) play in literacy development. In fact, this chapter intentionally blurs the distinction between these two types of adults so as to call attention to processes in *adult–child relationships* in which adults (teachers or parents or caregivers) activate, stimulate, and promote the development of literacy. In this regard, adults are *teachers* (of literacy skills) when they engage in interactions with children that involve processes contributing to the acquisition of literacy competencies; the word *teacher* is used to connote this broad meaning. This understanding of the teaching role helps explain the role that parents play in early (and ongoing) literacy development that in part also explains why parenting accounts for achievement gaps in literacy skills as children enter school (NICHD Early Childhood Research Network, 2002).

The second basic premise of the chapter is that, when considering the role that adult–

child relationships play in the complex process of acquiring proficiency in literacy, a developmental systems perspective is a useful heuristic because it provides conceptual tools that can be helpful to researchers and practitioners (Lyon, 2002; Pianta, in press; Snow et al., 1998). When using a developmental lens, a child can be viewed as housing many interacting subsystems that in turn interact with many contexts (Sameroff, 1995). A developmental systems perspective emphasizes the linkages between and among capacities and subsystems within the child (e.g., among emotion, language, and cognition systems) and between the child and the external world (e.g., how social relationships and interactions with adults and peers function in relation to the child's emerging skills). It is fundamental to this perspective that interactions and transactions between and among systems are a primary focus of inquiry and theory (Sameroff, 1995). The *literacy behavioral system* (i.e., the organization of cognition, language, speech, visual perception, etc., that produces reading in a functional manner) emerges from these interactions among component processes and transactions between these processes and the environment.

Interactions of Literacy Systems and Subsystems

Most readers will likely accept the premise that reading is made up of many component subsystems. A further distinction that is a consequence of taking a developmental systems perspective is that efforts to study, assess, or even change a process as complex as literacy (Lyon, 2002) are incomplete unless they take into consideration how the *unit of focus* at a given time or situation (e.g., whether a child knows letters) *functions within the multiple systems in which it is embedded* (e.g., the setting that calls for this skill). In a developmental systems view, the appropriate unit of analysis is the relationship or interaction of the skill domain in consideration (e.g., naming letters) with other systems or contexts (e.g., classrooms).

A core issue in theories of early literacy is the interrelation of two related but distinct components of literacy behaviors consistently identified in research: one involving meaning, language, interest, and understanding and a second involving phonological processing, metalinguistic, and cognitive

skills (e.g., Lonigan et al., 2000; Lyon, 2002; Sénéchal, LeFevre, Smith-Chant, & Colton, 2001; Snow & Tabors, 1996; Storch & Whitehurst, 2001). Much of the recent literature related to emergent literacy and acquisition of reading skills is concerned with the distinctness of these two subsystems within the literacy behavioral system, their relation to one another (e.g., sequential or coacting), and whether instructional approaches should focus more strongly on one relative to the other (Dickinson & Tabors, 2001; Foorman, Francis, Fletcher, Schatschneider, & Mehta, 1998; Morrison et al., 2003; Whitehurst & Lonigan, 1998; Yaden, Rowe, & MacGillivray, 1999). In this chapter, one goal is to examine more closely the interface of these two component subsystems of literacy and how they function developmentally in the context of adult–child (teacher–child) relationships.

Interactions with Contexts: Relationships and Distributed Competence

Young children's capacities to engage in a book-reading task is dependent on skills that are embedded in their experiences and interactions with personal and material resources in a variety of settings: with adults and peers at home, in child care, or in school. From a developmental systems perspective, children's interactions with these settings are active and dynamic exchanges of information, material, and energy (Ford & Ford, 1987). Developmental processes and growth, particularly in infancy and early childhood, are so dependent on these interactions that it is possible to view the developing child as having permeable "boundaries" such that competencies that appear to reside in the child are actually *distributed* across the child and the resources (personal and material) they engage within these various settings (Hofer, 1994; Resnick, 1994; Pianta, 1999). Given this point of view, it is not surprising to find that the most powerful and ubiquitous predictor of young children's functioning on skills related to social and academic competence as they enter school is the quality of interactions observed between mother and child during the preschool period (NICHD, 2002; Storch & Whitehurst, 2001; Whitehurst et al., 1994). Literacy behaviors displayed by children, even those at the level of skills involved in processing phoneme–grapheme associations, are embedded in these interactions and organized within adult–child relationships (Pianta, 2004).

Most comprehensive views of the development of literacy recognize the central role and function of child–adult relationships (Mikulecky, 1996), as evinced by the scores of articles on parent–child storybook reading (e.g., Bus, van IJzendoorn, & Pellegrini, 1995); child–teacher interactions and instructional practices in child care, preschool, and elementary school settings (e.g., Howes et al., 2004; NICHD, 2002); and intervention approaches that target parent–child interactions (e.g. Whitehurst et al., 1994). Relationships between children and adults are a central, and most likely *necessary*, conduit for energy and information that fuel developmental change in literacy. If one accepts this premise, then the issue becomes identifying the ways in which and the periods when relationships facilitate literacy development.

Relationship Processes and Literacy: Birth to Elementary School

Most considerations of adult–child relationships and early literacy focus on literacy and language as the medium of interaction and/or limit the time frame to the toddler or preschool age and older; this is particularly true when the role of the adult is defined as a teacher/educator. Pianta (2004) has argued for a more comprehensive view of how adult–child relationships function to support literacy competence, starting in early infancy and moving through the preschool early elementary period and involving systems other than language or phonological processing.

In his theory of development and the formative role of parent–child relationships, Sroufe (1989, 1996) describes the developmental themes around which interactions between children and caregiving adults (parents, child-care providers, teachers) are organized over time. Pianta (1999, 2004) extends this perspective by aligning these relational themes and processes with phases and processes in literacy development with a specific focus on the role of teachers. In considering the role of teacher–child relationships in literacy acquisition, two key starting points are the recognition that (1) the literacy behavioral system recruits skills and processes that

begin in infancy (Dickinson & Tabors, 2001; Hart & Risley, 1992; Lyon, 2002), and (2) the teacher–child interactions and transactions that take place around literacy-related skills and processes (such as sensitive stimulation of oral language) also support other developmental outcomes, such as social competence and self-regulation, some of which also support literacy skills. When discussing the role of teacher–child relationships in early literacy, the multilevel, reciprocal, dynamic nature of development is clearly both a challenge and an opportunity for deeper understanding.

Developmental progress in the increasing organization and complexity of relationships between children and adults can be characterized according to a set of relational themes described by Sroufe (1989, 1996). These adult–child relationship themes include: (1) regulation and modulation of physiological arousal, (2) formation of an effective attachment relationship, and (3) self-reliance, organization, and coordination of environmental and personal resources. The relational processes embedded in these themes, starting in infancy, are platforms and mechanisms that support activities such as dialogic reading, playing rhyming games, storybook reading, or learning vocabulary or letter names (Pianta, 1994). For example, if a mother fails to respond sensitively and responsively to the infants' interactive cues during feeding situations at 6 months, the ensuing problems with interacting cooperatively undermine the value of storybook reading or interactive rhyming games for supporting emergent literacy skills when the child is 2 or 3 (e.g., Bus et al., 1995). These relational themes and the developmental progression that characterizes the infancy–elementary period are described in the following section, with attention to the specific ways in which these themes contribute to literacy.

Infancy and Toddlerhood: Parents and Care Providers as Teachers

REGULATION OF AROUSAL

In the first 6 months of life, adult–child relationships and interactions are organized primarily around a theme of establishing and maintaining regulation and modulation of physiological arousal and joint attention. In these months the infant (and adult) must tolerate increasingly complex physical and social stimulation and maintain an organized state in the face of this increasing complexity. When established during episodes of interaction, this dyadic state supports periods of joint attention and mutuality, which in turn form the basis of exploration of the object and interpersonal world. Cycles driven primarily by the infant's physiological needs—sleep and alertness, feeding, interest, and arousal—all begin to become organized within the interactions the infant has with the caregiver very early on within this period (Hofer, 1994; Sroufe, 1996). Because the infant is not capable of establishing and maintaining organized states in response to cyclic physiological arousal and state variations on his or her own, interactions with a caregiver are *required* (Hofer, 1994; Sander, 1975).

When the dyad is functioning well, the infant responds to routines set by caregivers and, with caregivers, establishes regular rhythms of feeding, activity/alertness, and sleep in the context of smooth, regular, and predictable caregiving interactions marked by contingency upon infant cues. Over time, these fairly basic interactive patterns focused on physiological variation broaden to include domains such as interactive play (e.g., peekaboo games) and form a relational matrix that organizes the infant in the face of increasingly complex stimulation. This lays the foundation for processes related to communicative intent, function, and skill, key aspects of language that lay the groundwork for the early stages of reading (Dickinson & Tabors, 2001; Hart & Risley, 1992; Morrison et al., 2003; Snow et al., 1998). On the other hand, disordered child–caregiver interactions (e.g., Egeland, Pianta, & O'Brien, 1993; Cohn, Campbell, Matias, & Hopkins, 1990) disrupt the ways that adult–child interactions transmit knowledge and skill to children and affect literacy-specific interactions such as those that occur during book reading (Bus & van IJzendoorn, 1999). At later ages, well-regulated (e.g. sensitive, responsive) interactions between children and teachers in early elementary classrooms have been shown to predict improved growth in literacy functioning in prekindergarten (Howes et al., 2004) and first-grade classrooms (Connor, Son, Hindman, & Morrison, 2004), particularly for children who

already show problems in self-regulation (Hamre & Pianta, 2004).

Developmentally, this early phase of adult–child relationships has marked consequences for literacy outcomes and can be easily underestimated, which has particularly negative consequences for understanding and responding to the needs of poor readers in subsequent years (Dickinson, St. Pierre, & Pettingill, 2004; Pianta, 2004). If we acknowledge that the vast majority of language development supporting later literacy occurs within the home setting between birth and 3 years of age (Hart & Risley, 1992), that it is fairly stable through the preschool and early elementary years (e.g., Dickinson & Tabors, 2001; Snow, Barnes, Chandler, Goodman, & Hemphill, 1991; Sparling, 2004), and that it is predicated on these early interactive rhythms, communicative styles, and skills, then attempts to enhance literacy for underachieving children can only be strengthened by attending to the earliest patterns of dyadic regulation. Difficulties in establishing shared attention and engagement predict problems in behavioral and emotional regulation that have consequences for the level of enjoyment and information conveyed in joint book-reading interactions that take place later in toddlerhood and the preschool years (Bus et al., 1995). The quality of these early child–adult interactions affect whether the child will be a willing or skilled partner with parents or teachers in activities in which language and communication (either oral or print-based) are involved (Bus & van IJzendoorn, 1999; Foorman & Torgensen, 2001; Zevenbergen & Whitehurst, 2003).

ATTACHMENT

The next relational theme, emerging toward the end of the first year of life and continuing throughout childhood, involves the formation and maintenance of an effective attachment relationship. Effective attachment to an adult affords the child a sense of emotional security in the context of a relationship and provides the basis for early exploration of the object and interpersonal world (Howes & Ritchie, 2002). Attachment processes regulate emotions and behaviors when the child feels threatened and are critically important for the infant who is beginning to explore (Sroufe, 1996). Attachment processes recruit mechanisms related to attention, motor be-havior, fear and wariness, and signaling sys-tems between the caregiver and child. Adult responsiveness, emotional availability, and an effective signaling system are key aspects of determining the nature and quality of how these behaviors and processes are organized (Ainsworth, Blehar, Waters, & Wall, 1978), as are the adult's previous attachment expe-riences (Fonagy, Steele, & Steele, 1991; Main & Hesse, 1990; Zeanah et al., 1993).

The link between attachment and explora-tion advances cognitive skill through en-abling efficient and active exploration of, and attention to, information in the environ-ment. This is often called the "secure-base" function of attachment, by which the adult–child relationship serves as a conduit to in-formation. Whether a relationship functions as a secure base for exploration is related to the child's sense of emotional (and physical) safety and security; the effectiveness, depth, and complexity of communication and emo-tional expression between adult and child; and the adult's skilled integration of new information into ongoing interactive se-quences. One can easily see the linkage be-tween secure-base processes and language development and communicative skills.

Secure attachment predicts language de-velopment, emergent literacy and reading, aspects of cognition, and social interaction with peers and other adults (Bus & van IJzendoorn, 1988; Erickson, Sroufe, & Egeland, 1985; Sroufe, 1989). It figures prominently in the joint book-reading inter-actions of parents and children; children with secure attachments to an adult display more positive emotions during joint storybook-reading interactions and engage in more extended discussions of the book (Bus, Belsky, van IJzendoorn, & Crnic, 1997; Bus et al., 1995), whereas those with inse-cure attachments are less attentive and en-gaged (Bus & van IJzendoorn, 1997) and thus less able to make use of these book-reading sessions.

Preschool and Early Childhood: Parents at Home and Teachers in Schools

Starting in the toddler–preschool years and continuing throughout childhood, a key theme of child–adult interaction is the child's func-tional self-reliance and coordination of per-sonal and environmental resources in the context of relationships with adults. This theme in fact dominates interactions and re-lationships between children and teachers for most of a child's school career (Pianta, 1999). The child's use of her own and others' resources to engage information and tasks available to her to meet social and task-related demands is the hallmark of self-reliance, evident when the child enthusiasti-cally engages problems in the world, persists in using her own efforts to address the prob-lems and, before disengaging, signals for and uses resources from others (Pianta, 1999). In this period, adult–child interactions at home increasingly include more explicit literacy-related activities and interactions: listening to and telling stories, engaging in conversa-tions, participating in and attending to joint storybook reading, playing games with words and songs, and even starting to learn letters (e.g., Juel, 1998; Snow et al., 1991; Storch & Whitehurst, 2001). Such interac-tions also are more common in child care, preschool, and school settings (Dickinson et al., 2004). In fact by age 3 to 4, most chil-dren are enrolled in a preschool or other early education setting, and interactions with parents at home and teachers in those set-tings are increasingly focused on transmit-ting literacy skills.

A teacher and child looking at or reading a storybook one on one or in a small group is one of the main settings of literacy-supporting interaction that start in toddlerhood and ex-tend into early childhood. Children's motiva-tion to engage in interactions that teach reading-related skills, such as learning letter names and playing rhyming games, is culti-vated through joint storybook reading, be-cause through storybook reading they learn that understanding print is a tool for en-joyment and for learning (Scarborough & Dobrich, 1994). Storybook interactions also convey information about how oral and print forms of communication are integrated (Dickinson & Tabors, 2001; Juel, 1998; Snow et al., 1991), particularly when teach-ers call attention to connections that pro-vide cues to unlocking the phonetic code (Whitehurst et al., 1994). The child's willing-ness to explore and practice these abstract forms of language and cognition and to en-gage in the more instructionally focused in-teractions that they require is a consequence of the child's relationship experience with regard to prior relational themes of attachment and secure-base functioning.

A child's emotional experience in relationship with a teacher can be a key feature influencing the nature and extent of learning in early childhood. When the child experiences security, interactions are cooperative and responsive, reading together occurs more frequently (Bus & van IJzendoorn, 1995) and is more enjoyable and rewarding, and more literacy-related information is transmitted through instructional sequences (Bus & van IJzendoorn, 1988). It is widely accepted that teachers' emotional sensitivity and a child's sense of security are important elements of early childhood learning environments.

However, emotional security and sensitive responsiveness during this period, although perhaps *necessary* for establishing relationship-level functioning that supports ongoing enjoyment of reading and engagement in communication and language-focused activities, are not *sufficient* for competence as an independent reader (Baker et al., 2001; de Jong & Leseman, 2001; Foorman & Torgesen, 2001). Being emotionally warm is not enough if children are to acquire competence in decoding print, particularly for children whose prior experiences have understimulated language and literacy-related processes. The reason is that the complex and multicomponent processes involved in knowledge and mastery of receptive and expressive forms of print–sound correspondence, particularly at the level of phonemes, *requires explicit instruction from a teacher*, whether in the home or at school (e.g., Burgess et al., 2002; Foorman & Torgesen, 2001; Lyon, 2002; Morrison et al., 2003). Cleaving the instructional and emotional dimensions of teacher–child relationships is a somewhat unfortunate by-product of the differential attention these aspects of teaching have received over the years. From the standpoint of a relationship-systems perspective, emotionally sensitive interaction and appropriately stimulating instruction co-occur in adult–child relationships that are the most well suited for supporting children's skills—these aspects of interaction are not mutually exclusive in skilled teachers or parents (Pianta, Hamre, & Stuhlman, 2003). In one specific example of this in prekindergarten classrooms, emotional and instructional quality both contribute to growth in literacy skills (Howes et al., 2004).

The intentionally instructional component of teacher–child literacy-focused interaction, in which the adult provides cues to phoneme–grapheme relations and elicits the child's performance and practicing of these relations, is the mechanism by which the child learns decoding skills that enables him or her to read text independently and ultimately to understand print (e.g., Foorman & Torgesen, 2002; Haden, Reese, & Fivush, 1996; Hochenberger, Goldstein, & Haas, 1999; Lyon, 2002; Storch & Whitehurst, 2001). It is apparent now that such skills are taught, hopefully in the context of emotionally warm and sensitive teacher–child relationships. At the phase of literacy development at which learning decoding skills is critical, teacher–child interactions with print that once served social, communicative, and meaning-focused functions must become integrated with instructional elements of which the acquisition of skills related to phoneme–grapheme associations is the goal. In preschool, and certainly by the elementary years, the extent to which the explicitly skill-focused instructional dimension of interaction appears necessary for later reading is related to a range of prior conditions, some of which involve the themes of adult–child interaction discussed herein that predispose children for difficulty in learning to read.

The relationship transition that is perhaps the single most challenging aspect of adults' facilitation of children's growth in literacy skill occurs with introduction of a skill-focused, instructional component into adult–child interactions. This transition to incorporation of skill-focused interactions into adult–child communication patterns is difficult because it requires a transformation and reorganization of the relationship from one in which interactions are completely focused on communication of meaning with a primary focus on emotions and support to inclusion of a focus on instruction in challenging skills. In early childhood, how teacher–child relationships integrate the intentionally *instructional* dimension of interaction with the ongoing *support* dimension and balance phonological skill-focused interaction and instruction with enjoyment/meaning-focused interactions is a challenge that may determine whether or not the child will read competently (Mikulecky, 1996; Snow & Tabors, 1996).

Available data suggest that the challenge of integrating these two forms of interaction—(1) motivational and meaning/communication-focused and (2) instructional and skill-focused—continues throughout early childhood, with increasing prominence of instruction in the early elementary school years (Baker et al., 2001; Haden et al., 1996; Hochenberger et al., 1999; Whitehurst et al., 1994), particularly if children are having difficulty learning to read (Foorman & Torgesen, 2001). As noted before, this integration is an enormous challenge to teacher–child relationships. For example, nearly all teachers of reading from pre-K to third grade show enormous variation in the instructional component of literacy-related interactions with children, yet at the same time their social and emotional interactions are less variable and on average fairly positive (La Paro, Pianta, & Stuhlman, 2004; NICHD, 2002; Pianta, La Paro, Payne, Cox, & Bradley, 2002). This variation in the frequency, nature, and quality of teacher–child instructional interactions is evidence of the degree to which instruction challenges their relationships (e.g., NICHD, 2002; Whitehurst et al., 1994).

In short, teacher–child relationships have both support and instructional components that provide for the development of literacy through competencies related to communication, self-regulation, attention, understanding, and eventually print–sound correspondence. These components of relationships and of literacy have interrelated developmental sequences, and at the same time they coexist in parallel in a dynamic tension. These dynamics are what are observed in literacy-related interactions between teachers and children in classroom lessons and at home at bedtime. In the next section, a model reflecting these dynamics is presented and discussed.

Teacher–Child Relationships and Literacy: Dynamics of Instruction and Support

Many adults function as teachers of literacy; experiences that contribute to literacy development start at birth and are organized in the relationships between children and these adults. The review presented earlier suggests that adult–child relationships support literacy in two ways. First, they function as a *support* to the development of basic processes such as attention, conceptual development, communication, reasoning, motivation and interest, and help seeking, largely through oral language and gestural, nonverbal interactions. These interactions provide the communicative and motivational infrastructure for literacy growth; they enable the child to enjoyably attend to an adult teacher and cooperate in communication and interaction with that adult, and they ensure the adult's value as a transmitter of meaning and information. These capacities enhance the child's sense that reading can be a means of accessing meaningful information and can be enjoyable.

The second function served by adult–child relationships is *instructional* (Foorman & Torgesen, 2001) and intentional in that the adult focuses interaction in a directed and constrained manner (Pianta, 2003). One might consider this function explicitly teaching. In teacher–child interactions that serve this function, the adult calls explicit attention to grapheme–phoneme code in all its forms. For example, through instructional interactions during joint storybook reading, parents offer cues and clues to decoding: They point out letter–sound correspondence, rhyme, and sight words, all of which promote growth in code-breaking skills (Burgess et al., 2002; Foorman & Torgesen, 2001; Juel, 1998; Whitehurst et al., 1994).

Figure 11.1 provides an overview and summary of this theory of teacher–child relationships and the literacy behavioral system by organizing *relationship functions* (i.e., support or instruction) with *communicative modalities* (i.e., oral language or nonverbal communication or print). Critically, the intersections of relationship functions and communicative modalities are *literacy-related outcomes* (e.g., motivation or decoding). This framework is admittedly incomplete and oversimplified in relation to a process as complex as reading, but it does provide a way of thinking about the ways in which teacher–child interactions and relationships can focus on literacy and the kind of literacy-related outcomes that are produced as a result. In this way, this framework

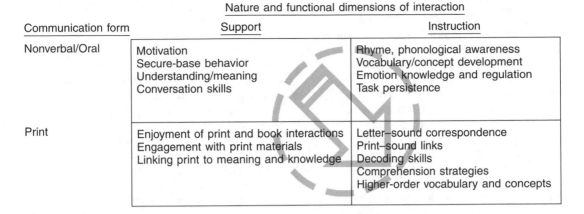

Nature and functional dimensions of interaction

Communication form	Support	Instruction
Nonverbal/Oral	Motivation Secure-base behavior Understanding/meaning Conversation skills	Rhyme, phonological awareness Vocabulary/concept development Emotion knowledge and regulation Task persistence
Print	Enjoyment of print and book interactions Engagement with print materials Linking print to meaning and knowledge	Letter–sound correspondence Print–sound links Decoding skills Comprehension strategies Higher-order vocabulary and concepts

FIGURE 11.1. Literacy-related outcomes produced by child–teacher relationships.

can be used as a tool for examining the ways that literacy is being promoted by the child–teacher relationship and for approaching decisions about what aspects of that relationship to emphasize in a specific classroom or with a specific child.

The dynamic association between these relationship components clearly has a basis in Vygotskian theory about the dual roles of support and challenge in promoting learning and development (see Pianta, 1999; see also Bodrova & Leong, Chapter 18, this volume). In fact, there are two directional patterns of movement in Figure 11.1 that correspond to developmental and contextual shifts that typically occur as children move through the phases of relational and literacy development that have been discussed. One directional pattern involves shifts that *challenge* the child and the child's relationship with his or her teacher; this type of movement was alluded to earlier. In Figure 11.1, when the focus of interaction shifts from supportive, emotion-focused interactions to instructional, skill-focused interactions, the relationship system is challenged by this "perturbation" (Sameroff & Emde, 1989) and over time will need to reorganize and integrate this form of interaction if it is to remain a viable context for supporting child competence. A second form of challenge or perturbation occurs when the nature of literacy-related input to teacher–child interactions shifts from nonverbal or oral communication to print-based input. As was the case for shifts to instructional interactions, interactions focus-

ing on print input of increasing complexity are likely to challenge or draw on the resources of the teacher–child relationship system. In systems in which there may be few resources to begin with, these shifts can lead to disengagement.

On the other hand, shifts can also take place that *restore* relationship resources. When, for example, the focus of interaction shifts from instructional challenges to providing support for emotional well-being, resources are restored to the teacher–child relationship. Similarly, restorative processes are activated when the literacy-related input around which interactions are focused shifts in complexity and abstraction from print to oral or even gestural form. This might take place when a teacher observes a child becoming disengaged or negative when the focus of interaction during storybook reading is on word identification and the teacher shifts to a focus on storytelling and vocabulary.

In many ways what I describe here is the balancing act that is "good teaching," viewed through the lens of a relationship system (Howes & Ritchie, 2002; Pianta, 1999, 2003). Gauging the difficulty of a task's demands and providing encouragement, as well as direct instruction and feedback, are all components of what a good teacher does and does in continuous and ongoing loops of interaction, often with many children simultaneously. The purpose of the model in Figure 11.1 is to make the relational and literacy-related dimensions more explicit and to identify the expected literacy-related outcomes associated with combinations of these dimensions.

From the standpoint of child–teacher relationships, there is a continual adjustment and readjustment process in relation to the shifts that challenge and restore relational resources. These shifts tend to be associated with more or less support and instruction and with more or less abstract literacy-related input. In Figure 11.1, the area identified within the dotted circle encompasses these typical movements and adjustments taking place within a teacher–child relationship. The arrow in this circle represents a more generalized directional tendency, in child–*teacher* relationships in early childhood and elementary school, toward increasing print-focused instructional interactions that produce decoding skills. This arrow represents the directional tendency, or *intentionality*, of child–teacher relationships (Pianta, 2004) with their goal of producing proficiency and independence in all aspects of sound–letter correspondence by the end of the early elementary grades. If one were to extend this model upward in developmental time, when the focus of literacy-related instruction is more dominated by understanding and meaning, then the model would need to be revised.

Intentionality is a concept that reflects the function of child–teacher relationships to produce skill development (MyTeachingPartner, 2004). Research examining teacher–child relationships and preschool children's literacy outcomes provides fairly clear evidence that literacy skills are improved when children are exposed to adult–child interactions that are characterized by warmth, emotional support, and sensitivity in *combination* with modeling, direct instruction, and feedback—in other words, intentionality (e.g., Bogner, Raphael, & Pressley, 2002; Burchinal, Peisner-Feinberg, Pianta, & Howes, 2002; Dolezal, Welsh, Pressley, & Vincent, 2003; NICHD, 2002; Storch & Whitehurst, 2001). Intentional teaching is characterized by high expectations for children, skills in management and planning, a learning orientation in the classroom, skills with which to engage children's attention with appropriate activities, and use of effective feedback in interactions with children that conveys warmth and acceptance (Pianta, 2003). Intentional teach-

ing tailors demands to the child's skill level and provides the child with individualized feedback and scaffolding support, always coupled with emotional sensitivity and warmth. When children are exposed to intentionality in classrooms and child–teacher interactions, social and academic functioning improves; when children experience sensitive, responsive teaching and are well regulated in their relationships and interactions with others, they are more attentive, cooperative, and able to benefit from what the teacher offers to them.

As was discussed earlier, it is important to emphasize that the support function of the teacher–child relationship provides a basis for the instructional function of the relationship but cannot replace instruction's unique importance for literacy growth. Attention to the dynamics of these two functions of teacher–child relationships may be particularly important for children who are likely to have difficulty learning to read when explicit instruction in phonological skills, emphasized in teaching interactions, may tend to come at the expense of interactions that enhance communication quality, motivation, and enjoyment (Foorman & Torgesen, 2001; Storch & Whitehurst, 2001). Thus the primary implication of this model for research and intervention in literacy is its focus on both the instruction and support functions in literacy interventions for poor readers. According to this model, interventions that embody both the support and instruction function provide greater resources for literacy acquisition than those focused only on one or the other. This is the case for two reasons. First, if the pathway to poor reading involves primarily cognitive, linguistic, or instructional deficits, then one could expect better performance when instructional interactions take place in a larger context of a supportive teacher–child relationship (e.g., Burchinal et al., 2002; Hamre & Pianta, 2004; Howes & Ritchie, 2002). On the other hand, if the pathway to poor reading involves compromised development in the basic adult–child relationship processes that support self-regulation, attention, communication, and motivation (e.g., the type of experiences that Pianta, 1999, describes as relational risk), then relationship support will be of paramount importance to provide the motivation for children to tolerate the challenges of explicit instruction.

Conclusions and Implications

Throughout this chapter the interconnected components of teacher–child relationships and literacy have been identified and emphasized. Several overriding themes and conclusions can be drawn from this discussion.

First, literacy is a behavioral system involving many subsystems of processes and functioning that starts at birth, the activation and continued stimulation of which is dependent on teacher–child interactions and relationships. Thus emotion regulation and secure-base functioning may be as important to the ultimate development of the ability to read as is letter–sound correspondence. Recognizing the interconnections among these subsystems and their organization within teacher–child relationships is a key aspect of a developmentally informed understanding of literacy.

Second, relationships between children and teachers promote literacy growth and development by serving two functional goals: (1) providing a base in motivation, interest, communication, and general knowledge and (2) instructing the child explicitly in the link between written and spoken language, particularly at the phonemic level. It is important, as research and theory move ahead, to recognize these two functions as separate, as well as interrelated.

Third, understanding the sequencing and intersection, in typically developing readers and poor readers, of the components of teacher–child relationships and the literacy-related focus of adult–child interactions (such as depicted in Figure 11.1) is essential to constructing theory-based interventions and prevention efforts for children in early education settings. These components and their interactions need further study in a wide range of populations and settings, both in descriptive and intervention studies. The model proposed of child–teacher relationships and literacy development provides a way to understand how the dimensions of interaction between children and teachers at home and in classrooms can be calibrated to respond appropriately to a child's social and instructional needs and still meet the goals of teaching this new and complex set of skills.

Acknowledgments

The work reported herein was completed under the Educational Research and Development Centers Program, PR/Award No. R307A60004, as administered by the Office of Educational Research and Improvement, U.S. Department of Education. However, the contents do not necessarily represent the positions or policies of the National Institute on Early Childhood Development and Education, the Office of Educational Research and Improvement, the Institute of Education Sciences, or the U.S. Department of Education, and readers should not assume endorsement by the federal government.

References

Ainsworth, M. D., Blehar, M. C., Waters, E., & Wall, D. (1978). *Patterns of attachment: A psychological study of the strange situation.* Hillsdale, NJ: Erlbaum.

Baker, L., Mackler, K., Sonnenschein, S., & Serpell, R. (2001). Parents' interactions with their first-grade children during storybook reading and relations with subsequent home reading activity and reading achievement. *Journal of School Psychology, 39*(5), 415–438.

Benjamin, L. A., & Lord, J. (Eds.). (1996). *Family literacy: Directions in research and implications for practice. Summary and Papers of a National Symposium (Washington, DC, September 7–8, 1995).* Washington, DC: Department of Education.

Bogner, K., Raphael, L., & Pressley, M. (2002). How grade 1 teachers motivate literate activity by their students. *Scientific Studies of Reading, 6*(2), 135–165.

Bowlby, J. (1982). *Attachment and loss: Vol. I Attachment* (2nd ed.). New York: Basic Books. (Original work published 1969)

Burchinal, M., Peisner-Feinberg, E., Pianta, R., & Howes, C. (2002). Development of academic skills from preschool through second grade: Family and classroom predictors of developmental trajectories. *Journal of School Psychology, 40*(5), 415–436.

Burgess, S. R., Hecht, S. A., & Lonigan, C. J. (2002). Relations of the home literacy environment (HLE) to the development of reading-related abilities: A one-year longitudinal study. *Reading Research Quarterly, 37*(4), 408–426.

Bus, A. G., Belsky, J., van IJzendoorn, M. H., & Crnic, K. (1997). Attachment and bookreading patterns: A study of mothers, fathers, and their toddlers. *Early Childhood Research Quarterly,* 12(1), 81–98.

Bus, A. G., & van IJzendoorn, M. H. (1988). Mother–child interactions, attachment, and emergent literacy: A cross-sectional study. *Child Development,* 59, 1262–1273.

Bus, A. G., & van IJzendoorn, M. H. (1995). Mothers reading to their 3-year-olds: The role of mother–child attachment security in becoming literate. *Reading Research Quarterly,* 30(4), 998–1015.

Bus, A. G., & van IJzendoorn, M. H. (1997). Affective dimension of mother–infant picturebook reading. *Journal of School Psychology,* 35(1), 47–60.

Bus, A. G., & van IJzendoorn, M. H. (1999). Phonological awareness and early reading: A meta-analysis of experimental training studies. *Journal of Educational Psychology,* 91, 403–414.

Bus, A. G., van IJzendoorn, M. H., & Pellegrini, A. D. (1995). Joint book reading makes for success in learning to read: A meta-analysis of intergenerational literacy. *Review of Educational Research,* 65, 1–21.

Cohn, J., Campbell, S., Matias, R., & Hopkins, J. (1990). Face-to-face interactions of postpartum depressed and non-depressed mother–infant pairs. *Developmental Psychology,* 26, 15–23.

Connor, C. M., Son, S. H., Hindman, A. H., & Morrison, F. J. (2004). *Teacher qualifications, classroom practices, and family characteristics: Complex effects on first-graders' vocabulary and early reading outcomes.* Manuscript submitted for publication.

de Jong, P. F., & Leseman, P. P. M. (2001). Lasting effects of home literacy on reading achievement in school. *Journal of School Psychology,* 39(5), 389–414.

Dickinson, D. K., Anastasopolous, L., McCabe, A., Peisner-Feinberg, E. S., & Poe, M. D. (2003). The comprehensive language approach to early literacy: The interrelationships among vocabulary, phonological sensitivity, and print knowledge among preschool-aged children. *Journal of Educational Psychology,* 93(3), 465–481.

Dickinson, D. K., St. Pierre, R. B., & Pettengill, J. (2004). High-quality classrooms: A key ingredient to family literacy programs' support for children's literacy. In B. Wasik (Ed.), *Handbook of family literacy* (pp. 137–154). Mahwah, NJ: Erlbaum.

Dickinson, D. K., & Tabors, P. O. (Eds.). (2001). *Beginning literacy with language: Young children learning at home and school.* Baltimore: Brookes.

Dolezal, S. E., Welsh, L. M., Pressley, M., & Vincent, M. M. (2003). How nine third-grade teachers motivate student academic engagement. *Elementary School Journal,* 103(3), 239–269.

Egeland, B., Pianta, R. C., & O'Brien, M. (1993). Maternal intrusiveness in infancy and child maladaptation in early school years. *Development and Psychopathology,* 5, 359–370.

Erickson, M. F., Sroufe, L. A., & Egeland, B. (1985). The relationship between quality of attachment and behavior problems in preschool in a high-risk sample. *Monographs of the Society for Research in Child Development,* 50, 1–2 (Serial No. 209).

Fonagy, P., Steele, H., & Steele, M. (1991). Maternal representations of attachment during pregnancy predict the organization of mother–infant attachment at one year of age. *Child Development,* 62, 891–905.

Foorman, B. R., Francis, D. J., Fletcher, J. M., Schatschneider, C., & Mehta, P. (1998). The role of instruction in learning to read: Preventing reading failure in at-risk children. *Educational Psychology,* 90(1), 37–55.

Foorman, B. R., & Torgesen, J. (2001). Critical elements of classroom and small-group instruction promote reading success in all children. *Learning Disabilities Research and Practice,* 16(4), 203–212.

Ford, D. H, & Ford, M. E. (1987). *Humans as self-constructing living systems.* Hillsdale NJ: Erlbaum.

Haden, C. A., Reese, E., & Fivush, R. (1996). Mothers' extratextual comments during storybook reading: Stylistic differences over time and across texts. *Discourse Processes,* 21, 135–169.

Hamre, B. K., & Pianta, R. C. (2004). *Can instructional and emotional support in the first grade classroom make a difference for children at risk of school failure?* Manuscript submitted for publication.

Hart, B., & Risley, T. R. (1992). American parenting of language-learning children: Persisting differences in family–child interactions observed in natural home environments. *Developmental Psychology,* 26(6), 1096–1105.

Hochenberger, E. H., Goldstein, H., & Haas, L. S. (1999). Effects of commenting during joint book reading by mothers with low-SES. *Topics in Early Childhood Special Education,* 19, 15–27.

Hofer, M. A. (1994). Hidden regulators in attachment, separation, and loss. *Monographs of the Society for Research in Child Development,* 59 (serial no. 240).

Howes, C., Burchinal, M., Pianta, R., Bryant, D., Early, D., Clifford, R., & Barbarin, O. (2004). *Ready to learn? Children's pre-academic achievement in pre-kindergarten programs.* Manuscript submitted for publication.

Howes, C., & Ritchie, S. (2002) *A matter of trust: Connecting teachers and learners in the early childhood classrooms.* New York: Teachers College Press.

Juel, C. (1998). What kind of one-on-one tutoring helps a poor reader? In C. Hulme & R. M. Joshi (Eds.), *Reading and spelling: Development and disorders* (pp. 449–471). Mahwah, NJ: Erlbaum.

La Paro, K. M., Pianta, R. C., & Stuhlman, M. (2004). Classroom Assessment Scoring System (CLASS): Findings from the pre-K year. *Elementary School Journal, 104*(5), 409–426.

Lonigan, C. J., Burgess, S. R., & Anthony, J. L. (2000). Development of emergent literacy and early reading skills in preschool children: Evidence from a latent-variable longitudinal study. *Developmental Psychology, 36*(5), 596–613.

Lyon, G. R. (Ed.). (2002). Reading development, reading difficulties, and reading instruction: Educational and public health issues [Special issue]. *Journal of School Psychology, 40*(1).

Main, M., & Hesse E. (1990). Is fear the link between infant disorganized attachment status and maternal unresolved loss? In M. Greenberg, D. Cicchetti, & M. Cummings (Eds.), *Attachment in the preschool years* (pp. 161–182). Chicago: University of Chicago Press.

Mikulecky, L. (1996). Family literacy: Parent and child interactions. In L.A. Benjamin & J. Lord (Eds.), *Family literacy: Directions in research and implications for practice. Summary and papers of a national symposium (Washington, DC, September 7–8, 1995)*. Washington, DC: Department of Education.

Morrison, F. J., Bachman, H. J., & Connor, C. M. (2003). *Improving literacy in America: Lessons from research*. New Haven, CT: Yale University Press.

Morrow, L. M, Rand, M. K., & Smith, J. K. (1995). Reading aloud to children: Characteristics and relationships between teachers and student behaviors. *Reading Research and Instruction, 35*(1), 85–101.

MyTeachingPartner. (2004). MyTeachingPartner: Building language, literacy, and social relationships. University of Virginia, Charlottesville, VA. Available online at www.myteachingpartner.com

NICHD Early Childhood Research Network. (2002). The relation of kindergarten classroom environment to teacher, family, and school characteristics and child outcomes. *Elementary School Journal, 102*(3), 225–238.

Pianta, R. C. (in press). Schools, schooling, and developmental psychopathology. In D. Cicchetti (Ed.), *Handbook of developmental psychopathology* (Vol. 2). New York: Wiley.

Pianta, R. C. (1994). Patterns of relationships between children and kindergarten teachers. *Journal of School Psychology, 32*, 15–32.

Pianta, R. C. (1999). *Enhancing relationships between children and teachers*. Washington, DC: American Psychological Association.

Pianta, R. C. (2003). *Standardized classroom observations from pre-K to 3rd grade: A mechanism for improving classroom quality and practices, consistency of P–3 experiences, and child outcomes* (Working paper). New York: Foundation for Child Development.

Pianta, R. C. (2004). Relationships among children and adults and family literacy. In B. Wasik (Ed.), *Handbook of family literacy* (pp. 175–192). Mahwah, NJ: Erlbaum.

Pianta, R. C, Hamre, B., & Stuhlman, M. (2003). Relationships between teachers and children. In W. Reynolds & G. Miller (Eds.), *Comprehensive handbook of psychology: Vol. 7. Educational psychology* (pp. 199–234). Hoboken, NJ: Wiley.

Pianta, R. C., La Paro, K. M., Payne, C., Cox, M. J., & Bradley, R. (2002). The relation of kindergarten classroom environment to teacher, family, and school characteristics and child outcomes. *Elementary School Journal, 102*(3), 225–238.

Resnick, L. B. (1994). Situated rationalism: Biological and social preparation for learning. In L. Hirschfield & S. Gelman (Eds.), *Mapping the mind: Domain specificity in cognition and culture* (pp. 474–493). Cambridge, UK: Cambridge University Press.

Sameroff, A. J. (1995). General systems theories and psychopathology. In D. Cicchetti & D.J. Cohen (Eds.), *Developmental psychology: Vol. 1. Theory and methods* (pp. 659–695). New York: Wiley.

Sameroff, A. J., & Emde, R. N. (1989). *Relationship disturbances in early childhood: A developmental approach*. New York: Basic Books.

Sander, L. (1975). Infant and caretaking environment: Investigation and conceptualization of adaptive behavior in a system of increasing complexity. In E. J. Anthony (Ed.), *Explorations in child psychiatry* (pp. 129–166). New York: Plenum Press.

Scarborough, H., & Dobrich, W. (1994). On the efficacy of reading to preschoolers. *Developmental Review, 14*, 245–302.

Sénéchal, M., LeFevre, J., Smith-Chant, B. L., & Colton, K. V. (2001). On refining theoretical models of emergent literacy: The role of empirical evidence. *Journal of School Psychology, 39*(5), 439–460.

Snow, C. E., Barnes, W. S., Chandler, J., Goodman, I. F., & Hemphill, L. (1991). *Unfulfilled expectations: Home and school influences on literacy*. Cambridge, MA: Harvard University Press.

Snow, C. E., Burns, M. S., & Griffin, P. (Eds.). (1998). *Preventing reading difficulties in young children*. Washington, DC: National Academy Press.

Snow, C., & Tabors, P. (1996). Intergenerational transfer of literacy. In L. A. Benjamin & J. Lord (Eds.), *Family literacy: Directions in research and implications for practice. Summary and papers of a national symposium (Washington, DC, September 7–8, 1995)*. Washington, DC: Department of Education.

Sparling, J. (2004). Earliest literacy: From birth to age 3. In B. Wasik (Ed.), *Handbook of family literacy* (pp. 45–56). Mahwah, NJ: Erlbaum.

Sroufe, L. A. (1989). Relationships and relationship

disturbances. In A. Sameroff & R. Emde (Eds.), *Relationship disturbances in early childhood* (pp. 97–124). New York: Basic Books.

Sroufe, L. A. (1996). *Emotional development: The organization of emotional life in the early years.* New York: Cambridge University Press.

Storch, S. A., & Whitehurst, G. J. (2001). The role of family and home in the literacy development of children from low-income backgrounds. In P. R. Britto & J. Brooks-Gunn (Eds.), *The role of family literacy environments in promoting young children's emerging literacy skills: New directions for child and adolescent development* (pp. 53–71). New York: Jossey-Bass.

Whitehurst, G. J., Arnold, D. S., Epstein, J. N., Angell, A. L., Smith, M., & Fischel, J. E. (1994). A picture book reading intervention in day care and home for children from low-income families. *Developmental Psychology, 30,* 679–689.

Whitehurst, G. J., & Lonigan, C. J. (1998). Child development and emergent literacy. *Child Development, 69,* 848–872.

Yaden, D. B., Jr., Rowe, D. W., & MacGillivray, L. (1999). *Emergent literacy: A polyphony of perspectives* (CIERA Report #1-005). Ann Arbor, MI: University of Michigan, School of Education.

Zeanah, C. H., Benoit, D., Barton, M., Regan, C., Hirschberg, L., & Lipsitt, L. (1993). Representations of attachment in mothers and their one-year-old infants. *Journal of the American Academy of Child and Adolescent Psychiatry, 32,* 278–286.

Zevenbergen, A. A., & Whitehurst, G. J. (2003). Dialogic reading: A shared picture book reading intervention for preschoolers. In S. A. Stahl, A. Van Kleeck, & E. B. Bauer (Eds.), *On reading books to children: Parents and teachers* (pp. 177–200). Mahwah, NJ: Erlbaum.

12

Environmental Supports for Language Acquisition

ERIKA HOFF

Children learn language by analyzing the speech they hear. The evidence for this assertion consists of the many findings that differences among children in the nature of the speech they hear create differences in their language development. Most obviously, children who hear English acquire English, children who hear Mandarin acquire Mandarin, and so on. Less obviously, but more important for the concerns of educators, children who hear a great deal of English (or any other target language) and whose exposure to their language includes exposure to a rich vocabulary and a wide variety of sentence structures are more advanced in acquiring the vocabulary and grammar of their language than are children who hear less speech or speech that uses a limited vocabulary and narrow range of sentence structures (e.g., Hoff & Naigles, 2002; Huttenlocher, Haight, Bryk, Seltzer, & Lyons, 1991; Huttenlocher, Vasilyeva, Cymerman, & Levine, 2002; Naigles & Hoff-Ginsberg, 1998).

This evidence that variability in environmental support creates variability among children in their language development provides one of the starting points of this chapter. Another starting point is the common observation, also supported by careful empirical study, that the variability among children in language skill is not randomly distributed in the population but varies sys-

tematically as a function of the socioeconomic status (SES) of the children's families. This chapter makes the argument that both individual and SES-related differences in children's language skill at school entry arise, in significant measure, from differences in children's earlier language learning experiences at home.

The outline of this chapter is as follows: First, I present data from a short-term longitudinal study of vocabulary growth in children from two different social strata that demonstrate that individual and SES-related differences in children's vocabulary are related to differences in the amount and nature of the speech they hear. Vocabulary is not all there is to oral language skill, but vocabulary size is a significant predictor of children's success in learning to read (Chall, Jacobs, & Baldwin, 1990; Snow, Burns, & Griffin, 1998). Second, I review the findings of other studies in the literature that corroborate the conclusion that differences among mothers in the way they use language with their young children create differences in the children's vocabulary growth and that these differences in experience systematically advantage children from higher socioeconomic strata. Third, I review the literature on environmental sources of individual and SES-related differences in aspects of language development other than vocabulary that are also related to literacy. Fourth, I consider the implications of the findings I present for optimizing all children's oral language skills and identify important directions for future work.

Environmental Predictors of Individual and SES-Related Differences in Children's Vocabularies

We assessed children's language experience and their vocabulary usage by videotaping conversations between 61 mothers and their 18- to 29-month-old children in their homes. We did this at two time points, 10 weeks apart. All of the talk that occurred was transcribed, and measures of the mothers' speech and the children's vocabulary growth were derived from these transcripts. We videotaped the mother–child interactions in the most naturalistic situations that it was feasible to observe. We taped a morning mealtime, mothers getting the children dressed for the day, and mother–child toy play. Together these settings yielded an average of 40 minutes of interaction.

All the children in the study were white, monolingual, and living with their families in the midwestern United States. All the mothers were native speakers of English, were the primary caregivers for their children, and were not employed outside of the home for more than 15 hours per week. Thirty-one of the children came from high-SES families in which both parents were college educated, and 30 children came from mid-SES families in which both parents were high-school educated. All fathers were employed with the exception of one mid-SES father, who was receiving disability payments. Only one high-SES and four mid-SES mothers were single mothers. None of these children would be considered to be living in poverty or at risk. Thus this sample provided the opportunity to investigate the effects of maternal education on the language environments mothers provide and on children's language development separate from the effects of poverty.

The high-SES group included 16 firstborn children and 17 later-born children. The mid-SES group contained 17 firstborns and 13 later-borns. As a result, the mean birth order of the high-SES children was higher than the mean birth order of the mid-SES children (1.8 and 1.5, respectively). In terms of gender composition, child age, and child mean length of utterance (MLU), the high and mid-SES groups of children were roughly equivalent. The high-SES group included 17 girls and 14 boys; the mid-SES group included 14 girls and 16 boys. For the high-SES children, the mean age was 20.8 months ($SD = 3.1$) and MLU was 1.26 ($SD = 0.12$); for the mid-SES children, the mean age was 21.6 months ($SD = 3.0$) and the mean MLU was 1.28 ($SD = 0.12$). Neither group difference in age or MLU approached significance, p's > .4.

We assessed two types of properties of mothers' language use in interaction with their children: (1) how language was used with respect to the engagement of the mother and child, and (2) the lexical and grammatical richness of the speech addressed to the child. Specifically, the indices of engagement were counts of *the number of utterances the mother produced when she and her child were in joint attention* (that is, focused on the same object or event), *the number of utterances that were topic-continuing replies to the child* (as opposed to unrelated to the child's speech), *the number of utterances intended to direct behavior* (this should be a negative indicator of mutual engagement), and *the number of utterances that were intended to elicit conversation from the child* (this should be a positive indicator of mutual engagement). The indices of the richness of the speech itself were *the number of word tokens produced* (i.e., the total number of words), *the number of word types produced* (i.e., the number of different words), and *the mean length of utterance (MLU)*. The measure of children's vocabulary was *the number of word types produced* in a sample of 90 utterances. These measures are listed in Table 12.1.

Properties of Input Predict Vocabulary Growth

The first findings, based on analyses of the whole sample, were that (1) the mothers varied in the nature of their language use with their children, (2) the 10-week interval between Time 1 and Time 2 was a period of significant vocabulary growth for the children, and (3) the children varied in how much their vocabularies grew during this period. These data are presented in Tables 12.2

TABLE 12.1. Measures of Maternal Speech and Child Vocabulary

Maternal speech measures
(based on full transcripts):

Indices of the data-providing properties of input
  Number of utterances
  Number of tokens (total number of words produced)
  Number of types (number of different words)
  Mean length of utterance (MLU)

Indices of the social-pragmatic features of input
  Number of utterances in joint attention
  Number of topic-continuing replies
  Number of behavior directives
  Number of conversation-eliciting questions

Child vocabulary measure (based on
90 utterances drawn from all three settings):

  Number of types

TABLE 12.3. Child Vocabulary Growth from Time 1 to Time 2

	Mean	Range
Time 1 word types	36.06	16–55
Time 2 word types	48.40	25–87

gagement in conversation were not related to vocabulary growth. These correlations are presented in Table 12.4. The properties of maternal speech that were related to child vocabulary growth were also related to each other, and therefore the predictive relations were not independent of each other. The best single predictor was MLU, which uniquely accounted for a significant 22% of the variance in children's vocabulary growth. This does not mean that the amount of speech and lexical richness were irrelevant, just that the mothers who talked a great deal also used a large vocabulary and also produced longer utterances.

In sum, these analyses of the relation of maternal speech to child vocabulary growth indicate that the process of vocabulary building is, to a significant degree, supported by an environment in which children hear a great deal of lexically rich and syntactically complex speech. It may be surprising to some that more complex speech is better for vocabulary development than simpler speech. This contradicts a once widely held view that mothers help their children acquire language by simplifying the speech children

and 12.3. The next finding is that some, but not all, of the measured properties of maternal speech predicted child vocabulary growth. The indices of the lexical and grammatical richness of maternal speech were significant positive predictors. Mothers who talked more (i.e., produced more word tokens), who used a richer vocabulary (i.e., more word types), and who produced longer utterances had children who grew in their productive vocabulary more than the children of mothers who talked less, used fewer different words, and spoke in shorter utterances. In contrast, the indices of mutual en-

TABLE 12.2. Properties of Maternal speech at Time 1

	Mean	Range
Data-providing properties		
Number of utterances	614	121–1,367
Number of tokens	1,182	311–4,502
Number of types	298	107–620
MLU	3.56	2.85–4.88
Social-pragmatic properties		
Utterances in joint attention[a]	101	17–291
Topic-continuing replies	130	26–284
Behavior directives	120	30–322
Questions	193	31–405

[a]Joint attention was coded only for the toy-play interaction because both the mother's and child's faces were not always visible in the other settings.

TABLE 12.4. Correlations between Measures of Maternal Speech at Time 1 and Child Vocabulary at Time 2

Data-providing features	
Number of utterances	.05
Number of word tokens	.21*
Number of word types	.22*
Mean length of utterance (MLU)	.55***
Social-pragmatic features	
Utterances in joint attention	.02
Topic-continuing replies	.18
Directives	−.05
Conversation-eliciting questions	−.03

Note. Removing variance attributable to the number of word types in child speech at Time 1.
*$p < .05$; ***$p < .001$.

hear. The present findings do not suggest that children should attend academic lectures to be exposed to complex speech. That is, the benefits of complexity that we found occurred within the naturally occurring range of complexity that appears in child-directed speech. The findings do suggest, however, that deliberate efforts to simplify for children are at best not necessary and perhaps not helpful.

Children cannot learn words they do not hear. Thus children who hear only a limited vocabulary will acquire only a limited vocabulary. Also, children appear to benefit from hearing vocabulary in the context of longer, rather than shorter, sentences. This may be because the structure of sentences provides clues to word meaning (Gillette, Gleitman, Gleitman, & Lederer, 1999; Naigles, 1990) or because other words in a sentence may provide clues to reference (e.g., *Can you use your spoon?* vs. *Can you use the spoon that's next to your plate?*). It may also be that longer sentences contain more content about word meaning (e.g., *Bats live in caves* vs. *Bats are animals that live in caves and sleep during the day*). In any case, children seem not to be confused by complex input but to be able to select that which they are ready to use. No doubt much gets wasted, but there is no reason for talk to children to be a scarce commodity.

There were no effects, in these data, of the indices of mutual engagement, although one would not argue from that null finding that mutual engagement in conversation is irrelevant to language development. A review of the literature suggests that mutual engagement may be more important for children under the age of 18 months than it is for older children (Hoff & Naigles, 2002). Together, the previous literature and the present findings suggest that the quality of the social interactions children experience very early in life set the stage for language development, and therefore differences among mothers and children in their skill at establishing mutually engaged social interaction between 9 and 18 months have effects on language development. By the age of nearly 2 years, however, most mothers and children are good at establishing mutual engagement, and thus the differences that matter at this point are in the richness of the language sample illustrated for children.

SES-Related differences in Mothers' Speech and Children's Vocabulary Growth

For the next analyses, we divided the sample of mothers into those with college educations (referred to as high-SES) and those with high school educations (referred to as mid-SES), and we found differences between these two groups of mothers in the properties of the speech they addressed to their children (Hoff-Ginsberg, 1991, 1998). Of particular relevance here is the comparison in terms of those properties that were related to child vocabulary: number of word tokens, number of word types, and MLU. The high-SES mothers used more words, more word types, and longer utterances than the mid-SES mothers. When the confounding effects of other variables were removed these differences were statistically significant.[1] These data are presented in Figures 12.1, 12.2, and 12.3. SES was also related to the children's vocabulary development, accounting for a statistically significant 5% of the variance in children's vocabulary size after other factors were removed.[2] The child vocabulary data are presented in Figure 12.4.

Mothers' Speech Is the Source of SES-Related Differences in Children's Vocabulary Growth

The finding that SES is related to the size of children's productive vocabularies raises the question of how SES exerts this influence. Socioeconomic status cannot directly affect the number of words a child knows. There must be some variable that mediates the relation, and the foregoing evidence of effects of

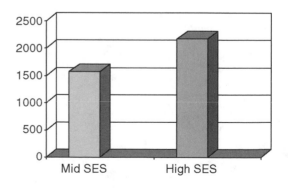

FIGURE 12.1. SES-related differences in word tokens in maternal speech at Time 1.

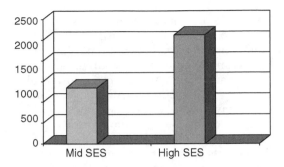

FIGURE 12.2. SES-related differences in word types in maternal speech at Time 1.

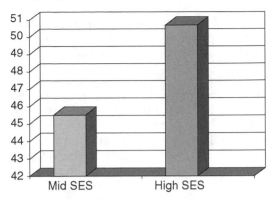

FIGURE 12.4. SES-related differences in children's productive vocabularies at Time 2.

maternal speech on child vocabulary and of SES-related differences in maternal speech suggest that maternal speech is that variable. The data suggest that the relation between SES and child vocabulary growth occurs because SES affects maternal speech and maternal speech, in turn, affects child vocabulary growth. This hypothesis is depicted in Figure 12.5.

The way in which one tests such a hypothesis is to statistically remove all the variance among the children that can be explained in terms of maternal speech and then ask whether any of the remaining variance is due to SES. If not, the SES difference must be the result of the effects of maternal speech on child vocabulary. When we conducted this analysis, we found that the mediation hypothesis was fully supported. SES, which accounted for 5% of the variance in child vocabulary when maternal speech was not considered, accounted for a nonsignificant 1% of the variance when the effects of ma-

ternal speech were removed. There is an important point in these results, which bears reiterating. The predictive properties of maternal speech identified in the present study accounted for 25% of the variance in child vocabulary and left 75% of the variance unexplained. Thus it is clear in these data that other factors besides maternal speech influence vocabulary development. But these other factors, whatever they turn out to be, are not part of the explanation for why the high-SES children in this study had larger vocabularies than the mid-SES children. Language experience is the full explanation.

Cautions in Interpreting These Findings

It is important to note that the conclusion that maternal speech fully explains the SES-related differences in children's productive vocabularies may not be generalizable outside the range of SES represented in the present sample. The participants in this study represented only a portion of the range of socioeconomic strata—a portion at the high

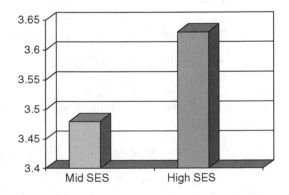

FIGURE 12.3. SES-related differences in the MLU of maternal speech at Time 1.

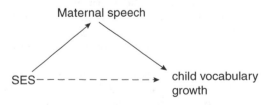

FIGURE 12.5. The hypothesized relations among SES, maternal speech, and child vocabulary growth: Maternal speech mediates the SES–child vocabulary growth relation.

end. In the population as a whole, the effect of SES is probably greater than in the present sample and mediated by other factors in addition to language experience. These cautions notwithstanding, the present findings argue that one of the reasons that children enter school with different oral language skills and one of the reasons that these language skills vary systematically as a function of family SES has to do with the language experiences children are provided at home.

Corroborating Evidence of Links Among SES, Experience, and Vocabulary Development

A substantial body of literature is consistent with the foregoing results and provides support for the conclusion that individual and SES-related differences in children's early vocabulary development reflect the influence of their differing language experiences. Other studies have similarly found that language experience predicts vocabulary development. In a middle-class sample, Huttenlocher et al. (1991) found that individual differences among mothers in the amount they spoke to their children predicted the children's growth in vocabulary. They also found that the frequency with which individual words appeared in input predicted the age of acquisition of those words. Clearly, vocabulary learning benefits from more input. In a low-income sample, Weizman and Snow (2001) found that mothers' use of rare words and the information mothers provided about word meaning when they produced new words predicted their children's vocabulary development. Both the Huttenlocher et al. (1991) and Weizman and Snow (2001) findings appeared within samples that were homogeneous with respect to SES.

Other findings in the literature also corroborate the present findings that when SES varies, so do maternal speech and child vocabulary development. Differences in language use are among the most reliably found SES-related differences in parent–child interaction (Hoff, Laursen, & Tardif, 2002). Findings particularly relevant to understanding children's vocabulary development are that higher SES mothers talk more, use a richer vocabulary, and provide more information about objects being labeled than lower SES mothers do (Hart & Risley, 1995; Lawrence & Shipley, 1996). And there is abundant evidence that children from higher SES families build their vocabularies at a faster rate than children from lower SES families (Hoff, 2004b). SES-related differences have been found when vocabulary is assessed on the basis of spontaneous speech samples (Hart & Risley, 1995) and in children's responses to examiner prompts (Wachs, Uzgiris, & Hunt, 1971) and have been measured by the MacArthur Communicative Development Inventory (Arriaga, Fenson, Cronan, & Pethick, 1998).

Environmental Support for Other Aspects of Oral Language Skill Related to Literacy

Evidence in the literature suggests that oral language skills other than vocabulary are also related to literacy and that early language experience influences the development of these aspects of language as well. The strongest oral language predictors of success in learning to read are skills in phonological processing—particularly phonological awareness, which is the ability to attend to the sound structure within spoken words (see, for example, Rayner, Foorman, Perfetti, Pesetsky, & Seidenberg, 2001; Snow et al., 1998; Wagner et al., 1997). Reading skill is also predicted by grammatical development, as measured by tests of children's ability to understand complex syntactic and morphological forms (Snow et al., 1998). Lastly, learning to read is easier for children if they are familiar with the way language is used in writing. Written language is stylistically different from spoken language; it is more formal than spoken language typically is (Ravid & Tolchinsky, 2002), and it is decontextualized (Snow, 1983; Watson, 2001). That is, there is no support for meaning interpretation from the nonlinguistic context, as there often is in face-to-face conversation.

The development of all of these aspects of oral language skill is related to the availability of environmental support. Children initially build their representations of the sounds of language on the basis of the speech they hear—as evidenced by findings that children exposed to different languages develop different phonological systems (Kuhl

& Meltzoff, 1997; Werker & Polka, 1993; Werker & Tees, 1984). The development of phonological awareness may be specifically supported by activities that manipulate language sounds, such as the rhymes in children's poetry and song. Among 3-year-old children, those who know more nursery rhymes also show higher levels of phonological awareness, even controlling for SES and IQ (MacLean, Bryant, & Bradley, 1987).

More rapid development of grammatical skill is associated with circumstances that lead to more one-to-one contact with adults, including attending a child-care center with a high teacher–child ratio and being the first-born child (NICHD Early Child Care Network, 2000; McCartney, 1984). Children whose mothers frequently ask questions and produce partial repetitions or expansions of their child's speech show more rapid syntactic development than children whose mothers produce speech in which these utterance types are less frequent (Hoff-Ginsberg, 1986; Nelson, Denninger, Bonvillian, Kaplan, & Baker, 1984; and see reviews in Hoff-Ginsberg & Shatz, 1982; Richards, 1994). Children who hear more complex structures in their mothers' speech both produce and understand more complex structures than children who hear fewer complex structures in their mothers' speech (Huttenlocher et al., 2002).

Children's experiences with book reading produce familiarity with the style of language use that characterizes written language. Children who are read to frequently thus have an advantage in this regard. In addition, some children's home language experience will make them more familiar with the "standard" or mainstream variety of language that tends to be used in writing than will other children's home language experience.

Many of these properties of language experience that shape phonological, grammatical, and stylistic aspects of language development vary as a function of SES. Higher SES children hear more speech than lower SES children. Also, higher SES mothers ask more questions, produce more partial self-repetitions and expansions, and expand their children's utterances more than lower SES mothers (Hoff-Ginsberg, 1986). Higher SES children also experience more joint book reading with an adult than do lower SES

children (U.S. Department of Education, 1998).

Not surprisingly, then, many aspects of language development show SES-related differences. Early phonological development seems least affected by SES (Dollaghan et al., 1999; Oller, Eilers, Basinger, Steffens, & Urbano, 1995), but by the time of school entry there are SES-related differences in reading readiness, and phonological skills are a large component of reading readiness (Snow et al., 1998). In the domain of grammatical development, children from higher social strata differ from children from lower social strata in producing shorter responses to adult speech (McCarthy, 1930), in scoring lower on standardized tests that include measures of grammatical development (Dollaghan et al., 1999; Morrisset, Barnard, Greenberg, Booth, & Spieker, 1990), and in producing less complex utterances in spontaneous speech as toddlers (Arriaga et al., 1998) and at ages 5 and 6 years (Snow, 1999; Huttenlocher et al., 2002).

There are also SES-related differences in what can be termed stylistic aspects of language use. Lower SES children have been described as differing from higher SES children in how they respond to questions and how they recount past events, for example (Heath, 1983; Michaels, 1981), and such stylistic differences may affect the acquisition of literacy. At various times and in various quarters it has been argued that the lower levels of literacy and school achievement of lower SES children compared with higher SES children is attributable, at least in part, to their lack of familiarity with the style of language use in school, although not everyone agrees with that contention (Ravid & Tochinsky, 2002).

The existence of SES-related differences in style of language use raises another knotty problem: All of the literature that uses spontaneous speech as a basis for assessing language development makes the implicit assumption that language use reflects language knowledge. Of course, this is not completely true. Language use reflects influences of the setting and conversational partner—as evidenced by the fact that the same speaker uses language differently depending on setting and conversational partner (Giles & Coupland, 1991; Pittam, 1994). This is true for both adults and children (Hoff, 2004a).

The concern in studying SES-related differences in language development is that consistent stylistic differences associated with SES produce differences in the complexity of language use in production that do not reflect differences in language knowledge. On the other hand, some of the studies that have found SES-related differences in language have used measures of language comprehension (Huttenlocher et al., 2002), suggesting that real differences do exist. And it would be surprising, given the literature just reviewed, if stylistic differences in maternal speech did not create differences in language knowledge in their children. Nonetheless, it is worth remembering that the language children produce is a function of many factors, and linguistic knowledge is only one of those factors.

Implications and Future Directions

This caveat notwithstanding, the foregoing evidence argues that in order to develop the oral language skills that provide the foundation for the acquisition of literacy, children require a supportive language-learning environment. The evidence further argues that when children differ in this aspect of preparedness for literacy, those differences arise to a significant degree from differences in the environments they have experienced. This evidence, which locates the source of SES-related differences in children's oral language skill in their differing language experiences, has an important implication: Enriching children's language experience should have beneficial effects on language development, even when other SES-related differences in children's environments remain unaddressed.

Questions for future research raised by these findings and by the concern to optimize all children's literacy preparedness revolve around how best to provide the experiences that support the foundational oral language skills. One question concerns the best target for intervention. Should intervention be aimed at phonological, lexical, syntactic, or stylistic aspects of language? Current intervention programs with dyslexic children target the phonological skill deficits that appear to be at the core of dyslexia (McCardle, Scarborough, & Catts, 2001; Rayner et al., 2001). However, there may be many children

with normal phonological processing skills who have problems in the acquisition of literacy that reflect more general inadequacies in language skills as a result of inadequate language experience. This possibility is suggested by the findings that among children with low language skills, phonological sensitivity predicts literacy less well than it does in children with normal language skills (Dickinson, McCabe, Anastasopoulos, Peisner-Feinberg, & Poe, 2003) and that among all but the lowest reading group vocabulary is the best predictor of reading, but that among the lowest 20% of readers in the fourth grade, phonological measures are the best predictors (Torgesen, Wagner, Rashotte, Burgess, & Hecht, 1997). Thus the appropriate target of intervention may be different for different children, and it may be important to identify and target children's specific areas of deficiency.

Another factor complicating the question of the best target of intervention concerns the interdependencies in development of the several domains of oral language competency. Phonological awareness, for example, is related not just to measures of articulation (Rvachew, Ohberg, Grawburg, & Heyding, 2003) but also to semantic and syntactic measures of oral language (Chaney, 1992), and there are arguments that both phonological and syntactic development depend on vocabulary development (Walley, 1993; Bates & Goodman, 1999). We need to know a great deal more about the basic processes of language development in order to make informed decisions about how best to support it.

A second sort of question concerns the best route for intervention (e.g.., through families, through programs outside the home) and the best form for such programs to take. The argument was made earlier that the specificity of the relation between properties of the environment and language development suggests that it should be possible to help the language and literacy development of disadvantaged children without solving all the societal problems that lead to disadvantage. Another aspect of the data, however, suggests that ultimately the best solution *is* in remedying societal inequality. The component of SES that predicted children's language experience was maternal education, and the differences in child-directed speech appeared to reflect not isolated parenting behaviors but more general differences in the mothers' habitual style of language use (Hoff, 2002; Hoff-Ginsberg, 1986). Thus the data suggest that, in the long run, the route to changing children's language experience at home is through providing higher levels of education to those who will become parents.

Notes

1. Because birth order was also related to maternal input and to child vocabulary growth and because the mid- and high-SES groups were not perfectly matched in birth order, effects of birth order were removed from these analyses.
2. See above.

References

Arriaga, R. J., Fenson. L., Cronan, T., & Pethick, S. J. (1998). Scores on the MacArthur Communicative Development Inventory of children from low- and middle-income families. *Applied Psycholinguistics, 19,* 209–223.

Bates, E., & Goodman, J. (1999). On the emergence of grammar from the lexicon. In B. MacWhinney (Ed.), *The emergence of language* (pp. 29–80). Mahwah, NJ: Erlbaum.

Chall, J. S., Jacobs, V. A., & Baldwin, L. E. (1990). *The reading crisis: Why poor children fall behind.* Cambridge, MA: Harvard University Press.

Chaney, C. (1992). Language development, metalinguistic skills, and print awareness in 3-year-old children. *Applied Psycholinguistics, 13*(4), 485–514.

Dickinson, D. K., McCabe, A., Anastasopoulos, L., Peisner-Feinberg, E. S., & Poe, M. D. (2003). The comprehensive language approach to early literacy: The interrelationsips among vocabulary, phonological sensitivity, and print knowledge among preschool-aged children. *Journal of Educational Psychology, 95,* 465–481.

Dollaghan, C. A., Campbell, T. F., Paradise, J. L., Feldman, H. H., Janosky, J. E., & Pitcairn, D. N. (1999). Maternal education and measures of early speech and language. *Journal of Speech, Language, and Hearing Research, 42,* 1432–1443.

Giles, H., & Coupland, N. (1991). *Language: Contexts and consequences.* Pacific Grove, CA: Brooks/Cole.

Gillette, J., Gleitman, H., Gleitman, L., & Lederer, A. (1999). Human simulations of vocabulary learning. *Cognition, 73,* 135–176.

Hart, B., & Risley, T.R. (1995*). Meaningful differ-*

ences in the everyday experience of young American children. Baltimore: Brookes.

Heath, S. E. (1983). *Ways with words.* Cambridge UK: Cambridge University Press.

Hoff, E. (2002). Causes and consequences of SES-related differences in parent-to-child speech. In M. H. Bornstein & R. H. Bradley (Eds.), *Socioeconomic status, parenting, and child development* (pp. 231–252). Mahwah, NJ: Erlbaum.

Hoff, E. (2004a, July). *Language use does not always reflect language knowledge.* Poster presented at the biennial meeting of the International Society for Research in Behavioural Development, Ghent, Belgium.

Hoff, E. (2004b). Poverty effects. In R.D. Kent (Ed.), *MIT encyclopedia of communication disorders* (pp. 369–371). Cambridge, MA: MIT Press.

Hoff, E., Laursen, B., & Tardif, T. (2002). Socioeconomic status and parenting. In M. H. Bornstein (Ed.) *Handbook of parenting* (2nd ed., pp. 231–252). Mahwah, NJ: Erlbaum.

Hoff, E., & Naigles, L. (2002). How children use input in acquiring a lexicon. *Child Development, 73,* 418–433.

Hoff-Ginsberg, E. (1986). Function and structure in maternal speech: Their relation to the child's development of syntax. *Developmental Psychology, 22,* 155–163.

Hoff-Ginsberg, E. (1991). Mother–child conversation in different social classes and communicative settings. *Child Development, 62,* 782–796.

Hoff-Ginsberg, E. (1998). The relation of birth order and socioeconomic status to children's language experience and language development. *Applied Psycholinguistics, 19,* 603–629.

Hoff-Ginsberg, E., & Shatz, M. (1982). Linguistic input and the child's acquisition of language. *Psychological Bulletin, 92,* 3–26.

Huttenlocher, J., Haight, W., Bryk, A., Seltzer, M., & Lyons, T. (1991). Early vocabulary growth: Relation to language input and gender. *Developmental Psychology, 27,* 236–248.

Huttenlocher, J., Vasilyeva, M., Cymerman, E., & Levine, S. (2002). Language input at home and at school: Relation to child syntax. *Cognitive Psychology, 45,* 337–374.

Kuhl, P. K., & Meltzoff, A. N. (1997). Evolution, nativism and learning in the development of language and speech. In M. Gopnik (Ed.), *The inheritance and innateness of grammars* (pp. 7–44). New York: Oxford University Press.

Lawrence, V., & Shipley, E. F. (1996). Parental speech to middle and working class children from two racial groups in three settings. *Applied Psycholinguistics, 17,* 233–256.

MacLean, M., Bryant, P. E., & Bradley, L. (1987). Rhymes, nursery rhymes and reading in early childhood. *Merrill-Palmer Quarterly, 33,* 255–282.

McCardle, P., Scarborough, H. S., & Catts, H. W.

(2001). Predicting, explaining, and preventing children's reading difficulties. *Learning Disabilities Research and Practice, 16,* 230–239.

McCarthy, D. (1930). *The language development of the preschool child.* Minneapolis: University of Minnesota Press.

McCartney, K. (1984). Effect of quality of day care environment on children's language development. *Developmental Psychology, 20,* 244–260.

Michaels, S. (1981). "Sharing time": Children's narrative styles and differential access to literacy. *Language in Society, 10,* 423–442.

Morrisset, D., Barnard, K., Greenberg, M., Booth, C., & Spieker, S. (1990). Environmental influences on early language development: The context of social risk. *Development and Psychopathology, 2,* 127–149.

Naigles, L. (1990). Children use syntax to learn verb meanings. *Journal of Child Language, 17,* 357–374.

Naigles, L., & Hoff-Ginsberg, E. (1998). Why are some verbs learned before other verbs? Effects of input frequency and structure on children's early verb use. *Journal of Child Language, 25,* 95–120.

National Institute of Child Health and Human Development Early Child Care Research Network. (2000). The relation of child care to cognitive and language development. *Child Development, 71,* 960–980.

Nelson, K. E., Denninger, M. M., Bonvillian, J. D., Kaplan, B. J., & Baker, N. D. (1984) Maternal input adjustments and nonadjustments as related to children's linguistic advances and to language acquisition theories. In A. D. Pellegrini & T. D. Yawkey (Eds.), *The development of oral and written languages: Readings in developmental and applied linguistics* (pp. 31–56). New York: Ablex.

Oller, D. K., Eilers, R. E., Basinger, D., Steffens, M. L., & Urbano, R. (1995). Extreme poverty and the development of precursors to the speech capacity. *First Language, 15,* 167–189.

Pittam, J. (1994). *Voice in social interaction.* Thousand Oaks, CA: Sage.

Ravid, D., & Tolchinsky, L. (2002). Developing linguistic literacy: A comprehensive model. *Journal of Child Language, 29,* 417–447.

Rayner, K., Foorman, B. R., Perfetti, C. A., Pesetsky, D., & Seidenberg, M. S. (2001). How psychological science informs the teaching of reading. *Psychological Science in the Public Interest, 2* (2).

Richards, B. J. (1994). Child directed speech and influences on language acquisition: Methodology and interpretation. In C. Gallaway & B. J. Richards (Eds.), *Input and interaction in language acquisition* (pp. 74–106). Cambridge, UK: Cambridge University Press.

Rvachew, S., Ohberg, A., Grawburg, M., & Heyding, J. (2003). Phonological awareness and phonemic perception in 4-year-old children with delayed expressive phonology skills. *American Journal of Speech-Language Pathology, 12,* 463–471.

Snow, C. E. (1983). Literacy and language: Relationships during the preschool years. *Harvard Educational Review, 53,* 165–189.

Snow, C. E. (1999). Social perspectives on the emergence of language. In B. MacWhinney (Ed.), *The emergence of language* (pp. 257–276). Mahwah, NJ: Erlbaum.

Snow, C. E., Burns, M. S., & Griffin, P. (Eds.). (1998). *Preventing reading difficulties in young children.* Washington, DC: National Academy Press.

Torgesen, J. K., Wagner, R. K., Rashotte, C. A., Burgess, S., & Hecht, S. (1997). Contributions of phonological awareness and rapid automatic naming ability to the growth of word-reading skills in second- to fifth-grade children. *Scientific Studies of Reading, 1,* 161–185.

U.S. Department of Education. (1999). *National Center for Education Statistics, 1999 National Household Education Survey.* Federal Interagency Forum on Child and Family Statistics, Table ED1. Available at aspe.hhs.gov

Wachs, T., Uzgiris, I., & Hunt, J. (1971). Cognitive development in infants of different age levels and from different environmental backgrounds: An explanatory investigation. *Merrill-Palmer Quarterly, 17,* 283–317.

Wagner, R. K., Torgesen, J. K., Rashotte, C.A., Hecht, S. A., Barker, T. A., Burgess, S. R., et al. (1997). Changing relations between phonological processing abilities and word-level reading as children develop from beginning to skilled readers: A 5-year longitudinal study. *Developmental Psychology, 33,* 468–479.

Walley, A. C. (1993). The role of vocabulary development in children's spoken word recognition and segmentation ability. *Developmental Review, 13,* 286–350.

Watson, R. (2001). Literacy and oral language: Implications for early literacy acquisition. In S. B. Neuman & D. K. Dickinson (Eds.), *Handbook of early literacy research* (pp. 43–53). New York: Guilford Press.

Weizman, Z. O., & Snow, C. E. (2001). Lexical input as related to children's vocabulary acquisition: Effects of sophisticated exposure and support for meaning. *Developmental Psychology, 37,* 265–279.

Werker, J. F., & Polka, L. (1993). Developmental changes in speech perception: New challenges and new directions. *Journal of Phonetics, 21,* 83–101.

Werker, J. F., & Tees, R. C. (1984). Cross-language speech perception: Evidence for perceptual reorganization during the first year of life. *Infant Behavior and Development, 7,* 49–63.

13

The Misunderstood Giant: On the Predictive Role of Early Vocabulary to Future Reading

MONIQUE SÉNÉCHAL
GENE OUELLETTE
DONNA RODNEY

Shared book reading is the best way that parents can prepare their children to learn to read (Anderson, Heibert, Scott, & Wilkerson, 1985). In the last 20 years, parents of young children have received this message from many sources. Public-awareness campaigns highlight the value of shared reading in posters and other forms of publicity; family-literacy practitioners promote book reading with low-literacy families; and kindergarten teachers send books home to encourage parents to read to their children. Given these strong encouragements, one would think that there would be robust evidence showing that reading books to young children is beneficial to reading acquisition. Recent evidence, however, suggests that shared reading enhances young children's language, not their early literacy skills (Jordan, Snow, & Porche, 2000; Sénéchal & LeFevre, 2002). Although the lack of a direct impact on early literacy might be surprising and disappointing, the positive effect on language should be very encouraging. Indeed, the positive effect of shared reading on early language development warrants a closer inspection of the relation between early differences in language skills and reading.

Most of the research on the benefits of shared reading has focused on the acquisition of oral vocabulary. Intervention studies clearly show that young children can learn new words from listening to adults read books to them (e.g., Hargrave & Sénéchal, 2000; Jordan et al., 2000; Lonigan & Whitehurst, 1998; Sénéchal, 1997; Whitehurst et al., 1988). Hence, shared book reading during the preschool years can be a source of learning vocabulary, which, in time, may facilitate reading.

In this chapter, we examine the predictive role of early individual differences in oral vocabulary in three types of child behaviors: phonological awareness, listening comprehension, and reading comprehension. Findings from longitudinal studies were reanalyzed to test the contribution of vocabulary knowledge measured in kindergarten to concurrent phonological awareness and listening comprehension, as well as to test the growth in these skills after 1 year. The role of kindergarten vocabulary in reading was also assessed after 1, 3, and 4 years of instruction.

Vocabulary and Phonological Awareness

Intervention studies have shown that improving children's phonological awareness has a direct impact on the development of reading skills (Bus & van IJzendoorn, 1999; Ehri et al., 2001). Presumably, children who can manipulate speech sounds more easily find it easier to understand how letters map onto speech sounds. Given these findings, researchers have been studying the development of early individual differences in phonological awareness (e.g., Lonigan, Burgess, & Anthony, 2000; Lonigan, Burgess, Anthony, & Barker, 1998; McBride-Chang, Wagner, & Chang, 1997; Thomas & Sénéchal, 2004). Although most of the attention has focused on the interplay between early literacy skills and phonological awareness, this research also shows a positive association between children's vocabulary and phonological awareness.

The positive association between vocabulary and phonological awareness has led researchers to posit that vocabulary growth during the preschool period results in a reorganization of how words are stored in memory, which, in time, will facilitate phonological awareness (Goswami, 2001; Metsala, 1999; Walley, Metsala, & Garlock, 2003). Specifically, they argue that words are initially represented as wholes but will become represented as segments of words (e.g., phonemes) as the number of words learned increases. Presumably, children who know more words will have richer and stronger representations of the constituent parts of words, and these richly represented segments will facilitate growth in phonological awareness. Therefore, a possible effect of vocabulary on future success in reading might be through its role in the development of phonological awareness. If that were the case, one would expect early vocabulary knowledge to predict children's phonological awareness concurrently and longitudinally after controlling for children's early literacy skills.

To test this possibility, archival data from Sénéchal and LeFevre (2002) were reanalyzed. Sénéchal and LeFevre (2002) reported the last phase of a longitudinal study examining the role of home literacy experiences on the acquisition of reading (see also Sénéchal, LeFevre, Thomas, & Daley, 1998). In this chapter, we analyzed these archival findings in a novel way to test whether children's vocabulary measured in kindergarten predicted children's phonological awareness

measured in kindergarten and in grade 1. This data set allowed more stringent tests of the predicted positive relation than have been reported (see the meta-analyses of Scarborough, 1998, 2001) because we controlled for a variety of variables that may account for the predicted relation.

The Sample

Two cohorts of children were tested at the beginning of kindergarten and grade 1. The children were English speaking and came mostly from middle-class homes. In the following analyses, a subset of the sample of children in Sénéchal and LeFevre's (2002) study was selected based on their kindergarten performance on a word-decoding task. Only the children who could read two or fewer words were included because of the known influence of reading skills on the development of phonological awareness. Most (67%) of the 84 children included could not read any words at all.

The Measures

At the beginning of kindergarten and grade 1, children completed language, phonological awareness, and early literacy tasks. The language measures included tests of receptive vocabulary and listening comprehension. For the vocabulary test, children were to select the picture that corresponded to a named item from an array of four pictures (Peabody Picture Vocabulary Test—Revised; Dunn & Dunn, 1981). The measure of listening comprehension required that children listen to 30 short stories that varied in length from a single sentence to five sentences. After each story, children were asked a question to assess their comprehension, either factual or inferential. Children answered by selecting a picture from an array of three pictures (the Listening to Stories subtest of the Stanford Early School Achievement Test; Psychological Corporation, 1989).

Children also completed a measure of phonological awareness in which they were to match words based on onsets or rimes (the Sound Categorization subtest of the Stanford Early School Achievement Test; Psychological Corporation, 1989). In this test, children were shown arrays of four pictures. For each array, the experimenter labeled each picture and then required children to choose from among the last three pictures, the item that either started with the same sound (i.e., onsets), or ended with the same rime as the first picture. For example, children were asked to select the picture that started with the same sound as *moth* from an array of pictures that included *hammer*, *thimble*, and *milk* or that ended with the same rime as *moon* from an array of pictures that included *stool*, *spoon*, and *pot*. (Sénéchal et al., 1998, p. 103)

The early literacy items measured knowledge of 15 letter names, decoding of 5 simple consonant–vowel–consonant words (e.g., *dog, hit*), and attempts at spelling 10 words. The spelling task, often called *invented spelling*, assessed children's attempts at capturing the phonological structure of words, albeit in unconventional ways (Mann, Tobin, & Wilson, 1987).

In addition to these measures, child and parent control variables were entered in the analyses when they were correlated with listening comprehension and vocabulary. The control variables included child cohort level (i.e., children tested in Year 1 or 2 of the study) and child analytic intelligence, measured with the Animal House subtest of the Weschler Preschool and Primary Scale of Intelligence—Revised (Weschler, 1989). Parent education and literacy levels were also assessed. Parent literacy levels were measured indirectly by assessing their knowledge of popular authors (Stanovich & West, 1989). The assumption underlying this measure is that parents who know more about popular adult fiction read frequently.

The Findings

Fixed-order hierarchical regression analyses were conducted because these analyses controlled for a series of other predictor variables before testing the contribution of vocabulary to phonological awareness. As indicated in Table 13.1, the regression for phonological awareness in kindergarten revealed that oral vocabulary explained 4% of unique variance in children's phonological awareness after controlling for parent literacy and child cohort level, as well as child early literacy. In this equation, children's alphabet knowledge and invented spelling were also statistically significant predictors of phonological awareness.

The next regression analysis predicted growth in phonological awareness from the beginning of kindergarten to the beginning of grade 1. In this analysis, relative growth was tested because phonological awareness in kindergarten was entered in the equation before the other kindergarten variables. This analysis showed that children's vocabulary explained a statistically significant 4% of variance in phonological awareness after controlling for parent literacy, child cohort level, and child alphabet knowledge, invented spelling, and listening comprehension in kindergarten. It is worth noting that alphabet knowledge was the only other kindergarten measure that was a statistically

TABLE 13.1 Hierarchical Regression Analyses Predicting Phonological Awareness in Nonreaders

Criterion Order	R^2	ΔR^2	ΔF	p
Phonological awareness in kindergarten ($n = 84$)				
Parent literacy and kindergarten cohort	.09	.09	4.30	.02
Alphabet knowledge in kindergarten	.33	.23	27.95	.00
Invented spelling in kindergarten	.36	.03	3.83	.05
Listening comprehension in kindergarten	.39	.03	3.79	.06
Vocabulary in kindergarten	.43	.04	5.65	.02
Phonological awareness in grade 1 ($n = 79$)				
Phonological awareness in kindergarten	.38	.38	46.95	.00
Alphabet knowledge in kindergarten	.43	.04	5.67	.02
Invented spelling in kindergarten	.43	.01	0.82	.37
Listening comprehension in kindergarten	.45	.01	1.96	.17
Vocabulary in kindergarten	.49	.04	5.54	.02

significant longitudinal predictor of phonological awareness.

The regression analyses provided rigorous
tests of the predictive role of oral vocabulary
knowledge to phonological awareness. The
obtained results extend previous findings
(Lonigan et al., 1998; McBride-Chang et al.,
1997; Thomas & Sénéchal, 2004; but cf.
Garlock, Walley, & Metsala, 2001) and are
consistent with theoretical claims about the
role of vocabulary in the development of
phonological awareness (e.g., Walley et al.,
2003). Moreover, the longitudinal results
showed that children who know more words
make greater gains in phonological awareness over 1 year as compared with children
who know fewer words.

Vocabulary and Listening Comprehension

Vocabulary might contribute to future success in reading because it provides the building blocks for the higher order thinking skills
necessary to comprehend texts. Children
who know more words and whose knowledge, consequently, is more complex in its
organization may find it easier to make inferences and to integrate story information into
a coherent whole. If that were the case, one
would expect early vocabulary knowledge to
predict children's listening comprehension
concurrently and longitudinally.

To test this possibility, archival data
from Sénéchal and LeFevre (2002) were
reanalyzed, as was done in the previous

section. In the following analyses, all kindergarten children were included, as it was
not necessary to control for word reading.
Hierarchical fixed-order regressions were
conducted to test whether vocabulary
would predict children's listening comprehension after controlling for a series of
variables. In the analyses, the measure for
children's early literacy consisted of factor
scores obtained from a factor analysis of
three variables: alphabet knowledge, decoding, and invented spelling.

The results are reported in Table 13.2. The
regression for listening comprehension in
kindergarten revealed that vocabulary explained 7% of unique variance in children's
listening comprehension after controlling for
parent literacy and child cohort level, as
well as child early literacy and phonological
awareness. In this equation, children's early
literacy and phonological awareness were
significant predictors of listening comprehension. A somewhat different pattern of results was obtained for the analysis predicting
growth in listening comprehension from the
beginning of kindergarten to the beginning
of grade 1. In this analysis, growth was
tested because listening comprehension in
kindergarten was entered in the equation before the other kindergarten variables. In this
analysis, children's vocabulary measured in
kindergarten explained a statistically significant 8% of variance in listening comprehension in grade 1 after controlling for parent
education and literacy, child cohort level,
child listening comprehension in kindergarten, and early literacy and phonological

TABLE 13.2. Hierarchical Regression Analyses Predicting Listening Comprehension

Criterion Order	R^2	ΔR^2	ΔF	p
Listening comprehension in kindergarten ($n = 103$)				
Parent literacy and kindergarten cohort	.17	.17	10.36	.00
Early literacy in kindergarten	.25	.08	10.45	.00
Phonological awareness in kindergarten	.29	.04	5.34	.02
Vocabulary in kindergarten	.35	.07	9.93	.00
Listening comprehension in grade 1 ($n = 95$)				
Parent education and literacy, kindergarten cohort	.10	.10	3.38	.02
Listening comprehension in kindergarten	.22	.12	13.63	.00
Early literacy in kindergarten	.22	.00	0.24	.62
Phonological awareness in kindergarten	.23	.01	1.14	.29
Vocabulary in kindergarten	.31	.08	10.20	.00

awareness in kindergarten. It is noteworthy that early literacy and phoneme awareness were not longitudinal predictors of listening comprehension.

The regression analyses provided conservative tests of the predictive role of vocabulary knowledge to listening comprehension. These results are consistent with the notion that early individual differences in lexical knowledge contribute to the development of listening comprehension. The analyses so far show that early individual differences in oral vocabulary are concurrently and longitudinally related to skills known to influence skilled reading and its acquisition. Through its relation with phonological awareness and listening comprehension, oral vocabulary makes—at the very least—an indirect contribution to skilled reading and its acquisition. Moreover, the findings from the concurrent analyses highlight the interrelations among early language, phonological, and literacy skills (Bowey, 1994; Chaney, 1998; Dickinson, Anastasopoulos, McCabe, Peisner-Feinberg, & Poe, 2003; Sénéchal, LeFevre, Smith-Chant, & Colton, 2001).

Vocabulary and Reading Comprehension

The ultimate goal of reading instruction is to ensure that children understand the texts that they read fluently. Text comprehension can be viewed as a complex process that involves fluent word recognition, as well as the activation of semantic and syntactic knowledge, making inferences, and integrating parts into a coherent whole (Lorch & van den Broek, 1997). Given this view of reading comprehension, children's vocabulary is one component of oral language that is necessary to reading comprehension (Perfetti, Marron, & Foltz, 1996). After all, a reader must understand words in order to comprehend text. Intervention studies with children in the elementary grades show that vocabulary instruction increases word knowledge (Biemiller, 1999). Most important, vocabulary instruction increases reading comprehension for texts containing the instructed words (Stahl & Fairbanks, 1986). The goal here, however, was to examine the predictive role of early differences in vocabulary to future reading comprehension.

There are few empirical studies that were especially designed to examine the association between oral vocabulary in kindergarten and future reading comprehension in the primary grades. More often, oral vocabulary measures are included as control variables in multivariate studies of early reading (e.g., Wagner et al., 1997). Nonetheless, the association between oral vocabulary and reading comprehension can be examined through reported zero-order correlations. Scarborough (1998, 2001) reported a median correlation coefficient of .38 between kindergarten vocabulary and reading achievement in her comprehensive review of 20 studies. Three examples of such studies are presented next.

In their longitudinal study, Roth, Speece, and Cooper (2002) reported a moderate correlation between performance on vocabulary tasks in kindergarten and subsequent reading comprehension in grade 1 ($r = .38$ and .53 for receptive vocabulary and oral definitions, respectively) and grade 2 ($r = .41$ and .70 for receptive vocabulary and oral definitions, respectively). Likewise, Share, Jorm, MacLean, and Matthews (1984), as well as Snow, Tabors, Nicholson, and Kurland (1995), reported a moderate correlation between performance on an oral definitions task in kindergarten and a standardized reading assessment that included comprehension tests in grade 1 ($r = .41$ and .44 for Share et al. and Snow et al., respectively). Taken together, these studies suggest that oral vocabulary development prior to formal literacy acquisition may be a significant predictor of future reading. These studies, however, did not include stringent tests of the relation between vocabulary and reading. Hence, it is not possible to ascertain whether the relation is direct or mediated through other variables, such as phonological awareness or listening comprehension. We conducted such rigorous tests as described next.

To assess the prospective role of early vocabulary knowledge to eventual differences in reading comprehension, two sets of archival data were reanalyzed. The first study reanalyzed the data reported in Sénéchal and LeFevre (2002), and the second study included data from Sénéchal (2004). The studies included conservative tests of the role of receptive vocabulary measured in kindergarten to reading comprehension at the end of grades 1, 3, or 4. Control variables included the education and literacy levels of the parents, child early literacy skills, phonological awareness, and listening comprehension.

Study 1

The children in Sénéchal and LeFevre's (2002) study were followed from the beginning of kindergarten to the end of grade 3. The children mostly came from middle-class homes. In addition to the variables described previously in the sections on phonological awareness and listening comprehension, reading comprehension was measured at the end of grade 1 (the Passage Comprehension subtest of the Woodcock-Johnson Psycho-Educational Battery—Revised; Woodcock & Johnson, 1989) and grade 3 (the Comprehension subtest of the Gates–MacGinitie Reading Tests, Level C, Form 3; MacGinitie & MacGinitie, 1992).

Hierarchical fixed-order multiple regressions were conducted to test whether vocabulary measured at the beginning of kindergarten would predict children's reading comprehension at the end of grades 1 and 3 after controlling for a series of variables. The control variables included those whose relations to reading have been well established in past research. In the analyses, the measure for children's early literacy consisted of factor scores obtained from a factor analysis of three variables: alphabet knowledge, decoding, and invented spelling.

The results are reported in Table 13.3. The regression for reading comprehension in grade 1 revealed that vocabulary did not predict any unique variance in children's reading comprehension after we controlled for parent education and literacy level, as well as child early literacy and phonological awareness. In this equation, children's early literacy and phonological awareness were significant predictors of reading comprehension.

A different pattern of results was obtained for grade 3. In grade 3, children's vocabulary measured in kindergarten explained a statistically significant 4% of variance in reading comprehension after we controlled for parent education and literacy level and child reading comprehension in grade 1, as well as early literacy, listening comprehension, and phonological awareness in kindergarten. In this analysis, the only other significant kindergarten predictor was listening comprehension.

The analyses in Study 1 provided a stringent test of the predictive role of vocabulary knowledge to reading comprehension. These tests revealed that vocabulary in kindergarten was a significant predictor of reading comprehension in grade 3, but not in grade 1. In fact, the pattern of results seems to support the well-documented finding that word recognition skills have to be well established before language comprehension skills can exert their full force. Archival data in Study 2 were analyzed to extend this pattern of findings by measuring reading fluency, as well as comprehension.

TABLE 13.3. Hierarchical Regression Analyses for Reading Comprehension in Grades 1 and 3 for Study 1

Criterion Order	R^2	ΔR^2	ΔF	p
Reading comprehension in grade 1 (n = 93)				
Parent education and literacy and child nonverbal intelligence	.25	.25	9.80	.00
Early literacy in kindergarten	.54	.29	56.59	.00
Listening comprehension in kindergarten	.54	.00	0.29	.59
Phonological awareness in kindergarten	.57	.03	5.66	.02
Vocabulary in kindergarten	.57	.00	0.08	.77
Reading comprehension in grade 3 (n = 66)				
Parent education	.05	.05	3.62	.06
Reading in grade 1	.37	.32	32.59	.00
Early literacy in kindergarten	.38	.01	0.87	.35
Listening comprehension in kindergarten	.45	.07	8.21	.01
Phonological awareness in kindergarten	.48	.02	2.87	.10
Vocabulary in kindergarten	.52	.04	4.99	.03

Study 2

Sénéchal (2004) followed a cohort of children from the end of kindergarten to the end of grade 4. In this chapter, we analyzed these archival data in a novel way to provide further evidence of the predictive relation between vocabulary and reading comprehension. The sample included 90 children who were tested at the end of kindergarten and the end of grade 1; 68 of these children were followed until the end of grade 4. The children were French speaking and attended French schools in the region of Ottawa, Canada.

At the end of kindergarten, children completed language and early literacy tasks. The language measures included a receptive vocabulary test (a French-Canadian version of the Peabody Picture Vocabulary Test—Revised; Dunn, Thériault-Whalen, & Dunn, 1993) and a measure of phonological awareness in which children were to delete a phoneme from a word in order to form another word. The early literacy measures included knowledge of letter names and decoding simple words. Finally, the reading measure included a test of word recognition in grade 1 (Mousty, Leybaert, Alegria, Content, & Morais, 1994), as well as tests of oral reading fluency (Lefavrais, 1967) and reading comprehension in grade 4 (Sarrazin, 1995). In addition to parent education levels, parent literacy was estimated indirectly by asking parents to indicate how many adult books they had at home. The assumption underlying this measure is that parents who have more books read more frequently than parents who have fewer books.

Hierarchical fixed-order multiple regressions were conducted to test whether vocabulary measured at the end of kindergarten would predict children's word recognition at the end of grade 1 and their reading comprehension at the end of grade 4 after controlling for a series of variables. In the analyses, the measure for children's early literacy consisted of factor scores obtained from a factor analysis of two variables: alphabet knowledge and decoding.

The results are reported in Table 13.4. The regression analysis in grade 1 revealed that vocabulary did not predict a statistically significant portion of unique variance in children's word recognition after we controlled for parent education and literacy level, as well as child early literacy and phonological awareness. In this equation, children's early literacy and phonological awareness were significant predictors of word recognition.

A different pattern of results was obtained for grade 4. In grade 4, children's vocabulary measured in kindergarten explained a statistically significant 15% of variance in reading comprehension after we controlled for parent education and literacy level, child reading fluency in grade 4, reading comprehension in grade 1, and early literacy and phonological awareness in kindergarten. It is worthy of mention that kindergarten vocabulary did not account for any variance in children's grade 4 reading fluency after we

TABLE 13.4. Hierarchical Regression Analyses for Reading Comprehension in Grades 1 and 4 for Study 2

Criterion Order	R^2	ΔR^2	ΔF	p
Word reading in grade 1 (*n* = 90)				
Parent education	.03	.03	3.11	.08
Early literacy at end of kindergarten	.32	.29	36.56	.00
Phonological awareness at end of kindergarten	.38	.06	8.36	.00
Vocabulary at end of kindergarten	.40	.02	2.29	.13
Reading comprehension in grade 4 (*n* = 68)				
Parent education and literacy	.13	.13	4.73	.01
Reading fluency at end of grade 4	.24	.11	9.25	.00
Reading at end of grade 1	.41	.17	18.29	.00
Early literacy at end of kindergarten	.48	.07	8.76	.00
Phonological awareness at end of kindergarten	.51	.02	3.07	.08
Vocabulary at end of kindergarten	.66	.15	27.09	.00

controlled for reading comprehension, as well as the other variables entered in the equation for reading comprehension. Kindergarten vocabulary seems associated specifically with reading comprehension in the middle-elementary grades.

The findings of Study 2 extend those of Study 1: Vocabulary in kindergarten was a significant predictor of reading comprehension in grade 4 after controlling for grade 4 reading fluency and grade 1 word reading, but it was not a predictor of differences in word reading in grade 1. Overall, the findings for English-speaking children in Study 1 and those for French-speaking children in Study 2 show a strikingly similar pattern of relations between early vocabulary and reading.

Taken together, the findings presented in this chapter are consistent with previous findings showing that early vocabulary skills are indirectly associated with reading during the first years of instruction (de Jong & van der Leij, 1999; cf. Share & Leiken, 2004) but that early vocabulary has a direct long-term relation to reading comprehension in grades 3 and 4 (Catts, Fey, Zhang, & Tomblin, 1999; Storch & Whitehurst, 2002).

Conclusion

Given the findings of the longitudinal studies presented here, it is clear that early individual differences in vocabulary can explain a reliable portion of variance in children's eventual success in reading comprehension. It can also play an indirect role on the acquisition of reading through its association with the growth in phonological awareness and listening comprehension. These findings provide additional evidence that early vocabulary is an important predictor of eventual success in reading (Snow, Burns, & Griffin, 1998; NICHD, 2000).

In all analyses presented in this chapter, a single measure of vocabulary was used. We measured the size of children's receptive vocabulary knowledge. There is reason to think, however, that a measure of receptive vocabulary may underestimate the strength of the relation between vocabulary and other variables for two reasons. First, some findings suggest that measures that tap expressive vocabulary yield stronger correlation co-

efficients than measures of receptive vocabulary (see the meta-analysis by Scarborough, 1998, 2001). Therefore, it might be the case that children's ability to speak known words is a better index of their vocabulary size. Second, Perfetti (1985) proposed that in addition to vocabulary size, the depth and organization of a child's semantic knowledge may also be predictive of reading (for a good example, see Nation & Snowling, 1998). Indeed, studies that include children's ability to orally define words—a measure of semantic depth—report slightly stronger relations between definitions and reading than between receptive vocabulary and reading (e.g., Roth et al., 2002). Future research could examine whether measures of vocabulary that assess the lexical breadth of expressive and receptive modes, as well as the depth and organization of semantic knowledge, provide a better understanding of the role of early vocabulary in the development of reading comprehension.

Just as intervention studies have been conducted to test the explanatory role of phonological awareness in the acquisition of word reading, intervention studies are needed to show how improving children's vocabulary prior to reading instruction could have beneficial short-term effects on their phonological awareness and listening comprehension, as well as long-term benefits on reading comprehension in grades 3 or 4. Shared book reading could certainly be used as the medium to promote such learning (e.g., Jordan et al., 2000).

Acknowledgments

This research was supported a research grant to Monique Sénéchal from the Social Sciences and Humanities Research Council of Canada.

References

Anderson, R. C., Heibert, E. H., Scott, J. A., & Wilkerson, I. A. (1985). *Becoming a nation of readers: The report of the commission on reading.* Washington, DC: National Institute of Education.

Biemiller, A. (1999). *Language and reading success.* Cambridge, MA: Brookline Books.

Bowey, J. A. (1994). Phonological sensitivity in novice readers and nonreaders. *Journal of Experimental Child Psychology, 58,* 134–159.

Bus, A. G., & van IJzendoorn, M. H. (1999). Phonological awareness and early reading: A meta-analysis of experimental training studies. *Journal of Educational Psychology, 91,* 403–414.

Catts, H. W., Fey, M. E., Zhang, X., & Tomblin, J. B. (1999t). Language basis of reading and reading disabilities: Evidence from a longitudinal investigation. *Scientific Studies of Reading, 3,* 331–361.

Chaney, C. (1998). Preschool language and metalinguistic skills are links to reading success. *Applied Psycholinguistics, 19,* 433–446.

de Jong, P. F., & van der Leij, A. (1999). Phonological abilities and reading acquisition: Results for a Dutch latent-variable longitudinal study. *Journal of Educational Psychology, 91,* 450–476.

Dickinson, D. K., McCabe, A., Anastasopoulos, L., Feinberg, E. S., & Poe, M. D. (2003). The comprehensive language approach to early literacy: The interrelationships among vocabulary, phonological sensitivity, and print knowledge among preschool-aged children. *Journal of Educational Psychology, 95*(3), 465–481.

Dunn, L., & Dunn, L. (1981). *Peabody Picture Vocabulary Test–Revised.* Circle Pines, MN: American Guidance Services.

Dunn, L. M., Thériault-Whalen, C. M., & Dunn, L. M. (1993). *Échelle de vocabulaire en images Peabody (EVIP).* Toronto, Ontario, Canada: Psycan.

Ehri, L. C., Nunes, S. R., Willows, D. M., Schuster, B. V., Yaghoub-Zadeh, Z., & Shanahan, T. (2001). Phonemic awareness instruction helps children learn to read: Evidence from the National Reading Panel's meta-analysis. *Reading Research Quarterly, 36,* 250–287.

Garlock, V. M., Walley, A. C., & Metsala, J. L. (2001). Age-of-acquisition, word frequency, and neighborhood density effects on spoken word recognition: Implications for the development of phoneme awareness and early reading ability. *Journal of Memory and Language, 45,* 468–492.

Goswami, U. (2001). Early phonological development and the acquisition of literacy. In S. B. Neuman & D. K. Dickinson (Eds.), *Handbook of early literacy research* (pp. 111–125). New York: Guilford Press.

Jordan, G. E., Snow, C. E., & Porche, M. V. (2000). Project EASE: The effect of a family literacy project on kindergarten students' early literacy skills. *Reading Research Quarterly, 35,* 524–546.

Hargrave, A. C., & Sénéchal, M. (2000). Book reading interventions with language-delayed preschool children: The benefits of regular reading and dialogic reading. *Early Childhood Research Quarterly, 15,* 75–90.

Lefavrais, P. (1967). *Test de l'Alouette.* Paris: Les Editions du Centre de Psychologie Appliquée.

Lonigan, C. J., Burgess, S. R., & Anthony, J. L. (2000). Development of emergent literacy and early reading skills in preschool children: Evidence from a latent-variable longitudinal study. *Developmental Psychology, 36,* 596–613.

Lonigan, C. J., Burgess, S. R., Anthony, J. L., & Barker, T. A. (1998). Development of phonological sensitivity in two- to five-year-old children. *Journal of Educational Psychology, 90,* 294–311.

Lonigan, C. J., & Whitehurst, G. J. (1998). Relative efficacy of a parent and teacher involvement in a shared-reading intervention for preschool children from low-income backgrounds. *Early Childhood Research Quarterly, 13,* 262–290.

Lorch, R. F., & van den Broek, R. (1997). Understanding reading comprehension: Current and future contributions of cognitive science. *Contemporary Educational Psychology, 19,* 199–216.

MacGinitie, W. H., & MacGinitie, R. K. (1992). *Gates–MacGinitie Reading Tests* (2nd Canadian ed.). Toronto, Ontario, Canada: Nelson Canada.

Mann, V. A., Tobin, P., & Wilson, R. (1987). Measuring phoneme awareness through invented spellings of kindergarten children. *Merrill-Palmer Quarterly, 33,* 365–391.

McBride-Chang, C., Wagner, R. K., & Chang, L. (1997). Growth modeling of phonological awareness. *Journal of Educational Psychology, 89,* 621–630.

Metsala, J. L. (1999). Young children's phonological awareness and non-word repetition as a function of vocabulary development. *Journal of Educational Psychology, 91,* 3–19.

Mousty, P., Leybaert, J., Alegria, J., Content, A., & Morais, J. (1994). *Batterie d'évaluation du langage écrit et de ses troubles.* Paris and Brussels: Laboratoire de Psychologie expérimentale.

Nation, K., & Snowling, M. J. (1998). Semantic processing and the development of word-recognition skills: Evidence from children with reading comprehension difficulties. *Journal of Memory and Language, 39,* 85–101.

NICHD: National Institute of Child Health and Human Development. (2000). *Report of the National Reading Panel. Teaching children to read: Reports of the subgroups.* Retrieved November 2005 from www.nichd.nih.gov/publications/nrp/report.htm

Perfetti, C. A. (1985). *Reading ability.* London: Oxford University Press.

Perfetti, C. A., Marron, M. A., & Foltz, P. W. (1996). Sources of comprehension failure: Theoretical perspectives and case studies. In C. Cornoldi & J. Oakhill (Eds.). *Reading comprehension difficulties: Processes and intervention* (pp. 137–165). Mahwah, NJ: Erlbaum.

Psychological Corporation. (1989). *Stanford Early School Achievement Test* (3rd ed.) San Antonio, TX: Harcourt Brace.

Roth, F. P., Speece, D. L., & Cooper, D. H. (2002). A longitudinal analysis of the connection between oral language and early reading. *Journal of Educational Research, 95,* 259–272.

Sarrazin, G. (1995). *Test de Rendement pour Franco-*

phones (TRF). Ottawa, Ontario, Canada: Harcourt Canada and The Psychological Corporation.

Scarborough, H. S. (1998). Early identification of children at risk for reading disabilities: Phonological awareness and some promising predictors. In B. K. Shapiro, P. J. Pasquale, & A. J. Capute (Eds.), *Specific reading disability: A view of the spectrum* (pp. 75–119). Timonium, MD: York Press.

Scarborough, H. S. (2001). Connecting early language and literacy to later reading (dis)abilities: Evidence, theory, and practice. In S. B. Neuman & D. K. Dickinson (Eds.), *Handbook of early literacy research* (pp. 97–110). New York: Guilford Press.

Sénéchal, M. (1997). The differential effect of storybook reading on preschooler's expressive and receptive vocabulary acquisition. *Journal of Child Language, 24,* 123–138.

Sénéchal, M. (2004). *Longitudinal relations among kindergarten literacy experiences and behaviors and grade 4 reading comprehension, fluency, and spelling.* Manuscript submitted for publication.

Sénéchal, M., & LeFevre, J. (2002). Parental involvement in the development of children's reading skill: A 5-year longitudinal study. *Child Development, 73,* 445–460.

Sénéchal, M., LeFevre, J., Smith-Chant, B. L., & Colton, K. (2001). On refining theoretical models of emergent literacy: The role of empirical evidence. *Journal of School Psychology, 39,* 439–460.

Sénéchal, M., LeFevre, J.-A., Thomas, E., & Daley, K. (1998). Differential effects of home literacy experiences on the development of oral and written language. *Reading Research Quarterly, 32,* 96–116.

Share, D. L., Jorm, A., MacLean, R., & Matthews, R. (1984). Sources of individual differences in reading achievement. *Journal of Educational Psychology, 76,* 1309–1324.

Share, D. L., & Leikin, M. (2004). Language impairment at school entry and later reading disability: Connections at lexical and supralexical levels of reading. *Scientific Studies of Reading, 8,* 87–110.

Snow, C. E., Burns, M. S., & Griffin, P. (Eds.). (1998). *Preventing reading difficulties in young children.* Washington, DC: National Research Council, National Academy Press.

Snow, C. E., Tabors, P. O., Nicholson, P. A., & Kurland, B. F. (1995). SHELL: Oral language and early literacy skills in kindergarten and first-grade children. *Journal of Research in Childhood Education, 10,* 37–48.

Stahl, S. A., & Fairbanks, M. M. (1986). The effects of vocabulary instruction: A model-based meta-analysis. *Review of Educational Research, 56,* 72–110.

Stanovich, K. E., & West, R. F. (1989). Exposure to print and orthographic processing. *Reading Research Quarterly, 24,* 402–433.

Storch, S. A., & Whitehurst, G. J. (2002). Oral language and code-related precursors of reading: Evidence from a longitudinal structural model. *Developmental Psychology, 38,* 934–945.

Thomas, E. M., & Sénéchal, M. (2004). Long-term association between articulation quality and phoneme sensitivity: A study from age 3 to age 8. *Applied Psycholinguistics, 25,* 513–541.

Wagner, R. K., Torgesen, J. K., Rashotte, C. A., Hecht, S. A., Barker, T. A., Burgess, S. R., et al. (1997). Changing relations between phonological processing abilities and word level reading as children develop from beginning to skilled readers: A 5-year longitudinal study. *Developmental Psychology, 33,* 468–479.

Walley, A. C., Metsala, J. L., & Garlock, V. M. (2003). Spoken vocabulary growth: Its role in the development of phoneme awareness and early reading ability. *Reading and Writing: An Interdisciplinary Journal, 16,* 5–20.

Weschler, D. (1989). *Weschler Preschool and Primary Scale of Intelligence—Revised.* San Antonio, TX: Psychological Corporation.

Whitehurst, G. J., Falco, F. L., Lonigan, C. J., Fischel, J. E., DeBaryshe, B. D., Valdez-Menchaca, M. C., & Caulfield, M. (1988). Accelerating language development through picture book reading. *Developmental Psychology, 24,* 552–559.

Woodcock, R. W., & Johnson, M. B. (1989). *Woodcock–Johnson Psycho-Educational Battery—Revised.* Allen, TX: DLM Teaching Resources.

IV
CULTURAL AND LINGUISTIC DIVERSITY

14

Effective Interventions for English Language Learners (Spanish–English) at Risk for Reading Difficulties

SHARON VAUGHN
SYLVIA LINAN-THOMPSON
SHAROLYN D. POLLARD-DURODOLA
PATRICIA G. MATHES
ELSA CÁRDENAS HAGAN

Reading First legislation (No Child Left Behind, 2002) has been fueled in no small part by the findings from ongoing reading research with monolingual English students that suggest that students at risk for reading problems benefit from interventions that are systematic and explicit (National Institute of Child Health and Human Development [NICHHD], 2000; Snow, Burns, & Griffin, 1998). Distinctly missing from these reports is a summary of the extent to which the findings generalize to students who are English-language learners (ELLs) or the extent to which there is research on effective practices with ELL students to support the transfer of the findings from monolingual English students to bilingual students. The National Reading Panel report states that "the panel did not focus on special populations such as children whose language is other than English" (NICHHD, 2000, p. 4-2).

Other analyses of early intervention research have reported few studies with English language learners. For example, Cavanaugh and colleagues (Cavanaugh, Kim, Wanzek, & Vaughn, 2004) synthesized all of the kindergarten intervention studies for students at risk for reading problems that yielded overall positive effects for students who participated in these interventions (effect sizes were in the moderate to high range). Further examination of these studies to determine whether any of them addressed ELL/English as a Second Language (ESL) students revealed that only two studies indicated that ELLs were included in their sample (Fuchs et al., 2002; O'Connor, Jenkins, & Slocum, 1995), and neither study disaggregated findings for this subgroup. Two of the studies specified criteria that excluded English-language learners (Brady, Fowler, Stone & Winbury, 1994; Torgesen et al., 1999).

The challenge for many states, but particularly states with large numbers of bilingual students such as Texas, California, New York, and Florida, is that there is little or no guidance for providing effective reading interventions for bilingual students at risk for reading problems. Furthermore, Reading First requires that school personnel base practices and educational decisions on scientifically based reading research—yet this research is not readily available.

The purpose of this chapter is to provide an overview of research on interventions designed to improve literacy outcomes for young students (kindergarten through third grade) at risk for reading difficulties. We review research from other interventions, then present findings from our intervention studies with bilingual students at risk for reading problems in Spanish and English.

Background on Interventions for English-Language Learners

The most hotly contested issues related to teaching young Spanish-speaking children have addressed language of instruction and timing of transition from native language to English. This has meant that the vast majority of writing and thinking in bilingual education has focused on the effectiveness of various types of bilingual programs (e.g., Garcia, 2000; Padilla, Fairchild, & Valadez, 1990; Ramirez, Yuen, & Ramey, 1991) and the amount of time students should be educated in their native language (for a review, see August & Hakuta, 1997). These discussions, and data to support their resolution, are critical to designing effective programs for youngsters who are English-language learners. But even if resolved—unlikely though that may be—they would still yield insufficient information about how to teach young students who are at risk for reading difficulties. Regardless of the effectiveness of core instruction and the quality of native-language instruction, some students will require interventions to improve their outcomes in reading and language. What do we know about effective interventions for ELLs with reading difficulties?

For the purpose of this review, we identified reading studies that were conducted with students who were in kindergarten through third grade and targeted students who were bilingual and were also identified as at risk for reading problems and for whom a supplemental reading intervention was provided to enhance their reading outcomes. To better interpret the findings, we have divided intervention studies into those that were conducted in English and those that were conducted in Spanish. Following a brief review of interventions for young bilin-

gual students, we provide an overview of the intervention we developed in English and Spanish for English-language learners who are Spanish-speaking and then preliminary findings from the interventions.

English Interventions

We identified four studies that were conducted as interventions for at-risk students in English. All were designed to improve the reading performance of at-risk students who were English-language learners. We focused our review on intervention studies, not those that addressed the core reading program. Each of the four studies had methodological strengths and challenges. Two of the studies used random assignment of participants to the intervention and control conditions and thus were true experimental designs (Gunn, Biglan, Smolkowski, & Ary, 2000; Denton, Anthony, Parker, & Hasbrouck, 2004). We discuss the findings from these two studies, followed by a study that provided treatment only without a control condition (Linan-Thompson, Vaughn, Hickman-Davis, & Kouzekanani, 2003), and finally a study that allowed teachers to select in which of two interventions they would participate (Stuart, 1999).

Gunn et al. (2000) randomly assigned early at-risk readers who were Hispanic to treatment and control groups. The precise number of intervention sessions provided to the treatment group was not specified; however, students (ELLs) in the treatment condition were provided a direct-instruction approach to reading in English for 25–30 minutes daily, for 5 months to 2 years. Students who participated for 2 years showed significant treatment effects for letter–word identification, word attack, reading vocabulary, and passage comprehension. There were no significant treatment effects for reading fluency. A relatively small subgroup of ELLs ($n = 19$) were identified as non-English speaking. The experimental students made significantly greater gains on words read per minute, but no statistically significant gains on other reading outcomes were recorded, though other measures were in the positive direction.

In this study, students were provided a very explicit and systematic reading instruction approach that had previously demonstrated significant gains for monolingual English-speaking students. The gains for the ELLs were statistically significant on one outcome in reading only—fluency. These gains seem modest when considering the length of time over which the intervention was provided.

The second study that featured random assignment of students to experimental and control groups conducted two types of intervention programs in English for students in second through fifth grades in a bilingual (Spanish–English) program (Denton et al., 2004). Students who scored below first-grade reading level were randomly assigned either to a systematic, explicit reading intervention using decodable text or to an untutored control group. Students who scored higher than first-grade reading level were randomly assigned to either a reading program that addressed fluency or to a control condition. Bilingual students were provided, on average, about 22 tutoring sessions conducted by undergraduates. Students in the systematic, explicit reading intervention significantly improved on word identification when compared with controls. Students in the fluency-only condition did not outperform control students.

The findings from both studies reported by Denton and colleagues (2004) yield only modest findings. Only one of the two studies yielded significant differences between treatment and control conditions: the first-grade explicit-instruction treatment group. Even for this group, significant findings were for word identification only. It is important to note that the treatment was provided for a relatively short period of time (22 sessions), thus contributing to reduced effects. It may also be that influencing the reading performance of bilingual students will take a more complex and multifaceted instructional design than typically used for monolingual English students. For example, it may be that modifications that include effective ESL strategies, oral skills, and critical linkages between native language and English need to be systematically designed within the intervention to more effectively influence outcomes.

A third study conducted an intervention in English for 26 ELLs who were second graders at risk for reading disabilities (Linan-Thompson et al., 2003). The study design was treatment-only with no control group.

Students were provided 58 sessions (35 minutes each) of supplemental intervention in group sizes of one to three. Students were followed for 4 weeks and 4 months after the intervention. Effect sizes (ES) were reported from pretest to posttest on word attack (ES = 0.49), passage comprehension (ES = 1.28), phoneme segmentation fluency (ES = 0.71), and oral reading fluency (ES = 1.61). The largest effect sizes were in the most complex and important outcomes of fluency and comprehension. Only three students showed less than 6 months' growth during the 3-month intervention. Oral-language proficiency in Spanish or English did not predict the performance of the three students who were low responders. In other words, many students with lower oral-language proficiency scores in Spanish and English performed well on the reading outcome measures. For the three students who made the least gains from the intervention, one student was fluent in Spanish but limited in English, one student was approaching fluency in English and had had very limited Spanish-language proficiency, and one student was limited in both languages. To appreciate the gains made by these at-risk ELL students who participated in the intervention, consider that they made more than two-words-per-week gains in fluency (on average), whereas on-level English monolingual readers make slightly above one-word-per-week gains in fluency (Hasbrouck & Tindal, 1992).

In terms of intervention, the study by Linan-Thompson and colleagues (2003) attended to many of the critical features of an intervention that appear to be associated with improved outcomes for ELLs with reading difficulties. The intervention was designed to capitalize on the best research from reading with monolingual students but also included ESL practices. Students were provided a more extensive intervention (58 sessions) and received it within relatively small groups, which gave students extensive opportunities to practice and obtain feedback from well-trained tutors. Students made significant gains from pretest throughout post- and follow-up testing; however, the findings are compromised by the lack of a control group.

The following study by Stuart (1999) was not for students who spoke Spanish but for those who spoke Sylheti. Though not technically an intervention study—all of the students in the classes were provided the intervention rather than identifying a subgroup of at-risk students—we have included the study in this review because most of the students were at risk for reading problems. Teachers volunteered to teach either Big Books or Jolly Phonics. Three teachers from three schools taught Jolly Phonics (57 5-year old students) and three teachers from one school taught Big Books (55 5-year old students). The intervention was provided for 12 weeks, 1 hour per day, beginning with whole-class and followed by small-group support. Testing occurred pre- and postintervention and 1 year later. Students in the Jolly Phonics program did not differ significantly from those students in the Big Books program on oral language, rhyme awareness, or phoneme discrimination at pre-, post-, or follow-up testing. For alphabetic knowledge, there were between-group differences in favor of Jolly Phonics at posttest only. For phonics recognition and recall and writing sounds, as well as for reading words and reading nonwords, Jolly Phonics significantly outperformed Big Books.

These studies suggest that students who are English-language learners can improve their word reading, fluency, and comprehension when provided systematic and explicit interventions that focus on the critical elements of reading (phonics, spelling, fluency, and comprehension) and also provide many opportunities to read text and interpret what they are reading. Interventions that had a more structured, systematic approach that includes phonics fared better than those without these elements.

Spanish Interventions

We examined interventions conducted in Spanish for students at risk for reading problems. Though interventions have been conducted in other alphabetic languages in other countries, such as French in Canada, the majority of students in the United States who speak a language other than English are ones whose native language is Spanish.

Beginning Reading Instruction in Spanish

Goldenberg, Reese, and Gallimore (1992) assigned Spanish-speaking kindergarten students by class to treatment or control conditions. Treatment students were introduced to a new book every 3 weeks by hearing the story read aloud several times and then taking the books home with a request for parents to enjoy the books with their children. In the control condition, the students received a comparable number of worksheet packets that focused on letters, sounds, and syllables. Parents were explicitly asked not to focus on decoding and accurate word reading at home. Observations at home indicated that decoding and word reading were the areas parents focused on most. Effect size for letters and sounds was 0.72, and for other literature measures, 0.86. Although students in the experimental group outperformed control students, no association was found between use of storybooks and reading achievement; but high association was found between use of worksheets and reading achievement.

In a related study with kindergarten students learning to read in Spanish, Goldenberg (1994) described a pilot study in six different Spanish-speaking kindergarten classrooms that participated in one of three different approaches (two classrooms per approach) conducted by classroom teachers for all kindergarten students (thus these were not interventions per se): (1) simple readers in Spanish sent home and used in class, (2) strong and direct academic focus on reading, and (3) general readiness. Students who participated in the condition of strong and academic focus on reading scored highest, and significantly higher than students in general readiness. The students who participated in the program in which simple readers in Spanish were sent home also significantly outperformed students in general readiness, but not on par with the condition of strong and academic focus on reading. In a subsequent study, when the storybook intervention was altered to include simple predictable storybooks plus direct instruction in letters and sounds, results were similar to the previous study. Students who participated in the more explicit instruction in letters and sounds (more academic classrooms) outperformed the readiness classrooms, particularly on word and sentence reading and individual subtests of letter names and sounds, identification of first syllables, decoding, and word writing. The academic instruction did not negatively influence liking to read or reading attitudes for participating students.

Two experimental studies were conducted in Spain that relate to the acquisition of Spanish literacy skills and thus are included in this review. Defior and Tudela (1994) conducted a particularly relevant study with an experimental design examining the effectiveness of phonological awareness training on first-grade students in Granada, Spain. Ninety-six children were assigned to one of four interventions or to a control group. The intervention was conducted for 6 months in groups of six children who received one training session (90 minutes) each week for 20 weeks. Each of the four treatment groups followed different training procedures, depending on the type of task used (phoneme vs. concept discrimination) and the way that the task was carried out (using or not using manipulative materials). The fifth group was used as a control. Findings indicated that training in phonological abilities in first grade positively influenced reading and writing outcomes when plastic letters were used during the phonological awareness training. This study provides support for the use of phonological awareness training but also provides an important link between sounds and letters that facilitates reading acquisition.

A second experimental design study was conducted in Spain with Spanish-speaking second- and third-grade students (Sanchez & Rueda, 1991). Fifteen students were randomly assigned to one of three programs of instruction: (1) adding phonemes (ADD), (2) training in segmentation and use of alphabetic code (WW), or (3) a control condition using perceptive and motor tasks. All intervention groups involved two sessions (1 hour per session) each week, for a total of 20 weeks or 40 hours of intervention. Both the ADD and WW groups improved relative to the control students in dictation but not in reading after training. The WW group, which used the application of phoneme-to-grapheme rules, was more effective than the ADD program in dictation. Again, connecting the sounds of language to print and the rules of reading print (phonics) yielded improved outcomes over phonemic instruction alone.

Reading Comprehension in Spanish

Echevarria (1995) and Muniz-Swicegood (1994) conducted studies with second- and third-grade students that addressed issues related to extending comprehension of text in students at risk for reading problems in Spanish. Echevarria examined proximal and distal effects of instructional conversations for five ELL students in second and third grades with reading difficulties. Target students were provided 25 lessons over 1 year, using instructional conversations for reading. The intervention focused on themes and expanded discussions with inferential comprehension and elaborated student dialogue. Three outcome measures were assessed in Spanish—oral retell (ES = 0.25), idea units (ES = -0.36), and literal recall (ES = -0.56)—yielding modest outcomes for participants.

In another comprehension intervention, Muniz-Swicegood (1994) conducted a study with 95 third-grade Spanish-speaking students who were randomly assigned to treatment and control conditions for 6 weeks. Though the instruction was not provided as an intervention, the findings may be relevant for the effective design of interventions. Students in the treatment condition read text from a third-grade Spanish reader and were taught to generate questions at the end of each paragraph. Students led dialogues in small groups, asking each other questions. Group sizes were reduced over time until students worked in pairs. Lastly, students generated questions on their own and discussed them with their teacher individually. English-reading effect size was 0.39, and Spanish-reading effect size was 0.22. Though only moderate effects were realized, an interesting outcome was that students who practiced comprehension activities with Spanish text were able to generalize the findings to English text.

Students learning to read in Spanish benefit from phonemic awareness training when explicit linkages to print are evoked and when they are provided with instruction in phonics and alphabetic principles and with explicit and systematic opportunities to practice reading words with correction and feedback. Also, students who were taught reading comprehension strategies in Spanish improved in their Spanish reading comprehension but also were able to generalize the comprehension strategies learned in Spanish to English reading. These findings are useful in guiding educators in developing interventions for students who are English-language learners at risk for reading problems and who are first learning to read in Spanish.

English and Spanish Interventions

In addition to the previous studies that were conducted in English and Spanish with young readers, two programs have initiated work in beginning reading for students with reading difficulties in Spanish: Success for All (Slavin & Madden, 1999, 2001) and Reading Recovery (Clay, 1993). Success for All has a Spanish-reading version, *Exito para Todos* (Slavin et al., 1996), that provides reading instruction in Spanish in first and second grades and then moves to English-only instruction. There is also a version for English-language development (ELD) with adaptations that provide additional support for vocabulary, concept, and language learning in English.

Borman, Hewes, Overman, and Brown (2003) conducted a systematic review of comprehensive school reform programs. Success for All (*Exito para Todos*) was the only program included within this review and designed specifically to improve reading, writing, and language arts performance that had a program for both English- and Spanish-speaking students. Success for All was also only one of three programs (no other with reading interventions in both English and Spanish) that met the highest standards of evidence and that could be expected to improve test scores. The mean weighted effect sizes for Success for All that represented studies with comparison groups was $d = 0.18$. Lipsey and Wilson (1993) concluded that these findings for educational interventions should not be considered trivial. The database for Success for All includes more than 42 separate studies, some of which include bilingual students and English-language learners (Slavin & Madden, 2001). Specific studies that compare the effects of *Exito para Todos* with those of other programs yield positive outcomes in favor of *Exito para Todos*.

Bilingual Cooperative Integrated Reading and Composition (BCIRC; Calderon, Hertz-Lazarowitz, & Slavin, 1998) is a bilingual adaptation of Cooperative Integrated Reading and Composition designed to enhance reading outcomes for students in second grade and above through cooperative learning groups (Stevens, Madden, Slavin, & Farnish, 1987). The BCIRC study was conducted with more than 200 Hispanic stu-dents in second and third grades from seven schools. Positive effects for reading and writing resulted for students who participated in the BCIRC when compared with control students.

Another example of a reading program originally developed in English and then in Spanish is *Descubriendo la Lectura* (Escamilla, 1994; Escamilla, Andrade, Basurto, & Ruiz, 1990–1991). Unlike Success for All, which is a school-wide model, *Descubriendo la Lectura* is a Spanish-reading intervention designed for at-risk readers in Spanish that is derived from Reading Recovery (Clay, 1993). Like Reading Recovery, *Descubriendo la Lectura* was designed as a one-on-one program (one highly trained teacher with one student) to provide an intervention program to return students to grade-level performance and keep them there. An examination of the effects of *Descubriendo la Lectura* was conducted by Escamilla (1994) and represented students in the lowest 20% of their class. Students who participated in the intervention ended their first-grade year with improved outcomes in Spanish reading. Findings from an extant database of *Descubriendo la Lectura* programs provided to first graders who were then followed into second and third grades (Escamilla, Loera, Ruiz, & Rodriguez, 1998) revealed that for those students identified as discontinued— those for whom the program was effective— students were performing on par with their peers. Though the percentage of ELL students in the treatment sample who were not "discontinued" is not identified, another study identifies them as more than 25% of the sample, which represents the students whose entry skills prior to treatment were the lowest in the group (Neal & Kelly, 1999). Neal and Kelly (1999) examined three groups of ELL students over 3 years who participated in Reading Recovery in either English or Spanish. The authors concluded that ELL students at risk for reading difficulties who were taught via Reading Recovery in English did not take longer to meet exit criteria than ELL students at risk for reading difficulties who were taught in Spanish via *Descubriendo la Lectura*.

Though these programs are noteworthy in their development, further experimental studies are needed of the effectiveness of these and other programs that specifically describe the effectiveness of interventions for at-risk students with reading problems who are learning to read in Spanish and English. There is a limited knowledge base for making decisions about the effectiveness of early interventions for bilingual students, including practice knowledge that could reduce the number of students later identified with reading problems and even long-term reading disabilities.

Findings from Our Intervention with Spanish-Speaking At-Risk Readers

We (Francis, Fletcher, Foorman, Goldenberg, & Vaughn, 2001) have been conducting a large-scale research project designed to examine the factors and conditions under which children who speak Spanish acquire proficiency in language and literacy skills. Approximately 1,400 Spanish-speaking students in 140 classrooms in schools from three geographical areas are participating in this longitudinal project. This study is not designed to evaluate the effectiveness of model types; therefore, the school sites were purposely selected to represent a range of language program models, including: (1) English-language immersion, (2) early exit from Spanish literacy instruction, (3) late exit from Spanish literacy instruction, and (4) dual-language instruction.

As part of our large-scale project to investigate the oral skills and literacy of young bilingual students (Francis, Fletcher, Foorman, Goldenberg, & Vaughn, 2000–2004), Vaughn and colleagues (Vaughn, Linan-Thompson, et al., in press; Vaughn, Mathes, et al., in press) conducted two studies with bilingual (Spanish–English) first-grade students at risk for reading disabilities. In both studies, students were selected from sites in Texas that represented large populations of Spanish–English-speaking students. All first-grade students from participating schools were screened for reading difficulties and were provided interventions matched to the language of their core instruction. Trained intervention teachers provided students whose core reading instruction in first grade was in Spanish with systematic and explicit daily Spanish reading and oral intervention in small groups. For students whose core reading instruction in first grade was in English, a

similar systematic and explicit intervention in reading and oral skills in English was provided to at-risk students in small groups. Both of these studies are in the implementation phase. Findings are available for the Spanish intervention only at this time and are described briefly here.

English-language learners identified as significantly at risk for later reading difficulties were randomly assigned by schools either to the researcher-implemented intervention for 50 minutes per day, 5 days per week (October through April), or to a comparison group not provided intervention by the research team. All students in the intervention and control groups continued with the core reading instruction provided by their classroom teachers in Spanish.

Participants, Intervention, and Findings

School sites for the intervention study were purposely selected because they represented population areas where large numbers of bilingual students attend school, because they included schools that were considered effective for bilingual students (80% or more of students passed the state-level reading assessment), and because large numbers of ELLs attended kindergarten and first grades at these schools (75–100%).

Students at risk for reading difficulties were identified through a screening completed with all first-grade students at the beginning of the school year that used letter identification and word-reading measures. Sixty-four students from 21 teachers' classes were randomly assigned to the intervention group ($n = 32$) and the control group ($n = 32$).

The intervention for this study was in Spanish and was derived from research on effective reading instruction in English for native English speakers with reading difficulties, on the sequence and development of Spanish literacy acquisition, on principles of effective instruction, on and language acquisition in bilingual students. The interventions in Spanish and English were related in terms of instructional design and delivery but were different in terms of sequence of instruction and focus of critical features of instruction. Students were taught to recognize phonemes in Spanish and to map them to letters. They were taught to read syllables within a few lessons and taught letter–sound correspondences by sounding out syllables and then reading them as a whole and reading multisyllable words. By the seventh day of instruction, students were reading connected text daily. Fluency and comprehension skills were promoted from the beginning of the program (Mathes et al., 2003). Additionally, we built a 10-minute oral-skills lesson into every daily lesson that included identifying key words in expository books, teaching the words, reading the stories, and providing students opportunities to use the words and to retell stories (Hickman, Pollard-Durodola, & Vaughn, 2004).

Findings from the study revealed that although there were no significant pretest differences between the treatment and control conditions, there were intervention effects for almost all Spanish outcome measures at posttest. Treatment students outperformed control students on phonemic awareness, word attack, word reading, reading comprehension, fluency, and overall language in Spanish. Interesting in this study are the gains in comprehension, fluency, and overall Spanish language—often difficult to realize with at-risk students with reading difficulties. These findings suggest that the students who participated in the intervention are better prepared for the rigors of reading in second grade and above and are likely to have improved transitions from Spanish to English. To determine whether indeed this is true, we intend to follow these students through third grade to determine their success in transitioning to English and maintaining Spanish reading.

Implications for At-Risk ELL Readers

Though systematic and carefully conducted research with ELLs is a necessary next step to further our understanding of best practices for effective instruction, this review of extant research reveals that there are some findings to inform our decision making. Following are several principles from the research that may be used to guide reading instruction for ELL students who are at risk for reading problems.

1. *Use the many commonalities between reading instruction in English and Spanish to design reading programs.* Gersten and Geva

(2003) acknowledge that although there may be features of instructional practices that differ, reading instruction in other alphabetic languages such as Spanish is similar to reading instruction in English. For example, instruction in areas such as oral language and reading comprehension are important to ELLs as well (Scarborough, 2002).

2. *Consider ways to instruct students in all of the critical elements of beginning reading initially and then in the elements most clearly related to effective outcomes as they become more mature readers.* Gersten and Geva (2003) identify six instructional practices in reading that are effective for beginning ELLs: (1) explicit teaching, (2) English-language learning, (3) phonemic awareness and decoding, (4) vocabulary development, (5) interactive teaching that maximizes student engagement, and (6) instruction that produces opportunities for accurate responses. The foundation skills of phonemic awareness and phonics are more critical in the very beginning stages of reading and less important as students become readers of connected text. Improving vocabulary and word knowledge is an important part of reading and of all content learning throughout the school years. Improving listening comprehension is initially important, as is then transferring these comprehension skills to text understanding.

3. *Recognize that English is a more difficult language to learn to read and that many of the foundation skills of phonics and word reading that come readily in Spanish need more explicit instruction in English.* Seymour, Aro, and Erskine (2003) conducted a study across 12 alphabetic languages that vary in orthographic complexity to determine the influence of orthography on rates of acquisition of the foundation skills in reading. Languages with deep orthographies are those languages whose written forms have many inconsistencies and complexities. English is the language with the most complex orthography. Shallow orthographies are those with highly consistent phoneme–grapheme correspondence, such as Spanish. In a study of the connection between the depth of orthography and the acquisition of beginning word-reading skills, the rate of development of foundation skills in English (a deep orthography) was found to be more than twice as slow as for those languages that are shallow (e.g., Finnish, Spanish, Ital-

ian). The data from the Seymour et al. (2003) study support the hypothesis of Katz and Frost (1992) regarding orthographic depth and learning to read. They suggest that shallow orthographies allow students to learn to read more easily because they follow a single process grounded on the alphabetic principle of mapping phonemes to graphemes. However, more complex orthographies such as English make learning to read more difficult because they require students to learn two systems: alphabetic (decoding) and logographic (storage of word recognition and familiar words).

4. *Make connections between what students know in one language and its application to the second language.* If students are literate prior to learning to read in English, the level of orthographic complexity of the language in which they are literate will influence their metalinguistic knowledge and how that knowledge will transfer to English. For example, if students are literate in an alphabetic language, such as Spanish, that is orthographically shallower than English, students will need to be taught that some of the rules in English reading are alphabetic (using examples that link their current literacy skills and English) and some of the rules in English are logographic (again selecting examples from their current literacy skills and from English). Second, if students are acquiring literacy skills in English and another language at the same time, pointing out similarities and differences in the application of the alphabetic process between the two languages will be useful. Third, if students are acquiring literacy skills in English as a second language but have few if any literacy skills in their primary language, then students would benefit from beginning with sounds and words that are regular (decodable) and from being taught practices for decoding these words. Irregular words are taught by applying those decodable skills that work (e.g., the /d/ sound in *done* applies) and then being taught how the irregular word is spelled and written. For example, the teacher would say, "*Done* is an irregular word. The first sound is decodable, /d/, and the rest of the word is said like this: /un/. We spell it *d-o-n-e*. Let's look at the word, say it, spell it, and then write it." Thus students are clearly taught both the alphabetic process and the logographic process and taught when and how to use both of them.

5. *Promote opportunities to use oral language during instruction and give opportunities for students to engage in addressing higher order questions.* ELL students who often have limited opportunities to use oral language during instruction and few opportunities to address challenging higher order questions. Many of the questions posed allow for one- or two-word answers, limiting their opportunity to use oral language. Opportunities for structured use of both conversational and academic language are needed. For example, oral participation can be facilitated by providing scaffolding in the form of sentence stems that offer students a structure for responding orally to challenging questions. To assist students in addressing higher order questions, teachers may initially model more complex syntactic structures and fade out support as students become more proficient in English. Although learning the academic vocabulary of English is necessary for school success, many English-language learners may not have access to this vocabulary outside of the school setting, making it difficult to become truly proficient in academic English (Corson, 1997). However, academic language can be encouraged through planned discussions in which students have a specific role and rotate their responsibilities, through small-group or paired cooperative-learning activities, and through development of prior knowledge (O'Malley & Chamot, 1999).

6. *Capitalize on all opportunities to teach and engage in vocabulary and concept building.* Vocabulary development is an essential feature of reading, comprehension, and content learning for ELLs. Students will be required to learn new words to understand expository and narrative texts (e.g., *civil, equity, molecule*), as well as to learn the meaning of descriptive words to fully appreciate and interpret what they are reading (e.g., *worried, marvelous, eagerly*). All of this vocabulary and concept development cannot occur through context alone. Explicit instruction is beneficial when teaching core vocabulary, and students require strategies for encountering less frequent words in context (Coady, 1993). Students will require highly organized, focused, and repeated opportunities to learn these words well enough to both understand their meaning in context and apply them in their own language use. Second-language learners benefit from vocabulary

instruction when words and knowledge acquired in the first language are associated with new words and concepts presented in English, so that students understand new information by relating it to what they already know (McLaughlin, 1994; Nagy, 1988). Young English-language learners may focus on cognates, morphographic elements, semantic feature analysis of words with shared features, words with multiple meanings, synonyms and antonyms, and activities that emphasize semantic relationships between new words and familiar words. However, vocabulary development for ELLs may present additional challenges when focusing on words that are not in the student's oral or reading vocabulary and for which the student does not have an available concept. Such words can be classified as either those that represent a concept that can be easily developed and those for which a concept cannot be easily developed. Graves (1984) refers to these words, respectively, as Type III and IV, and suggests that these words might be taught within specific concepts or content matter, with the latter sometimes requiring more than one day to develop. Ulanoff and Pucci (1999) suggest that students benefit from previewing important concepts and vocabulary in their primary language (Spanish) prior to listening to stories read in English and then reviewing key concepts in Spanish. In conclusion, English vocabulary development for ELLs may sometimes be augmented by providing support in their primary language (Spanish).

7. *Organize effective use of peer pairing and cooperative groups to enhance learning.* There is considerable evidence that peer pairing and structured group activities hold promise for ELLs acquiring proficiency in English (Klingner & Vaughn, 1996; Klingner & Vaughn, 2000) and Spanish (Muniz-Swicegood, 1994). Peer pairing or cooperative grouping provide intensive individualized instruction for students from varied literacy backgrounds (Fuchs, Fuchs, Mathes, & Simmons, 1997) by increasing the amount of time spent in academic engagement and by providing immediate feedback (e.g. reading errors, pacing, etc.) from peers. Cooperative grouping may especially benefit ELLs by presenting opportunities for them to take greater risks in using language for both academic and social purposes (Larsen-Freeman, 2001). Students may attempt to use more complex language structures and vocabulary when working with peers in cooperative groups than during conventional interactions with the teacher in which they feel their responses are being evaluated.

Future Directions for Beginning ELLs with Reading Difficulties

Considerable work is needed to better understand beginning reading instruction for ELLs. Our focus in this chapter is on those students whose initial skills in reading at the beginning of first grade place them at risk for reading difficulties. The interventions we have designed are time-consuming (50 minutes per day for 7 months), and it may be challenging for schools to obtain adequate resources to implement them. Fortunately, there is some evidence that these interventions can be implemented well by highly prepared teaching assistants (Grek, Mathes, & Torgensen, 2003). It would be interesting to determine whether effective outcomes can be achieved for students at risk for reading problems with less intensive interventions that are implemented for briefer periods.

Future research on beginning reading for ELL students might address the effectiveness of interventions that assist students in transitioning from reading in their primary language (e.g., Spanish) to reading in English. There are still many unaddressed questions about when this transition is best made and whether the timing for transition is the same for very able readers as it is for students with reading difficulties.

We are also interested in the role of language competence in Spanish and English and its influence on reading in each language. By 2050, 40% of students in public schools in the United States will speak a language that is not English (Lindholm-Leary, 2000). Although one would agree that for most children, good instruction is the most adequate means of preventing reading failure (Snow et al., 1998), the reality is that teachers of ELLs are often ill prepared for what they encounter in the classroom (August & Hakuta, 1997; Calderon, 2001). We need to conduct research that helps classroom teachers provide the most effective instruction for all students—many of whom will be English-language learners.

Acknowledgments

This research was funded by a grant from the National Institute of Child Health and Human Development and by a grant award from the Institute of Educational Sciences (No. PO1 HD 39521, Development of English Literacy in Spanish-Speaking Children).

References

August, A., & Hakuta, K. (Eds.). (1997). *Improving schooling for language-minority children: A research agenda*. Washington, DC: National Academy Press.

Borman, G. D., Hewes, G. M., Overman, L. T., & Brown, S. (2003). Comprehensive school reform and achievement: Meta-analysis. *Review of Educational Research, 73*, 125–230.

Brady, S., Fowler, A., Stone, B., & Winbury, N. (1994). Training phonological awareness: A study with inner-city kindergarten children. *Annals of Dyslexia, 44, 26–59.*

Calderon, M. (2001). Curricula and methodologies used to teach Spanish-speaking limited English proficient students to read in English. In R. E. Slavin & Calderon (Eds.), *Effective programs for Latino students* (pp. 251–305). Mahwah, NJ: Erlbaum.

Calderon, M., Hertz-Lazarowitz, R., & Slavin, R. E. (1998). Effects of bilingual cooperative integrated reading and composition on students making the transition from Spanish to English reading. *Elementary School Journal, 99*(2), 153–165.

Cavanaugh, C. L., Kim, A., Wanzek, J., & Vaughn, S. (2004). Kindergarten reading intervention for at-risk students: Twenty years of research. *Learning Disabilities: A Contemporary Journal, 2*(1), 9–21.

Clay, M. M. (1993). *Reading Recovery*. Auckland, New Zealand: Heinemann.

Coady, J. (1993). Research on ESL/EFL vocabulary acquisition: Putting it in context. In T. Huckin, M. Haynes, & J. Coady (Eds.), *Second language reading and vocabulary learning* (pp. 3–23). Norwood, NJ: Ablex.

Corson, D. (1997). The learning and use of academic English words. *Language Learning, 47*, 671–718.

Defior, S., & Tudela, P. (1994). Effects of phonological training on reading and writing acquisition. *Reading and Writing: An Interdisciplinary Journal, 6*, 299–320.

Denton, C. A., Anthony, J. L., Parker, R., & Hasbrouck, J. (2004). Effects of two tutoring programs on the English reading development of Spanish–English bilingual students. *The Elementary School Journal.*

Escamilla, K. (1994). *Descubriendo la lectura:* An early intervention literacy program in Spanish. *Literacy Teaching and Learning, 1*(1), 57–70.

Escamilla, K., Andrade, A., Basurto, A., & Ruiz, O. (1990–1991). *Descubriendo la lectura:* An early intervention Spanish language literacy project. *National Association for Bilingual Education Annual Conference Journal*, 31–43.

Escamilla, K., Loera, M., Ruiz, O., & Rodriguez, Y. (1998). An examination of sustaining effects in *descubriendo la lectura* programs. *Literacy Teaching and Learning: An International Journal of Early Reading and Writing, 3*(2), 59–78.

Eschevarria, J. (1995). Interactive reading instruction: A comparison of proximal and distal effects of instructional conversations. *Exceptional Children, 61*, 536–552.

Francis, D., Fletcher, J., Foorman, B., Goldenberg, C., & Vaughn, S. (2000–2004). Oracy/literacy development of Spanish-speaking children. Grant award by the National Institute of Child Health and Human Development and the Institute of Education Sciences (P01 HD 39521). Development of English Literacy in Spanish-Speaking Children. Unpublished raw data.

Frost, R. and Katz, L., (Eds.). (1992). *Orthography, phonology, morphology, and meaning*. Amsterdam: Elsevier North Holland Press.

Fuchs, D., Fuchs, L. S., Thompson, A., Al Otaiba, S., Yen, L., & Yang, N. J., Braun, M., & Connor, R. (2002). Exploring the importance of reading programs for kindergartners with disabilities in mainstream classrooms. *Exceptional Children, 68*, 295–311.

Garcia, G. E. (2000) Bilingual children's reading. In M. L. Kamil, P. B. Mosenthal, P. D. Pearson, & R. Barr (Eds.), *Handbook of reading research* (Vol. 3, pp. 813-834). Mahwah, NJ: Erlbaum.

Gersten, R., & Geva, E. (2003, April). Teaching reading to early language learners. *Educational Leadership, 60*(7), 44–49.

Goldenberg, C. (1994). Promoting early literacy development among Spanish-speaking children: Lesson from two studies. In E. Hiebert & B. M. Taylor (Eds.), *Getting reading right from the start: Effective early literacy interventions* (pp. 272–299). Boston: Allyn & Bacon.

Goldenberg, C., Reese, L., & Gallimore, R. (1992). Effects of literacy materials from school on Latino children's home experiences and early reading achievement. *American Journal of Education, 100*(4), 497–536.

Graves, M. F. (1984). Selecting vocabulary to teach in the intermediate and secondary grades. In J. Flood (Ed.), *Understanding reading comprehension* (pp. 245–260). Newark, DE: International Reading Association.

Grek, M. L., Mathes, P., & Torgesen, J. K. (2003). Similarities and differences between experienced teachers and trained paraprofessionals: An observational analysis. In S. Vaughn & K. Briggs (Eds.), *Reading in the classroom: Systems for the observation of teaching and learning* (pp. 267–294). Baltimore: Brookes.

Gunn, B., Biglan, A., Smolkowski, K., & Ary, D.

(2000). The efficacy of supplemental instruction in decoding skills for Hispanic and non-Hispanic students in early elementary school. *Journal of Special Education, 34*(2), 90–103.

Hasbrouck, J. E., & Tindal, G. (1992). Curriculum-based oral reading fluency norms for students grades 2 through 4. *Teaching Exceptional Children, 24*(3), 41–44.

Hickman, P., Pollard-Durodola, S., & Vaughn, S. (2004). *Storybook reading: Improving vocabulary and comprehension for English language learners. Reading Teacher, 57*(8), 720–730.

Katz, L., & Frost, R. (1992). Reading is different in different orthographies: The orthographic depth hypothesis. In R. Frost & L. Katz (Eds.), *Orthography, phonology, morphology, and meaning* (pp. 67–84). Amsterdam: Elsevier North Holland.

Klingner, J. K., & Vaughn, S. (1996). Reciprocal teaching of reading comprehension strategies for students with learning disabilities who use English as a second language. *Elementary School Journal, 96*(3), 275–293.

Klingner, J. K., & Vaughn, S. (2000). The helping behaviors of fifth-graders while using collaborative strategic reading during ESL content classes. *TESOL Quarterly, 34*(1), 69–98.

Larsen-Freeman, D. (2001). *Techniques and principles in language teaching.* New York: Oxford University Press.

Linan-Thompson, S., Vaughn, S., Hickman-Davis, P., & Kouzekanani, K. (2003). Effectiveness of supplemental reading instruction for second-grade English language learners with reading difficulties. *The Elementary School Journal, 103*(3), 221–238.

Lindholm-Leary, K. (2000). *Biliteracy for a global society: An idea book on dual language education.* Washington, DC: National Clearinghouse for Bilingual Education.

Lipsey, M. W., & Wilson, D. B. (1993). The efficacy of psychological, educational, and behavioral treatment: Confirmation from meta-analysis. *American Psychologist, 48*, 1181–1209.

Mathes, P., Linan-Thompson, S., Pollard-Durodola, S. D., Hagan, E. D., & Vaughn, S. (2003). *Lectura proactiva para principantes: Intensive small group instruction for Spanish-speaking readers.* Grant award by the National Institute of Child Health and Human Development, (HD 99 012). Development of English Literacy in Spanish-speaking Children. Unpublished raw data.

Mathes, P. G., Torgesen, J. K., Wahl, M., Menchetti, J. S., & Grek, M. L. (1999). *Proactive beginning reading: Intensive small group instruction for struggling readers.* Grant award by the National Institute of Child Health and Human Development, (R01 HD). Prevention and Remediation of Reading Disabilities. Unpublished raw data.

McLaughlin, B. (1994). First and second language literacy in the late elementary grades. In B. McLeod (Ed.), *Language and learning: Educating linguistically diverse students* (pp. 179–198). Albany: State University of New York Press.

Muniz-Swicegood, M. (1994). The effects of metacognitive reading strategy training on the reading performance and student reading analysis strategies of third grade bilingual students. *Bilingual Research Journal, 18*(102), 83–97.

Nagy, W. E. (1988). *Teaching vocabulary to improve reading comprehension.* Newark, DE: International Reading Association.

National Institute of Child Health and Human Development. (2000). *Report of the National Reading Panel: Teaching children to read: An evidence-based assessment of the scientific research literature on reading and its implications for reading instruction* (NIH Publication No. 00-4769). Washington, DC: U.S. Government Printing Office.

Neal, J. C., & Kelly, P. R. (1999). An examination of sustaining effects in *Descubriendo la Lectura* programs. *Literacy Teaching and Learning: An International Journal of Early Reading and Writing, 4*(2), 81–108.

O'Connor, R. E., Jenkins, J. R., & Slocum, T. A. (1995). Transfer among phonological tasks in kindergarten: Essential instructional content. *Journal of Educational Psychology, 87*, 202–217.

O'Malley, J. M., & Chamot, A. U. (1999). *Learning strategies in second language acquisition.* New York: Cambridge University Press.

Padilla, A. M., Fairchild, H. H., & Valadez, C. M. (1990). *Bilingual education: Issues and strategies.* Newbury Park, CA: Sage.

Ramirez, J. D., Yuen, S., & Ramey, D. (1991). *Longitudinal study of structured English immersion strategy, early-exit and late-exit transitional bilingual education programs for language-minority children* (Vols. 1–2). San Mateo, CA: Aguirre International.

Sanchez, E., & Rueda, M. I. (1991). Segmental awareness and dyslexia: Is it possible to learn to segment well and yet continue to read and write poorly? *Reading and Writing: An Interdisciplinary Journal 3*, 11–18.

Scarborough, H. (2001). Connecting early language and literacy to later reading (dis)abilities: Evidence, theory, and practice. In S. B. Neuman & D. K. Dickinson (Eds.), *Handbook of early literacy research* (pp. 97–110). New York: Guilford Press.

Seymour, P. H. K., Aro, M., & Erskine, J. M. (in collaboration with COST Action A8 Network). (2003). Foundation literacy acquisition in European orthographies. *British Journal of Psychology, 94*, 143–174.

Slavin, R. E., & Madden, N. A. (1999). Effects of bilingual and English as a second language adaptations of Success for All on the reading achievement of students acquiring English. *Journal of*

Education for Students Placed at Risk, 4, 393–416.

Slavin, R., & Madden, N. (2001). Effects of bilingual and English-as-a-second-language adaptations of Success for All on the reading achievement of students acquiring English. In R. E. Slavin & M. Calderon (Eds.), *Effective programs for Latino students* (pp. 207–250). Mahwah, NJ: Erlbaum.

Slavin, R., Madden, N. A., Dolan, L. J., Wasik, B. A., Ross, S., Smith, L., & Dianda, M. (1996). Success for all: A summary of research. *Journal of Education for Students Placed at Risk, 1,* 41–76.

Snow, C. E., Burns, M. S., & Griffin, P. (Eds.). (1998). *Preventing reading difficulties in young children.* Washington, DC: National Academy Press.

Stevens, R., Madden, N., Slavin, R., & Farnish, A. (1987). Cooperative integrated reading and composition: Two field experiments. *Reading Research Quarterly, 22,* 433–454.

Stuart, M. (1999). Getting ready for reading: Early phoneme awareness and phonics teaching improves reading and spelling in inner-city second-language learners. *British Journal of Educational Psychology, 69,* 587–605.

Torgesen, J. K., Wagner, R. K., Rashotte, C. K., Rose, E., Lindamood, P., Conway, T., et al. (1999). Preventing reading failure in young children with phonological processing disabilities: Group and individual response to instruction. *Journal of Educational Psychology, 91,* 579–593.

Ulanoff, S. H., & Pucci, S. L. (1999). Learning new words from books: The effects of read aloud on second language vocabulary acquisition. *Bilingual Research Journal, 23*(4), 409–421.

U.S. Department of Education, Office of Elementary and Secondary Education. (2002).*No Child Left Behind: A Desktop Reference.* Washington, DC: Author.

Vaughn, S., Linan-Thompson, S., Mathes, P. G., Cirino, P. T., Carlson, C. D., Pollard-Durodola, S. D., Cárdenas Hagan, E., & Francis, D. J. (in press). Effectiveness of Spanish intervention for first-grade English language learners at risk for reading difficulties. *Journal of Learning Disabilities.*

Vaughn, S., Mathes, P. G., Linan-Thompson, S., Cirino, P. T., Carlson, C. D. , Pollard-Durodola, S. D., Cárdenas Hagan, E., & Francis, D. J. (in press).First-grade English language learners at-risk for reading problems: Effectiveness of an English intervention. *Elementary School Journal.*

15

Recent Research on the Language and Literacy Skills of African American Students in the Early Years

HOLLY K. CRAIG
JULIE A. WASHINGTON

Far too many African American students entering kindergarten this year will experience significant difficulty learning to read as they progress through the elementary grades. By fourth grade, when students need to use their reading skills to comprehend academic content, many African American students evidence considerable difficulty understanding the general purpose of the text and are unable to elaborate the theme with details, or to connect it to their own real-life experiences. This problem is not new. Despite measurable progress across the past few decades, elementary-grade African American students nationwide continue to read at levels significantly below their mainstream peers (Donahue, Daane, & Grigg, 2003).

For more than a decade, our research program has been focusing on issues related to the language and literacy development of African American students. A decade ago, when we began this work, very little information was available about the oral language skills of this large minority population. Whereas good oral language skills are foundational to good reading skills, the lack of information about the language skills of African American students represented a critical shortcoming in identifying those factors supporting academic success and those that were barriers to achievement.

In this chapter we provide a brief discussion of the black–white achievement gap as a way to frame the problem in reading. Likely the factors contributing to the black–white achievement gap are many, varied, and overlapping. Two major hypotheses for persistence of the gap are discussed in the extant literature: early literacy experiences and poverty and its associated problems. We hypothesize that a neglected variable in recent decades is the role of language in the reading failure of many African American students. To make this point, we foreground information gathered primarily from our research program over the last decade that focuses on the sociolinguistic regularities characterizing child African American English (AAE), followed by a discussion of the roles of early literacy experiences and poverty in perpetuating the black–white achievement gap. We conclude by discussing implications and by identifying important new directions for future advancement of this line of research.

The Black–White Achievement Gap

Performance differences between African American and mainstream students are known as the "black–white test score gap" (Jencks & Phillips, 1998), or more broadly as the black–white achievement gap. Fishback and Baskin (1991) observed that this gap is long standing, with the performance disparity noted as early as 1910. Today, African American students remain much more likely than their white peers to perform at the lowest levels on standardized tests of reading achievement: 60% compared with 25% on the 2003 administration of the National Assessment of Educational Progress (NAEP; Donahue et al., 2003). In contrast, majority students are much more likely than African American students to read at or above basic levels: 75% compared with 40%. Failure to develop prerequisite reading skills can seriously curtail a student's ability to achieve across the academic content areas. Not surprisingly, therefore, on a national level, African American students perform significantly lower than their mainstream peers in science, math, and geography (Braswell, Daane, & Grigg, 2003; O'Sullivan, Lauko, Grigg, Qian, & Zhang, 2003; Weiss, Lutkus, Hildebrant, & Johnson, 2002). The black–white test score gap is apparent at school entry (West, Denton, & Reaney, 2000) and shows little improvement across the elementary grades or high school (Phillips, Crouse, & Ralph, 1998).

The persistence of the gap over the past century has negatively affected the quality of life for many African Americans compared with the white citizenry in the United States. Lower levels of academic achievement for African American students can translate into lower adult literacy levels and contribute to cross-generational cycles of poverty due to lower earnings and higher levels of unemployment (Hoffman & Llagas, 2003; Sable, 1998). The year 2004 marked the 50th anniversary of *Brown v. Board of Education* (1954). Unfortunately, for many African American students and adults, academic success and its many consequent benefits remain separate and unequal from that of white America.

One of the earliest hypotheses about the underlying basis for the black–white achievement gap focused on the role of dialect. Many African American students residing in large urban centers speak AAE at school entry (Battle, 1993; Craig & Washington, 2002; Manning & Baruth, 2000). AAE is a rule-governed variation of English spoken by many African Americans (Baugh, 2001; Craig & Washington, 2004b), and it is characterized by an expansive set of morphological, syntactic, semantic, phonological, and discourse features that differ systematically from the ways that the same meanings would be expressed in Standard American English (SAE). SAE, however, is the mainstream dialect in this country, and a formal version of SAE, known as Mainstream Classroom English (MCE) or School English (SE), is the language of classrooms, the curriculum, tests, and texts.

The role of AAE in reading acquisition was an early focus in the study of language and literacy skills of African American students. Borrowing from lessons learned in the study of second-language acquisition, scholars questioned whether reading achievement for African American students was negatively affected by dialect interference (Piestrup, 1973; Troutman & Falk, 1982), in which first-language (dialectal) forms intrude in the production of spoken and written English during literacy acquisition. With rare exceptions (Bartel & Axelrod, 1973), the general consensus of these studies was that students produced AAE features during oral reading tasks but that the dialect was unrelated to reading comprehension. This finding was robust across studies for students as early as first grade and extending through ninth grade (e.g., Rystrom, 1973–1974; Steffensen, Reynolds, McClure, & Guthrie, 1982). Dialect appeared unrelated in studies focusing on morphosyntactic features only (Gemake, 1981; Simons & Johnson, 1973; Steffensen et al., 1982), on phonological features only (Hart, Guthrie, & Winfield, 1980; Melmed, 1973; Rystrom, 1973–1974; Seymour & Ralabate, 1985), or on both (Goodman & Buck, 1973; Harber, 1977). Further, methods were recommended to avoid penalizing a student's production of features while reading aloud, using a system of credits (Harber, 1982) for widely used formal tests of reading such as the Gray Oral Reading Test (Gray & Robinson, 1967). Not surprisingly, in the context of so much agreement and failure to find important relationships between AAE features and reading performances, little additional research has focused explicitly on the potential role of AAE in reading since the mid-1980s.

The research heuristic in this early work was to probe for associations between specific dialect features and reading outcomes. The work was hampered greatly by dependence on the adult AAE feature system as the analytic base. At the time, what was known about AAE derived from studies of adolescents or adults when the research imperative was to refute prevailing assumptions that AAE was an inferior form of SAE (Dillard, 1972; Wolfram & Fasold, 1974). Literature has since shown the fallacy of making research assumptions about what children do linguistically based simply on adult data (Bloom, 1970; Brown, 1973), and more child-centered strategies have been adopted. The early research on reading, unfortunately, had no alternatives. Further, these early studies selected only a circumscribed subset of features, so it was not clear whether the lack of association between AAE and reading was valid or an artifact of the specific features chosen for study. This research would have benefited both from a child AAE feature system and a more holistic system-based rather than isolated feature-driven analysis.

The Language and Literacy Skills of African American Students

Until recently, very little was known about the AAE spoken by many African American children. A rich and extensive literature existed that characterized adult AAE, but important information about the dialectal features used by children, the developmental course of acquiring and using these features, and the relationships between AAE and literacy development were scarce. In the absence of information about child AAE, the foremost task was to identify and describe the features used by children.

The Child AAE Feature Inventory

The inventory of features that characterize child AAE is now fairly complete for the morphosyntactic and phonological feature systems (Craig, Thompson, Washington, & Potter, 2003; Craig & Washington, 2004b; Green, 2002; Labov, Baker, Bullock, Ross, & Brown, 1998; Seymour & Ralabate, 1985; Washington & Craig, 1994, 2002). Table 15.1 identifies and provides examples of the 34 features produced by the more than 1,000 students enrolled in our research program over the past decade (Craig et al., 2003; Washington & Craig, 1994, 2002). Although the linguistic conventions used to identify these features may be unfamiliar to some readers, it is hoped that all readers can see how rich a system this is, characterized by approximately three dozen rule-governed variations from SAE, and how predictable and principled these variations are. It is also hoped that the reader can appreciate that these are not minor variations, as is often the case in other dialects within the United States—for example, the dropping of r in some east coast communities. In combination, these AAE features can make an appreciable difference in the way an African American student talks compared with a mainstream peer.

Major lines of research are using this inventory to continue to advance understanding of child AAE. As an important example, AAE has much to offer to the linguistic goal of writing a Universal Grammar (UG), and one important line of research has been to focus on improving understanding of distinctive forms of AAE. Seymour, Roeper, and colleagues have generated meticulous descriptions of the special features of AAE that make the dialect distinct from SAE (Green, 2002; Seymour & Ralabate, 1985; Seymour & Roeper, 1999; Seymour & Seymour, 1981). Notably, these include contrastive features such as aspectual "be" ("she be workin'"), which communicates a habitual meaning and that has no morphosyntactic equivalent in SAE (Green, 1998, 2000; Seymour & Roeper, 1999), and noncontrastive features such as negative concord ("he don't have no friends"), which communicates a single negative meaning between two negative elements within a clause and that does have morphosyntactic equivalents in SAE ("he doesn't have any friends," "he has no friends"; Coles-White, 2004). This line of research contributes significantly to linguistic theory building and provides strong counterevidence to lingering negative attitudes that AAE is a deficient form of SAE.

In contrast to research programs framed within theoretical linguistics, our research program has adopted a sociolinguistic perspective. We have adopted a sociolinguistic approach because we are primarily interested in the importance of AAE for understanding the student more holistically as

TABLE 15.1. Morphosyntactic and Phonological Features of Child AAE

Morphosyntactic definitions	Examples
Ain't Ain't used as a negative auxiliary in have + not, do + not, are + not, and is + not constructions	"And the cars *ain't* gonna move."
Appositive pronoun Both a pronoun and a noun, or two pronouns, used to signify the same referent	"And this *girl she* has on a flower."
Completive *done* or *did* *Done* or *did* are used to emphasize a recently completed action	"I *done* broke this off." "They *did* fell."
Double marking Multiple agreement markers for regular nouns and verbs, and hypercorrection of irregulars	"But somebody *broked* it." "Here's *theirs* cars."
Double copula/auxiliary/modal Two modal auxiliary forms are used in a single clause	"Why *does* Ken *don't hafta* put on his yet?"
Existential *it* *It* is used in place of *there* to indicate the existence of a referent without adding meaning	"And *it's* a lot of people outside."
Fitna/sposeta/bouta Abbreviated forms coding imminent action	"I'm *fitna* get her something." "Her *bouta* go to the movies with her mama." "We *sposeta* push this so the cars can go?"
Had Preterite *had* appears before simple past verbs	"They *had* fell down."
Indefinite article *A* is used regardless of the vowel context	"Yeah her house is *a* island."
Invariant *be* Infinitival *be* coding habitual actions or states	"This car *be* fast."
Multiple negation Two or more negatives used in a clause	"She *don't* have *no* shoes."
Noninverted question Subject and auxiliary not inverted in direct questions, including those involving *wh-* forms	"What he's gonna do with this?"
Regularized reflexive pronoun *Hisself, theyself, theirselves* replace reflexive pronouns	"Then the other boy hurt *hisself* on the head."
Remote past *been* *Been* coding action in the remote past	"I *been* knew how to swim."
Subject–verb agreement* Subjects and verbs differ in marking of number	"And he *have* a lunchbox."
Undifferentiated pronoun case Pronoun cases used interchangeably	"*Her* said stop."
Zero article Articles are variably included	"She got _ purse too."
Zero copula/auxiliary Copula and auxiliary forms of the verb *to be* are variably included	"____ this the baby's shoe?" "No I ____ goin' in."

(continued)

TABLE 15.1. *(continued)*

Morphosyntactic definitions	Examples
<u>Zero -*ing*</u> Present progressive -*ing* is variably included	"Are you lay____ down?"
<u>Zero modal auxiliary*</u> *Will*, *can*, *do*, and *have* are variably included as modal auxiliaries	"How ____ you put it on?"
<u>Zero past tense*</u> -*ed* markers are variably included on regular past verbs and present forms of irregulars are used	"Look a Barbie's shoe *fall* off." "She already comb____ her hair."
<u>Zero plural*</u> -*s* is variably included to mark number	"They are pig_."
<u>Zero possessive*</u> Possession coded by word order so -*s* is deleted or the case of possessive pronouns is changed	"And that was *they* son." "Somebody_ coat fell on the ground."
<u>Zero preposition</u> Prepositions are variably included	"And what happened ____ the tree?"
<u>Zero *to*</u> Infinitival *to* is variably included	"And the little girl trying ____ help him up."

Phonological definitions	Examples
<u>Postvocalic consonant reduction*</u> Deletions of consonant singles following vowels	"envelope" /ɛnvəlo/ for /ɛnvəlop/
<u>*g* dropping</u> Substitutions of /n/ for /ŋ/ in final word positions	"sledding" /slɛdɪn/ for /slɛdɪŋ/
<u>Substitutions for /θ/ and /ð/</u> /t/ and /d/ substitute for /θ/ and /ð/ in prevocalic positions, /f, t/ and /v/ substitute for /θ/ and /ð/ in intervocalic positions, and in postvocalic positions	"their" /deɚ/ for /ðeɚ/ "mouth" /maʊf/ for /maʊθ/ "without" /wɪtaʊt/ for /wɪθaʊt/
<u>Consonant cluster reduction*</u> Deletion of phonemes from consonant clusters	"ground" /graʊn/ for /graʊnd/
<u>Consonant cluster movement</u> Reversal of phonemes within a cluster, with or without consonant reduplication	"ask" /æks/ for /æsk/
<u>Devoicing final consonants</u> Voiceless consonants substitute for voiced following the vowel	"crossing guard" /krɔsɪŋ gaɚt/ for /krɔsɪŋ gaɚd/
<u>Syllable deletion</u> Reduction of an (unstressed) syllable in a multisyllabic word	"became" /kem/ for /bikem/
<u>Syllable addition</u> Addition of a syllable to a word, usually as a hypercorrection	"stopped" /staptɪd/ for /stapt/
<u>Monophthongization of diphthongs</u> Neutralization of diphthong	"side" /sad/ for /saɪd/

Note. Asterisks indicate those features that might be considered either a morphosyntactic or phonological form, depending on the particular lexical context (Craig et al., 2003; Labov et al., 1998).

a speaker of AAE who is trying to learn in particular social–linguistic contexts. The following section summarizes findings from a number of school-based studies we have undertaken to examine relationships between child AAE and performances in authentic testing and learning contexts.

Distributional Properties of Child AAE

In order to begin this work, we developed a metric for comparing and contrasting levels of feature production and probed for systematic variations among students related to this measure. Accordingly, the Dialect Density Measure (DDM; Craig, Washington, & Thompson-Porter, 1998) divides the frequency of AAE features produced in a sample by the number of words in the sample. DDM helps to stabilize variance in feature production rates due to variations in sample lengths and captures how much feature production characterizes a student's discourse.

Major findings to date for distributional relationships between feature production rates as measured by DDMs relate to grade/age and to context. Developmentally, production of AAE features is highly variable (Washington & Craig, 1994; Washington, Craig, & Kushmaul, 1998), from a high of 1 feature per 4 words to only 1 feature per 91 words for kindergartners and from 1 feature per 5 words to zero for first to fifth graders (Craig & Washington, 2004a). In other words, practitioners may find that young students, at school entry, produce many more AAE features than their older schoolmates. Also at school entry, boys produce more AAE features than do girls (Craig & Washington, 2002; Washington & Craig, 1998; Washington et al., 1998), but these differences disappear in later grades (Craig & Washington, 2004a; Thompson, Craig, & Washington, 2004). Further, at school entry, students from low socioeconomic status (LSES) homes produce higher rates of AAE features than those from middle socioeconomic status (MSES) homes (Washington & Craig, 1998), but again these differences disappear in later grades (Craig & Washington, 2004a; Thompson et al., 2004).

Across grades, for many (approximately two thirds) but not all students, AAE feature production during spoken discourse shifts dramatically downward at first grade (Craig & Washington, 2004a). A second major downward shift in feature production rates occurs for oral reading in third grade (Craig, Thompson, Washington, & Potter, 2004). Sensitivity to MCE increases significantly between kindergarten and first grade but then remains the same at second grade (Charity, Scarborough, & Griffin, 2004), suggesting that the downward shift for production of AAE features at first grade corresponds to an upward shift in sensitivity. These observations are important because they indicate that language skills, particularly dialect shifting abilities, increase spontaneously for many students and are associated with substantially better reading outcomes. This relationship is considered again in the next section of this chapter.

AAE varies in systematic ways by context. AAE is spoken by many African American students living both in large urban centers and in midsize central cities (Craig & Washington, 2002; Manning & Baruth, 2000). However, students residing in urban-fringe communities produce higher rates of AAE features than students in midsize central cities (Craig & Washington, 2004a). Discourse genre also influences feature production rates so that more features occur during semistructured picture descriptions than during spontaneous free-play interactions (Washington et al., 1998). AAE features occur during oral reading of SAE text and during spontaneous writing, but again at lower levels than during picture descriptions (Thompson et al., 2004). Further, writing facilitates student shifts between AAE and MCE productions (Thompson et al., 2004).

Overall, these findings underscore the value of considering child AAE from a sociolinguistic perspective. Variable rates of feature production characterize the African American student's discourse, and this variability is orderly and predictable. Both intrinsic child variables—in particular, gender and SES—and extrinsic variables—especially grade, community, and discourse context—relate systematically to the production of child AAE features.

Bidialectalism

Across the elementary grades, some children develop bidialectal skills, learning to shift to SAE renderings of what were initially produced as AAE forms. This shift to SAE provides closer alignment to the MCE of classrooms and to language and literacy testing contexts and is advantageous. Dialect shifting is evidence of a child's increasing bidialectal competence and can occur as a by-product of formal schooling in the absence of explicit instruction (Adler, 1992; Battle, 1996; Bountress, 1983; Craig & Washington, 2004b; Manning & Baruth, 2000). Many African American adults are bidialectal, and this linguistic competence can translate into improved economic and social mobility (Baron, 2000; Doss & Gross, 1994; Hoover, 1978).

Our data reveal that approximately two-thirds of African American elementary-grade students dialect shift away from AAE toward the MCE of classrooms without explicit instruction (Craig et al., 2003; Craig & Washington, 2004a; Thompson et al., 2004). African American students who dialect shift have measurably better reading performances than nonshifters (Craig & Washington, 2004a). Significantly better reading abilities also are associated with greater sensitivity to SE (Charity et al., 2004). Even in the later grades, however, many students continue to use AAE features during spoken discourse, and approximately one-third may show no evidence of dialect shifting (Craig & Washington, 2004a). The reading performances of the nonshifting group are poor and consistent with the national data for African American students who perform in the low normal range on most standardized tests (Donahue et al., 2003).

We know very little else about the acquisition of bidialectal skills by African American students. As discussed earlier in this chapter, examination of feature-specific linkages to reading outcomes was not fruitful when pursued in the research programs of the 1970s and early 1980s, and it was largely abandoned. Although empirical study was discontinued, scholars continued to acknowledge that AAE must play a contributing role; Rickford (1999) said the following:

> The factor . . . which has led many linguists (like myself) to get involved in this issue, is the depressingly poor record of American schools in helping African American students to read and write well, and to succeed in school more generally. While other factors (such as teacher expectations and school facilities) are involved in this failure, the distinctive, systematic vernacular which many African American students speak (AAVE or Ebonics)[1] is certainly relevant, especially teachers' negative and prejudicial attitudes toward it, and their failure to take it into account in helping students master the art of reading and writing in the standard variety. (p. 344)

Armed now with a better understanding of child AAE and a metric for exploring AAE relationships to academic achievements using the DDM, future research must probe the potential influences of a student's status as a dialect speaker and his or her reading performances. This seems particularly important in the context of two studies, published within a short time of each other, that show that shifting to MCE forms of AAE features in spoken discourse and greater sensitivity to the forms of MCE both bear marked and positive relationships to reading achievement outcomes (Charity et al., 2004; Craig & Washington, 2004a).

Our recent research stands in sharp contrast to prior studies that failed to find an important relationship between AAE and reading achievement. Prior research failed to find feature-specific influences on reading outcomes that had explanatory potential for understanding the black–white achievement gap. Our own work has the advantage of a child AAE feature inventory and a metric for capturing whole-system rather than isolated feature-level effects. The unresolved and high levels of reading failure experienced by so many students in this large segment of U.S. society and the advantages of new information and measures make a compelling case for revisiting the relationship between language and literacy for African American students.

Many students are becoming bidialectal across the early elementary grades (Craig & Washington, 2004a). However, many African American students living in the same communities, attending the same schools, and enrolled in the same classes fail to make this shift. Why? What are the factors that support a child's increasing sensitivity to MCE and the development of bidialectal skills? At what level does dialect production most affect performance—decoding, spelling, reading comprehension, or writing? Should teachers encourage SAE, and how would one do so in constructive and respectful ways? What is the relative importance of bidialectal competence compared with other important contributing factors? Answers to many important questions remain forthcoming.

Early Literacy Experiences and the Impact of Poverty

No consideration of the black–white achievement gap can ignore the importance of early literacy experiences and the role of poverty in the lives of many African American students. These two variables are widely discussed and influence early literacy skill development and academic achievement in fundamental ways.

Prior to school entry, many African American students have primary exposure to literacy practices that differ from those of their mainstream peers. Therefore, early classroom instruction may teach foundational reading skills using literacy materials and interactive methods unfamiliar to the African American child, for which he or she has limited prior preparation. Storytelling in African American homes often takes the form of oral, collaborative, fictionalized narratives (Heath, 1983; Vernon-Feagans, 1996), and this distinctive style helps preserve cultural identity (Heath, 1983; Ogbu, 1988). Not surprisingly, therefore, African American preschoolers likely own fewer books and may not be read to on a daily basis (Federal Interagency Forum on Child and Family Statistics [FIFCFS], 2003; Nettles & Perna, 1997). For many young African American children, environmental print (e.g., names on signs, trademarks, etc.) represents a first and key form of literacy experience (Craig & Washington, 2004b; Purcell-Gates, 1996).

In contrast, mainstream peers are more likely to engage in frequent storybook reading in the home (DeTemple, 2001; Whitehurst & Lonigan, 2001), and these opportunities are positive predictors of later reading skills (Bus, van IJzendoorn, & Pellegrini, 1995; Scarborough & Dobrich, 1994; Scarborough, Dobrich, & Hager, 1991). Home-based storybook reading is characterized by question–response routines between parent and child that are a good fit to the early literacy activities of classrooms (Anderson-Yockel & Haynes, 1994; Hammer, 1999; Pellegrini, Perlmutter, Galda, & Brody, 1990). As a whole, these findings indicate that family literacy practices for African American and mainstream students differ considerably and that the family practices of mainstream students are more congruent with those of early literacy instruction in schools.

Recent research indicates that a better alignment between home and school practices can be achieved fairly readily with significant positive benefits. Of particular importance, minority parents read with their children the books that are sent home from school (Connor, 2002; Robinson, Larsen, & Haupt, 1996). Home book programs for minority children increase both the number of books in the home, which is a key positive predictor of later reading achievement (Chall, Jacobs, & Baldwin, 1990; Yaden et al., 2000), and the overall frequencies of literacy activities experienced by children at home (Robinson et al., 1996). It will be important for future research to improve our understanding of other ways in which home and school can work together to improve the young African American student's readiness for the literacy practices of schools.

Unlike the positive associations that seem possible with early literacy for African American students, the resolution of poverty is less hopeful, and poverty has a huge adverse effect on student achievement. Whereas African American children are more likely than white children to grow up in impoverished households (30% vs. 9%; FIFCFS, 2003), family socioeconomic status must be considered in any attempt to understand the black–white achievement gap. Poverty is not a circumscribed factor but alternatively is associated with covariables that bear a negative relationship to achievement. Low income levels are frequently associated with lower educational levels and poor adult literacy levels in the home (Hoffman & Llagas, 2003; McLoyd, 1990, 1998). Poor families may have limited access to health care, generally poorer nutrition, increased exposure to environmental hazards, and other negative neighborhood influences that may increase the prevalence of medical and developmental problems compared with mainstream children (Brooks-Gunn, Duncan, Klebanov, & Sealand, 1993; Fazio, Naremore, & Connell, 1996). Paired with sparse books, infrequent reading opportunities, and single-parent heads of households (Hoffman & Llagas, 2003; Nettles & Perna, 1997), the cumulative effects of these covariables place African American children living in poverty at increased risk for literacy failure.

Fortunately, there is a burgeoning scientific base identifying the core characteristics of early educational programs that can beat these odds. High-quality preschool experiences and targeted early intervention programs both yield impressive positive results for at-risk students. The understanding of what constitutes high-quality early schooling has increased dramatically in recent years and can be characterized in part by low teacher–student ratios (Biddle & Berliner, 2002; Wasley, 2002), strong teacher qualifications (Dickinson, 2001), high teacher expectations (Chall et al., 1990; Gill & Reynolds, 1999), effective use of paraprofessionals (Schepis, Reid, Ownbey, & Parsons, 2001), and cognitively challenging decontextualized talk during pretend play (Dickinson & Smith, 1994). Clearly, more research of this type is needed. How can these characteristics of high-quality preschool programs be maximized and generalized to benefit all African American students?

A number of large-scale prevention programs have convincingly demonstrated that a focus on critical early literacy skills such as phonological awareness (Torgesen, 1998; Vellutino, Scanlon, & Tanzman, 1998) relates to significant improvements in later outcomes for children at risk (Brown & Felton, 1990; Foorman, Francis, Fletcher, Schatschneider, & Mehta, 1998; Torgesen et al., 1999; Vellutino et al., 1996; Whitehurst et al., 1994). Further, for AAE-speaking students and/or economically disadvantaged preschoolers, direct explicit instruction rather than implicit strategies may be especially beneficial (Connor, 2002; Foorman & Torgesen, 2001). These positive findings are hopeful signs that some of the negative influences of poverty can be ameliorated, at least in part, with early, high-quality instructional programs that target foundational literacy skills. Whereas African American students are disproportionately living in low-income homes, this segment of U.S. schoolchildren stands to benefit the most from making high-quality instructional programs the norm across the country.

Implications and Future Directions

Our research program has made a number of significant contributions to current understanding of the African American student. In other work, research in theoretical linguistics has demonstrated that AAE features occur within specific linguistic contexts on a rule-governed basis. Our sociolinguistic studies provide complementary evidence that variations between children are also systematic and reflect a fairly complex set of intrinsic and extrinsic child factors.

The inventory of morphosyntactic and phonological features of child AAE has been established and represents an important advancement. This inventory provides a firm foundation for ongoing research about the linguistic parameters that govern specific features. In addition, the inventory is sufficiently comprehensive that distributional relationships between the density of dialect feature production and language and literacy relationships are now possible. Both of these lines of research are critical to understanding African American students and must be vigorously pursued.

Unfortunately, the data necessary to define appropriate programmatic responses to the positive relationships between bidialectal skill and reading outcomes are simply not yet available. When available, this information will have important practical implications. For example, it may prove possible to teach dialect shifting to African American students in the early grades and gain the same improvements for reading achievement as experienced by students who learn bidialectal skills without formal instruction. At this time, it is not at all clear how practitioners interested in working on bidialectal skill development should proceed. Where does a teacher start? Should the focus be on phonological features, morphosyntactic features, or both, or should this be determined by grade and general language developmental level? Many important questions, therefore, remain unanswered.

In conclusion, understanding of the challenges faced by African American students has increased dramatically in recent years and has raised new questions. Interest in improving the outcomes for African American students is at an all-time high, and many promising new directions are apparent. For researchers and practitioners interested in improving the achievement levels of African American students in the early grades, this is an exciting and promising time.

Note

1. AAVE (African American Vernacular English) and Ebonics are terms that also refer to AAE and often are the preferred terminology of linguists.

References

Adler, S. (1992). *Multicultural communication skills in the classroom*. Boston: Allyn & Bacon.

Anderson-Yockel, J., & Haynes, W. (1994). Joint picture-book reading strategies in working-class African American and white mother–toddler dyads. *Journal of Speech, Language, and Hearing Research, 37,* 583–593.

Baron, D. (2000). Ebonics and the politics of English. *World Englishes, 19,* 5–19.

Bartel, N. R., & Axelrod, J. (1973). Nonstandard English usage and reading ability in Black junior high students. *Exceptional Children, 39,* 653–655.

Battle, D. E. (1993). *Communication disorders in multicultural populations*. Boston: Andover Medical.

Battle, D. E. (1996). Language learning and use by African American children. *Topics in Language Disorders, 16,* 22–37.

Baugh, J. (2001). Coming full circle: Some circumstances pertaining to low literacy achievement among African Americans. In J. Harris, A. Kamhi, & K. Pollock (Eds.), *Literacy in African American communities* (pp. 277–288). Hillsdale, NJ: Erlbaum.

Biddle, B. J., & Berliner, D. C. (2002). Small class size and its effects. *Educational Leadership, 59*(5), 12–23.

Bloom, L. (1970). *Language development: Form and function in emerging grammars*. Cambridge, MA: MIT Press.

Bountress, N. G. (1983). Effect of segregated and integrated educational settings upon selected dialectal features. *Perceptual and Motor Skills, 57,* 71–78.

Braswell, J., Daane, M., & Grigg, W. (2003). *The nation's report card: Mathematics highlights 2003* (NCES No. 2004–451). Washington, DC: U.S. Department of Education, Institute of Education Sciences, National Center for Education Statistics.

Brooks-Gunn, J., Duncan, G. J., Klebanov, P. K., & Sealand, N. (1993). Do neighborhoods influence child and adolescent development? *American Journal of Sociology, 99,* 353–395.

Brown v. Board of Education, 347 U.S. 483 (1954).

Brown, I. S., & Felton, R. H. (1990). Effects of instruction on beginning reading skills in children at risk for reading disability. *Reading and Writing, 2,* 223–241.

Brown, R. (1973). *A first language: The early stages*. Cambridge, MA: Harvard University Press.

Bus, A. G., van IJzendoorn, M. H., & Pelligrini, A. D. (1995). Joint book reading makes for success in learning to read: A meta-analysis on intergenerational transmission of literacy. *Review of Educational Research, 65,* 1–21.

Chall, J. S., Jacobs, V. A., & Baldwin, L. E. (1990). *The reading crisis: Why poor children fall behind*. Cambridge, MA: Harvard University Press.

Charity, A. H., Scarborough, H. S., & Griffin, D. M. (2004). Familiarity with School English in African American children and its relation to early reading achievement. *Child Development, 75,* 1340–1356.

Coles-White, D. (2004). Negative concord in child African American English: Implications for specific language impairment. *Journal of Speech, Language, and Hearing Research, 47,* 212–222.

Connor, C. M. (2002). *Preschool children and teachers talking together: The influence of child, family, teacher, and classroom characteristics on children's developing literacy*. Unpublished doctoral dissertation, University of Michigan, Ann Arbor.

Craig, H. K., Thompson, C. A., Washington, J. A., & Potter, S. L. (2003). Phonological features of child African American English. *Journal of Speech, Language, and Hearing Research, 46,* 623–635.

Craig, H. K., Thompson, C. A., Washington, J. A., & Potter, S. L. (2004). Performance of elementary grade African American students on the Gray Oral Reading Tests. *Language, Speech, and Hearing Services in Schools, 35,* 141–154.

Craig, H. K., & Washington, J. A. (2002). Oral language expectations for African American preschoolers and kindergartners. *American Journal of Speech–Language Pathology, 11,* 59–70.

Craig, H. K., & Washington, J. A. (2004a). Grade-related changes in the production of African American English. *Journal of Speech, Language, and Hearing Research, 47,* 450–463.

Craig, H. K., & Washington, J. A. (2004b). Language variation and literacy learning. In C. A. Stone, E. R. Silliman, B. J. Ehren, & K. Apel (Eds.), *Handbook of language and literacy: Development and disorders* (pp. 228–247). New York: Guilford Press.

Craig, H. K., Washington, J. A., & Thompson-Porter, C. (1998). Average c-unit lengths in the discourse of African American children from low income, urban homes. *Journal of Speech, Language, and Hearing Research, 41,* 433–444.

DeTemple, J. M. (2001). Parents and children reading books together. In D. K. Dickinson & P. O. Tabors (Eds.), *Beginning literacy with children:*

Young children learning at home and school (pp. 31–51). Baltimore: Brookes.

Dickinson, D. K. (2001). Putting the pieces together: Impact of preschool on children's language and literature development in kindergarten. In D. K. Dickinson & P. O. Tabors (Eds.), *Beginning literacy with language* (pp. 257–287). Baltimore: Brookes.

Dickinson, D. K., & Smith, M. W. (1994). Long-term effects of preschool teachers' book readings on low-income children's vocabulary and story comprehension. *Reading Research Quarterly, 29*, 104–122.

Dillard, J. L. (1972). *Black English: Its history and usage in the United States.* New York: Random House.

Donahue, P., Daane, M., & Grigg, W. (2003). *The nation's report card: Reading highlights 2003* (NCES No. 2004–452). Washington, DC: U.S. Department of Education, Institute of Education Sciences, National Center for Education Statistics.

Doss, R. C., & Gross, A. M. (1994). The effects of Black English and code-switching on intraracial perceptions. *Journal of Black Psychology, 20*, 282–293.

Fazio, B., Naremore, R. C., & Connell, P. J. (1996). Tracking children from poverty at risk for specific language impairment: A 3-year longitudinal study. *Journal of Speech and Hearing Research, 39*, 611–624.

Federal Interagency Forum on Child and Family Statistics. (2003). *America's children: Key national indicators of well-being.* Washington, DC: U.S. Government Printing Office.

Fishback, P. V., & Baskin, J. H. (1991). Narrowing the black-white gap in child literacy in 1910: The roles of school inputs and family inputs. *Review of Economics and Statistics, 73*, 725–728.

Foorman, B. R., Francis, D. J., Fletcher, J. M., Schatschneider, C., & Mehta, P. (1998). The role of instruction in learning to read: Preventing reading failure in at-risk children. *Journal of Educational Psychology, 90*, 37–55.

Foorman, B. R., & Torgesen, J. (2001). Critical elements of classroom and small-group instruction promote reading success in all children. *Learning Disabilities Research and Practice, 16*, 203–212.

Gemake, J. S. (1981). Interference of certain dialect elements with reading comprehension for third graders. *Reading Improvement, 18*, 183–189.

Gill, S., & Reynolds, A. J. (1999). Educational expectations and school achievement of urban African American children. *Journal of School Psychology, 37*, 403-424.

Goodman, K. S., & Buck, C. (1973). Dialect barriers to reading comprehension revisited. *Reading Teacher, 27*, 6–12.

Gray, W. S., & Robinson, H. M. (1967). *Gray Oral Reading Test.* Indianapolis, IN: Bobbs-Merrill.

Green, L. J. (1998). Remote past and states in African-American English. *American Speech, 73*, 115–138.

Green, L. J. (2000). Aspectual *be*-type constructions and coercion in African American English. *Natural Language Semantics, 8*, 1–25.

Green, L. J. (2002). *African American English: A linguistic introduction.* Cambridge, UK: Cambridge University Press.

Hammer, C. S. (1999). Guiding language development: How African American mothers and their infants structure play. *Journal of Speech, Language, and Hearing Research, 42*, 1219–1233.

Harber, J. R. (1977). Influence of presentation dialect and orthographic form on reading performance of black, inner-city children. *Educational Research Quarterly, 2*(2), 9–16.

Harber, J. R. (1982). Accepting dialect renderings of extant materials on black-English speaking children's oral reading scores. *Education and Treatment of Children, 5*, 271–282.

Hart, J. T., Guthrie, J. T., & Winfield, L. (1980). Black English phonology and learning to read. *Journal of Educational Psychology, 72*, 636–646.

Heath, S. B. (1983). *Ways with words.* Cambridge, UK: Cambridge University Press.

Hoffman, K., & Llagas, C. (2003). *Status and trends in the education of Blacks* (NCES No. 2003-034). Washington, DC: U. S. Department of Education, National Center for Education Statistics.

Hoover, M. R. (1978). Community attitudes toward Black English. *Language in Society, 7*, 65–87.

Jencks, C., & Phillips, M. (Eds.). (1998). *The black–white test score gap.* Washington, DC: Brookings Institution Press.

Labov, W., Baker, B., Bullock, S., Ross, L., & Brown, M. (1998). *A graphemic–phonemic analysis of the reading errors of inner city children.* Unpublished manuscript. Retrieved June 6, 2001, from www.Ling.upenn.edu/~wlabov/Papers/GAREC/GAREC.html

Manning, M. L., & Baruth, L. G. (2000). *Multicultural education of children and adolescents* (3rd ed.). Boston: Allyn & Bacon.

McLoyd, V. C. (1990). The impact of economic hardship on black families and children: Psychological distress, parenting, and socioemotional development. *Child Development, 61*, 311–346.

McLoyd, V. C. (1998). Socioeconomic disadvantage and child development. *American Psychologist, 53*, 185–204.

Melmed, P. J. (1973). Black English phonology: The question of reading interference. In J. L. Laffey & R. W. Shuy (Eds.), *Language differences: Do they interfere?* (pp. 70–85). Newark, DE: International Reading Association.

Nettles, M. T., & Perna, L. W. (1997). *The African American education data book: Vol. II. Preschool through high school.* Ann Arbor, MI: Frederick D. Patterson Research Institute of College Fund/UNCF.

Ogbu, J. (1988). Cultural diversity and human development. *New Directions for Child Development*, 42,11–28.

O'Sullivan, C. Y., Lauko, M. A., Grigg, W. S., Qian, J., & Zhang, J. (2003). *The nation's report card: Science 2000* (NCES No. 2003-453). Washington, DC: U.S. Department of Education, Institute of Education Sciences, National Center for Education Statistics.

Pellegrini, A., Perlmutter, J., Galda, L., & Brody, G. (1990). Joint reading between black Head Start children and their mothers. *Child Development*, 61, 443–453.

Phillips, M., Crouse, J., & Ralph, J. (1998). Does the black–white test score gap widen after children enter school? In C. Jencks & M. Phillips (Eds.), *The black–white test score gap* (pp. 229–272). Washington, DC: Brookings Institution Press.

Piestrup, A. (1973). *Black dialect interference and accommodation of reading instruction in first grade* (Language-Behavior Research Laboratory Monograph No. 4). Berkeley, CA: University of California.

Purcell-Gates, V. (1996). Stories, coupons, and the TV Guide: Relationships between home literacy experiences and emergent literacy knowledge. *Reading Research Quarterly*, 31, 406–428.

Rickford, J. R. (1999). *African American Vernacular English: Features, evolution, educational implications*. Malden, MA: Blackwell.

Robinson, C. C., Larsen, J. M., & Haupt, J. H. (1996). The influence of selecting and taking picture books home on the at-home reading behaviors of kindergarten children. *Reading Research and Instruction*, 35, 249–259.

Rystrom, R. (1973–1974). Perceptions of vowel letter–sound relationships by first-grade children. *Reading Research Quarterly*, 2, 170–185.

Sable, J. (1998). The educational progress of black students. In J. Wirt, T. Snyder, J. Sable, S. P. Choy, Y. Bae, J. Stennett, A. Gruner, & M. Perie (Eds.), *The condition of education 1998* (No. NCES 98-013, pp. 2–10). Retrieved August 14, 2002, from the U.S. Department of Education, National Center for Education Statistics, website: nc   es.ed.gov/pubs98/98013.pdf

Scarborough, H. S., & Dobrich, W. (1994). On the efficacy of reading to preschoolers. *Developmental Review*, 14, 245–302.

Scarborough, H. S., Dobrich, W., & Hager, M. (1991). Preschool literacy experience and later reading achievement. *Journal of Learning Disabilities*, 24, 508–511.

Schepis, M. M., Reid, D. H., Ownbey, J., & Parsons, M. B. (2001). Training support staff to embed teaching within natural routines of young children with disabilities in an inclusive preschool. *Journal of Applied Behavior Analysis*, 34, 313–327.

Seymour, H. N., & Ralabate, P. K. (1985). The acquisition of a phonologic feature of Black English.

Journal of Communication Disorders, 18, 139–148.

Seymour, H. N., & Roeper, T. (1999). Grammatical acquisition of African American English. In O. L. Taylor & L. Leonard (Eds.), *Language acquisition across North America: Cross-cultural and cross-linguistic perspectives* (pp. 109–152). San Diego, CA: Singular.

Seymour, H. N., & Seymour, C. M. (1981). Black English and Standard American English contrasts in consonantal development of 4- and 5-year-old children. *Journal of Speech and Hearing Disorders, 46,* 274–280.

Simons, H. D., & Johnson, K. R. (1974). Black English syntax and reading interference. *Research in the Teaching of English, 8,* 339–358.

Steffensen, M. S., Reynolds, R. E., McClure, E., & Guthrie, L. F. (1982). Black English Vernacular and reading comprehension: A cloze study of third, sixth, and ninth graders. *Journal of Reading Behavior, 14,* 285–298.

Thompson, C. A., Craig, H. K., & Washington, J. A. (2004). Variable production of African American English across oracy and literacy contexts. *Language, Speech, and Hearing Services in Schools, 35,* 269–282.

Torgesen, J. K. (1998, Spring-Summer). Catch them before they fall: Identification and assessment to prevent reading failure in young children. *American Educator, 32–39.*

Torgesen, J. K., Wagner, R. K., Rashotte, C. A., Rose, E., Lindamood, P., Conway, T., et al. (1999). Preventing reading failure in young children with phonological processing disabilities: Group and individual responses to instruction. *Journal of Educational Psychology, 91,* 579–593.

Troutman, D. E., & Falk, J. S. (1982). Speaking Black English and reading: Is there a problem of interference? *Journal of Negro Education, 51,* 123–133.

Vellutino, F. R., Scanlon, D. M., Sipay, E. R., Small, S. G., Pratt, A., Chen, R., et al. (1996). Cognitive profiles of difficult to remediate and readily remediated poor readers: Early intervention as a vehicle for distinguishing between cognitive and experiential deficits as basic causes of specific reading disability. *Journal of Educational Psychology, 88,* 601–638.

Vellutino, F. R., Scanlon, D. M., & Tanzman, M. S. (1998). The case for early intervention in diagnosing specific reading disability. *Journal of School Psychology, 36,* 367–397.

Vernon-Feagans, L. (1996). *Children's talk in communities and classrooms.* Cambridge, MA: Blackwell.

Washington, J. A., & Craig, H. K. (1994). Dialectal forms during discourse of urban, African American preschoolers living in poverty. *Journal of Speech and Hearing Research, 37,* 816–823.

Washington, J. A., & Craig, H. K. (1998). Socioeconomic status and gender influences on children's dialectal variations. *Journal of Speech, Language, and Hearing Research, 41,* 618–626.

Washington, J. A., & Craig, H. K. (2002). Morphosyntactic forms of African American English used by young children and their caregivers. *Applied Psycholinguistics, 23,* 209–231.

Washington, J. A., Craig, H. K., & Kushmaul, A. J. (1998). Variable use of African American English across two language sampling contexts. *Journal of Speech, Language, and Hearing Research, 41,* 1115–1124.

Wasley, P. A. (2002). Small classes, small schools: The time is now. *Educational Leadership, 59*(5), 6–10.

Weiss, A. R., Lutkus, A. D., Hildebrant, B. S., & Johnson, M. S. (2002). *The nation's report card: Geography 2001* (NCES No. 2002-484). Washington, DC: U.S. Department of Education, Office of Educational Research and Improvement, National Center for Education Statistics.

West, J., Denton, K., & Reaney, L. (2000). *The kindergarten year: Findings from the Early Childhood Longitudinal Study, kindergarten class of 1998–99* (NCES No. 2001-023). Washington, DC: U.S. Department of Education, Office of Educational Research and Improvement, National Center for Education Statistics.

Whitehurst, G. J., Epstein, J. N., Angell, A. L., Payne, A. C., Crone, D. A., & Fischel, J. E. (1994). Outcomes of emergent literacy intervention in Head Start. *Journal of Educational Psychology, 86,* 542–555.

Whitehurst, G. J., & Lonigan, C. L. (2001). Emergent literacy: Development from prereaders to readers. In S. B. Neuman & D. K. Dickinson (Eds.), *Handbook of early literacy research* (pp. 11–29). New York: Guilford Press.

Wolfram, W., & Fasold, R. (1974). *The study of social dialects in American English.* Englewood Cliffs, NJ: Prentice Hall.

Yaden, D. B., Jr., Tam, A., Madrigal, P., Brassell, D., Massa, J., Atlamirano, L. S., et al. (2000). Early literacy for inner-city children: The effects of reading and writing interventions in English and Spanish during the preschool years. *Reading Teacher, 54,* 186–189.

16

Cultural Diversity in Early Literacy: Findings in Dutch Studies

PAUL P. M. LESEMAN
CATHY VAN TUIJL

Despite their own expectations and eagerness to learn, many children entering primary school each year will experience difficulties with acquiring basic skills, particularly reading. Although learning disabilities may be involved with endogenous primary causes in roughly 5–10% of the cases in each cohort of children, in most of today's Western societies a much bigger part of the problem is sociocultural in origin. Learning to read in primary school, which begins in first grade at age 6 or 7 in most countries, seems to depend on knowledge and skills that all children should already have acquired to some extent, but unfortunately many still lack these prerequisite skills. National and international comparative studies, such as the recent Programme for International Student Assessment (PISA 2000; Organisation of Economic Cooperation and Development, 2002) and Progress in International Reading Literacy Study (PIRLS 2001; Mullen, Martin, Gonzalez, & Kennedy, 2003), consistently show that students from lower socioeconomic background and from ethnic and sociolinguistic minority families obtain lower reading and writing scores than same-age peers from other family backgrounds. Particularly compelling are research findings, for instance from the United States (Stipek, 2001) and the Netherlands (Tesser & Iedema, 2001), showing that differences between students in reading skill at the end of primary school can be traced directly to differences in a variety of cognitive, language, and preliteracy skills at the time of primary school entrance, which thus appear to be remarkably stable over time. In spite of the fact that this pattern of sociocultural disadvantages has been found repeatedly and in many countries and that it concerns, in most countries, significant numbers of minority students, little yet is known about the nature and causes of this persistent socioeconomic and cultural diversity in the developmental pathways of reading skill, which are already present in the preschool period. This chapter discusses results of studies designed to help illuminate the causes of early differences in development that are associated with sociocultural factors.

In this chapter we discuss results of two longitudinal studies of early language and literacy development of young preschool children in the Netherlands that followed the oral language and preliteracy development of 3- to 4-year-old children (study 1) and 4- to 7-year-old children (study 2). The studies were conducted in samples of middle- and low-income Dutch families and low-income families from the largest ethnic minority groups in the Netherlands; the Surinamese Dutch and Turkish Dutch. Turkish immigrants constitute the largest non-Western ethnic minority group in the Netherlands. Most immigrant Turkish parents in the Netherlands originate from poor rural areas in Turkey and have low levels of schooling and literacy, especially among the women. In the majority of Turkish families, Turkish is still the most important conversational language; as a consequence, most preschool Turkish children are bilingual, with Turkish as their stronger language when they enter primary school. Immigrants from Surinam are the descendants of African slaves and Indian and Indonesian contract laborers. They constitute the second largest ethnic minority group in the Netherlands. Surinam is a former Dutch colony; almost all Surinamese immigrants are familiar with the Dutch culture, went to schools modeled on the Dutch school system, and speak the Dutch language, but the Surinamese culture and associated parenting practices are still quite distinct from those of the Dutch. Many Surinamese Dutch children, and about one third of the present samples, are bilingual, speak Dutch as their predominant language as well as a traditional Surinamese language (Sranan Tongo or Sarnami Hindu). Some details about the studies' design and measurements are briefly presented in Table 16.1; for more details the reader is referred to Leseman and van den Boom (1999) and Leseman and de Jong (1998). The comparative design of our studies systematically varied socioeconomic, linguistic and cultural background factors in order to help disentangle the impact of these variables on children's acquisition of literacy.

Biases in Early Literacy Research

Research into early reading acquisition in school and into the development of its precursors has been strongly focusing on the development of phonological skills, memory skills (working memory and rapid naming), and letter knowledge (Scarborough, 1998). Strong predictive relationships have been found between these precursor skills and initial reading achievement, with these relationships mainly found for learning to decode—that is, learning the "technics" of reading—and with later reading comprehension, because access to the code is conditional on access to the content. Except for pioneering work (Dickinson & Snow, 1987), only recently has interest in the role of vocabulary and oral text comprehension, as predictors and explanatory constructs, gained a prominent place in early literacy research (Bus, 2001; Dickinson, McCabe, Anastasopoulos, Peisner-Feinber, & Poe, 2003; Sénéchal & LeFevre, 2002; Storch & Whitehurst, 2002). This emphasis on the phonological and orthographic technics of reading reflects a bias in the pertinent research toward explaining endogenous reading disabilities that become manifest in initial reading in primary school. It also, as a consequence, reflects a lack of interest in the specific problems of children from lower socioeconomic status (SES) and ethnic minority backgrounds, who may not initially attract attention as seriously disabled readers despite performing below average. Furthermore, it has biased the study of sociocultural factors in literacy development by making literacy central in a narrow sense (e.g., interaction with printed materials, shared book reading), overlooking as a consequence other potential contributions to the rise of social–cultural differences in reading.

There is now broad scientific and societal consensus about the importance of supporting early language and preliteracy development in the preschool period in order to enhance (later) learning to read and write in primary school and to prevent severe reading problems. Starting joint book reading at an early age seems to be the most effective way in which families can foster preliteracy skill development in their children, including phonological skills, letter knowledge, awareness of the conventions, functions and uses of print, and specialized vocabulary and grammatical skills that are typical for literacy. Several review studies have concluded that children who were read to frequently from a very young age are doing relatively well in primary school in reading, writing, and math (cf. Bus, van Ijzendoorn, & Pellegrini, 1995; Whitehurst & Lonigan, 1998). Subsequent studies have detailed the effective mechanisms of joint book reading as a "literacy acquisition device." Basically, three facets seem to stand out in distinguishing optimal from less optimal literacy-supporting environments (cf. Bus, 2001; de Jong & Leseman, 2001; Hammett, van Kleeck, & Huberty, 2003; Rebello Britto & Brooks-Gunn, 2001; Vernon-Feagans, Scheffner

TABLE 16.1. Overview of Design and Measurements of the Dutch Home Language and Literacy Studies Reported in This Chapter

Study 1	Measurement occasions		
Average age in years	3	3½	4
Sample size	143	137	125
Semistructured interviews with mothers			
• Background characteristics (SES, etc.)	×		
• Symbolic (literacy) job demands	×		
• Parents' uses of literacy	×		
• Childrearing beliefs	×		
• Exposure to language and literacy events	×	×	×
Observations of social interactions at home			
• Shared book reading	×	×	×
• Joint problem solving	×	×	×
Tests (administered at home)			
• Nonverbal intelligence	×		
• First and second language vocabulary	×	×	×
• Premath concepts	×	×	×

Study 2	Measurement occasions				
Average age in years	4	5	6	7	9
Sample size	155	143	119	95	72
Semistructured interviews with mothers					
• Background characteristics (SES, etc.)	×				
• Symbolic (literacy) job demands	×				
• Parents' uses of literacy	×				
• Childrearing beliefs	×				
• Exposure to language and literacy events	×	×	×		
Observations of social interactions at home					
• Shared book reading	×	×	×		
• Joint problem solving	×	×	×		
Tests (kindergarten, primary school)[a]					
• Nonverbal intelligence	×	×			
• Phonological skills		×	×		
• Rapid naming		×	×		
• Working memory span		×	×		
• Letter knowledge		×	×		
• Dutch vocabulary		×	×	×	
• Dutch oral text comprehension		×	×		
• Technical reading (recoding speed)				×	×
• Reading comprehension				×	×

Note. "×" indicates time of measurement.
[a]In collaboration with de Jong and van der Leij, University of Amsterdam.

Hammer, Miccio, & Manlove, 2001). The first facet concerns the exposure to literacy products and literacy uses in everyday life, including as a subfacet of special interest, the frequency or amount of special opportunities for shared caregiver–child book reading. The second facet relates to the informal instruction that is embedded in literacy-related social interactions, with a subfacet of special interest being the ways in which children are learning phonological skills, letter knowledge, and complex cognitive–linguistic skills through shared book reading (Sénéchal &

LeFevre, 2002). The third facet concerns the affective context of literacy-related social interactions in everyday life, again with the affective quality of shared book reading as a subfacet of special interest (Bus, 2001).

In addition to the multifaceted approach, research has broadened the original narrow focus on directly print related social interactions to include other social interactions in nonliteracy situations as well. Thus, in addition to shared book reading (most often studied), studies have also addressed other forms of literacy interaction with a less official literate appearance (e.g., Purcell-Gates, 1996), informal conversations, play and problem-solving situations, and everyday household chores (Baker, Mackler, Sonnenschein, & Serpell, 2001; Leseman & de Jong, 1998; Snow & Kurland, 1996). In this way, the study of early literacy development has (re)connected to the study of cognitive and language development in general (cf. Gauvain, 2001) and to older work on social inequalities in education that emphasized the role of particular styles, or "codes," of language use. As a matter of fact, concepts such as oral literacy (Olson, 1991) and linguistic literacy (Ravid & Tolchinsky, 2002) or decontextualized language (Dickinson & Snow, 1987) typically cross the boundaries between oral and written language while referring to a more basic dimension of literacy. What is this basic dimension of literacy? To give a preliminary answer to this question, it may useful to introduce the concepts of genre and register from linguistics. Given the theme of this chapter, we limit the discussion to school literacy, acknowledging that there exist several other "literacies" (Purcell-Gates, 1996).

Early Literacy and Academic Language Skill

Reading (and writing) in school is about certain types of texts that form particular genres. In addition to narrative texts (such as storybooks), there are instructional texts, expository knowledge texts, and analytical texts, just to mention the most important genres. Moreover, these texts become increasingly domain-specific, marked by highly specific technical jargon, as in math, science, or history texts. A particularly interesting feature of school literacy is that reading (and writing) texts are embedded in related oral discourse—for example, when the teacher explains a text, gives verbal instruction in a particular domain, when previously read stories are discussed in the class, or when a student gives a talk about a particular topic for which he or she consulted magazines, books, and web pages. Comic books, advertisments, interpersonal talk, gossip, or teasing are *not* typical genres of (oral) school literacy, although they may frequently occur in the school context. Generally, texts should be appreciated as an authoritative account from an expert point of view, as truthful within

the situation that is referred to, and as containing a cognitively complex proposition or argument. By the same token, in writing or speaking, a writer or speaker is expected to construct in language "authority," "point of view," "reference," "coherence," and "truth," "plausibility," or "possibility" by making explicit the speaker's or writer's epistemological attitude towards the possible—historical, abstract-theoretical, or future-world that is referred to. In order to be able to do this, different linguistic structures are needed from those commonly used in interpersonal communication. The concept of *academic language register* (Halliday, 1994) is useful as an overarching concept that captures the interrelatedness of complex cognitive goals (e.g., teaching about the Industrial Revolution), text genres, social expectations, and the lexical and grammatical structures needed to realize the cognitive goals and social expectations.

Seen this way, the basic dimension of (school) literacy may not be the technics of recoding letters into sounds and blending them into words and sentences (however important for actual reading texts of all kinds of genres) but mastery of the academic language register and its associated specialized vocabulary and grammar.

Static versus Developmental Approaches to Early Literacy

To determine what constitutes early literacy skill, different perspectives are possible (Thomas & Karmiloff-Smith, 2002). The currently predominant "static" cognitivist approach is based on an information processing model of the reading process, derived from skilled readers, that specifies a number of processing components, including visual analysis, phonological short-term storage, working memory, orthographic long-term memory (for letters and words), semantic knowledge, grammatical knowledge, and world knowledge. This model, only very roughly outlined here, is reasonably adequate as a descriptive or heuristic model, but it may fall short from a developmental perspective. For instance, while working within this approach, a focus on the technics of reading is likely to result because problems with phonemic analysis and word recognition are the main forms in which difficulties with beginning reading acquisition manifest themselves in the first place. Before reading instruction starts, and parallel with reading instruction, children may exhibit several other problems or knowledge deficits, but these do not specifically affect beginning reading. Reading problems that arise from lack of knowledge of rare, specialized vocabulary (Weizman & Snow, 2001) or complex grammatical structures (e.g., verb tense, causal and logical connectives; Snowling, Bishop, & Stothard, 2000) are not likely to become apparent as early as grade 3 or 4 normally, because the reading tasks and the assessments of reading achievement are linguistically rather simple until then (De Jong & Leseman, 2001).

The second perspective is developmental and views reading skill as a dynamic structure of hierarchically integrated component skills (e.g., phonological perception and short-term storage, retrieval of grammatical and semantic representations, motivation) that adapt to changing situations with changing demands, supports, and rewards. Instead of presuming a fixed architecture of information processing modules, the developmental process is seen as flexibly adapting to specific situational demands, bound by certain constraints, and using all available resources (social support, intrinsic motivation) to perform—that is, to read, understand, interpret, evaluate, memorize— optimally in that situation. Reading skill varies structurally according to the specific reading tasks at hand, as do the relevant developmental trajectories that lead to reading skill regarding these tasks.

Phonological skills provide an interesting case to illustrate the developmental perspective, because they attracted so much research effort within the cognitivist approach. Children who develop normal oral language skills in interaction with language input in the family, including normal vocabulary, show *implicit* mastery knowledge of the syllabic and phonemic structure of the language. For instance, they can accurately differentiate between *cat* and *bat* or between *hit* and *him* upon hearing these sound strings at an early age. Explicit awareness of large phonological units, predominantly words, also arises early due to the functional relevance of the word in early everyday communication and to properties of the statistical distribution of phoneme combinations that serve to mark the beginnings and the ends of syllables and words in speech strings (Mattys & Jusczyk, 2001). However, the development of explicit awareness of smaller units requires different kinds of language experiences from mere everyday conversation. For instance, *awareness of onset–rime* (recognition and discrimination of beginning and following sounds of a word) and skill in rhyme recognition and production has been found to be related to the practice of singing nursery rhymes in the preschool age, in which part of the pleasure and functionality for young children lies in the funny, systematic variations of onset–rime combinations, that are so typical for nursery rhymes (Goswami, 2001; Raz & Bryant, 1990). Similarly, the development of *phonemic awareness*—usually defined in operational terms as the ability to manipulate consciously the phonemes of a word to form a different word or to identify single phonemes in a word—seems to depend strongly on yet another particular type of language interaction. This form of interaction is initial reading instruction, a form of interaction that also may start informally in the family context, long before school, as parents help children learn letters and how to write their names (Goswami, 2001).

Following the static cognitive model approach, phonemic awareness is seen as a core module of reading skill. Early phonemic awareness strongly predicts reading achievement in school; a deficit in phonemic awareness is seen as a major proximal cause of dyslexia in children, and this in turn may often result from genetically induced atypical brain development (Vellutino, Fletcher, Snowling, & Scanlon, 2004). Implicitly or explicitly, a strong version of innate modularity is presupposed, which is currently criticized as neurobiologically implausible (Goswami, 2003; Thomas & Karmiloff-Smith, 2002; Vellutino et al., 2004). According to the developmental approach, the emergence of phonemic awareness reflects the situated construction of a new special skill, integrating, among others, visuoperceptual, attention, and memory skills (e.g., for perceiving, discriminating, and storing printed letters in memory) and well-established implicit phonological skill, to meet the new demands posed by formal or informal reading instruction. The construction and consolidation of the new phonemic skill may proceed faster in learning situations if the child's basic implicit phonological skill has already differentiated into a more specialized "branch" of onset–rime awareness due to extensive experience with nursery rhymes (Raz & Bryant, 1990), but do not automatically emerge. Basically, we assume that there is no intrinsic reason for the developing mind to develop phonemic awareness except to deal with written language.

Similarly, academic language skill—the ability to use the appropriate lexical and grammatical structures of one's language to produce or apprehend typical school texts—can be viewed as a new, increasingly sophisticated special skill that emerges when the developing child is confronted with these or similar text genres, at home or in school, and adapts to the demands posed by these texts (cf. Crain-Thoreson, Dahlin, & Powell, 2001). Academic language skill goes beyond everyday interpersonal communication skill regarding the linguistic demands. For instance, to establish or co-construct a shared frame of reference that does not coincide with the immediate situation, a speaker must use explicit references to time and place, make clear from whose point of view the information is given, and provide this information in an economic way by using lexically dense noun and prepositional phrases. If some kind of expert knowledge is involved, specific "technical" (often infrequent) vocabulary should be used (Snow & Kurland, 1996) and in order to make a complex report or argument understandable, a coherent and logically structured discourse is needed, which requires the use of devices to establish cohesion between sentences, and causal and logical connectives (Haden, Haines, & Fivush, 1997).

Literacy Development as Cultural Canalization: Starting Points in Infancy

Cultural diversity in early literacy, we propose, can be best approached from a developmental perspective. Presuming normal (since we do not focus on neurobiologically atypical cases) and largely unspecified starting points, the first question is how the most important developmental context of the young child, that is, the family, "orchestrates" successive experiences—confronta-

tions with particular situational demands requiring new adaptations—so as to *channel* children's skill development toward school literacy. The second question is how socioeconomic and cultural factors operate in these contexts and how they may explain differences in cultural canalization that lead to differences in literacy learning in school. We address these questions in the remainder of this chapter.

Ideally, the study of cultural diversity in early literacy development should start very early in the child's life. For instance, research in caregiver–child attachment has shown that children in the first year of life develop different "working models" of social relationships and feelings of security that influence both cooperation in joint learning situations and the child's exploratory behavior. Bus (2001) argues that both the age of onset and the frequency and interaction quality of joint book reading depend on feelings of security and mutual affective satisfaction based in secure early attachment. According to this view, the caregiver's sensitivity and responsiveness is essential in this early developmental process and is negatively influenced by socioeconomic stresses, acculturation problems and collectivistic cultural ideas about childrearing (Harwood, Miller, & Irizarry, 1995).

Related to this is the development in the first year of joint attentional focus or intersubjectivity, considered a basic constituent of human cultural learning and communicative development and found to be strongly related to language development (Mundy & Gomes, 1998; Trevarthen & Aitken, 2001). Intersubjectivity, defined as mutual self–other consciousness, emerges according to present theory (Trevarthen & Aitken, 2001) from early caregiver–child proto-conversations in the first 6 months of life, involving mutual imitation of facial expressions, eye-pointing, gestures, hand signs, and vocalizations in a conversation-like pattern of turn taking. This developmental system can be disturbed by the caregiver's failure to respond appropriately to the infants cues with well-timed, lively emotional expressions. Depression in the caregiver, which is found to be related to socioeconomic stresses and cultural factors, such as single parenthood, subordinate position and social isolation of the female caregiver (García Coll &

Magnuson, 2000), generally presents a serious risk for normal development of intersubjectivity in the child's first year and for cognitive, communicative, cooperative, and prosocial behaviors later in life (Field, 1998). Cultural differences in patterns of childrearing in the first year of life are reported in several studies, revealing among other things, a basic division in caregiver's attribution of intentionality or "selfhood" to infants, which is presupposed to influence their engagement in proto-conversations, joint attention episodes, and cooperative play (Sigel & Kim, 1996). However, to our knowledge, detailed research into the consequences for intersubjectivity and subsequent cultural learning ability is lacking.

Although literacy development starts very early with the development of multiple domain-general skills that feed forward into the later development of language and literacy skills, the narrowing down or specialization to trajectories that lead to (school) literacy have been mostly studied beginning in the third or fourth year of life. It is during this period when most children have become autonomous explorers of their environments without constant supervision by the caregiver, motivating them and their caregivers to share memories about situations and events of which the caregivers have only partial knowledge (Gauvain, 2001). Their linguistic skills, particularly their grammatical and discourse skills, become increasingly creative and productive after a period of "syntactical conservatism" up to age 2½–3 years, enabling them to participate in extended discourse (Lieven, Behrens, Speares, & Tomasello, 2003). It is also the period during which, at least in mainstream middle-class families, shared picture-book reading with active dialogical involvement of the child (Bus et al., 1995; Whitehurst & Lonigan, 1998).

Culturally Diverse Language and Literacy Environments in Early Childhood

Several studies have reported on socioeconomic and cultural differences in home language and literacy environments, usually focusing on only one facet (mostly exposure), but sometimes on two, such as exposure and

instruction (for overviews, see Leseman & de Jong, 1998; Whitehurst & Lonigan, 1998). Furthermore, only a few, mostly ethnographic, studies have detailed the wider social and cultural context of diversity in home language and literacy (cf. Heath, 1983). In our studies with multiethnic samples in the Netherlands we have tried to address all of these different topics of interest together. We discuss the findings hereafter that reveal the culturally diverse canalizations of early literacy development of children then relate these facets to a range of socioeconomic and cultural context factors. Finally, we address their effects on cognitive, language, and reading development.

Exposure to Academic Genres of Literacy and Talk.

The home provides the developing child with different kinds of opportunities for contact with literacy to different degrees. The presence of literacy is certainly not all or none, as became clear in studies into the role of environmental print in early literacy learning (Anderson & Stokes, 1984; Purcell-Gates, 1996). Even in homes that can be regarded as functionally illiterate, because the parents can hardly read and write or almost never do so, printed language invades regularly via free advertisement papers, instructions for use on packings, the television guide, or the Bible.

In our study of a sample of Dutch, Surinamese Dutch, and Turkish Dutch families with 3-year-old children, we found strong differences between these cultural groups in the reported frequency of literacy events such as shared book reading and the caregiver's reading a book or a newspaper or writing a letter or postcard in the presence of the child; but we found no or only small and statistically insignificant differences in the frequency of the caregiver leafing through a magazine or advertising paper, or reading the instructions for use of a certain product (see Figure 16.1). Cultural differences pertained to situations of educational and recreational use of literacy, but not to situations of instrumental use (cf. Heath, 1983). The pattern of differences remained remarkably stable over time and was also found in the second longitudinal study in Dutch, Surinamese Dutch and Turkish Dutch families with 4-year-old children who were followed until age 7 (with

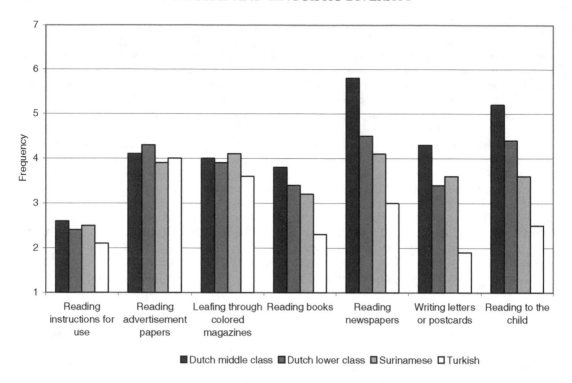

FIGURE 16.1. Frequency of exposure of 3-year-old children to different genres of oral language use in the family (1 = never, 7 = once or more per day), by socioeconomic and ethnic–cultural background.

an additional follow-up in third grade, at age 9; see the following discussion). Although this study's reported frequency of shared book reading decreased in all groups over time, between-group differences remained rather constant. Moreover, the decrease was the least strong in the Dutch middle-class families, which already had the highest frequency of shared book reading.

The preschool home environment provides other experiences that are potentially relevant for literacy development, including cognitive experiences that are foundational for the semantic and world knowledge components of complex literacy skill (e.g., reading comprehension). For the present purpose, we will focus on oral language experiences. In the aforementioned studies with 3- to 4-year-olds and 4- to 7-year-olds, caregivers were also asked to report in a personal interview with a semi-structured questionnaire the frequency of several typical oral language situations. Once again, we found no big overall differences between the cultural groups in the reported total amount of talking to or in the presence of the child.

However, for the type or genre of oral language exchange, typical patterns of cultural differences became evident. Cultural differences were comparatively strong for mealtime talk and increased active involvement of the child in mealtime talk, for sharing past experiences and telling true stories to the child (e.g., social remembering, family stories; cf. Gauvain, 2001), and for explaining the working of an apparatus or the principles of a household routine. The reported occurrence of these genres of family talk was, overall, highest in Dutch middle-class families and lowest in the Surinamese Dutch and Turkish Dutch families in our studies, with the Dutch-lower class families falling in between. However, there were no group differences in the reported frequency of intimate, affectionate child–caregiver talk, in caregivers' talking with other adults during social meetings with the child being present, and in telling funny, fictitious stories and jokes to the child (see Figure 16.2). Again, the pattern of differences in the most prominent genres of family talk appeared to be rather stable over time.

Although mere exposure to particular genres of oral and written language is perhaps uninformative as to what children may learn from it, we presuppose that these situations provide all kinds of affordances and challenges for cognitive–linguistic processing. For instance, social remembering at the dinner table or sharing true stories require participants to construct explicit reference, to use a narrative format to share experiences, and to use linguistic devices to establish discourse cohesion (Gauvain, 2001; Haden et al., 1997). Likewise, explaining the working of an apparatus affords the use of technical vocabulary and complex sentences (Snow & Kurland, 1996). In the next section we discuss how cognitive–linguistic experiences like these are mediated or scaffolded by the caregivers.

Instruction of Complex Cognitive–Linguistic Skill in Shared Reading

A second facet of cultural differences in the canalization of children's development towards literacy skills concerns the specific cognitive and linguistic skills that develop in and through the particular types of social interactions that are provided, while coping with the particular demands of these situations and being supported by an experienced other. Observational studies of literate and oral language interactions and of play and problem-solving interactions have focused on several aspects. In literacy interactions, shared book reading in particular, the studied aspects included instruction in the formal characteristics of printed language ("print talk"), explanations of word meanings, scaffolding of text comprehension, and stimulation of representational or abstract cognition (van Kleeck, Gillam, Hamilton, & McGrath, 1997). In observations of oral language interactions, in particular mealtime conversations, instruction in word meaning (cf. Weizman & Snow, 2001), sociolinguistic styles of expressive versus referential talking (cf. Blake, 1993), and input of grammatical structures have been studied (cf. Hoff & Naigles, 2002; Lieven et al., 2003). Finally, play and problem-solving interactions were mainly studied from the perspective of abstract talk or conceptual instruction, representational cognition (Sigel, Stinson, & Kim, 1993), and cognitive skill level (Mayo &

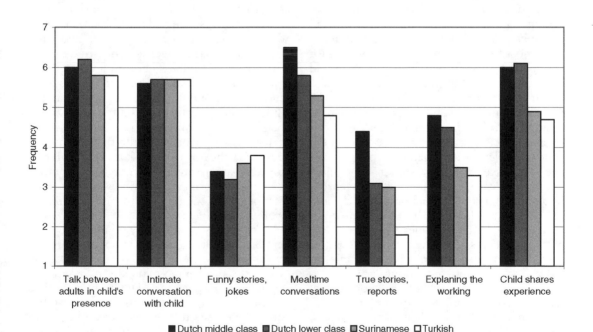

FIGURE 16.2. Frequency of exposure of 3-year-old children to different genres of oral language use in the family (1 = never, 7 = once or more per day), by socioeconomic and ethnic–cultural background.

Leseman, 2004). Socioeconomic and cultural differences have been reported in a number of studies, revealing, from the perspective of emergent school skills, a significant advantages for children reared in mainstream middle-class families compared with children from low-income minority families (cf. Laosa, 1982; Mayo & Leseman, 2004).

In our study with 3-year-old children, observations of mother–child pairs reading unfamiliar picture books, the most important statistically significant cultural differences concerned the proportion of utterances by the mother and, as a consequence, by the child who was stimulated by the mother, to answer challenging questions. Such exchanges included those that contained explanations of word meanings; affective evaluations of the story or of events described in the story; extensions to the child's personal experience; and extensions of the story by adding new events, by anticipating which events would come next, and by relating the topic of the story to general world knowledge (Leseman & van den Boom, 1999). This pattern was most frequently observed in Dutch middle class families, and least frequently in Turkish Dutch families, the other groups falling in between. In contrast, labeling and describing pictures, repeating (or asking to repeat) just-read sentences and pausing to let the child complete a sentence were most frequently observed in the Turkish Dutch and Surinamese Dutch families, and least often in Dutch middle-class families.

The results for the second cohort, with the 4- to 7-year-olds, were similar (Leseman & de Jong, 1998). Again, the most striking difference concerned the use of pauses to let the child complete a sentence or repeat a just-read sentence, which was even more pronounced in this second cohort. It occurred frequently in the Surinamese Dutch and Turkish Dutch families, but was almost absent in the Dutch families. Moreover, the patterns were stable over time. We interpreted the overall pattern of both studies as indicating a significant cultural divide between, on the one hand, a meaning-oriented, text-comprehension scaffolding approach and, on the other hand, a print-as-sacred, recitational approach (Leseman & de Jong, 1998). The latter qualification refers to religious reading practices such as Qur'an recitation which for most of the Turkish Dutch

mothers and for about half of the Surinamese Dutch mothers, who were Muslim as well, probably was the most familiar cultural practice of reading.

Instruction of Complex Cognitive–Linguistic Skill in Joint Problem Solving.

We have argued that shared book reading is but one genre of family interactions that may contribute to the development of literacy. In our studies with Dutch, Surinamese Dutch, and Turkish Dutch families we also observed mother–child interactions in a problem-solving situation. The problem solving involved a categorization task in which a number of pictures of familiar objects had to be grouped in three according to their conventional superordinate. We looked specifically at the conceptual level of instruction given by the mother in the form of statements, questions, suggestions, and directives. On the lowest level, instructions were either simple behavioral directives to pick an item and place it at a certain location, and instructions to categorize on the basis of irrelevant characteristics (e.g., color). The next level concerned instructions to assemble pictures according to thematic relationships (co-occurrence in space and time based on everyday personal experience, e.g., fork, milk, and bread go together because you see them on the breakfast table). The third level included more abstract instructions and suggestions, such as to group items according to a shared hidden function (e.g., edibility) or to membership of the same conventional taxonomic category (e.g., fruits). In addition, the use of labels for the objects (*knife, fork, spoon*) and for the superordinates (*cutlery*) and utterances that presented defining semantic characteristics or contained formal definitions were counted.

In the study with the 3-year-olds, the most important cultural differences were found at the start of the problem-solving session, when the mothers explained the task to the children. On average, Dutch middle-class mothers explained the task with most frequent reference to the abstract and conventional semantic principles that should guide assembling of the items. Turkish Dutch mothers did this least frequently and instead used irrelevant instructions most frequently; the other groups fell in between. The results of the second study with the 4- to 6-year-olds were similar and the pattern of differences showed stability over time.

Affective–Motivational Aspects.

Joint book reading and problem solving are not only cognitive–linguistic but also affective events. We examined this by evaluating the emotional and motivational quality of the observed book-reading and problem-solving interactions in our two samples, using the rating scales of Erickson, Sroufe, and Egeland (1985). More specifically, we evaluated mother's emotional support for the child's development (a combined measure of highly intercorrelated scores for supportive presence, nonintrusiveness, clarity of instruction, and confidence in the child) and children's motivation (a combined measure of children's scores for persistence in task performance and sustained attention, expressed enthusiasm, and experienced competence based on successful contributions and received praise). The results of both studies were remarkably similar and stable over time (Leseman & van den Boom, 1999; Leseman & de Jong, 1998, 2001; de Jong & Leseman, 2001). Overall, the highest emotional support was found in Dutch middle-class families, the lowest in the Surinamese Dutch and Turkish Dutch families. The Dutch lower-class families were ranked in between, but the mean score for these families was close to that of the Dutch middle-class families. The "cultural divide" amounted to roughly 0.7– 1.0 SD. This pattern of between-group differences was found for both shared book reading and joint problem solving. Similarly, in both studies, Dutch middle- and lower-class children obtained the highest motivation ratings (with only small differences in favor of the middle-class children), whereas Surinamese Dutch and Turkish Dutch children obtained the lowest motivation ratings (with no consistent differences between these two groups).

The cultural nature of the observed differences in shared book reading between Dutch, Surinamese Dutch, and Turkish Dutch mother–child pairs was further explored in a subsample of low-income families only that were strictly matched for SES to rule out SES differences as a possible ex-

planation (Bus, Leseman, & Keultjes, 2000). The results underscored the multidimensional nature of cultural differences in early home literacy, revealing an instructional dimension that referred to scaffolding of text comprehension and extensions beyond the story content, and an emotional dimension that referred to mothers' supportive presence, nonintrusiveness, clarity of instructions, and confidence in the child. The frequency of exposure dimension (see above) was not included, but might have added a third dimension for discriminating between the groups. Interestingly, in this SES-matched low-income sample, Surinamese Dutch and Turkish Dutch families showed different profiles. Whereas Turkish Dutch families differed most strongly from the other families in instruction quality, Surinamese Dutch families differed most strongly in emotional quality.

Contextual Constraints of Language and Literacy Environments

To explain the cultural differences in the canalization of young children's literacy development, we examined several structural and cultural contextual factors. In addition to the caregivers' education and SES, seen as "structural background factors," we explored the relationships of the informal early literacy curriculum at home with the caregivers' own uses of literacy (cf. Heath, 1983), the degree of literacy use in their jobs (cf., Kohn & Schooler, 1983), and their cultural childrearing beliefs (cf. Sigel & Kim, 1996). We found big differences in both studies between the four groups in SES based on the parents' educational level (due to the deliberate sampling of socioeconomically distinct groups), job content, parents' own literacy use, and childrearing beliefs. The degree of literacy, numeracy and information technology use in the jobs of the parents differed strongly between the four groups. For instance, most Turkish fathers and mothers (if working) had unskilled or semiskilled jobs requiring them to work manually or with heavy tools and machinery, but hardly ever with symbolic materials and modern information technology. To determine parents' own uses of literacy, we asked them to rate how often they read books, newspaper and magazine articles, and other literacy products of different genres (cf. Heath, 1983). The strongest difference between the groups concerned the frequency of use of literacy for entertainment and educational purposes, which was high in the Dutch middle-class group and very low in the Turkish Dutch group, with the other two groups falling in between (for more details, see Leseman & de Jong, 1998). Finally, Surinamese Dutch and Turkish Dutch parents held collectivistic and authoritarian childrearing beliefs, valuing obedience and respect for authority, and seeing learning and development as a result of biological maturation and behavioral modeling. The parents in both Dutch groups (with no statistically significant difference between middle and lower class) more strongly adhered to individualistic beliefs, valuing the early development of an independent self in the child, emphasizing the importance of active self-discovery and guided constructivist learning, and of exploration of social boundaries. The results reported in this section are based on our second study with the 4- to 7-year-olds, but in the younger cohort highly similar results were found.

The frequency of exposure to interactions with academic literacy correlated moderately strongly with SES, symbolic job content, and the caregivers' cultural childrearing beliefs (correlations were in the $r = .40$ to $r = .50$ range; $p < .001$), and strongly ($r = .61$, $p < .000$) with the caregivers' own use of literacy at home for work, education, and entertainment. A similar pattern of correlations of roughly the same size was found for the frequency of shared book reading, as a subfacet of literacy opportunities. The multivariate R^2's were .47 ($p < .000$), and .48 ($p < .000$) respectively; the amount of variance solely explained by job content, cultural beliefs, and caregivers' own literacy was .46 ($p < .000$) and .44 ($p < .000$), with no significant additional effects of SES or cultural minority status. The frequency of opportunities for talking and playing correlated less strongly with the family background characteristics. Caregivers' symbolic job content, literacy, and cultural beliefs correlated in the $r = .25$ to $r = .35$ range ($p < .05$); SES was not statistically significantly correlated with opportunities for talking and playing. In multiple regression analyses, caregivers' literacy and cultural beliefs predicted an amount of variance of $R^2 = .14$ ($p < .01$) in opportunity for talking and $R^2 = .15$ ($p < .01$) in opportunity for play. Furthermore, there remained small direct effects of cultural minority status that apparently were not mediated by job content, caregivers' literacy, caregivers' childrearing beliefs, or SES. The conclusion is that unknown or unmeasured cultural factors were at work, limiting time for talking and playing with the young child—perhaps customs that were not fully revealed by the cultural childrearing beliefs questionnaire.

The instruction quality of shared book reading and joint problem solving also correlated moderately strongly with SES, symbolic job content, the caregivers' cultural beliefs and the caregivers' own literacy use, with correlations ranging between $r = .43$ to $r = .52$ ($p < .000$). The multivariate R^2's were .39 ($p < .000$) for book reading and .39 ($p < .000$) for problem solving, with symbolic job content, cultural childrearing beliefs, and caregivers' literacy solely predicting .28 ($p < .000$) and .34 ($p < .000$) of the variance, respectively. In the case of book reading instruction quality, additional direct effects of minority status, Surinamese and Turkish alike, were found that could not be accounted for by the included family characteristics. The correlations found for the affective quality (mothers' emotional support) of shared book reading and problem solving were similar, being in the $r = .38$ to $r = .54$ range ($p < .000$). The degree of symbolic job content (also seen as a factor determining the value parents attach to socialization of independence and self-actualization in children; Kohn & Schooler, 1983) and caregivers' cultural childrearing beliefs correlated most strongly with affective quality; caregivers' literacy was less strongly related to this facet. The R^2's were .42 ($p < .000$) and .41 ($p < .000$) for shared book reading and joint problem solving, respectively. Again, small direct effects, not explained by the currently employed measures of minority status remained, in particular for Surinamese Dutch.

To conclude this section, language and literacy practices at home are part of wider ecological systems. These systems include a society's distribution of educational opportunities and jobs, adults' leisure practices and cultural lifestyles, and cultural communities' beliefs systems. In the reported studies, these systems seem to orchestrate profound cultural differences in children's preschool language and literacy environments. A final question remains: How do these differences affect children's developmental pathways to literacy?

Effects of Early Language and Literacy Environments

The effects of all these different facets of the educational preschool home environment on children's language and (pre)literacy skills were examined in a number of papers (Leseman & de Jong, 1998, 2001, 2004; de Jong & Leseman, 2001). Leseman and de Jong (2004) provide the most comprehensive account, with the outcome measures including early phonological skills, working memory capacity, rapid naming skill, letter knowledge, and vocabulary in addition to standard reading achievement measures. We briefly review the main findings.

By the end of kindergarten, a few months before the start of reading instruction in first grade, there were important differences in preliteracy skills between the four groups of children. Dutch middle-class children showed a big advantage on all measures. The other groups did not differ strongly except with respect to vocabulary and oral text comprehension, where a big disadvantage was present, especially for the Turkish Dutch children and to a lesser extent for the Surinamese Dutch children.

Reading achievement was assessed at two time points, at the end of first and third grades, with tests of recoding speed (using a test that required students to read as many one-, two- and three-syllable words of increasing phonotactic difficulty as they could in 1 minute), referred to hereafter as "technical reading," and reading comprehension (using a number of short narrative and expository-knowledge texts with questions about the content). The tests came from a widely used student-monitoring system developed by the Dutch national educational testing service. Again, Dutch middle-class students were far ahead of all other students on all tests at both measurement times. The differences on technical reading tended to become smaller from first to third grade; in particular, Surinamese Dutch and Turkish Dutch students appeared to catch up. For in-

stance, the difference between Dutch middle-class students and Turkish Dutch students decreased from 0.95 SD in first grade to 0.69 in third grade (which, of course, is still a big difference). A similar decrease of the initial disadvantage was found for the Surinamese Dutch students. However, regarding reading comprehension, the initial differences tended to become bigger, apparently due to a strong growth of reading comprehension skill among the Dutch middle-class students with which the other students could not keep pace.

We examined whether the home language and literacy environments could explain the differences in cognitive and language skills and in reading achievement. The characteristics of the home language and literacy environment that we discussed earlier (exposure, instruction quality, affective quality), were combined into composite measures that were then aggregated over measurement occasions (for details of the scale construction, see Leseman & de Jong, 1998; de Jong & Leseman, 2001). Three kinds of composite measures were thus constructed, representing, respectively, (1) the degree of exposure to academic oral and printed discourse genres (e.g., shared book reading, reading newspapers in the child's presence, involvement in mealtime talk, telling true stories, explaining the working of an apparatus); (2) the use of explanations, evaluations, and extensions beyond the story by the mother in shared reading and the use of conceptual semantic–taxonomic instructions by the mother in shared problem solving; and (3) the degree of emotional support by the mother in book reading and problem solving interactions. The correlations of the composite home characterics with children's cognitive, language, and literacy skill measures are presented in Table 16.2. They reveal two interesting patterns. First, there were no clear (i.e., at least moderately strong) relationships between the cultural home environments and the children's cognitive skills. For instance, almost all correlations with nonverbal IQ, working-memory capacity, and rapid naming were close to zero, but there were rather strong and consistent relationships with letter knowledge (which correlated substantially with home measures, indicating effects of exposure and instruction), with vocabulary and oral text comprehension, and with

TABLE 16.2. Correlations of Home Language and Literacy Facets With Cognitive and Linguistic Precursors of Reading in the Preschool Age (Ages 5–6 Years) and With Reading Achievement in First (Age 7) and Third Grades (Age 9)

Reading (precursor) skills by age in years	Frequency of shared reading	Frequency of shared talking	Instructional quality of reading	Instructional quality of problem solving	Affective quality of reading	Affective quality of problem solving	Dominant home language
Phonological skill 5–6	.21	.18	.14	.33**	.24*	.24*	.19
Rapid naming 5–6	.10	.21	.04	.19	.14	.18	.22*
Working memory 5–6	.11	.13	.14	.25*	.19	.24*	.10
Nonverbal intelligence 5–6	.19	.07	.04	.10	.06	.08	.10
Letter knowledge 5–6	.29**	.19	.26**	.41**	.27*	.34**	.30**
Dutch vocabulary 5–6	.31**	.26**	.29**	.27*	.22*	.23*	.57**
Dutch vocabulary 7	.32**	.20	.42**	.41**	.46**	.42**	.71**
Technical reading 7	.37**	.29**	.27*	.41**	.26*	.29**	.30**
Reading comprehension 7	.29**	.20	.08	.27*	.13	.18	.31**
Technical reading 9[a]	.09	.10	.19	.26*	.11	.13	.12
Reading comprehension 9[a]	.23*	.10	.28*	.49**	.12	.35**	.29*

[a]$n = 72$.
$p < .10$; * $p < .05$; ** $p < .01$.

the reading achievement measures obtained in primary school. The use of Dutch as the predominant language in a range of communicative situations normally occurring at home instead of Turkish or Sarnami and Sranan (Surinamese languages), not surprisingly, correlated strongest with Dutch vocabulary. But the frequency of experiences with particular genres of literacy (shared book reading, reading newspapers in the child's presence) and oral language use (mealtime conversations, true storytelling), and the instruction and affective quality of shared book reading and problem solving was also moderately strongly related to children's language and literacy development. Note, for instance, the remarkable correlation of the instruction quality of problem solving in the preschool period with reading comprehension in third grade, that is, four years later, of $r = .49$ ($p < .001$).

We further examined with hierarchical multiple regression analyses the separate contributions of cognitive characteristics and home language and literacy experiences to developing reading skill. For brevity, we summarize the main findings here (for detailed accounts, see de Jong & Leseman, 2001; Leseman & de Jong, 2004). The results indicated a two fold developmental trajectory of literacy skills, a "technical" and "language comprehension" route (cf. Storch & Whitehurst, 2002). Cognitive skills predicted initial technical reading and reading comprehension, with only indirect effects of home language and literacy experiences via letter knowledge, vocabulary, and oral text comprehension. In third grade technical reading was solely predicted by technical reading in first grade, with no additional effects of cognitive skills, language skills, or home language and literacy experiences. In contrast, however, reading comprehension in third grade, controlling for technical reading and reading comprehension in first grade, still appeared to depend on previous home language and literacy experiences. In addition to the indirect effects via letter knowledge, vocabulary, and oral text comprehension—all moderately to strongly related to home language and literacy experiences—we found substantial additional direct effects (up to $R^2 = .10$; $p < .01$). These effects were related in particular to the instruction quality of shared reading and problem solving in the preschool period (de Jong & Leseman, 2001; Leseman & de Jong, 2004). We interpreted this pattern as indicating a more general cognitive-linguistic effect of the home environment which became more influential (and visible) with the increasing cognitive–linguistic demands of the reading comprehension tasks in third grade as opposed to first grade, and that especially benefited Dutch middle-class students with ample academic language and literacy experiences at home compared to Dutch lower-class and ethnic minority students.

Our findings not only are consistent with the abundant evidence for the central role of early cognitive skills (phonological skills, working memory capacity, rapid naming) in initial reading, but also showed that this role was limited to the initial stage of reading acquisition. After this initial stage, a new special skill has been formed integrating these cognitive skills with implicit language knowledge for the special purpose of recoding and word recognition in reading. This finding has been discussed elsewhere in the context of the fairly regular, transparent orthography of Dutch as compared, for instance, with English (de Jong & Van der Leij, 1999; Goswami, 2003) and the predominant use of intensive phoneme-based reading instruction methods in Dutch primary education (de Jong & Leseman, 2001), which seem to help socioculturally disadvantaged students to overcome initial reading difficulties. So the finding may be limited to regular orthographies and effective reading instruction practices. However, one can also argue that the Dutch situation (regular orthography, phoneme-based reading instruction) provides a particularly appropriate context within which to unravel the specific difficulties of lower-class and minority students in becoming literate. Although early socioeconomic and cultural differences in this particular sample related to almost all cognitive and language precursors of reading achievement, sociocultural differences were strongest for oral language skills and letter knowledge, and through these skills and knowledge for reading comprehension in third grade, when reading texts had become cognitively more complex and linguistically more demanding.

Conclusions

To understand cultural diversity in early literacy development, we need to adopt a broad view on literacy (Dickinson et al., 2003). Narrowing down literacy to the technics of phoneme-grapheme analysis and printed word recognition, and focusing on problems with reading acquisition in the initial stage reflect a bias in (English-language) research. This bias conceals the specific problems of lower-class and cultural minority students that become manifest in later grades with the increasing cognitive and linguistic complexity of the reading (and writing) tasks they have to deal with in several subject areas, in examinations, and in international comparative studies like PISA and PIRLS. These students, on average, grow up in environments that provide them with ample experience with many kinds of language use, including instrumental and social uses of literacy, but that fall short in providing them with comparable exposure to genres of oral and literate language that are linguistically closely related to the genres of academic language use in school settings. Moreover, these students experience less emotional and cognitive–linguistic support in dealing with these more demanding genres.

The precise mechanisms, that is, the kind of cognitive–linguistic and social-emotional skills that are involved, are still largely unknown. There is in the extant literature growing awareness that, for instance, the beneficiary effects of shared book reading and nonimmediate talk about past events at the dinner table consist in the scaffolded experience with complex grammatical structures (for instance, frequent use of long sentences with main and subordinate clauses, lexically dense noun phrases, connectives, etc.) and rare technical vocabulary that characterize even very simple young children's books and everyday nonimmediate mealtime talk (Gauvain, 2001; van Kleeck et al., 1997; Weizman & Snow, 2001). A growing body of evidence within the functional usage-based language acquisition research program supports the idea that the acquisition and creative use of complex grammar is strongly dependent upon the token and type frequencies of these structures in the input children receive (Lieven et al., 2003).

In addition, and partly overlapping because linguistic structures are used for cognitive representation, the effect of these scaffolding experiences may also consist in the general cognitive-representational skills that are fostered in everyday social interactions. For example, in another study we observed mothers and their 3-year-old children solving a construction task with wooden blocks and analyzed verbal and nonverbal actions with a coding scheme based on Fischer's skill theory (Fischer & Bidell, 1998), focusing on the coordination and integration of lower-level sensorimotor behaviors (looking at and picking up a block) and single representations (e.g. labeling, instruction of a single sensorimotor action) into higher-level compounded representations (descriptions, extended action plans) and systems of representation (explanations referring to hidden causes, forces or processes, verbal reasoning). Already at age 3, big differences were found with respect to the average cognitive skill level between Dutch middle-class, Dutch lower-class, Surinamese Dutch, and Turkish Dutch children, and these differences tended to increase over the course of one year. This effect could be explained by the ways the mothers engaged in the joint task (Mayo & Leseman, 2004). Differences in the rate of development of representational skill may explain differences in language comprehension and reading comprehension when the contents of oral and printed discourses in instruction situations and textbooks become more abstract and hypothetical.

We found strong cultural differences in the affective experience of shared book reading and problem solving. Although the results may reflect a cultural bias in the observation scheme used to evaluate the affective dimension of mother-child interaction, which was rooted in the attachment theory (cf. Harwood et al., 1995), the related measures of children's overt motivation and subjective competence may be seen as universally valid indications of the affective quality of these particular interaction episodes. The consequences may be manifold. Bus (2001) presupposes that a lower affective quality of shared book reading and, consequently, a higher degree of negative experiences on part of the child, decreases the frequency of subsequent shared book reading episodes since a positive motivating force is lacking. Based on evidence in other studies, we can propose that lower affective quality decreases the efficiency of the microdevelopmental processes in social interaction episodes by decreasing motivation and cooperation, so that a lower skill level results (Fischer & Bidell, 1998). Leseman and de Jong (1998) reported significantly more difficulties with mother-

child cooperation in shared book reading in Surinamese Dutch and Turkish Dutch families with 4-year-old children than in Dutch families; difficulties with cooperation sometimes led to a breakdown of the shared book reading session and predicted unique variance in first-grade vocabulary and reading achievement. Finally, the affective quality of the mother–child relationship may also influence the affective quality of children's subsequent social relationships with teachers and peers in kindergarten and primary school and thus affect school achievement (Pianta, Nimetz, & Bennett, 1997).

References

Anderson, A. B., & Stokes, S. J. (1984). Social and institutional influences on the development and practice of literacy. In H. Goelman, A. Oberg, & F. Smith (Eds.), *Awakening to literacy* (pp. 24–37). London: Heinemann.

Baker, L., Mackler, K., Sonnenschein, S., & Serpell, R. (2001). Parents' interactions with their first-grade children during storybook reading and relations with subsequent home reading activity and reading achievement. *Journal of School Psychology, 39*(5), 415–438.

Blake, I. (1993). The social-emotional orientation of mother–child communication in African American families. *International Journal of Behavioral Development, 16*(3), 443–463.

Bus, A. G. (2001). Joint caregiver–child storybook reading: A route to literacy development. In S. B. Neuman & D. K. Dickinson (Eds.), *Handbook of early literacy research* (pp. 179–191). New York: Guilford Press.

Bus, A. G., Leseman, P. P. M., & Keultjes, P. (2000). Joint book reading across cultures: A comparison of Surinamese-Dutch, Turkish-Dutch, and Dutch parent–child dyads. *Journal of Literacy Research, 32*(1), 53–76.

Bus, A. G., van IJzendoorn, M. H., & Pellegrini, A. D. (1995). Joint book reading makes for success in learning to read. A meta-analysis on intergenerational transmission of literacy. *Review of Educational Research, 65*, 1–21.

Crain-Thoreson, C., Dahlin, M. P., & Powell, T. A. (2001). Parent–child interaction in three conversational contexts: Variations in style and strategy. *New Directions for Child and Adolescent Development, 92*, 23–37.

de Jong, P. F., & Leseman, P. P. M. (2001). Lasting effects of home literacy on reading achievement in school. *Journal of School Psychology, 39*(5), 389–414.

de Jong, P. F., & Van der Leij, A. (1999). Specific contributions of phonological abilities to early reading acquisition: Results from a Dutch latent variable longitudinal study. *Journal of Educational Psychology, 91,* 450–476.

Dickinson, D. K., McGabe, A., Anastasopolous, L., Peisner-Feinberg, E. S., & Poe, M. D. (2003). The Comprehensive Language Approach to early literacy: The interrelationships among vocabulary, phonological sensitivity, and print knowledge among preschool aged-children. *Journal of Educational Psychology, 95*(3), 465–481.

Dickinson, D. K., & Snow, C. E. (1987). Interrelationships among prereading and oral language skills in kindergartners from two social classes. *Early Childhood Research Quarterly, 2,* 1–15.

Erickson, M. F., Sroufe, L. A., & Egeland, B. (1985). The relationship between quality of attachment and behavior problems in preschool in a high-risk sample. *Monographs of the Society for Research in Child Development, 50*(1/2, Serial No. 209).

Field, T. M. (1998). Maternal depression effects on infants and early intervention. *Preventative Medicine, 27,* 200–203.

Fischer, K. W., & Bidell, T. R. (1998). Dynamic development of psychological structures in action and thought. In W. Damon & R. M. Lerner (Eds.), *Handbook of child psychology (5th ed.): Vol. 1. Theoretical models of human development* (pp. 467–561). New York: Wiley.

García Coll, C., & Magnuson, K. (2000). Cultural differences as sources of developmental vulnerabilities and resources. In J. P. Shonkoff & S. J. Meisels (eds.), *Handbook of early childhood intervention* (2nd ed., pp. 94–114). Cambridge, UK: Cambridge University Press.

Gauvain, M. (2001). *The social context of cognitive development.* New York: Guilford Press.

Goswami, U. (2001). Early phonological development and the acquisition of literacy. In S. B. Neuman & D. K. Dickinson (Eds.), *Handbook of early literacy research* (pp. 111–125). New York: Guilford Press.

Goswami, U. (2003). Why theories about developmental dyslexia require developmental designs. *Trends in Cognitive Sciences, 7*(12), 534–540.

Haden, C. A., Haines, R. A., & Fivush, R. (1997). Developing narrative structure in parent–child reminiscing across the preschool years. *Developmental Psychology, 33*(2), 295–307.

Halliday, M. A. K. (1994). *An introduction to functional grammar (2nd ed.).* London: Edward Arnold.

Hammett, L. A., van Kleeck, A., & Huberty, C. J. (2003). Patterns of parents' extratextual interactions with preschool children: A cluster analysis study. *Reading Research Quarterly, 38*(4), 442–467.

Harwood, R. L., Miller, J. G., & Irizarry, N. L. (1995). *Culture and attachment: Perceptions of the child in context.* New York: Guilford Press.

Heath, S. B. (1983). *Ways with words.* Cambridge, UK: Cambridge University Press.

Hoff, E., & Naigles, L. (2002). How children use input to acquire a lexicon. *Child Development, 73*(2), 418–433.

Kohn, M. L., & Schooler, C. (1983). *Work and personality: An inquiry into the impact of social stratification.* Norwood, NJ: Ablex.

Laosa, L. M. (1982). Families as facilitators of children's development at 3 years of age. In L. M. Laosa & I. E. Sigel (Eds.), *Families as learning environments for children* (pp. 79–135). New York: Plenum Press.

Leseman, P. P. M., & de Jong, P. F. (1998). Home literacy: opportunity, instruction, cooperation, and social-emotional quality predicting early reading achievement. *Reading Research Quarterly, 33*(3), 294–318.

Leseman, P. P. M., & de Jong, P. F. (2001). How important is home literacy for acquiring literacy in school? In L. Verhoeven & C.E. Snow (Eds.), *Literacy and motivation: Reading engagement in individuals and groups* (pp. 71–93). Hillsdale, NJ: Erlbaum.

Leseman, P. P. M., & de Jong, P. F. (2004). Förderung der Sprach- und Präliteralitätsentwicklung in der Familie und Vorschule [Promoting language and preliteracy development in the family and preschool]. In G. Faust, M. Götz, H. Hacker & H.-G. Rossbach (Eds.), *Anschlussfähige Bildungsprozesse im Elementar- und Primarbereich* (pp. 168–189). Bad Heilbrunn, Germany: Julius Klinkhardt Verlag.

Leseman, P. P. M., & van den Boom, D. C. (1999). Effects of quantity and quality of home proximal processes on Dutch, Surinamese-Dutch, and Turkish-Dutch preschoolers' cognitive development. *Infant and Child Development, 8,* 19–38.

Lieven, E., Behrens, H., Speares, J., & Tomasello, M. (2003). Early syntactic creativity: A usage-based approach. *Journal of Child Language, 30,* 333–370.

Mattys, S. L., & Jusczyk, P. W. (2001). Phonotactic cues for segmentation of fluent speech by infants. *Cognition, 78,* 91–121.

Mayo, A. Y., & Leseman, P. P. M. (2004). *Developmental changes in cognitive co-construction in Dutch, Surinamese-Dutch and Turkish-Dutch mother–child problem solving interactions.* Manuscript submitted for publication.

Mullen, I. V. S., Martin, M. O., Gonzalez, E. J., & Kennedy, A. M. (2003). *PIRLS 2001 international report.* Boston: International Study Center, Boston College.

Mundy, P., & Gomes, A. (1998). Individual differences in joint attention skill development in the second year. *Infant Behavior and Development, 21*(3), 469–482.

Organisation of Economic Cooperation and Development. (2002). *PISA 2000.* Paris: Author. Available online at www.pisa.oecd.org

Olson, D. R. (1991). Literacy as metalinguistic activity. In D. R. Olson & N. Torrance (Eds.), *Literacy and orality* (pp. 251–270). Cambridge, UK: Cambridge University Press.

Pianta, R. C., Nimetz, S. L., & Bennett, E. (1997). Mother–child relationships, teacher–child relationships, and school outcomes in preschool and kindergarten. *Early Childhood Research Quarterly, 12,* 263–280.

Purcell-Gates, V. (1996). Stories, coupons, and the TV guide: Relationships between home literacy experiences and emergent literacy knowledge. *Reading Research Quarterly, 31,* 406–428.

Ravid, D., & Tolchinsky, L. (2002). Developing linguistic literacy: A comprehensive model. *Journal of Child Language, 29,* 417–447.

Raz, I. T., & Bryant, P. (1990). Social background, phonological awareness and children's reading. *British Journal of Developmental Psychology, 8,* 209–225.

Rebello Britto, P., & Brooks-Gunn, J. (2001). Beyond shared book reading: Dimensions of home literacy and low-income African American preschoolers' skills. *New Directions for Child and Adolescent Development, 92,* 73–89.

Scarborough, H. S. (1998). Early identification of children at risk for reading disabilities: Phonological awareness and some other promising predictors. In B. K. Shapiro, P. J. Accardo, & A. J. Capute (Eds.), *Specific reading disability. A view of the spectrum* (pp. 75–119). Timonium, MD: York Press.

Sénéchal, M., & LeFevre, J. A. (2002). Parental involvement in the development of children's reading skill: A five-year longitudinal study. *Child Development, 73*(2), 445–460.

Sigel, I. E. & Kim, M., (1996). The answer depends on the question. A conceptual and methodological analysis of a parent belief–behavior interview regarding children's learning. In S. Harkness & C. M. Super (Eds.), *Parents' cultural belief systems: Their origins, expressions, and consequences* (pp. 83–120). New York: Guilford Press.

Sigel, I. E., Stinson, E. T., & Kim, M. (1993). Socialization of cognition: The distancing model. In R.H. Wozniak & K. W. Fischer (Eds.), *Development in context: Acting and thinking in specific environments* (pp. 211–224). New York: Erlbaum.

Snow, C. E., & Kurland, B. (1996). Sticking to the point: Talk about magnets as a preparation for literacy. In D. Hicks (Ed.), *Child discourse and social learning: An interdisciplinary perspective* (pp. 189–220). New York: Cambridge University Press.

Snowling, M., Bishop, D. V. M., & Stothard, S.E. (2000). Is preschool language impairment a risk factor for dyslexia in adolescence? *Journal of Child Psychology and Psychiatry, 41*(5), 587–600.

Stipek, D. J. (2001). Pathways to constructive lives: The importance of early school success. In A. Bohart & D. Stipek (Eds.), *Constructive and destructive behavior: Implications for family, school, and society* (pp. 291–316). Washington, DC: American Psychological Association.

Storch, S. A., & Whitehurst, G. J. (2002). Oral language and code-related precursors to reading: Evidence from a longitudinal structural model. *Developmental Psychology, 38*(6), 934–947.

Tesser, P. T. M., & Iedema, J. (2001). *Rapportage Minderheden 2001. Deel I Vorderingen op school* [Minorities Report 2001. Part I: School achievements] The Hague, The Netherlands: SCP.

Thomas, M., & Karmiloff-Smith, A. (2002). Are adult developmental disorders like cases of adult brain damage? Implications from connectionist modelling. *Behavioral and Brain Sciences, 25,* 727–750.

Trevarthen, C., & Aitken, K. J. (2001). Infant intersubjectivity: Research, theory, and clinical applications. *Journal of Child Psychology and Psychiatry, 42*(1), 3–48.

van Kleeck, A., Gillam, R., Hamilton, L., & McGrath, C. (1997). The relationship between middle-class parents' book sharing discussion and their preschoolers' abstract language development. *Journal of Speech, Language, and Hearing Research, 40,* 1261–1271.

Vellutino, F. R., Fletcher, J. M., Snowling, M. J., & Scanlon, D. M. (2004). Specific reading disability (dyslexia): What have we learned in the past four decades? *Journal of Child Psychology and Psychiatry, 45*(1), 2–40.

Vernon-Feagans, L., Scheffner Hammer, C., Miccio, A., & Manlove, E. (2001). Early language and literacy skills in low-income African American and Hispanic children. In S. B. Neuman & D. K. Dickinson (Eds.), *Handbook of early literacy research* (pp. 192–210). New York: Guilford Press.

Weizman, Z. O., & Snow, C. E. (2001). Lexical input as related to children's vocabulary acquisition: Effects of sophisticated exposure and support for meaning. *Developmental Psychology, 37*(2), 265–279.

Whitehurst, G. J., & Lonigan, C. J. (1998). Child development and emergent literacy. *Child Development, 69*(3), 848–872.

17

Considering Culture in Research-Based Interventions to Support Early Literacy

STUART McNAUGHTON

This chapter focuses on the literacy achievement of children from culturally and linguistically diverse communities; specifically, children from those communities traditionally not well served by mainstream schools. Since colonization in New Zealand, these have often been Māori children (the indigenous people of New Zealand), but more recently they also include children of immigrant families from Pacific nations such as Samoa, Tonga, Niue, and the Cook Islands. Longitudinal studies show that many of these children enter school with relatively low scores on school-based measures of early literacy, such as concepts about print or word recognition. Often they have lower scores than other children on standardized measures of English language, such as receptive or expressive vocabulary (McNaughton, Phillips, & MacDonald, 2003). Thereafter, their progress is typically lower than that of other children after one year at school, and differences in literacy achievement become accentuated over the following years, particularly in the areas of text comprehension and writing quality (McNaughton, et al., 2003). This pattern parallels the experiences of children from families with "minority" status in other countries (Snow, Burns, & Griffin, 1998).

The issue addressed in this chapter is how these children's early literacy development might be supported so that the transition to conventional literacy instruction at school and the early development of conventional school literacy is enhanced. In keeping with the overall focus of this volume, this chapter explores how research-based interventions might contribute to the early development of literacy for these children. This exploration focuses on the role of cultural and linguistic identity in the design of effective support.

Culture and Early Literacy Development: Basic Premises

Our goal for enhancing early literacy development for Māori and Pacific nations' children in New Zealand has two components. The first of these components is descriptive. This descriptive component plots local patterns of development and socialization in early literacy, analyzing literacy-related events as cultural practices both within family settings and over the transition to school. The rationale for the significance of this component is that research-based interventions in families and schools become considerably better informed and more effective by knowing about current practices of literacy in families. The second component has been systematic interventions in family, early childhood education, and school settings using the descriptive information provided by the first component.

Literacy Practices at Home and at School

Several premises underpin the intervention logic. One concerns the variability of literacy and language practices in different cultural groups in Western industrialized societies, including the groups of most concern in this chapter. Cultural groups, that is, groups having common practices and meanings associated with those practices (Greenfield & Cocking, 1994), may differ from each other in terms of the characteristics of their language and literacy practices, both in the types of activities that form their practices and in the frequency of occurrence of those activities (Greenfield, 1994). But cultural groups are internally heterogeneous with respect to those activities and their occurrences. That is, family literacy activities are variable in terms of type and occurrence of particular activities, so that within any given cultural group families differ one from another (McNaughton, 1996; Neuman, Hagedorn, Celano, & Daly, 1995). Additionally, individual families within a cultural group may use different practices at different times. For example, parents might vary the ways in which they read a text with a preschool child, depending on such things as the type of text and the ideas they hold about the purposes for reading different types of texts (Heath, Branscombe, & Thomas, 1986). Or they may shift practices as they access new information, for example, about book reading and school practices (Whitehurst & Lonigan, 2001).

The reason for the variability in literacy activities is that socialization practices are structured but are also dynamic. On the one hand, parents' ideas and actions guide children, creating "channels" of development for children that increase the likelihood of some activity settings for children occurring and decrease the probability of others (Valsiner, 1988). Within these channels, development is coconstructed by the children as active learners engaging in these settings with family members, with others, and by themselves. Children develop expertise that is situated in recurring activity settings, which involves coming to know the goals, the actions, and the conditions relevant to those activities (Gee, 2001; Rogoff, 1990). On the other hand, children and caregivers are not passive, and their ideas and actions change. New ideas and ways of acting are con-

structed from messages available from family, community, and institutional sources. Both the commonalities and the diversity of practices within cultural groups can be attributed to the dynamic nature of the ideas and actions of both socialization agents and children (McNaughton, 1996).

A second premise concerns relationships between family practices and the instructional activities at school that define conventional school literacy practices, such as the activities within which instruction for decoding and comprehension occur. Some family practices are more directly developmentally linked with school practices than others, and use of specific activities by families may enhance the development of aspects of conventional literacy both before school and when a child goes to school (Heath, 1983). For example, developmental relationships between particular sets of knowledge and skills before school and subsequent progress at school can be linked to specific family activities, such as how books are read with children (Whitehurst & Lonigan, 2001).

Given that literacy practices reflect and construct cultural identity, there is a dilemma in any intervention with families. The dilemma is that the act of intervention is a cultural act, insofar as it changes family practices (Greenfield, 1994). A further premise, therefore, is that there are some circumstances under which interventions with families to adopt new practices associated with greater success in mainstream schools will be more effective. One is basing the intervention on the feature of heterogeneity of cultural practices without undermining current practices. A second is that interventions should enable families to add to their repertoire of practices and, in so doing, increase the range of uses of texts to achieve different purposes (McNaughton, 1995; Gutierrez & Rogoff, 2003).

There is a further premise underlying the intervention logic. In addition to interventions with families, it is possible for school practices to be modified to create stronger developmental links with aspects of family practices that heretofore may have had limited relationships with school practices (Lee, Spencer, & Harpalani, 2003). The rationale for this parallels the concepts of family practices and their variability outlined previously. In schools, curriculum statements specify and officially sanction a set of beliefs about social practices (Gee, 1998). That is, they impose constraints on and definitions of expertise for children that promote some forms of literacy and reduce the likelihood of others. They provide detailed expectations about sequences of learning. In this respect, teachers are like parents, although a curriculum and its associated practices are likely to provide more rigid channels for development than those practices that occur at home.

However, teachers also apply their expertise in changing social and professional environments. Historical, community, professional, and personal contexts, together with the ongoing changes in the children they teach, all provide sources for the reconstruction of their ideas and actions (Olson & Bruner, 1996). So teachers' ideas about cultural practices in families and the nature of children's development can change. Modifying school practices to incorporate more of the diversity in children's language and literacy experiences, therefore, is possible but is dependent on the degree of flexibility in school curricula and practices (Dyson, 2001; Lee et al., 2003; McNaughton, 2002).

The Transition to School

Our research has focused on the transition to school (see also Morrison, Connor, & Bachman, Chapter 27, this volume). This focus follows from theoretical considerations of developmental transitions in general and from a consideration of the significance of this particular transition. In Western industrialized societies such as New Zealand, going to school creates a developmental transition through a predictable age-related change in childrearing (Bronfenbrenner, 1986). Shifts in developmental tasks; in the roles of teachers, students, and families; and in the goals of socialization are compressed into a short period of time. Theoretical predictions about such transitions, therefore, suggest that in the months just prior to going to school and in the months immediately after starting school literacy development is particularly malleable and therefore more open to outside guidance and instruction (McNaughton, 1995). Under optimal conditions, this period can lead to changes in developing skills and expertise. In less than optimal conditions, however, children begin to struggle. This is the case for many children from cultural groups with "minority" status.

In the following sections, I describe the two components of the research program: descriptions of family literacy activities and planned interventions over the transition to school. I end the chapter with a summary of the attributes of effective interventions for children from diverse cultural and linguistic communities who are "at risk" in mainstream schools.

Component One: Plotting Local Patterns of Development and Socialization

Family Activities and Cultural Identity

A detailed research base exists that describes features of literacy events in different families and communities in terms of cultural and social practices (e.g., Gee, 2001). In these descriptions, family members are described as using written language in particular ways to achieve certain purposes. These ways both express and construct cultural and social identity (Heath, 1983). For older family members, practices serve a range of roles and purposes, including the role of socialization agent. Their socialization practices involve specific activity settings, which are selected, arranged, and deployed by family members. In these activity settings participants' actions are goal directed, and they occur as conventionalized but dynamic types of participation.

Activities provide vehicles for learning and development to take place through processes that can be described using current tutorial models such as scaffolding (Wood, 1998) and guided participation (Rogoff, 1990). These processes enable expertise with written language, situated in the activities, to develop. A basic assumption about the nature of these activities is that shared understandings of goals and ways of acting need to develop so that the activities become fully effective vehicles for personal development (Rogoff, 1990; Wertsch, 1991).

When fully articulated in research accounts, descriptions of literacy as social practices draw relationships between the characteristics of the observed events and the ideas and goals families have. They also draw explicit connections between the literacy events and the cultural meanings and values that practices express and construct for children. An example from our work is the analysis of reading books to preschool children in Māori, Pacific nation, and Pakeha (Anglo-European) families (summarized in McNaughton, 1995).

Although book reading events are widespread in New Zealand, there are differences in frequency, differences in types of book used across families, and differences in how activity settings are constituted. Of interest here are descriptions of three patterns of exchanges used when reading narrative texts that create distinctive tutorial styles and that constitute three distinct activities. The exchanges themselves are not necessarily exclusively used; even with the same book, families can switch between styles to meet different purposes (McNaughton, 1995). But each style can be analyzed in terms of how the patterns create tutorials, of how particular ways of participating develop, of how particular goals are associated with the activity, and of how forms of expertise develop within the activity. These in turn can be mapped onto cultural beliefs and meanings.

In one of these styles, child and reader are focused on the narrative and life-to-text relationships. The interactions are more like conversations, and the scaffolding that is provided by the reader guides the child through clarifying, elaborating, and negotiating meanings at different semantic levels in the text. Often the setting is one-to-one, with the child becoming able to initiate dyadic exchanges that can challenge both the meaning and forms of reading using the text (Phillips & McNaughton, 1990). These features can be linked with beliefs and meanings about literacy as an individual possession and the development of intentionality (Wolf & Heath, 1992).

The properties of this narrative style have been identified repeatedly in research studies. The style has been seen as canonical (McNaughton, 1995) because of its demonstrated relationships with progress in reading at school, its formal similarities with the "linguistically contextualized" literacy of school, and its association with Anglo-European middle-class families (Bus, 2002; Gee, 1998; Whitehurst & Lonigan, 2002; Wolf & Heath, 1992).

But there are other styles. A second style develops children's capabilities of reciting portions of the text. The tutorial structure involves systematic modeling and imitation of sentence text segments with successive shifts to the child's own independent performance. When these are Māori or Pacific nation families the event more often is found to involve multiparty settings, and the readers can be older siblings and members of the wider family (Wolfgramm, 1991). The pedagogy that this pattern represents has widespread presence in indigenous families, in families with less exposure to or experience with mainstream Westernized schooling (Gallimore & Goldenberg, 1993; Greenfield, 1994), and in educational and religious contexts other than those of mainstream Westernized schooling (Wagner & Spratt, 1987). This style also can be linked to significant beliefs and meanings, which include beliefs about group cohesion, about texts being authoritative and needing to be represented accurately, and about how personal knowledge carries group responsibilities (see McNaughton, 1998).

A third style is concerned with displays of items of knowledge such as colors, letters, or labels. Skills in referential speech, as well as specific item knowledge, develop through questioning routines initially controlled by the reader but shifting over time to the child. This style has formal similarities with what Cazden (2001) described as the default condition of classroom discourse, exchanges that involve teacher-initiated questions, a student response, and teacher evaluation. We have not found that this style is particularly predominant in any cultural group in studies of 4-year-olds' reading of narrative texts. But in studies that have focused on picture-book reading, and especially with younger children, this style has been found in middle-class Anglo-European families (Heath, 1983; Ninio & Bruner, 1978; Pelligrini & Galda, 1998)

It is important to qualify statements in these summaries. The variation within a cultural group in its uses of different styles can be greater than the variation between groups (McNaughton, 1996). However, in New Zealand, our studies of 4-year-old children reading narrative texts indicate a tendency for Anglo-European families to be more exclusive in their use of the narrative style and for Māori families and Pacific nation families to be more dexterous by using different styles.

We developed the notion of "textual dexterity" from descriptions of a group of

Māori and Pacific nation parents reading to preschoolers (McNaughton, 1995). These were families in which there was an older sibling who was a high-progress reader at school. The families could switch between different patterns of reading books to their preschool children depending on how the families perceived the task. This switching occurred under the control of the family and illustrates a choice in styles to suit different needs.

Over time and with familiar books, these styles provide the basis for particular sorts of expertise. The narrative style, for example, is associated with comprehension strategies similar to those valued at school. The performance style is associated with (among other things) recitation memory; and the display style, particularly with young children, with learning about referents and referencing (McNaughton, 1995; Ninio & Bruner, 1978; Wagner & Spratt, 1987).

Similar evidence for varied expertise situated within particular activities can be found in intensive studies of writing before school. The same conclusions can be drawn. Early writing activities within and between families in different cultural groups cover a range of forms and purposes, and there are relationships between the forms and functions and specific cultural beliefs and meanings (Goodridge & McNaughton, 1995).

Parents' Ideas about Activities

We also need to consider the ideas participants hold about activities. Family members construct ideas about the nature of children's development and appropriate forms of teaching and learning. These include beliefs about developmental goals and stages. The ideas can be seen as part of activities (Wertsch, 1991) but, as noted earlier, they are not static. They change over the course of child-rearing and across generations, a process that contributes to cultural shifts. Like their children, parents' ideas develop through processes of personal construction from ambient events, through personal problem solving, and through coconstruction in joint activities with others.

For example, studies of children's writing before school in New Zealand (McNaughton, Kempton, & Turoa, 1994) have found that Anglo-European parents tended to adopt explicit developmental goals; for example, expecting their children to learn to write their names, before they begin school, which in New Zealand is typically on a child's fifth birthday. They spoke of the need to prepare children for school, hence conferring what they expressed as an "advantage" to their children. This was associated with an increase in writing activities in the last months before school, marked by a focus on applying the child's existing knowledge to school-like tasks. For example, there was an increased frequency of copying and writing letters of the alphabet in contexts such as writing names. Some families bought exercise books and taught children the mechanics of writing, such as the spacing and alignment of letters, which they assumed was what would be required in the new entrant classrooms.

In contrast, Māori parents and Samoan parents more often expressed "readiness" views about children's development, noting that children would learn such things as writing their names when they were ready. Also, they believed that promoting such writing was not a family responsibility but the primary responsibility of the educational professionals. Related to this belief was an ambivalent view about school-based knowledge and appropriate forms of teaching and learning.

Parents in families from the Pacific nation communities in New Zealand, such as Samoan parents, typically have placed a different emphasis on the respective roles of teachers and parents than have Anglo-European caregivers (Research Solutions, 1999). Their ideas tend to differentiate the roles of teaching and caregiving. Although families in general in New Zealand believe education to be important, Pacific nation families more often say they don't know how to help their children in schoolwork. This is associated with a trust of and deference to school professionals and an assumption that as long as children go to school they will learn what they need to know. Parents from Pacific nation families are more likely to express reservations about teaching children if one is not a schoolteacher than are other cultural groups.

The significance of parents' ideas about socialization and literacy raises an issue that bears directly on children's transition to school. It is the access that families might have to privileged professional knowledge about specific activities and what that access might enable caregivers to do. In Goodridge and McNaughton's (1994) descriptions of Māori, Samoan, and Anglo-European families in relatively poor urban communities, mothers were asked to provide examples of their 4 1/2-year-old children's writing. Initially, they could provide very few instances. When the request was pursued by asking for drawings, scribbling, joint activities, and other emergent writing attempts, many examples were received. Initially, the parents did not hold the same views of the developmental significance of these activities as the researchers did, but they could quickly find examples of writing activities given a shared view. The research intention had been to collect naturalistic descriptive data over the months before school, but the process of asking was highly reactive, at least in a methodological sense. That is, the families viewed these forms of emergent writing in a very different light from the way they had previously, and they became more interested and supportive of them as important educationally relevant activities. The effectiveness of communication between educators and families about home support for literacy, therefore, is likely to depend on shared understanding of concepts and beliefs about the nature of teaching and learning and what might count as being effective.

Family Activities as a Basis for Interventions

These descriptions of family activities and parental beliefs have a general, as well as a local, significance for interventions. Generally, we know that different communities can take on different forms and functions of literacy. But locally, knowing patterns of literacy practices signals how to build new activities into the existing repertoire of family activities. The presence of intrafamily and interfamily variation in cultural practices challenges descriptions that homogenize cultural groups or that describe cultural practices as static, fixed in time, and standard across settings.

The ways in which families can use and develop different activity structures when reading with children were demonstrated in a study of Samoan families living in Samoa and in New Zealand (Tagoilelagi, 1995).

When reading the Bible (in Samoan), there was no variation across families and across countries. Families used a standard performance style by which children learned to recite verses through modeling and imitation routines. Some families also adopted this style exclusively when reading narrative texts in Samoan and English. Others used mixtures of styles, and some did not use the performance style at all but used combinations of the narrative and item styles. The performance style of reading the Bible and its use in the reading other texts can be attributed to long-standing pedagogical practices and language activities in the Samoan culture. The other styles may have parallels in traditional cultural practices also, but reflect access to messages and practices associated with contemporary childrearing and schooling practices in New Zealand and elsewhere.

Differences between families show heterogeneity within a cultural group and the dynamic nature of cultural practices in these communities. This heterogeneity can provide a basis for interventions by adapting a program of teaching to particular families' repertoires. An example from our research involved eight Tongan mothers whose children attended a Tongan language preschool (a preschool that is registered and monitored by the New Zealand Ministry of Education, in which early childhood education follows national guidelines and is delivered through the Tongan language and culture). We hoped to increase the narrative focus style described earlier, also analyzed by Dickinson and Tabors (2001) as "nonimmediate" talk. We identified exchanges of this sort in some mothers' transcripts. We found that, when these exchanges were identified as significant for the development of conventional school forms of literacy, these and other mothers were able to increase the frequency of use of this style.

Component Two: Interventions

There is a growing literature on interventions that aim to support early literacy for children typically at risk in mainstream schools. Here, I identify three distinct forms of educational enhancement to achieve this aim when optimizing the transition to school.

Modifying Family Practices

One form of intervention is to modify family literacy practices in ways that enhance the skills and knowledge needed for more effective engagement in the literacy instruction and discourse of schools. Examples include increasing the frequency or the style of reading (typically narrative) texts with children before school (e.g., Pellegrini & Galda, 1998; Whitehurst & Lonigan, 2001). In some instances, this has been done in the home language of a minority language group (Gallimore & Goldenberg, 1993; Wolfgramm, Afeaki, & McNaughton, 1997; Yaden et al., 2000). Other interventions have adopted a broader focus by extending literacy activities to include writing and oral storytelling or by creating intergenerational family literacy programs (Morrow, 1995).

This research has shown that family members can be taught to increase the use of specific activities such as reading to children and that this can have a positive impact on beginning reading instruction at school (Whitehurst & Lonigan, 2001). But difficulties have been reported, including sustaining patterns within families. Gallimore and Goldenberg (1993) report an intervention to increase the educational success of children in Hispanic families. Immigrant families in Los Angeles were given specially written beginning reading texts that they could read with their kindergarten-level children. The families had not typically read storybooks with children, so with these specially designed texts they were asked to read for enjoyment together and to concentrate on the story.

The researchers found that sending linguistically and culturally appropriate narrative texts home did not result in the predicted increase in targeted exchanges that had the features of elaborating, extending, and negotiating meanings. Rather, families' interactions were like the performance and item style. Parents interpreted the task in terms of their ideas about appropriate school pedagogy and how they had learned to read. The researchers, reflecting on this outcome, argue that the ideas and beliefs held by participants in educational programs were important determinants of how activity settings develop. Other researchers have noted the significance of developing shared understanding in interactions between family members and researchers in research contexts (Edwards, 1995; Renshaw, 1992)

Similarly, studies in New Zealand have shown that through specific training programs, mothers in Pacific nation communities can add, or increase the frequency of, exchanges that focus on text meaning by using language that elaborates and extends (Wolfgramm et al., 1997). The research shows that parents can develop ideas about differential uses of exchanges across texts to suit different purposes they might have for their children's reading, thus developing their "textual dexterity."

Modifying Classroom Practices

A second strategy for optimizing instruction for children whose cultural and linguistic identities mean that they are at risk in classrooms is to modify classroom practices. The view is to increase continuities between forms of literacy and discourse patterns across settings with those in school (Cazden, 2001). Tharp and Gallimore (1988) and Au (1993) report how classroom discourse patterns were systematically modified so that a culturally preferred style of talking by indigenous Hawaiian children could be used in effective comprehension instruction.

But there are difficulties in this hypothesis of continuity, which include precisely defining the nature of discontinuities and sustaining the effects of increased continuity (McNaughton, 2002; Reese & Gallimore, 2000; Tharp, Estrada, Dalton, & Yamauchi, 2000). To overcome these difficulties, we have attempted to explain the processes that might produce more effective teaching and learning in two ways. The first is to focus on how activity settings inside school and outside school are related. The framework outlined earlier suggests that effective modification of school activity settings involves creating activities that enable more incorporation of the expertise children have on entry to school. And the second is to help children solve the mismatches between current knowledge and skills and how they have been learned and what is required in school (Gee, 1998).

However, like other aspects of teaching, the ability to identify and act on children's existing expertise is determined by the ideas that teachers hold (Olson & Bruner, 1996). The overarching frameworks that teachers can hold reflect the major traditions of thinking about the nature of learning and development (Case, 1996; Olson & Bruner, 1996), and these lead to different views of the nature and significance of children's out-of-school emergent expertise. Constructivist ideas about early literacy tend to be associated with a view that in general children's literacy development follows a predictable and unitary sequence because endogenous processes direct acquisition. Other frameworks, such as sociocultural theorizing, are more likely to be associated with a view that literacy development can take multiple pathways that reflect the patterns of guidance and definitions of expertise associated with different communities, including those of schools (McNaughton, 1999).

The ideas teachers hold are important to interventions focusing on improving connections between home and school cultures. In the case of the transition to school, if the views that teachers hold differ in the ways described previously, teachers will define their starting points with learners differently, and instructional patterns will take on different properties. If teachers have an understanding of children's diverse forms of expertise, as well as the markers of conventional school literacy, they will be more effective at identifying and building on those forms.

Teachers' ideas, therefore, about early literacy can be examined in terms of the degree of awareness they have of children's diversity in cultural and social practices and associated forms of expertise. It is not sufficient to know that children's literacy in general might have a number of features; rather, it is important to know that these features might or might not apply to individual new entrant students. From a research perspective, considering a teacher's current awareness of diversity provides a way of understanding how their ideas about children relate to the specific actions they take to gain personalized knowledge about each student. Given that teachers' ideas are dynamic, this is a basis for modifying practices because they are able to modify their practices by reflection on their actions with learners (McNaughton, 2002).

Research into the ideas held by new-entrant teachers in the schools serving communities in the lowest employment and in-come levels in New Zealand shows that they differ one from another in the kinds of things they would look for in a new student to establish a child's existing literacy knowledge and skills (McNaughton, 2001). But in general, despite their children's communities being composed of diverse cultural and language groups, they seldom refer to the potential for variations between children in knowledge and skills that develop through family literacy activities. They focus almost exclusively on the presence or absence of specific aspects of school-related knowledge and skills in their children, and this can reinforce low expectations about what children know or can do (McNaughton, 2002).

But it is possible to change the ideas and practices of teachers with children from diverse cultural and linguistic backgrounds in the first months at school so that effective modification of activities occurs. In one study professional development sessions focused on helping teachers manage the mismatches between children's current expertise and the classroom requirements in early literacy instruction (Phillips, McNaughton, & MacDonald, 2004). One third of the 73 teachers were Māori or from Pacific nation communities, with a wide variety of teaching experience, and the majority of their children were from Māori families, Pacific nation families, or families who identified as both, living in communities with the lowest employment rates and income levels in New Zealand. Within the general classroom program there was a specific focus on small-group instruction over the first 6 months at school in four literacy activities. These were reading to children, instructional reading (to guide children to accurately and speedily decode words from the texts), coconstructing a language base for writing expository and narrative accounts, and instruction in writing that shared language.

The teachers developed greater awareness of children's understanding of school tasks and of the relevance of children's experiences and knowledge on entry to school. Through sensitive observation, they developed ways of incorporating children's strengths into classroom activities. They worked on more effective instruction to help children make connections between school literacy and their own world knowledge. The teachers also learned how to monitor their own uses of language and literacy in activities with children.

The quasi-experimental design with cross-sectional and longitudinal components had a baseline phase (McNaughton et al., 2003). This phase provided a description of the current progress of children's literacy and language at 5.0 years (on entry to school), 5.6 years, and 6.0 years against which progress of different experimental groups could be plotted. The initial profile of children's development, together with descriptions of teaching, added information about teaching and learning on which the professional development programs could be based. The profiles were used in professional development sessions to challenge beliefs about the sources of low achievement and the inevitability of low progress and to set goals for teaching. Ideas about and descriptions of family literacy practices and emergent literacy in community settings were also introduced, emphasizing concepts of diversity and dexterity.

Process measures indicated changes in literacy activities consistent with the intervention focus, as well as changes in teacher expectations and understanding of child development. Children made significantly more progress over the first year at school on all the literacy and language measures compared with the controls. They were reading at or close to nationally expected distributions in most areas. Especially significant were the high levels of achievement in reading texts and writing. This outcome was educationally significant compared with nationally expected levels.

Combined Interventions

A third strategy involves a combination of family and school-based interventions, systematically increasing the articulation between teaching, learning, and development in specific activities in both settings. Heath's (1983) classic ethnographic study in which descriptions of the discourse patterns at home and at school were shared between family and teachers represents an early action research approach; so do more extensive case studies of collaboration between communities and schools in designing ways of teaching and learning at home and at school (Delgado-Gaitan, 1990).

In the current research, we have combined interventions in community early childhood centers in which families participate with the school-based interventions described earlier. The interventions before school have taken place in a range of early childhood centers, including "language nests" run by mothers from community groups. More than half of the center adults were Māori or from Pacific nation backgrounds. Like the professional development program with schoolteachers, the 10 early childhood professional development sessions aimed to elaborate ideas about children's literacy and language and about teaching, learning, and development. Specific literacy activities that had similarities with school activities were targeted. These were reading texts to children using exchanges that focused on text meaning and elaborated and extended the text, guidance with emergent writing, and developing coherence and elaboration in children's telling and retelling of stories.

We examined the effects of the early childhood interventions combined with the effects of the interventions in the first 6 months at school (Phillips, McNaughton, & MacDonald, 2001). We found that the combined program was associated with significantly greater progress in measures of story retelling and receptive language and in literacy concepts compared with the schoolteaching program alone after 6 months at school (effect sizes ranged from 0.42 to 1.00). But after 1 year the children who had received both components were similar to children who had received the teacher development component only in most of the specific literacy measures, suggesting that the primary teachers were teaching early decoding accuracy and fluency in ways that effectively built on different levels of conventional school knowledge on entry to school.

It will be important to plot continued progress in interventions such as this (Keogh, 2004). Other studies suggest a longer term effect on levels of comprehension in subsequent years at school if more complex language (such as elaborated language use and vocabulary size) has been more developed on entry to school (Dickinson & Tabors, 2001; Dickinson, McCabe, Anastasopoulos, & Peisner-Feinberg, 2003; Storch & Whitehurst, 2002). Also, this intervention highlighted how little information there is on how interventions might affect bilingual and biliteracy development (Tabors & Snow, 2001), and further research-based interventions have been implemented that plot the development of bilingual and biliteracy development at school for Pacific nations children (Tagoilelagi-Leota, McNaughton, Mac-Donald, & Farry, 2003).

Summary

This chapter has argued that successful interventions need to recognize children's cultural and linguistic identity. One reason concerns the dynamic and potentially heterogeneous nature of cultural practices (Greenfield, 1994). Interventions need to add value to existing practices, increasing the potential for textual dexterity in family practices. Another reason is the central role of ideas in socialization and the need for interventions to develop shared understandings about the nature of teaching, learning, and development. In essence, interventions involving families contain at least two sets of interacting developmental systems (Bronfenbrenner, 1986). The focal system for researchers and educators usually is that involving the child and family members interacting in literacy activities. But a second system is that created by interactions between educators or researchers and those family members that are part of the intervention. Just like the primary system, the development of shared understanding is necessary to a fully functioning system.

Similarly, we need to support effective interventions for teaching at school. For teachers, adding to or capitalizing on their knowledge of linguistic and cultural backgrounds provides a means of both incorporating children's expertise and pointing to how instructional settings are likely to be confusing for children and how these confusions might be solved.

Teachers need to adapt and build on children's cultural and linguistic backgrounds on entry to school. In addition, they need to help children disambiguate the requirements of classroom instruction. But curricula that closely specify what has to be learned, how it is to be learned, and in what sequence it has to be learned can restrict the degree to which it is possible to recognize and build on chil-dren's existing literacy skills and knowledge (Dyson, 2001). Teachers also need to recognize how culture influences teaching, learning, and development (Olson & Bruner, 1996). Considering culture in research-based interventions depends on pedagogical frameworks that recognize the significance of culture in literacy for teaching, learning, and development.

References

Au, K. H. (1993). *Literacy instruction in multicultural settings.* Fort Worth, TX: Harcourt Brace.

Bronfenbrenner, U. (1986). Ecology of the family as a context for human development. *Developmental Psychology, 22,* 723–742.

Bus, A. D. (2001). Joint caregiver–child storybook reading: A route to literacy development. In S. B. Neuman & D. K. Dickinson (Eds.), *Handbook of early literacy research* (pp. 179–191). New York: Guilford Press.

Case, R. (1996). Changing views of knowledge and their impact on educational research and practice. In D. R. Olson & N. Torrance (Eds.), *The hand book of education and human development: New models of learning, teaching and schooling* (pp. 75–99). Cambridge, UK: Blackwell.

Cazden, C. (2001). *Classroom discourse* (2nd ed.). Portsmouth, NH: Heinemann.

Delgado-Gaitan, C. (1990). *Literacy for empowerment: The role of parents in children's education.* London: Falmer Press.

Dickinson, D., & Tabors, P. O. (Eds.). (2001). *Beginning literacy with language: Young children learning at home and at school.* Baltimore: Brookes.

Dickinson, D. K., McCabe, A., Anastasopoulos, L., & Peisner-Feinberg, P. M. (2003). The comprehensive language approach to early literacy: The interrelationships among vocabulary, phonological sensitivity and print knowledge among preschool-aged children. *Journal of Educational Psychology, 95,* 465–481.

Dyson, A. H. (2001). Writing and children's symbolic repertoires: Development unhinged. In S. B. Neuman & D. K. Dickinson (Eds.), *Handbook of early literacy research* (pp. 126–141). New York: Guilford Press.

Edwards, P. A. (1995). Combining parents' and teachers' thoughts about storybook reading at home and at school. In L. M. Morrow (Ed.), *Family literacy: Connections in schools and communities* (pp. 54–69). Newark, DE: International Reading Association.

Gallimore, R., & Goldenberg, C. (1993). Activity settings of early literacy: Home and school factors in children's emergent literacy. In E. A. Forman,

N. Minick, & C. A. Stone (Eds.), *Contexts for learning: Sociocultural dynamics in children's development* (pp. 315–335). New York: Oxford University Press.

Gee, J. P. (1998). Foreword. In L. I. Bartolome (Ed.), *The misteaching of academic discourses: The politics of language in the classroom* (pp. ix–xvi). Boulder, CO: Westview Press.

Gee, J. P. (2001). A sociocultural perspective on early literacy development. In S. B. Neuman & D. K. Dickinson (Eds.), *Handbook of early literacy research* (pp. 30–42). New York: Guilford Press.

Goodridge, M. J., & McNaughton, S. (1994, May). *How families and children construct writing expertise before school: An analysis of activities in Maori, Pakeha and Samoan families.* Paper presented at the New Zealand Reading Association Conference, Auckland, NZ.

Greenfield, P. M. (1994). Independence and interdependence as developmental scripts: Implication for theory, research and practice. In P. M. Greenfield & R. C. Cocking (Eds.), *Cross-cultural roots of minority child development* (pp. 1–37). Hillsdale, NJ: Erlbaum.

Greenfield, P. M. & Cocking, R. C. (Eds.). (1994). *Cross-cultural roots of minority child development.* Hillsale, NJ: Erlbaum.

Gutierrez, K. D., & Rogoff, B. (2003). Cultural ways of learning: Individual traits or repertoires of practice. *Educational Researcher, 32*(5), 19–25.

Hannon, P. (2004). Family literacy programmes. In N. Hall, J. Larson, & J. Marsh (Eds.), *Handbook of early childhood literacy* (pp. 99–111). London: Sage.

Heath, S. B. (1983). *Ways with words: Language, life and work in communities and classrooms.* Cambridge, UK: Cambridge University Press.

Heath, S. B., Branscombe, A., & Thomas, C. (1986). The book as a narrative prop in language acquisition. In B. Schieffelin & P. Gilmore (Eds.); *The acquisition of literacy: Ethnographic perspectives* (pp. 16–34). Norwood, NJ: Ablex.

Keogh, B. K. (2004). The importance of longitudinal research for early intervention practices. In P. McCardle & V. Chhabra (Eds.), *The voice of evidence in reading research* (pp. 81–102). Baltimore: Brookes.

Lee, C. D., Spencer, M. B., & Harpalani, V. (2003). "Every shut eye ain't sleep": Studying how people live culturally. *Educational Researcher, 32*(5), 6–13.

McNaughton, S. (1995). *Patterns of emergent literacy: Processes of development and transition.* Auckland, New Zealand: Oxford University Press.

McNaughton, S. (1996). Ways of parenting and cultural identity. *Culture and Psychology, 2,*(2) 173–201.

McNaughton, S. (1998). Why there might be several ways to read storybooks to preschoolers in Aotearoa/New Zealand: Models of tutoring and sociocultutral diversity in how families read books to preschoolers. In M. K. de Oliviera & J. Valsiner (Eds.), *Literacy in human development* (pp. 123–143). Stamford, CT: Ablex.

McNaughton, S. (1999). Developmental diversity and literacy instruction over the transition to school. In J. S. Gaffney & B. J. Askew (Eds.), *Stirring the waters: The influence of Marie Clay* (pp. 3–16). Portsmouth, NH: Heinemann.

McNaughton, S. (2001). Co-constructing expertise: The development of parents' and teachers' ideas about literacy practices and the transition to school. *Journal of Early Childhood Literacy, 1*(1), 40–58.

McNaughton, S. (2002). *Meeting of minds.* Wellington, New Zealand: Learning Media.

McNaughton, S., Kempton, M., & Turoa, L. (1994, June–July). *Tutorial configurations in an early writing activity at home.* Paper presented to the meeting of the International Society for the Study of Behavioral Development, Amsterdam.

McNaughton, S., Phillips, G. E., & MacDonald, S. (2003). Profiling teaching and learning needs in beginning literacy instruction: The case of children in "low decile" schools in New Zealand. *Journal of Literacy Research, 35*(2), 703–730.

Morrow, L. (Ed.). (1995). *Family literacy: Connections in schools and communities.* Newark, DE: International Reading Association.

Neuman, S. B., Hagedorn, T., Celano, D., & Daly, P. (1995). Toward a collaborative approach to parent involvement in early education: A study of teenage mothers in an African-American community. *American Educational Research Journal, 32*, 801–827.

Ninio, A., & Bruner, J. S. (1978). The achievement and antecedents of labelling. *Journal of Child Language, 5*, 5–15.

Olson, D. R., & Bruner, J. S. (1996). Folk psychology and folk pedagogy. In D. R. Olson & N. Torrance (Eds.), *The handbook of education and human development: New models of learning, teaching and schooling* (pp. 9–27). Cambridge, UK: Blackwell.

Pellegrini, A., & Galda, L. (1998). *The development of school-based literacy: A social ecological perspective.* London: Routledge.

Phillips, G., & McNaughton, S. (1990). The practice of storybook reading to preschool children in mainstream New Zealand families. *Reading Research Quarterly, 25*(3), 196–212.

Phillips, G. E., McNaughton, S., & MacDonald, S. (2001). *Picking up the pace: Effective literacy interventions for accelerated progress over the transition to decile 1 schools. Report to the Ministry of Education.* Wellington, New Zealand: Ministry of Education.

Phillips, G., McNaughton, S., & MacDonald, S. (2004). Managing the mismatch: Enhancing early literacy progress for children with diverse language and cultural identities in mainstream urban schools in New Zealand. *Journal of Educational Psychology, 96,* 309–323.

Reese, L., & Gallimore, R. (2000). Immigrant Latinos' cultural model of literacy development: An evolving perspective on home–school discontinuities. *American Journal of Education, 108,* 103–134.

Renshaw, P. D. (1992). Reflecting on the experimental context: Parent's Interpretations of the education motive during teaching episodes. In L. T. Winegar & J. Valsiner (Eds.), *Children's development within social context* (Vol. 2, pp. 53–74). Hillsdale, NJ: Erlbaum.

Research Solutions. (1999). *Benchmark research into the attitudes of various ethnic groups to helping their children to learn.* Wellington: New Zealand Ministry of Education.

Rogoff, B. (1990). *Apprenticeship in thinking: Cognitive development in social context.* Oxford, UK: Oxford University Press.

Snow, C. E., Burns, S., & Griffin, P. (1998). *Preventing reading difficulties in young children.* Washington, DC: National Academy Press.

Storch, S., & Whitehurst, G. J. (2002). Oral language and code-related precursors to reading: Evidence from a longitudinal structural model. *Developmental Psychology, 38,* 934–947.

Tabors, P. O., & Snow, C. E. (2001). Young bilingual children and early literacy development. In S. B. Neuman & D. K. Dickinson (Eds.), *Handbook of early literacy research* (pp. 159–178). New York: Guilford Press.

Tagoilelagi, F. F. (1995). *The role of the Samoan culture (fa'a Samoa) in the development of its children's literacy skills.* Unpublished master's thesis, University of Auckland, NZ.

Tagoilelagi-Leota, F., McNaughton, S., MacDonald, S., & Farry, S. (2003, October). *The precious threads: Bilingual and biliteracy development over the transition to school.* Paper presented at Language Acquisition Forum, Ministry of Education, Wellington, NZ.

Tharp, R. G., Estrada, P., Dalton, S. S., & Yamauchi, L. A. (2000). *Teaching transformed: Achieving excellence, fairness, inclusion, and harmony.* Boulder CO: Westview Press.

Tharp, R. G., & Gallimore, R. (1988). *Rousing minds to life: Teaching, learning, and schooling in social context.* Cambridge, MA: Cambridge University Press.

Valsiner, J. (1988). Ontogeny of co-construction of culture within socially organized environmental settings. In J. Valsiner (Ed.), *Child development within culturally structured environments* (Vol. 2, pp. 283–296). Norwood, NJ: Ablex.

Wagner, D. A., & Spratt, J. E. (1987). Cognitive consequences of contrasting pedagogies: The effects of Quranic pre-schooling in Morocco. *Child Development, 58,* 1207–1219.

Wertsch, J. V. (1991). *Voices of the mind: A sociocultural approach to mediated action.* Cambridge, MA: Harvard University Press.

Whitehurst, G. J., & Lonigan, C. J. (2001). Emergent literacy: Development from prereaders to readers. In S. B. Neuman & D. K. Dickinson (Eds.), *Handbook of early literacy research* (pp. 11–29). New York: Guilford Press.

Wolf, S. A., & Heath, S. B. (1992). *The braid of literature: Children's worlds of reading.* Cambridge, MA: Harvard University Press.

Wolfgramm, E. (1991). *Becoming literate: The activity of book reading to Tongan preschoolers in Auckland.* Unpublished master's thesis, University of Auckland, NZ.

Wolfgramm, E., Afeaki, V., & McNaughton, S. (1997). Story-reading in a Tongan language group. *Set Special: Language and Literacy, 7,* 1–4.

Wood, D. (1998). *How children think and learn* (2nd ed.). Oxford, UK: Blackwell.

Yaden, D. B., Tam, A., Madrigal, P., Brassell, D., Massa, J., Altamirano, S., & Armendariz, J. (2000). Early literacy for inner-city children: The effects of reading and writing interventions in English and Spanish during the preschool years. *Reading Teacher, 54,* 186–190.

V

SUPPORTING LITERACY
IN PRESCHOOL CLASSROOMS

18

Vygotskian Perspectives on Teaching and Learning Early Literacy

ELENA BODROVA
DEBORAH J. LEONG

For several reasons, the topics of literacy acquisition and its promotion in young children fit perfectly into a discussion of the principles of Vygotsky's cultural—historical theory and the applications of this theory in the classroom. First, literacy, as a system of signs that is collectively developed and culturally transmitted, was used by Vygotsky as the prime example of "cultural tools" that transform the course of human development—on the scale of the entire history of humankind, as well as in the course of ontogenesis of an individual child. Second, learning to read and write figures prominently in Vygotsky's conceptualization of the relationship between development, teaching, and learning. Third is the success of instructional practices based on the Vygotskian approach and applied to the teaching of early literacy competencies by post-Vygotskians of the second, third, and now fourth generations, including D. B. Elkonin, V. V. Davydov, G. A. Zuckerman, and others.

However, it seems that there still is a large gap between the richness of the Vygotskian tradition, in terms of what it can offer to education, and how much is known in the West about the work done by Vygotsky, by his colleagues, and by his students in the area of early literacy. One of the reasons is that many of the theoretical and practical contributions to the cultural–historical theory

were made by post-Vygotskians in Russia, especially when we consider the topics of learning and development of young children in general and literacy acquisition in particular. Unfortunately, many of these works are virtually unknown to Western audiences. In some cases, when translations are available, understanding of the methodology used and the scope of practical applications of specific instructional strategies is still not an easy task: One needs to be aware of vast differences in cultural contexts—from the use of terminology to the traditional ways of teaching certain academic subjects to what are considered acceptable parenting practices—that affect many aspects of work done within the Vygotskian paradigm. If we add another layer of the differences—phonological, orthographical, morphological, and syntactical—between the Russian and English languages, then the chances of the Vygotskian approach having a positive effect on literacy instruction in American classrooms do not look hopeful.

As a result, the general perception of the Vygotskian approach continues to be more as a philosophy that may provide educators with inspiration and perhaps general guidance but that is not very helpful in designing practical solutions to classroom problems. In this role, the Vygotskian approach produced a strong following in the West, with many theorists proposing changes in educational practice based on such ideas as the zone of proximal development, scaffolding, socially shared learning, and the sign-mediated activity (see, e.g., Moll, 1990; Daniels, 1993, Dixon-Krauss, 1996; Lee & Smagorinsky, 2000). However, most attempts to replicate some of the original instructional methods developed by the post-Vygotskians did not succeed at all (see, e.g., Wilder, 1972) or ended up reducing an integrated system of instruction to a collection of isolated teacher tricks, as is the case with the "Elkonin blocks" widely used in remedial reading programs (e.g., Clay, 1993).

Following the old adage that "nothing is more practical than a good theory," we have examined the Vygotskian approach to find answers to the questions of today's early childhood educators. What we found fits another popular saying—everything new is well-forgotten old. Since the 1920s, first Vygotsky himself and later his students have been dealing with the issues that continue to face educators in the 21st century: Is it developmentally appropriate to start teaching reading and writing in preschool? Why can we not use the methods of formal instruction designed for older students with 4- and 5-year-olds? Can we expect children to learn to read and write as spontaneously as they learn to talk? What is school readiness and how do we assess it?

As we were trying to help preschool and kindergarten teachers struggling with similar issues (see Bodrova & Leong, 1996, 2001, 2003), we realized that it would be virtually impossible to simply design a Vygotsky-based literacy curriculum (or math curriculum, for that matter) without completely changing the way teachers see their students. In the classrooms in which we pilot tested some of our Vygotsky-based literacy strategies, we ended up giving teachers "Vygotsky's eyes" to watch how preschoolers and kindergartners play, communicate, concentrate, get distracted, remember, and forget. As a result, we discovered that the greatest gains in literacy were made in the classrooms in which teachers focused primarily on supporting the development of deliberate and intentional behaviors defined by Vygotsky as higher mental functions (see Bodrova & Leong, 1998, 2001, 2003; Bodrova, Leong, Norford,

& Paynter, 2003). In the present day, when the "literacy wars" have reached our youngest students, we believe that the Vygotskian approach holds great potential for providing truly developmental perspectives on learning in early childhood and on teaching children in this age group.

In this chapter, we focus on several principles of the Vygotskian approach that we consider largely overlooked by the Western scholars of early literacy and on the applications of these principles to early literacy instruction. Most of the research discussed in this chapter was conducted in Russia, and so were the classroom applications; however, we attempt to illustrate Vygotsky's ideas and concepts using practices already used in American classrooms or those that were designed specifically to fit this context.

Vygotsky's Views on Children's Learning of Written Language in the Context of His Cultural Historical Theory

- *Principle 1. Mental development in children results from a complex "interlacing" of two processes: their natural development and their cultural development.* The core idea of Vygotsky's cultural–historical theory is that the history of human development (ontogeny as well as phylogeny) involves a complex interplay between the processes of natural development that are determined biologically and the processes of cultural development brought about by the interactions of the growing individuals with other people and cultural artifacts. What happens as the result of these interactions is more than simply acquisition of values, expectations, or competencies promoted by a specific culture; the entire system of naturally determined mental functions gets restructured to produce what Vygotsky described as higher mental functions:

> When the child enters into culture, he not only takes something from culture, assimilates something, takes something from outside, but culture itself profoundly refines the natural state of behavior of the child and alters completely anew the whole course of his development. (1997, p. 223)

The idea of cultural origins of child development is reflected in the position Vygotsky took in regard to the childrearing practices in general and school education in particular. Arguing with the proponents of "following child's lead," he wrote:

> The old point of view . . . assumed that it was necessary to adapt rearing to development (in the sense of time, rate, form of thinking and perception proper to the child, etc.). It did not pose the question dynamically.
>
> The new point of view . . . takes the child in the dynamics of his development and growth and asks where must the teaching bring the child, but it answers the question differently. It says that in lessons with pupils [in lower classes], it would be folly not to consider the concrete and graphic nature of their memory, which must be relied on; but it would also be folly to cultivate this type of memory. This would be to keep the child at a lower step of development and to fail to see that the concrete type of memory is only a transitional step to a higher type, that concrete memory must be overcome in the process of teaching. (1997, p. 224)

What Vygotsky wrote in this paragraph about different types of memory can also be applied to many other mental competencies—perception, attention, reasoning, and so forth. All of these processes initially develop according to the laws of maturation, but at a certain point they become transformed by specific cultural practices and can no longer be explained exclusively in terms of their biological foundations. In his writings, Vygotsky repeatedly cautioned against reducing mental development to the development of the brain and ignoring the social origin of higher mental functions. With new advances in neuroscience, the danger of overemphasizing the role of the brain in the development of complex cognitive behaviors (including reading and writing) becomes a reality, and Vygotsky's caution remains as relevant today as it was 70 years ago.

• *Principle 2. The formation of higher mental functions is the major development of early childhood.* Lower (or "natural") mental functions, in Vygotsky's view, are carried out by physiological mechanisms that are similar for humans and other mammals.

These functions can be measured and manipulated using the stimulus–reaction paradigm. Vygotsky often referred to how memorization can occur (in humans as well as in animals) simply by repeated association of stimuli as an example of a "natural" mental function. Learning that occurs through the use of lower mental functions is to a great degree dependent on the factors external to the learner (e.g., whether stimuli were repeated enough times or whether they were novel enough to attract attention).

In contrast, higher (or "cultural") mental functions are uniquely human and are acquired by individuals through social interactions and through learning to use specific cultural tools. When a learner possesses higher mental functions, he or she can control the process and outcome of learning and no longer depends on environmental factors. For memory, it means being able to remember on demand after only a few repetitions of the stimuli or even after a single repetition. It becomes possible if the learner uses specific memory aids to assist the process of remembering. These aids vary from scribbles and pictures used by young children to elaborate mnemonic devices employed by adults (Vygotsky, 1997).

Human babies are born equipped with the lower mental functions only; however, as soon as they engage in their first interactions with their caregivers, the formation of higher mental functions begins, facilitated by language and other cultural tools. The early years are the period during which the formation of higher mental functions goes through its initial stages, when children's use of oral language continues to transform their perceptions and begins to transform their attention, memory, imagination, and thinking. Examples of these transformations include children's emerging ability to attend or remember on demand by verbalizing the important components of these attention or memory tasks through self-directed or "private" speech (Vygotsky, 1987, 1997).

With children's acquisition of literacy, numeracy, and other symbolic systems, the transformation of mental functions continues into school age, culminating in development of conscious awareness and volition, which Vygotsky considered major developmental accomplishments of the primary school years (Vygotsky, 1934/1987). Vygotsky pointed out the reciprocal relationship that exists between the nature of higher mental functions as deliberate and sign-mediated processes and the demands of formal schooling that requires children to engage in purposeful behaviors mostly involving operations on signs and symbols. Thus higher mental functions become both a prerequisite and an outgrowth of schooling, presenting us with a new way to approach the very definition of school readiness— readiness that may be fully evaluated only *after* a child has had a chance to encounter the real demands of a classroom (see Carlton & Winsler, 1999, for discussion of the implications of Vygotsky's approach to school readiness).

One of the essential characteristics of higher mental functions is their deliberateness— whereas lower ("natural") behaviors such as associative memory or reactive attention place children under the control of environmental stimulation, new, higher mental functions such as focused attention and deliberate memory liberate children from this dependence, making them "masters of their own behaviors."

We cannot overstate the importance of this deliberateness in learning to read and write: Unlike many other skills that young children master in the first years of their lives, acquiring literacy means dealing with many things that are counterintuitive and simply arbitrary. Letter names do not always match letter sounds, small words denote large objects, and even small variations in letter orientation change the way a letter is read. Of course, it is possible to memorize all this through endless repetitions, but focused attention and deliberate memory make learning of this kind of material much more productive.

What we can learn from Vygotsky's concept of higher mental functions is that many of the difficulties young children face when learning to read and write may not necessarily be attributable to the deficiencies in their processing of visual or auditory information or to their lack of background knowledge and experience in reading; they may instead stem from these children's inability to engage in purposeful and deliberate mental behaviors. It might be that this approach will help

us deal with children who seem to be resistant to content-specific literacy interventions (see, e.g., Torgeson, Morgan, & Davis, 1992).

For Vygotsky, higher mental functions have yet another important feature: Unlike lower or natural mental functions, these culture-specific mental behaviors originate as interindividual, or shared behaviors and become individual only in their final stages of development. Consistent with the spirit of the entire cultural–historical approach, this principle emphasizes the importance of social context for the development of higher mental functions:

> Every function in the cultural development of the child appears on the stage twice, in two planes, first, the social, then the psychological, first between people as an intermental category, then within the child as intramental category. This pertains equally to voluntary attention, to logical memory, to the formation of concepts, and to the development of will. (1997, p. 106)

The idea of the transformation of higher mental functions from interindividual ("intramental" in Vygotsky's words) to intra-individual (or "intramental") became very popular in the West, and various models of peer collaboration became one of the most common applications of Vygotsky's theories, though, in most cases, any kind of interaction is assumed beneficial for children's learning and development. More detailed analysis of what exactly is "shared" and what exactly is eventually internalized is essential for designing effective learning opportunities for cooperative learning (for examples of this analysis and its instructional applications, see Rubtsov, 1991; Slobodchikov & Tsukerman, 1992; Zuckerman, 2003).

Vygotsky's idea that what we share in the process of learning is not limited to the content but also includes the very psychological functions helps us better understand why certain early literacy practices are especially effective. Book reading to young preschoolers in one-on-one or small-group settings is known to have a positive effect on their oral language development and some of their later literacy skills, especially when adult– child interaction is structured as a series of dialogic exchanges (see, e.g., Lonigan, Anthony, Bloomfield, Dyer, & Samwell, 1999; Whitehurst et al., 1999). In addition to the child's exposure to and practice in appropriate "book talk," this practice seems to have an added benefit of promoting the child's focused attention—a competency essential for learning of any academic subject, including reading. During the book-reading session, attention is initially shared between children and an adult, with the adult modeling how to pay attention to certain elements of the book and supporting children's focusing on the book by guiding questions and prompts. For young children who lack other opportunities to practice focused attention (which is often the case with at-risk youngsters), these small-group or individual sessions are more effective than sessions involving the entire class.

• *Principle 3. The main mechanism of children's "cultural development" is their acquisition of cultural tools.* "Cultural tools" is a metaphor used by Vygotsky to describe a specific category of auxiliary devices or signs that humans create to gain control over their own behavior. Similar to the way mechanical tools expand humans' physical abilities, these cultural tools expand humans' metal abilities, allowing for greater memory, more focused attention, more productive reasoning, and so forth. Vygotsky's great insight was that these tools, although existing outside the human organism, nevertheless have an impact on its internal functioning: "Man introduces artificial stimuli, signifies behavior, and with signs, acting externally, creates new connections in the brain" (1997, p. 55).

Vygotsky discussed several examples of the use of cultural tools. Many of these examples described young children gaining control of their external behavior through the use of self-directed speech, by developing deliberate memory through the use of drawing and writing, and by performing arithmetic computation by counting on their fingers. In all these instances, tools help children solve problems that require engaging in mental processes at levels not yet available to them (e.g., tasks that call for deliberate memorization or for focused attention). In a modern classroom we can see many cases of children using various tools to aid their learning, such as using alphabet charts to remind them of the associations between letter sounds and letter symbols or singing the "ABC" song to prompt their memory of the order of letters in the alphabet.

External operations with cultural tools later become internalized by an individual, resulting in new internal operations characteristic of higher mental functions—deliberate, sign-mediated behaviors that may take different forms depending on specific cultural context. In teaching literacy to older students, we often assume that they already have deliberate sign-mediated behaviors necessary for composing a text or monitoring reading comprehension. However, to acquire such internal strategies, children have to be introduced at an earlier age to more specific and often more primitive cultural tools that help them to gradually gain control of their attention, memory, and thinking.

Vygotsky's theory of cultural development describes how children acquire higher mental functions through interaction with others. In his paper "The Problems of the Cultural Development of the Child" (Vygotsky, 1994), he described a four-stage process that leads to the transformation of children's "natural" behaviors into the "cultural" ones. This model can be applied to children's learning of a specific cultural behavior (such as learning the letters of the alphabet), as was done by Mason and Sinha (1993), but it can also be applied to the overall transformation of children's learning processes that takes place in the context of instruction.

The first stage of this process is characterized by the dominance of "natural behaviors," when learning takes place through establishing "associative or conditional reflexive connections between the stimuli and reactions" (Vygotsky, 1929/1994, p. 60). One can see this type of learning as the dominant one in preschool children whose attention, memory, and interest are completely controlled by the environment: Children tend to learn certain content if and when it is presented to them through multiple repetitions (such as singing the "ABC" song day after day) or in attention-grabbing engaging format (*Sesame Street* and similar shows).

At the second stage, children are introduced to symbols and tools that are specific to the context in which these children's learning is taking place. (Vygotsky and his close collaborator Alexander Luria's pioneering research on cultural differences in learning, led the way to a great number of studies both within and outside of the cultural–historical paradigm.) Vygotsky pointed out an interesting aspect of the beginning steps of the use of the tool by children: At first, children practice new skills and concepts unconsciously and spontaneously, and only later do they gain conscious control over their own behaviors. This second stage is dominated by shared or "intersubjective" behaviors that are often referred to as adult's scaffolding of children's learning (e.g., Wood, Bruner, & Ross, 1976).

In the third stage, children begin using symbols or tools independently and with increased deliberateness. However, at this stage, similar to the previous one, the tool remains external to a child, thus limiting the range of its usage. In our attempt to describe the use of cultural tools in a classroom (Bodrova & Leong, 1996), we refer to these tools as "external mediators," referring to Vygotsky's distinction between tool-mediated behaviors and immediate behaviors governed by the laws of conditioning (Vygotsky, 1978). Thus children require prompts such as an alphabet chart to remember what sound a letter makes.

Finally, at the fourth stage, the internalization of the tool occurs, and the child "starts to use the inner schemes, tries to use as signs of his remembrances, the knowledge he formerly acquired" (Vygotsky, 1929/1994, p. 66). At this point, external tools are no longer needed, and new behavior—now mediated by a more sophisticated mental tool—often reaches a qualitatively new level. Vygotsky described such qualitative change when he wrote about children making the transition to silent reading (Vygotsky, 1978). Similar to the way private speech loses its function as a tool and becomes abbreviated and finally transformed into inner speech, reading aloud serves as a temporary support for the processing of visual symbols and is abandoned by a more proficient reader.

It is in this context of discussing the role of mental tools and the developmental trajectory of their acquisition by young children that it seems appropriate to turn to the Elkonin boxes—probably the best known

contribution of Vygotskians to the field of early literacy instruction. In fact, Elkonin boxes (a schematic representation of the phonemic composition of a word) present only a small part of an innovative language arts curriculum designed for the primary grade students and later expanded to include children ages 3–6. The main goal of this curriculum (that until recently has been limited to a handful of lab schools but that now is gaining popularity in Russia and abroad) is to instill in young children a theoretical approach to the structure and function of language. Learning to encode and decode comes as an added benefit, whereas the major emphasis is put on building awareness of the elements of written language and the rules applied to them. By using various external mediators and later replacing them with private and eventually inner speech, children learn about sound composition of the words, about changes in the words' meaning caused by a change in a specific consonant or vowel, and about other relationships between components of a single word or a sentence (Elkonin, 1963).

• *Principle 4. To be effective, instruction should be aimed in the child's zone of proximal development.* The concept of the zone of proximal development (ZPD; Vygotsky, 1978) is undoubtedly the best known Vygotskian concept (see Chaiklin, 2003, for a comprehensive review of literature on this topic). The innovative approach to the definition of development contained in the notion of the ZPD led to the appearance of multiple interpretations of what this zone is and even to multiple names for it. We attempted to summarize some of these interpretations in our book (Bodrova & Leong, 1996), but many new interpretations have appeared, since the 1990s, making it difficult to proceed from the discussion of this idea to its practical implementation. For this reason, we decided to include the original definition of the ZPD given by Vygotsky:

> What we call the Zone of Proximal Development . . . is a distance between the actual developmental level determined by individual problem solving and the level of development as determined through problem solving under guidance or in collaboration with more capable peers. (1978, p. 86)

Skills and competencies contained in a child's ZPD have not yet fully emerged but are still "at the edge of emergence," and the child needs a little assistance in order to exhibit them. Therefore, these skills and competencies do not determine the child's developmental level but rather his or her learning potential. In the absence of aforementioned guidance or collaboration, this potential might not be realized, and consequently a higher developmental level will be never attained.

Unfortunately, the full potential of teaching within each child's ZPD is seldom realized, even by teachers who want to build their practices on Vygotskian ideas. We see the reason for this in two questions (spoken or unspoken). The first is the question of how to deal with the endless variability between the ZPDs of individual children; various ranges and levels of ZPD within a single classroom make it practically impossible to address each child's individual zone.

The second is the question of the transition from assisted to independent performance after a child demonstrates a higher level of performance "under guidance or in collaboration": even when a teacher finds the right method of assisting a child and brings this child's performance to a higher level, there always remains a question of how to withdraw this assistance without sacrificing this high level of performance. As a result of this seeming impracticality of the use of ZPD in a classroom, most research on the interactions within the child's zone is limited to one-on-one interactions examined in a laboratory setting or in a family context.

Our experience in implementing Vygotskian theory in early childhood classrooms shows us that the first question will never be answered as long as the assumption remains that an adult is the only source of assistance and that—short of cloning this adult—there is no other way to support higher levels of functioning in several children simultaneously. However, if we expand our notion of assistance to include social contexts (such as make-believe play or specifically designed group activity), various aids and instruments, and behaviors that children can use to self-assist (such as using private speech, writing, or drawing), then the idea of having the entire class functioning at the highest levels of performance no longer sounds unrealistic.

By answering the first question, we also answer the second one. From other-assistance to self-assistance and finally to independence, designing appropriate scaffolding means planning to start withdrawing support from the very moment this support is first provided. Children who use assistance other than direct teacher support are already one step closer to becoming completely independent; children who act independently are now ready to be challenged with a more difficult task and provided new assistance. By orchestrating the quantity and quality of assistance to fit each child's individual needs and strengths, it is possible to maximize each child's learning potential.

• *Principle 5. For preschool and kindergarten children, make-believe play creates the zone of proximal development.* Although it seems a little off the subject to write about play in a chapter on early literacy, the link between play and written language was, for Vygotsky, an obvious one. In his analysis of the development of writing in children (Vygotsky, 1997), Vygotsky pointed out repeatedly that children would learn to read and write only if these activities became meaningful for them (in fact, he wrote "as meaningful as play"). This emphasis on play in early childhood is not accidental; Vygotsky saw many parallels between what happens in children's play and what constitutes the very core of cultural development:

> Play also creates the zone of proximal development of the child. In play the child is always behaving beyond his age, above his usual everyday behavior; in play he is, as it were, a head above himself. Play contains in a concentrated form, as in the focus of magnifying glass, all developmental tendencies; it is as if the child tries to jump above his usual level. The relationship of play and development should be compared to the relationship between instruction and development. (1933/1978, p. 74)

Whereas Vygotsky's insights about the effects of play on development may appear more metaphoric than specific, the works of Vygotsky's colleague and student Daniel Elkonin make it clear exactly how play (meaning fairly advanced role-play or sociodramatic play but not other play-like activities such as manipulating toys or engaging in movement games) elevates children's performance to the highest levels of their zones of proximal development. Elkonin has identified four principal ways in which play influences child development, all of them important for preparing the foundations for subsequent learning that takes place in primary grades (Elkonin 1977, 1978). Elkonin expects play to affect the child's development through:

1. Effecting the child's motivation. In play, children develop a more complex hierarchical system of immediate and long-term goals than the one they use in nonplay settings. In fact, play becomes the first context in which young children demonstrate their ability to delay gratification, thus moving in the direction of gaining control of their behavior and making behavior more deliberate and purposeful.
2. Facilitating cognitive "decentering." The ability to take other people's perspectives is critical for coordinating multiple roles and negotiating play themes and the use of props. In addition, assigning different "pretend" functions to the same object involves cognitive decentering. This newly acquired competency will later enable children to coordinate their cognitive perspectives with those of their learning partners and teachers and eventually will be turned inward, leading to the development of reflective thinking and metacognition.
3. Advancing the development of mental representations. This development occurs as a result of child's separating the meaning of objects from their physical form. First, children use replicas to substitute for real objects; then they proceed to use new objects that are different in appearance, although they can perform the same function as the object prototype; and, finally, most of the substitution takes place in a child's speech with no objects present. This ability to use words to assign new meanings to objects was considered by Vygotsky a critical prerequisite for learning to write (Vygotsky, 1978).
4. Fostering the development of deliberate behaviors—physical and mental voluntary actions. The development of deliberateness in play becomes possible due to the child's need to follow the rules of play

and because of the fact that play partners constantly monitor each other following these rules (a child playing "mommy" is not supposed to talk in the same way as the child playing "baby"). Following the laws of internalization, regulation of physical and social behaviors later extends to mental processes such as memory and attention.

One can easily see how these outcomes of play can contribute to the development of behaviors critical for the acquisition of literacy competencies. However, difficulties of studying (and assessing) play result in our limited knowledge about specific connections between the "active ingredients" of play and specific literacy outcomes. Evidence available from the studies conducted within the Vygotskian tradition is largely anecdotal or has been collected from populations with different age characteristics (large numbers of children in Russia do not enter school until age 7). With the imminent danger of play disappearing from preschool (it has already all but disappeared in kindergarten), it is critical to establish the true value of play for learning and development.

In an attempt to increase the literacy content of early childhood curricula, early childhood teachers are often advised to incorporate pretend (or real) reading and writing into the play themes of 3- and 4-year-old children. From our experience with supporting play in children of this age, it seems that children would truly benefit from these new literacy opportunities only after their play reaches a certain level (e.g., using multifunctional and unstructured materials instead of realistic props, taking on and maintaining a variety of coordinated roles, and engaging in extended verbal exchanges). Focusing on the support afforded by play to the underlying cognitive, social, and language skills seems to be a higher priority than simply adding new literacy-laden materials.

• *Principle 6. Early stages in the development of written speech include play and drawing.* The central part of Vygotsky's approach to early writing is the idea that children learn to employ the instrumental function of written speech to expand their mental capacities:

The development of written language belongs to the . . . most obvious line of cultural development because it is connected with the mastery of an external system of means developed and created in the process of cultural development of humanity. (1997, p. 133)

Studies conducted by Alexander Luria in connection with Vygotsky's general research program demonstrated a gradual progression in children's ability to use written symbols as memory aids (Luria, 1998). Some of Luria's findings (such as the ability of 3-year-old children to reliably "read" and "reread" their idiosyncratic scribbles) made their way into Western literature and inspired researchers to study early forms of writing that appear prior to the onset of formal schooling (see, e.g., Ferreiro & Teberosky, 1982)

Another, less known component of Vygotsky's theory of early writing is the idea that writing originates from two activities that often do not even look like writing: drawing and make-believe play. In both these activities, children learn to associate sign and the meaning of this sign. In play, it occurs through the use of gestures indicating the new or changing function of a play prop. In drawing, a gesture results in making a mark that later becomes a representation of a word or a phrase:

A child's symbolic play may . . . be understood as a very complex system of speech aided by gestures that supplement and indicate the meaning of individual toys. Only on the basis of indicating gestures does the toy gradually acquire its meaning precisely as drawing, supported at first by a gesture, becomes an independent sign. (1997, p. 135)

Repeated naming and renaming of toys in play helps a child master the symbolic nature of words and eventually realize the unique relationship that exists between words and the objects they signify—in other words, to develop metalinguistic awareness, which is frequently associated by contemporary researchers with children's mastery of written language. At the same time, drawing provides a nonwriting child with a temporary means to record his or her own stories and messages. Vygotsky found many indications that early drawings are linked to children's oral speech—from the frequent increases

in self-directed speech observed as children were engaged in drawing to the similarities between children's drawings and their verbal concepts, both of which convey only essential and constant characteristics of objects. From that, Vygotsky concluded that young children's drawings are "a unique graphic speech, a graphic story about something . . . more speech than representation" (Vygotsky, 1997, p. 138). Learning letters supplies the final component to move the child from idiosyncratic forms of "drawing speech" to a conventional way of recording speech in written words. Early writing (as well as early reading) still depends on oral speech. The dependence is later overcome by experienced readers and writers:

The initial written symbols serve as a sign of verbal symbols. Understanding written language is done through oral speech, but gradually this path is shortened, the intermediate link in the form of oral speech drops away, and written language becomes a direct symbol just as understandable as oral speech. (1997, p. 143)

Discussing the methods of teaching writing, Vygotsky emphasized that "teaching must be set up so that reading and writing satisfy the child's need" and that the goal of the instruction should be "to teach a child written language and not writing the alphabet." In the absence of play and self-initiated drawing, children who learn to write master merely the skills of letter formation. They do not use written language the way it is supposed to be used in the culture; as a means of communication with others and with oneself. Vygotsky uses an example of perfect handwriting produced by 4-year-olds attending Montessori schools. The content of their letters indicated that they did not use writing to express their own thoughts or feelings; they had written what the teachers dictated to them or copied the teacher's messages (coincidentally, make-believe play has never been and still is not a part of the traditional Montessori curriculum).

At the same time, Vygotsky advocated early (at age 3–4) instruction in writing that emphasizes the communicative and instrumental function of written language and not the mechanics of its production. True to his own belief that good instruction should lead development and not follow it, Vygotsky explained the value of learning to write early not in the context of preparing children for formal schooling but in the broader context of using cultural tools for supporting the development of higher mental functions.

Implementing Vygotskian Approaches in an American Classroom

In our attempts to implement Vygotskian ideas in the United States (Bodrova & Leong, 1996, 1998, 2001, 2003), we came to the conclusion that we could not import even effective instructional practices developed in a different social context. Instead, we ended up designing new instructional practices that were based on the same theoretical and methodological principles but that addressed the unique needs of an American classroom. The use of these practices by preschool and kindergarten teachers in a variety of settings proved successful (see, e.g., Bodrova & Leong, 2001, Bodrova, Leong, Norford, & Paynter, 2003 for the description of the implementation), thus confirming our belief that Vygotsky's ideas may be not only inspiring but also practical. Next we provide a brief description of several instructional strategies we developed with reference to specific Vygotskian ideas used in them.

Mystery Word

The use of external mediators to assist children's emergent ability to discriminate between individual phonemes in a word was extremely successful in Elkonin's literacy curriculum, mentioned earlier in the chapter. However, to use similar strategies in an American preschool or even in kindergarten, we had to make adjustments to the social context of activities and the format of their presentation. Elkonin's specific instructional strategies for introducing activities in this curriculum were designed for Russian schools with an old tradition of whole-class instruction and with children who entered first grade later than their American counterparts. Because of the differences inherent in English and Russian, Elkonin boxes must be adapted to meet both the linguistic differences and the differences in the social context.

The Mystery Word game uses modified Elkonin boxes adapted for the situation in which children practice sound analysis with minimal adult guidance (Bodrova, Leong, Paynter, & Hughes, 2002). Children gather at a pocket chart (because the activity is usually scheduled during transition time, the number of children interacting is naturally limited to no more than 4 or 5) that has several pictures of objects, each accompanied by its sound model (Elkonin boxes matching the number of phonemes in the word pictured). One word is a clue, and children have to use this clue to choose between two or three other words. If the objective is to isolate the beginning sound, the first box under the "clue" is shaded, and question marks are written in the first boxes of all mystery words. Depending on the children's progress, the teacher uses the same format to have children practice isolation of ending sounds, of middle sounds, rhyming, blends, and so forth. Visual representations of separate sounds within a word serve as a temporary tool helping children to develop phonemic awareness prior to learning more conventional markers for the separate phonemes—the letters.

Scaffolded Writing

The Scaffolded Writing method (Bodrova & Leong 1998, 2001, 2003) is an example of how multiple levels and multiple forms of assistance can be provided in a regular classroom setting. During Scaffolded Writing sessions, a teacher helps a child plan his or her own message by drawing a line to stand for each word the child says. The child then repeats the message, pointing to each line as he or she says the word. Finally, the child writes on the lines, attempting to represent each word with some letters or symbols. During the first several sessions, the child may require some assistance and prompting from the teacher. As the child's understanding of the concept of a word grows, the child becomes able to carry the whole process independently, including drawing the lines and writing words on these lines.

The lines separated by spaces represent the existence of individual words and their sequence in a sentence, thus creating a visual model of this sentence. Thus the lines themselves act as universal assistance: for some children, they are reminders of the length of their message; for others, they indicate that the message will contain some words that are longer than others; and for yet other children, the lines have not yet acquired the meaning of placeholders for future words. These children use the lines in their own idiosyncratic way, similar to the participants in Luria's (1998) study of emergent writing.

In addition, when Scaffolded Writing is used during a designated writing period (such as a Writers' Workshop), we encourage teachers to individualize their assistance to incorporate the variations in the mastery of the early writing skills. Among the additional ways to assist emergent writers is the use of a picture alphabet chart and/or a chart with children's names. Children quickly learn to search for the letter on the chart to match the sound they want to represent in their writing. An alphabet chart and the teacher's modeling of ways to use it provide a way for the children to self-assist in searching for the right letter. Children who are still having trouble finding the letter symbol on the alphabet chart sometimes use extra self-assistance as they sing the "ABC" song, pointing to the symbols on the chart until they come to the one they need.

Private speech (Vygotsky, 1987; Berk & Winsler, 1995) is another strategy children learn to use to self-assist during Scaffolded Writing sessions. Private speech seems to support writing in at least three ways. First, when a child talks to herself when writing, it helps her remember more words from her initial message. Second, as a child repeats the word and draws a line, she practices voice-to-print correspondence, thus reinforcing the emergent concept of a word. Finally, with lines reminding her of other words of the message, the child can concentrate on repeating any word as many times as may be necessary to come up with more accurate phonemic representations.

For the children who tend to forget their messages before attempting to write them down or who change their messages constantly, drawing a picture provides yet another form of assistance. At the earliest stages of writing, the very process of drawing

and later the pictorial representation helps children keep the message in memory longer (Luria, 1998).

In addition to these strategies for self-assistance, Scaffolded Writing sessions provide children with an opportunity to assist each other in prompting the words of the intended message or helping to find the letter on the alphabet chart. All these strategies relieve the teacher from the burden of being the only source of help. Now the teacher can observe children to determine who needs to be challenged and who might benefit from additional support. The teacher can also interact with one or several children, giving them the luxury of undivided attention so rare in a typical early childhood classroom.

The analysis of writing samples over several months indicates that children begin to write in a more advanced manner compared with how they were able to write prior to its introduction. After having used Scaffolded Writing for some time, children internalize the procedure of planning the sentence so that they gradually give up, first, the teacher assistance and eventually, the lines themselves, as the quality of their writing continues to improve (Bodrova & Leong, 1998, 2001).

Figure 18.1 provides an example of the use of Scaffolded Writing by a 4-year-old Head Start student in the context of the play-planning procedure described next. The plan says, "I am going to make an animal cracker zoo."

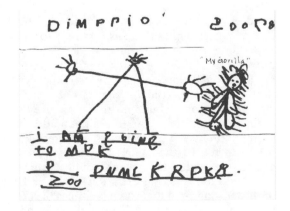

FIGURE 18.1. Play plan with Scaffolded Writing used.

Play Plans

It has been documented in numerous studies that children as young as 3 and 4 can use writing meaningfully. However, most of these studies were conducted in home settings, where children's first attempts at writing were provided maximum assistance. In a typical preschool classroom, few teachers have expectations of all of their 4-year-olds being able to form recognizable letters other than the letters in their names, let alone read their own writing days after it was completed.

In designing the method of play planning (Bodrova & Leong, 2001; Bodrova et al., 2001), we have drawn on Vygotsky's ideas about the origins of early writing. Therefore, we introduced writing in the context of play, making sure that both the process of writing and its product were maximally meaningful for children. In addition, we introduced writing through drawing, allowing for a stage at which drawing, not writing, represented the message.

During a play-planning session, children make plans for the next 40–50 minutes, which they will spend in the centers acting out a play scenario, doing an art project, listening to books on tape, or playing on a computer. The purpose of the plan is to help children remember what they intend to do when they get to the center. It is not meant to guide all of the play at the center but to begin the play. All children state their plans orally, which allows friends going to the same center to work out the details of their play and allows a teacher to make suggestions to the children who seem to run out of ideas. The next stage of planning takes different forms depending on the developmental level of an individual child: Some children indicate their choice by marking on paper with a marker that matches the color of the sign at a specific center; some children draw a picture of their plan; and yet others attempt to add to their picture by writing letters or letter-like forms to record their plan. Children's plans are also recorded by a teacher who verifies the message by taking dictation—even children who can read their own scribbles or letters do not always make them readable by an adult. With play being the most motivating activity for young children, writing about play is always meaningful, especially because

making a detailed drawing or writing a recognizable word helps avoid conflicts over an attractive toy or a desirable role to play.

With an emphasis on the use of written language and not just on its production, children's mastery of writing progresses rapidly. However, this progress in writing (and in subsequent reading of one's own and each other's plans) would not occur if the play in the centers were not exciting and if children's oral language remained stifled. Following the developmental trajectory of early writing and supporting each stage on this trajectory yields higher results than speeding up the learning to write at the cost of not paying enough attention to the earlier prerequisite competencies.

*　*　*

Vygotsky's view on early literacy instruction is that this instruction cannot be reduced to having children memorize letter names and copy letter symbols. For Vygotsky, early literacy instruction cannot be disentangled from the development of the child's mental processes. The very act of instruction and learning contributes not only to "reading" and "writing" but also to the development of the mind itself through the formation of higher mental functions. With increasing demands on children's ability to regulate their social, emotional, and cognitive behaviors, an emphasis on promoting intentional deliberate behavior seems to become an essential part of school readiness (see, e.g., Blair, 2002), thus placing more value on the development of underlying behaviors than on acquisition of any one content-specific skill. As for literacy acquisition, Vygotsky's position on this issue sounds counterintuitive, but it is nevertheless consistent with the other principles of the cultural–historical approach. According to Vygotsky, a child enters school not having all the prerequisites for learning academic subjects fully developed:

> The child begins to learn to write when he does not yet have the mental functions that are required for written speech. It is for precisely this reason that instruction in written speech calls these functions to life and leads their development. This is true of all productive instruction. (1987, p. 213)

And this will be the implication of the Vygotskian approach for early literacy instruction: Productive instruction should aim not at the functions that are fully developed but at the ones that are still within the child's zone of proximal development, utilizing multiple forms of assistance to arm children with cultural tools and call to life higher mental functions.

References

Berk, L. E. & Winsler, A. (1995). *Scaffolding children's learning: Vygotsky and early childhood education* NAEYC Research and Practice Series, 7. Washington, DC: National Association for the Education of Young Children.

Blair, C. (2002). School readiness: Integrating cognition and emotion in a neurobiological conceptualization of children's functioning at school entry. *American Psychologist, 57*(2), 111–127.

Bodrova, E., & Leong, D. J. (1996). *Tools of the mind: The Vygotskian approach to early childhood education.* Englewood Cliffs, NJ: Merrill/Prentice Hall.

Bodrova, E., & Leong, D. J. (1998). Scaffolding emergent writing in the zone of proximal development. *Literacy Teaching and Learning, 3*(2), 1–18.

Bodrova, E., & Leong, D. J. (2001). *The Tools of the Mind Project: A case study of implementing the Vygotskian approach in American early childhood and primary classrooms.* Geneva, Switzerland: UNESCO, International Bureau of Education.

Bodrova, E., Leong, D. J., Paynter, D. E., & Hughes, C. (2002). *Scaffolding literacy development in a kindergarten classroom.* Aurora, CO: McREL.

Bodrova, E., & Leong, D. J. (2003). Learning and development of preschool children: The Vygotskian perspective. In A. Kozulin, B. Gindis, V. Ageev, & S. Miller (Eds.), *Vygotsky's educational theory in cultural context* (pp. 156–176). New York: Cambridge University Press.

Bodrova, E., Leong, D., Norford, J., & Paynter, D. (2003). It only looks like child's play. *Journal of Staff Development, 24*(2), 47–51.

Bodrova, E., Leong, D. J., Paynter, D. E., & Hensen, R. (2001). *Scaffolding literacy development in a preschool classroom.* Aurora, CO: McREL.

Carlton, M., & Winsler, A. (1999) School readiness: The need for a paradigm shift. *Psychology Review, 28* (3), 338–353.

Chaiklin, S. (2003). The zone of proximal development in Vygotsky's analysis of learning and instruction. In A. Kozulin, B. Gindis, V. Ageev, & S. Miller (Eds.), *Vygotsky's educational theory in cultural context* (pp. 39–64). New York: Cambridge University Press.

Clay, M. (1993). *Reading Recovery: A guidebook for teachers in training.* Portsmouth, NH: Heinemann.

Daniels, H. (Ed.). (1993). *Charting the agenda: Educational activity after Vygotsky.* New York: Routledge.

Dixon-Krauss, L. (Ed.). (1996). *Vygotsky in the classroom: Mediated literacy instruction and assessment.* White Plains, NY: Longman.

Elkonin, D. (1977). Toward the problem if stages in the mental development of the child. In M. Cole (Ed.), *Soviet Developmental Psychology.* White Plains, NY: M. E. Sharpe. (Original work published in 1971)

Elkonin, D. (1978). *Psychologija igry [The psychology of play].* Moscow: Pedagogika.

Elkonin, D. B. (1963). The psychology of mastering the elements of reading. In B. Simon & J. Simon (Eds.), *Educational psychology in the U.S.S.R.* London: Routledge & Kegan Paul, (pp. 165–179).

Ferreiro, E., & Teberosky, A. (1982). *Literacy before schooling.* Exeter, NH: Heinemann.

Lee, C., & Smagorinsky, P. (Eds.). (2000). *Vygotskian perspectives on literacy research.* New York: Cambridge University Press.

Lonigan, C. J., Anthony, J. L., Bloomfield, B. G., Dyer, S. M., & Samwell, C. S. (1999). Effects of two shared-reading interventions on emergent literacy skills of at-risk preschoolers. *Journal of Early intervention, 22,* 306–322.

Luria, A. R. (1998). The development of writing in the child. In M. Kohl de Oliveira & J. Valsiner (Eds.), *Literacy in human development* (pp. 15–56). Stamford, CT: Ablex.

Mason, J. M., & Sinha, S. (1993). Emerging literacy in the early childhood years: Applying a Vygotskian model of learning and development. In B. Spodek (Ed.), *Handbook of research on the education of young children* (pp. 137–150). New York: Macmillan.

Moll, L. C. (Ed.). (1990). *Vygotsky and education: Instructional implications and applications of sociohistorical psychology.* New York: Cambridge University Press.

Rubtzov, V. V. (1991). *Learning in children: Organization and development of cooperative actions.* New York: Nova Science Publishers.

Slobodchikov, V. I. & Tsukerman, G. A. (1992). The genesis of reflective consciousness at early school age. *Journal of Russian and East European Psychology, 30*(1), 65–81.

Torgeson, J. K., Morgan, S. T., & Davis, C. (1992). Effects of two types of phonological awareness training on word learning in kindergarten children. *Journal of Educational Psychology, 84*(3), 364–370.

Vygotsky, L. (1978). *Mind in society: The development of higher psychological processes.* Cambridge, MA: Harvard University Press. (Original work published 1933)

Vygotsky, L. (1987). Thinking and speech. In R. W. Reiber & A. S. Carton (Eds.), *The collected works of L. S. Vygotsky: Vol. 1. Problems of general psychology* (N. Mimic, Ttrans.; pp. 39–285). New York: Plenum Press. (Original work published 1934)

Vygotsky, L. (1994). The problem of the cultural development of the child. In R. v. d. Veer & J. Valsiner (Eds.), *The Vygotsky reader* (pp. 57–72). Cambridge, MA: Blackwell. (Original work published 1929)

Vygotsky, L. (1997). The history of the development of higher mental functions. In R. W. Rieber (Ed.), *The collected works of L. S. Vygotsky* (M. J. Hall, Trans., Vol. 4). New York: Plenum Press.

Whitehurst, G. J., Zevenbergen, A. A., Crone, D. A., Schultz, M. D., Velting, O. N., & Fischel, J. E. (1999). Outcomes of an emergent literacy intervention from Head Start through second grade. *Journal of Educational Psychology, 91,* 261–272.

Wilder, L. (1972). *Analysis training: Failure to replicate Elkonin.* Technical Report #202. Madison, WI: University of Wisconsin Research and Development Center for Cognitive Learning ERIC #ED070067.

Wood, D., Bruner, J. C., & Ross, G. (1976). The role of tutoring in problem solving. *Journal of Child Psychology and Psychiatry 17,* 89–100.

Zuckerman, G. (2003). The learning activity in the first years of schooling: The developmental path toward reflection. In A. Kozulin, B. Gindis, V. Ageev, & S. Miller (Eds.) *Vygotsky's educational theory in cultural context* (pp. 177–199). New York: Cambridge University Press.

19

Preschool Classroom Environments and the Quantity and Quality of Children's Literacy and Language Behaviors

DALE C. FARRAN
CANAN AYDOGAN
SHIN JI KANG
MARK W. LIPSEY

This chapter addresses how prekindergarten classrooms can be used as intervention settings for language and literacy development with children from low-income families. We review the importance of language development for predicting later literacy and school success, using findings from a large-scale curriculum research project currently under way. In addition, we focus on the difficulty of determining what language facilitating activities should be included in today's preschool classrooms.

Importance of Language Development for Poor Children

Predictive Significance for School Success

Considerable evidence exists that young children who score lower on cognitive measures are at greater risk for later school failure (Lee, Loeb, & Lubeck, 1998; Stevenson & Newman, 1986) and that such scores are more likely among children from disadvantaged backgrounds (Coley, 2002; Stipek & Ryan, 1997; see Neuman, Chapter 2, and Morrison, Connor, & Bachman, Chapter 26,

this volume). Reading is an especially important early school achievement that is based on perceptual, language, and cognitive skills (Ball, 1993; Bradley & Bryant, 1985; Torgesen & Mathis, 1999; Vellutino & Scanlon, 1988). For example, the development of a lexical basis for reading requires sufficient vocabulary so that new words may be learned from context (Weizman & Snow, 2001), and syntactic knowledge is necessary for children to predict the meaning of sentences based on form and known words.

Longitudinal studies have shown preliteracy and language-related variables, along with basic cognitive skills, to be among the strongest predictors of academic outcomes during the early school years (Chew & Lang, 1990; Kontos, 1988; LaParo & Pianta, 2000; NICHD Early Child Care Network, 2004; Reynolds, 1989; Stevenson & Newman, 1986). Kurdek and Sinclair (2000) found that verbal readiness at kindergarten entry was the strongest predictor of first-through fifth-grade standardized test scores and grades in math and reading. Torgesen and colleagues (1999) found that the strongest kindergarten predictors of second-grade

reading comprehension included rapid naming and general verbal ability. Pianta and
McCoy (1997) demonstrated that language
skills at kindergarten entry differentiated
children who were retained in a grade, were
placed in special education, and scored low
on achievement tests in the second grade.
Other longitudinal studies have produced
similar findings.

Language and communication skills represent an important intersection between cognitive and social-behavioral domains. Children
with low language skills, particularly boys,
are more likely to have deficits in social skills
stemming from difficulties using language in
peer-play interactions to mediate conflicts, to
gain entry into social groups, and to comprehend and respond to instruction (Brinton &
Fujiki, 1999; Kaiser, Hancock, Cai, Foster,
& Hester, 2000). More generally, children
who have difficulty using language in everyday communicative interactions with adults
and peers are at increased risk for both
behavior problems and school failure (Kaiser
& Hester, 1997; Lonigan et al., 1999).

Children growing up in poverty generally
have poorly developed language skills (Hart
& Risley, 1995; Qi, Kaiser, Milan, Yzquierdo,
& Hancock, 2003). Poor language skills are
thus a significant part of the reason children
from disadvantaged families are at risk for
school failure. Moreover, given the centrality
of reading and verbal ability to school performance, there is little doubt that early
language-related skills have causal influence
on later school success. Reading and writing
competencies are major school achievement
outcomes in their own right, so it is not surprising that those cognitive skills related to
language and family literacy background are
good predictors of school success. Language
and communication variables are also related to behavior problems and poor peer relations, however, which are themselves significant risk factors for school failure and
appear to be connected to liking for school
and achievement motivation as well.

Specific Aspects of Language Development

STRUCTURAL ASPECTS OF READING
AND WRITING

Many studies of young children's concepts
and skills in literacy show that preschoolers

generally know a great deal about written
language and the processes and purposes
of reading and writing (Einarsdottier &
Johanna, 1996; Hiebert, 1981; Hiebert,
Cioffi, & Antonak, 1984; Lomax & McGee,
1987; Morgan, 1987; Weir, 1989). Hiebert
(1981) found that even 3-year-old children
show some proficiency in letter naming, visual discrimination, and auditory discrimination, as well as in some understanding of
the processes and purposes of using print,
and that children's knowledge of print and
reading-related skills increased significantly over the preschool period. In addition,
Hiebert (1981) suggested that the preschool
period is a particularly active time for print-
related learning. Hiebert et al.'s research
(1984) demonstrated that preschoolers' proficiency in the reading-related skills of letter
naming, visual discrimination, and auditory
discrimination preceded knowledge of the
purposes and processes of reading.

As noted earlier, children from low-
income families tend to begin school with
significantly poorer academic skills than
children from middle-income families do. In
particular, Raz and Bryant (1990) suggested
that the performance of children from
middle-income families was especially superior to those from low-income families in the
skill areas of understanding prose and phonological awareness. Moreover, this tendency is stronger and the disparities are
wider for poor children in the United States
than in other countries (Case, Griffin, &
Kelly, 2001).

MEANING ASPECTS
OF LANGUAGE: VOCABULARY

A focus on specific literacy-related skills,
such as phonemic awareness, represents a
relatively narrow approach to literacy. Reading is a complex process made up of multiple
components that should be promoted together (Byrnes, 2001). Students must first
learn to decode, and for that, phonemic
awareness and rapid naming are strong predictors (Rayner, Foorman, Perfetti, Pesetsky,
& Seidenberg, 2002; Ashby & Rayner,
Chapter 4, this volume). However, those
skills by themselves do not show much relationship to reading comprehension, a skill
that is critical for children's progress in
school (Schatschneider, Carlson, Francis,

Foorman, & Fletcher, 2002; Torgesen et al., 1999).

The language variable that does predict reading comprehension is vocabulary (Snow, Burns, & Griffin, 1998). A longitudinal study of young children's exposure to language in their homes and child-care settings found that reading comprehension in the fourth and seventh grades was predicted by measures of receptive vocabulary and oral language taken in kindergarten (Tabors, Snow, & Dickinson, 2001). Snow et al. (1998) also reported that focused instruction to improve vocabulary has been shown to increase children's reading comprehension. Interestingly, the type of instruction effective for this purpose was not drill and practice but involved providing children with conceptual understanding of the words. This finding parallels work on vocabulary acquisition by young children (Booth & Waxman, 2002; Waxman & Booth, 2001), indicating that children as young as 3 years old acquire and retain vocabulary based on conceptual information and connections, something Booth and Waxman (2002) term a "dramatic and uniquely human process" (p. B20).

Preschools as Intervention Sites for Language Development

Since at least 1964, classrooms have been used as intervention sites for helping children from poor families transition to school and formal learning. Debates about what were the most important experiences to prepare children for later success began immediately and have not been resolved (Englemann, 1999; Goffin, 1994; Schweinhart, Weikart, & Larner, 1986). Recently more language and reading-specific interventions have been developed and assessed.

Examples of this new approach can be found in Whitehurst et al. (1999), who evaluated a literacy program added to the regular Head Start curriculum. Their program consisted of sound- and letter-awareness activities with interactive reading at home and in the classroom. Positive effects were found at the end of the preschool year on emergent literacy skills that lasted through kindergarten but not through the first and second grades. Similarly, Blachman, Tangel, Ball, Black, and McGraw (1999) assessed an intervention to develop phonological aware-

ness and word recognition skills for kindergarten children from low-income families. At the end of first grade, children who received treatment outperformed the control group on phonological awareness, letter name and sound knowledge, and word recognition, and they were still superior on word recognition at the end of the second grade.

In contrast to focusing on specific emergent literacy skills, the preschool literacy program that might have stronger and more lasting effects on educational achievement is one that emphasizes vocabulary growth and language in a way that connects concepts to children's experiences. But vocabulary growth has been more difficult to effect in preschool classrooms. An example of attempts to link vocabulary and preschool behaviors can be found in the study reported by Dickinson (2001) and Smith (2001). Their longitudinal investigation explored the specific aspects of the preschools that predicted end-of-kindergarten performance in vocabulary and print awareness. Dickinson created a composite variable called Extended Teacher Discourse, made up primarily of teaching strategies observed in use by teachers during large group instruction. These included both linguistic and behavioral strategies. Literacy-related behaviors included the amount of "cognitive extending" the teacher used with conversational topics (talking about past, future, and the hypothetical), as well as the amount of time spent in analyzing the text during book reading. The behavioral strategy included in this composite was one Dickinson (2001) termed Group Focusing. It related to how effectively the teacher managed and controlled behaviors during large-group instruction. This composite variable predicted end-of-kindergarten measures of receptive vocabulary and emergent literacy.

Smith (2001) examined the amount of time children were observed in small-group instruction and the quality of the writing program and found both to be related to later vocabulary outcomes. In contrast, Smith found that none of the general variables associated with a social-emotional philosophical focus—teachers believing that the function of preschool was to help socialize children—was related to later literacy outcomes including more time in free play and higher Early Childhood Environmental Rating Scale (ECERS) scores.

Classroom Environmental Effects on Engaging Children in Literacy Activities

A number of studies have examined environmental factors in classrooms and their associations with literacy use. Various researchers have actually manipulated aspects of the classroom literacy environment and examined their effects on children's behaviors; they have discovered that designing an enriched play environment by displaying literacy materials in play centers stimulated children's literacy behaviors (Christie & Enz, 1992; Morrow, 1991; Morrow & Rand, 1991; Morrow & Schickedanz, Chapter 20, this volume; Nel, 2000; Neuman & Roskos, 1990; Wasik & Bond, 2001). In an experimental study, Morrow and Rand (1991) found that the number of literacy behaviors demonstrated by children in a classroom with general or thematic literacy-related materials was greater than the number of literacy behaviors demonstrated by children in the control classroom. Similarly, Morrow (1991) found correlations between the presence of specific literacy materials and the frequency of literacy behaviors during free play. Results indicated that the number of books, the number of different kinds of recording materials (e.g., paper, computer), and the number of recording tools (e.g., pencils, crayons) and labels in the classroom were closely related to the frequency of children's reading and writing. Inserting literacy props related to a theme, such as library, post office, office, and kitchen, were found not only to make literacy more situated and interactive but also to induce a greater number of literacy demonstrations in a play context (Neuman & Roskos, 1990).

Intervening in preschools, Christie and Enz (1992) found that adding the theme-related literacy materials increased children's functional play. Wasik and Bond (2001) conducted a similar but more structured strategy of intervention. They added books on specific themes or topics and concrete objects that represented the topics so that books and props could collaborate to help children build vocabulary on the corresponding topics.

Access to books is an environmental factor strongly related to children's literacy development (DeTemple, 2001; Neuman, 1996; Neuman, 1999; Neuman & Gallagher, 1994; Raz & Bryant, 1990; Whitehurst & Lonigan, 1998). Some preschool intervention programs have been designed to provide books for children from low-income communities to enhance their early literacy skills (Neuman, 1999, Wasik & Bond, 2001). Results indicated correlations between the frequency of literacy behaviors during free play and the number of books in the class, print segments written in children's home language, and functional labels.

The teacher, of course, is an essential part of the preschool classroom environment. Studies of teacher behavior have usually been separate from studies of the effects of materials in the environment. Vukelich (1991) compared the amount of time children spent in literacy behaviors in three different sessions: before teacher modeling of the use of literacy materials, during teacher modeling, and after teacher modeling. Her results showed that the percentage of time children engaged in literacy behaviors increased significantly during teacher modeling and decreased after teacher modeling to nearly the same level or even lower than the level it had been before teacher modeling. This outcome suggests the importance of ongoing teacher mediation in engaging literacy behavior.

Christie and Enz (1992) compared the effects of the presence of literacy-related materials and teacher-provided instruction on children's literacy play patterns and their achievement of literacy skills. They found that literacy skills improved similarly for children who played with literacy materials alone and for those who played with the materials with teachers. The pattern of play, however, differed for the two groups, suggesting that teacher interaction could influence the type of play with literacy materials in which children were engaged. Children who experienced teacher mediation engaged in more imaginative dramatic play and less repetitive motor play than did children who did not experience teacher mediation.

These studies suggest that preschool classrooms are complex environments for engaging children with literacy materials. Clearly, the actual presence of books, environmental print, writing materials, and the like serves to stimulate children's literacy behaviors. In addition, it appears that teacher attention to literacy through instruction also stimulates children's literacy behavior. As the next section demonstrates, it is difficult to know which aspects of teachers' language might best facilitate children's language interactions.

Language Interactions in Preschool Classrooms

In order to determine the possibly important teacher-language variables to observe in preschool classrooms, we examined what is known about home environmental effects on children's language development. Parental effects on language development are difficult to ascertain—children are not randomly assigned to families. However, the preponderance of evidence suggests that families have important influences on children's language development and that one important mediator of their impact is maternal responsiveness (Goldfield, 1987; Tamis-LeMonda, Bornstein, Baumwell, & Damast, 1996). During routinized and jointly engaged mother–child activities, the timing of mothers' responses is important for children to discern the meanings of words. Maternal responsiveness creates contiguity between children's attentional focus and maternal input, which helps children understand that the adult verbalization refers to the action or object that they are mutually focused on.

Most studies, however, examined the effect of maternal responsiveness only on children from upper- and middle-income families. There are a few studies that compare mother–child interactions in low-income families with those in middle- and upper-middle-income families, and those tend to show that mothers in higher income families are more responsive to their children's verbalizations than are mothers in lower income families (Hoff, Laursen, & Tardif, 2002). For example, Hoff-Ginsberg (1991) designed a study that included 30 working-class and 33 upper-middle-income mothers having 18- to 29-month-old children. She reported that upper- and middle-income mothers used more topic-continuing replies to their children than did working-class mothers.

The amount of maternal talk addressed to children is another dimension of the family-provided verbal environment that is associated with children's rates of vocabulary growth (Anderson & Freebody, 1981; Hart & Risley, 1995; Huttenlocher, Haight, Bryk, Seltzer, & Lyons, 1991). The more mothers talk, the more frequently children are exposed to the words. This is important for children to acquire vocabulary (Huttenlocher et al., 1991). Frequent exposure to words influences children's acquisition of those words (Hoff & Naigles, 2002). Indeed, children need to hear the same words repeatedly so that they can establish sound–meaning relations.

Research has also shown that family income and education are related to differences in the amount of maternal talk (Hart & Risley, 1995; Hoff, 2003a, 2003b; Hoff et al., 2002; Hoff-Ginsberg, 1991), which may then account for individual differences in the rate of children's vocabulary growth (Hart & Risley, 1995; Hoff & Naigles, 2002; Huttenlocher et al., 1991; Naigles & Hoff-Ginsberg, 1998). Comparisons of mothers from lower income families with those from higher income families revealed that the former talked less frequently to their children (Hoff et al., 2002). Hart and Risley (1995) estimated the number of words children in their study would have heard during the first 4 years of life. They found that children of professional parents would have heard nearly 45 million words, whereas children of working-class parents would have heard 26 million words and children of parents on welfare would have heard merely 13 million words. This estimation showed that the gap among income and education groups would have become greater over time. Although their calculations relied on assumptions, they provided a "best guess" about the amount of verbal experience children of different family backgrounds might bring to preschool at age 4.

Total amount of talk is important, as is exposure to low-frequency words, two aspects of language input that tend to be related to each other. Corroboration of the importance of exposure to low-frequency vocabulary can be found in a study by Weizman and Snow (2001). They audiotaped mother–child interactions during a home visit when children were 5 years old while mothers and children were engaging in five different activities. They identified the maternal use of low-frequency words based on the Dale–Chall word list, which comprises the 3,000 words that teachers judge as known to most fourth graders. Weizman and Snow found that the low-income children's early exposure to low-frequency words predicted approximately one-third of the variation in their Peabody Picture Vocabulary Test—Revised (PPVT-R) scores in kindergarten and second grade. Beals and Tabors (1995) also used the Dale–Chall word list as their list of common words, through which they identified low-frequency words produced by mothers. They found that low-income mothers' use of low-frequency words during toy play when their children were 3 years old correlated with children's PPVT-R scores at age 5. Thus both studies found a strong relationship between mothers' use of low-frequency words and children's later vocabulary outcomes. Moreover, it appears that children from low-income homes are exposed to less talk overall and fewer low-frequency words in particular. These differences in language input may be related to the relatively low language skills that poor children exhibit at school entry and therefore should be an important focus in preschool intervention.

Vocabulary acquisition is the aspect of language learning perhaps most related to input characteristics; children need to establish a social link with their caregivers for successful vocabulary acquisition. Overall vocabulary input at home substantially contributes to children's vocabulary outcomes. Taken together, studies demonstrate the relationship between the family verbal environments and children's vocabulary development; linguistically stimulating home environments positively influenced young children's comprehensive and productive vocabulary development.

The specific positive aspects of the home language environment that might be exportable to preschool classrooms to promote children's vocabulary acquisition include adult input that (1) follows children's attentional focus, (2) is responsive to children's verbalizations, (3) provides opportunities for frequent exposure to new words within different situations or settings during face-to-face

interactions, and (4) exposes children to low-frequency words starting in the early years. The issue is whether, in fact, the processes that operate in families are the same ones that operate in classroom groups.

Preschool Intervention Projects

To examine the benefit of preschool intervention, we have conducted two recent studies on different aspects of the preschool classroom environment and their impact on children's literacy and language behaviors in the classrooms. The following sections describe each study briefly and how it contributes to a better understanding of interventions in preschool settings.

Classroom Literacy Environments and Children's Literacy Behaviors

Within a larger study focusing on early childhood curricula, we investigated whether the presence of literacy-related materials and the instructional emphasis of the teacher in 34 classrooms influenced the degree to which children were involved with literacy materials in the classroom (Kang, 2003). Our interest was in determining whether the previously established relationship described for heterogeneous classrooms might also hold for prekindergarten programs serving low-income children and whether the presence of materials or the instructional efforts of the teacher was more strongly related to children's literacy behaviors in the classroom.

Curriculum Implementation Checklist

In order to assess literacy-related material and instructional environments, 133 literacy items were extracted from the combined version of the Curriculum Implementation Checklist.[1] These items were divided between those that were associated with literacy-related material environments and those associated with the literacy-related instructional environments. Items related to physical and material features included the availability of literacy-related materials (e.g., books, pencils, puppets, listening materials), the presence of environmental print (e.g., labels, alphabet displayed on the wall, daily schedule displayed), and the organization of literacy-related materials and environmental print (e.g., organization of literacy materials on low shelves to promote independent use, displaying environmental print low). Items related to the instructional features included teachers' verbal interactions (e.g., asking open-ended questions, making suggestions, describing actions or events) and teachers' guidance in literacy learning (e.g., reading books, encouraging retelling stories using props, modeling the writing process). Sixty-five items assessed the literacy-related physical environment, and 68 items addressed the literacy-related instructional environment. Each classroom therefore was given both a score for the literacy-related material environment and a score for the literacy-related instructional environment.

CLASSROOM OBSERVATION PROTOCOL

One child literacy behavior coded from the Child Observation in Preschools (COP; Culp & Farran, 1989; Farran, Kang, & Plummer, 2003) involved a description of materials with which the child was engaged. Initially a narrative format was used to describe what materials a child was engaged with or what activity the child was doing if he or she had no materials. Codes were developed from the narrative descriptions to characterize the materials with which the children were engaged. The frequency of children's engagement with literacy materials was calculated as a percentage of children's overall involvement with literacy materials relative to their involvement with other types of materials. The criteria for coding children's engagement with literacy materials was based on Morrow and Rand's (1991) definition of literacy behavior: reading, writing, and paper handling.

Reading materials included books, sequencing cards that tell a story, View masters, ABC puzzles, magnetic alphabet letters, letter bingo, letter stamps, name tags, name cards, and others. Writing materials incorporated pencils, markers, crayons, chalk, and so forth. All kinds of papers that could be handled by children, such as magazines and note pads, were regarded as literacy-related materials. Other materials, such as puppets, flannel boards, and songbooks, were also categorized as literacy materials. A computer was characterized as a literacy material if it was used for literacy activities such as reading stories or playing games involving the alphabet (Farran, Kang, & Plummer, 2003).

A child's looking at, holding, talking about, or carrying any of the materials described was coded as a literacy engagement. In other words, literacy behavior was defined as engagement with literacy materials—having literacy materials in hand, being attentive visually to literacy materials, or talking about literacy materials that somebody else was holding.

Involvement level measures how focused and engaged the child is in whatever activity he or she is doing; in other words, the quality of the child's involvement. Involvement is measured on a rating scale coded low, medium low, medium, medium high, or high every time the child is observed.

For example, if a child was observed when he or she was carrying a book but not paying attention to it, the description was coded as literacy engagement, but the level of involvement was rated as low. Therefore, children's engagement with literacy materials was captured from the codes used for the materials, and the quality of the child's engagement was judged by rating involvement level.

VARIABLES FOR ANALYSIS

Two variables were obtained from the checklists: (1) the degree of literacy emphasis in the physical classroom environment and (2) the degree of emphasis on literacy in the teacher-provided instruction. Two variables were taken from the COP: (1) the number of times a child was observed holding or attending to a literacy material or activity and (2) the level of involvement or degree of engagement the child showed in that activity or material.

The results of our study indicated that in classrooms with a strong literacy-related physical environment, children's engagement with materials was high. Children differed dramatically in their activity level with materials. Types of materials and teacher behavior correlated modestly with the amount of time children used literacy materials during free-choice time. More interesting, the literacy emphases in the classroom (both materials present and instruction) were highly positively correlated with how involved children were with the literacy materials. Children actively responded to materials that teachers cared most about, as evidenced by their choices of activities during free-play time and the degree of their involvement with the materials.

Language Interactions in Preschool Classrooms

In our second study (Aydogan, 2004), we examined the language characteristics of teachers in the preschools using variables comparable to the factors found to be related to language growth in the home. In this study, we examined the relationship of these language variables on children's linguistic behavior in the classrooms.

CURRICULUM IMPLEMENTATION CHECKLIST

In order to assess teachers' emotional warmth, responsive language, and small-group and one-on-one instructions, 63 items were extracted from the combined version of the Curriculum Implementation Checklist. These items were divided among those that were associated with teachers' emotional warmth, those associated with teachers' responsive language, those associated with small-group instruction, and those associated with one-on-one instruction.

Items related to teachers' emotional warmth included teachers' demonstration of affection and caring for each child (e.g., smiling, comforting distressed child, touching, holding), teachers' interest in children's activities and efforts, teachers' creating a positive social environment, and teachers' efforts to enhance children's self-esteem and confidence. The Teacher Warmth scale was composed of 17 items; the variable used in analyses for this study was the percentage of warmth items implemented averaged across the three observational time periods.

The teachers' responsive language scale was divided into three subcategories: quantity and quality of teacher language, teacher language that encourages children's expressive language development, and teacher language that promotes children's vocabulary development. Items related to quantity and quality of teacher language demonstrated

how frequently teachers verbally interacted with children and asked open-ended questions to elicit conversation from children. Items related to teacher language that encourages children's expressive language development included teachers' attempts to follow children's leads and teachers' encouragement of children's conversation initiations. Items related to teacher language that promotes children's vocabulary development included teachers' use of low-frequency words and teachers' practices that provide children with frequent exposure to new words in different activities and that help children derive meaning from texts that they are read. The Responsive Language scale included 38 items scored for the percentage implemented and averaged across the three observational time periods.

Four items related to small-group instruction included teachers' use of small-group activities in their schedules and teachers' use of this instructional context to meet children's interests and needs. Four items related to one-on-one instruction included teachers' allocation time for one-on-one interaction with children and teachers' valuing this instructional context. These eight items were combined to yield a variable called smaller group instruction; they were scored for percentage implemented and averaged across the three observational time periods.

CHILD OBSERVATION IN PRESCHOOLS

The verbal category on the COP measured whether the child was speaking or listening and to whom. Therefore, this category captured both the child's verbal behavior and the target to whom the child was talking or listening. Every time the child was observed, the child's verbal level was coded.

Results indicated the coherence between the language environment presented by the teachers and young children's language behavior. When teachers were rated as warmer and using more responsive language that also included the introduction of new vocabulary, children were more likely to be observed listening and talking to them, with the strongest effects observed on the intensity of the children's interactions. Positive language environments promoted more intense linguistic involvement on the part of the children. These findings are similar to the ones obtained for the contribution of the literacy environment to children's behavior. To understand the relationships, it appears to be important to observe the quality of children's behavior, not just the quantity.

Summary and Directions for Future Research

By their very nature, classrooms, even those for young children, are different language learning environments from homes, as Hemphill and Snow (1996) and Wells (1978) have pointed out. For example, at home, mothers and children are mostly engaged in one-on-one interactions, in which mothers are highly responsive to children's interests and transmit new meanings of words to children through joint activities in a reciprocal relationship. But at preschool, teachers tend to do most of the talking. As a result, there may be less opportunity for children to contribute to classroom activities. Further, the size of the group and daily routines at preschool may not afford children the opportunities to engage in one-on-one interaction with the teacher. Dialogue rules tend to be different in classrooms than in the home; children are expected to provide information to the teacher in a ritual turn-taking routine, and the focus is generally on the known, not new, material.

It is important to examine in detail the characteristics of preschool classrooms as learning environments for children from low-income families. These children are likely to enter the classrooms with quite different language experiential histories from children of higher income backgrounds. Evidence shows clearly that by formal school entry, the language skills of the two groups of children are quite divergent, and the differences are ones likely to make a difference in school achievement. The two studies reported here have begun to disentangle the relationship between the classroom environments and children's behavioral responses. In both cases, stronger effects were obtained between positive characteristics of the environment and the intensity of various types of children's involvement. They provide clear evidence that learning begins with engagement, especially for young children. The next steps will be to

determine the relationship between the classroom environment, children's behaviors, and later school success.

Note

1. This checklist was created by combining two curriculum implementation measures: one developed by the Charlotte–Mecklenburg School System for their *Bright Beginnings* curriculum (Smith, Pellin & Agruso, 2003) and the *Curriculum Implementation Checklist* developed by Teaching Strategies (Dodge, Colker, & Heroman, 2002).

References

Anderson, R. C., & Freebody, P. (1981). Vocabulary knowledge. In J. T. Guthrie (Ed.), *Comprehension and teaching: Research reviews* (pp. 77–117). Newark, DE: International Reading Association.

Aydogan, C. (2004). *The relationship between teachers' emotional warmth and teachers' responsive language and preschoolers' vocabulary development.* Unpublished master's thesis, Vanderbilt University.

Ball, E. W. (1993). Assessing phoneme awareness. *Language, Speech and Hearing Services in Schools, 34,* 130–139.

Beals, D., & Tabors, P. (1995). *Arboretum, bureaucratic, and carbohydrates*: Preschoolers' exposure to rare vocabulary at home. *First Language, 15,* 57–76.

Blachman, B. A., Tangel, D. M., Ball, E. W., Black, R., & McGraw, C. K. (1999). Developing phonological awareness and word recognition skills: A two-year intervention with low-income, inner-city children. *Reading and Writing: An Interdisciplinary Journal, 11,* 239–273.

Booth, A., & Waxman, S. (2002). Word learning is "smart": Evidence that conceptual information affects preschoolers' extension of novel words. *Cognition, 84,* B11–B22.

Bradley, L., & Bryant, P. (1985). *Rhyme and reason in reading and spelling.* Ann Arbor: University of Michigan Press.

Brinton, B., & Fujiki, M. (1999). Social interactional behaviors of children with specific language impairment. *Topics in Language Disorders, 19,* 49–69.

Byrnes, J. P. (2001). *Minds, brains, and learning: Understanding the psychological and educational relevance of neuroscientific research.* New York: Guilford Press.

Case, R., Griffin, S., & Kelly, W. M. (2001). Socioeconomic differences in children's early cognitive development and their readiness for schooling. In

S. L. Golbeck (Eds.), *Psychological perspectives on early childhood education* (pp. 37–63). Mahwah, NJ: Erlbaum.

Chew, A. L., & Lang, W. S. (1990). Predicting academic achievement in kindergarten and first grade from prekindergarten scores on the Lollipop Test and DIAL. *Educational and Psychological Measurement, 50*, 431–437.

Christie, J. F., & Enz, B. (1992). The effects of literacy play interventions on preschooler's play patterns and literacy development. *Early Education and Development, 3*, 205–219.

Coley, R. (2002). *An uneven start: Indicators of inequality in school readiness.* Princeton, NJ: Educational Testing Service.

Culp, A. M., & Farran, D. C. (1989). *Manual for observation of play in preschools.* Unpublished manuscript, University of North Carolina–Greensboro.

DeTemple, J. M. (2001). Parents and children reading books together. In D. K. Dickinson & P. O. Tabors (Eds.), *Beginning literacy with language* (pp. 31–51). Baltimore: Brookes.

Dickinson, D. (2001). Putting the pieces together: Impact of preschool on children's language and literacy development in kindergarten. In D. Dickinson & P.Tabors (eds.), *Beginning literacy with language* (pp. 257–287). Baltimore: Brookes.

Dodge, D. T., Colker, L. J., & Heroman, C. (2002). *The creative curriculum for preschool* (4th ed.). Washington, DC: Teaching Strategies.

Einarsdottir, J. (1996). Dramatic play and print. *Childhood Education, 72*, 352–357.

Engelmann, S. (1999). How sound is High/Scope research? *Educational Leadership, 56*, 83–84.

Farran, D. C., Kang, S., & Plummer, C. (2003). *Child observation in preschool manual.* Unpublished manuscript, Vanderbilt University.

Goffin, S. (1994). *Curriculum models and early childhood education.* New York: Merrill.

Goldfield, B. (1987). The contributions of child and caregiver to referential and expressive language. *Applied Psycholinguistics, 8*, 267–280.

Hart, B., & Risley, T. R. (1995). *Meaningful differences in the everyday experience of young American children.* Baltimore: Brookes.

Hemphill, L., & Snow, C. (1996). Language and literacy development: Discontinuities and differences. In D. Olson & N. Torrance (Eds.), *The handbook of education and human development* (pp. 173–201). Cambridge, MA: Blackwell.

Hiebert, E. H. (1981). Developmental patterns and interrelationships of preschool children's print awareness. *Reading Research Quarterly, 16*, 236–259.

Hiebert, E. H., Cioffi, G., & Antonak, R. F. (1984). A developmental sequence in preschool children's acquisition of reading readiness skills and print awareness concepts. *Journal of Applied Developmental Psychology, 5*, 115–126.

Hoff, E. (2003a). Causes and consequences of SES-related differences in parent-to-child speech. In M. H. Bornstein & R. H. Bradley (Eds.), *Socioeconomic status, parenting, and child development* (pp. 147–160). Mahwah, NJ: Erlbaum.

Hoff, E. (2003b). The specificity of environmental influence: Socioeconomic status affects early vocabulary development via maternal speech. *Child Development, 74*(5), 1368–1378.

Hoff, E., Laursen, B., & Tardif, T. (2002). Socioeconomic status and parenting. In M. H. Bornstein (Ed.), *Handbook of parenting* (2nd ed., pp. 231–252). Mahwah, NJ: Erlbaum.

Hoff, E., & Naigles, L. (2002). How children use input in acquiring a lexicon. *Child Development 73*(2), 418–433.

Hoff-Ginsberg, E. (1991). Mother–child conversation in different social classes and communicative settings. *Child Development, 62*, 782–796.

Huttenlocher, J., Haight, W., Bryk, A., Seltzer, M., & Lyons, T. (1991). Early vocabulary growth: Relation to language input and gender. *Developmental Psychology, 27*(2), 236–248.

Kaiser, A. P., Hancock, T. B., Cai, X., Foster, E. M., & Hester, P. P. (2000). Parent-reported behavior problems and language delays in boys and girls enrolled in Head Start classrooms. *Behavioral Disorders, 26*, 26–41.

Kaiser, A. P., & Hester, P. P. (1997). Prevention of conduct disorders through early intervention: A social-communicative perspective. *Behavioral Disorders, 22*, 117–130.

Kang, S. J. (2003). *The relationship between literacy related environments of preschool classrooms and low SES children's engagement with literacy materials.* Unpublished master's thesis, Vanderbilt University.

Kontos, S. (1988). Development and interrelationships of reading knowledge and skills during kindergarten and first grade. *Reading Research and Instruction, 27*, 13–28.

Kurdek, L., & Sinclair, R. (2000). Psychological, family, and peer predictors of academic outcomes in first through fifth-grade children. *Journal of Educational Psychology, 92*, 449–457.

La Paro, K., & Pianta, R. (2000). Predicting children's competence in the early school years: A meta-analytic review. *Review of Educational Research, 70*, 443–484.

Lee, V. E., Loeb, S., & Lubeck, S. (1998). Contextual effects of prekindergarten classrooms for disadvantaged children on cognitive development: The case of Chapter 1. *Child Development, 69*, 479–494.

Lomax, R. G., & McGee, L. M. (1987). Young children's concepts about print and reading: Toward a model of word reading acquisition. *Reading Research Quarterly, 22,* 237–256.

Lonigan, C. J., Bloomfield, B. G., Anthony, J. L., Bacon, K. D., Phillips, B. M., & Samwel, C. S. (1999). Relations among emergent literacy skills, behavioral problems, and social competence in preschool children from low- and middle-income backgrounds. *Topics in Early Childhood Special Education, 17,* 40–53.

Morgan, A. L. (1987). The development of written language awareness in black preschool children. *Journal of Reading Behavior, 19,* 49–66.

Morrow, L. M. (1991). Relationships among physical design of play centers, teacher's emphasis on literacy in play, and children's literacy behaviors during play. In J. Zutell & S. McCormick (Eds.), *Learner factors/teacher factors: Issues in literacy research and instruction: Fortieth yearbook of the National Reading Conference* (pp. 127–140). Chicago: National Reading Conference.

Morrow, L. M., & Rand, M. (1991). Promoting literacy during play by designing early childhood classroom environments. *Reading Teacher, 44,* 309–402.

Naigles, L. R., & Hoff-Ginsberg, E. (1998). Why are some verbs learned before other verbs? Effects of input frequency and structure on children's early verb use. *Journal of Child Language, 25,* 95–120.

Nel, E. M. (2000). Academics, literacy, and young children. *Childhood Education, 76,* 136–141.

Neuman, S. B. (1996). Children engaging in storybook reading: The influence of access to print resources, opportunity, and parental interaction. *Early Childhood Research Quarterly, 11,* 495–513.

Neuman, S. B. (1999). Books make a difference: A study of access to literacy. *Reading Research Quarterly, 34,* 286–311.

Neuman, S. B., & Gallagher, P. (1994). Joining together in literacy learning: Teenage mothers and children. *Reading Research Quarterly, 29,* 383–401.

Neuman, S. B., & Roskos, K. (1990). Play, print, and purpose: Enriching play environments for literacy development. *Reading Teacher, 44,* 214–221.

NICHD Early Child Care Research Network. (2004). Multiple pathways to early academic achievement. *Harvard Educational Review, 74,* 1–29.

Pianta, R. C., & McCoy, S. (1997). The first day of school: The predictive validity of early school screening. *Journal of Applied Developmental Psychology, 18,* 1–22.

Qi, C., Kaiser, A., Milan, S., Yzquierdo, Z., & Hancock, T. (2003). The performance of low-income, African American children on the Preschool Language Scale—3. *Journal of Speech, Language, and Hearing Research, 46,* 576–590.

Rayner, K., Foorman, B., Perfetti, C., Pesetsky, D., &

Seidenberg, M. (2002). How should reading be taught? *Scientific American, 286,* 84–91.

Raz, I. S., & Bryant, P. (1990). Social background, phonological awareness and children's reading. *British Psychological Society, 8,* 209–225.

Reynolds, A. J. (1989). A structural model of first-grade outcomes for an urban, low socioeconomic status, minority population. *Journal of Educational Psychology, 81,* 594–603.

Schatschneider, C., Carlson, C., Francis, D., Foorman, B., & Fletcher, J. (2002). Relationship of rapid automized naming and phonological awareness in early reading development: Implications for the double-deficit hypothesis. *Journal of Learning Disabilities, 35,* 245–256.

Schweinhart, L., Weikart, D., & Larner, M. (1986). Consequences of three curriculum models through age 15. *Early Childhood Research Quarterly, 1,* 15–45.

Smith, E. J., Pellin, B. J., & Agruso, S. A. (2003). *Bright Beginnings: An effective literacy-focused pre-K program for educationally disadvantaged four-year-old children.* Arlington, VA: Educational Research Service (*www.ers.org*).

Smith, M. (2001). Children's experiences in preschool. In D. Dickinson & P. Tabors (Eds.), *Beginning literacy with language* (pp. 149–174). Baltimore: Brookes.

Snow, C. E., Burns, M. S., & Griffin, P. (Eds.). (1998). *Preventing reading difficulties in young children.* Washington, DC: National Research Council.

Stevenson, H. W., & Newman, R. S. (1986). Long-term prediction of achievement and attitudes in mathematics and reading. *Child Development, 57,* 646–659.

Stipek, D., & Ryan, R. (1997). Economically disadvantaged preschoolers: Ready to learn but further to go. *Developmental Psychology, 33,* 711–723.

Tabors, P., Snow, C., & Dickinson, D. (2001). Homes and schools together: Supporting language and literacy development. In D. Dickinson & P. Tabors (Eds.), *Beginning literacy with language* (pp. 313–334). Baltimore: Brookes.

Tamis-LeMonda, C. S., Bornstein, M. H., Baumwell, L., & Damast, A. M. (1996). Responsive parenting in the second year: Specific influences on children's language and play. *Early Development and Parenting, 5,* 173–183.

Teaching Strategies. (2002). *The creative curriculum for preschool implementation checklist.* Washington, DC: Teaching Strategies.

Torgesen, J., Wagner, R., Rashotte, C., Rose, E., Lindamood, P., Conway, T., & Garvan, C. (1999). Preventing reading failure in young children with phonological processing disabilities: Group and individual responses to instruction, *Journal of Educational Psychology, 91,* 579–593.

Torgesen, J. K., & Mathes, P. (1999). What every

teacher should know about phonological awareness. In *Consortium on Reading Excellence* (CORE, pp. 54–61). Novato, CA: Arena Press.

Vellutino, E. R., & Scanlon, D.M. (1988). Phonological coding, phonological awareness, and reading ability: Evidence from a longitudinal and experimental study. In K. E. Stanovich (Ed.), *Children's reading and the development of phonological awareness* (pp. 77–119). Detroit, MI: Wayne State University.

Vukelich, C. (1991). Materials and modeling: Promoting literacy during play. In J. Christie (Eds.), *Play and early literacy development* (pp. 215–231). Albany: State University of New York Press.

Wasik, B. A., & Bond, M. A. (2001). Beyond the page of a book: Interactive book reading and language development in preschool classrooms. *Journal of Educational Psychology, 93,* 243–250.

Waxman, S., & Booth, A. (2001). On the insufficiency of evidence for a domain-general account of word learning. *Cognition, 78,* 277–279.

Weir, B. (1989). A research base for prekindergarten literacy programs. *Reading Teacher, 42,* 456–460.

Weizman, Z. O., & Snow, C. E. (2001). Lexical input as related to children's vocabulary acquisition: Effects of sophisticated exposure and support for meaning. *Developmental Psychology, 37*(2), 265–279.

Wells, G. (1978). Talking with children: The complementary roles of parents and teachers. *English in Education, 12,* 15–38.

Whitehurst, G., & Lonigan, C. (1998). Child development and emergent literacy. *Child Development, 69,* 848–872.

Whitehurst, G. J., Zevenbergen, A. A., Crone, D. A., Schultz, M. D., Velting, O. N., & Fischel, J. E. (1999). Outcomes of an emergent literacy intervention from Head Start through second grade. *Journal of Educational Psychology, 91,* 261–272.

20

The Relationships between Sociodramatic Play and Literacy Development

LESLEY MANDEL MORROW
JUDITH A. SCHICKEDANZ

More than ever before, literacy development is a major goal for preschool education. The 2002 No Child Left Behind legislation includes preschool among its many literacy initiatives. This legislation provides funding for Early Reading First for the purpose of developing excellent models of literacy instruction for 3- and 4-year-olds (see also Roskos & Vukelich, Chapter 22, this volume). In addition, states are currently developing early learning standards in language, literacy, and mathematics. These efforts reflect the growing interest in improving children's school readiness skills in the very earliest years. Validating previous syntheses of research, including the National Research Council's *Preventing Reading Difficulties* (Snow, Burns, & Griffin, 1998) and the position statement of the International Reading Association (IRA) and National Association for the Education of Young Children (NAYEC) (1998), the most recent National Early Literacy Panel (2004) identified variables associated with early literacy development:

- Oral language: expressive and receptive vocabulary.
- Alphabetic code: alphabet knowledge, phonological/phonemic awareness, invented spelling.
- Print knowledge: environmental print, concepts about print.
- Other skills: rapid naming of letters, num-

bers, visual memory, and visual perceptual abilities.

Against this backdrop there is good reason for the concerns of many early childhood educators and researchers that the role of play, including dramatic play, may be overlooked in our effort to ensure that children receive more explicit language and literacy instruction in the preschool setting. It is noteworthy that play has been reaffirmed by the NAEYC in its most recent accreditation standards (NAEYC, 2004). It is important that our understanding of play is integrated into our developing understanding of school readiness. In this chapter we seek to address this need by reviewing research on dramatic play and literacy, describing what we know about the relationships between play and literacy development and the impact of classrooms and teachers on the nature and quality of children's play.

As will become apparent, most of the research to date clearly describes the relationship between play, environmental supports, and literacy development. But it does not describe a causal connection between them. The current situation reflects the fact that theories of play have undergone several major shifts in points of view regarding the appropriateness of adult support for child's development through play. We begin by briefly outlining these changing theoretical perspectives on play, indicating how these points of view have shaped research. We then turn to studies that have explicitly examined the relationship of play with literacy as we review (1) studies that have examined literacy behavior exhibited by preschoolers in their spontaneous dramatic play; (2) studies of the effects on children's literacy development of access to literacy-enriched environments in preschool classrooms; (3) studies of the variations in, and effects of, roles assumed by teachers who participate in children's dramatic play; (4) studies of the added benefit to children's engagement in literacy-related behavior of teacher mediation and support of play; and (5) studies of the benefits of conversations between teachers and children during play. This research suggests the important relationships between literacy and play, helping to inform next steps in this line of inquiry.

A Brief History of Theories about Play

Prior to the 1970s, psychoanalytic theory dictated the use of play in classrooms and, as a result, teachers limited their involvement in children's play so as not to interfere with their emotional problem solving and catharsis (Johnson, Christie, & Yawkey, 1987). Piaget's (1962) theory of play, which began to replace or at least augment the psychoanalytic view by the 1970s, stressed play's relationship to cognition. Specifically, Piaget viewed pretend play as a kind of symbolic activity, with objects and imagined roles representing something else. From a Piagetian perspective, development in play entails increases in decontextualization and decentration, which means that there is an increase in the distance of play behavior from the child's daily experiences in reality. For example, a younger child might use an empty play cup in pretending to take a drink of water, whereas an older child might position his or her hand as if holding an imaginary cup. A Piagetian observer would note that the older child's play shows more decontextualization than the younger child's. Similarly, a younger child might pretend to eat or drink, activities engaged in quite often by the child in real life, whereas an older child might pretend to be a firefighter, a doctor, or a nurse, all roles

the child has observed but never occupied in reality. A Piagetian would say that the older child's play shows greater decentration than the younger child's.

The Piagetian view of play opened the door to consideration of the relationship between pretend play and overall cognitive and language development and play's possible role in furthering development in these areas. It did not, however, change the adult's role in the child's play, given that Piaget's stage theory assumes that changes in development result from the interplay between maturation and the child's autonomous interactions with the world. As noted by Haight and Miller (1992), Piaget omitted "information about the social context of early pretending, with the implication that pretend play develops regardless of whether anyone pretends with the child" (pp. 331–332). It was Vygotsky's (1967, 1978) theory of cognitive development that gave a central role in play to a partner who tutors. Such a partner must be a more experienced other, often an adult or an older child, and sometimes a more skilled peer.

Research on the relationship between pretend play and language and literacy development has been framed in ways that reflect the prevailing theories about the nature and functions of play. Thus the shift from psychoanalytic views of play to more cognitive views prompted some researchers to examine children's ability to engage in symbolic, representational play (e.g., Fein, 1975). Research done in this tradition has provided important insight into the development of children's abilities to represent experience symbolically through play. For example, Bondioli (2001) described the progressive development of children's ability to decontextualize their object use, to decenter their role in their play, and to integrate play schemes. The trend in development of object use is from prototypical objects to substitute objects (i.e., objects that do not resemble physically their assigned function in play), to imaginary objects.

Based on a Piagetian perspective, adult participation in children's play typically was not a central variable. Although relatively little is known about the effects of particular types of adult input to the children's general cognitive development, research on adult intervention in play has revealed variations in the quality of children's play that are related to adult styles of interaction in play. Specifically, when adults' behavior in the play setting involved give and take, the symbolic quality of the child's play is enhanced, and when the adult's behavior is directive rather than reciprocal, the child's play becomes less symbolic (Fein & Fryer, 1995; Haight & Miller, 1992).

Smilansky and Shefatya (1990) and Bondioli (2001) have also attempted to understand strategies that adults can use that support children's engagement in play. Bondioli (2001) summarized this work when she outlined what is required of the adult who hopes to foster pretend-play abilities in children. She stated that the adult should take a maieutic role, with a high level of curiosity and with the ability to withstand uncertainty. The adult must scaffold the play, but within the child's zone of proximal development. The adult must also keep in mind the characteristics of play, such as "denotative license, referential freedom, affective meaning, and shared symbolism" (p. 128). Ideally, the tutor does not predetermine roles, content, or the direction of play; rather, he or she "must pay attention to 'what happens and when it happens' and stimulate children to develop play scripts or themes by themselves" (p. 114).

Research on adult input in toddler play (Bornstein & Tamis-LeMonda, 1995; Haight & Miller, 1992; Slade, 1987) also has been limited to studying the quality of toddlers' play with and without an adult partner. Overall, results of adult interventions to support play show that levels of play, as defined by a Piagetian framework (i.e., decentration and decontextualization), are altered positively by adult participation. In the toddler research, play episodes involving adult partners were also more frequent and longer than when children played independently.

The adult behavior that supports the development of play behaviors in the dramatic play context shares essential features with adult behavior known to facilitate other aspects of development. For example, reciprocity in parent–child interactions predicts the development of a secure attachment relationship (Ainsworth et al., 1978; Isabella & Belsky, 1991; Lamb, 1992), whereas intrusiveness, indifference, and other kinds of insensitive behavior predict anxious attach-

ments. Similarly, sensitive and reciprocal verbal interactions by parents predict competence in children's skill in relating autobiographical narratives (McCabe & Peterson, 1991; Peterson, Jesso, & McCabe, 1999), whereas lack of sensitivity and reciprocity on the part of the parent inhibits the development of narrative competence.

In sum, throughout the 20th century theories of child development changed dramatically, and with these shifts have come varied views of the nature and functions of play, changes in notions about the role of adults in supporting play, and shifts in the priorities of researchers. Distinct bodies of research examined play, with the result being a relatively diffuse body of literature showing that children's play goes through predictable development stages and that adults can play a role in nurturing development (Hart & Risley, 1995; Morrow, 2005).

Play as Literacy Behavior

In the final decades of the 20th century reading researchers began serious study of the origins of literacy, and some began to investigate the intersection between early literacy and play. Studies carried out by researchers with primary interest in literacy have also shifted focus from early examination of children's literacy behaviors to contextual factors that affect children's uses of print during play.

Inventories of Children's Literacy Behavior in Spontaneous Play

The early research dealing with children's literacy behavior in spontaneous play was motivated by a concern that adult-centered, decontextualized probes (i.e., tests) underestimate preschoolers' actual literacy knowledge and skill. In one study of this kind, free-play data were collected for 50 children over a 2-month period in two preschool settings (Neuman & Roskos, 1991). The literacy demonstrations isolated in play protocols were analyzed for functions served by the child's literacy behavior and for evidence of children's knowledge of various features of print (e.g., letter names, orientation of print). Results showed that preschoolers had considerable knowledge about literacy functions and also readily displayed knowledge about print features in functional contexts.

A second study of this kind provided a similar inventory of preschoolers' literacy demonstrations as they occurred naturally in the context of children's pretend play (Roskos, 1991). Literacy-related videotaped episodes were analyzed and inventoried as instances of activities, skills, and knowledge. The inventory demonstrated that preschoolers knew a lot about literacy and revealed that knowledge readily in the dramatic play context. These two descriptive studies established that existing pretend-play contexts in preschools elicited literacy behavior from preschool children and provided situations in which literacy behavior, especially functional routines, could be practiced.

Given that these settings were not furnished with an abundance of literacy-related materials, researchers wondered whether preschoolers would engage in more literacy behavior if the typical dramatic play areas of their classrooms were enriched. This curiosity led naturally to additional studies of enriched dramatic play environments and shifted the focus of researchers from viewing play as a window through which to learn what preschoolers already understand about literacy to viewing it as a potential context for promoting literacy learning.

Enriching Dramatic-Play Contexts with Literacy Materials to Enhance Engagement

In one study of this kind the researchers redesigned the physical environments of two urban preschool classrooms to create four dramatic-play areas: a kitchen, a post office, an office, and a library (Neuman & Roskos, 1990). Literacy props appropriate to each play theme (e.g., paper, pencils, envelopes, and books) were added. Prior to adding literacy props to the areas, each child's literacy behaviors were observed and videotaped over a 2-week period during free play in the four dramatic-play centers. Each child's print concepts were measured with the Concepts about Print test (Clay, 1979). Four weeks after the addition of literacy props, children's behavior was again observed during free play and videotaped in the four dramatic-

play contexts, and the Concepts about Print test was administered as a posttest.

The average number of literacy demonstrations per child almost doubled following the intervention, and children also made significant gains in print concepts. Literacy demonstrations also increased in length and density and became more unified in the enriched-play centers. Given the small number of classrooms and the absence of a comparison group, there could be other explanations for increases in children's print concepts. Yet the study demonstrated that literacy-enriched dramatic-play contexts alter children's literacy behavior in beneficial ways.

In a subsequent study, Neuman and Roskos (1992) assigned classrooms from two day-care centers to two conditions. At the intervention site (B), three existing play areas were defined physically and enriched with literacy materials to create a library, a kitchen/house, and an office. At the nonintervention site (A), no changes were made. Prior to intervention, the Test of Early Reading Ability (TERA; Reid, Hresko, & Hammill, 1981) established that groups did not differ in their literacy knowledge. Children's literacy behavior was observed and videotaped at both sites prior to the intervention to obtain information about the literacy demonstrations spontaneously engaged in by children during play.

Following the changes made at Site B, children's behavior during free play was videotaped weekly for 6 months. In Site A (nonintervention), contexts for videotaping included the housekeeping area, a book corner, a small-manipulatives area, and the arts and crafts table. In Site B (intervention), the contexts included the house/kitchen, library, and office play areas. Each child's spontaneous play behavior was observed during the final 2 weeks of the study.

Significant differences were found on all types of literacy demonstrations (handling, reading, and writing) in favor of the intervention group. In fact, children at Site B engaged in 10 times as many literacy demonstrations as children at Site A, and these demonstrations were longer and more complex.

Two additional studies, one by Morrow (1990) and another by Neuman and Roskos (1993b), also investigated the effects of literacy-enriched dramatic-play settings. In these studies, researchers also manipulated adult support for play, which is discussed separately in the next section of this chapter. Here, we consider the studies' effect of enriching play contexts with literacy-related materials.

In Morrow's (1990) study, 13 preschool classrooms were randomly assigned to a control group and three experimental groups (E1, E2, and E3). The kitchen play areas in the three E1 classrooms were enriched with literacy materials. In the four E2 classrooms and the three E3 classrooms, the preintervention kitchen play area was transformed into a veterinarian's office. Many literacy props related to a veterianian's job were added to the play area. The E2 and E3 conditions differed in terms of levels of adult support, but not in their physical design or in the literacy materials available.

Children were observed during free play prior to the intervention to obtain data on children's engagement in literacy activities. One week after the changes were made, observation data on children's literacy activity were again collected during free play. Following a 1-month period during which observations were not made, children's engagement with literacy activities was observed for a third time. All three experimental groups differed significantly from the control group on three literacy behaviors (paper handling, reading, and writing). The study demonstrated that enriching dramatic-play areas with literacy materials increases preschoolers' literacy behavior.

In the second study, eight Head Start classrooms were randomly assigned to three groups (Neuman & Roskos, 1993b). In Group 1 and Group 2 classrooms, a literacy-enriched office was created. Groups 1 and 2 differed in terms of adult participation in play (discussed in the next section), but were identical in terms of literacy-enrichment of an office-play context. No changes were made in the two control classrooms (Group 3).

Children's behavior during free play was observed before the intervention, and the Test of Early Reading Ability (Reid et al., 1981) established that groups were initially similar in terms of their literacy knowledge and skill. After 1 month of the intervention, children's free play was videotaped weekly.

The play behavior of children was also observed 8 weeks into the intervention, and again during the last 2 weeks of the intervention. After the 5-month intervention ended, children were tested on an environmental word-reading task and a print-functions task. Children in intervention classrooms engaged in a greater number of literacy-related interactions during free play, both during and after the intervention, than children in the control group; and children in the intervention classrooms also did significantly better than the control group on the environmental word-reading task and the labeling-of-items portion of the print-functions task.

This line of inquiry established very clearly that literacy-enhanced dramatic-play settings can significantly increase preschoolers' engagement with literacy functions and routines and also that dramatic play is a context in which children can learn about environmental print and basic print concepts. To explore further how children demonstrate their literacy knowledge and how they adapt literacy tools to fit situations encountered in play, a study was conducted with two groups of children in one Even Start classroom (Neuman & Roskos, 1997). Three play settings, all representing contexts familiar to the children, were created (doctor's office, restaurant, and post office). Many literacy-related materials and objects were provided in each context (about 20 in each play setting). Over the 7-month course of the study, children's play was videotaped weekly during a 30-minute free-play period. The number of children who played in each setting was recorded in a log of the videotaping. The researchers also observed children's behavior in the play contexts once each week to judge whether the play areas were engaging children sufficiently and to inform themselves about the need to add new literacy materials.

Literacy-play episodes were identified on the videotapes, transcribed, resituated within the various play contexts, and then analyzed again. These analyses yielded insights as to how children used their knowledge of literacy in relation to specific situations. A major finding was that the purposes evident in children's literacy behavior "varied dramatically across settings" (p. 32). This study indicated that not only do literacy-enriched dramatic-play areas serve as contexts for learning what children know about literacy, but they are also places where children can practice what they already know and participate in critical cognitive work in literacy. The researchers noted, however, that providing authentic contexts in which children can practice literacy routines and skills does not address how "print conventions and literacy skills are formed by young children" (p. 30). The investigators suggested that adult support in these literacy-enriched play contexts might enhance children's literacy learning (Neuman & Roskos, 1997).

Adult Behavior and Children's Literacy Behavior in Pretend Play

In this section we review studies that provide descriptive information about teacher styles of interaction and delineate how these styles link to effects on children's play behavior (Enz & Christie, 1997; Neuman & Roskos, 1993a; Schrader, 1990). We also look at the effects of adult mediation and guidance on children's engagement in learning from literacy-enriched dramatic-play contexts (Morrow, 1990; Neuman & Roskos, 1993b). The commonality among the studies is that all discuss the effects of adult behavior on children's literacy behavior in play contexts (Glaubman, Kashi, & Koresh, 2001).

Teacher Interactive Styles in Literacy-Enriched Dramatic-Play Contexts

Three descriptive studies provide useful information about adult styles or roles in children's literacy-enriched dramatic play. The first study, conducted by Schrader (1990), involved four preschool teachers in a university laboratory preschool and two private preschools. Before the study began, teachers were provided training in early literacy development. Teachers were instructed to first ascertain a child's intentions and then to provide support in the form of comments, questions, demonstrations, and suggestions during play. After the training, the teachers' behavior was observed in three dramatic-play settings (post office, office, and house), each enriched with many literacy-related materials. Data on interactive teacher behavior in these contexts were obtained from videotapes and audiotapes of teacher–child in-

teractions, from the teachers' written observations of their experiences, and from children's writing samples. Data were coded in terms of extending or redirecting behaviors. *Extending* behaviors supported the child's intentions while also taking a child's idea beyond where the unassisted child might have gone with them. *Redirecting* behaviors ignored the child's intentions by introducing an idea unrelated to the child's intentions. All teachers exhibited both extending and redirecting type behaviors, and all teachers used the extending style more than the redirecting style. Teachers varied somewhat in terms of the number of behaviors captured by the two styles defined for use in the study.

In a second study of teacher roles in children's literacy-enriched dramatic play, Neuman and Roskos (1993b) collected data on six preschool teachers. Data consisted of teachers' journal entries of their interactions with children in three literacy-enriched play settings; interviews (audiotaped and transcribed) conducted by one of the researchers with the teachers to discuss their journal entries; and field notes of teacher interactions in the play settings. Through a process of data analysis and reduction, characteristics of teacher behavior were identified, and three distinct roles emerged: onlooker, player, and leader. In the role of *onlooker*, a teacher created "a sense of benign and accepting presence" and "celebrated children's literacy triumphs" (p. 86). In the role of *player*, a teacher played along as "a member of the team" (p. 87). In the role of *leader*, the teacher introduced specific literacy-related ideas into the play and used play opportunities to teach children about literacy. All teachers interacted quite similarly in children's play.

In a third study on teacher roles in play, Enz and Christie (1997) identified six styles/roles among four preschool teachers working in three early childhood classrooms: (1) uninvolved, (2) interviewer, (3) stage manager, (4) coplayer, (5) play leader, and (6) director/instructor. These styles/roles provide a continuum of interaction that ranges from uninvolved to highly directive behavior.

Enz and Christie (1997) found specific effects associated with the various styles of interaction on the children's play behavior. Styles/roles from the middle of the continuum (stage manager, coplayer, and play leader) promoted children's play. The play lasted longer, and children did not leave the scene. Teacher styles/roles from the extremes (*interviewer* and *director/instructor*) either ended the pretend play in reaction to the teacher's direction and control or allowed the play to fizzle or disintegrate into disputes over roles and materials (*uninvolved*). The four teachers used a distinct style that was related to their experience and training. For example, a less experienced teacher trained in family counseling used the interviewer style 41% of the time. The most experienced teacher, who had extensive training in early childhood, occupied the coplayer role 51% of the time.

The styles/roles identified by Enz and Christie (1997) have features in common with the styles identified by researchers studying parental styles of interaction in toddler play (Bornstein & Tamis-LeMonda, 1995; Haight & Miller, 1992; Slade, 1987) and with parental styles identified by researchers studying infant attachment (Ainsworth et al., 1978; Cassidy & Berlin, 1994; Isabella & Belsky, 1991; Magai & McFadden, 1995). The behaviors characteristic of the most effective roles allow for a measure of responsiveness to the child's current behavior. This behavior is neither neglectful nor controlling, but responsive, allowing for reciprocal influences between children and the adult.

Effects of Adult Support of Children's Literacy-Enriched Dramatic Play

The two studies reviewed here differ from the descriptive studies in that adult engagement or support of dramatic play was varied systematically. Although quite different in the kinds of support adults provided, both studies found that adult support of play affects positively the literacy outcomes for children who have access to enriched dramatic-play environments.

One study on adult support was conducted by Morrow (1990). Recall from our previous discussion of this study that each experimental classroom (E1, E2, and E3) had literacy-enriched dramatic-play areas, whereas a control classroom did not. E2 and E3 classrooms provide the comparison of in-

terest because the same physical changes were made in classrooms assigned to these conditions (addition of a literacy-rich veterinarian office), but level of adult support for play was varied. In E2 classrooms, teachers introduced the literacy materials in the new play area and made suggestions for their use *only* on the first day the new play area was available. In E3 classrooms, teachers introduced literacy items in the enriched-play area and suggested possible uses on *every day* of the 4-week intervention. Observational data collected for 3 weeks prior to the intervention and for the last 3 weeks of the intervention were analyzed and placed in literacy demonstration categories (i.e., handling, reading, and writing). Significant differences were found among groups for both reading and writing demonstrations, with more of each occurring in the E2 classrooms. This study demonstrated that adult support for literacy-enriched dramatic play, provided outside of the play itself, can have beneficial effects on children's literacy-related play behavior (Morrow, 2005).

In a second study on adult support of play conducted by Neuman and Roskos (1993a), adult involvement and support of children's play in a literacy-enriched dramatic-play area was contrasted with physical enrichment alone without adult support during play. In this study, parent volunteers served as "parent/teachers" in eight Head Start classrooms. In three classrooms (Group 1), parent/teachers were instructed to join children in ways that were responsive as they played in a literacy-enriched office area. A literacy-enriched office-play area was also provided in the three classrooms comprising Group 2, but parent/teachers in these classrooms were asked to refrain from joining with children in their play (i.e., to adopt an *onlooker* role). The two classrooms assigned to Group 3 (control) continued, as usual, without an enriched office-play area or specific instructions to teachers about engagement in children's dramatic play.

No differences were found among groups on literacy skills prior to the intervention. During the preintervention period, children's play behaviors were observed to identify literacy demonstrations (i.e., handling, reading, and writing), and the researchers met separately with the parent/teachers in each intervention group to explain expectations for their behavior with respect to the literacy-enriched office-play setting (i.e., responsive participation in Group 1; no participation in Group 2).

After the intervention, the researchers videotaped on a weekly basis to capture children's interaction in the office-play setting, and data were collected on individual children's behavior in the new play setting at the end of the first 8 weeks of the intervention and then again during the last 2 weeks of the intervention. Immediately after the 5-month intervention, children were assessed individually to determine their knowledge of the functions and uses of office-play print objects (e.g., a page from a telephone book, a stamp, a calculator, and so on) and their ability to read words drawn from the environmental print displayed in the office-play area (e.g., *office, exit, open, closed*).

Literacy demonstrations (i.e., handling, reading, and writing behaviors) increased in the two intervention groups (Groups 1 and 2), but not in Group 3 (control group), after 2 months of the intervention. At the end of the 5-month period, Group 1 (intervention with adult participation), but not Group 2 (intervention without adult participation), showed additional gains. There were also significant differences on environmental word reading between Group 1 and Group 3, Group 2 and Group 3, and Group 1 and Group 2, indicating that adult interaction provided a benefit above the benefit of mere physical enrichment of a play space. Other results obtained in the study included a significant difference in the number of children who participated in the office-play setting and in the duration of their interactions with peers, with Group 1 again ahead of Group 2 in each case.

Conversations in Play and Literacy Development

The studies of adult engagement in dramatic play that we have reviewed do not discuss in detail the content or course of conversation that occurred during play. They simply describe and define in broad terms the role taken by the teacher. Another approach to examining the relationships between play and development has been taken by researchers whose primary interest has been language development (Glaubman et al., 2001). This work, which is consistent with Vygotskian theory, has examined sociodramatic play during which children enact scenarios that they create and negotiate themselves, using knowledge of real-life situations they have experienced or observed. Investigators (Dickinson & Tabors, 2001; Heath, 1983; Pellegrini, 1980, 1982, 1985; Pellegrini & Galda, 1993; Sachs, 1980) who have examined preschool children's engagement in such play have concluded that engagement in sociodramatic play prompts children to use language to convey meaning, interpret ideas, and appreciate the role or perspective of others.

Research conducted by Dickinson (2001b), and studies reported in Dickinson, St. Pierre, and Pettengill (2004) emphasize the need for high-quality language and literacy preschool programs to have a high level of teacher–child verbal interaction, with special emphasis on narrative conversation. Strong relationships have been found between the types of conversations engaged in by teachers and children and literacy behavior assessed at the end of kindergarten. Conversations in which teachers use rare words, limit how much they talk relative to how much the child talks, and listen to what children say benefit children's language development the most.

Further evidence of the power of conversations to affect language outcomes comes from home studies of parents and children. In one home study (McCabe & Peterson, 1991) designed to enhance children's narrative conversation through parent interaction with children during play parents were asked to:

1. Talk to your child frequently and consistently about past experiences.
2. Spend a lot of time talking about each topic.
3. Ask lots of *wh-* questions, such as "Where . . .?" and "When . . .?" Ask few yes or no questions.
4. Listen to what your child says and encourage elaboration.
5. Encourage your child to say more than one sentence at a time by repeating what your child has just said.
6. Follow your child's lead by talking about what he or she wants to talk about.

Parents in the treatment group increased the types of utterances they had been taught to include in their conversation with their children. After the intervention, children in the experimental group increased in vocabulary. At 12 months, when tested, they showed improvement in all areas.

Studies carried out to determine whether preschools provide the type of instruction or setting needed for language and literacy to flourish have found that few children are receiving the support needed, especially those who already have limited language ability (Tizard & Hughes, 1984). In observational studies of interactive talk between teachers and children during free play and at other times during the school day, researchers have found that little conversation occurs (Chall & Dale, 1995; Wilcox-Herzog & Kontos, 1998; Dickinson, 2001b). Studies in preschools have also found that the number of different words and the different types of words used by teachers is limited and that little explicit or intentional vocabulary development takes place. Researchers have suggested that teachers think about increasing the frequency and complexity of language interactions with children and also about the settings in which this might best take place. Even the positioning of the teacher in relation to the child to encourage talk is a consideration (Galda, Pellegrini, & Cox, 1989).

A study by Dickinson (2001a, pp. 239–240) gives us a glimpse into a preschool classroom during dramatic play when a teacher engages the children in a conversation about their dramatic play, which involved sharks.

TEACHER: Oh, so you're going to get the sharks. Do you need to kill them, or do you move them to a different place so they can't hurt anybody?

CASEY: Kill them.

TEACHER: Kill them. You have to kill them?

BRYAN: Yeah.

CASEY: There's water already in the cage.

TEACHER: Oh, so they're in cages that are filled with water?

BRYAN: Yeah, it's a water cage.

TEACHER: And they don't get to eat spinach. Do you think sharks miss eating spinach?

CASEY: Sharks think they could get out with spinach.

TEACHER: You must be a very brave and daring man to go down there and take all these sharks back to this special place.

CASEY: We're protecting them.

TEACHER: Do you have to wear special suits? What kind do you wear in the water?

BRYAN: I wear climbing.

TEACHER: A climbing suit?

CASEY: Yeah.

TEACHER: What do you wear?

CASEY: A shark suit.

TEACHER: Those things on your back, are those the oxygen tanks? To help you breathe underwater?

BRYAN: They can breathe underwater.

TEACHER: Wow, that's special trick to learn how to do.

In this conversation the teacher repeats ideas discussed by the children to help them make their own concepts clear. For example, she repeats "Oh, so you're going to get the sharks." She clarifies what they eat and repeats the novel words *spinach* and *oxygen*. She helps children clarify what the oxygen tanks use. The teacher listened to the children and then spoke to them about the topic of their play, she used words that were rare for them, and she explicitly repeated new ideas and words in sentences (Dickinson, 2001a, p. 250). Dickinson found that conversations of this type, sampled when children were 4, were correlated with children's language development a year later at the end of kindergarten.

Clearly, we need to study conversations in play in more depth. For example, studies are needed in which teachers are trained in conversations that are designed to help support children's language and literacy development during dramatic play, after which their conversations are compared with conversations of teachers in a control group. The quality and content of teachers' verbal behavior in relation to children's must be measured, and we must measure children's language and literacy achievement in the short and long term.

Conclusion

At this time, although the relationships between play and literacy development have been documented, we still lack information for making causal connections between the two. In terms of the four categories of learning identified by the National Early Literacy Panel (2004), research on play in literacy-enriched dramatic-play contexts seems to contribute, and perhaps has the potential to contribute, to print knowledge (i.e., knowledge of environmental print and concepts about print) and oral language (i.e., receptive and expressive vocabulary). The lack of causal evidence linking play to literacy development must be viewed within the context of the shifting theories of play and associated limitations in available research. Many potentially productive questions remain to be addressed. For example, researchers have yet to explore the relationship between children's increased engagement in literacy behavior during dramatic play and their interest in and attentiveness to teacher-directed and explicit literacy instruction provided in the children's school day. It seems likely that playing with literacy objects and routines might indeed make explicit treatments of literacy in teacher-directed contexts more interesting to young children. If this were the case, might there also be some long-term consequences for children's reading and writing achievement? Future research on dramatic play in literacy-enriched contexts needs to probe for such relationships, in the short term and over the long haul.

Research might also help us learn how to give children more to *take to* their play, and perhaps benefit more from it. We know that children practice in play what they already know about literacy functions and features and that literacy-enriched play settings increase this kind of behavior. We also know that supportive adult participation in play leads to gains in knowledge of environmental print and print concepts. The evidence is limited, however, on the causal connections to children's knowledge of environmental print and literacy functions. We also have no information about possible effects of supportive adults participating with children in play on children's relationships to their teachers and the possible benefit this might bestow on children's learning in other contexts, such as story reading. We need to study how close attachments to teachers influence play behavior, similar to research conducted by Adriana Bus (2001).

In the discussion section of their 1997 study, Neuman and Roskos commented that "children's actions and routines did not appear to significantly change or become more embellished over the 7-month period of the study" (p. 32). They continued by suggesting that teacher support in play (not a focus in the 1997 study) might prompt more "active knowledge construction" (p. 32). In their concluding comments, however, they suggest that "both situated learning and formal school learning" are needed to provide sufficient support for preschoolers' literacy learning. We concur wholeheartedly.

If we are to develop comprehensive and integrated early literacy preschool programs, we need the benefit of evidence-based research demonstrating whether and how literacy-enriched play environments benefit children's literacy learning, how various styles of teacher interaction in play affect children's language and literacy learning, how teacher-directed literacy activities outside of play might leverage children's literacy learning in play, and how teacher–child relationships are affected by different styles of teacher participation. We also need to study the content and course of conversations between teachers and children during play and how variations in conversations affect language and literacy development.

Researchers also must pursue more play and literacy connections using randomized experimental and control groups, and they must probe for a wider range of possible benefits to literacy development, including children's interest in literacy learning. Moreover, studies must include longitudinal designs, to determine what happens, in time, to any near-term benefits identified. Longitudinal designs would also uncover "sleeper effects"—benefits in the long, but not the near, term.

Unless randomized controlled trials are used to examine literacy from play, we run the risk of losing a traditional component of preschool programming as problems with school readiness continue to alarm us. This would be a loss, for reasons both related and unrelated to literacy. Such a loss would be devastating if it were to occur as a consequence of what benefits play might hold for language and literacy development in our youngest children.

References

Ainsworth, M. C., Blehar, M. D., Waters, E., & Wall, S. (1978). *Patterns of attachment*. Hillsdale, NJ: Erlbaum.

Bondioli, A. (2001). The adult as a tutor in fostering children's symbolic play. In A. Goncu & E. L. Klein (Eds.), *Children in play, story, and school* (pp. 107–131). New York: Guilford Press.

Bornstein, M. H., & Tamis-LeMonda., C.S. (1995). Parent–child symbolic play: Three theories in search of an effect. *Developmental Review, 15,* 382–400.

Bus, A. G. (2001). Joint caregiver–child storybook reading: A route to literacy development. In S. B. Neuman & D. K. Dickinson (Eds.), *Handbook of early literacy research* (pp. 179–191). New York: Guilford Press.

Cassidy, J., & Berlin, L. J. (1994). The insecure/ambivalent pattern of attachment: Theory and research. *Child Development, 65,* 971–991.

Chall, J., & Dale, P. (1995). *Readabilty revisited: The new Dale–Chall readability formula*. Cambridge, MA: Brookline Books.

Clay, M. (1979). *The early detection of reading difficulties: A diagnostic survey with recovery procedures*. Portsmouth, NH: Heinemann.

Dickinson, D., & Tabors, P. (2001). *Beginning literacy with language: Young children learning at home and school*. Baltimore: Brookes.

Dickinson, D. K. (2001a). Large-group and free-play times: Conversational settings supporting language and literacy development. In D. Dickinson & P. Tabors (Eds.), *Beginning literacy with language* (pp. 223–256). Baltimore: Brookes.

Dickinson, D. K. (2001b). Putting the pieces together: Impact of preschool on children's language and literacy development in kindergarten. In D. Dickinson & P. Tabors (Eds.), *Beginning literacy with language* (pp. 257–288). Baltimore: Brookes.

Dickinson, D. K., St. Pierre, R. G., & Pettengill, J. (2004). High-quality classrooms: A key ingredient to family literacy programs' support for children's literacy. In B. H. Wasik (Ed.), *Handbook of family literacy* (pp. 137–154). Mahwah, NJ: Erlbaum.

Enz, B., & Christie, J. (1997). Teacher play interaction styles: Effects on play behavior and relationships with teacher training and experience. *International Journal of Early Childhood Education, 2,* 55–69.

Fein, G. G. (1975). The transformational analysis of pretending. *Developmental Psychology, 11*(3), 291–296.

Fein, G. G., & Fryer, M. G. (1995). Maternal contri- butions to early symbolic play competence. *Developmental Review, 15,* 367–381.

Heath, S. B. (1983). *Ways with words*. Cambridge, UK: Cambridge University Press.

International Reading Association & National Association for the Education of Young Children. (1998). Learning to read and write: Developmentally appropriate practice. *Reading Teacher, 52,* 193–216.

Isabella, R. A., & Belsky, J. (1991). Interactional synchrony and the origins of infant-mother attachment: A replication study. *Child Development, 62*(2), 373–384.

Johnson, J. E., Christie, J. F., & Yawkey, T. D. (1987). *Play and early childhood development*. Glenview, IL: Scott, Foresman.

Lamb, M.E. (1992). Parent–infant interaction, attachment, and socioemotional development in infancy. In R. M. Emde & R. J. Harmon (Eds.), *The development of attachment and affiliative systems* (pp. 195–211). New York: Plenum Press.

Magai, C., & McFadden, S. H. (1995). *The role of emotions in social and personality development: History, theory and research*. New York: Plenum Press.

McCabe, A., & Peterson, C. (1991). Getting the story: A longitudinal study of parental styles in eliciting narratives and developing narrative skill. In A. McCabe & C. Peterson (Eds.), *Developing narrative structure* (pp. 217–252). Hillsdale, NJ: Erlbaum.

Morrow, L. M. (1990). Preparing the classroom environment to promote literacy during play. *Early Childhood Research Quarterly, 5,* 537–554.

Morrow, L. M. (2005). *Literacy development in the early years: Helping children read and write* (5th ed.). Boston, Allyn & Bacon.

National Association for the Education of Young Children (2004). *NAEYC Academy for Early Childhood Program Accreditation*. Retrieved from http://www.naeyc.org/accreditation/academy.asp

National Early Literacy Panel Report. (2004). Washington, DC: National Institute for Literacy.

Neuman, S. B., & Roskos, K. (1990). The influence of literacy-enriched play settings on preschoolers' engagement with written language. *National Reading Conference Yearbook, 39,* 179–187.

Neuman, S. B., & Roskos, K. (1991). Peers as literacy informants: A description of young children's literacy conversations in play. *Early Childhood Research Quarterly, 6,* 233–248.

Neuman, S. B., & Roskos, K. (1992). Literacy objects as cultural tools: Effects on children's literacy behaviors in play. *Reading Research Quarterly, 27*(3), 202–225.

Neuman, S. B., & Roskos, K. (1993a). Access to print for children of poverty: Differential effects of adult mediation and literacy-enriched play settings on environmental and functional tasks. *American Educational Research Journal, 30*(1), 95–122.

Neuman, S. B., & Roskos, K. (1993b). Descriptive observations of adults' facilitation of literacy in young children's play. *Early Childhood Research Quarterly, 8,* 77–97.

Neuman, S. B., & Roskos, K. (1997). Literacy knowledge in practice: Contexts of participation for young writers and readers. *Reading Research Quarterly, 32*(1), 10–32.

Pellegrini, A. D. (1980). The relationship between kindergarteners' play and achievement in pre-reading, language, and writing. *Psychology in the Schools, 17,* 530–535.

Pellegrini, A. D. (1982). The construction of cohesive text by preschoolers in two play contexts. *Discourse Process, 5,* 101–108.

Pellegrini, A. D. (1985). The relations between symbolic play and literate behavior: A review and critique of the empirical literature. *Review of Educational Research, 55*(1), 107–121.

Pellegrini, A. D., & Galda, L. (1993). Ten years after: A reexamination of symbolic play and literacy research. *Reading Research Quarterly, 28,* 162–175.

Peterson, C., Jesso, B., & McCabe, A. (1999). Encouraging narratives in preschoolers: An intervention study. *Journal of Child Language, 26,* 49–67.

Piaget, J. (1962). *Play, dreams, and imitation in childhood.* New York: Norton. (Original work published 1945)

Reid, D. K., Hresko, W. P., & Hammill, D. D. (1981). *The test of early reading ability.* Los Angeles: Western Psychological Services.

Roskos, K. (1991). An inventory of literate behavior in the pretend play episodes of eight preschoolers. *Reading Research and Instruction, 30*(3), 39–52.

Sachs, J. (1980). The role of adult–child play in language development. In K. Rubin (Ed.), *Handbook of child psychology: Socialization, personality and social development* (pp. 33–48). San Francisco: Jossey-Bass.

Schrader, C. T. (1990). Symbolic play as a curricular tool for early literacy development. *Early Childhood Research Quarterly, 5,* 79–103.

Slade, A. (1987). Quality of attachment and early symbolic play. *Developmental Psychology, 23*(1), 78–85.

Smilansky, S., & Shefatya, L. (1990). *Facilitating play: A medium for promoting cognitive, socio-emotional and academic development in young children.* Gaithersburg, MD: Psychosocial and Educational Publications.

Snow, C., Burns, M. S., & Griffin, P. (1998). *Preventing reading difficulties.* Washington, DC: National Research Council.

Tizard, B., & Hughes, M. (1984). *Young children learning.* Cambridge, MA: Harvard University Press.

Vygotsky, L. (1967). Play and its role in the mental development of the child. *Soviet Psychology, 5,* 6–18. (Original work published 1933)

Vygotsky, L. (1978). *Mind in society: The development of higher psychological processes.* Cambridge, MA: Harvard University Press.

Wilcox-Herzog, A., & Kontos, S. (1998). The nature of teacher talk in early childhood classrooms and its relationship to children's play with objects and peers. *The Journal of Genetic Psychology, 159*(1), 30–44.

21

Encouraging Young Children's Language Interactions with Stories

MARGARET G. McKEOWN
ISABEL L. BECK

The characterization of reading to children as "a cornerstone of literacy development and classroom practice for over a century" (Brabham & Lynch-Brown 2002, p. 465) would probably not be considered an overstatement. We begin this chapter by briefly reviewing the research on reading aloud, focusing on the extent to which it has been shown to facilitate literacy development and on the identification of components of read-aloud interactions that have been found to be most effective. We also consider two aspects of oral language development—the amount of language heard in the home and children's participation in conversational interactions—and come to focus on their intersection with reading aloud. In the remainder of the chapter, we trace the development of an instructional approach in which we attempted to capture the benefits of read-alouds.

Positive correlations between being read to and eventual reading achievement have been published in journals for over 50 years (Teale, 2003). Listening to read-alouds offers children exposure to new vocabulary and new language forms, as well as opportunities to learn information and acquire cultural literacy. Listening to stories read brings children in touch with story structures and literary conventions that are prerequisite for understanding text (Cochran-Smith, 1984)

and exposes children to grammatical structures and discourse forms that are not typically found in conversational language (Bus, van IJzendoorn, & Pellegrini, 1995).

Bus, van IJzendoorn, and Pellegrini (1995) examined whether the potential that reading aloud seems to hold for children's literacy has the expected payoff by conducting a quantitative meta-analysis of 29 studies of parents reading aloud to their children. Key variables in the studies were either frequency of reading aloud or a composite of qualitative components of reading that included reading aloud. The researchers concluded that reading aloud is moderately to strongly related to language growth, emergent literacy, and reading achievement.

However, the conclusions of Bus and colleagues (1995) stand in contrast to those of Scarborough and Dobrich (1994), who also conducted a review of studies, those done between 1960 and 1993, on reading aloud. Their conclusion was that the effects are much more modest than is traditionally assumed. They suggest that large effects credited to reading aloud may actually have been due to other influences of the home environment, such as parental language ability, books in the home, or level of language in the home. Indeed, it seems as though such components may be the very ones that coexisted with reading aloud to create a composite in many of the studies that Bus et al. (1995) examined.

What about Reading Aloud Enhances Literacy Development?

It seems, then, that there is something within the sphere of reading aloud that affects literacy outcomes, but the specifics were not revealed through meta-analyses. Studies that took the issues into classrooms began to shed light on aspects of the reading-aloud situation itself that are productive for literacy outcomes. Researchers who observed teacher–student read-aloud interactions identified talk surrounding reading as the most valuable aspect of the activity for enhancing children's language development. Cochran-Smith (1984), Heath (1983), and Snow and her colleagues (Snow, 1993; Snow & Dickinson, 1991; Snow, Tabors, Nicholson, & Kurland, 1995) all highlight the role of the talk that surrounds book reading in becoming literate. Snow et al. (1995) and Dickinson and Tabors (1991) found evidence that preschool children's participation in talk about book reading enhances the growth of children's literacy skills. Further evidence for the role of talking about books comes from studies by Morrow (1992) and Freppon (1991), both of which compared literature-oriented and skills-oriented classrooms. In each study the researchers concluded that "talk surrounding the text" (Morrow, 1992, p. 253) or "getting children to think about what was going on in the story" (Freppon, 1991, p. 144) were key to literacy growth.

Of course, the nature and quality of talk accompanying text reading can be wide ranging. Researchers who have explored teachers' reading-aloud interactions in classrooms have identified a variety of styles and noted their differential effects on children's understanding (Dickinson & Smith, 1994; Teale & Martinez, 1996). From their observations of reading aloud in preschool classrooms, Dickinson and Smith (1994) initially identified three styles of reading aloud— coconstructive, didactic–interactional, and performance. They found that children whose teachers' styles had been categorized as "performance" had higher vocabulary scores a year later as kindergartners. But

Dickinson and Smith's (1994) more fine-grained examination revealed that certain features of interactions were more meaningful than holistic categories. Specifically, they found that interactions that occurred as the story was read, that involved both children and teachers, and that were analytic in nature led to positive effects on both vocabulary and story comprehension in kindergarten. Talk that was "analytic in nature" required children to reflect on the story content or language.

Teale and Martinez (1996) described the read-aloud styles of six teachers, each of whom was somewhat distinct in her approach to the text content and the kinds of interactions that she encouraged. The style of one teacher led to better story retelling by children. The teacher focused attention on important story information before and after the story, as well as during reading, and elicited responses from the children about the story episodes.

Teale and Martinez (1996) also pointed out some features of teachers' styles that may have interfered with comprehension. Chiefly, these included less effective ways of dealing with children's responses, such as allowing children to stray well beyond the storyline, or circumscribing the situation to allow only brief, literal responses, with the teacher quickly supplying answers if children hesitated. Their discussion suggested that the most effective encouragement of children's responses involves focusing on important story ideas and allowing children opportunities to reflect rather than expecting a quickly retrieved answer. Thus Teale and Martinez's (1996) and Dickinson and Smith's (1994) ideas about the most effective read-aloud strategies seem quite consistent.

Brabham and Lynch-Brown (2002) took the notion of styles of reading aloud a step further by conducting an intervention study to examine effects of teaching teachers to deliver read-alouds in a read-only, a performance, or a coconstructive interactive style. Their results showed the interactive style to be the most effective and the just-reading condition least effective for vocabulary and comprehension gains. They concluded that teacher explanations and student discussions were critical factors allowing students to derive benefits from texts read aloud.

Whitehurst and his colleagues developed an approach to read-alouds for young preschoolers that uses an interactive style (Whitehurst et al, 1988). Called dialogic reading, its intent is for the child to learn to become the storyteller over time. The adult's role is to ask open-ended questions and expand the child's verbalizations. Numerous studies have indicated that dialogic reading enhances expressive language and emergent literacy skills in children from all socioeconomic-status groups, even after relatively brief—for example, 4-week—interventions (see, for example, Crain-Thoreson & Dale, 1999; Whitehurst et al., 1994; Whitehurst et al., 1999).

Learning to Build Meaning through Talk

The finding of the importance of not just reading and not just talk, but also interactional talk requiring attention and response from the children, dovetails strongly with other current understandings about learning. First and most generally, current understandings of the learning process make it clear that successful learning requires more than mere exposure to information. Rather, learning requires attention to incoming information, connection of pieces of information and integration of new information and prior knowledge (see, for example, Brown, Bransford, Ferrara, & Campione, 1983; Sternberg, 1979, 1982).

More specific is what the field has discovered about child language learning over the past decade. Hart and Risley's (1995) longitudinal, in-depth research has shown that children's language learning depends on their exposure to and involvement in language, with amount of talk being the key to higher language achievement. Hart and Risley studied children learning to talk by recording the talk in children's homes from the time they spoke their first words. The researchers found that the number of words to which children were exposed in their homes made profound differences in their language development at age 3 and was subsequently related to their accomplishment in literacy in school at age 9. Such language features as using a positive tone and asking children and giving them choices rather than telling them

were associated with higher literacy accomplishments at school ages.

As Hart and Risley (1999) probed their data further, they found that the children whose language continued to develop most productively in the early years were those who not only heard language spoken but who also learned to take part in that talk through the conversational interaction of listening to and responding to another. Hart and Risley had found that the families they studied had devoted similar amounts of talk to major activities such as socializing children and getting them fed and dressed. But talkative families engaged in added talk that concerned topics beyond the necessities of everyday life. In these families, parents provided more language experience before age 3 and involved their children in a reciprocity of everyday interactions that blended the amount of parent talk and the amount of child practice talking.

Hart and Risley (1999) found that the amount of reciprocal, conversational interaction between parent and child per hour was profoundly related to children's verbal and cognitive competence. They reasoned that these advantages accrued because, in conversations, each partner must say something related to a shared topic and respond immediately with an utterance that enables conversation to continue. In order to continue their role in the conversation, children need to listen for vocabulary content and attempt utterance forms so they can construct responses. Being involved in conversation familiarizes children with what might be said in the language and prompts them to practice selecting what can be said appropriately in the immediate circumstances.

As Hart and Risley (1999) imply, learning to engage in interactive conversation is a language learning task on a higher cognitive level than the initial accomplishments of acquisition. The children they observed all successfully began speaking and could make themselves understood and communicate their needs, wants, and so forth. Yet long after this point, the researchers note, only gradually do children learn how to take something someone says and use it to answer that person in a way that converts turn-taking to conversation. The notion of transforming turn-taking into conversation has significant implications for classroom learning, especially for learning from discourse surrounding text and, in the present case, text read aloud.

The Challenge of Decontextualized Language

The content of text represents a new aspect of language for young listeners. Book language is decontextualized, removed from everyday tangible and familiar experiences within the immediate context. In order to make sense of text they hear, listeners need to build ideas from words alone. Participating in decontextualized language, forming ideas about what was in a book, and expressing them in ways that make sense to others are the ingredients of building communication competence. Because facility with decontextualized language underlies literacy competence, getting children involved in talking about the ideas in stories they hear promotes literacy growth. The involvement in talk that will promote literacy needs to exhibit certain characteristics. Hart and Risley's (1999) distinction between turn-taking and conversation can help build a representation of what productive, literacy-promoting talk looks like. Although the labels *interactive talk* and *coconstructive talk* have become familiar in the literature, what they really represent may not yet have become clear. Encouraging children to talk about a story's ideas, acknowledging their responses, and moving on does not fulfill the prescription for engaging children in talk and in thinking about ideas.

The literature on reading aloud documents that the most effective practices are far from the most common ones. Dickinson, McCabe, and Anastasopoulos (2003) and Teale (2003) reached this conclusion from their long-term research in the area. Other researchers have also found lack of the practices identified as effective. These studies include Lickteig and Russell's (1993) discussion of studies showing that 90% of teachers read for entertainment and enjoyment rather than for instructional purposes and Hoffman, Roser, and Battle's (1993) study of 537 teachers in which they found that discussion virtually never took place during reading and that few teachers evoked children's responses to the literature. However, we in the field of reading aloud cannot think our work is done if we simply turn classroom read-aloud time into talking time—not even if the talk is always about story ideas and children get to contribute as the story moves along.

With the foregoing perspectives on reading aloud and talk as background, we turn to considering our attempt to capture the benefits of read-alouds through promoting talk about books, Text Talk. We describe early implementations of the approach in which teachers began to prompt students to talk. But our focus in this chapter is on how, through continued feedback and support of the teachers, the talk shifted from turn-taking to conversation that engaged students in ideas and scaffolded their building of meaning. Our purpose is to show the effort it takes to get to that level of talk and, more important, how distinct it is from more shallow talk and thus how important for influencing literacy development.

Text Talk

Text Talk is a read-aloud approach designed to engage children in talking about the ideas in a story as the story is read (Beck & McKeown, 2001; McKeown & Beck, 2003). Our motivation for developing Text Talk was our reading of the literature and our own classroom observations, which were consistent with those described in the literature (Dickinson & Smith, 1994; Teale & Martinez, 1996). At the start of our Text Talk work, we observed kindergarten and first-grade teachers reading to their classrooms and found that they tended not to involve children in focusing on and discussing major story ideas. Often there was no interaction when the story was read, and when there was, it revolved around simple questions asking children to retrieve a text idea that had just been presented (e.g., "What did Terrance find in his room?" "His missing shoe"). The most frequent pattern we observed was the teacher reading the story from start to finish without any input from the children.

After the teacher finished reading, she often engaged students in brief discussions that focused mainly on whether they had liked the story and whether they had ever experienced anything that was similar to some event in the story. What was not present in these discussions was a sense of what the children actually had understood about the story. Our observations of such lessons prompted us to question whether children had followed the story well enough to have constructed a coherent representation of its events and ideas.

Text Talk was developed to scaffold children's comprehension of a story as the events and ideas unfold. Toward that end, the teacher poses interspersed questions that ask children to consider the ideas in the story and connect them as the story moves along. For instance, "What's happening now?" asks children to describe an event from the story. Given that stories are basically structured on a chain of events, describing an event is important for building a representation. A question such as "What do we know so far about their family?" requires children to put together several pieces of information, which may or may not come from different parts of a story. The question, "How have things changed?" represents a linchpin in comprehension of a story, because changes in characters or actions typically drive the plot of stories. The descriptions and integration of story ideas that emerge in response to such questions model the development of a coherent text representation.

Beyond building comprehension of the specific story, the questions asked in Text Talk enhance children's language development because they encourage children to articulate their thinking and put together ideas from the story. Consider the amount of language and the complexity of ideas that were elicited from kindergarten and first-grade children in June, after being involved in Text Talk since the beginning of the school year.

Example 1: Kindergarten

TEACHER: Why are his parents happy [that his blanket is now a handkerchief]?

STUDENT: Because he don't have to drag it around no more like babies drag their stuff around and get it dirty.

Example 2: First grade

TEACHER: What does Livingstone Mouse have to do?

STUDENT: His mom says you're getting too big for my nest and then she said you got to go live by yourself and make your own nest.

These examples represent the general finding from a study of four Text Talk classrooms in which children's responses from read-aloud discussions before the teacher began using Text Talk were compared with Text Talk discussions. We found that in baseline lessons, children's responses averaged 2.1 words in length, whereas Text Talk responses averaged 7.65 words (McKeown & Beck, 2003). It is important to emphasize that these examples and data came from classrooms in which Text Talk had been ongoing for most of the school year. But as children are first asked to interact with a text by articulating story ideas, their responses are often limited.

Children's Early Responses to Text

When asked a question about a text, the most common type of response children give is to parrot part of the text that has just been read. Although such verbatim responses are most often relevant to the question asked, they do not represent the kind of thinking that we want children to develop, the kind of thinking that even young children are quite capable of—with some practice.

Other tendencies that characterize children's early interactions with text are to respond with ideas other than those asked about and to address the text ideas being considered in an incomplete way. We consider these two tendencies next.

Another Road Taken

Sometimes when children are asked a question about text ideas or events, their response takes the conversation down another road. An example of this that has become a classic for us happened as the teacher began reading *Curious George Takes a Job* (Rey, 1975), which starts as follows: "This is George. He lived in the zoo. He was a good little monkey and always very curious. He wanted to find out what was going on outside the zoo." At this point the teacher asked, "What do we know so far about George?" and the first response was "He likes bananas." Given that George is a monkey, he probably does like bananas. But the point of the teacher's probe was to get students to start thinking about what is going on in the story.

It seems quite clear that the "bananas" response comes from prior knowledge, perhaps from a previously read story about Curious George or general knowledge about what monkeys like to eat. We found that prior knowledge was a common source for children's responses because, we surmised, it was easier for them to access their knowledge base than to focus on the decontextualized information about characters and events that were newly presented to them from a text.

Another road children went down as a source for their responses was to take information from an earlier part of a text that had already been established through discussion. Consider a section in *Harry the Dirty Dog* (Zion, 1984) in which Harry decides to return home because he's tired and hungry after his day romping around and getting dirty. To establish that Harry is now on his way home, the teacher asks, "Now what is Harry up to?" and a child responded, "He got all dirty." It seems likely that this response was offered because Harry's getting dirty had been the subject of earlier discussion, and thus the information was easily accessible to the child. In contrast, switching gears to Harry's deciding to go home would have been more difficult because those ideas represented newly presented information that had not yet been dealt with.

On the Road, but Not in the Lane

In contrast to responses that are not based on the text information asked about, another type of limited response *is* based on relevant text information but does not fully address the essence of the question that was asked. As such, we think of these as "on the road, but not in the lane." Consider the beginning of the story *Brave Irene* (Steig, 1986), in which Irene's mother has just finished making a dress for the duchess for that evening's ball but is feeling too ill to deliver the dress. The teacher asks, "What problem does Mrs. Bobbin have?" and a child replies, "She's sick." That response is correct and text based; however, it doesn't establish the effect of being sick on how the story unfolds. The problem of the story is that Mrs. Bobbin is feeling too ill to deliver the dress, which is the initiating event for the storyline. That is, Irene takes it upon herself to deliver the dress, with adventures along the way.

Another way that children can be on the road but not in the lane is illustrated by a response to an early section in *Dr. DeSoto* (Steig, 1982), when an ailing fox comes to Dr. DeSoto, the mouse dentist, for treatment. The fox is told, " 'I cannot treat you, sir,' " and referred to the sign outside the office, which reads "Cats & other dangerous animals not accepted for treatment." The teacher asks, "Why did Dr. DeSoto say, 'I cannot treat you, sir?' " and a child responds "Because he's a fox." Although a teacher might well surmise that the child understands and is implying that being a fox makes him a dangerous patient for Dr. DeSoto, the response as articulated does not explicitly make that connection.

The Need for Teacher Follow-Up: Round 1

The limited nature of children's early responses means that the job of constructing meaning often does not get done in one question-and-response turn. So there is need to follow up children's initial responses with prompts for elaboration and completion. Doing so turns out to be the most challenging aspect of implementing Text Talk for teachers because there seem to be two almost reflexive reactions that get in the way.

One common reaction is to accept children's limited responses. That is, when a child responds with some text information, albeit information that only partially addresses a question, teachers often have some difficulty recognizing that such a response is incomplete. Rather, it is not uncommon for teachers to accept such responses as sufficient and continue on. For instance, in the previous Dr. DeSoto example, consider the child's response, "because he's a fox," to the question about why Dr. De Soto said "I cannot treat you, sir." It would be easy to accept such a response, surmising that the child understood the danger that a fox would present to a mouse. But it would serve several functions to follow up by inquiring, "And why might that be a problem for Dr. DeSoto?"

One function is to ensure that the child does indeed understand the hazards of a relationship between a fox and a mouse dentist.

Second, prompting the child to fill in the connection can help develop children's ability to articulate ideas; and third, making the full idea public can promote the comprehension of other children in the classroom who may not have understood that connection.

Similarly, in the example presented earlier from *Brave Irene,* the child's response, "She's sick" to the question "What problem does Mrs. Bobbin have?" does not establish the significance of that information to the story. That significance could be developed by directly asking, "Why is being sick such a problem for Mrs. Bobbin right now?"

Another common way for teachers to react to children's contributions that do not fully respond to an issue at hand is to take over the task and fill in the needed information. Consider the earlier example from *Harry the Dirty Dog,* in which a child responded with prior text information that Harry had gotten dirty, rather than about the current event in the story. In this case, the teacher said, "We already talked about how Harry got dirty, but the part we just read is about Harry being worried about his family and wanting to go home," thus providing the information herself. But the teacher might have gotten the children to provide that information if after she acknowledged what the child had given—"Yes, we know Harry likes to get dirty"—she provided a prompt that invited the children to address the issue at hand, such as, "But what's Harry up to now?"

We viewed teachers' reacting to incomplete responses by providing the salient information themselves as teachers' attempts to "fix" things for children, driven by a motivation to help them, to support them, and not to let them flounder. But here's the rub—giving children information in cases such as those discussed is not as helpful as getting them to figure out and articulate the information themselves, because a major purpose of read-aloud discussion is to develop children's ability to make sense of and respond to decontextualized language.

The Need for Teacher Follow-Up: Round 2 and Beyond

The foregoing examples suggested that salient ideas could be developed with one round of follow-up conversation between teacher and children. It is often the case, however, that a follow-up question still does not bring forth a completely expressed idea. The teacher may need to go in again and again to elicit and build complete ideas. When that happens, the resulting conversations are messier than the ones we have provided so far. Let us consider an example of that messier domain.

The following example is from a first-grade class's discussion about the story *Space Case* (Marshall, 1980), in which an alien comes to earth on Halloween and starts trick-or-treating with a group of children. The focus of this part of the discussion is the following text:

> *Trick or treat beeped the thing.*
> *"There's something weird about that new kid," whispered Lily.*

The teacher wants to draw children's attention to the alien's nonhuman characteristic. Notice her first question and a student's response:

TEACHER: What made Lily say "There's something weird about that new kid"?

STUDENT: Because he said "Trick or treat" and he sounded like an alien.

This student is in the right ballpark because he understands that the "new kid" is not saying "trick or treat" like a normal child, but the heart of the issue is that, rather than speaking, the alien can only beep.

Notice in the following that the teacher acknowledges the student's response by repeating it, but then questions a part of it by asking the children to focus on whether the alien actually *said* "trick or treat."

TEACHER: Wait a minute, [the student] said he said "Trick or treat" and he said it like an alien. Did he say "Trick or treat"? How did he say it like an alien? What does that mean, "say it like an alien"?

STUDENT: He said it beeping.

This student brings in the beeping, and as shown next the teacher acknowledges the response. Then she goes on to ask for a connection with the issue of "something weird about that new kid."

TEACHER: Exactly. He beeped "trick or treat." Why was that weird?

STUDENT: 'Cause a kid ain't supposed to beep it. They're supposed to say it.

This child explains weird by contrasting beeping with speaking. The teacher repeats the idea but elaborates it slightly, giving the idea more articulate expression.

TEACHER: OK, a person doesn't beep "trick or treat"; they say it. He didn't talk, he made a funny sound.

Notice what the teacher did in these exchanges. Throughout the discussion she monitored the responses, evaluated what had been said and what still needed to be added, and then figured out a way to provide some direction for children's responses. She did not, however, fill in and provide the information for them.

Filling in Is Not Following Up

Analogously, as children need practice to build facility in providing thoughtful responses to text, teachers also need to become accustomed to dealing with student–text interactions in a different way. An early response that teachers have is that students have too great a difficulty responding to the kind of open questions that are characteristic of Text Talk. Consider what a teacher, Ms. K., wrote in her Text Talk journal (which all collaborating teachers kept) early in her work with Text Talk.

> The questions that say, "So, what is George doing now?" they don't understand. However, if I reword the question and coax them along, they do much better. They have trouble answering "What happened just now?" questions.

Note from the transcript that follows that what Ms. K. means by "coax them along" is to go through a text piece by piece rather than helping the children to connect ideas. As such, she is taking ideas apart rather than supporting the children in putting them together. In the following transcript, Ms. K.'s class is reading a *Curious George* story, and at this point in the discussion Ms. K. apparently wants the children to notice that

George is about to get into some trouble because of his curiosity. The text under consideration is:

> George stopped working and pressed his nose against the window. Two painters were working inside. George was fascinated. Painting looked a lot more fun than washing windows.

Notice in the following exchanges that Ms. K. starts with an open question in an attempt to draw attention to the idea that George is getting bored with what he's doing and becomes distracted by something that probably is going to get him into trouble. But as soon as she gets the first student's limited response, her follow-up invites another limited response:

TEACHER: How do things look now for George?

STUDENT: Terrible.

TEACHER: Terrible, because what's getting ready to go on?

Although Ms. K.'s follow-up is conceptually in a useful arena—to get the student to elaborate on why things look terrible—the wording narrows down the response space rather than providing an open invitation to develop the idea. The wording of the question sets forth an expectation of a very specific response. A question that would, in contrast, leave more space for children to develop a response might be, "What do you mean things look terrible?" Next we return to the discussion as it unfolded it the classroom.

STUDENT: He's looking . . . he's curious.

TEACHER: He's about to become curious, about what?

Here, rather than prompting the student to explain George's curiosity, Ms. K. merely asks her to fill in the blank, which, as can be seen, she does:

STUDENT: Painting.

TEACHER: About painting. He's about to become curious about painting. And is he supposed to become curious about painting?

After Ms. K. has made explicit the connection between painting and being curious, her next question allows only a yes or no response.

CLASS: No.

TEACHER: What is he supposed to be doing?

It is not relevant that George has stopped his assigned job of washing windows; what's relevant is that George has been distracted by the painters.

STUDENT: Washing the windows.

TEACHER: So, it looks like George might be getting ready to get into some . . .

CLASS: Trouble.

In comparison with the earlier transcript from the discussion of *Space Case*, in which the teacher encouraged the students to develop what they were saying by elaborating and connecting ideas, in the *Curious George* transcript the teacher's questioning limits students' responses.

From our experiences working with teachers, it appears that teachers' skepticism about the extent to which children can articulate ideas on their own is partly responsible for the kind of questioning in the *George* transcript. And because the children provide very limited responses to begin with, teachers' skepticism about children's ability is reinforced. Thus when the limited responses come forth, teachers very quickly resort to stepping out the ideas in a piecemeal fashion or filling in the ideas for the children. Recall Ms. K.'s journal entry, noted earlier, that suggested that she felt she needed to provide the children with very specified question prompts.

Principles toward Effective Interactions

In the course of our early work with Text Talk, we observed teachers' initial efforts to prompt children to respond to text ideas and noted issues that arose at meetings and in teachers' journals as they reflected on their lessons. As we shared our observations and worked with the teachers, several principles for most effectively developing children's ability to respond emerged, which we discuss in the next sections.

Keeping the Purpose in Mind and Models in Sight

Teachers' past experiences with talk about stories are, characteristically, that children are well able to answer questions that require simple responses or literal details and that, indeed, they are eager to do so. Teachers are encouraged when they witness many hands go up in response to such questions as "So, what is George getting into?" and "Where is George now?" In contrast, teachers can become discouraged when they see more tentative reactions to open questions. Because teachers may not be immediately presented with a sea of raised hands, they may interpret that children are less involved. But immediate and easy responses only indicate involvement at a surface level. Developing children's ability to get to a deeper, more meaningful level takes time and effort. Yet if teachers limit their questions to ones children can already answer with ease, this development is unlikely to take place.

Two ways to mediate teachers' early discouragement are to reinforce the purpose of Text Talk and to provide positive models. First, we found it important to keep reminding teachers that the purpose of Text Talk is not merely to get questions answered but also to develop students' abilities to construct meaning by interacting with story events and ideas through elaboration. Second, the most effective way we were able to persuade teachers to withhold their skepticism was to provide concrete evidence that children with similar backgrounds to their students had learned to respond in richer ways. We were able to provide them with many examples that contrasted children's responses to constrained questions, which inherently limit responses to a few words, with the richer ways children could respond to open questions. These examples came from our early pilot work, in which we observed typical read-alouds in kindergarten and first-grade classrooms and modeled Text Talk lessons in those same classrooms. Table 21.1 presents the kinds of examples we shared with teachers. The two sets of questions and responses, constrained and open, come from discussions of *Harry the Dirty Dog* (Zion, 1984) in two classrooms.

TABLE 21.1. Examples of Children's Responses to Constrained Questions and Open Questions

Constrained questions	Responses
As they started scrubbing, what came off?	dirt
Harry liked everything except _____.	a bath
Is Harry glad to be home?	yes
How did the family feel when they couldn't find Harry?	sad

Open questions	Responses
How does what Harry did fit in with what we already know about him?	He doesn't really want to get clean, he just wants to stay dirty.
When the family looked out and said, "There's a strange dog in the backyard," why did they call Harry a strange dog?	Because when he got all dirty, his family didn't know who he was.
What's Harry up to now?	He decided to dig a hole and get the brush so he could wash and then they would recognize him.
They called Harry "this little doggie." What does that tell us?	That means that they don't know that it's their doggie. They don't know its name, so they just call him little doggie.
Why do you think the children shouted, "Come quick"?	Because the kids knowed that that's the dog they had.

Easy Back-and-Forth between Teacher and Student

Even as teachers' skepticism was allayed by a model of what to aim for and examples of language that children could produce, making it happen was not straightforward. Rather, it required developing new ways of responding to students' responses. One feature that helped set a new response pattern in place was a conversational style of interaction. The aims of Text Talk—encouraging children's language production and building meaning from story content—are well served by a conversational style of teacher-led talk. It is formed around easy back-and-forth between teacher and student, as illustrated in the following excerpt:

TEACHER: Can the wind really talk?

STUDENT: NO!

STUDENT: The wind wants the dress.

TEACHER: But we just said the wind can't really talk, so what's happening?

STUDENT: Wait—can you repeat the question?

TEACHER: If the wind really can't talk, what's happening?

STUDENT: She's hearing things.

TEACHER: So, do you mean she's just thinking that's what she hears?

The essence of using this conversational pattern is that it changes the relationship of teacher response to students from evaluation of a response's accuracy to consideration of the content of the response itself. In doing so, the teacher attempts to uncover the student's thinking that led to the response and can then provide scaffolding to encourage elaboration, connection, or, if needed, modify the ideas.

Drawing on the Language of Students' Responses

When a teacher's response uses the content of a student's comment, it keeps the conversation going in a coherent direction and invites the next participant to connect to what is being said. Repetition of ideas is a characteristic of real conversation. It is a way of letting our conversation partners know that they have been heard and lets them know where our next move in the conversation will go. Consider the example below:

TEACHER: What's happening to Hansel and Gretel?

STUDENT: They're getting lost.

TEACHER: How did that happen to Hansel and Gretel?

STUDENT: They walked in the woods

TEACHER: So they went for a walk in the woods? And how did that connect with what [the student] said about getting lost?

STUDENT: They were walking, walking, and it got dark.

TEACHER: OK, so they walked until it was dark. So they couldn't find their way any more; they were lost.

Notice how the teacher's first response implicitly reflected the idea of getting lost from the student's response and asked students to take it farther (How did *that* happen . . .?). In her subsequent responses the teacher restated what the student had said and connected it back to the idea of getting lost until the complex event of walking in the woods until dark and not being able to find their way was developed.

Making the Best of Scarce Resources: Modeling and Pursuing

As indicated earlier, using the children's comments as connective tissue that provides focus for a discussion of story ideas works very well—as long as there is something to grab onto in what students contribute. But in many cases children's responses are very sparse—merely a word or two—or have little relevance to story ideas; what to do then? Two directions that can work are teacher modeling of comments about the story and doggedly pursuing whatever sparse fuel there is. Following are examples of each.

The following example of modeling comes from a first-grade discussion of the story *The Cow Who Wouldn't Come Down* (Johnson, 1993), an improbable tale of a stubborn cow who insists on flying about. The teacher is trying to establish why the cow's flying is a problem for its owner, Miss Rosemary, after reading the following:

TEACHER: *Miss Rosemary knew Gertrude had a mind of her own. Even so, the day*

that Gertrude took to flying, it put Miss Rosemary in something of a tizzy.

"This won't do. It just won't do!" she fussed and stewed. There was no telling what people would say. Besides, Miss Rosemary hadn't the slightest notion how to milk a flying cow.

TEACHER: How does Miss Rosemary like having a flying cow?

STUDENT: Good.

TEACHER: She thinks it's good? Listen to that part again.

"This won't do. It just won't do!" she fussed and stewed. There was no telling what people would say. Besides, Miss Rosemary hadn't the slightest notion how to milk a flying cow.

So, how does Miss Rosemary like having a flying cow?

STUDENT: Sad.

STUDENT: Mad.

TEACHER: Well, I think she's worried because she doesn't know how to milk a flying cow.

Notice that children had very little insight about Miss Rosemary's problem. The first child provides the opposite interpretation for Miss Rosemary's reaction to her cow's mobility. The teacher then regroups, asks the question again, but gets no more of a response than if she had simply provided a fill-in-the-blank probe. The teacher then presents her own thoughts on the topic. Although she does, in essence, provide the answer for the children, the point is that she gave two opportunities for children to see the types of questions she wanted them to consider, and then modeled how such a question would be responded to.

Another tack that teachers have taken is to pursue meaning, going back to children for further responses, even though the responses are sparse, recasting the ideas in the question and eventually getting something developed. The following is such an example, from a kindergarten class reading the story *Harriet* (Inkpen, 1998), about a pet hamster who escapes her cage and wanders off into the great outdoors. The teacher is trying to establish the point that the sounds and smells outside are new to Harriet because she has not been outdoors before. The text under discussion is as follows:

> *Above her, giant plants spread their leafy fingers. And over them all stretched the blue sky. Harriet's whiskers quivered. Her nose twitched. The air was full of new sounds and smells.*

TEACHER: New sounds and new smells. What do you think that tells us?

STUDENT 1: Hearing something.

TEACHER: Yes, she heard something, but what does it mean, new sounds and new smells Why's it say that?

STUDENT 2: New sounds.

TEACHER: Why do you think the story calls them new sounds? What's that about? It's new. Well, tell me, what does that mean about Harriet? What does that tell you about Harriet?

STUDENT 1: He eat, he hears cows.

STUDENT 2: It's a she!

TEACHER: It's a she, yes. But it's talking about new sounds and new smells? What's that tell you?

STUDENT 3: It's new, new (*inaudible—noise*).

TEACHER: Hmm? It's new? Why do you think they're new? They're new for Harriet? Think about what we already know about Harriet?

STUDENT 1: New sounds.

TEACHER: Why are they new?

STUDENT 2: Cause . . . cause um, cause they um just moved in.

TEACHER: She just moved in? What do we know about Harriet? Why are they new for her?

STUDENT 3: Because she's been in her cage for a long long time.

TEACHER: Ooh yes!

STUDENT 3: It's old. The cage is old.

TEACHER: She's been in her cage for a long long time, so she probably didn't hear a lot of these things or smell a lot of these things. I think you got it exactly right. This is all new to her outside. Good thinking.

Notice how the teacher kept the ideas of "new sounds and new smells" in play the en-

tire time and also kept asking children to consider that notion in conjunction with what they knew about Harriet. So the teacher was essentially pointing out the relevant pieces with which the children could make meaning from the text segment that had just been read.

Reread Text as Often as Needed

There is a clear need to help children keep the text in mind if they are to think about text ideas in meaningful ways. This may seem pretty obvious, but we have found it frequently the case that once the text is read, it is not returned to. If children have difficulty responding to a question, the teacher is often more likely to provide extra information for children than to go back and reread a relevant part of the text to prompt children's thinking.

Because working to make sense of decontextualized language is rather new for young children, it makes sense that they may need to meet that language more than once in order to deal with it successfully. Going back to the text to reread also models for children that dealing with text is not a linear process, but that in the course of reading, a reader returns to the text as a resource for building meaning. Such modeling may prevent habits we have seen some young readers develop when, in response to a question about what they are reading, they look off into space as if they are thinking hard— rather than checking the text and using that to develop their ideas. We suspect that many young readers think of it as "cheating" to look back at the text if they don't know how to answer rather than seeing the text as the fundamental material with which they are working. Rereading portions of text helps children build the understanding that to successfully comprehend text a reader needs to deal with what is in the text rather than guessing and verbalizing associations that come to mind.

Another characteristic of rereading that makes it a good strategy for teachers to use is that the text is always there. If a question brings no response from children or information that is garbled, off-target, or otherwise puzzling, coming up with a useful follow-up question can be difficult for a teacher. But it can be very effective to simply say "Let's think about that again" and reread a portion of text to ground the discussion.

Final Comments

The messages that can be taken from the work we've described deal with the kind of talk that promotes children's language growth, ways that teachers can encourage that kind of talk, the pitfalls involved in making it happen, and the value of such talk. Previous work has emphasized that it is not just talk about a story that matters; it is thoughtful talk about the important ideas in a story that is key. We have tried to demonstrate that producing such talk requires "growing" it. That is, just asking thoughtful question does not produce rich, meaningful responses from young children, at least not at first. Rather, the teacher needs to skillfully deal with responses, aiming to get children to explain, elaborate, and connect their ideas. This is a difficult task because there can be a fine line between providing children some direction that helps them elaborate their ideas and filling in information that in essence does the work for them. Especially when children's initial responses are sparse or garbled, it is hard to know how much information to give and how to leave the meat of the work for children to do.

Achieving the right balance between providing direction and leaving space is as much an issue of keying into the language of children's interactions as to the text ideas. That is, it requires really listening to and understanding the content of children's responses. Teachers we have worked with indicated that in order to scaffold children's responses, they have needed to learn to listen to what children are saying in more attentive and active ways. And they have noted that such listening takes a lot of effort, especially at first. So why do it? Because of the importance of prompting children to interact with text ideas in ways that help them think, organize their thoughts, and produce language. Such talk is an essential component of guiding children to make sense of decontextualized language. And it must be emphasized that comprehension of decontextualized language—written texts—is a major source of learning and thus is at the center of academic achievement.

References

Beck, I. L., & McKeown, M. G. (2001). Text Talk: Capturing the benefits of read-aloud experiences for young children. *Reading Teacher, 55*(1), 10–20.

Brabham, E. G., & Lynch-Brown, C. (2002). Effects of teachers' reading-aloud styles on vocabulary acquisition and comprehension of students in the early elementary grades. *Journal of Educational Psychology, 94*(3), 465–473.

Brown, A. L., Bransford, J. D., Ferrara, R. A., & Campione, J. C. (1983). Learning, remembering, and understanding. In J. H. Flavell & E. M. Markman (Eds.), *Handbook of child psychology* (4th ed.): Vol. 3. *Cognitive development* (pp. 420–494). New York: Wiley.

Bus, A., van IJzendoorn, M., & Pellegrini, A. (1995). Joint book reading makes for success in learning to read: A meta-analysis on intergenerational transmission of literacy. *Review of Educational Research, 65,* 1–21.

Cochran-Smith, M. (1984). *The making of a reader.* Norwood, NJ: Ablex.

Crain-Thoreson, C., & Dale, P. S. (1999). Enhancing linguistic performance: Parents and teachers as book reading partners for children with language delays. *Topics in Early Childhood Special Education, 19,* 28–39.

Dickinson, D. K., McCabe, A., & Anastasopoulos, L. (2003). A framework for examining book reading in early childhood classrooms. In A. van Kleeck, S. A. Stahl, & E. B. Bauer (Eds.), *On reading books to children* (pp. 95–113). Mahwah, NJ: Erlbaum.

Dickinson, D. K., & Smith, M. W. (1994). Long-term effects of preschool teachers' book readings on low-income children's vocabulary and story comprehension. *Reading Research Quarterly, 29,* 104–122.

Dickinson, D. K., & Tabors, P. O. (1991). Early literacy: Linkages between home, school, and literacy achievement at age five. *Journal of Research in Childhood Education, 6,* 30–46.

Freppon, P. A. (1991). Children's concepts of the nature and purpose of reading and writing in different instructional settings. *Journal of Reading Behavior: A Journal of Literacy, 23,* 139–163.

Hart, B., & Risley, T. (1995). *Meaningful differences.* Baltimore: Brookes.

Hart, B., & Risley, T. (1999). *The social world of children learning to talk.* Baltimore: Brookes.

Heath, S. B. (1983). *Ways with words.* Cambridge, UK: Cambridge University Press.

Hoffman, J. V., Roser, N. L., & Battle, J. (1993). Reading aloud in classrooms: From the modal to a "model." *Reading Teacher, 46,* 496–503.

Inkpen, D. (1998). *Harriet.* New York: Hodder Children's Books.

Johnson, P. B. (1993). *The cow who couldn't come down.* New York: Orchard Books.

Lickteig, M., & Russell, J. (1993). Elementary teachers' read-aloud practices. *Reading Improvement, 30,* 202–208.

Marshall, E. (1980). *Space case.* New York: Penguin Books.

McKeown, M. G., & Beck, I. L. (2003). Taking advantage of read alouds to help children make sense of decontextualized language. In A. van Kleeck, S. A. Stahl, & E. B. Bauer (Eds.), *Storybook reading* (pp. 159–176). Mahwah, NJ: Erlbaum.

Morrow, L. M. (1992). The impact of a literature-based program on literacy achievement, use of literature, and attitudes of children from minority backgrounds. *Reading Research Quarterly, 27,* 250–275.

Rey, H. A. (1975). *Curious George takes a job.* Boston: Houghton Mifflin.

Scarborough, H. S., & Dobrich, W. (1994). On the efficacy of reading to preschoolers. *Developmental Review, 14,* 245–302.

Snow, C. E. (1993). Families as social contexts for literacy development. In C. Daiute (Ed.), *The development of literacy through social interaction* (No. 61, pp. 11–24). San Francisco: Josey-Bass.

Snow, C. E., & Dickinson, D. K. (1991). Some skills that aren't basic in a new conception of literacy. In A. Purves & T. Jennings (Eds.), *Literate systems and individual lives: Perspectives on literacy and schooling* (pp. 175–213). Albany, NY: State University of New York Press.

Snow, C. E., Tabors, P. O., Nicholson, P. A., & Kurland, B. F. (1995). SHELL: Oral language and early literacy skills in kindergarten and first-grade children. *Journal of Research in Childhood Education, 10,* 37–47.

Steig, W. (1982). *Doctor DeSoto.* New York: Farrar, Straus & Giroux.

Steig, W. (1986). *Brave Irene.* New York: Farrar, Straus & Giroux.

Sternberg, R. J. (1979). The nature of mental abilities. *American Psychologist, 34,* 214–230.

Sternberg, R. J. (1982). A componential approach to intellectual development. In R. J. Sternberg (Ed.), *Advances in the psychology of human intelligence* (Vol. 1, pp. 413–463). Hillsdale, NJ: Erlbaum.

Teale, W. H. (2003). Reading aloud to young children as a classroom instructional activity: Insights from research and practice. In A. van Kleeck, S. A. Stahl, & E. B. Bauer (Eds.), *On reading books to children* (pp. 114–139). Mahwah, NJ: Erlbaum.

Teale, W. H., & Martinez, M. G. (1996). Reading aloud to young children: Teachers' reading styles and kindergartners' text comprehension. In C. Pontecorvo, M. Orsolini, B. Burge, & L. B. Resnick (Eds.), *Children's early text construction* (pp. 321–344). Mahwah, NJ: Erlbaum.

Whitehurst, G. J., Arnold, D. S., Epstein, J. N., Angell, A. L., Smith M., & Fischel, J. E. (1994). A picture book reading intervention in day care and home for children from low-income families. *Developmental Psychology, 30*(5), 679–689.

Whitehurst, G. J., Falco, F., Lonigan, C. J., Fischel, J. E., DeBaryshe, B. D., Valdez-Menchaca, M. C., & Caulfield, M. (1988). Accelerating language development through picture-book reading. *Developmental Psychology, 24,* 552–558.

Whitehurst, G. J., Zevenbergen, A. A., Crone, D. A., Schultz, M. D., Velting, O. N., & Fischel, J. E. (1999). Outcomes of an emergent literacy intervention from Head Start through second grade. *Journal of Educational Psychology, 91,* 261–272.

Zion, G. (1984). *Harry the dirty dog.* New York: HarperCollins.

22

Early Literacy Policy and Pedagogy

KATHLEEN ROSKOS
CAROL VUKELICH

Early literacy policy is a new topic in the field of early childhood policy. Through a number of initiatives, early literacy has become a flash point for change in early childhood education. The timing is right, as substantial research indicates that early exposure to oral language and readiness skills (e.g., phonological awareness) place children at an advantage for later reading achievement (Hart & Risley, 1995; Snow, Burns, & Griffin, 1998; Shonkoff & Phillips, 2000). Faced with a perceived crisis in students' reading achievement (NCES, 1998), a variety of policy makers (e.g., government agencies, professional organizations, think tanks, foundations and trusts) encouraged curricular change in early childhood education programs. Beginning with the 1998 Head Start reauthorization, early literacy pedagogy has moved toward center stage, culminating with its own policy initiative—Early Reading First, a component of the No Child Left Behind Act of 2001 (Public Law 107-110). At the same time, early literacy pedagogy was increasingly incorporated into states' standards-based education reform. Between 2000 and 2003, for example, the number of states with early reading standards had more than doubled, from 16 to 34 states (Neuman, Roskos, Vukelich & Clements 2004).

In this chapter, we trace the recent history and potential influences of early literacy policy on early literacy pedagogy. Such informa-tion can help to create a historical context for early literacy policy research, a very new topic of study in the early childhood field. We begin with a brief description of the genesis of early literacy policy ideas, rooted in the standards movement that originated in states around the mid-1980s. We next review the recent history of early literacy policy recorded in the 1998 Head Start reauthorization and the conversations regarding its reauthorization in 2003 and early reading initiatives of the Bush administration, including Good Start, Grow Smart and Early Reading First. We then examine these early literacy policies through the lens of policy-oriented research in the K–3 English language arts standards to gain insights about the potential of early literacy policy for influencing early literacy pedagogy in diverse early education and care settings. Reflecting on lessons learned from K–3 reading policy research, we close the chapter with recommendations for early literacy policy research toward the goal of establishing a high-quality early literacy education system in the United States.

The Genesis of Early Literacy Policy

The current standards movement began in response to the *A Nation at Risk* report prepared by the National Commission on Excellence in Education in 1983. Its presence, however, had already been felt in scientific curriculum making and the rise of social efficiency in the early 1900s (Kliebard, 1995). A "rising tide of mediocrity" in the schools, the commissioners warned, threatened the nation's place in the world, and high standards were urgently needed to restore strength, rigor, and direction in public education.

States' response to the report was immediate and swift, as many set about developing rigorous standards to stem the rising tide. The movement gained momentum in 1989, when the nation's governors met in Charlottesville, Virginia, and established eight education goals for the nation aimed at improving public education (see Table 22.1). The eight goals launched a multiyear, multipronged campaign to improve schooling across the full range of educational services and to raise student achievement in the core disciplines of language arts, mathematics, sci-

ence, and social studies. Galvanized by bipartisan support in the early 1990s and backed by federal funding by the mid-1990s (Goals 2000: Educate America Act, 1994), the standards movement dominated school reform for the remainder of the 20th century.

By the late 1990s, the movement was in full swing as states engaged in massive restructuring efforts to lay the foundations of state-level standards-based education. Given the incentive of Goals 2000 funding, most states were actively engaged in drafting academic content and performance standards for all students through a consensus-reaching process that included key stakeholders (professional organizations, educators, business and community leaders, parents). To receive federal funds, however, states had to meet three additional requirements in their reform plans: (1) development of reliable state assessments at three grade spans; (2) alignment

TABLE 22.1. Goals 2000

Goal area	Goal
School readiness	All children in America will start school ready to learn.
School completion	The high school graduation rate will increase to at least 90%.
Student achievement and citizenship	All students will leave grades 4, 8, and 12 having demonstrated competency over challenging subject matter, including English, mathematics, science, foreign languages, civics and government, economics, arts, history, and geography, and every school in America will ensure that all students learn to use their minds well, so they may be prepared for responsible citizenship, further learning, and productive employment in our Nation's modern economy.
Teacher education and professional development	The Nation's teaching force will have access to programs for the continued improvement of their professional skills and the opportunity to acquire the knowledge and skills needed to instruct and prepare all American students for the next century.
Mathematics and science	United States students will be first in the world in mathematics and science achievement.
Adult literacy and lifelong learning	Every adult American will be literate and will possess the knowledge and skills necessary to compete in a global economy and exercise the rights and responsibilities of citizenship.
Safe, disciplined, and alcohol- and drug-free schools	Every school in the United States will be free of drugs, violence, and the unauthorized presence of firearms and alcohol and will offer a disciplined environment conducive to learning.
Parental participation	Every school will promote partnerships that will increase parental involvement and participation in promoting the social, emotional, and academic growth of children.

Note. From www.ed.gov/legislation/GOALS2000/TheAct/sec102.html.

of local curricula to state standards and assessments; and (3) a broad-scale effort to educate teachers and the general public about the states' standards. Beneath the surface of standards making per se, these constituted a profound, tectonic shift in public education. For nearly a century, people at the local school level had determined goals, expectations, and their own sense of how well their schools were doing. Creating a state-level standards-based education system, however, shifted responsibility from local schools to the state, threatening to erode local control of schooling as traditionally held. By 2004, all but one state (Iowa) had adopted K–12 academic content and performance standards. Of the 49 states with standards, only Rhode Island had not adopted standards in all core content areas by 2004.

The passage of the No Child Left Behind Act in 2001 tightened the grip of the standards movement on state-level education reform by holding students and schools accountable for meeting the states' academic content standards. The act required the implementation of achievement tests from grade three through high school to assess students' success in meeting state standards in reading, mathematics, and science by 2007–2008, and an accountability system that holds students and the education system (schools and districts) responsible for *all* students' achievement (Education Commission of the States, [ECS], 2000).

Thus in a relatively short period of time (about 15 years), the idea of national educational goals as useful guideposts for state action that had been discussed and debated by state governors in 1989 had led to fairly well-defined, standards-based systems in many states by 2004 that included academic content standards, achievement tests, and large-scale professional development efforts. (See, for example, *Quality Counts*, 2004). Early literacy policy entered the educational arena in this historical context. In the next section we describe how the standards and accountability framework began to give voice to early literacy policy and pedagogy.

Recent History of Early Literacy Policy

Publication of *Learning to Read and Write: Developmentally Appropriate Practices for Young Children,* a joint statement of the International Reading Association (IRA) and the National Association for the Education of Young Children (NAEYC; 1998), was a milestone in the evolution of early literacy as a recognized domain of development from birth to 5 years of age. From the 1970s on, mounting research evidence pointed to an "emergent literacy" phase of literacy acquisition that prepared the way for decoding written language and using it as a source of meaning. Children's recognition of alphabet letters and grasp of book and print concepts, along with a phonological sensitivity to sounds in words, showed strong positive relationships to their later reading achievement in the primary grades (e.g., Bryant, MacLean, Bradley, & Crossland, 1990; Ehri, 1994; Juel, 1991; Richgels, 1995; Whitehurst et al., 1994). But the position statement not only summarized this research; it also laid out a set of benchmarks for early literacy learning from preschool through grade 3, along with broad recommendations for policy makers, educators, and parents.

The IRA/NAEYC position was approved at the same time as the National Research Council published a synthesis of early reading research, titled *Preventing Reading Difficulties in Young Children* (Snow, et al., 1998). The research report identified early risk factors, such as vocabulary deficits, that significantly increased chances for children's reading failure—a condition already linked to broader social and economic problems (e.g., crime, poverty, joblessness). The significance of the early years, not only for learning to read and write but also for learning in general, was well documented in two subsequent reports of the National Research Council: *From Neurons to Neighborhoods* (Shonkoff & Phillips, 2000), which synthesized scientific knowledge about the nature of early development and the role of early experiences, and *Eager to Learn* (Bowman, Donovan, & Burns, 2001), which reviewed and synthesized the knowledge base on early childhood pedagogy. This trio of reports, commissioned by the National Research Council, made a strong case for high-quality early childhood education and care for all children. Together, they sounded the call for a comprehensive early education system that was not only well resourced but also well aligned with K–12 expectations, which subsequently grafted early literacy pedagogy to the momentum of K–12 school reform.

Thus, at the beginning of the Bush administration in 2000, research on children's rapidly developing brains in the first years of life, on their emerging print knowledge and skills, and on the influence of rich early literacy experiences (e.g., being read to) on later reading achievement indicated that learning to read and write begins before school. Even as this significant finding illuminated the larger scope of literacy development, it also laid bare a difficult social problem. Although some infants, toddlers, and preschoolers receive quality, education-oriented care filled with literacy experiences at home or in child care that prepare them for school and successful reading achievement, many others do not, and these children enter school with deficits (e.g., weak vocabulary) that are extremely difficult to remedy and that put them at risk for long-term reading failure. The psychological, social, and economic consequences of reading failure are many, and no complex society can endure such a loss of human capital for long (Heckman, 2002). High-quality early literacy instruction for all young children, therefore, was increasingly seen as a preventive measure that might reduce this societal risk—a key message of the seminal book *Preventing Reading Difficulties in Young Children* (Snow et al., 1998).

The presence of this compelling problem (the need to prepare children to read and succeed in school), coupled with a potential solution (early literacy instruction) in a favorable political environment (standards-based reading reform), opened what is referred to as a "policy window" (Kingdon, 1995)—a golden opportunity for new policy ideas and change. Spurred by strong early literacy advocacy groups (academics, interest groups, professional organizations, government agencies, think tanks), policy makers crafted two prominent federal early reading policies at this propitious time: Good Start, Grow Smart and Early Reading First. They also used the opportunity to introduce policy change into Head Start, an early childhood education mainstay. In the following, we describe these policies more fully as to their purposes, policy implementation tools, and influences on early literacy pedagogy.

Good Start, Grow Smart

In March 2002, President Bush outlined a plan to strengthen early learning, increasingly seen as foundational for school success and overall quality of life. Titled Good Start, Grow Smart, the early learning plan was multipronged, addressing three major areas of early childhood education: (1) strengthening Head Start and other child-care programs; (2) partnering with states to improve early childhood education; and (3) providing information to teachers, caregivers, and parents. Though providing no additional funding, this initiative outlined an ambitious plan, given the patchwork system of early education and care funding and practice in the United States. Early childhood services vary considerably as to accessibility, program quality, teacher quality, cost, and curriculum within and between states (see, for example, Schumacher, Irish, & Lombardi, 2003).

At its core the Bush plan argued that to better prepare children for school, especially in the key areas of language, early literacy, and mathematics, a stronger, more coordinated and better aligned system of early education and care was needed at federal and state levels. But to achieve this, several obstacles needed to be overcome, such as lack of alignment between preschool and primary grade education; lack of accountability in early childhood programs for children's school readiness; and lack of information for parents, caregivers, and teachers about the importance of early learning and what they can do to help children prepare for school.

To address these weaknesses or disconnects in the system, multiple methods were developed to strengthen, improve, inform, connect, stretch, and expand early childhood literacy education programs. Four were chief among them and especially relevant to early literacy education: (1) setting quality criteria for early childhood education (e.g., early learning content standards); (2) establishing a national reporting system for Head Start programs on children's early literacy, language, and numeracy skills; (3) providing professional development and training in early literacy (e.g., Head Start's Summer Teacher Education Program, or Project

STEP); and (4) identifying the most effective prereading and language curricula and teaching strategies for early education through rigorous experimental methods. By 2004 these approaches were being vigorously applied at different points in the early childhood education system (federal and state), but not without considerable resistance in the professional community. Project STEP, for example, launched in the summer of 2002 to prepare early literacy specialists in early literacy curriculum, was received with some skepticism in the Head Start community, but it gained momentum as specialists received more support and training for their mentoring role (National Head Start Training and Technical Assistance Resource Center, *www.hsnrc.org*; see also *www.stepnetportal.org*).

Around the same time, the National Association for the Education of Young Children (NAEYC) and the National Association of Early Childhood Specialists in State Departments (NAECS/SDE) issued a joint position statement on early learning content standards titled *Early Learning Standards: Creating the Conditions for Success (2002)* that described four factors of quality early learning standards, including (1) supportive systems, (2) significant content, (3) informed, inclusive processes, and (4) appropriate, ethical implementation. Informed inclusive processes of standard setting, for example, were seen as "essential to high quality standards." How early learning standards are developed is "at least as important as what those standards are about" (p. 9). A subsequent report conducted by the SERVE Center for Continuous Improvement, University of North Carolina–Greensboro, indicated that standard setting was being actively pursued in the field, was typically led by state education agencies in collaboration with a broad spectrum of stakeholders, and was a lengthy, complex process heavily influenced by existing K–12 standards. At the time of the report, standards making in states was indeed inclusive and also informed to the extent that groups consulted existing early childhood frameworks in language and literacy domains (e.g., the Head Start Child Outcomes Framework) and other states' prekindergarten standards (Scott-Little, Kagan, & Frelow, 2003).

Good Start, Grow Smart policy attempted to bring a more cognitive focus to many early childhood programs. Although the 1998 reauthorization of Head Start mandated learning standards in early literacy, language, and numeracy skills as program goals, it did not provide a road map for how to effectively and fully implement learning standards in local practice. The Good Start, Grow Smart initiative attempted to make the standards-based route clearer by requiring a new accountability in Head Start, more intensive professional development and training in language and literacy instruction for teachers and providers, and stronger state-level commitment to school readiness in funded early childhood programs. Such bold steps toward the policy goal of all children achieving school readiness introduced dramatic change into early childhood educational practices: testing young children's early reading and math skills; the application of research-based methods in teaching and caring for young children; and collecting and analyzing data to make judgments about the children's literacy learning, as well as teachers' needs for professional development in literacy pedagogy. These plans for early education practice set a high bar that seriously challenged traditional approaches to early learning, as well as cherished views about the fundamental nurturing purposes of early education and care.

Early Reading First

Established in the No Child Left Behind Act of 2001 (NCLB), Early Reading First was designed to prepare children, especially those at risk and those with disabilities and limited English proficiency, to enter kindergarten with the necessary cognitive, language, and early literacy skills for success in school. The early childhood counterpart of Reading First, which targeted the improvement of primary-grade reading instruction grounded in scientifically based reading research, Early Reading First set its sights on the prevention of later reading difficulties. Toward this end, the program used a competitive grant process designed to turn existing preschool programs into preschool centers of educational excellence by improving classroom environments and instruction through scientific research-based practices in language, cognition, and early reading.

More specifically, the program had five purposes: (1) to enhance preschoolers' language, cognitive, and early reading development by using scientifically based teaching strategies and professional development; (2) to create high-quality language and print-rich environments so children learn fundamental language and literacy skills; (3) to implement research-based language and literacy activities into practice for development of oral language, phonological awareness, print awareness, and alphabet knowledge; (4) to assess and monitor children's progress; and (5) to integrate an early reading curriculum based on scientifically based reading research into preschool programs.

From a practice perspective, Early Reading First required a more literacy-oriented classroom environment than before, with abundant print materials, well-stocked libraries, writing centers, and literacy-enriched play settings. It required a research-based early literacy curriculum, which meant more systematic, intentional instruction of essential prereading skills—that is, letter recognition; rhyming, blending, and segmenting sounds; complex vocabulary; and print concepts. It required reliable, valid reading assessment for purposes of screening and progress monitoring, thus moving beyond informal observational approaches (e.g., checklists). And above all, it called for intensive professional development in a "scientific approach" to early literacy pedagogy—one that taught teachers how to implement scientifically based reading research knowledge, including assessments, in their everyday teaching practice.

Modestly funded compared with other NCLB legislation ($75 million in 2002), Early Reading First nonetheless gave substance and form to what early literacy instruction might look like in high-quality early childhood education programs. In this respect, it presented a new image of language and literacy pedagogy into the early childhood field and upped the ante for what was expected of children and of their teachers. It is too early in its history to determine whether or to what extent these grants will change preschool practice.

Head Start Reauthorization

The 1998 Head Start reauthorization changed Head Start's purpose from providing comprehensive developmental services for America's low-income children to "[promoting] school readiness by enhancing the social and cognitive development of low-income children" (SEC.648c). This signaled the beginning of a new emphasis on children's *education* (as well as care) within the traditional Head Start structure of providing comprehensive developmental services.

In its initial proposal for reauthorization of Head Start, the Bush policy remained consistent with its broader Good Start, Grow Smart goals—strong science, strong content standards, strong assessment, strong accountability—with the added incentive of flexibility. To strengthen Head Start and improve preschool programs, the policy proposed to allow up to eight states to coordinate federal and state funds to promote school readiness, thus giving states the opportunity to integrate Head Start with other-funded preschool programs, such as Title I, special education, child care block brants, and state-funded initiatives. It proposed to allow states to develop coordinated early education and care *systems*, thereby allowing states to take the bulk of the responsibility for early education and care.

Policy adaptations in the reauthorization language from 1998 to 2003 also reflect an increasing (and narrowing) emphasis on the language, literacy, and numeracy components of this educational goal. The 1998 reauthorization, for example, included *phonemics, print, oral language, vocabulary, appreciation of books* and *numeracy*, along with *children's emotional development*, in describing Head Start instructional content, whereas the 2003 reauthorization streamlined this description to *prereading, language skills*, and *numeracy* skills instruction using *scientifically based programs that promote school readiness*. The focus on children's emotional development was eliminated in the description of content to be learned. Rather, *supporting children's social development* was described in reference to the development of teacher capacity to ensure school readiness.

This narrower focus on language, literacy, and mathematics content reflects what might be characterized as the slow, steady importing into early education of the traditional "3Rs," which first appeared in the kindergarten curriculum in the mid-20th century (see, for example, *We Begin,* the readiness book of the Macmillan Reading Program, 1966, which combined word discrimination, letter matching, practicing left-to-right sequence, and fine motor coordination). Although at this point the reauthorization has not been finalized, both Republicans and Democrats acknowledge the need for additional emphasis on the academic skills. No longer will Head Start likely focus as singularly as in the past on social-emotional development to the exclusion of cognitive skills.

Our legislative synopses outline the documented history of early literacy policy that began in a new century, rooted in K–12 standards-based reform in the 1980s and 1990s. A number of "turning point" policy ideas were introduced into the early education field via these federal initiatives and programs that attempted to steer early childhood practice in new directions.

The content of early literacy, for example, was identified and described to include oral language (expressive and receptive language, vocabulary development), phonological awareness, print awareness, and alphabet knowledge and was subsequently codified in states' early learning standards, in response to both the requirements of the Good Start, Grow Smart initiative and the states' larger (and relentless) pursuit of K–12 standards-based reform. Ensuring the scientific research base in instructional programs, materials, and teaching techniques was increasingly required as the signator of high quality in early education programs. Assessment assumed a much larger role in determining school readiness skills of children and program effectiveness.

The key policy idea for implementing these pedagogic changes was intensive professional development that ensured that teachers were knowledgeable about early literacy development and learning and sufficiently skilled to create the kinds of learning conditions that get results—not just for a few children, but for all children. Although professional development made sense as a policy implementation tool, it also faced a daunting set of deployment challenges. Mobilizing sufficient expertise for high-quality professional development on a large scale, for example, presented states with difficult resource issues and problems (Gallup Organization, 2003; Maxwell, Field, & Clifford, 2004). Differentiating instruction to meet the range of educational needs in a largely undereducated workforce further exacerbated these resource issues and dilemmas (Breunig, Brandon, & Maher, 2004).

Lessons Learned from K–3 Policy-Oriented Reading Research

The extent to which early literacy policy ideas, such as *centers of educational excellence* in Early Reading First, will translate into actual practice is not yet clear. We can, however, explore the potential of early literacy policy for fostering change in early literacy pedagogy from traditional practices to newer ones driven by scientifically based reading research. Drawing on policy-oriented reading research aimed at primary-grade reading instruction—also filled with the hope and promise of stemming reading failure—we can examine lessons learned that might also apply to relationships between early literacy policy and practice. Understanding some of this history may help the early childhood field avoid mistakes of the past in achieving their future goal of high-quality early literacy education for all young children.

In the next section, we describe reading policy research that examines three key areas of educational reform: (1) the quality of reading standards setting, (2) the implementation of standards-based reading instruction in districts and schools, and (3) connections between policy-driven reading instruction in primary-grade classrooms and student achievement. We focus our analysis on a few key policy-related studies in primary-grade reading whose findings are instructive when considering the interplay of federal policy and improvement in early literacy practices.

The Quality of Reading Standards

Several groups have conducted analyses of state K–12 standards based on different sets of criteria for judging their quality, such as the American Federation of Teachers (1995), the Fordham Foundation (2000), and the Council of Basic Education (1998). Specific to beginning reading, Wixson and Dutro (1999) examined the reading and language arts standards of 42 states from two perspectives—what is known about standards and what is known about beginning reading. Using criteria established by the Council of Chief State School Officers (CCSSO) in collaboration with nine other educational organizations, they analyzed a sample of reading and language arts standards from 14 states that provided grade-by-grade information for grades K–3. They addressed the complexity (organization of the standard) and level of detail (number of benchmarks within an area) of the reading–language arts standards documents. A content analysis addressed content coverage (the curricular path and learning areas covered) and appropriateness (degree of inclusion of inappropriate content and exclusion of appropriate content).

The twofold analysis of standards documents led to several conclusions about quality features of primary-grade reading standards. First, standards often were not sufficiently detailed to clearly describe expectations, and as a result important content to be learned was overlooked. Second, reading standards were conceptualized and arranged in highly varied ways that caused confusion in the field for purposes of implementation and reporting (e.g., some identify reading apart from the language arts; some do not). Third, standards seemed too general, thus failing to offer sufficient guidance, or too specific, thereby choking local flexibility in the development of curricula, instruction and assessment practices, and policies. Fourth, and a potentially fatal flaw, the specification of a standard often did not appear to provide a viable curricular path across grade levels that continuously develops student knowledge and skill to higher levels of reading performance. Finally, some standards seemed to require inappropriate content, and others ignored essential content, which, in either case, jeopardizes students' learning to read.

These results regarding the quality of K–3 standards making are instructive in meeting the Good Start, Grow Smart policy regarding voluntary state guidelines on literacy, language, and prereading skills aligned with state K–12 standards in that they offer a research-based set of criteria for judging early learning standards. Based on Wixson and Dutro's (1999) analysis, well-formulated, well-structured, and well-specified standards should focus on skills that young children should know and be able to do. They should be research-based, built on a solid foundation of information about child development and language and early literacy learning domains to ensure that skills are reasonably achievable for all prekindergarten children, age appropriate, and necessary for school readiness. They should be clearly written for multiple audiences to understand. They should be comprehensive, representing the knowledge and skills essential for achievement, yet manageable and realistic given the constraints of time. Finally, standards should establish a clear, consistent, age-appropriate curricular path that takes into account the rapid, uneven development of young children and the interrelatedness of their development (Neuman & Roskos, 2004).

Different analyses of states' early learning standards have used some or all of these criteria to examine their quality for guiding curriculum and instruction (Bodrova, Leong, Paynter, & Semenov, 2000; Burns, Midgette, Leong, & Bodrova, 2001; Scott-Little et al., 2003; National Institute for Early Education Research, 2004; Neuman & Roskos, 2005) and thus provide an early test of the strength of the Good Start, Grow Smart policy for influencing practice at this level. That 34 states put early learning standards into place between 2000 and 2004, and that many of them produced fairly strong standards in this first round, indicates that standards-based reform is indeed moving into early childhood (Neuman et al., 2004).

The Quality of Standards Implementation

The critical question will be how well policy implementation educates teachers about standards as a change strategy (solution) for achieving higher student performance. A policy's intentions do not necessarily relate to its implementation. Quality standards, therefore, are no guarantee for use in everyday practice.

To track reading standards policy further into the world of practice, Dutro, Fisk, Koch, Roop, and Wixson (2002) undertook a 2-year study of standards-based professional development to promote the newly adopted Michigan English Language Arts standards, supported by federal Goals 2000 funding. Their goal was to use the "policy occasion" (the call for academic content standards) to help districts strategize local reform, help teachers implement standards-based reading and language arts instruction, and argue for a constructivist model of professional learning in a standards-based context. Specifically, they focused on how a statewide reform initiative affected teachers' capacities to become change agents in their own classrooms and districts and how district contexts supported or constrained their capacities to do so.

They assembled a group of administrators (two per district) and teachers (10 per district) from four representative districts, creating a network of learning communities to serve as future disseminators of standards-based reform to other Michigan districts. The professional development design incorporated three features thought critical to educational change: networking individuals and groups; establishing new values, beliefs, and norms (reculturing); and supporting new roles and structures for change (restructuring). Several principles, anchored in constructivist and developmental educational theory, guided the implementation of the design—principles such as experiential learning, inquiry, collaborative working, expert mentoring, and environmental supports (e.g., time to practice). Thematic analyses of interview data showed changes in teachers' views of themselves as change agents, as learners, and as literacy models and reflective practitioners, as well as the interplay of district environmental characteristics (e.g., size and structure; readiness for change; history) on the nature of teacher change. All in all, the standards project demonstrated policy affecting practice in positive and informative ways, attributable in large measure, the researchers argue, to the inclusion of teachers "as partners in the construction of policy and research-based practice" (Dutro et al., 2002, p. 808).

Three implications from this study offer insights for federal policy aimed at strengthening effective early literacy pedagogy through professional development. One is an apparent "readiness" factor by which local programs are already primed to use their resources (time, money, teacher expertise, leadership) to maximize professional development opportunities. Another refers to a multipronged approach in which professional development occurs at different program tiers (administration, teachers, paraprofessionals), sending a consistent message and developing common pedagogic understandings and skills (e.g., in storybook reading). The third involves capacity building, by which professional development activity strategically uses extant resources (e.g., site history, teacher knowledge) to develop more capacity in the system that builds toward change.

These insights shed light on Project STEP (Summer Teacher Education Program) as an implementation strategy of early literacy policy. The purpose of Project STEP was to train Head Start teachers in early literacy curriculum topics, such as phonemic awareness, a literacy-rich environment, and literacy-related materials (U.S. Department of Education, 2002). Conducted in summer 2002, the project used a "trainer of the trainers" model in which national experts trained 2,500 Head Start teachers and child-care providers as early literacy specialists who, in turn, were slated to train teachers in their respective programs. The model offered 32 hours of training in early literacy pedagogy at four regional training sessions across the country. The model was also designed to include follow-up mentoring and coaching at the classroom level, but unfortunately the effort was curtailed due to other priorities.

Although the policy implementation strategy paid attention to building capacity at the local level through the strategic use of existing personnel (a trained early literacy specialist), it did not create local networks of communication and understanding about early literacy pedagogy. It failed to build up a local leadership to create a shared vision of early literacy teaching and, most important, to garner resources (e.g., time for professional learning) to meet that vision. Lacking this, the potential of the policy strategy for affecting everyday practice was substantially reduced, because no matter how well trained, individual early literacy specialists cannot affect lasting, systemic change by themselves; they need strong and stable leadership to ensure sufficient resources in order to do the job.

The Quality of Reading Instruction for Improved Learning Outcomes

Implicit in early literacy policy is the idea that higher teaching quality will lead to improved early reading skills and overall school readiness for all children. Policy-related studies in elementary-grade reading, however, indicate that obtaining wide-scale higher teaching quality is difficult, even when policy implementation strategies (e.g., professional development) are effective.

A 3-year study conducted by the Consortium for Policy Research in Education (CPRE), for example, examined the premise that organizational changes, such as grouping practices, team teaching, and cross-age classrooms, are the catalysts for improved instructional practice. Not so, as 3 years' worth of evidence revealed only a "weak, problematic and indirect relationship" between changing organizational structures and changing teaching practices (Elmore, Peterson, & McCarthy, 1996, p. 237). Focused on governance, a 4-year study of participative decision-making found an interesting relationship between kind of teacher involvement and reading achievement gains (Smylie, Lazarus, & Brownlee-Conyers, 1996). When teachers' participation in decision making included curriculum and instruction issues (e.g., assessments, integrated language arts units) along with management issues, students' reading achievement test scores improved significantly. Conversely, low teacher participation on matters of curriculum and instruction did not yield such results. The process of participative decision making, in sum, appeared less influential than the kinds of decision making undertaken. Those decisions closest to the "front line" of instruction weighed more heavily on teachers' practice"thus producing changes in it"than those concerned with larger administrative issues (e.g., staffing). These policy studies caution that structural changes promoted by early literacy policy, such as raising the degree requirements for staff (Head Start reauthorization) and voluntary early learning guidelines (Good Start, Grow Smart), are starting points for change rather than potentially powerful forces for bringing about improvements in teaching practice at the local level.

Studies of statewide reading policy implementation further demonstrate how local contexts—the human capital, the quantity and quality of resources, the instructional culture—shape policy and its realization in instructional practice. Longitudinal studies of two Michigan school districts followed the implementation of state policy to the district level, documenting how the districts aligned curriculum, materials, and assessments to the new state reading policy and prepared their teachers to implement it (Spillane, 1994, 1998). Findings showed the development of a coherent policy environment at the district level as a result of the interplay between the state policy and local administrator interpretations of it. The district response, in other words, shaped the state policy, just as the state policy prompted local ideas and thinking toward a consistent view. But the findings also showed that a coherent district policy (morphed from the state policy) was insufficient to improve practice at the classroom level, even though well aligned across the essential tools of professional work, that is, curriculum, materials, and assessment. Teachers needed more opportunity (and more time) to fully understand the reading policy in order to accurately recognize what it should look like in material resources, as well as in their own practice.

Reading policy implementation in California tells a story of coherent policy gained and lost (Carlos & Kirst, 1997). Over a 10-year period the state built up an interrelated system of policies around an English–language arts curriculum framework that included textbook adoption criteria and the California Learning Assessment System, aligned with the framework. Although pockets of high-quality professional development occurred in line with curricular change and with good results, wide-scale, high-powered professional development to help teachers change their practice toward policy goals was lacking. As it turned out, California's students were last in the nation in reading achievement in 1992 and 1994—a turn of events that precipitated intervention by the state legislature across the latter part of the 1990s in the direction of skills-based academic content standards, fundamental skills instruction, class size reductions, and skills-oriented academic content standards. Caught in the dismantling of one system and the building up of another philosophically very different, California teachers were on their own to make sense of state policy in their daily reading instruction.

Lessons learned from these K–3 reading policy studies suggest that powerful policy strategies, even when applied jointly and consistently, may not be enough to help practitioners do a better job. Standards, for example, brought new order to instruction, but they did not teach practitioners how to *use* them as a means to more powerful instruction. Reporting requirements do ensure accountability, but they do not help educators understand why it is essential nor tell them how to obtain meaningful assessment information from families and children that make it worthwhile. Professional development may reach some, but not enough, of the teaching force. Like all reading policy, the historical evolution of early literacy policy must rely on leadership to make clear the limits of policy and the responsibilities of practice. What early literacy policy accomplishes in the next decades depends not only on the structures placed on and in settings and programs but also on people who act on those structures to create patterns of activity that can either advance, resist, or stall change.

The Need for Early Literacy Policy Research

In summary, our survey showed that policy-related inquiry in early literacy education (standards, curriculum, assessment, professional development) consists primarily of nonresearch articles (e.g., policy briefs or recommendations of panels) and reviews (e.g., research syntheses) that frequently embed early literacy in a broader treatment of issues. The National Association of Early Childhood Specialists in State Departments of Education (NAEYC & NAECS/SDE) position on early childhood curriculum, child assessment, and program evaluation titled *Building an Accountable and Effective System for Children Birth through Age Eight* is one example (2003). A few professional groups and think tanks have issued policy-related information specific to early literacy, such as the Educational Testing Service (ETS)

report titled *Early Literacy Assessment Systems: Essential Elements,* which describes the need for a "coordinated system of monitoring children's literacy development" that incorporates early learning standards, multiple assessment measures, strong leadership, and ongoing professional development of teachers (Jones, 2003, p. 10).

Evaluation-oriented research has also referenced early literacy policy implementation in critical reviews of state early learning standards (e.g. Bodrova et al., 2000; NIEER, 2004; Neuman, et al., 2004; Scott-Little et al., 2003), for example, and evaluation requirements of Early Reading First grants for annual reporting (U.S. Department of Education, 2004). At the very least, these two types of inquiry describe early literacy policy and, at the very most, inform it, but both lack scientifically research-based evidence as defined by the National Research Council (Shavelson & Towne, 2002) for actually improving early literacy policy and for educating its enactors in the best sense (Stanovich & Stanovich, 2003). For "good" early literacy policy in critical areas of teacher development, program quality and effectiveness, curriculum and assessment alignment, professional development models, and overall teaching quality, research that meets scientifically based research standards is critical and necessary (Education Sciences Reform Act, 2002; Eisenhart & Towne, 2003). Policy, early childhood, and early literacy researchers need to conduct rigorous research, to collaborate, and to synthesize research information, not only to support the formulation of strong early literacy policy but also to provide implementation strategies better calculated to produce real change in local practice toward optimal learning conditions for all young children.

Several key areas await this important and necessary empirical work. Among them is the need to interpret early literacy policy clearly and align it with everyday practice. For high expectations to be met, teachers must understand policies at the classroom level. Another is the need to conduct solid evaluations of early literacy initiative outcomes using large enough samples and standards-based assessments. The Early Reading First initiative provides this opportunity, through which a consortium of grantees might collaborate on and standardize their evaluation and research designs, thus enlarging the sample and increasing the data pool for examining child and teaching quality outcomes via this intervention.

Policy researchers can develop tools to examine the validity of data from (1) standards-based assessments; (2) data-driven decision making at multiple levels of implementation; and (3) quality indicators related to program, including standards, assessments, curriculum, and instruction. Program monitoring tools to assess fidelity of curriculum implementation, for example, have been found to be not only valuable sources of formative data but also effective feedback mechanisms for project implementors and teachers (Landry, 2004). Researchers can conduct studies on the cost effectiveness of specific early literacy initiatives, such as professional development or curriculum models, to determine whether the investment realizes sufficient gain to improve early literacy instruction. And they need to take on the complexities of designing evaluation studies that examine the interdependencies among variables (e.g., teacher credentials, site readiness for change, leadership styles, curriculum) from a systemic growth perspective and shed light on the supports and constraints in developing a "system" of early literacy education at local and state levels.

Conclusion

This chapter described a number of initiatives and recent policies. In our account we described the origins of early literacy policy and the key legislation that defined it at the turn of the century. And, in light of this historical context, we identified several fruitful areas for research that might inform and improve policy making toward more effective early literacy pedagogy in the nation's early education and care system. Our aim was to highlight where we are in the early literacy policy-to-practice relationship, where we believe the most fruitful directions might be for the future, and the directions to which we seem to be tending, in the hopes that a historical description may help us to more thoughtfully determine what to do and how to do it in the future.

References

American Federation of Teachers. (1995). *Setting strong standards: AFT criteria for high-quality standards*. Washington, DC: Author.

Bodrova, E., Leong, D. J., Paynter, D. E., & Semenov, D. (2000). *A framework for early literacy instruction: Aligning standards to developmental accomplishments and student behaviors*. Aurora, CO: Mid-Continent Research for Education and Learning Lab.

Bowman, B. T., Donovan, M. S., & Burns, M. S. (2001) *Eager to learn: Educating our preschoolers*. Washington, DC: National Research Council.

Breunig, G. S., Brandon, R., & Maher. E. J. (2004, February). *Counting the child care workforce: A catalog of state data sources to quantify and describe child caregivers in the fifty states and the District of Columbia*. Paper presented at the Workshop on Defining and Measuring Professional Development and Training in the Early Childhood Workforce, Washington, DC.

Bryant, P. E., McLean, M., Bradley, L., & Crossland, J. (1990). Rhyme and alliteration, phoneme detection and learning to read. *Developmental Psychology, 26*, 429–438.

Burns, M. S., Midgette, K., Leong, D., & Bodrova, E. (2001). *Prekindergarten benchmarks for language and literacy: Progress made and challenges to be met*. Aurora, CO: Mid-Continent Research for Education and Learning Lab.

Carlos, L., & Kirst, M. W. (1997). *California curriculum policy in the 1990's: "We don't have to be in front to lead."* Paper presented at the meeting of the American Education Research Association, Chicago, IL.

Council of Basic Education. (1998). *Great expectations: Defining and assessing rigor in state standards for mathematics and English language arts*. Washington, DC: Author.

Dutro, E., Fisk, M. C, Koch, R., Roop, L. J., & Wixson, K. K. (2002). When state policies meet local district contexts: Standards-based professional development as a means to individual agency and collective ownership. *Teachers College Record, 104*(4), 787–811.

Education Commission of the States. (1998, March). *Designing and implementing standards-based accountability systems*. Denver, CO: Author.

Education Sciences Reform Act of 2002, Pub. L. No. 107–279, 20 U.S.C.

Ehri, L. (1994). Development of the ability to read words: Update. In R. Ruddell, M. R. Ruddell, & H. Singer (Eds.), *Theoretical models and processes of reading* (4th ed., pp. 323–358). Newark, DE: International Reading Association.

Eisenhart, M., & Towne, L. (2003). Contestation and change in national policy on "scientifically based" education research. *Educational Researcher, 32*, 31–38.

Elmore, R. F., Peterson, P. L., & McCarthy, S. J. (1996). *Restructuring in the classroom: Teaching, learning and school organization.* San Francisco: Jossey-Bass.

Fordham Foundation. (2000). *The state of state standards 2000.* New York: Author.

Gallup Organization. (2003). *A survey of child care quality indicators in four Midwestern states.* University of Nebraska Center on Children, Families and the Law.

Goals 2000: Educate America Act. H.R. 1804; 103d cong. (1994). Retrieved July 2004 from *www.ed.gov/legislation/GOALS2000/TheAct/index.html*

Hart, B., & Risley, T. (1995). *Meaningful differences in the everyday experience of young American children.* Baltimore: Brookes.

Heckman, J. (2002). *Human capital: Investing in parents to facilitate positive outcomes in young children.* In *The first eight years: Pathways to the future* (pp. 6–15). Washington, DC: The Head Start Bureau, Mailman School of Health and Society for Research in Child Development.

International Reading Association & National Association for the Education of Young Children. (1998). *Learning to read and write: Developmentally appropriate practices for young children.* Newark, DE: International Reading Association.

Jones, J. (2003). *Early literacy assessment systems: Essential elements.* Princeton, NJ: Educational Testing Service.

Juel, C. (1991). Beginning reading. In R. Barr, M. Kamil, P. Mosenthal, & P. D. Pearson (Eds.), *Handbook of reading research* (Vol. 2, pp. 759–788). New York: Longman.

Kingdon, J. W. (1995). *Agendas, alternatives and public policies* (2nd ed). New York: Harper-Collins.

Kliebard, H. M. (1995). *The struggle for the American curriculum* (2nd ed.). New York: Routledge.

Landry, S. (2004, June). *Evaluating preschool curricula for children from low-income families: Issues and outcomes.* Paper presented at the annual Head Start Research Conference, Washington, DC.

Maxwell, K. L, Field, C. C., & Clifford, R. M. (in press). How are professional development and training defined and measured in research? An overview. In I. Martinez-Beck & M. Zaslow (Eds.), *Early childhood professional development and children's successful transition to elementary school.* Baltimore: Brookes.

National Association for the Education of Young Children & National Association of Early Childhood Specialists in State Departments of Education. (2002). *Early learning standards: Creating the conditions for success.* www. naeyc.org/resources/position_statements/position_statement.pdf

National Association for the Education of Young Children & National Association of Early Childhood Specialists in State Departments of Education. (2003). *Building an Accountable and Effective System for Children Birth Through Age Eight.*

National Center for Education Statistics. (1998). *NAEP 1998: Reading report card for the nation and the states* (NCES Publication No. 1999-50). Washington, DC: Author.

National Commission on Excellence in Education. (1983). *A Nation at Risk: The Imperative for Educational Reform: A Report to the Nation and the Secretary of Education, United States Department of Education.* Washington, DC: U.S. Government Printing Office.

Neuman, S. B., & Roskos, K. (2004, February). *A methodology for assessing the quality of early learning standards.* Paper presented at annual meeting of the NAEYC and NAECS/SDE. Washington, DC.

Neuman, S. B, & Roskos, K. (2005) *The state of state pre-kindergarten in standards.* Paper presented at the annual meeting of the American Education Association, Montreal, Canada.

National Institute for Early Education Research (2004). *Child outcomes standards in preschool programs: What is needed to make them work?* Retrieved July 2004 from *www.nieer.org*

No Child Left Behind Act of 2001. Pub. L. No. 107-110, 107th Cong. (2001). Retrieved from *www.nclb.org*

Quality counts 2004: Count me in: Special education in an era of standards. (2004, January). Washington, DC: Education Week.

Richgels. D. (1995). Invented spelling ability and printed word learning in kindergarten. *Reading Research Quarterly, 30,* 96–109.

Scott-Little, C., Kagan, S., & Frelow, V. S. (2003). *Standards for preschool children learning and development.* Greensboro, NC: SERVE Center for Continuous Improvement, University of North Carolina–Greensboro. Retrieved July 2004 from *www.serve.org*

Schumacher, R., Irish, K., & Lombardi, J. (2003). *Meeting great expectations: Integrating early education program standards and child care.* Washington, DC: Center for Law and Social Policy.

Shavelson, R. J., & Towne, L. (Eds.). (2002). *Scientific research in education.* Washington, DC: National Academy Press.

Shonkoff, J. & Phillips, D. (2000). *From neurons to neighborhoods: The science of early childhood development.* Washington, DC: National Academy Press.

Smylie, M. A., Lazarus, V., & Brownlee-Conyers, J. (1996). Instructional outcomes of school-based participative decision making. *Educational Evaluation and Policy Analysis, 18*(3), 181–198.

Snow, C., Burns S., & Griffin, P. (Eds.). (1998). *Preventing reading difficulties in young children.* Washington, DC: National Academy Press.

Spillane, J. P. (1994), How districts mediate between state policy and teachers' practice. In R. Elmore, & S. H. Fuhrman (Eds.), *The governance of curriculum* (pp. 167–185). Alexandria, VA: Association for Supervision and Curriculum Development.

Spillane, J. P. (1998). State policy and the non-monolithic nature of the local school district: Organizational and professional considerations. *American Educational Research Journal, 35,* 33–64.

Stanovich, P. J., & Stanovich, K. E. (2003, May). *Using research and reason in education.* Washington, DC: National Institute of Child Health and Human Development, Partnership for Reading, National Institute for Literacy, U.S. Department of Education.

U.S. Department of Education. (2002, April). *Good Start, Grow Smart.* Washington, DC: Author.

U.S. Department of Education Office of Elementary and Secondary Education. (2004). *Application for new grants for the early reading first program.* Washington, DC: Author.

We Begin. (1966). New York: Macmillan.

Whitehurst, G., Arnold, D., Epstein, J., Angell, A., Smith, M. & Fischel., J. (1994). A picture book reading intervention in day care and home for children from low-income families. *Developmental Psychology, 30,* 679–689.

Wixson, K. K., & Dutro, E. (1999) Standards for primary-grade reading: An analysis of state frameworks. *The Elementary School Journal, 100*(2), 89–110.

VI
PROGRAMMATIC INTERVENTIONS DURING THE PRESCHOOL YEARS

23

Reading Ahead:
Effective Interventions for Young Children's
Early Literacy Development

PIA REBELLO BRITTO
ALLISON S. FULIGNI
JEANNE BROOKS-GUNN

Over the past decade we have witnessed a renewed interest in early years of life, given the links between early experiences and later development. Evidence from several sources has converged to suggest that the stimulation and support provided in the home during infancy and the toddler years is an important influence on later preschool cognitive and language development and on intellectual skills when children enter elementary school. Parents and key caregivers are critical in terms of providing these stimulating experiences to promote this early literacy learning and development, through activities such as looking at books, singing nursery rhymes, and encouraging communication (Bradley, 1995; Snow, 1993; Trehub & Trainor, 1998). The foundation for sustained and sound literacy development is laid during the early years, and a tremendous degree of predictability is noted between early and later reading achievement (Baydar, Brooks-Gunn, & Furstenberg, 1993; Francis, Shaywitz, Stuebing, Shaywitz, & Fletcher, 1996; also see Landry & Smith, Chapter 10, this volume).

Proficiency in reading and writing skills is fundamental to achieving success in today's world, especially given the recent rapid tech-nological advancements in our society. Ironically, national early literacy rates are not keeping up with the rising demand for competence in literacy skills. Indicators of children's emergent literacy skills suggest that fewer than one third (29%) of first-time kindergartners are proficient in recognizing beginning letter sounds, a component of early literacy skills (West, Denton, & Germino-Hausken, 2000). These statistics are further exacerbated for children from low socioeconomic backgrounds, as these children tend to perform below normative standards on school, state, and national assessments of reading achievement (for further exploration of the effects of poverty, see Neuman, Chapter 2, this volume).

The twin thrusts of (1) recognizing the importance of early learning environments and the association between the entry-level skills and later academic performance and (2) concern over the lower literacy and educational achievement of children from a low socio-economic background have stimulated and supported the field of early literacy intervention (National Assessment of Educational Progress, 1998; Neuman & Dickinson, 2001; Snow, Burns, & Griffin, 1998; Whitehurst,

1997). Response to these juxtaposed issues has been manifested in the creation of several models of early intervention programs designed to enhance language, literacy, and school-related outcomes for low-income young children. However, the relationships between socioeconomic status (SES), early literacy, and intervention programs are complex (see also Hoff, Chapter 12, this volume). In an attempt to unravel these complexities, in this chapter we explore influences on the literacy development of young children from low-SES families and the effectiveness of early intervention efforts to enhance that development. The chapter is organized around four central issues:

- What is early literacy development and how is it most commonly measured?
- How are inequalities in socioeconomic status reflected in influences on early literacy development?
- What are the different early intervention program models and for whom, under what circumstances, and for what outcomes are these programs effective?
- How does our knowledge about literacy development and program effectiveness translate into developing sustainable early literacy programs?

What Is Early Literacy and How Is It Commonly Measured?

The word *literacy*, derived from Latin, means "marked with letters." According to the widely respected National Academy of Science Report on Preventing Reading Difficulties in Young Children, the term literacy is broader than reading and encompasses writing and other creative or analytic skills (Snow et al., 1998). In other words, literacy development can be understood in terms of the acquisition of a set of complex multidimensional skills that take place on a developmental continuum, with its origins early in life. Beginning at birth, oral language and literacy interactions set the stage for early literacy development, the end point of which is not linked to chronological age or school entry, but rather the point at which literacy skills are mastered.

In the mid-1980s the term *emergent literacy* gained prominence as a theory for ex-

plaining the genesis of children's reading skills (Mason & Allen, 1986; Teale & Sulzby, 1986). Emergent literacy consists of skills, knowledge, and attitudes that are developmental precursors to conventional forms of reading and writing (Whitehurst & Lonigan, 1998). Emergent literacy is based on the notion that children acquire literacy skills not only as a result of direct instruction but also as a product of a stimulating and responsive environment, in which children are exposed to print, observe the functionality and uses of print, and are motivated and encouraged to engage with print.

Whitehurst and Lonigan (1998) have crafted one of the most widely used typologies of skills for understanding the components of emergent literacy. In brief, the typology of skills is grouped according to two distinct processes: "outside-in" and "inside-out." Outside-in processes refer to the children's understanding of the context within which the writing they are trying to read (or write) occurs. The three components of outside-in processes are language, conventions of print, and emergent reading. Inside-out processes comprise skills that represent children's knowledge of the rules for translating the particular writing that they are trying to read into sounds. Inside-out processes are composed of the following components: linguistic awareness, phoneme–grapheme correspondence, and emergent writing.

Measurement of Early Literacy

The measurement of early literacy skill development is complex and multifaceted. Presently there is debate over the effectiveness and policy implications of formal, standardized child assessments versus more informal methods and measures (Johnston & Rogers, 2001; Salinger, 2001; Wagner, 2003). The measurement of preliteracy development of infants and toddlers in large-scale national and longitudinal initiatives is relatively uncommon (Brooks-Gunn, Fuligni, & Berlin, 2003). Most assessments of child outcomes measure a range of skills and abilities, such as language development and cognitive development, that are broadly associated with emerging literacy skills. Initiatives that serve preschool-age children tend to use more comprehensive measures of emergent literacy outcomes.

The Bayley Scales of Infant Development (Bayley, 1969, 1991–1993), appear to be the most commonly used standardized measure for outcomes for children from birth to 3 years of age in several nationally recognized early childhood initiatives, such as the National Evaluation of the Early Head Start (EHS) program, the Comprehensive Child Development Program (CCDP) and Infant Health and Development program (IHDP), and the NICHD Early Child Care Study (NICHD). Even though the Bayley Scales (as they are commonly referred to) are primarily measures of children's cognitive development, results from factor analyzing the measure indicate significant loadings of this scale for receptive language and vocabulary as early as 24 months of age (Brooks-Gunn, Liaw, & Klebanov, 1992). Other standardized assessments of language development for infants and toddlers, in national initiatives, have most commonly included the Peabody Picture Vocabulary Test (PPVT-R; 3, Dunn & Dunn, 1981); McArthur Communicative Developmental Inventories (Fenson, Dale, Reznick, Thal, & Reilly, 1991); and Bracken Basic Concept Scale (BBCS; Bracken, 1984; Naglieri & Bardos, 1990). Given the prevalence of these measures across large-scale national initiatives, it appears that the primary method of assessing early childhood literacy during infancy and toddlerhood is via oral language development. Theoretically, given the strong links between oral language and reading ability (Stone, Silliman, Ehren, & Apel, 2004), these measures tap into one of the primary constructs underlying early literacy development; however, they fall short of measuring literacy skills comprehensively. Ideally, known precursors and predictors of later achievements should be assessed (National Institute of Child Health and Human Development [NICHD], 2002).

How Is Socioeconomic Status Reflected in Family Support for Early Literacy?

We define SES in terms of income poverty and levels of educational attainment or human capital. Income and education, in addition to occupation, individually or in some weighted combination, are among the most commonly used indicators of SES (Brooks-Gunn, Duncan, & Britto, 1999). It is a well-established fact that the literacy gap is associated with SES differences, with some estimates suggesting that at school entry, children from disadvantaged backgrounds are already a couple of years behind their more advantaged peers (Snow et al., 1998). However, in order to comprehensively understand the associations between SES and academic achievement, we need to move beyond the dire predictions and associations to tease apart the influences on early literacy development. Three levels of influences have been implicated in the acquisition of early literacy skills (Snow et al., 1998). First, there are influences at the level of the child. These include cognitive ability, sensory capacity (such as hearing impairments, attention deficit problems), and physical and clinical conditions such as early language impairment and the like. The second level of influences includes family-level factors such as income, the home literacy environment, maternal education, and human capital. The third level of influences takes into account school, neighborhood, and community. In this section, we discuss the latter two levels of influences as they pertain to literacy development for young children from low socioeconomic backgrounds.[1] In particular, we look at the following sets of family-level influence: income, education or human capital, and the home literacy environment. These influences are interlinked (for instance, income increments are associated with enhanced material resources), but we discuss them individually to clarify the unique contribution of each influence on young children's early literacy skills. In the next section we turn our attention to the third level of influences, i.e., school, neighborhood, and community.

Income Poverty

In the United States, income poverty is defined in terms of a family income failing to meet a federally established absolute threshold, living at or below which signifies that the family lacks basic financial resources and, consequently, adequate access to food, health care, and shelter (Brooks-Gunn, Britto, & Brady, 1999; Leventhal & Brooks-Gunn, 2002). The United States' child poverty rate is at least two to three times higher than in most other major Western industrial-ized nations. In 2001, almost 12 million chil-dren (16%) lived in families in which the parents' income was at or below the poverty level (U.S. Census Bureau, 2002). For chil-dren under the age of 6, the rate was even higher (18.5%), and for those living in a female-headed household, the rate was al-most 49%. Whichever way we slice the pie, poverty data clearly demonstrate that large numbers of children in the United States are living in economically impoverished condi-tions.

The literature documenting the conse-quences of poverty on children's develop-ment is extensive and constantly expanding. The several salient issues in understanding poverty consequences include duration, ex-tent, and timing of the poverty experiences. The dynamic nature of poverty experiences can be attributed to multiple factors, such as changes in life situations (divorce, death of earning member of family, employment changes) and/or changes in the social and economic environment of the country (e.g., economic recessions; Brooks-Gunn, 1995; Brooks-Gunn, Britto, & Brady, 1999; Corcoran & Chaudry, 1997). Persistent pov-erty (continuing for many years) is poten-tially more deleterious for child outcomes than transient poverty (lasting only for a short period of time), and living in deep pov-erty (50% or less than the poverty threshold) appears to be more noxious than hovering near the poverty threshold.

Investigations into the timing of poverty have provided evidence for the relative im-portance of income deprivation on academic achievement, literacy development, and cog-nitive ability when experienced in the first few years of life, compared with later child-hood and adolescence (Duncan & Brooks-Gunn, 1997; Duncan, Yeung, Brooks-Gunn, & Smith, 1998). Results from nonexperi-mental studies have shown income effects for children's language and literacy development as measured by standardized test scores of verbal ability, which are stronger when pov-erty is experienced during early childhood and for children experiencing persistent pov-erty (Klebanov, Brooks-Gunn, McCarton, & McCormick, 1998; Whitehurst, 1997). Ex-perimental welfare and antipoverty pro-grams examining the effects of enhanced in-come through both increased employment

and earning supplements indicate positive and significant impacts for preschool-age children. Family income model estimates suggest that for children between 2 and 5 years of age, a $1,000 increase in annual in-come corresponds to approximately a 1-point increase in a standardized test score (Morris, Duncan, & Rodrigues, 2005). However, the gains are still modest in terms of effect sizes.

Not all social scientists conclude that fam-ily income is important for child outcomes. Many see income as a proxy for other char-acteristics, such as a strong work ethic, or hypothesize that other family characteristics not typically included in income-effect mod-els may also account for the poverty–well-being link (Blau, 1999; Shea, 2000). Mayer (1997) has made this argument by testing for omitted variable bias. Income effects are vastly reduced in her models, lending sup-port for the hypothesis that family income may not matter as much, as is suggested by income models, for child outcomes. From a selection point of view, even though some models might be overestimating the effects of income, just as the Mayer models might be underestimating these effects, we interpret these different sets of findings as a demon-stration that income does matter. The ques-tion is the degree to which it matters.

Human Capital

Mother and child literacy skills have been closely linked (Chall, Jacobs, & Baldwin, 1990). Parental education, maternal level of education in particular, has emerged as a strong predictor of children's verbal abil-ity and academic performance (Bornstein, Hahn, Suwalsky, & Haynes, 2003; Haveman & Wolfe, 1995; Willms, 1999). Not surpris-ingly, due to these strong links and other fac-tors such as ease of measurement[2] and stabil-ity in adulthood, maternal education is one of the most commonly used indicators of SES (Ensminger & Fothergill, 2003). Despite the robust findings linking maternal education and child outcomes, little work has exam-ined the causal nature of the association, such as motivation for higher education, ge-netic differences, and the like (Duncan & Magnuson, 2003). In this section we specu-late on three potential pathways between maternal education and children's early literacy development: maternal modeling of literate behaviors and verbal skills; expectations, beliefs, and attitudes; and parent and child interactions.

MODELING READING AND WRITING

It is hypothesized that parents, by modeling reading and writing behaviors, inculcate attitudes valuing these behaviors in their children. Children who see their parents reading and writing purposefully and enjoying the activity are more likely to engage in such behaviors themselves (Edwards, 1994; Mikulecky, 1996). In addition to adult book reading, many naturally occurring daily activities, such as making grocery lists and paying bills, also expose children to parental modeling of print use (Morrow, Paratore, Gaber, Harrison, & Tracey, 1993; Purcell-Gates, 1996; Taylor, 1983). Because these activities are not staged for the child's benefit nor adjusted to the child's ability, they provide children opportunities to observe authentic uses of literacy, and children's level of understanding of these events provides a means to assess children's understanding of the adult uses of literacy (Neuman & Gallagher, 1994).

Adults vary in the extent to which they recognize the potential value of their own modeling of the uses of literacy. Interviews conducted with over 100 parents with differing reading proficiency levels indicated differences in the importance that they attached to their modeling of literacy behaviors (Fitzgerald, Spiegel, & Cunningham, 1991). Parents with lower literacy levels (an eighth grade reading level or lower) saw child-focused events, such as the child listening to stories or the child reciting the alphabet, as more important than adult-focused events, such as reading a book themselves or following directions or a recipe. However, the parents with a college or higher reading grade level viewed themselves as literacy role models for their children and mentioned the importance of their children seeing them engage in literacy behaviors. On a cautionary note, Edwards's work (1989) suggests that young low-income mothers with lower reading levels do see themselves as their children's first teacher and role model. However, they might be inhibited in stating their views due to their own limited reading ability.

GOALS, BELIEFS, AND ATTITUDES

More recently, parents' educational goals for their children and beliefs and attitudes toward literacy are being considered a potential pathway for understanding the link between parental educational achievement and child educational outcomes (Davis-Kean, 2005). One explanation put forth is that educational expectations and aspirations often dictate parents' style of interacting with their children (DeBaryshe, 1995; Goldenberg, Reese, & Gallimore, 1992; Lancy, Draper, & Boyce, 1989). For instance, it has been noted that mothers with higher educational expectations for their children tend to use more conversational styles and decontextualized language[3] during book reading (De Temple & Tabors, 1994). Parents with higher levels of educational attainment also appear to have higher expectations for their children's educational achievement (Dauber, Alexander, & Entwisle, 1996; Davis-Kean & Magnuson, 2005). For better educated parents, there appears to be a correspondence between expectations for child educational achievement and actual school performance (Alexander, Entwisle, & Bedinger, 1994).

Several explanations have been advanced to explain the lack of correspondence between less educated parents' goals for their children and their behavior supporting those goals. First, even though many parents have high educational goals for their children, they feel that they do not possess the requisite educational skills to assist their children to achieve these goals and, as a result, have a lowered sense of efficacy (Edwards, 1989; Gadsden, 1995). Second, skills valued at home may not be in keeping with more academic types of skills valued at school (Auerbach, 1989; Boyd, Brock, & Rozendal, 2004; Ogbu, 1981; Sonnenschein, Brody, & Munsterman, 1996; Taylor, 1997). Third, despite the fact that the parents are highly interested and value their children's academic success, stressful living conditions, such as inadequate housing, lack of money, and unsafe neighborhoods, often impede parents' efforts to assist their children's literacy progress (Brody et al., 1994; McLoyd, 1990; McLoyd & Wilson, 1991). On the other hand, higher levels of education might enhance parent's ability to seek out advice, information, and opportunities to improve their children's educational outcomes (Davis-Kean & Magnuson, 2005).

PARENT–CHILD INTERACTIONS

The literature on the links between parent's level of education and parent–child interactions is replete with examples of parents with higher levels of education engaging in a diversity of stimulating interactions with their infants and toddlers (Britto, Fuligni, & Brooks-Gunn, 2002; Custodero, Britto, & Brooks-Gunn, 2003) and exposing their children to richer verbal language (Hoff, 2003) and higher levels of warmth, supportiveness, and responsivity (Klebanov, Brooks-Gunn, & Duncan, 1994; see also Hoff, Chapter 12, this volume). Given that parent and child interactions are an integral aspect of the family literacy environment, this aspect is discussed more fully in the ensuing section.

Home Literacy Environment

The home environment has been cited as a significant influence for the development of young children's literacy and school readiness skills (Britto & Brooks-Gunn, 2001; Snow, Barnes, Chandler, Hemphill, & Goodman, 1991; Sugland et al., 1995). Most investigations of home literacy environments have focused on the language and verbal interactions in the home as the critical component for developing early literacy skills.[4] The structural aspect of this dimension has typically been investigated in terms of the presence and availability of printed matter in the home, and the functional aspect in terms of language interactions, such as during shared book reading.

STRUCTURAL ASPECT

Availability and exposure to print in the home, such as the presence of books, newspapers, magazines, crayons, and coloring books, has been found to be associated with enhanced literacy skills in children (National Center for Education Statistics, 1992). Availability of printed and learning materials has primarily been assessed through parental report and semistructured observation, using measures such as the Home Observation for Measurement of the Environment, or HOME inventory (Bradley & Caldwell,

1988; Leventhal, Martin, & Brooks-Gunn, 2004). More recently researchers have also begun looking at exposure to print via television viewing (Clarke & Kurtz-Costes, 1997; Neuman, 1991; Purcell-Gates, 1996). Without underestimating the concern over media influences on children's development, there is evidence and optimism regarding its potential for improving children's literacy skills, primarily via adult-mediated educational programs (Naigles & Mayeux, 2001; Singer & Singer, 2001).

FUNCTIONAL ASPECT

In terms of print-related interactions in the home, joint parent and child book reading has received the most attention, primarily due to the focus on verbal interaction, being socially interactive and fairly commonplace in most homes (Baker, Serpell, & Sonnenschein, 1995; Beals, De Temple, & Dickinson, 1994; Bus, van IJzendoorn, & Pellegrini, 1995; Payne, Whitehurst, & Angell, 1994; Sulzby & Teale, 1991; Toomey & Sloane, 1994). Being read to at home is associated with higher school achievement, language development, and reading skills for children (Bus et al., 1995; Ewers & Brownson, 1999; Saracho, 1997; Sénéchal & LeFevre, 2001; Snow, et al., 1998; Whitehurst & Lonigan, 1998). The most commonly used indicator to measure children's exposure to book reading is the frequency of shared book reading experiences. Based on a national survey of over 2,000 families with young children, only one fifth of parents reported reading to their infants (12 months and younger) and two fifths reported reading to their toddlers on a daily basis (Britto, Fuligni, & Brooks-Gunn, 2002). Similar differences in frequency of daily reading were noted in a national evaluation of the Early Head Start (EHS) program, in which mothers were asked about the frequency of book reading when their children were 14, 24, and 36 months of age (Raikes et. al., in press). Mothers reported reading on a daily basis to 14-month-olds 48% of the time compared with 55% of the time to 24-month-olds; thus at age 2 this practice is found only in a small majority of these low-income homes. Data indicate that children from low-income families are read to less frequently when compared with their middle-class peers (Britto et al., 2002; Vernon-Feagans, Hammer, Miccio, & Manlove, 2001). These early SES-related differences are likely to be significant, because the results from the EHS evaluation indicate that weekly and daily reading to infants as young as 14 months of age is associated with higher language scores on standardized language assessments, such as the McArthur Communicative Developmental Inventories (Raikes et. al., in press).

In addition to frequency of book reading, variation in book reading styles may affect the degree to which this activity supports literacy development. Aspects of book reading patterns that have been studied with young children include the role of routines, degree of maternal engagement, language use, and cognitive demand placed on the child (Britto, Brooks-Gunn, & Griffin, in press; De Temple, 2001; Haden, Reese, & Fivush, 1996; Reese & Cox, 1999; Sénéchal et al., 1997; Whitehurst et al., 1999). For example, four reading patterns have been identified in a sample of urban African American mothers reading to their 13- to 18-month-old toddlers (Hammer, 2001). A "modeling" pattern was characterized by mothers' modeled reading behaviors, such as pointing to and labeling pictures in the book, which they expected their child to imitate. In the "different styles for different texts" pattern, mothers (mostly from the middle-income group) varied their reading behaviors based on the type of book. For picture books, these mothers used more pointing and labeling, and for more text-oriented books, they combined it with reading of the text. In the third reading pattern, "reading from the text," the mothers primarily did a straight read of the book. The fourth reading pattern, marked by a low interest in the book reading activity, was labeled as a "limited periods of joint attention" style. Differences in maternal reading patterns have been associated with variability in child outcomes, namely language usage, word recall, and story comprehension (Britto & Brooks-Gunn, 2004; Pellegrini, Galda, Jones, & Perlmutter, 1995; Sénéchal & LeFevre, 2001).

Besides book reading, researchers also have examined verbal interactions during other activities in the home, such as mealtimes and playtime. Conversations among family members about past and future events during such times as mealtimes provide children with the exposure and opportunity to improve their own vocabulary and to learn and practice the structure of event narratives (Beals et al., 1994; Dickinson & Beals, 1994). Parent's conversational styles and language complexity appear to vary across a range of interactions, from shared book reading to playing with toys, and accounts for differences in children's language outcomes, with parents tending to use more complex language during playtime than during shared book reading (Crain-Thoreson, Dahlin, & Powell, 2001).

What Are Influences on Early Literacy Development Beyond the Home?

We now turn to the next level of influence on children's early literacy development—school, neighborhood, and community. Taken collectively, there appears to be a strong correlation between school- and community-level influences and child literacy outcomes. This association is attributable to several factors. Children from low-SES families tend to reside in primarily low-income communities and are more likely to attend substandard schools (Puma et al., 1997; Snow et al., 1998). From a measurement point of view, when SES is taken as an aggregate, measured at the school or community level, the result is a strong association with school achievement. In some cases even stronger effects are found for this aggregate set of factors than are found for family-level characteristics, which are measured at the individual level (Bryk & Raudenbush, 1992; White, 1982). This finding suggests that SES effects could be attributed more to residing in communities and attending schools with children from a similar low-SES background than to individual family factors. In this section we attempt to understand these community-level influences by examining child-care effects and the impact of neighborhood and communities on the development of early literacy.

Early Care

Economic and policy trends, such as a greater number of working mothers and expansion of federal child-care vouchers, to name a few, have led to a rapid rise in early-child-care attendance, not just in terms of the number of children attending but also in an increase in the amount of time spent in such educational programs. An overwhelming majority of children begin experiencing regular non-maternal care before 3 years of age and more than 50% of 3-year-olds spend over 30 hours per week in nonmaternal care (NICHD Early Child Care Research Network, 2001). Consequently, the relevance and importance of child-care settings for young children's literacy development is growing.

Aspects of quality early care and learning environments critical for literacy development have been studied in two categories: structural/physical and interactional (caregiver and child). Structural aspects are typically indexed by the quality of the facility, availability of developmentally appropriate materials, and types of child activities (Family Daycare Rating Scale [FDCRS], Early Childhood Environment Rating Scale [ECERS]; Harms, Clifford, & Cryer, 1997). The quality of caregiver–child interaction has been measured in terms of responsivity and sensitivity toward the child, stimulation for development, positive regard, attentiveness, and warmth (Observational Record of the Caregiving environment [ORCE]; Arnett Scale of Caregiving Behavior; Child Care Observational System [C-COS]; Arnett, 1989; NICHD & Duncan, 2003).

The link between high-quality child-care and other early educational settings and enhanced child outcomes has been well documented (NICHD Early Child Care Research Network, 1997, 1999, 2001; Peisner-Feinberg & Burchinal, 1997; Yoshikawa, 1995), especially for children from low-income backgrounds (Burchinal et al., 2000; Dickinson & Sprague, 2001). For instance, a 5-year multistate investigation of the effects of child care on young children's language and cognitive development in low-income communities provides robust evidence for the influence of quality of care on child outcomes (Loeb, Fuller, Kagan, & Carrol, 2004). In particular, caregiver sensitivity and responsivity appeared to be significantly linked with children's language development after controlling for other influences on development such as maternal language use and education. However, early-child-care settings that are available to poor children

vary widely in program quality (Phillips, Voran, Kisker, Howes, & Whitebook, 1994), with many centers providing less than adequate language and learning environments (Snow et al., 1998). Poor-quality early learning settings appear to have a lasting effect on children's academic achievement by placing them at risk for poor educational outcomes (Pianta, 1990). However, this literature has been criticized as overestimating developmental outcomes of child care quality by not accounting for demographic and family-level characteristics and not controlling for selection bias (NICHD & Duncan, 2003).

Neighborhood and Community

Income-poor families are often constricted in their choice of neighborhood of residence and tend to reside in poor neighborhoods characterized by social disorganization (e.g., crime, unemployment) and few resources (e.g., playgrounds, health care facilities) for optimal development of their young children (Sampson & Morenoff, 1997; Wilson, 1987). We examine neighborhood and community influences on early literacy development via the family environment and child-care settings.

In our research examining indirect effects of neighborhoods on children through the family context, we have found that residing in poor and ethnically diverse neighborhoods is associated with a poorer physical and less cognitively stimulating home environment, which in turn is associated with children's lowered verbal ability (Klebanov, Brooks-Gunn, Chase-Lansdale, & Gordon, 1997). Consequently, neighborhoods with a higher density of low-income families could be considered detrimental for young children's literacy and school-related outcomes.

The relationship between neighborhood affluence and type and quality care appears to be curvilinear, with the largest number of centers and best quality of care in the richest and poorest communities, and the lowest number and lower quality centers in lower-middle-income neighborhoods (Loeb, Fuller, & Strath, 2001). In low-income communities, it appears that state-mandated and federally funded initiatives provide higher quality early-care programs (Fuller et al., 2003). Less is known about the associations between neighborhood characteristics and parental choice about type of care. Nascent work on child care choices, using the data from the Project on Human Development in Chicago Neighborhoods (PHDCN), also supports this pattern. The data indicate that parents are more likely to select center-based care if they live in communities with a lower density of friends and relatives and a lower sense of trust and shared values among community members. At the same time, parents from communities with higher structural advantages in terms of availability of institutional resources tend to select center-based care (Burchinal, Nelson, Carlson, & Brooks-Gunn, forthcoming).

In summary, from an ecological perspective, family-, school- and community-level inputs or influences are significantly linked with early literacy outcomes. The research reviewed suggests that the quality of some of these influences—for example, type of parent and child verbal interactions—may be compromised for children from low-SES backgrounds. In an attempt to improve the quality of family and school influences, several literacy intervention program models have been developed. We now review the effectiveness of these programs.

What Are the Effects of Early Intervention Program Models?

In recognition of patterns of school difficulties for children from low-income families and neighborhoods, many early childhood intervention program models have been designed over the past 40 years to provide young children with enhanced learning experiences and other forms of support. These intervention experiences are generally intended to prepare children to enter school with the skills and motivation necessary to promote later academic success. Such programs for economically disadvantaged children and families originally focused on the years just prior to formal school entry (e.g., 3 to 5 years). A classic example is the Head Start program, a federally funded preschool program for children from low-income families designed to help reduce disparities between lower and higher income children upon school entry. As the amassed body of evidence has demonstrated the importance of very early experiences and development for

later cognitive and linguistic child outcomes, intervention programs have begun to address the educational needs of very young children in poverty; therefore, we review intervention programs for low-income families with children from birth to 3 years of age. We organize our discussion using one of the key defining aspects of early intervention programs, the location or type of services provided to the children (i.e., home-visiting programs, center-based programs, and a combination of home- and center-based services).

One service model often utilized in programs with very young children is a home-visiting model. These programs are designed to begin before or shortly after the birth of the child and often serve the family during the child's infancy and toddler years. Home-visiting programs are often parent focused, with a professional or paraprofessional visiting the home regularly to provide social support and services in the form of direct assistance, training, information, and/or referrals. For example, educational home-visiting programs strive to teach parents intellectually stimulating ways of interacting with their young children, often by demonstrating the uses of books, toys, or other materials. A very different service model is the center-based model, such as that employed by Head Start and other preschools. Center-based early childhood programs for economically disadvantaged children are often more formal and school-like to provide children with learning and socialization experiences. These are most typically preschool-type programs for children age 3 to 5 years and operate either part-time or all-day. However, center-based models do also exist for infants and toddlers, providing them with group socialization experiences in an age-appropriate classroom environment. In a third service model, some programs combine center-based and home-visiting services, often in conjunction with other family support services, to provide a comprehensive program to multiple family members.

In Table 23.1, we provide examples of early intervention programs for children birth to age 3, focusing on programs that have published evaluation data pertaining to their effectiveness in improving the early literacy and school readiness skills of participating children. Home-visiting programs re-

TABLE 23.1. Efficacy of Early Intervention Programs for Young Children's Early Literacy Development

Program name	Description of intervention program	Description of research design	Outcomes	
			Literacy inputs[a]	Child outcomes[b]
Home-based programs				
Hawaii Healthy Start and Healthy Families America (Duggan et al., 1999)	Mothers of newborns considered to be at high risk for child abuse and neglect; expanded nationally as Healthy Families America, providing home-visiting services to families with children from birth to age 5 years	Randomized trial; $n = 684$ (T = 373; C = 270); six sites	n.s.	n.s.
Parents as Teachers (Wagner & Clayton, 1999)	Low-income and primarily minority families; birth to age 3 years, half-hour to hourly monthly visits by paraprofessionals; early childhood education; service referrals	Randomized trial; $n = 707$ (T = 529; C = 178); four sites; multimeasure	n.s.	*Cognitive:* T > C
Nurse Home Visiting (Olds et al., 1999)	Prenatal to age 2 years; service delivery by nurses weekly during 1st 6 weeks to 1 visit every 6 weeks at 20–24 months; average length of visit 1 hour	Randomized trial; $n = 400$ (T = 216; C = 184); one site; longitudinal, multimethod assessment	*Language stimulation and materials* T > C	n.s.
Center-based programs				
Abecedarian (Campbell & Ramey, 1994).	Intensive curriculum; focus on cognitive and linguistic development; 8–9 hours per day, 5 days per week, 50 weeks per year, until age 3 years	Random assignment: $n = 111$ (T = 57; C = 54); African American; high risk; multimethod assessments every 6 months for 1st 54 months of participation	n.s.	Cognitive development: T > C
Mixed approach				
Infant Health and Development Program (Gross, Spiker, & Hayes, 1997)	Birth to age 3 years; experimental demonstration for low birthweight; < 1 year: weekly home visits; 2–3 years: biweekly home visits; at least 5 half-days of preschool per week; bimonthly parent group meetings	Random assignment; $n = 856$; assessment of child literacy outcomes at 36 months, 6½, and 8 years	*Observed parent–child interactions:* At 30 months, T > C on maternal quality of assistance during problem solving and on mother–child "mutuality"	*Receptive vocabulary:* Age 3 years T > C on PPVT-R scores

Program	Description[a]	Sample/Design	Parenting/home outcomes[b]	Child outcomes[b]
Early Head Start (EHS) (Love et al., 2002)	Prenatal to age 3 years; federally funded for low-income families; two-generational approach; integrated and intensive services; either center based, home based, or mixed approach	17 competitively selected sites with *n* = 150–200 participants per site based on inclusivity criteria (total *n* = approx. 3,000); multimethod assessment of child literacy outcomes at 14, 24, and 36 months	*Parenting attitudes, knowledge, and quality of home environment:* At 3 years, T > C on HOME; T = C on maternal childrearing knowledge and attitudes *Observed parent–child interactions:* At 36 months, T > C on maternal supportiveness during semistructured play task *Parenting attitudes, knowledge, and quality of home environment:* T > C on HOME total score and HOME support for language and learning subscale; T > C on parent report of daily reading to child	*IQ:* Age 3 years T > C on Stanford–Binet scores Age 8 years T > C on WISC-R scores for heavier birthweight *Cognitive scores:* T > C at 24 and 36 months on Bayley MDI scores *Receptive vocabulary:* T > C at 24 and 36 months
Comprehensive Child Development Program (St. Pierre & Layer, 1999)	Federally funded programs; low-income children; comprehensive developmental and health screenings; biweekly 30-minute home visits during the first 3 years of life, health care services, and parenting education and adult education	21 CCDP sites; program families *n* = 2,213; control families *n* = 2,197; multimethod data, including standardized assessment of literacy outcomes collected annually during home visit with family	*Observed parent–child interactions, parenting attitudes, knowledge, and quality of home environment:* T = C, no significant differences.	*Receptive vocabulary, cognition:* T = C, no significant differences
Parent Child Development Centers (Houston PCDC) (Andrews et al., 1982)	Federally funded demonstration; low-income families; year 1: 30 1½-hour home visits; year 2: 12 hours/week for 8 months; educational center-based child care plus classes for parents	Random assignment; *n* = 216 families; standardized assessments at 12, 24, and 36 months	*Observed parent–child interaction/relationship quality:* At posttest, T > C on parenting measures *Parenting knowledge, attitudes, and home environment:* At 36 months, T > C on HOME	*Cognitive scores:* T > C at 24 months

Note. T, treatment group; C, comparison group; n.s., not significant.
[a]Only those inputs that have been discussed in the body of the chapter are listed in this column.
[b]Only literacy-related outcomes are listed in this column.

viewed include Hawaii Healthy Start (and its expanded version, Healthy Families America), Parents as Teachers (PAT), and the Nurse–Family Partnership. The Abecedarian Project is reviewed as an example of a center-based program for children under age 3, and mixed-approach programs reviewed include the Infant Health and Development Program (IHDP), Early Head Start (EHS), the Comprehensive Child Development Program (CCDP), and the Houston Parent–Child Development Centers (PCDC). All of the programs described have been evaluated via rigorous impact studies. Several reviews of such research have summarized these findings (Barnett, 1995; Bryant & Maxwell, 1997; Farran, 2000; Fuligni & Brooks-Gunn, 2000, 2004; Halpern, 2000; Yoshikawa, 1995; see also Barnett, Chapter 25, this volume). Historically, intervention evaluations have focused on program impacts on cognitive and linguistic functioning, as these have been considered the most important elements in improving disadvantaged children's later school success. However, the special challenges of conducting research with infants and toddlers, combined with a broadening conception of the skill domains needed for success in school (Fuligni & Brooks-Gunn, 2000; National Education Goals Panel, 1998), have pushed program evaluations to address young children's social and emotional functioning and learning-related motivations and behaviors.

Program Outcomes for Children from Birth to 3 Years

Table 23.1 summarizes the research findings for the eight programs featured in this chapter, specifically focusing on outcomes related to program impact on home literacy environments (or inputs) and child language and preliteracy-related outcomes. Program providing home-visiting services without a center-based early education component report the fewest effects on child IQ and cognitive and language development. Home-based services tend to target parental well-being and mental health and improved parent–child relationships. These types of programs may have stronger effects on parents while providing an indirect influence on children (Berlin, O'Neal, & Brooks-Gunn, 1998; Yoshikawa, 1995). On the other hand,

center-based programs, by providing educational services directly to children, are more likely have direct effects on children's cognitive and linguistic development.

Although some home-visiting programs have been followed to assess their long-term effects, no long-term child IQ or cognitive development effects have been documented (Olds & Kitzman, 1993; Olds et al., 1999). The Nurse–Family Partnership home-visiting model has been the focus of several rigorous experimental trials. Consistent with the major goals of the program, evaluation has revealed program effects on maternal outcomes, such as reducing subsequent births, reducing welfare use, and decreasing child abuse and neglect (Kitzman et al., 2000; Olds et al., 1999). Other documented outcomes for children include long-term decreases in criminal and antisocial or delinquent behaviors at age 15 and less experience of maltreatment (Olds et al., 1998). The only documented child cognitive benefit of the program was increased cognitive development at a single site among the children of smokers (Olds et al., 1999).

The Hawaii Healthy Start program provided intensive home visiting to parents at risk for abusing their newborn infants. This initiative resulted in more positive parenting attitudes and child–parent interactions at 6 and 12 months but showed no program effects on the children's scores on cognitive measures (McCurdy, 1996). The Hawaii Healthy Start home-visiting program model was expanded both within Hawaii and nationally, based on initial pilot study findings that participating families had extremely low incidence of child neglect and no instances of child abuse following the program. However, in a randomized, controlled evaluation study, there were no program effects on parenting, home learning environment, parent–child interaction, or child development and no impact on child maltreatment (Duggan et al., 1999). Similarly, in a set of randomized controlled evaluations of the PAT home-visiting program, program impact in the areas of parent knowledge and behavior and of child development and health was small and not consistent across different program sites (Wagner & Clayton, 1999). However, one PAT program showed impact in some measures of cognitive and social development for children of Latina mothers but not of non-

Latina mothers, and especially for children of Spanish-speaking Latinas (Wagner & Clayton, 1999).

Center-based programs starting in infancy have documented larger effects on child IQ. For example, children who had participated in the Abecedarian Project preschool program since age 4 months or younger exhibited higher IQ scores than control-group children by 18 months of age (Campbell & Ramey, 1994), and children who participated in the Infant Health and Development Program showed significantly higher IQ scores and receptive language scores than the control group at age 3, when intervention was completed (Brooks-Gunn et al., 1994; Infant Health and Development Program [IHDP], 1990).

The mixed-approach service model has also yielded mixed results. The CCDP case-management and home-visiting model was evaluated in a randomized experiment and found no effects overall on children's developmental outcomes (St. Pierre, Layzer, Goodson, & Bernstein, 1997). However, site-level analyses showed program effects on children's motor, cognitive, and language development at sites where the parenting education was "more intense" based on the average number of home visits received (Brooks-Gunn, Burchinal, & Lopez, 2001). Furthermore, children whose families participated in CCDP for 3 or more years exhibited higher cognitive and language scores than control-group children. The scarcity of program effects has been interpreted as potential evidence that case management may not result in increasing families' receipt of direct services (St. Pierre et al., 1997).

The Houston PCDC has published follow-up results of evaluation of the low-income Mexican American children participating in the program and age-matched comparison children. Program effects were noted in the areas of reducing teacher-rated behavior problems at ages 8–11 years (Johnson & Walker, 1987) and some evidence of improved intelligence test scores at ages 4–6 and 6–9 years (Walker & Johnson, 1988).

The Infant Health and Development Program (IHDP) has reported significant impact on mothers' provision of support during parent–child problem-solving tasks at 2½ years, improved home environment, and positive effects on children's language and IQ scores at age 3 (Gross, Spiker, & Haynes, 1997). Following the children several years after the completion of the intervention program, IHDP reported smaller, but still significant, effects on IQ for the heavier group of low-birth-weight infants at age 8 (McCarton et al., 1997).

The Early Head Start (EHS) national evaluation, with a randomized controlled design, found overall program effects for children's cognitive development on the Bayley Scales of Infant Development, and Mental Development Index, on receptive language measured with the Peabody Picture Vocabulary Test (PPVT-III), on reduced aggressive behavior reported by parents, and on reduced negative behavior toward parents during a videotaped play task. In addition, several program effects were found relative to parents' provision of a cognitively stimulating home environment. EHS increased parents' scores on a subset of HOME items representing support for language and learning, increased rates of parental daily reading to their children, and increased use of nonphysical discipline strategies (Love et al., 2002). However, differential program effects were found relative to the type of services each program provided. Programs providing center-based early childhood services demonstrated effects on children's cognitive and social-emotional development and on parenting outcomes, but the home-based programs exhibited a weaker pattern of program effects favoring parenting outcomes (such as reducing parenting stress) over child development outcomes. Finally, EHS programs providing a combination of center-based and home-based services showed the most consistent pattern of effects on children's language development, social-emotional development, and parenting behaviors.

Because EHS program services vary by site, the EHS evaluation findings support the pattern of findings for the multiple infant/toddler programs reported previously. The domain of program effects (e.g., parenting versus child development) is associated with the focus and recipient of intervention services. Children are most likely to benefit directly from child-focused (often center-based) services.

The evidence from the Abecedarian, IHDP, and EHS studies together argue for the importance of child-focused services even during infancy and toddlerhood. Similarly, the weaker findings with respect to children's cognitive and language development from the home-visiting approaches suggest that using the parent as the indirect pathway for program effects is not a sufficient strategy in and of itself. Many programs rightly acknowledge the important role of the parent as the child's first teacher and the home environment as a critical context for early literacy development. However, the research suggests that targeting these contexts alone may not constitute a sufficiently intense intervention to meaningfully change children's early learning.

How Do We Develop Effective and Sustainable Programs?

Home, school, and community influences appear to play an important role in the development of young children's literacy skills. The review of the intervention literature indicates that certain aspects of intervention programs have proven to be successful in improving early literacy. In this section, we marry these two bodies of work to present a set of recommendations for early intervention programs.

Provision of Intensive Services to Children

Family-level influences clearly indicate that providing optimal developmental experiences, especially language experiences, is central for early literacy development. Most of the referenced program models have a parenting component targeted at supporting child development and improving the quality of stimulation provided to young children. However, given short-lived outcomes of most of the programs, it appears that the provision of services might need to be intensified or altered to also provide services to the children, in addition to the family.

Recent program evaluations have highlighted the role of intensity and duration of program participation, also known as "dose effects," as one of the most potentially important aspects of program implementation. For instance, even though the results of the home-visiting intervention programs (PAT

and Home Instruction Program for Preschool Youngsters [HIPPY]) have not been strong, evaluations of service intensity and exposure analyses indicate that greater receipt of home visits was associated with improved developmental outcomes for children, averaging a 1-month developmental advantage per 10 home visits (Wagner & Clayton, 1999). Similarly, for mixed-service models, such as IHDP, long-term sustained effects on children's cognitive scores were associated with high levels of participation in the program (Hill, Brooks-Gunn & Waldfogel, 2002).

Meeting Individual Family Needs

Implementing intervention efforts with vulnerable populations is a tremendous challenge (Halpern, 2000). Early intervention initiatives need to consider methods for meeting individual family needs (including those of ethnic minority and immigrant families) and supporting retention of families in programs. The association between program effects and participant characteristics could be graphed in the form of a bell-shaped curve, with families with moderate levels of risk factors reaping greater benefits from intervention programs then families with fewer risk factors or with multiple risk factors (Fuligni & Brooks-Gunn, 2000). This curvilinear relationship has been demonstrated in several program evaluations, such as PAT, IHDP, and Parent–Child Demonstration Centers (Brooks-Gunn et al., 1992; Brooks-Gunn, Klebanov, Liaw, & Spiker, 1993; Farran, 2000; Wagner & Clayton, 1999). These results indicate that program effects are not uniform across participants due to heterogeneity within the populations served. Consequently, programs need to be flexible enough to serve a diverse population and to intensify services for children at high risk for low literacy. Related to meeting individual family needs is the notion of participant retention in the program. For instance, high attrition rates are not uncommon in home-visiting and some mixed-service model programs (Baker, Piotrkowski, & Brodes-Gunn, 1999; Wagner & Clayton, 1999; Walker & Johnson, 1988). High program retention rates lead to stronger effects on both families and children, as program participation is a more or less uniform experience for the families.

In Search of New Child Literacy Outcomes

As we noted earlier, very few intervention programs use measures of literacy development per se. Most outcomes for the studies we have reviewed fell under a broad definition of literacy that includes associated skills and abilities, such as cognitive development and language skills. Alternative approaches to assessing literacy outcome are required, such as those that have been explored in the Home School Study of Language and Literacy Development (Dickinson & Tabors, 2001); the New Chance Evaluation (De Temple & Tabors, 1994); and the Newark Young Family Study (Britto & Brooks-Gunn, 2001). These approaches have relied on observational data taken during adult and child print-related interactions to obtain language samples from young children. One of the most commonly observed interactions concerns shared book reading, in large part due to the strong links between verbal interactions during such activities and subsequent literacy development (Britto & Brooks-Gunn, 2001; Ewers & Brownson, 1999; Saracho, 1997; Sénéchal & LeFevre, 2001; Snow et al., 1998). Similar alternative approaches to assessing child literacy outcomes are also being explored in a few of the sites participating in the national EHS research and evaluation project. The results of those evaluations are awaited.

Another important issue in the measurement of early literacy development among low-income families is literacy development among children whose first language is not English. Large-scale research projects have not yet come to agreement on the best way to measure the development of language and preliteracy skills among children of immigrants, who are overrepresented among low-income samples. Questions of how to compare standardized language assessments of bilingual children with monolingual children, as well as the appropriate norming practices, must be addressed.

In summary, we have attempted to understand the links between family-level and community-level influences on early literacy development for children from low-SES backgrounds. We separated out these influences as far as possible to understand the contribution of each individual factor. Given that learning begins at birth and children from low-SES backgrounds are at risk for low literacy development at a very early age, we reviewed the effectiveness of early intervention efforts for children from birth to 3 years of age. Some of the interventions have shown evidence of promise in raising children's academic and literacy-related skills. The increase in intervention programs and associated research studies focusing on the zero-to-3 age group promises to move the field toward providing appropriate and effective interventions. We hypothesize that improvements in program design and implementation that target key issues such as increasing program intensity, retaining participants in the program, and developing more sensitive and nuanced measures of literacy will lead to more efficacious efforts to enhance children's early literacy development.

Notes

1. We do not address the child-level influences, as the interventions aimed to ameliorate physical and clinical conditions are beyond the scope of the present chapter.
2. However, more recently researchers have argued for more sensitive measures of maternal education beyond number of years of schooling to include aspects such as quality of schooling (Davis-Kean & Magnuson, 2005).
3. Decontextualized language, which has been defined as an ability to talk about nonpresent objects with little reliance on the shared physical context (Snow, 1991) and its presence in adult–child activities such as book reading is linked to child outcomes (Britto & Brooks-Gunn, 2001) and strongly predictive of later-developing literacy skills (Dickinson, De Temple, & Hirschler, 1992).
4. Other dimensions include the learning environment, the warmth in the home, the physical environment, and so forth (Britto & Brooks-Gunn, 2001).

References

Alexander, K. L., Entwisle, D. R., & Bedinger, S. D. (1994). When expectations work: Race and socioeconomic differences in school performance. *Social Psychology Quarterly, 57*(4), 283–299.

Andrews, S. R., Blumenthal, J. B., Johnson, D. L., Kahn, A. J., Ferguson, C. J., Lasater, R. M., et al. (1982). The skills of mothering: A study of parent child development centers. *Monographs of the Society for Research in Child Development, 47*(6, Serial No. 198).

Arnett, J. (1989). Caregivers in day-care centers: Does training matter? *Journal of Applied Developmental Psychology, 10,* 541–552.

Auerbach, E. (1989). Toward a social-contextual approach to family literacy. *Harvard Educational Review, 59*(2), 165–181.

Baker, A., Piotrkowski, C., & Brooks-Gunn, J. (1999). The Home Instruction Program for Preschool Youngsters (HIPPY). *Future of Children, 9*(1), 116–133.

Baker, L., Serpell, R., & Sonnenschein, S. (1995). Opportunities for literacy learning in the homes of urban preschoolers. In L. Morrow (Ed.), *Family literacy: Connections in schools and communities* (pp. 236–252). Newark, DE: International Reading Association

Barnett, W. S. (1995). Long-term effects of early childhood programs on cognitive and school outcomes. *The Future of Children, 5,* 25–50.

Baydar, N., Brooks-Gunn, J., & Furstenberg, F. F., Jr. (1993). Early warning signs of functional illiteracy: Predictors in childhood and adolescence. *Child Development, 64*(3), 815–829.

Bayley, N. (1969). *Bayley Scales of Infant Development: Manual.* New York: Psychological Corporation.

Bayley, N. (1991–1993). *Bayley Scales of Infant Development* (2nd ed., standardization version). New York: Psychological Corporation.

Beals, D. E., De Temple, J. M., & Dickinson, D. K. (1994). Talking and listening that support early literacy development of children from low-income families. In D. Dickinson (Ed.), *Bridges to literacy: Children, families, and schools* (pp. 19–42). Cambridge, MA: Blackwell.

Berlin, L. J., O'Neal, C. R., & Brooks-Gunn, J. (1998). What makes early intervention programs work?: The program, its participants, and their interaction. In L. J. Berlin (Ed.), Opening the black box: What makes early child and family development programs work? [Special issue]. *Zero to Three, 18,* 4–15.

Blau, D. M. (1999). The effect of income on child development. *Review of Economics and Statistics, 8,* 261–276.

Bornstein, M. H., Hahn, C., Suwalsky, J. T. D., & Haynes, O. M. (2003). Socioeconomic status, parenting, and child development: The Hollingshead Four Factor Index of Social Status and the Socioeconomic Index of Occupation. In M. H. Bornstein & R. F. Bradley (Eds.), *Socioeconomic status, parenting, and child development* (pp. 29–81). Mahwah, NJ: Erlbaum.

Boyd, F. B., Brock, C. H., & Rozendal, M. S. (Eds.). (2004). *Multicultural and multilingual language and literacy: Contexts and practices.* New York: Guilford Press.

Bracken, B. A. (1984). *Bracken Basic Concept Scale.* San Antonio, TX: Psychological Corporation.

Bradley, R. H. (1995). Environment and parenting. In M. Bornstein (Ed.), *Handbook of parenting* (Vol. 2, pp. 235–261). Hillsdale, NJ: Erlbaum.

Bradley, R., & Caldwell, B. (1988). Using the HOME Inventory to assess the family environment. *Pediatric Nursing, 14,* 97–102.

Britto, P. R., & Brooks-Gunn, J. (Eds.) (2001). *New directions for child and adolescent development: The role of family literacy environments in promoting young children's emerging literacy skills.92.* San Francisco: Jossey Bass.

Britto, P. R., & Brooks-Gunn, J. (2004). *The "before" and "after" of shared book reading: Observations of young African-American mothers' reading to their preschoolers.* Manuscript submitted for publication.

Britto, P. R., Brooks-Gunn, J., & Griffin, T. (in press). Maternal reading and teaching patterns: Associations with school readiness in low income, African American families. *Reading Research Quarterly.*

Britto, P. R., Fuligni, A. S., & Brooks-Gunn, J. (2002). Reading, rhymes and routines: American parents and their young children. In N. Halfon, M. A. Schuster, & K. T. McLearn (Eds.), *Child rearing in America: The conditions of young children in American families* (pp 117–145). Cambridge, MA: Cambridge University Press.

Brody, G. H., Stoneman, Z., Flor, D., McCary, C., Hastings, L., & Conyers, O. (1994). Financial resources, parent psychological functioning, parent co-caregiving, and early adolescent competence in rural two-parent African-American families. *Child Development, 65,* 590–605.

Brooks-Gunn, J., Klebanov, P. K., Liaw, F., & Spiker, D. (1993). Enhancing the development of low birth weight, premature infants: Changes in cognition and behavior over the first three years. *Child Development, 64*(3), 736–753.

Brooks-Gunn, J. (1995). Strategies for altering the outcomes of poor children and their families. In P. L. Chase-Lansdale & J. Brooks-Gunn (Eds.), *Escape from poverty: What makes a difference for children?* (pp. 87–117). New York: Cambridge University Press.

Brooks-Gunn, J., Britto, P. R., & Brady, C. (1999). Struggling to make ends meet: Poverty and child development. In M. E. Lamb (Ed.), *Parenting and child development in "non-traditional" families* (pp. 279–304). Mahwah, NJ: Erlbaum.

Brooks-Gunn, J., Burchinal, M., & Lopez, M. (2001). *Enhancing the cognitive and social development of young children via parent education in the Comprehensive Child Development Program.* Manuscript submitted for publication.

Brooks-Gunn, J., Duncan, G., & Britto, P. (1999). Are socioeconomic gradients for children similar to those for adults?: Achievement and health in the United States. In D. P. Keating & C. Hertzman (Eds.), *Developmental health and the wealth of nations: Social, biological and educational dynamics* (pp. 94–124). New York: Guilford Press.

Brooks-Gunn, J., Fuligni, A. S., & Berlin, L. J. (2003). *Early child development in the 21st century: Profiles of current research initiatives.* New York: Teachers College Press.

Brooks-Gunn, J., Liaw, F., & Klebanov, P.K. (1992). Effects of early intervention on low birth weight preterm infants: What aspects of cognitive functioning are enhanced? *Journal of Pediatrics, 120,* 350–359.

Brooks-Gunn, J., McCarton, C., Casey, P., McCormick, M., Bauer, C., Bernbaum, J., et al. (1994). Early intervention in low birth weight, premature infants: Results through age 5 years from the Infant Health and Development Program. *Journal of the American Medical Association, 272,* 1257–1262.

Bryant, D., & Maxwell, K. (1997). The effectiveness of early intervention for disadvantaged children. In M. J. Guralnick (Ed.), *The effectiveness of early intervention* (pp. 23–46). Baltimore: Brookes.

Bryk, A. S., & Raudenbush, S. W. (1987). Application of hierarchical linear models to assessing change. *Psychological Bulletin, 101*(10) 147–158.

Bryk, A. S., & Raudenbush, S. W. (1992). *Hierarchical Linear Models for social and behavioral research: Applications and data analysis methods.* Newbury Park, CA: Sage.

Burchinal, M. R., Nelson, L., Carlson, M., & Brooks-Gunn, J. (submitted). *Community and family selection factors in child care choices: The Project on Human Development in Chicago neighborhoods.*

Burchinal, M. R., Roberts, J. E., Riggins, Jr., R., Zeisel, S. A., Neebe, E., & Bryant, D. (2000). Relating quality of center-based child care to early cognitive and language development longitudinally. *Child Development, 71,* 339–357.

Bus, A. G., van IJzendoorn, M. H., & Pellegrini, A. D. (1995). Joint book reading makes success in learning to read: A meta-analysis on intergenerational transmission of literacy. *Review of Educational Research, 65,* 1–21.

Campbell, F., & Ramey, C. (1994). Effects of early intervention on intellectual and academic achievement: A follow-up study from low-income families. *Child Development, 65,* 684–698.

Chall, J. S., Jacobs, V. A., & Baldwin, L. E. (1990). *The reading crisis: Why poor children fall behind.* Cambridge, MA: Harvard University Press.

Clarke, A. T., & Kurtz-Costes, B. (1997). Television viewing, educational quality of the home environment and school readiness. *Journal of Educational Research, 90*(5), 279–285.

Corcoran, M.E. & Chaudry, A. (1997). The dynamics of childhood poverty. *The Future of Children,* 7(2), 40–54.

Crain-Thoreson, C., Dahlin, M. P., & Powell, T. A. (2001). Parent–child interaction in three conversational contexts: Variations in style and strategy. In P. R. Britto & J. Brooks-Gunn (Eds.), *New directions for child and adolescent development: Vol. 92. The role of family literacy environments in promoting young children's emerging literacy skills* (pp. 23–38). San Francisco, CA: Jossey-Bass.

Custodero, L., Britto, P., & Brooks-Gunn, J. (2003). Musical lives: A collective portrait of American parents and their young children. *Journal of Applied Developmental Psychology, 24*(5), 553–572.

Dauber, S. L., Alexander, K. L., & Entwisle, D. R. (1996). Tracking and transitions through middle grades: Channeling educational trajectories. *Sociology of Education, 69,* 290–307.

Davis-Kean, P. E. (2005). The influence of parent education and family income on child achievement: The indirect role of parental expectations and the home environment. *Journal of Family Psychology.*

Davis-Kean, P. E., & Magnuson, K. (2005). *The influence of parents' educational attainment on child development.* Unpublished manuscript.

DeBaryshe, B. D. (1995). Maternal belief systems: Linchpin in the home reading process. *Journal of Applied Developmental Psychology, 16,* 1–20.

De Temple, J. (2001). Parents and children reading books together. In D. Dickinson & P. O. Tabors (Eds.), *Beginning literacy with language: Young children learning at home and school* (pp. 31–52). Baltimore: Brookes.

De Temple, J. M., & Tabors, P. O. (1994, December). *Styles of interaction during a book reading task: Implications for literacy intervention with low-income families.* Paper presented at the annual meeting of the National Reading Conference, San Diego, CA.

Dickinson, D. K., De Temple, J. M., & Hirschler, J. A. (1992). Book reading with preschoolers: Co construction of text at home and school. *Early Childhood Research Quarterly, 7,* 323–346

Dickinson, D. K., & Beals, D. E. (1994). Not by print alone: oral language supports for early literacy development. In D. F. Lancy (Ed.), *Children's emergent literacy: From research to practice.* (pp. 29–40). Westport, CT: Praeger.

Dickinson, D. K., & Sprague, K. E. (2001). The nature and impact of early childhood care environments on the language and early literacy development of children from low-income families. In S. B. Neuman & D. D. Dickinson (Eds.), *Handbook of early literacy research* (pp. 263–280). New York: Guilford Press.

Dickinson, D. K., & Tabors, P. O. (2001). *Beginning*

literacy with language: Young children learning at home and school. Baltimore, MD: Brookes.

Duggan, A. K., McFarlane, E. C., Windham, A. M., Rohde, C. A., Salkever, D. S., Fuddy, L., et al. (1999). Evaluation of Hawaii's Healthy Start Program. *The Future of Children, 9*(1), 66–90.

Duncan, G., & Brooks-Gunn, J. (Eds.). (1997). *Consequences of growing up poor.* New York: Russell Sage.

Duncan, G. J., & Magnuson, K. (2003). Off with Hollingshead: Socioeconomic resources, parenting, and child development. In M. H. Bornstein & R. H. Bradley (Eds.), *Socioeconomic status, parenting, and child development* (pp. 83–106). Mahwah, NJ: Erlbaum.

Duncan, G. J., Yeung, W. J., Brooks-Gunn, J., & Smith, J. R. (1998). How much does childhood poverty affect the life chances of children? *American Sociological Review, 63,* 406–423.

Dunn, L. M., & Dunn, L. M., (1981). *Peabody Picture Vocabulary Test–Revised.* Circle Pines, MN: American Guidance Service.

Edwards, P. A. (1989). Supporting lower SES mothers' attempts to provide scaffolding for book reading. In J. Allen & J. Mason (Eds.), *Risk makers, risk takers, risk breakers: Reducing the risks for young literacy learners* (pp. 222–250). Portsmouth, NH: Heinemann.

Edwards, P. A. (1994). Responses of teachers and African-American mothers to a book-reading intervention program. In D. K. Dickinson (Ed.), *Bridges to literacy: Children, families, and schools* (pp. 175–210). Cambridge, MA: Blackwell.

Ensminger, M., & Fothergill, K. (2003). A decade of measuring SES: What it tells us and where to go from here. In M. H. Bornstein & R. H. Bradley (Eds.), *Socioeconomic status, parenting, and child development* (pp. 13–27). Mahwah, NJ: Erlbaum.

Ewers, C. A., & Brownson, S. M. (1999). Kindergarteners' vocabulary acquisition as a function of active vs. passive storybook reading, prior vocabulary, and working memory. *Reading Psychology, 20,* 11–20.

Farran, D. C. (2000). Another decade of intervention for children who are low income or disabled: What do we know now? In J. P. Shonkoff & S. J. Meisels (Eds.), *Handbook of early childhood intervention* (2nd ed., pp. 510–548). New York: Cambridge University Press.

Fenson, L., Dale, P. S., Reznick, J. S., Thal, D., & Reilly, J. S. (1991). *Technical Manual for MacArthur Communicative Development.* San Diego, CA: San Diego State University.

Fitzgerald, J., Spiegel, D. L., & Cunningham, J. W. (1991). The relationships between parental literacy level and perceptions of emergent literacy. *Journal of Reading Behavior, 23*(2), 191–213.

Francis, D. J., Shaywitz, S. E., Stuebing, K. K.,

Shaywitz, B. A., & Fletcher, J. M. (1996). Developmental lag versus deficit model of reading disability: A longitudinal, individual growth curve analysis. *Journal of Educational Psychology, 88,* 3–17.

Fuligni, A. S., & Brooks-Gunn, J. (2004). Early childhood intervention in family literacy programs. In B. H. Wasik (Ed.), *Handbook of family literacy* (pp. 117–136). Mahwah, NJ: Erlbaum.

Fuligni, A. S., & Brooks-Gunn, J. (2000). The healthy development of young children: SES disparities, prevention strategies, and policy opportunities. In B. D. Smedley & S. L. Syme (Eds.). *Promoting health: Intervention strategies from social and behavioral research.* (pp. 170–216). Washington, DC: National Academy of Sciences.

Fuller, B., Holloway, S. D., Bozzi, L., Burr, E., Cohen, N., & Suzuki, S. (2003). Explaining local variability in child care quality: State funding and regulation in California. *Early Education and Development, 14,* 47–66.

Gadsden, V. L. (1995). Literacy and poverty: Intergenerational issues within African-American families. In H. E. Fitzgerald, B. M. Lester, & B. Zuckerman (Eds.), *Children of poverty: Research, health, and policy issues* (pp. 85–124). New York: Garland.

Goldenberg, C., Reese, L., & Gallimore, R. (1992). Effects of literacy materials from school on Latino children's home experiences and early reading achievement. *American Journal of Education, 100,* 497–537.

Gross, R. T., Spiker, D., & Haynes, C. W. (Eds.) (1997). *Helping low birth weight babies: The Infant Health and Development Program.* Stanford, CA: Stanford University Press.

Haden, C. A., Reese, E., & Fivush, R. (1996). Mothers' extra textual comments during storybook reading: Stylistic differences over time and across texts. *Discourse Processes, 21,* 135–169.

Halpern, R. (2000). Early intervention for low-income children and families. In J. P. Shonkoff & S. J. Meisels (Eds.), *Handbook of early childhood intervention* (2nd ed., pp. 361–386). New York: Cambridge University Press.

Hammer, C. S. (2001). "Come sit down and let mama read": Book reading interactions between African-American mothers and their infants. In J. L. Harris, A. G. Kamhi, & K. E. Pollock (Eds.), *Literacy in African-American communities* (pp. 21–43). Mahwah, NJ: Erlbaum.

Harms, T., Clifford, R., & Cryer, D. (1997). *Published ECERS and FDCRS scales.* New York: Teachers College Press.

Haveman, R., & Wolfe, B. (1995). The determinants of children's attainments: A review of methods and findings. *Journal of Economic Literature, 23,* 1829–1878.

Hill, J., Waldfogel, J., & Brooks-Gunn, J. (2002).

Assessing the differential impacts of high-quality child care: A new approach for exploiting post-treatment variables. *Journal of Policy Analysis and Management, 21*(4), 601–627.

Hoff, E. (2003). Causes and consequences of SES-related differences in parent-to-child speech. In M. H. Bornstein & R. H. Bradley (Eds.), *Socioeconomic status, parenting, and child development* (pp. 145–160). Mahwah, NJ: Erlbaum.

Infant Health and Development Program. (1990). Enhancing the outcomes of low-birthweight, premature infants. *Journal of the American Medical Association, 263*, 3035–3042.

Johnson, D. L., & Walker, T. (1987). Primary prevention of behavior problems in Mexican-American children. *American Journal of Community Psychology, 15*(4), 375–385.

Johnston, P. H., & Rogers, R. (2001). Early literacy development: The case for "informed assessment." In S. B. Neuman & D. D. Dickinson (Eds.), *Handbook of early literacy research* (pp. 377–389). New York: Guilford Press.

Kitzman, H., Olds, D. L., Sidora, K., Henderson, C. R., Hanks, C., Cole, R., et al. (2000). Enduring effects of nurse home visitation on maternal life course. *Journal of the American Medical Association, 283*, 1983–1989.

Klebanov, P. K., Brooks-Gunn, J., Chase-Lansdale, L., & Gordon, R. (1997). Are neighborhood effects on young children mediated by features of the home environment? In J. Brooks-Gunn, G. Duncan, & J. L. Aber (Eds.), *Neighborhood poverty: Context and consequences for children.* (Vol. 1, pp. 119–145). New York: Russell Sage.

Klebanov, P. K., Brooks-Gunn, J., & Duncan, G. J. (1994). Does neighborhood and family poverty affect mothers' parenting, mental health, and social support? *Journal of Marriage and the Family, 56*(2), 441–455.

Klebanov, P. K., Brooks-Gunn, J., McCarton, C., & McCormick, M. C. (1998). The contribution of neighborhood and family income to developmental test scores over the first three years of life. *Child Development, 69*, 1420–1436.

Lancy, D. F., Draper, K. D., & Boyce, G. (1989). Parental influence on children's acquisition of reading. *Contemporary Issues in Reading, 4*(1), 83–93.

Leventhal, T., & Brooks-Gunn, J. (2002). Poverty and child development. *International encyclopedia of the social and behavioral sciences, 3*(14), 11889–11893.

Leventhal, T., Martin, A., & Brooks-Gunn, J. (2004). The Home Observation for Measurement of the Environment (HOME) Inventory–Early Childhood: Across five national datasets in the third to fifth year of life. *Parenting, 4* (2/3), 99–114.

Loeb, S., Fuller, B., Kagan, S. L., & Carrol, B. (2004). Child care in poor communities: Early learning effects of type, quality, and stability. *Child Development, 75*, 47–65.

Loeb, S., Fuller, B., & Strath, A. (2001). *Explaining the national distribution of child-care workers.* Stanford, CA: Stanford University.

Love, J. M., Kisker, E. E., Ross, C. M., Schochet, P. Z., Brooks-Gunn, J., Paulsell, D. et al. (2002). *Making a difference in the lives of children and families: The impacts of Early Head Start programs on young children and their families.* Washington, DC: U.S. Department of Health and Human Services.

Mason, J. M., & Allen, J. (1986). A review of emergent literacy with implications for research and practice in reading. In C. J. Rothkopf (Ed.), *Review of research in education* (Vol. 13, pp. 3–48). Washington, DC: American Educational Research Association.

Mayer, S. E. (1997). *What money can't buy: Family income and children's life chances.* Cambridge, MA: Harvard University Press.

McCarton, C. M., Brooks-Gunn, J., Wallace, I. F., Bauer, C. R., Bennett, F. C., Bernbaum, J. C., et al. (1997). Results at age 8 years of early intervention for low-birth-weight premature infants: The Infant Health and Development Program. *Journal of the American Medical Association, 277*, 126–132.

McCurdy, K. (1995). *Homevisiting.* Washington, DC: National Resource Center on Child Abuse and Neglect.

McCurdy, K. (1996). *Intensive home visitation: A randomized trial, follow-up and risk assessment study of Hawaii's Healthy Start Program: Executive Summary.* Report submitted to Administration for Children, Youth and Families, U.S. Department of Health and Human Services.

McCurdy, K. (2001). Can home visitation enhance maternal social support? *American Journal of Community Psychology, 29*, 97–112.

McLoyd, V. C. (1990). The impact of economic hardship on Black families and children: Psychological distress, parenting, and socioemotional development. *Child Development, 61*, 311–346.

McLoyd, V. C., & Wilson, L. (1991). The strain of living poor: Parenting, social support, and child mental health. In V. C. McLoyd & C. A. Flanagan (Eds.), Economic stress: Effects on family life and child development. *New Directions for Child Development, 46*, 49–69.

Mikulecky, L. (1996). Family literacy: Parent and child interactions. In L. A. Benjamin & J. Lord (Eds.), *Family literacy: Directions in research and implications for practice* (pp. 55–63). Washington, DC: U.S. Department of Education.

Morris, P., Duncan, G. J., & Rodrigues, C. (2005). *Does money really matter: Estimating impacts of family incomes on children's achievement with data from random-assignment experiments.* Unpublished manuscript.

Morrow, L. M., Paratore, J., Gaber, D., Harrison, C., & Tracey, D. (1993). Family literacy: Perspective and practices. *Reading Teacher, 47*(3), 194–200.

Naglieri, J. A., & Bardos, A. N. (1990). Bracken Basic Concept Scale. *Diagnostique, 15*, 41–50.

Naigles, L. R., & Mayeux, L. (2001). Television as incidental language teacher. In D. Singer & J. Singer (Eds.), *Handbook of children and the media* (pp. 135–152). Thousand Oaks, CA: Sage.

National Assessment of Educational Progress. (1998). *1996 reading report card for the nation and the states.* Washington, DC: U.S. Department of Education.

National Center for Education Statistics. (1992). *National assessment of education progress: 1992 trends in academic progress.* Washington, DC: U.S. Department of Education.

National Education Goals Panel. (1998). *The National Education Goals report: Building a nation of learners.* Washington, DC: U.S. Government Printing Office.

Neuman, S. B. (1991). *Literacy in the television age.* Norwood, NJ: Ablex.

Neuman, S. B., & Dickinson, D. D. (Eds.). (2001). *Handbook of early literacy research.* New York: Guilford Press.

Neuman, S. B., & Gallagher, P. (1994). Joining together in literacy learning: Teenage mothers and children. *Reading Research Quarterly, 29*(4), 383–401.

National Institute of Child Health and Human Development. (2002, June). *Early childhood education and school readiness: Conceptual models, constructs, and measures.* Workshop proceedings, Washington, DC.

NICHD Early Child Care Research Network. (1997). Poverty and patterns of child care. In G. Duncan & J. Brooks-Gunn (Eds.), *Consequences of growing up poor* (pp. 100–131). New York: Russell Sage.

NICHD Early Child Care Research Network. (1999). Child outcomes when child care classes meet recommended standards for quality. *American Journal of Public Health, 89*, 1072–1077.

NICHD Early Child Care Research Network. (2001). Nonmaternal care and family factors in early development: An overview of the NICHD Study of Early Child Care. *Journal of Applied Developmental Psychology, 22*(5), 457–492.

NICHD & Duncan, G. J. (2003). Modeling the impacts of child care quality on children's preschool cognitive development. *Child Development, 74*, 1454–1475.

Ogbu, J. U. (1981). Origins of human competence: A cultural–ecological perspective. *Child Development, 52*, 413–429.

Olds, D., Henderson, C. R., Cole, R. E., Eckenrode, J. J., Kitzman, H. J., Luckey, D., et al. (1998). Long-term effects of nurse home visitation on children's criminal and antisocial behavior: 15-year follow-up of a randomized controlled trial. *Journal of the American Medical Association, 280*, 1238–1244.

Olds, D. L., Henderson, C. R., Kitzman, H. J., Eckenrode, J. J., Cole, R. E., & Tatelbaum, R. C. (1999). Prenatal and infancy home visitation by nurses: Recent findings. *The Future of Children, 9*, 44–64.

Olds, D. L., & Kitzman, H. (1993). Review of research on home visiting for pregnant women and parents of young children. *The Future of Children, 3*, 53–92.

Payne, A. C., Whitehurst, G. J., & Angell, A. L. (1994). The role of home literacy environment in the development of language ability in preschool children from low-income families. *Early Childhood Research Quarterly, 9*, 427–444.

Peisner-Feinberg, E. S., & Burchinal, M. R. (1997). Relations between preschool children's child-care experiences and concurrent development: The cost, quality and outcomes study. *Merrill-Palmer Quarterly, 43*, 451–477.

Pellegrini, A. D., Galda, L., Jones, I., & Perlmutter, J. (1995). Joint reading between mothers and their Head Start children: Vocabulary development in two text formats. *Discourse Processes, 19*, 441–463.

Phillips, D. A., Voran, M., Kisker, E., Howes, C., & Whitebook, M. (1994). Child care for children in poverty: Opportunity or inequity? *Child Development, 65*, 231–246.

Pianta, R. C. (1990). Widening the debate on educational reform: Prevention as a viable alternative. *Exceptional Children, 56*, 306–311.

Puma, M., Karweit, N., Price, C., Ricciuti, A., Thompson, W., & Vaden-Kieran, M. (1997). *Prospects: Final report on student outcomes.* Washington, DC: U.S. Department of Education, Planning and Evaluation Services.

Purcell-Gates, V. (1996). Stories, coupons, and the *TV Guide*: Relationships between home literacy experiences and emergent knowledge. *Reading Research Quarterly, 31*(4), 406–428.

Raikes, H., Pan, B., Tamis-Lemonda, C., Brooks-Gunn, J., Wshiard, A., et al. (in press). Parent child book reading. *Child Development.*

Reese, E., & Cox, A. (1999). Quality of adult book reading affects children's emergent literacy. *Developmental Psychology, 20*, 20–28.

Salinger, T. (2001). Assessing the literacy of young children: The case for multiple forms of evidence. In S. B. Neuman & D. D. Dickinson (Eds.), *Handbook of early literacy research* (pp. 390–418). New York: Guilford Press.

Sampson, R., & Morenoff, J. (1997). Ecological perspectives on the neighborhood context of urban poverty: Past and present. In J. Brooks-Gunn, G. J. Duncan, & J. L. Aber (Eds.), *Neighborhood poverty: Conceptual, methodological, and policy approaches to studying neighborhoods* (Vol. 2, pp. 1–23). New York: Russell Sage.

Saracho, O.N. (1997). Perspectives on family literacy. *Early Child Development and Care, 127–128*, 3–11.

Schweinhart, L. J., Barnes, H. V., & Weikart, D. P. (1993). *Significant benefits: The High/Scope Perry preschool study through age 27.* Ypsilanti, MI: High/Scope Press.

Sénéchal, M. (1997). The differential effect of storybook reading on preschoolers' acquisition of expressive and receptive vocabulary. *Journal of Child Language, 24*, 123–138.

Sénéchal, M., & LeFevre, J. (2001). Storybook reading and parent teaching: Links to language and literacy development. In P. R. Britto & J. Brooks-Gunn (Eds.), *The role of family literacy environments in promoting young children's emerging literacy skills* (Vol. 92, pp. 39–52). San Francisco, CA: Jossey-Bass.

Shea, J. (2000). Does parents' money matter? *Journal of Public Economics, 77*, 155–184.

Singer, D., & Singer, J. (Eds.) (2001). *Handbook of children and the media.* Thousand Oaks, CA: Sage.

Snow, C. E. (1993). Families as social contexts for literacy development. In C. Daiute (Ed.), *The development of literacy through social interaction* (pp. 11–24). San Francisco: Jossey-Bass.

Snow, C. E., Burns, S. M., & Griffin, P. (Eds.). (1998). *Preventing reading difficulties in young children.* Washington, DC: National Academy Press.

Snow, C. E., Barnes, W. S., Chandler, J., Hemphill, L., & Goodman, I. F. (1991). *Unfulfilled expectations: Home and school influences on literacy.* Cambridge, MA: Harvard University Press.

Sonnenschein, S., Brody, G., & Munsterman, K. (1996). The influences of family beliefs and practices on children's early reading development. In L. Baker, P. Afflerbach, & D. Reinking (Eds.), *Developing engaged readers in school and home communities.* (pp. 3–20). Mahwah, NJ: Erlbaum.

St. Pierre, R. G., & Layzer, J. I. (1999). Using home visits for multiple purposes: The Comprehensive Child Development Program. *Future of Children, 9*, 134–151.

St. Pierre, R. G., Layzer, J. I., Goodson, B. D., & Bernstein, L. S. (1997). *National impact evaluation of the Comprehensive Child Development Program: Final report.* Cambridge, MA: Abt.

Stone, C. A., Silliman, E. R., Ehren, B. J., & Apel, K. (Eds.) (2004). *Handbook of language and literacy: development and disorders.* New York: Guilford Press.

Sugland, B. W., Zaslow, M., Smith, J. R., Brooks-Gunn, J., Coates, D., Blumenthal, C., et al. (1995). The Early Childhood HOME Inventory and HOME—Short Form in differing racial/ethnic groups: Are there differences in underlying structure, internal consistency of subscales, and patterns of prediction? *Journal of Family Issues, 16*, 632–663.

Sulzby, E., & Teale, W. (1991). Emergent literacy. In R. Barr, M. Kamil, P. Mosenthal, & P. D. Pearson (Eds.), *Handbook of reading research* (Vol. 2, pp. 727–758). New York: Longman.

Taylor, D. (1983). *Family literacy: Young children learning to read and write.* Portsmouth, NH: Heinemann.

Taylor, D. (Ed.). (1997). *Many families, many literacies: An international declaration of principles.* Portsmouth, NH: Heinemann.

Teale, W. H., & Sulzby, E. (Eds.). (1986). *Emergent literacy: Writing and reading.* Norwood, NJ: Ablex.

Toomey, D., & Sloane, J. (1994). Fostering children's early literacy development through parental involvement: A five-year program. In D. Dickinson (Ed.), *Bridges to literacy: Children, families and schools* (pp. 129–149) Cambridge, MA: Blackwell.

Trehub, S. E., & Trainor, L. J. (1998). Singing to infants: Lullabies and playsongs. *Advances in Infancy Research, 12*, 43–77.

U.S. Census Bureau. (2002, March) Current population surveys, 1976–2002. Available online at www.census.gov/prod/2003pubs/p60-222.pdf

Vernon-Feagans, L., Hammer, C. S., Miccio, A., & Manlove, E. (2001). Early language and literacy skills in low-income African-American and Hispanic children. In S. B. Neuman & D. K. Dickinson, (Eds.), *Handbook of early literacy Research* (pp. 192–210). New York: Guilford Press.

Wagner, R. K. (2003). Sketching a framework for assessment: Prospects for moving beyond first principles to practice. *Measurement: Interdisciplincary research and perspectives, 1*, 88–91.

Wagner, M. M., & Clayton, S. L. (1999). The Parents as Teachers program: Results from two demonstrations. *The Future of Children, 9*, 91–115.

Walker, T., & Johnson, D. L. (1988). A follow-up evaluation of the Houston Parent–Child Development Center: Intelligence test results. *Journal of Genetic Psychology, 149*(3), 377–381.

West, J., Denton, K., & Germino-Hausken, E. (2000). America's kindergartners: Finding from the early childhood longitudinal study, kindergarten class of 1998–99, Fall 1998 (NCES Report No. 2000-070). Washington, DC: National Center for Education Statistics.

White, K. R. (1982). The relation between socioeconomic status and academic achievement. *Psychological Bulletin, 91*, 461–481.

Whitehurst, G. J. (1997). Language processes in context: Language learning in children reared in poverty. In L.B. Adamson & M.A. Romski (Eds.), *Research on communication and language disorders: Contribution to theories of language development* (pp. 233–266). Baltimore, MD: Brookes.

Whitehurst, G. J., & Lonigan, C. J. (1998). Child development and emergent literacy. *Child Development*, 69(3), 848–872.

Whitehurst, G. J., Zevenberger, A. A., Crone, D. A., Schultz, M. D., Velting, O. N., & Fischel, J. E. (1999). Outcomes of emergent literacy intervention from Head Start through second grade.

Journal of Educational Psychology, 91, 261–272.

Willms, J. D. (1999). Quality and inequality in children's literacy: The effects of families, schools, and communities. In D. P. Keating & C. Hertzman (Eds.), *Developmental health and the wealth of nations* (pp. 72–93). New York: Guilford Press.

Wilson, W. J. (1987). *The truly disadvantaged: The inner city, the underclass, and public policy.* Chicago: University of Chicago Press.

Yoshikawa, H. (1995). Long-term effects of early childhood programs on social outcomes and delinquency. *The Future of Children*, 5(3), 51–75.

24

A Pediatric Approach to Early Literacy

ROBERT NEEDLMAN
PERRI KLASS
BARRY ZUCKERMAN

Since the description in 1895 of "congenital word blindness" by a Scottish ophthalmologist, the traditional medical approach to literacy has focused on literacy problems, and specifically on identifying and treating brain-based reading disability. Recently, however, pediatricians[1] have begun to pay more attention to the normative aspects of literacy development and to incorporate promotion of reading aloud into their standard health supervision routine. The catalyst for this change has been a program called Reach Out and Read (ROR). In the ROR model, at each health supervision visit (i.e., well-child check) from 6 months through 5 years of age, the doctor offers the parent individualized guidance about reading aloud and provides a new, developmentally and culturally appropriate picture book. Furthermore, in many clinics, in addition to a well-stocked bookshelf and displays about reading, community volunteers are scheduled to read aloud in the waiting rooms with the children, demonstrating to parents effective ways to use picture books with young children.

First piloted in Boston in 1989, ROR has now been adopted by more than 2,000 clinics serving lower-income children, including most academic pediatric and family-practice training programs. There are ROR clinics in all 50 states, as well as in Italy, Great Britain, and Israel. A growing body of evidence sug-gests that the approach is effective, particularly for children who are at greatest risk of developing reading problems. This chapter describes the rationale for making reading aloud a focus of routine medical encounters, reviews the evidence of the approach's efficacy, and explores the implications of these clinic-based interventions for future program development and research.

Rationale and Program Operation

The rationale for making literacy a target of pediatric intervention is threefold. First, the medical community is increasingly aware that illiteracy constitutes a *health* risk. Second, pediatricians understand that experience shapes synaptic development, providing a biological rationale for efforts to enhance the early learning environment. Finally, the pediatric health supervision encounter (informally, the "checkup") provides an opportune context in which to promote reading aloud and other parenting practices that support literacy development.

Medical risks associated with low literacy have been extensively documented in adult populations and to a lesser degree in children (Weiss, Hart, & Pust, 1991; Kefalides, 1999). Adults with limited literacy face increased risk of illness and hospitalization and higher health care costs, even after controlling for socioeconomic status and other potential confounding factors (Weiss, Hart, & McGee, 1992; Baker et al., 1996). The medical risks extend from difficulty reading prescription labels and poison warnings to inability to read and comprehend complex statements of the risks and benefits of participation in medical research (Golstein, Frasier, Curtis, Reid, & Krecher, 1996; Mrvos, Dean, & Krenzelok, 1993). The labyrinthine hallways of a large medical center constitute a physical barrier to care: Patients who cannot read the signs are apt to become lost, arrive late at appointments, or simply give up (Baker et al., 1996).

Children whose parents have low literacy face similar hurdles. In contemporary practice, a great deal of information is conveyed to parents through handouts and pamphlets, but these are often written at a level far higher than the average reading ability of the parents (Davis, Crouch, Wills, Miller, & Abdehou, 1990). Patients and parents with limited literacy may avoid asking questions if they think the information might appear in printed material they have just been handed, because to do so would risk exposing their illiteracy (Parikh, Parker, Nurss, Baker, & Williams, 1996). Instead, they may guess at doses, timing of medications, indications for telephoning the office, and so on (Baker et al., 1996).

Another way in which reading problems become medical problems for children arises from the link between educational failure and risk-taking behavior. Children who fail at reading may be more likely to leave school before earning their diplomas, more likely to engage in risky sexual behavior leading to pregnancy, and more likely to engage in illegal activities resulting in injury and incarceration. The evidence connecting early reading failure and later medical morbidity is suggestive, but not conclusive. It is known, for example, that the incidence of premature sexual activity and pregnancy is lower among college-bound girls and that the prevalence of educational disability is higher among incarcerated youths than among their nonincarcerated peers (Haigler, Harlow, O'Connor, & Campbell, 1994). Prospective studies have shown that children who receive intensive early educational interventions are less likely to experience later legal troubles (Ramey et

al., 1992). Promoting early reading success may therefore reduce later social and medical morbidity.

Over the past decade pediatricians, along with the rest of society, have been fascinated by advances in developmental neurobiology. The demonstration that experience plays a crucial role in directing synaptic development provides a compelling biological rationale for early intervention (Klass, Needlman, & Zuckerman, 2003). The existence of sensitive periods after which specific neural systems become relatively resistant to further modification lends a sense of urgency. Although there is no evidence of a biologically sensitive period for literacy per se, the neural systems underlying auditory perception, attention, and language are developing rapidly during the first 5 years of life (see also Dickinson, McCabe & Essex, Chapter 1, this volume). Experiences that strengthen these emerging systems, such as participation in reading aloud, may facilitate later literacy acquisition (also see Pugh, Sandak, Frost, Moore, & Mencl, Chapter 5, this volume).

The final rationale for incorporating literacy into pediatric primary care is that the current system of health supervision visits readily lends itself to the promotion of reading aloud. As improved immunizations, safety regulations, and other public health measures have reduced the burden of illness and injury, developmental and behavioral concerns have become increasingly prominent components of primary health care for children (Dinkevich & Ozuah, 2002). The level of pediatrician's expertise in dealing with these concerns has risen over the past decade, largely as a consequence of new requirements for training in developmental and behavioral issues. Parents expect pediatricians to provide not only reassurance of their children's physical well-being but also guidance about their learning and emotional development (Regalado & Halfon, 2001; Dworkin, 1993; Nelson, Wissow, & Cheng, 2003). The American Academy of Pediatrics' schedule for health supervision establishes multiple opportunities for pediatricians to counsel parents on such issues, recommending a dozen routine visits before the child's 6th birthday. Visits are scheduled every 2 to 3 months during the first year of life, stretching to 6 months by the end of the second year and annually after that. Most of these checkups are linked to specific immunizations, adding an incentive for parental participation. Nationally, approximately 80% of children receive a full set of immunizations; very few receive no immunizations at all (Barker & McCauley, 2004). Thus pediatricians have frequent access to parents during the period when reading aloud can often be successfully established. The structure of the routine health encounter provides multiple opportunities for literacy promotion, as described next.

Program Implementation

In the clinics that provide care for many lower-income families, children and parents regularly wait for an hour or more before being seen. The waiting room, therefore, becomes a potential context for literacy intervention. By turning waiting rooms into print-rich environments with interventions targeting children and parents, clinics can include at least an element of literacy promotion in every visit. The most novel intervention, which has been an element of several of the published studies on program efficacy, is the availability of volunteer readers. In many ROR programs, there is a special area set aside for reading, demarcated by a rug or a child-sized table and chairs. A reader, typically a community volunteer or a student assigned to perform service learning, sits down and opens a canvas bag full of books. Within minutes, most of the children old enough to walk have gravitated to this fascinating newcomer. And as the reader begins to look at the books with the children, inviting their active participation through pointing, labeling, joining in, and embellishing their own stories, the parents who are observing from the sidelines acquire information about effective techniques for reading aloud and are able to note their own children's interest in being read to. Clinics and practices for which waiting-room volunteer readers are not practical (family practice clinics, for example, which may see only a relatively small number of children a day, or practices with very short waiting times) have shown initiative in developing waiting-room displays on literacy-related subjects, making used books available to waiting children, playing read-aloud videotapes, and in other ways enhancing the waiting-room environment with print, books, and literacy promotion. A comprehensive program manual published by the ROR National Center includes a curriculum for reader training, as well as instructions and guidelines for other aspects of program implementation (see Appendix).

During the health supervision visit, parents typically spend between 10 and 20 minutes face-to-face with the pediatrician. The medical evaluation begins with the physician eliciting parental concerns. Once these have been addressed, the doctor asks a series of probes or "trigger questions" intended to uncover important issues, such as whether an infant sleeps face down (a risk for sudden infant death syndrome) or whether a toddler is over-reliant on the milk bottle. Trigger questions about reading aloud include, for example, "Have you begun looking at picture books with Johnny yet?" or "What do you do with Olivia to help her get ready for bed?" The pediatrician tailors these questions and the ensuing discussion to the individual strengths and challenges of each family.

The agenda for health supervision visits is long, including topics such as nutrition, sleep, safety, discipline, and the parents' emotional state (Committee on Psychosocial Aspects of Child and Family Health, 1997). The competition among diverse issues for scarce visit time means that physicians have to choose which topics to cover. Pediatricians are unlikely to adopt any intervention unless it can be delivered quickly. In the service of efficiency, literacy-related guidance is often combined with information on other relevant topics. For example, in talking with a mother about why it is appropriate for her 6-month-old infant to chew on the new board book, the doctor may also point out that young children need to explore the world with their mouths, leading to a discussion of prevention of choking and poisoning. The topic of regular times for reading leads seamlessly to bedtime routines. Evidence of the efficacy of literacy intervention, discussed later, has swayed many pediatricians to place a high priority on literacy promotion.

The anticipatory guidance provided by the doctor focuses on helping young children grow up loving books, rather than teaching children to read early. The importance of physical closeness and shared enjoyment is stressed. Parents are urged to engage their babies in back-and-forth conversation, rather than sticking to the words on the page, and clinicians are trained to model such book interactions. This approach is informed by Whitehurst's concept of dialogic reading (Whitehurst et al., 1988). "Reading aloud" thus refers to an activity that all parents can successfully undertake, regardless of their reading ability.

The third component of the ROR model, in addition to the waiting-room demonstration and individualized guidance, is the distribution of a free, developmentally and culturally appropriate picture book at each health supervision visit from 6 months through 5 years of age. The books are purchased at substantial discount, so that the pediatrician can provide high-quality books that might have list prices of $5 or more. If a typical child receives 10 picture books over the first 5 years of life, the total cost is still less than that of a single chest X-ray. Unlike pamphlets, which are easily lost, the books persist in the home, reinforcing the messages conveyed by the rest of the clinic experience. The use of new books, rather than second-hand ones, communicates to the parents the high value placed on reading. The books purchased for ROR programs tend to feature children and parents who look like the families in the clinic. A wide selection is available in English, Spanish, or both languages together on the page. A smaller but still considerable number are available in multiple languages, including, for example, Portuguese, Russian, and a variety of East Asian languages. Books with racist, sexist, and other stereotypes are explicitly excluded.

ROR model programs, although conceptually simple, present logistical challenges. Administrative tasks include training physicians and readers, book ordering and inventory, and fund-raising. Leadership is often shared between the medical staff and collaborating service organizations and/or libraries. Supporting the individual centers are a growing number of regional and statewide ROR coalitions. The ROR National Center, provides technical support and quality control and coordinates advocacy at the national level. For the past several years, the national ROR program has received funding from the federal government, most of which has been distributed to local sites in the form of start-up and continuation grants. The rapid expansion of the ROR model has been fueled to a large extent by the accumulation of research showing that clinic-based literacy interventions do make a difference. These studies are reviewed next.

Evidence of Efficacy

The ROR model has distinguished itself from other primary-care psychosocial interventions by the volume of evidence demonstrating its efficacy. At present, 12 articles have appeared in peer-reviewed journals documenting a number of positive outcomes associated with ROR-model programs. The findings include more positive parent and child attitudes toward reading aloud; more frequent reading aloud in general, and specifically at bedtime; and greater book ownership and presence of picture books in the home. Studies have also found improvements in child expressive and receptive vocabulary, both by parent reports and by standardized testing (see Table 24.1). The methodological strengths and limitations of this body of evidence have recently been reviewed (Needlman & Silverstein, 2004). The following paragraphs review details of the more important studies, looking first at parent attitudes and behaviors and second at evidence of changes in children's verbal abilities.

Parent Attitudes and Behaviors

ATTITUDES TOWARD READING ALOUD

Several studies have looked at parent and child attitudes toward reading aloud. In the pilot evaluation of the original ROR program, 79 parents of children ages 6–60 months were interviewed in the waiting room of a clinic serving a low-income clientele in Boston, at a time when the program was not yet universally implemented by the clinic doctors (Needlman, Fried, Morley, Taylor, & Zuckerman, 1991). The study employed open-ended questions to minimize potential overreporting of reading aloud due to social desirability bias. Parents were asked

TABLE 24.1. Study Designs, Samples, and Main Findings

Study	Design	Sample size; location; national origin; and education[a]	Main findings
Needlman (1991)	Cross-sectional, retrospective	$n = 79$; Boston; 51% born outside United States; 25% < high school education	4×[b] increase in Literacy Orientation among parents given books
High (1998)	Pre- and postintervention	$n = 151$; Providence, RI; 30% born outside United States; 37% Latino, 17% African American; 37% < high school education	Approximately 4×[b] increase in child-centered literacy orientation in the intervention group
Golova (1999)	Prospective, quasi-randomized controlled study	$n = 135$; Providence, RI; 92% born outside United States; 90% Spanish speaking at home; 55% single; 57% < high school education	10×[b] increase in reading aloud ≥ 3 nights/week; trend for higher receptive vocabulary in children > 18 months old
High (2000)	Prospective, quasi-randomized controlled study	$n = 205$; Providence, RI; 60% born outside United States; 74% Hispanic; 41% < high school education	Parent-reported receptive vocabulary up 40%, expressive up 80%, in children > 18 months
Jones (2000)	Prospective, quasi-randomized controlled study	$n = 352$; Louisville, KY; 85% African American; 90% single; 91% high school graduates, but < 10% with more than high school education	2× increase in proportion listing reading as favorite activity; physician "helpfulness" and parent "receptiveness" rated higher
Sanders (2000)	Cross-sectional, retrospective	$n = 122$; Palo Alto, CA; 90% Latino; 63% < high school education	3.6×[b] increase in book sharing at least 3 times/week
Mendelsohn (2001)	Cross-sectional, between-clinics comparison	$n = 122$; New York; 28% born outside United States; 40% < high school education	Receptive vocabulary up 8.6 points; expressive up 4.3 points on standardized tests
Sharif (2002)	Cross-sectional, between-clinics comparison	$n = 200$; New York; 53% Latino, 46% African American; 64% < high school education	Receptive vocabulary up 7.2 points on standardized test
Silverstein (2002)	Pre- and postintervention	$n = 180$; Seattle; 57% English *not* the primary language; mean education of non-English speakers = eighth grade	2.4× increase in reading aloud as a favorite activity; 1.7× increase in regular bedtime reading
Fortman (2003)	Cross-sectional, between-clinics comparison	$n = 165$; Midwest; middle-class, predominantly white, and college-educated	No significant difference associated with intervention
Theriot (2003)	Cross-sectional, retrospective	$n = 64$; Louisville, KY; 88% African American	Language scores correlated with number of books given by clinic × number purchased by parents
Weitzman (2004)	Cross-sectional, retrospective	$n = 100$; New Haven, CT; 83% African American or Hispanic	Child Home Literacy Index (CHLI) correlated to number of ROR visits ($r = .318$)

[a] Combining intervention and control groups.
[b] Odds ratio.

to name their three favorite parenting activities and to report all activities they had engaged in with their child over the previous 24 hours, using time-of-day cues to improve recall. "Literacy orientation" was scored as positive if parents included reading aloud or looking at books among their favorites, or if they reported reading aloud in the past 24 hours. At the close of the interview, parents were asked whether they had received a book from their child's doctor at a previous visit, had been counseled about reading aloud, or had observed waiting-room readers.

Of the 36 parents who had received at least one book at a previous visit, 53% scored positive for literacy orientation (as defined earlier), compared with 32% of those who had not received a book ($p < .06$). After correcting for potential confounding factors, including child age, parental years of schooling, welfare status, and ethnicity, parents who had reported receiving a book were four times more likely to include reading aloud as a favorite activity or to report having read aloud to their child within the past 24 hours (odds ratio = 4.05, $p < .03$, 95% confidence interval = 1.12–14.6). Although "literacy orientation" combined parent attitudes (favorite activities) and behaviors (reading aloud in last 24 hours), the attitude question alone accounted for the significant difference that was found (Needlman, 1991, unpublished data). Neither parental report of having observed readers in the waiting room nor having talked with the doctor about reading aloud was associated with literacy orientation, although in a subsequent study, guidance by the pediatrician was *more* strongly associated with positive parental attitudes toward reading aloud than was simply receiving a book (Sharif, Reiber, & Ozuah, 2002b).

Questions about "favorite activities" were also used in three studies by High and her colleagues. One hundred parents were interviewed after they had received at least two books from their clinic doctors at well-child visits between 6 and 36 months of age (High, Hopman, LaGasse, & Linn, 1998). The parents also received guidance from the physician about reading aloud, along with a simple pamphlet on the same topic. The comparison group comprised 51 parents interviewed before the institution of the pro-

gram. Parents in the intervention group were significantly more likely to include reading aloud as one of their child's three favorite activities (21% vs. 8%, $p = .04$); to include reading aloud as one of their *own* favorite parenting activities (42% vs. 22%, $p = .01$); and to read aloud at bedtime 6 or 7 nights per week (35% vs. 20%, $p = .05$). These three questions were combined into a single variable labeled Child Centered Literacy Orientation (CCLO). A significant between-group difference was found for CCLO, in the expected direction (69% vs. 33%, $p < .001$). In stratified analyses, similar between-group differences were observed among both younger (12–23 months) and older (24–38 months) children (odds ratios = 3.6, $p = .007$, and 6.9, $p = .004$, respectively, controlling for parental education); among both parents with less than high school educations and parents who had completed high school (odds ratios = 7.1, $p = .002$, and 3.0, $p = .03$, respectively, controlling for child age); and among Hispanic and non-Hispanic white parents, but not among African American parents (odds ratios = 5.4, $p = .01$; 4.7, $p = .02$; and 1.8, $p = .5$, respectively, controlling for child age and parental education). However, the latter subgroup contained only 25 parents.

In a prospective trial at two urban health centers serving predominantly Hispanic families, 65 children ages 5–11 months were assigned to receive books and guidance at two consecutive well-child visits; 70 comparable children who arrived in the clinic on alternate days were assigned to receive usual care (Golova, Alario, Vivier, Rodriguez, & High, 1999). The groups were similar in child age and gender and in parental age, education, country of origin, language and literacy abilities, and employment. At study entry, the percentage of parents in each group who included reading aloud as a favorite activity was comparably low, 3% in the intervention group versus 1% in the control group. At study completion, the percentages were 43% in the intervention group versus 13% in the control group ($p < .001$). In a multiple logistic regression model, controlling for child age and for parent age, education, reading habits, and English-language proficiency, intervention-group parents were six times more likely to include reading aloud as one of their child's favorite activities (odds ratio

= 5.9, 95% confidence interval = 2.3–14.9, $p < .001$).

A similar prospective controlled study carried out in four urban health centers serving a low-income multiethnic clientele replicated and extended these findings (High, LaGasse, Beeker, Ahlgren, & Gardner, 2000). Children were enrolled at 7 months of age on average and were assigned on alternate days to receive either books and guidance ($n = 76$) or standard care ($n = 77$). At follow-up, at average age 18.5 months, more intervention parents included reading aloud among the child's favorite activities (27% vs. 12%, $p = .02$) and the parent's favorite activities (57% vs. 33%, $p = .003$.) Using paired t-tests, significantly more intervention parents demonstrated a change in attitude over the course of the study, newly citing reading aloud as a favorite child activity (23% vs. 9% in the control group, $p = .04$) or as a favorite parent activity (43% vs. 18%, $p < .01$).

Four other studies (Jones et al., 2000; Silverstein, Iverson, & Lozano, 2002; Sharif, Reiber, & Ozuah, 2002a; Theriot et al., 2003) also found positive associations between ROR-like interventions and parents considering reading aloud a favorite activity for themselves, their children, or both. One of these (Silverstein et al., 2002) was notable for enrolling a culturally very diverse study population. Two studies (Sanders, Gershon, Huffman, & Mendoza, 2000; Fortman, Fisch, Phinney, & Defor, 2003) failed to replicate this finding. However, both were methodologically weaker than the studies discussed previously. The Sanders et al. study was a cross-sectional retrospective study, relying on parent recall of having received books (similar in design to Needlman et al.'s 1991 pilot). The Fortman et al. study was a cross-sectional comparison between comparable clinics; however, 41% of parents at *control* clinics reported having received books from their doctors, suggesting that contamination may have played a significant role in that negative finding.

In summary, eight studies have employed open-ended questions about parents' and/or children's favorite activities as a gauge of attitudes toward reading aloud, and all have reported positive associations in the predicted direction. Among these studies were two prospective controlled trials, a methodology that is generally considered relatively resistant to error and bias. These were not, however, truly *randomized* controlled trials, as children were assigned to treatment or control groups on alternate days. Nonetheless, the confluence of evidence across diverse clinical samples and study designs suggests that the observed association is not likely to be erroneous.

The external validity of the "favorite activities" questions, however, is less readily established. To date, no published intervention study has utilized a more detailed measure of parental beliefs about literacy development. However, one cross-sectional study (Celano, Hazzard, McFadden-Garden, & Swaby-Ellis, 1998) reported a moderate correlation between a 43-item measure of parents' literacy-related beliefs (DeBaryshe & Binder, 1994) and a composite measure composed of three questions: parent's favorite activities, reading aloud included in the bedtime routine, and the child having looked at a book in the past 24 hours ($r = .40$, $p < .001$).

FREQUENCY OF READING ALOUD

Of the nine studies that looked at parent-reported frequency of reading aloud, seven documented positive associations with the ROR-like intervention. Among these are three studies that were described previously. As noted, High et al. (1998), found a higher percentage of parents reporting frequent bedtime reading after institution of the clinic program. In Golova et al. (1999) there was no difference in the percentage of parents who reported reading aloud at least 3 days per week at baseline (24% vs. 23%), but quite a large difference at follow-up (66% among intervention parents, 24% among controls; $p < .001$). On average, intervention parents reported reading aloud 3.6 days per week compared with 2.0 days per week among controls ($p < .001$). In the multiple logistic regression analysis (described earlier), intervention parents were 10 times more likely to report reading aloud on 3 or more days per week (odds ratio = 10.1, 95% confidence interval = 4.0–25.6, $p < .001$).

Similarly, in High et al. (2000), more intervention parents reported reading aloud at bedtime at least 6 nights per week (32% vs. 13%, $p = .006$) and reading aloud during the daytime three or more days per week (78% vs. 46%, $p < .001$). The average number of bedtimes with reading aloud was greater (4.3 vs. 2.8, $p < .001$), as was the average number of days with reading aloud (3.4 vs. 2.1, $p = .004$). In paired t-test analyses, parents in the intervention group were significantly more likely to report positive changes from baseline to follow-up in frequency of reading aloud at bedtime and during the day.

Significant increases in bedtime and daytime reading aloud were also documented by Silverstein et al. (2002) in a study of 85 parents interviewed before institution of an ROR-like program in a Seattle clinic, compared with 95 parents interviewed 14 months after the program was started. The children were 6 months to 5½ years in age. Notably, 29% of the study population gave Somali as their primary language; 9%, Spanish; 7%, Vietnamese; 12%, other languages; and only 43%, English. Among English-speaking parents, more of those exposed to the intervention reported reading aloud at least once per week (93% vs. 63% of preintervention parents, $p = .05$), but no difference was noted in bedtime reading aloud (93% vs. 98%). Among parents whose primary language was not English, program exposure was associated with increased reading aloud at bedtime (56% vs. 36%, $p = .04$), with a trend toward increased reading aloud at other times (76% vs. 60%, $p = .07$).

Sharif et al. (2002a) interviewed 100 caretakers (primarily mothers; henceforth "parents") in a federally funded health center in the South Bronx that had an established ROR program, comparing them with 100 parents in a similar clinic in the same area that had not implemented ROR. At the ROR clinic, 5% of parents reported that they "never" read to their children, compared to 15% at the control clinic ($p = .01$). ROR-exposed children were also more likely to be read to by someone other than the parent interviewed (80% vs. 63%). However, there was no difference in the average days per week of parental reading aloud (1.25 vs. 1.12), nor in the percentage of parents reporting bedtime reading aloud (19% vs. 12%, $p = .17$). At neither clinic did any parent confess to not reading well, despite well-documented low literacy among similar populations of adults. Parents at the ROR clinic were more likely to report reading for their own pleasure (73% vs. 53%, $p < .003$).

These last findings may reflect the potential for social desirability to color parents' responses related to literacy.

In contrast to the previous study, Mendelsohn et al. (2001) used a similar study design (described in detail later) and found significantly more average days per week of reading aloud among 49 parents interviewed in a clinic with ROR compared with parents in a comparison clinic (4.6 vs. 3.7, $p = .04$). The one study that failed to find any differences in frequency of reading aloud was the one by Fortman et al. (2003). However, as noted earlier, this study suffered from extensive contamination of the control group, 43% of whom had received books from their doctors.

HOME LITERACY ENVIRONMENT

Seven studies used the number of children's books in the home as an indicator of an environment supportive of literacy development. Golova et al. (1999), in the well-controlled prospective study described previously, documented an increase in the reported number of children's books in the home. At baseline, the intervention and control groups were comparable, with 12% and 11% reporting five or more children's books, respectively. Following the intervention (in the course of which they were given three books), 52% of intervention parents reported having five or more picture books at home, compared with 19% of controls ($p < .001$). Similarly, in High's (2000) prospective, controlled trial, 61% of parents exposed to the ROR-like intervention reported having 10 or more children's books at home, compared with 45% of unexposed parents ($p = .04$). In Sharif's (2002a) study, ROR-exposed parents reported having an average of 2.63 children's books at home, compared with 2.14 books among unexposed parents ($p = .01$). In Silverstein et al.'s (2002) multicultural study, exposure to the intervention was associated with a higher percentage of households with 10 or more children's books among parents whose primary language was not English (49% in the exposed vs. 31% in the unexposed group, $p = .05$), but not among parents who were native English speakers (98% vs. 93%, $p = .9$). These studies have not distinguished between books obtained from the doctors and books purchased by parents or received as gifts. Anecdotally, parents report that once reading aloud becomes a regular activity, they begin to find picture books to buy for their children. More systematic evidence that this process takes place is, however, lacking.

The concept of environmental supports for reading development clearly encompasses more than simply a count of the number of children's books in the home. Weitzman, Roy, Walls, and Tomlin (2004) utilized a 10-item battery termed the Child Home Literacy Index (CHLI), which had as one component the number of children's books. Home visits were conducted with parents of 100 children ages 18–30 months, who were enrolled in the pediatric clinic at Yale–New Haven Hospital, 83% of whom were either African American or Hispanic, and 90% of whom received Medicaid. At each home visit, interviewers observed the number of children's books visible, whether the books were accessible to the child, whether the child approached the parent with a book during the interview, and whether the parent provided the child with a book. Also asked were questions about bedtime routines, frequency of reading aloud, favorite activities, and whether the parent had purchased books for the child. The CHLI score, created by combining these variables, was found to be correlated with the number of ROR encounters ($r = .318$, $p = .005$), as well as the score on a widely accepted measure of the home environment (the HOME scale; Bradley & Caldwell, 1984) and parent's educational level. In a hierarchical linear regression model, controlling for HOME score, parent education and a measure of parent reading ability, the number of ROR encounters explained 4.7% of the variance in CHLI scores ($F = 4.7$, $p < .05$). However, the data on children's book ownership were not presented separately.

Two studies failed to find associations between the ROR-like intervention and children's book ownership. The Sanders et al. study (2000), reviewed earlier, was potentially weakened by its reliance on parent recall of having received a book from the doctor. Mendelsohn et al. (2001) also found no significant difference in book ownership. Among parents exposed to their ROR pro-

gram, the average number of children's books reported was 28.5, compared with 23.4 among nonexposed parents ($p = .18$). The very high standard deviations associated with these means (21.3 and 20.7, respectively) contribute to the lack of statistical significance for this comparison. This study, which looked primarily at language outcomes, is described in detail later.

In summary, evidence from a variety of studies, including prospective controlled trials, consistently shows parent attitudes and reported literacy-related behaviors responding as expected to clinic-based interventions. Typically, the effects appear clinically meaningful, as well as statistically significant, with odds ratios ranging from 1.5 to 10. There is no evidence that the effects of the intervention are limited by child age, sex, or ethnicity. The diversity of study designs and outcome measures precludes more formal meta-analysis (Needlman & Silverstein, 2004). The few negative findings that have made their way into the published literature come from among the *less* methodologically sound studies. Nonetheless, important limitations need to be recognized. The studies have focused on a relatively narrow set of parent attitudes; parents cannot be expected to report the frequency of reading aloud and numbers of children's books with great precision or accuracy; and social desirability bias cannot be entirely excluded from parental reports, despite efforts to minimize its impact. Finally, detailed information about the quality of parent–child–book interactions is not available from current studies. These limitations raise questions about the effectiveness of the program, questions that are to a degree addressed by the findings discussed in the next section.

Effects on Language Development

Among the dozen published ROR outcome studies, five have included measures of child language. The linkages between early exposure to reading aloud and enhanced language development and between preschool vocabulary and later literacy are well documented (Moerck, 1985; Whitehurst & Lonigan, 1998; Walker, Greenwood, Hart, & Carta, 1994; Snow, 1991.) As an outcome measure, child language ability offers the additional advantage of being readily testable and thus relatively impervious to potential inflation by parents eager to provide socially desirable answers.

The prospective controlled trials by Golova et al. (1999) and High et al. (2000), described earlier, both used a modified version of the MacArthur Communicative Development Inventories Short Form (MCDI), a standardized parent-report measure. Fifty words were chosen from the MCDI, supplemented by 50 words found in the books that were given to the children as part of the intervention. Following MCDI administration guidelines, parents were asked to identify words their children used (expressive vocabulary) and understood (receptive). Spanish versions of the inventory were used when appropriate.

Golova et al. (1999) found only a limited effect of their brief intervention on children's language. However, as described earlier, many of the children were still infants, making changes in language difficult to observe. Among children older than 18 months (the top half of the age distribution), intervention-group children scored significantly higher only for the words contained in the books given out, not for the words drawn from the standard MCDI (data not given in the published report). More extensive differences were found, however, in the study by High et al. (2000), which looked at an older sample of children. Intervention-group children scored significantly higher for receptive vocabulary (mean score, 51.0 vs. 39.3, p = .004), but not for expressive vocabulary (mean score, 22.1 vs. 15.9, p = .11). However, among children 18 months and older (the upper half of the distribution, n = 88), significant differences were documented for both receptive and expressive vocabulary (mean scores, 54.8 vs. 38.3 and 32.1 vs. 17.5, p = .004 and p = .01, respectively). Moreover, significant differences in receptive and expressive scores were observed both within the list of standard MCDI words and within the word list drawn from the distributed books. In multiple linear regression analyses, controlling for child age and parent education, country of origin, and language proficiency, the intervention accounted for 6% of the receptive language score among the older children and 4% of the expressive score. With days per week of reading aloud added to the model, the intervention no longer carried unique variance, suggesting that the intervention was mediated by increased frequency of reading aloud.

The most direct evidence of efficacy with respect to children's vocabulary appears in the study by Mendelsohn et al. (2001). Parents of 122 children, ages 2–5.9 years, were recruited in two pediatric clinics in New York, both serving a predominantly low-income clientele. Only Latino and African American caretakers speaking English, Spanish, or a combination of those languages were included. One clinic (intervention) had had an ongoing ROR program for the previous 3 years; the other clinic (control) had instituted its ROR program just 3 months previously. Consistent with standard ROR practice, books were provided in English, in Spanish, or in both languages on the same page. Books with few words were used, and parents were encouraged to talk about the pictures rather than stick to the printed words.

The families enrolled at the two clinics were similar in virtually all respects, including child age, gender, and preschool attendance; parent immigrant status and high school graduation; SES; ethnicity; English-language proficiency; and government assistance. On the Receptive One-Word Picture Vocabulary Test, children in the intervention group (n = 49) had standard scores on average 9.7 points—more than one half standard deviation—higher than those in the comparison group (n = 73; p = .001, 95% confidence interval = 4.5–15.0 points). On the Expressive One-Word Picture Vocabulary Test, the between-group difference did not reach statistical significance. However, in analyses restricted to Latino families (n = 86), who received books in English or Spanish or both, and who were tested in their language of greatest comfort, the receptive score was 10.5 points higher in the intervention group, and the expressive score was 5.3 points higher (p = .001 and p = .04, respectively.) In multivariate analyses correcting for 10 potential confounding variables, including child's age and gestational age and mother's ethnicity, primary language, educational level, and reading ability, among others, the adjusted mean receptive score was 93.9 in the intervention group versus 85.2 in the control group (95% confidence interval =

3.3–14.0, $p = .002$). The adjusted mean expressive score was 85.2 in the intervention group, versus 80.9 in the controls (95% confidence interval = 0.04–8.6, $p < .05$). When the total number of literacy-promoting contacts—the number of times parents recalled having received books, guidance, or participated in waiting-room reading—was added to the model, a dose effect was observed, whereby each such contact was associated with a 0.4-point increase in the receptive vocabulary score and a 0.2-point increase in the expressive score ($p = .02$ and $p = .07$, respectively).

A similar dose effect was observed by Theriot et al. (2003) in an uncontrolled cross-sectional study of 3-year-old children attending routine well-child visits. In the clinic's well-established literacy program, books and guidance were given starting at the 2-month visit. Children could thus receive up to 10 books over their first 3 years; records were kept of all books given. A convenience sample of 64 children was enrolled and tested using the Peabody Picture Vocabulary Test III—(a measure of receptive vocabulary) and the Expressive and Receptive One-Word Picture Vocabulary Tests. Parents were asked to estimate the number of picture books they had purchased for their children. In a multivariate model, the interaction between the number of books given and the number of children's books purchased by parents predicted receptive and expressive scores ($r^2 = .17$, $p < .001$ and $r^2 = .25$, $p = .03$, respectively). Data showing the influence of ROR-like intervention visits, independent of parental picture book purchases, were not presented. Nor was account taken of potential confounding factors, such as family income or parental education, that might have been associated with both more consistent attendance at well-child visits and more advanced child vocabulary. Nonetheless, the study represents a replication of sorts of Mendelsohn et al.'s (2001) more methodologically sound findings.

In summary, a substantial body of evidence supports the efficacy of ROR-like programs in promoting positive attitudes toward reading aloud, increasing the frequency and regularity of parent–child reading, and—probably as a result of these changes—stimulating vocabulary growth. Furthermore, the program seems to be most effective for children at greatest risk of developing reading problems, including children from low-income households and Latino children in particular. Limitations of the data must be acknowledged, however. Although the evidence includes two carefully done, prospective controlled trials, neither employed truly random group assignment. However, it seems unlikely that the alternate-day group-assignment scheme used could result in the substantial findings reported. On the other hand, social desirability bias threatens to undermine findings based on parental report. For parents who have been urged repeatedly by their doctors to read aloud, the temptation to report frequent reading aloud must be substantial. Given this concern, Mendelsohn et al.'s (2001) findings are particularly important, because it is hard to see how social desirability could affect children's vocabulary test results. Finally, the available studies do not directly address the question of whether clinic-based interventions that promote reading aloud actually reduce problems of reading acquisition or promote reading comprehension.

Implications for Program Development

Clinic-based literacy interventions are becoming the standard of pediatric care (AAP, 1997). As these programs grow in number, so do the opportunities for collaboration with other programs that incorporate a literacy agenda. For example, home-visiting programs designed to promote child health and safety could—and probably should—harmonize the messages they give parents about reading aloud with the messages given in the clinic. Child-care centers could do the same. Libraries are increasingly seeking to broaden their services and bring them to a wider audience, offering parent–child play groups, for example, or lending materials for play-based language learning. ROR programs offer a ready way for such libraries to attract new families. In turn, the libraries can offer a range of expertise, as well as substantive help with storage and other logistical challenges (Feldman & Needlman, 1999). Colleges can be a ready source of waiting-room readers, and the waiting rooms provide a valuable site for service learners to acquire experience interacting with parents and children. Questions by pediatricians about parental reading habits may lead to referrals to adult literacy programs. As pediatricians and other health providers become more personally engaged in promoting early learning, they are apt to become more sensitive to and supportive of the efforts of other professionals in their communities.

Implications for Research

The growing presence of clinic-base literacy interventions poses a challenge for researchers seeking to evaluate related programs. Increasingly, it will be important for researchers to ascertain whether study participants are receiving books and guidance about literacy from outside sources (i.e., their doctors). The focus of attention will have to broaden to include not only discrete programs but also systems of programs.

Pediatric literacy programs raise many questions of practical importance. For example: What methods of encouraging reading aloud are most effective? How should clinicians adapt their approach to different parents, children, and cultures? What training do physicians need in order to implement such interventions? What space should literacy-related guidance fill within the well-child care agenda, already packed with issues of physical health, safety, nutrition, and parenting?

Programs that target literacy development during the early years also raise questions that are less directly linked to program operation. How does very early exposure to reading aloud relate to concurrent or later changes in brain function or structure? What are the effects of promoting developmentally appropriate reading aloud on the establishment of daily routines, on parental sensitivity and verbal interactions, or on the parent–child relationship generally? It seems likely that the quality of parent–child attachment, for example, affects the quality of the reading-aloud interaction (Bus, 2001), but it remains to be seen whether the causality can flow in the opposite direction. As physicians broaden the scope of their work with parents and young children to include early literacy experiences, they open opportunities for research collaboration with professionals from other disciplines.

Appendix: Reach Out and Read

The Reach Out and Read (ROR) national office in Boston provides a wide range of materials to participating programs, including a comprehensive program handbook, posters, pamphlets, research summaries, a pocket guide for developmental assessment (with a focus on language and literacy development), and videotapes. Through a collaboration with Scholastic, Inc., ROR produces a catalog of books for young children, representing diverse cultures and languages, available at substantial discounts. The catalog allows ROR programs to obtain books for $2 to $3 apiece. Through public–private partnerships, ROR is able to provide grants, in the form of book credits, to assist with program start-up and continuation. The ROR website, www.reachoutandread.org, provides additional information.

Note

1. Throughout the chapter, *pediatricians* is meant to include the full spectrum of professionals providing primary health care for children, including family doctors, nurse practitioners, and others—all of whom have successfully implemented Reach Out and Read.

References

Baker, D. W., Parker, R. M., Williams, M. V., Pitkin, K., Parikh, N. S., Coates, W., et al. (1996). The health care experience of patients with low literacy. *Archives of Family Medicine, 5,* 329–334.

Barker, L., & McCauley, M. (2004). National, state, and urban area vaccination coverage among children aged 19–35 months—United States, 2003. *Morbidity and Mortality Weekly Report, 53,* 65–661.

Bradley, R. H., & Caldwell, B. M. (1984). The relation of infants' home environments to achievement test performance in first grade: A follow-up study. *Child Development, 55,* 803–809.

Bus, A. (2001). Parent-child book reading through the lens of attachment theory. In L. Verhoeven & C. Snow (Eds.), *Literacy and motivation: Reading engagement in individuals and groups* (pp. 39–53). Mahwah, NJ: Erlbaum.

Celano, M., Hazzard, A., McFadden-Garden, T., & Swaby-Ellis, D. (1998). Promoting emergent literacy in a pediatric clinic: Predictors of parent–child reading. *Children's Health Care, 27,* 171–183.

AAP Committee on Psychosocial Aspects of Child and Family Health. (1997). *Guidelines for health supervision (Vol. 3).* Elk Grove Village, IL: American Academy of Pediatrics.

Davis, T. C., Crouch, M. A., Wills, G., Miller, S., & Abdehou, D. M. (1990). The gap between patient reading comprehension and the readability of patient education materials. *Journal of Family Practice 31*, 533–538.

DeBaryshe, B.,& Binder, J. (1994). Development of an instrument for measuring parental beliefs about reading aloud to young children. *Perceptual and Motor Skills, 78*, 1303–1311.

Dinkevich, E., & Ozuah, P. O. (2002). Well-child care: Effectiveness of current recommendations. *Clinical Pediatrics (Philadelphia), 41*, 211–217.

Dworkin, P. H. (1993). Ready to learn: A mandate for pediatrics. *Journal of Developmental and Behavioral Pediatrics, 14*, 192–196.

Feldman, S., & Needlman, R. (1999). Take two board books and call me in the morning. *School Library Journal, 45*, 30–33.

Fortman, K. K., Fisch, R. O., Phinney, M. Y. & Defor, T. A. (2003). Books and babies: Clinical-based literacy programs. *Journal of Pediatric Health Care, 17*, 295–300.

Goldstein, A. O., Frasier, P., Curtis, P., Reid, A., & Kreher, N. E. (1996). Consent form readability in university-sponsored research. *Journal of Family Practice, 42*, 606–611.

Golova, N., Alario, A., Vivier, P., Rodriguez, M., & High, P. (1999). Literacy promotion for Hispanic families in a primary care setting: A randomized, controlled trial. *Pediatrics, 103*, 993–997.

Haigler, K., Harlow, C., O'Connor, P., & Campbell, A. (1994). *Literacy behind prison walls*. Washington, DC: U.S. Department of Education, National Center for Education Statistics.

High, P., Hopman, M., LaGasse, L., & Linn, H. (1998). Evaluation of a clinic-based program to promote book sharing and bedtime routines among low-income urban families with young children. *Archives of Pediatrics and Adolescent Medicine, 152*, 459–465.

High, P., LaGasse, L., Becker, S., Ahlgren, L., & Gardner, A. (2000). Literacy promotion in primary care pediatrics: Can we make a difference? *Pediatrics, 104*, 927–934.

Jones, V. F., Franco, S. M., Metcalf, S. C., Popp, R., Staggs S., & Thomas A. E. (2000). The value of book distribution in a clinic-based literacy intervention program. *Clinical Pediatrics (Philadelphia), 391**, 535–541.

Kefalides, P. T. (1999). Illiteracy: The silent barrier to health care. *Annals of Internal Medicine, 130*, 333–336.

Klass, P. E., Needlman, R., & Zuckerman, B. (2003). The developing brain and early learning. *Archives of Disease in Childhood, 88*(8), 651–654.

Mendelsohn, A., Mogliner, L., Dreyer, B. P., Forman, J. A., Weinstein, S. C., Broderick, M., et al. (2001). The impact of a clinic-based literacy intervention on language development in inner-city preschool children. *Pediatrics, 107*, 130–134.

Moerck, E. L. (1985). Picture-book reading by mothers and young children and its impact upon language development. *Journal of Pragmatics, 9,* 547–566.

Mrvos, R., Dean B. S., & Krenzelok, E. P. (1993). Illiteracy: A contributing factor to poisoning. *Veterinary and Human Toxicology, 35*, 466–468.

Needlman, R. (1991). *Additional analyses of clinic-based intervention data* (Unpublished raw data).

Needlman, R., Fried, L., Morley, D., Taylor, S., & Zuckerman, B. (1991). Clinic-based intervention to promote literacy. *American Journal of Diseases of Children, 145*, 881–884.

Needlman, R., & Silverstein, M. (2004). Pediatric interventions to support reading aloud: How good is the evidence? *Journal of Developmental and Behavioral Pediatrics, 25*, 352–363.

Nelson, C. S., Wissow, L. S., & Cheng T. L. (2003). Effectiveness of anticipatory guidance: Recent developments. *Current Opinion in Pediatrics, 15*, 630–635.

Parikh, N., Parker, R., Nurss, J., Baker, D., & Williams, M. (1996). Shame and health literacy: The unspoken connection. *Patient Education and Counselling, 27*, 33–39.

Ramey, C. T., Bryant, D. M., Wasik, B. H., Sparling, J. J., Fendt, K. H., & LaVange, L. M. (1992). Infant health and development program for low birth weight, premature infants: Program elements, family participation, and child intelligence. *Pediatrics, 89*, 454–465.

Regalado, M., & Halfon, N. (2001). Primary care services promoting optimal child development from birth to age 3 years: Review of the literature. *Archives of Pediatrics and Adolescent Medicine, 155*, 1311–1322.

Sanders, L. M, Gershon, T. D, Huffman, L. C., & Mendoza, F. S. (2000). Prescribing books for immigrant children. *Archives of Pediatrics and Adolescent Medicine, 154*, 771–777.

Sharif, I., Reiber, S., & Ozuah, P.O. (2002a). Exposure to Reach Out and Read and vocabulary outcomes in inner city preschoolers. *Journal of the National Medical Association, 94*, 171–177.

Sharif, I., Rieber, S., & Ozuah, P. O. (2002b). The pediatric forum: Effective elements of literacy intervention: Book, talk, or both? *Archives of Pediatrics and Adolescent Medicine, 156*, 518–519.

Silverstein, M., Iverson, L., & Lozano, P. (2002). An English-language clinic-based literacy program is effective for a multilingual population. *Pediatrics, 109*, e76.

Snow, C. (1991). The theoretical basis for relationships between language and literacy development. *Journal of Research in Childhood Education, 6*, 5–10.

Theriot, J. A., Franco, S. M., Sisson, B. A., Metcalf, S. C., Kennedy, M. A., & Bada, H. S. (2003). The impact of early literacy guidance on language skills of 3-year-olds. *Clinical Pediatrics (Philadelphia), 42*, 165–172.

Walker, D., Greenwood, C., Hart, B., & Carta, J. (1994). Prediction of school outcomes based on early language production and socioeconomic factors. *Child Development, 65*, 606–621.

Weiss, B. D., Hart, G., & Pust, R. E. (1991). The relationship between literacy and health. *Journal of Health Care for the Poor and Underserved, 1,* 351–363.

Weiss, B. D., Hart, G., McGee, D. L ., & D'Estelle, S. (1992). Health status of illiterate adults: Relation between literacy and health status among persons with low literacy skills. *Journal of the American Board of Family Practice, 5*, 257-264.

Weitzman, C. C., Roy, L., Walls, T., & Tomlin, R. (2004). More evidence for Reach Out and Read: A home-based study. *Pediatrics, 113*, 1248–1253.

Whitehurst, G. J., Falco, F. L., Lonigan, C. J., Fischel, J. E., DeBaryshe, B. D., Valdez-Menchaca, M. C., et al. (1988). Accelerating language development through picture book reading. *Developmental Psychology, 24*, 552–559.

Whitehurst, G. J., & Lonigan, C. J. (1998). Child development and emergent literacy. *Child Development, 69*, 848–872.

25

Emergent Literacy of Low-Income Children in Head Start: Relationships with Child and Family Characteristics, Program Factors, and Classroom Quality

NICHOLAS ZILL
GARY RESNICK

Head Start is an early childhood education program that, despite debates about its efficacy, has been expanded several times over its 36-year history. Much of the criticism of Head Start has been based on anecdotal impressions, rather than on systematic study of children's activities in Head Start and what skills they do or do not acquire over the course of their participation in the program. In this chapter we report results on emergent literacy skills from a nationwide longitudinal study of a representative sample of families and children attending Head Start. The Head Start Family and Child Experiences Survey (FACES) assessed the quality of Head Start child-care and educational services and the extent to which Head Start enhances the intellectual, social, and emotional development of children who attend the program. The FACES study also collects descriptive information about Head Start procedures and services and the characteristics of program participants.

In this chapter, we answer questions about Head Start children's acquisition of emergent literacy skills by the time they leave Head Start. We identify factors, such as classroom quality, teacher experience and qualifica-

tions, sociodemographic characteristics of Head Start families, and family backgrounds, that are associated with the levels of children's skills and with their gains. Among the questions we addressed in FACES were the following: How much variation was there from program to program in children's emergent literacy skills? And, if there was substantial variation in children's skills, was it associated with differences in program quality, classroom or teacher factors, or characteristics of the children and families? Beyond these questions about whether Head Start "works," the results have implications for such methodological and theoretical questions as the measurement of emergent literacy and the linkages between emergent literacy and early childhood education interventions in general.

The chapter begins with a brief sketch of the history of the Head Start program and its efforts to identify its effects on children's emergent literacy. We then provide a conceptual framework that guided the choice of measures and the subsequent analyses of the data. Next, the chapter summarizes the key research questions addressed by FACES and gives a brief description of the research methods, including sample, measures, and analytic plan. The research findings are structured according to the initial research questions. The chapter concludes with a discussion of the implications of the findings for Head Start and of how the findings speak to the underlying theory and research into interventions designed to improve children's emergent literacy.

Background Conceptual Framework, and Research Questions

In this section we briefly describe the national Head Start program and its goals in relation to improving disadvantaged children's emergent literacy. We then describe the Family and Child Experiences Survey (FACES) and present a conceptual framework that guides the FACES research effort. The conceptual framework then leads into the research questions that are the focus of data presented in this chapter.

Head Start and Emergent Literacy

PROGRAM DESIGN AND DEVELOPMENT

Head Start is an early childhood education program that has its roots in the War on Poverty of the 1960s. When it was founded in 1965, the basic premise underlying its establishment was that children from low-income families often did not get the same intellectual stimulation and encouragement of learning before starting school that children from middle- and upper-income families received. Furthermore, parents in low-income families had fewer resources for obtaining high-quality child care and early education services for their children. Publicly funded preschool and kindergarten programs were not widely available in the 1960s, nor were private programs, at least not at prices that low-income families could afford. Lack of stimulation at home and lack of access to early education programs outside the home were presumed to impair children's achievement in elementary school and beyond. The intention of the founders was to establish a federal program that would fund local agencies to run centers that would furnish some of the early learning experiences that low-

income children were not getting either at home or outside the home; that would instruct parents in educational activities they could carry out with their preschoolers; and that would provide other essentials that poor families often could not afford for their children, such as nutritious meals and health checkups.

The design of Head Start was not based on an extensive body of research. However, subsequent research has provided support for several of the premises underlying the program. Evidence that low-income families tend to provide less intellectual stimulation to their young children than do higher-income families has been found in both large-scale studies of probability samples of the U.S. child population (Bradley et al., 1989; Zill, Moore, Smith, Stief, & Coiro, 1995; Zill, Collins, West, & Hausken, 1995; Zill, 1999; Nord, Lennon, Liu, & Chandler, 1999) and in smaller scale, in-home observational studies (Beals, 1993; Hart & Risley, 1995; Dickinson & Tabors, 2001). Several longitudinal studies showed that high-quality, intensive early childhood education programs could be effective at improving children's cognitive, language, and social outcomes. Head Start rapidly became one of the most widely recognized and popular federal programs, and in 2003 Head Start provided services to approximately 900,000 children and their families each year, at an annual cost of nearly $6 billion. The program was reauthorized by Congress in 1998, and in the following year it received an additional $1 billion in annual appropriations to provide services to still more children and improve the quality of those services.

In addition to serving many more children, the Head Start program has undergone a philosophical shift, from an early emphasis on enhancing children's cognitive and language development to placing more stress on bolstering children's social skills. There has also been movement away from promotion of heavily didactic activities, such as teaching children letters and numbers, toward encouragement of more play-oriented and discovery-learning activities. In recent years, some have criticized Head Start for going so far in the socialization, whole-language, and discovery-learning directions that it neglected to give children any grounding in print awareness, phonemic sensitivity, or word-decoding skills. As part of the Head Start reauthorization legislation in 1998, Congress mandated a set of preliteracy skills that children should accomplish by the end of their participation in the program. These skills, modeled on the developmental accomplishments of literacy acquisition for 3- to 4-year-olds given in the report of the National Academy of Sciences Committee on the Prevention of Reading Difficulties in Young Children (Snow, Burns, & Griffin, 1998, Table 2.1, p. 61), included the ability to identify 10 letters of the alphabet. This chapter presents evidence from a nationally representative, longitudinal sample of programs, families, and children in Head Start of the extent to which Head Start programs are meeting these mandated goals.

EVALUATION OF EFFECTIVENESS

Despite the rapid growth and size of the program, there has been surprisingly little large-scale research on Head Start's quality or on the outcomes for children and families, although numerous smaller scale studies examined questions of Head Start's efficacy. In 1985, the Head Start Evaluation, Synthesis and Utilization Project (McKey et al., 1985), reporting the results of a meta-analysis of over 75 Head Start research studies, found that Head Start produced immediate, meaningful gains in all areas of cognitive development, as well as in social behavior, achievement motivation, and health status. However, the cognitive and socioemotional gains of Head Start children appeared to fade over time.

Largely in response to questions about the efficacy of Head Start and to collect data for program improvement, the Head Start Family and Child Experiences Survey (FACES) was established by the Administration on Children, Youth, and Families of the U.S. Department of Health and Human Services in 1996. FACES is a major activity within the Head Start Performance Measurement Center (HSPMC), which helps to monitor the quality and effectiveness of Head Start and to guide agency efforts to improve program performance. FACES assesses the quality of Head Start services and the intellectual, social, and emotional development of children

who attend the program and collects descriptive information about Head Start procedures and services and the characteristics of program participants.

The ultimate goal of Head Start is to promote the school readiness of children (Administration on Children, Youth, and Families, 1997). FACES measures school readiness using a "whole child" perspective (Goal One Technical Planning Group, 1991, 1993) that sees school readiness as a multifaceted phenomenon comprising five developmental domains: (1) physical well-being and motor development, (2) social and emotional development, (3) approaches to learning, (4) language usage and emerging literacy, and (5) cognition and general knowledge. The battery of measures being used in FACES covers all of these domains and recognizes their interrelatedness.

Conceptual Framework

The conceptual framework that has guided analyses of FACES data is a multilevel, multicausal model of the influences that shape children's emergent literacy and cognitive development, including the role of children's experiences in Head Start in moderating or compensating for deficiencies in children's home environments (see Figure 25.1). Emergent literacy is defined as the skills, knowledge, and attitudes that are considered to be the developmental precursors to reading and writing and, more broadly, to school achievement (Whitehurst & Lonigan, 1989). Children's emergent literacy and school readiness are viewed as reflecting influences of the Head Start program, center, and classroom levels and of their interaction with family backgrounds and home environments, recognizing that child outcomes reflect the combined effects of classroom and program quality (see Dickinson, McCabe, & Essex, Chapter 1, and Farran, Aydogan, Kang, & Lipsey, Chapter 19, this volume), and family and community factors (see Britto, Fuligni, & Brooks-Gunn, Chapter 23, and Landry & Smith, Chapter 10, this volume). The nature and quality of the learning environment depends on the training and experience of teachers; the availability of resources such as facilities, materials, and teaching assistants; the educational philoso-

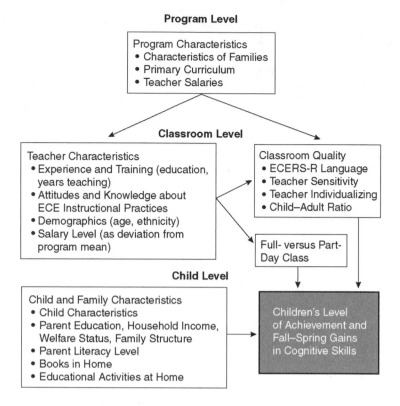

FIGURE 25.1. Analytical model of multilevel factors predicting classroom quality and children's achievement and gains in the Head Start year.

phy; and the curriculum used. Children are expected to do better in programs that employ well-thought-out curricula that are comprehensive and integrated in terms of educational activities and assessment methods. This is especially the case if the program is able to provide teachers with adequate training and support in the curriculum. At the same time, children's progress in a given area depends on whether the program's basic philosophy and curriculum of choice are supportive of efforts to bolster that aspect of child development.

Research Questions

FACES uses multilevel modeling to test hypotheses about early childhood education program characteristics hypothesized to be associated with enhanced cognitive growth in preschool children. Research questions that have been addressed include the following:

1. What emergent literacy skills and knowledge do children have when they enter Head Start programs and at the end of their Head Start year, and how do their skills compare with national norms?
2. Do children make significant gains in literacy during the Head Start year in comparison with national norms, and how do these gains vary across emergent literacy skill domains?
3. Are there differences in the gains in emergent literacy skills between children who attended Head Start for 2 years compared to those who attended for 1 year?
4. How do the emergent literacy levels that children reach at graduation and the literacy gains made over their Head Start year vary across Head Start programs, centers, and classes?
5. Are the graduation levels and gains in emergent literacy skills related to socioeconomic characteristics of programs,

differences in program quality or curriculum, or differences in teacher experience, credentials, or knowledge and beliefs?

The analyses presented here are based on children who were assessed in English in both the fall and spring of the Head Start year. Information about the skills and knowledge of children whose knowledge of English was insufficient for testing in English in the fall (and thus were initially assessed in Spanish) is available in other FACES reports (e.g., Administration on Children, Youth, and Families, 2003). Additionally, although the children in the FACES sample were followed into the spring of their kindergarten year, we report here only fall-to-spring gains during their time in Head Start. Results showing the gains made by Head Start children when they are in kindergarten can be found in the fourth progress report of the Administration on Children, Youth, and Families (2003) and in conference presentations (Zill & Sorongon, 2004; Sorongon, 2004).

Methods

In this section we briefly describe the sample, measures, and analytic plan of FACES. Readers are also encouraged to find detailed descriptions of the sample, measures, procedures, and analytic methods in the fourth progress report (Administration on Children, Youth, and Families, 2003).

Study Sample

The first cohort of FACES began in the fall of 1997 and consisted of a nationally representative sample of 3,200 children and their families, measured in fall 1997 and spring 1998 of the children's Head Start year, and on entry into kindergarten, spring 1999 and spring 2000, and first grade, spring 2001 for some children.[1] New national cohorts of FACES were launched in 2000 and 2003. In the fall of 2000, a second national cohort, called FACES 2000, was initiated and consisted of 2,800 children and their families in 43 different Head Start programs across the nation.[2] A third national cohort, FACES 2003, began in fall of 2003 with a nation-

ally representative sample of approximately 2,800 3- and 4-year-old children and their families from 50 different Head Start programs. This chapter focuses on findings from the second FACES cohort, FACES 2000.

The Head Start children for FACES 2000 were selected as a two-stage sample. The first-stage sampling units were Head Start programs; the second-stage units were classes within sampled programs. In each sampled classroom, all eligible children in their first year of Head Start were taken into the sample. A sample of 45 programs was initially selected for FACES 2000, but two were later discovered to be ineligible because they had been defunded, which resulted in a total of 43 sampled programs, 286 classrooms, and 2,790 first-year children and their families.

Measures

EMERGENT LITERACY

This chapter focuses specifically on the emergent literacy and cognitive measures from the FACES child assessment battery and measures of classroom quality. Brief descriptions of each measure is available in prior FACES reports (cf. Administration on Children, Youth, and Families, 2003).

The literature has distinguished between two interdependent sets of skills and processes that are necessary for the development of both emergent literacy and later language abilities; "outside-in" and "inside-out" skills (Whitehurst & Lonigan, 1989). *Outside-in* skills refer to children's general knowledge of the outside world and oral language skills, including knowledge of vocabulary, oral grammar, and narrative or story conventions. *Inside-out* skills refer to the ability to decode written text into spoken sounds, words, and phrases, using knowledge of phonics, punctuation, spelling, and conventions of English print. The "inside" knowledge of written text letters forming phonemes, words, and sentences is brought "outside" through decoding processes (see Chapters 3 and 6–10, this volume, for additional discussion). The FACES child assessment battery consists of tasks assessing both types of skills.

The measures in the FACES battery include both norm-referenced and criterion-referenced tests, both of which have been shown to predict later school achievement, especially of later reading proficiency and oral language skills (Horn & Packard, 1985; Snow, Tabors, Nicholson, & Kurland, 1995; Snow, Barnes, Chandler, Goodman, & Hemphill, 1991; Pianta & McCoy, 1997). Standard scores are generally reported for the norm-referenced tests, as these are adjusted for the child's age and are useful for comparing children from Head Start programs with other children on a nationwide basis. The criterion-referenced measures do not have national norms and cover areas that are often included in assessments of children's school readiness and progress. When FACES began, there were few good criterion-referenced measures available that had good reliability and validity data. Additionally, when FACES 2000 was developed, there were few good norm-referenced tests appropriate to 3- and 4-year-old children from a Head Start population. Thus a number of tasks were created specifically for FACES by Zill and Resnick (1998a, 1998b) based on tasks in the *CAP Early Childhood Diagnostic Instrument* (Mason & Stewart, 1989). These tasks underwent a thorough series of piloting and pretesting to determine validity and reliability, and the results from the national field test, as well as the first cohort

of FACES, proved their value as measures of children's abilities (Administration on Children, Youth, and Families, 2001a; Administration on Children, Youth, and Families, 2003).

In general, the tasks in the FACES assessment battery can be plotted according to skill area (inside-out–outside-in–numeracy) and test type (norm- vs. criterion-referenced, Table 25.1.

Spanish-speaking children in the FACES sample were assessed in Spanish unless their teachers reported that they had sufficient command of English to be assessed in that language. By spring 2001, language-minority children in most Head Start programs were assessed in English. Results of Spanish-only and bilingual child assessments are described in the third and fourth progress reports (Administration on Children, Youth, and Families, 2001a, 2003). Finally, all child assessors were trained and monitored periodically by research staff. In general, the direct child assessment required 30–40 minutes per child.

PROGRAM AND CLASSROOM QUALITY

In FACES 2000, specially trained observers were present in each sample classroom throughout one full Head Start day and com-

TABLE 25.1. Summary of FACES Child Assessment Battery Subtasks by Skill Area and Test Type

Skill area	Type of test	
	Norm-referenced	Criterion-referenced
Outside-in emergent literacy skills	• Peabody Picture Vocabulary Test, Third Edition (PPVT-III; Dunn & Dunn, 1997)	• Story and Print Concepts Task (FACES) • Social Awareness (FACES) • Color Names section of the Color Names and One-to-One Counting task (FACES)
Inside-out emergent literacy skills	• Letter–Word Identification and Dictation tasks of the Woodcock–Johnson Psycho-Educational Battery—Revised (WJ-R; Woodcock & Mather, 1989)	• McCarthy Draw-A-Design from the McCarthy Scales of Children's Abilities (McCarthy, 1972)
Emergent numeracy skills	• Applied Problems subtask of the Woodcock–Johnson Psycho-Educational Battery—Revised (WJ-R; Woodcock & Mather, 1989)	• Counting section of the Color Names and One-to-One Counting task (FACES)

pleted several standardized and widely used instruments designed to assess the quality of child-care and early education classroom environments. The measures included: the Early Childhood Environment Rating Scale—Revised (ECERS; Harms, Clifford, & Cryer, 1998) and the ECERS-R Language Scale; the Scheduling, Learning Environment and Individualizing Scales of the Assessment Profile for Early Childhood Programs: Research Edition I (Abbott-Shim & Sibley, 1987); the Arnett Caregiver Interaction Scale (Arnett, 1989); and the Child:Adult Ratio, calculated from two separate enumerations made by observers during the classroom day. Lead teachers in Head Start classrooms were interviewed to collect teacher-background information (experience and qualifications) and more detailed information about their curricula, classroom activities, and attitudes and knowledge about early childhood education practices, with the latter constructs measured using 10 items adapted from the Teacher Beliefs Scale (Burts, Hart, Charlesworth, & Kirk, 1990).

On the observational measures of quality, agreement between two independent observers in a sample of classrooms during fall 2000 averaged 93.5% for the Assessment Profile Scheduling Scale, 87.9% for the Assessment Profile Learning Environment Scale, and 86.7% for the Assessment Profile Individualizing Scale. Percent agreement across all ECERS scales (which includes direct hits and being off by 1 on a 7-point scale) averaged 79.5%, agreement on the ECERS-R Language subscale averaged 85.7%, and agreement on the Caregiver Interaction Scale averaged 93.9%.

ANALYSIS METHOD

To determine skills and knowledge of children when they enter Head Start and at the end of their Head Start year, we used the standard scores of tests in vocabulary (Peabody Picture Vocabulary Test, Third Edition PPVT-III), early writing (Woodcock–Johnson dictation task), letter identification (Woodcock–Johnson Letter–Word Identification task), and early math (Woodcock–Johnson Applied Problems task). To find whether children make significant gains in knowledge and skills during the Head Start year, children's gain scores during their Head Start year were calculated as the differences between the fall and spring mean standard scores.[3] Fall-to-spring gain scores were tested for significance using dependent-samples *t*-tests. Effect sizes estimate how meaningful these gains are because, in studies of large samples, it is often the case that differences may be statistically significant, but the size of the effect may be too small to be meaningful from an educational programming perspective[4] (see Cohen, 1995, or Rosenthal & Rosnow, 1984, for details on effect size). In all analyses, statistical tests were carried out on weighted data using WesVar-PC software (Brick & Morganstein, 1997) that adjusts standard errors for effects of sample clustering and differential sampling rates and allows for interpretation of the results for the population of Head Start children as a whole.

To answer the remaining research questions regarding associations between Head Start program and class characteristics and children's cognitive development, multilevel, linear regression modeling using the SAS PROC MIXED computer program (Singer, 1998; Bryk & Raudenbush, 1992) was conducted. Multilevel modeling shows how the average achievement scores of a sample of classes, schools, or other educational units relate to characteristics of those units, such as measures of program demographics and classroom quality. Simultaneously, this type of modeling can examine how the achievement scores of individual children relate to a set of child-level characteristics, such as child demographics and home literacy activities. This method provides a numerical estimate of how sizable the program-to-program and class-to-class variation in average scores is, relative to the child-to-child variation in scores within classes.

Findings

In this section, results of the analyses are presented according to the key research questions, moving from reporting descriptive findings to analyses that relate child growth to program- and classroom-related factors, as well as factors associated with family sociodemographic characteristics, which were significantly predictive of variation in children's scores.

Children's Emergent Literacy Skills in Head Start and Comparison with National Norms

The majority of children who entered Head Start in fall 2000 came into the program with early literacy and numeracy skills that were less developed than those of most children of the same age (Table 25.2). Based on the standard scores (with an overall mean of 100 and a standard deviation of 15), the literacy and number skills of the average Head Start child entering the program were from half a standard deviation to a full standard deviation below national averages. On the criterion-referenced tasks, children scored in the middle range of the one-to-one counting task rating (2.5 out of a possible 5), indicating that they could count but made several non-self-correcting errors. They also scored in the middle range on the color naming and social awareness tasks. However, their scores were low on the book-knowledge score of the story and print concepts task (1.6 out of a possible 5).

Earlier studies have found that the standard scores of low-income children without preschool experience on tests such as the PPVT are typically in the 82 to 85 range (Haskins, 1989; McKey et al., 1985; White, 1986). For some especially disadvantaged low-income populations, average standard scores of preschool children in the high 70s have been reported (Abt Associates, 1997). Thus the average entry-level scores of children in the Head Start FACES 2000 sample were at these levels for the PPVT and the Woodcock–Johnson dictation tasks but were somewhat higher for the Woodcock–Johnson applied problems and were closer to the national norms for letter–word identification.

Although most children had below-average literacy skills, FACES 2000 found considerable diversity in the Head Start population. For the highest quarter of children entering Head Start, the means were at national averages in vocabulary, letter recognition, early math, and early writing skills (Table 25.2). These students would rank slightly above the 50th percentile when compared with all U.S. preschoolers. On the other hand, mean standard scores for the lowest quarter of Head Start children were two standard deviations or more below national averages, particularly in vocabulary and early writing skills. These scores would rank within the bottom quarter of Head Start students and in the lowest 2% of all U.S. preschoolers. Table 25.2 also displays the fall and spring scores and the gain scores from fall to spring for the FACES sample and provides the relevant effect sizes for the differences.

TABLE 25.2. Fall 2000, Spring 2001, and Fall–Spring Difference Scores for Head Start Children

Skill area	Sample size	Fall 2000 Mean (SD)	Bottom quartile	Top quartile	Spring 2001 Mean (SD)	Fall–spring difference Mean	Effect Size
Norm-referenced measures							
Vocabulary	1,801	85.3 (14.6)	62.6	101.1	89.1 (14.3)	3.8	0.26
Letter–Word Identification	833	92.4 (9.6)	82.7	103.9	92.9 (12.0)	0.5 (n.s.)	0.05
Early Writing	799	85.1 (13.6)	70.9	100.8	87.1 (14.3)	2.0*	0.15
Early Math	859	87.9 (15.2)	68.8	104.7	89.0 (17.1)	1.2*	0.08
Criterion-referenced measures							
Book Knowledge	1,876	1.6 (1.3)	0.5	2.7	2.5 (1.3)	0.9	0.67
Color Naming	1,893	11.3 (7.3)	1.7	19.3	15.7 (5.9)	4.4	0.60
Design Copying	1,914	2.9 (1.3)	1.5	4.5	3.6 (1.7)	0.6	0.47
One-to-One Counting	1,848	2.5 (1.2)	1.7	3.8	3.3 (1.4)	0.7	0.59
Social Awareness	1,893	3.4 (1.7)	1.3	4.8	4.1 (1.5)	0.6	0.38

Note. All fall–spring difference scores are significant at $p < .0001$ except where indicated.
*$p < .05$

Children's Gains in Emergent Literacy during Head Start

Children in Head Start showed significant advances in some emergent literacy skills between the beginning and end of the program year, but they continued to lag behind national norms. Table 25.2 displays the fall-to-spring difference score and the associated effect size for the difference. Among the norm-referenced scores, the strongest gain was for a measure of outside-in skills, namely, vocabulary. By contrast, the only score with no significant change from fall to spring was on a measure of inside-out skills, namely, the letter–word identification task. Another key inside-out skill, early writing, showed a significant but relatively small gain. The gain for early math skills was smaller still.

Among the criterion-referenced measures, moderate gains from fall to spring were found for the book-knowledge scores (story and print concepts task), color naming, and one-to-one counting. The smallest gain among the criterion-referenced measures was for social awareness scores. Although effect sizes of the gains appear larger for the criterion-referenced than for the norm-referenced tests, the actual differences are due to the inclusion in the criterion-referenced tests of changes due to maturation combined with any gains attributable to Head Start.

Most of the gains in the norm-referenced measures were relatively modest in magnitude but fell within the range that has been deemed "educationally meaningful" (Rosenthal & Rosnow, 1984). "Educationally meaningful" results are those that explain a sufficiently large amount of the variation in scores to have meaningful programmatic or policy implications. The gains were also in line with earlier findings on the immediate effects of Head Start on children's intellectual performance (Haskins, 1989; McKey et al., 1985).

On the other hand, the vocabulary gains found in Head Start were about half the size of standard-score gains in IQ and achievement that have been obtained in some earlier studies of more intensive interventions with children from disadvantaged families (Barnett, 1998). Barnett (1998), citing studies from the intervention literature by White and Casto (1985), McKey et al. (1985), and Ramey, Bryant, and Suarez (1985), reported gains of one half of a standard deviation, or approximately 8 standard-score points. Barnett (1998) concludes that the short-term effects are larger for intensive, high-quality, and well-designed interventions compared with child-care programs.

It is interesting to note that the measures in which children scored closer to national norms upon entry into Head Start—letter–word recognition, early writing, and early math—were also the measures showing the least amount of change from fall to spring. This suggests the possibility that the stronger gains found for the other measures reflect the fact that children who scored in the lowest range upon program entry made the strongest gains.[5] A comparison of the lowest and highest quarters of children, based on their fall baseline scores, revealed that children who came to Head Start with lower early literacy and math skills made greater gains in the program than those who came with average or above-average skills (Table 25.3). On the PPVT, children in the lowest quartile in the fall gained an average of more than half of a standard deviation, or 8.4 standard-score points, compared with the overall average gain of 3.8 points. By contrast, children who were in the highest quarter of the distribution in the fall showed no gain (mean change = –0.5) in their vocabulary standard scores by spring.

With respect to letter recognition, there was evidence of a slight but significant increase in standard scores for children in the lowest quartile in the fall and no change for children in the highest quartile. In early writing and math skills, whereas children in the lowest quarter showed gains of 7.0 and 5.9 standard scores, respectively, those in the highest quarter showed slight declines. The same pattern was found across all of the criterion-referenced tests, with children in the lowest quartile showing statistically significant gains in raw scores while those in the highest quarter showed no change or slight declines.

The preceeding pattern may suggest the possibility of a regression-to-the-mean effect, a statistical artifact of comparing scores pretest to posttest. However, the results for children in the highest and lowest quarters were different; those in the lowest quarters gained, while those in the highest quarters stayed about the same and did not show a reduc-

TABLE 25.3. Fall 2000 to Spring 2001 Mean Gain Scores for FACES Assessment Measures

Skill area	Sample size	Mean gain score		
		Overall	Bottom quartile	Top quartile
Norm-referenced measures				
Vocabulary	1,801	3.8	8.4	–0.5
Letter–Word Identification	833	0.5	1.3	–0.6
Early Writing	799	2.0	7.0	–2.7
Early Math	859	1.2	5.9	–3.2
Criterion-referenced measures				
Book Knowledge	1,876	0.9	1.5	–0.2
Color Naming	1,893	4.4	7.8	–0.4
Draw-a-Design	1,914	0.6	1.3	0.1
One-to-One Counting	1,848	0.7	1.2	0.1
Social Awareness	1,893	0.6	1.9	–0.4

tion, as would be expected by regression to the mean, suggesting that the gains are more likely to be a meaningful contrast in relative growth in skills. This was particularly true for the one test score closest to national norms—letter–word identification—in which no significant gains from fall to spring were found. Whereas the letter-recognition standard scores averaged fall-to-spring gains of 0.5 of a standard score, children in the lowest quartile showed over double that size of gain (1.3 standard scores). Despite the gains shown by children who entered in the lowest quartile of the Head Start population, these children ended the year with skills that were well below average. Most children left Head Start with vocabulary, early writing, and numeracy skills below national averages.

*Differences in Gains for Children
Who Attended Head Start for 2 Years
versus 1 Year*

Analyses were conducted on children who entered Head Start for the first time in fall 2000 and graduated in spring 2001, the 1-year graduates, and those who graduated the following year, in spring 2002, the 2-year graduates. Three-way analyses of covariance (ANCOVA) were conducted with length of Head Start attendance (1 year vs. 2 years) predicting gains in child assessment scores while controlling for child's age and assessment score in fall 2000 (i.e., at baseline).[6]

Children who attended Head Start for 2 years showed greater progress than their peers who attended for 1 year (Table 25.4). The effect sizes were relatively large, even after controlling for the child's age and baseline scores, with Cohen's d ranging from 0.29 standard deviation to slightly less than 1 standard deviation. When we look at the rate of gain, by dividing the average gain scores by the number of months for which the gains were measured, the prorated rate of gain across the two periods of time was similar for both groups of children (Table 25.4). The achievement of the 2-year Head Start children were significantly higher than those of children who attended only 1 year, both at graduation from Head Start and at the end of kindergarten (Administration on Children, Youth, and Families, 2003). Effects of 2 years versus 1 year of Head Start are much larger than those reported in the literature (Reynolds, 1995; Sprigle & Schaefer, 1985; White, 1986) and provide support for the benefits of 2 years in Head Start, although we cannot be sure whether it is due to the children's age or to the length of exposure to the intervention. If the differences were due to the children's age at entry, it is possible that 3-year-olds enrolled in Head Start may be more needy and possibly more disadvantaged and that their gains over 2 years reflect movement from a much lower starting point than to the 4-year-old children. Further, factors such as parental involvement may favor children with 2 years of the intervention whose parents were highly involved

TABLE 25.4. Comparing "Entry-to-Graduation" Gain Scores between 1-year and 2-year Head Start Graduates

Skill area	1-year graduates			2-year graduates			Effect size (Cohen's d)[b]	Significance of the mean comparison
	Mean gain	SD	Growth rate (per month)[a]	Mean gain	SD	Growth rate (per month)		
PPVT-III	3.4	9.6	0.49	7.7	12.1	0.41	0.29	$F(1, 1388) = 12.4^*$
Book Knowledge	0.8	1.4	0.11	1.6	1.5	0.08	0.55	$F(1, 1450) = 68.4^{**}$
Color Naming	3.9	5.3	0.56	9.4	6.6	0.55	0.92	$F(1, 1463) = 202.9^{**}$
Design Copying	0.7	1.8	0.10	1.9	1.8	0.10	0.67	$F(1, 1474) = 128.9^{**}$
One-to-One Counting	0.8	1.5	0.11	1.7	1.4	0.09	0.62	$F(1, 1425) = 92.5^{**}$
Social Awareness	0.6	1.5	0.09	1.7	1.7	0.09	0.69	$F(1, 1450) = 134.7^{**}$

$p < .001$; $^{**}p < .0001$.
[a]Growth rates prorated on a per-month basis by dividing mean gain by 7 months for 1-year graduates and by 19 months for 2-year graduates.
[b]Effect size uses Cohen's d, calculated from differences between mean gains divided by mean sample standard deviation, and expressed in standard deviation units.

(Reynolds, 1995). Thus, in general, the FACES results are suggestive of beneficial effects associated with 2 years in Head Start.

Variation in Emergent Literacy Levels across Head Start Programs and Classes

To determine how much Head Start programs and classrooms differed in children's emergent literacy, the total variability in child assessment scores (entry, graduation, and gains) was divided into three components: (1) the variation between programs in the average child assessment scores for the entire sample (between-program variation), (2) the variation between classrooms in the average child assessment scores for a given program (between-classroom variation), and (3) the variation among children in their assessment scores within the same classroom (within-classroom variation, otherwise known as the residual). If children with differing levels of initial achievement were randomly distributed across Head Start programs and classrooms, one would expect that 90% or more of the variation in initial achievement would fall into the residual, within-classroom component and that only a small

proportion would fall into the between-program or between-classroom components. On the other hand, if some process were systematically sorting children into different programs or classes according to their initial achievement levels, or if programs and/or class-rooms differed substantially in the efficacy of their instructional activities, then, based on previous research, one might expect one fifth or more of the variation to fall into the between-programs (if program variation was important) or the between-classrooms (if classroom variation was critical) components (Bryk & Raudenbush, 1992).

Thus, using the national sample from 43 programs, each analytic model tested three components of variation in the dependent variables, as follows:

1. The proportion of variation in average assessment scores or average gain scores across programs expressed as deviations of the program means from the overall mean score for the entire sample,
2. the proportion of variation in classroom means from the overall program means, and

3. the proportion of variation in individual children's scores or gain scores around the classroom means (Singer, 1998).

We first look at the unconditional three-level model, in which no independent variables at the child, classroom, or program levels are entered. This serves as the baseline for identifying the degree to which variation in children's scores are due to the between-program and between-classroom components. Once the amount of variation due to these two components is present in the unconditional model, we then test the three-level model that adds variables from all three levels as predictors and determine the degree to which these factors add to the amount of variation in children's scores explained.

The Three-Level Unconditional Model

In general, the largest proportion of variation in children's emergent literacy was found for the within-classroom component, indicating that, without the use of controls, scores vary most among children within the same classrooms (Table 25.5). Approximately 80–95% of the variation in children's scores at entry, at graduation, and in fall-to-spring gains was due to the within-classroom component, indicating a relatively strong residual error component to the scores for different Head Start programs and classrooms.

However, there are several notable exceptions, suggesting that programs or class-rooms within the same programs show substantial disparities in children's scores, in which systematic differences related to instructional activities, program management, classroom quality, or demographic factors of the program participant population may be operating. Entry and graduation scores on the PPVT-III showed relatively large amounts of variation due to the between-programs component (25.9% for entry scores and 23.5% for graduation scores). Similarly, between-program variation at entry and at graduation explained a large amount of total variation in book-knowledge and social-awareness scores. These findings suggest that there are some disparities in program-related factors that enhance or constrain children's abilities, particularly at graduation. Looking further at the fall-to-spring gain scores, we see little between-program variation but a large component of between-classroom variation for the PPVT-III and book-knowledge scores, suggesting that children in some classrooms, even within the same programs, are showing greater gains on these measures compared with other children.

The between-classroom component also appears to account for a relatively large proportion of variation in other scores at entry and graduation and, to some extent, in gain scores. On the PPVT-III, a further 13.4% (at entry) and 11.5% (at graduation) of the variation in scores could be explained by factors at the level of the classroom. The same holds

TABLE 25.5. Percent Distribution of Variance in Children's Assessment Scores at Program Entry, Head Start Graduation, and Fall–Spring Gains, by Skill Area

| | Proportion of overall variance in dependent variable | | | | | | | | |
| | Entry | | | Graduation | | | Gain | | |
Skill area	Between programs	Between classes	Within classes	Between programs	Between classes	Within classes	Between programs	Between classes	Within classes
PPVT-III	25.9	13.4	60.7	23.5	11.5	65.0	3.7	16.8	79.5
WJR Letter–Word ID	5.3	6.5	88.2	7.0	13.7	79.3	4.0	17.2	78.8
WJR Applied Problems	7.5	12.9	79.6	7.7	14.7	77.6	0.0	2.0	98.0
WJR Dictation	4.3	6.9	88.8	0.6	12.1	87.3	3.3	5.1	91.6
Book Knowledge	8.6	7.2	84.2	9.4	12.3	78.3	0.9	14.6	84.5
Color Naming	11.4	10.1	78.5	4.2	6.4	89.4	6.4	11.7	81.9
Design Copying	2.8	9.3	87.9	0.4	8.9	90.7	0.3	4.9	94.8
One-to-One Counting	2.7	11.0	86.3	0.8	5.3	93.9	0.2	8.2	91.6
Social Awareness	8.3	6.3	85.4	13.2	5.8	81.0	2.6	4.6	92.8

true particularly for the graduation scores on letter–word identification, early math, early writing, and book knowledge. In all of these measures, at graduation, there were relatively strong between-classroom proportions, explaining from 11.5–14.7% of the variation in scores. Relatively strong proportions of between-classroom variance were also found for fall-to-spring gain scores, including the PPVT-III, letter–word identification task, book knowledge, color naming, and one-to-one counting.

These findings suggest that classrooms within the same programs varied in some potentially systematic ways in children's average scores at graduation and in the gains made from fall to spring. Further, when comparing the relatively strong amounts of variance accounted for by the between-classroom component with the much smaller proportions of variance accounted for by the between-program component on most gain scores, it would appear that classrooms within the same programs may be more divergent in children's gains compared with typical classrooms across different programs. Most important, even in the same programs, in which there is one administrative structure and one management system and set of policies, generally dictating both teacher salaries, staff hiring, and choice of curriculum, classrooms differ in the gains children are making.

Table 25.5 allows a comparison of changes in the proportions of variation across entry and graduation that were attributable to the between-program and between-classroom components. In some cases, the proportion of variance due to between-program and between-classroom components diminishes from entry to graduation, whereas for other areas the proportions increase or stay the same. These patterns may identify emergent literacy skills that appear most influenced by program and classroom characteristics.

Results for color naming reveal a reduction in variance accounted for by programs from entry to graduation, falling from 11.4% of variation at entry to only 4.2% of the total variation at graduation. A similar pattern was observed for the between-classroom component. These shifts indicate that, over the course of the Head Start year, differences in average scores across programs and classrooms were reduced or leveled out, suggesting an influence of programs

on this skill that may help children who are behind to catch up with those who are more advanced. Similar patterns of reductions in the amount of variation due to between-program differences were found for early writing, design copying, and one-to-one counting. Thus, in these areas, preexisting differences between programs diminished by graduation, and children from different programs tended to perform more comparably by the time they left Head Start.

By contrast, in other skill areas, notably letter–word identification, the proportion of total variance explained by the between-program and between-classroom components increased from entry to graduation. For letter–word identification scores, the proportion of total variation explained by the between-program component increased from 5.3% to 7%, and the proportion explained by the between-classroom component almost doubled, from 6.5% to 13.7%. Here, the effect may be one of greater differentiation; children in some classes and programs are learning their letters, whereas children in other classes and programs are not. A similar pattern was found for book knowledge, in which the proportion of the total variance due to the between-program component increased slightly but the proportion of variance due to the between-classroom component increased markedly.

In other skill areas, such as vocabulary and early math, the amount of variation explained by the between-program and between-classroom components remained approximately the same. By the end of the Head Start year, there were still significant differences in average scores among programs or between classrooms within the same programs for early math skills, but these were similar to those that were present at program entry. Head Start seems to be having neither an equalizing effect nor a differentiating effect on vocabulary and early math skills.

Overall, these proportions are comparable to the between-schools variations in achievement that have been found in studies conducted at the high school level. According to Bryk and Raudenbush (1992), "results typically encountered in cross-sectional studies of school effects . . . [are that] 10% to 30% of the achievement variability is between schools" (p. 188). However, Bryk and

Raudenbush (1992) also report that high school studies find that larger proportions of the variations in gains occur between schools. This was not the case for Head Start programs.

The Three-Level Model Combining Child, Classroom, and Program Factors

The foregoing unconditional models indicate that some of the differences in children's scores may be due to elements of programs and classrooms, but they do not identify the sources of these differences. We now discuss analyses that examined the contributions of program, classroom, and child factors for predicting entry, graduation, and gain scores (Table 25.6).

Results indicated that the combined three-level models explained a significant amount of total variance in the emergent literacy and numeracy scores at entry and graduation and in fall-to-spring gains (Table 25.7). At entry, total variance explained by the models ranged from 17% (letter–word identification) to 54% (vocabulary). At graduation, total variance explained by the models was slightly lower but still substantial, ranging from 15% (design copying and one-to-one counting) to 51% (vocabulary). Total variance explained for the gain scores was substantially less, ranging from 10% (one-to-one counting) to 37% (vocabulary). For predictions of fall-to-spring gains, the models explained the most variation in vocabulary, color naming, and letter-recognition gain scores. Conversely, the three-level models explained the least total variation for gains in design copying, one-to-one counting, and book knowledge.

Program and Classroom Factors Associated with Head Start Children's Emergent Literacy Skills

Having shown substantial variation across Head Start programs and classrooms in children's emergent literacy skills at program entry, at graduation, and in gain scores, three-level analyses were used to ascertain whether the socioeconomic composition of the program's student population, measures of pro-

TABLE 25.6. Summary of Predictors at Each Level in the Multilevel Hierarchical models, FACES 2000

Program level	Classroom level	Child level
Program mean parent education level	Average ECERS language score	Parent education level (deviation)
Program mean family income level	Average child–adult ratio	Family income level (deviation)
High/Scope Curriculum	AP Individualizing score	Welfare status
Creative Curriculum	Teacher BA or AA	Age of child in months
Mean teacher salary level	Years teaching experience	Sex of child
Proportion language-minority children	Black teacher	Disability status
Proportion nonminority children	Hispanic teacher	Black child
	Teacher salary deviation score	Hispanic child
	Teacher DAP beliefs score	Language-minority family
	Average lead teacher Arnett score	Mother–father family
	Class parent education level (deviation)	Neither birth parent in home
	Class family income level (deviation)	Parent literacy standard score (KFAST)
	Proportion language minority (deviation)	Books in home
	Class proportion nonminority (deviation)	Frequency of reading to child
	Part-day class	Not at all
		One or twice
		Every day
		One-year Head Start graduate

Note. All deviations are expressed as deviations from the program average.

TABLE 25.7. Summary of the Variation Accounted for by between-Program, between-Classroom, within-Classroom, and Total Variance Components in Three-Level Models of Emergent Literacy and Numeracy Skills in Head Start.

| | Proportion of variance explained by combined three-level model, and total variance explained, for entry, graduation, and gain scores | | | | | | | | | | | |
| | Entry | | | | Graduation | | | | Fall-to-spring gains | | | |
Dependent variable	Between-program	Between-class	Within-class	Total explained variance	Between-program	Between-class	Within-class	Total explained variance	Between-program	Between-class	Within-class	Total explained variance
Vocabulary	100%	65%	32%	54%	98%	53%	34%	51%	85%	72%	28%	37%
Letter–Word Identification	73%	100%	8%	17%	95%	69%	10%	24%	100%	57%	7%	20%
Early Math	100%	79%	18%	32%	100%	66%	14%	28%	< 0[a]	100%	17%	19%
Early Writing	100%	100%	17%	26%	100%	100%	13%	24%	100%	86%	7%	14%
Book Knowledge	82%	75%	11%	22%	86%	41%	10%	21%	100%	36%	8%	11%
Color Naming	94%	66%	18%	31%	77%	59%	12%	18%	94%	72%	17%	28%
Design Copying	100%	56%	16%	22%	100%	44%	12%	15%	< 0[a]	58%	10%	12%
One-to-One Counting	78%	66%	14%	21%	100%	39%	13%	15%	100%	37%	8%	10%
Social Awareness	100%	68%	10%	21%	91%	83%	13%	28%	100%	75%	10%	16%

Note. Between-program and between-classroom variances are expressed as percentages of the total explained variance. If between-program variation is 100%, then this means that 100% of the total explained variance is due to between-program factors.

[a] The amount of total variance explained by the between-program component for these unconditional models is too low to obtain reliable estimates.

361

gram quality and curriculum, and teacher experience, credentials, and knowledge or belief were associated with the variation in assessment scores. All models included controls for the number of years of participation in Head Start, as this was an important predictor of gains in the preceding analysis.

For each dependent variable, three separate models were tested (entry, graduation, and gain), with each model testing the three components of variation in the dependent variables (between-program, between-class, and within-class variation). The results are summarized according to whether a combined three-level model controlling for all independent variables did a better job at predicting entry, graduation, and gain scores than the unconditional child-level model. Results showed significant and substantial differences in average literacy and numeracy levels across Head Start programs and classes at program entry, at graduation, and, to a lesser extent, in gains across the Head Start program year. The addition of the program- and classroom-level variables significantly contributed to the prediction of all nine assessment scores at entry into Head Start, increasing the variance accounted for by the model by approximately 1–7% (Table 25.8). The addition of the program- and classroom-level variables significantly contributed to the prediction of eight of the nine

graduation scores, increasing the variance accounted for in these models by approximately 2–9%. Finally, the addition of the program- and classroom-level variables significantly contributed to the prediction of six of the nine gain scores, increasing the variance accounted for in these models by approximately 1.6–4.3%.

The multilevel regression analyses showed that there were significant relationships between some of the program and class characteristics identified earlier and variations in children's emergent literacy gains (see Administration on Children, Youth, and Families, 2003 for details). We now discuss factors that were significant predictors of children's scores.

Children in programs that employed the High/Scope curriculum were found to have higher scores at Head Start graduation and made greater gains while at Head Start than children in programs that did not employ one of the two integrated curricula that are most widely used by local Head Start programs. After adjusting for the influence of related variables, children in programs using the High/Scope curriculum had significantly greater vocabulary skills on the PPVT-III at graduation from Head Start than children in programs that employed other curricula. They also showed significantly greater early writing skills on the Woodcock–Johnson dic-

TABLE 25.8. Percentage of Variance Accounted for by the Child-Level Model and the Combined Model with Program-, Classroom-, and Child-Level Factors, and the Difference in the Proportions

	Proportion of variance in dependent variable accounted for								
	Entry			Graduation			Gain		
Dependent variable	Child-level model	Combined model	Additional variance	Child-level model	Combined model	Additional variance	Child-level model	Combined model	Additional variance
PPVT-III	51.2	54.1	2.9****	47.7	51.0	3.3****	35.5	37.1	1.6*
WJR Letter–Word ID	10.0	17.1	7.1****	15.2	23.7	8.5****	15.4	19.7	4.3**
WJR Applied Problems	26.1	31.8	5.7****	20.2	28.0	7.8****	15.8	18.7	2.9**
WJR Dictation	20.3	26.3	6.0**	14.9	24.2	9.3**	10.1	13.9	3.8*
Book Knowledge	19.6	21.9	2.3****	15.4	20.8	5.4****	7.4	11.0	3.6**
Color Naming	29.0	31.5	2.5****	15.7	18.0	2.3****	25.9	28.3	2.4****
Design Copying	20.9	22.0	1.1**	13.3	14.9	1.6	11.1	12.5	1.4
One-to-One Counting	19.1	21.4	2.3***	12.7	15.4	2.7***	8.4	10.2	1.8
Social Awareness	18.3	20.8	2.5****	25.2	27.6	2.4****	13.6	15.8	2.2

Note. χ^2 test of significance with the following significance levels: *p .05; **p .01; ***p .001; ****p .0001.

tation task, significant gains in letter recognition skills on the Woodcock–Johnson—Revised letter–word identification task, and gains in social awareness scores.

Children attending Head Start programs with higher average teacher salary levels made greater progress at graduation and from entry to graduation for letter-recognition scores, early writing skills, and social-awareness scores. In some cases, the differences between programs was substantial; for example, the difference in letter–word identification scale scores associated with each $10,000 increment in average teacher salaries, adjusted for the influence of related variables, was 4.17 scale-score points.

Teacher education also was important, as children in Head Start classes taught by lead teachers with bachelor's or associate's degrees showed greater gain scores from entry to graduation on the color-naming task compared with children in programs with teachers who did not have such a degree.

The length of the classroom day was also an important factor. As of the 2000–2001 school year, the majority of children who attended Head Start participated in part-day classes that were conducted in morning or afternoon sessions only. Compared with children who attended for part of a day, children who attended full-day Head Start programs made greater gains in early writing, book-knowledge, and color-naming skills.

Some indicators of classroom quality proved not to be significant predictors of children's emergent literacy or numeracy skills, despite evidence from the literature suggesting their potential role (Peisner-Feinberg & Burchinal, 1997). Higher scores for the classroom teacher that indicated sensitivity, warmth, and responsiveness were associated with higher early writing skills at graduation but not with greater fall–spring gains in early writing skills. The other indicator of classroom quality, the ECERS-R Language scale, also was not associated with higher graduation scores or greater entry-to-graduation-gain scores on any of the cognitive outcome measures. Counterintuitively, higher quality scores on the ECERS-R Language scale were related to lower dictation scores. The ECERS-R Language score was not associated with any other cognitive outcomes. Finally, some independent variables did not show relationships to children's gains or graduation scores that were hypothesized, such as child-to-staff ratio, the Individualizing scale of the Assessment Profile, and the teacher's attitudes and knowledge about early childhood educational practices.

Contribution of Program and Classroom Predictors to Children's Outcomes

Because the final, combined models with all three levels of predictor variables explained a significant amount of variation in a number of emergent literacy areas, particularly at children's graduation from Head Start, an important question is the degree to which specific subgroupings of predictors were responsible for these results. Specifically, we were interested in whether the results could be explained entirely by demographic and socioeconomic characteristics of program participant population or whether program quality and process factors contributed significantly to the predictions.

A series of analyses were conducted in which process and quality factors were removed from the combined models. The factors at the program level that were removed were High/Scope curriculum, creative curriculum, and mean teacher salary. The classroom-level factors removed consisted of average ECERS-R language score, average child–adult ratio, Assessment Profile Individualizing score, teacher bachelor's associate's degree, years teaching experience, teacher minority status (African American or Hispanic), teacher salary deviation score, teacher early childhood education beliefs score, lead teacher Arnett score, and full-versus part-day class. Thus the models were left with demographic and socioeconomic characteristics of the program participant population (at the program and classroom levels), or families and children (at the child level). The proportion of total variance explained by the Program/Classroom SES Differences component was then compared with the proportion of total variance explained by a combined model that added program and classroom process and quality. Significance tests determined whether additional variance of the process and quality component explained a significant amount of variation, over and above that explained by program and class SES characteristics (Table 25.9).

TABLE 25.9. Comparison of Combined Models with and without Program- and Classroom-Level Process Factors, Differences in Proportion of Variance Explained

Dependent variable	Entry			Graduation			Gain		
	Program/classroom SES differences	Program/classroom SES + quality/process	Additional variance explained by quality/process	Program/classroom SES differences	Program/classroom SES + quality/process	Additional variance explained by quality/process	Program/classroom SES differences	Program/classroom SES + quality/process	Additional variance explained by quality/process
PPVT-III	53.6	54.1	0.5	50.2	51.0	0.8	36.2	37.1	0.9
WJR Letter–Word ID	14.0	17.1	3.1*	18.4	23.7	5.3*	16.3	19.7	3.5
WJR Applied Problems	28.6	31.8	3.2†	24.6	28.0	3.4†	17.1	18.7	1.6
WJR Dictation	22.6	26.3	3.7*	18.4	24.2	5.9*	11.8	13.9	2.1
Book Knowledge	20.9	21.9	1.0	18.3	20.8	2.6*	8.9	11.0	2.1†
Color Naming	30.0	31.5	1.4	16.8	18.0	1.2	26.9	28.3	1.5
Design Copying	21.3	22.0	0.7	14.0	14.9	0.9	11.6	12.5	0.9
One-to-One Counting	20.4	21.4	1.0	14.1	15.4	1.3	8.8	10.2	1.4
Social Awareness	19.8	20.8	1.0	26.1	27.6	1.5	14.1	15.8	1.7*

Column group header: Proportion of total variance in dependent variable accounted for

Note. χ^2 test of significance with the following significance levels: †$p < .10$; *$p < .05$.

The models of greatest interest are those that predict graduation and gains scores, because program- and class-level process and quality factors are mainly expected to influence scores after children have benefited from their exposure to Head Start.[7] In the models predicting to graduation scores, the program and classroom process/quality variables explained a significant amount of variation for letter-word identification, early writing, and book knowledge. Thus, in these areas, program quality and management processes appeared to make the greatest difference in explaining the variation of children's scores.

There were few significant effects of program quality and processes in predictions of children's gain scores, with only predictions to social awareness scores reaching levels of statistical significance and predictions to book knowledge gain scores reaching a nonsignificant trend level.

Role of More Frequent Parental Reading to Children

Children are in preschool programs for only a limited time, but preschool programs may extend their influence by encouraging parents to engage in more frequent and more effective educational activities at home with their children. Analyses of the impact of the reported frequency of reading controlled for parent education level, the mother's score on a measure of adult literacy (the K-FAST), and an indicator of the presence of books in the home. The three-level regression analyses showed that more frequent parental reading in the fall was associated not only with higher initial achievement for children as they entered the program but also with larger gains during the program year. Larger gains were observed for children whose parents read to them every day. Smaller gains were observed for children who were read to only once or twice a week or not at all. More frequent parental reading to children was associated with higher scores for receptive vocabulary, letter-word identification, book knowledge, dictation, and design copying at graduation from Head Start. On all five measures, children whose parents reported reading to them only once or twice per week had significantly lower mean scores at graduation compared with children whose parents reported reading three to six times per week.

Children whose parents reported reading once or twice per week revealed lower gain scores for letter-word identification and book-knowledge scores, but not for vocabulary, dictation, and design copying, compared with children whose parents reported reading three to six times per week. Further, children whose parents reported reading every day had significantly higher vocabulary scores at graduation and higher gains in vocabulary and book knowledge compared with children whose parents reported reading three to six times per week.

Finally, children whose parents reported not reading to them at all had mean social awareness scores at graduation that were significantly lower compared with children whose parents reported reading three to six times. In terms of gain scores from entry to graduation, the children whose parents reported not reading to them at all in the previous week had gain scores that were significantly lower than those whose parents reported reading to them three to six times per week.

Summary of Multilevel Hierarchical Models

The findings suggest that children in Head Start do make some gains in emergent literacy, but these gains are relatively modest and are limited. It would appear that outside-in skills such as vocabulary, book knowledge, and color naming are those most likely to show improvement among Head Start children compared with the inside-out skills, such as letter-word identification, psychomotor tasks, and early writing (these latter two skills showed improvement but not at the same level as the outside-in skills). Although numeracy skills also showed gains from fall to spring, these were relatively modest. Further, significant variation in the average scores of programs and classrooms at graduation and in fall-to-spring gains for the outside-in skills appeared due to factors between programs and between classrooms within the same programs. Thus the skills that appeared to show the most movement also appeared to be those most likely to have been affected by instructional, management, and program/classroom processes such as the hiring of experienced teachers, teacher sensitivity and responsiveness, and classroom quality. Fewer of the inside-out skills, in the multilevel models, revealed potential effects of differences in quality or instructional efficacy between programs and classrooms. However, there were significant relationships between program/classroom factors and achievement of letter identification skills.

Evidence from the multilevel models supports the notion that family and child characteristics interact with program-related factors, such as program quality, curriculum, teacher experience and qualifications, and the sociodemographic milieu in which the Head Start programs operate to influence children's emergent literacy at graduation from Head Start and the short-term gains they made while in the program. Program quality provides modest but significant prediction to gains, as well as somewhat stronger predictions to entry and graduation levels, but these effects appeared to occur for some skill areas and not others. Skill areas most affected by program quality and process factors at the program and classroom levels include letter–word identification, book knowledge, and early writing. The significant amount of variation explained by between-program and between-classroom components for these skills indicates that the systematic differences in children from different programs and even in different classrooms within the same programs shown by these results may be at least partially due to variations in program quality. That is, children in higher quality programs begin Head Start with higher levels on some skills and finish their Head Start year also at higher levels on these skills, even though children at the lowest quarters within these classrooms and programs make the larger gains.

The multilevel analyses also revealed a number of significant predictors of children's scores. Children's scores at graduation and, to a lesser extent, their fall-to-spring gains were related to programs using an integrated curriculum, particularly the High/Scope curriculum; programs having higher teacher salaries; teachers having bachelors' or associates' degrees; children attending full-day rather than part-day classes; and parents reporting that they read to their children more frequently. The multilevel analyses showing key predictors of children's scores also provides potential reasons that Head Start children may not be reaching, upon graduation,

the same high levels on letter recognition and numeracy as they do on vocabulary or book-knowledge skills. Several factors identified by the multilevel models may explain these differential findings. For example, children may not have been in classrooms with skilled and sensitive teachers or may not have been exposed to the curricula and learning environment for a sufficient length of time (based on the results of regression analyses favoring 2 years of Head Start over 1 year) nor to reading in the home. However, it is also possible that some skills (letter recognition and numeracy) may not have been emphasized in specific types of curricula.

The use of an integrated, systematic curriculum such as High/Scope and, to a lesser extent, Creative Curriculum, predicted both higher levels at graduation after adjusting for age and family–child characteristics and gains from fall to spring. Although children were making more progress in Head Start in the important prereading skill of letter recognition, the result shows that Head Start programs still have a way to go in bringing children closer to or even up to national norms. The Early Childhood Longitudinal Study of the Kindergarten class of 1998 found that a majority of U.S. children knew the letters of the alphabet upon entering kindergarten (Zill & West, 2001). Preliminary findings from randomized intervention studies conducted in Head Start programs in Long Island, New York, as part of the Head Start Quality Research Consortium studies suggest that children in Head Start can make strikingly larger gains in letter recognition and related skills with certain research-based, literacy-focused curricula (Fishel, Storch, Spira, & Stolz, 2003).

Conclusions

The gains made by Head Start children are smaller than those reported in the literature for more intensive, "model" research and demonstration programs, such as the Perry Preschool Project. However, many writers have noted these differences when comparing studies involving model research and demonstration programs from established, government-funded, large-scale programs. Many of the effects of early childhood education programs may be attributed to the intensity and control available in a model program. The dissemination of a promising program model to a larger scale at the state or national levels often results in what Heather Weiss termed the "demonstration dilution effect" (Weiss, Resnick, & Hausman, 1987). Thus it is possible that the discrepancy between Head Start and model programs could be due to the greater intensity and quality of the model programs, as well as the fact that children start earlier and spend a longer time in these programs than children in Head Start. On the other hand, many studies that tested model demonstration programs began their research during the early years of program implementation, when programs may not have been fully operational (Reynolds, 1995). Head Start represents an established program that, although perhaps lacking in the resources that many model demonstration programs have, does have an extensive implementation history and can tailor its services to the needs of children and families. Clearly, the contexts in which model programs operate compared with established large-scale programs are important to understanding the potentially conflicting research evidence. FACES represents a broad-based effort at studying an established, large-scale, government-funded program, and its benefits may not be comparable to the often-cited model research and demonstration projects.

The notion that children in lower quality programs do not appear to completely make up the gaps relative to their peers in higher quality programs leads to some speculation about the intersection between program quality and characteristics of the population served by Head Start. The effects of classroom process and structural quality on children's emergent literacy and numeracy skills were relatively modest. In interpreting this finding, it is important to keep in mind the restricted range of quality found in Head Start programs. Prior FACES reports have shown that quality in Head Start falls mainly within the "good" range and that there is a more limited range of quality than that seen in child-care centers and preschools in several other national studies (Administration on Children, Youth, and Families, 2003). Strong between-program and between-classroom effects suggest systematic differences in the types of children who are en-

rolled in different Head Start programs, as well as the sociodemographic characteristics of the population served by these programs. Program quality may also be influenced by these factors, as shown by the FACES finding that program-level factors such as the sociodemographic characteristics of the participant population influence quality in the classroom (Resnick & Zill, 2003). These findings support Barnett's (1998) hypothesis that the size of program effects may be a function of the distance between the quality of the learning environment provided by Head Start and the quality of the learning environment in the child's home and community. Children's emergent literacy skills may improve either by increasing the quality of Head Start programs or by targeting more severely disadvantaged families.

In recent years, there have been a variety of initiatives within the federal government aimed at improving the quality of Head Start programs, and there is a renewed emphasis on enhancing children's learning of emergent literacy and numeracy skills (Administration on Children, Youth, and Families, 2001a). However, as Resnick and Zill (2003) noted, variations in the quality of Head Start classrooms may be explained by characteristics of the families and children they serve, by the curriculum used in the program, and by teacher attitudes and knowledge about early childhood education practice. Thus improvements in quality at the classroom level may be limited without changes at the level of the Head Start program. But these changes require resources in order to institute integrated curricula, improve educational qualifications of teaching staff, and provide for higher quality learning environments in the classrooms. Perhaps lower quality Head Start programs do not have sufficient resources to make the changes required to bring their quality up to the level of the higher quality programs and, indeed, to the level required to approach the quality found in model programs.

Another strategy toward enabling Head Start children to reach national norms on key emergent literacy skills may focus on involving the most severely disadvantaged families in the program. The multilevel analyses showed that socioeconomic characteristics of families attending Head Start are the most significant predictors, particularly of the children's levels at graduation. We found that programs, and classrooms within programs, vary systematically on some key characteristics that influence children's emergent literacy, such as differences in socioeconomic backgrounds of families. That is, there may be a self-selection effect in which families who have sufficient resources and knowledge to register their children in Head Start are those most likely to have children who score better on their emergent literacy skills initially and maintain their higher standing at the end of their Head Start year. By relying on natural variation in participation rates—that is, self-selection by parents into Head Start programs—we cannot distinguish between the effects of the program and the effects of family characteristics that influence families' enrollment decisions (Barnett, 1998). A recent study of families eligible for Head Start who do not enroll their children supports this hypothesis. Recruitment efforts by Head Start staff were not always successful, and there was little consistency across programs in the actual process of selecting families, with the final decision for selecting families for enrollment left to an individual or to a committee (Administration on Children, Youth, and Families, 2001b). Thus, to improve children's emergent literacy scores in Head Start, programs should focus their recruitment efforts on identifying families who are the neediest and most severely disadvantaged.

However, we should also be clear on the limitations of the FACES study. Without a rigorous experimental design using random assignment to intervention and no-intervention groups, it is difficult to amass the necessary counterfactual evidence to establish what would have happened if these children were not attending Head Start. FACES was not intended to estimate program effectiveness per se, but rather to link variations in program quality with variations in children's emergent literacy skills and to describe the skill levels of a nationally representative sample of Head Start children compared with national norms. Another national study initiated by the Administration for Children and Families (ACF), the national Head Start Impact Study (HSIS), will answer the effectiveness question. The study's goals are to find out how Head Start affects the school readiness of children participating in the program as compared with children not enrolled in Head Start and to determine under which conditions Head Start is most effective (see www.acf.dhhs.gov/programs/core/ongoing_research/hs/impact_intro.html).

Additional FACES reports that go beyond the scope of this chapter suggest significant long-term benefits after the children they leave Head Start. Based on follow-up of the 1997–1998 cohort, Head Start graduates showed further progress toward national averages during kindergarten (Administration on Children, Youth and Families, 2003; Zill & Sorongon, 2004). Briefly, gains of between one third to more than one half standard deviation were observed in vocabulary, math, and writing skills during kindergarten. Graduates made more substantial or comparable gains toward national norms between the end of Head Start and the end of kindergarten on all of the emergent literacy measures (Zill & Sorongon, 2004). Head Start graduates were essentially at national norms in early reading and writing. Graduates were about one third standard deviation below national norms in vocabulary, general knowledge, and early math. Other analyses reveal positive effects with respect to grade repetition, another indicator of preschool success. Lower early literacy and early math skills have been found to be associated with repeating kindergarten, with the strongest predictor being design copying scores. With every unit increase in design copying scores, children were 32% less likely to repeat kindergarten (Sorongon, 2004).

Taken as a whole, the short-term results reported in this chapter showing relatively modest gains in emergent literacy and numeracy, along with other FACES reports citing significant longer term gains made by Head Start children in kindergarten, suggest that greater gains in emergent literacy and numeracy might well be achieved while children are in Head Start. Potential sources of gains might include the use of an integrated curriculum, improving program quality through greater resources for lower quality programs, and upgrading teacher training and qualifications. Future expansion of Head Start to serve all eligible children, combined with additional funding to support current quality improvement initiatives would go a long way toward achieving these gains and thereby improving emergent literacy and numeracy outcomes for all disadvantaged children.

Acknowledgments

The FACES research project was sponsored by the Administration for Children and Families, U.S. Department of Health and Human Services (DHHS) under Contract No. HHHS-105-96-1912, Head Start Quality Research Consortium's Performance Measurement Center.

We are grateful for the continuing support of the Federal Project Officers for this study: Louisa B. Tarullo, EdD, and Michael Lopez, PhD, Child Outcomes Research and Evaluation, Office of Planning, Research and Evaluation, Administration for Children and Families, U.S. Department of Health and Human Services, Washington, DC.

We also acknowledge key members of the FACES project team, including Peggy Hunker, Kwang Kim and Alberto Sorongon, Westat, Ruth Hubbell-McKey (Co-Project Director), Shefali Pai-Samant and Cheryl Clark, Xtria, and Robert O'Brien and Mary Ann D'Elio, the CDM Group.

We also wish to thank the statistical programming assistance provided by members of Westat's programming group, including John Brown (manager), Ban Cheah, and Kristen Madden.

Some results discussed in this chapter were previously presented at the Society for Research in Child Development Biennial Meeting in Tampa, Florida, April 24–27, 2003.

Notes

1. Details of the first cohort design, measures, and findings are described in Head Start FACES: Longitudinal findings on program performance: Third progress report (Administration on Children, Youth, and Families, 2001a), available from the following website: www.acf.hhs.gov/programs/core/ongoing_research/faces/faces_pubs_reports.html
2. Details of the second cohort design, measures, and findings are available in Head Start FACES 2000: A whole child perspective on program performance: Fourth progress report (Administration on Children, Youth, and Families, 2003). Available from the following website: www.acf.dhhs.gov/programs/core/ongoing_research/faces/faces00_4thprogress/faces00_title.html
3. According to Willet (1988), the reliability in the difference score can be quite high under some conditions, particularly those favored by large-scale population-based survey methods.
4. The effect size is defined as an estimate of the magnitude of the relationship or difference between two or more variables. Effect sizes of approximately .20 are considered "small" (see Cohen, 1977 for details); moderate effect sizes of .50 are differences large enough to be clearly visible in behavior or attitudes. Large effect sizes are those above .80.
5. It is possible that some of the gain that children made occurred early in the Head Start year, before the FACES baseline assessment was administered.
6. Because the Woodcock–Johnson—Revised subtests (letter–word identification, applied problems, and dictation) are administered only to children 4 years old or older, very few children who attended Head Start for 2 years have baseline data from fall 2000. As a result, gain scores were not calculated for these subtests.
7. It is recognized that a counterargument can be made for examining predictions to entry scores, because there may be systematic grouping of children by skill levels or factors related to family demographics at program entry. For this reason, the entry-level predictions are included in Table 25.7.

References

Abbott-Shim, M. S., & Sibley, A. N. (1987). Assessment Profile for Early Childhood Programs. Atlanta: Quality Assist, Inc.

Abt Associates, Inc. (1997). Comprehensive child development program evaluation report. Prepared for the Administration for Children and Families, U.S. DHHS.

Administration on Children, Youth, and Families. (2001b). *Reaching out to families: Head Start recruitment and enrollment practices.* Washington, DC: U.S. Department of Health and Human Services. Retrieved November 2004 from www.acf.dhhs.gov/programs/core/ongoing_research/faces/reaching_out_families/reaching_title.html

Administration on Children, Youth, and Families. (1997). *First progress report on the Head Start program performance measures.* Washington, DC: U.S. Department of Health and Human Services. Retrieved November 2004 from www.acf.dhhs.gov/programs/core/pubs_reports/faces/meas_one_toc.html

Administration on Children, Youth, and Families. (2001a). *Head Start FACES: Longitudinal findings on program performance. Third progress report.* Washington, DC: U.S. Department of Health and Human Services. Retrieved November 2004 from www.acf.dhhs.gov/programs/core/pubs_reports/faces/meas_99_intro.html

Administration on Children, Youth, and Families. (2003). *Head Start FACES 2000: A whole child perspective on program performance: Fourth* progress report. Washington, DC: U.S. Department of Health and Human Services. Retrieved November 2004 from www.acf.dhhs.gov/programs/core/ongoing_research/faces/faces00_4thprogress/faces00_title.html

Arnett, J. (1989). Caregivers in day-care centers: Does training matter? *Journal of Applied Developmental Psychology. 10,* 541–552.

Barnett, W. S. (1998). Long-term effects on cognitive development and school success. In W. S. Barnett & S. S. Boocock (Eds.). *Early care and education for children in poverty* (pp. 11–44). Albany, NY: State University of New York Press.

Beals, D. E. (1993). Explanations in low-income families' mealtime conversations. *Applied Psycholinguistics, 14*(4), 489–513.

Bradley, R. H., Caldwell, B. M., Rock, S. L., Ramey, C. T., Barnard, K. E., Gray, C., et al. (1989). Home environment and cognitive development in the first 3 years of life: A collaborative study involving six sites and three ethnic groups in North America. *Developmental Psychology, 25*(2), 217–235.

Brick, J. M., & Morganstein, D. (1997). Computing sampling errors from clustered unequally weighted data using replication: WesVarPC. *Bulletin of the International Statistical Institute, Proceedings, 1,* 479–482.

Bryk, A. S., & Raudenbush, S. W. (1992). *Hierarchical linear models: Applications and data analysis methods.* Newbury Park, CA: Sage.

Burts, D. C., Hart, C. H., Charlesworth, R., and Kirk, L. (1990). A comparison of frequencies of stress behaviors observed in kindergarten children in classrooms with developmentally appropriate versus developmentally inappropriate practices. *Early Childhood Research Quarterly, 5,* pp. 407–423.

Cohen, J. (1977). *Statistical power analysis for the behavioral sciences* (rev. ed.). New York: Academic Press.

Dickinson, D. K., & Tabors, P. O. (Eds.). (2001). *Beginning literacy with language.* Baltimore: Brookes.

Dunn, L., & Dunn, L. (1997). *Peabody Picture Vocabulary Test, Third Edition.* Circle Pines, MN: American Guidance Service.

Fishel, J. E., Storch, S. A., Spira, E. G., & Stolz, B. M. (2003, April). *Enhancing emergent literacy skills in Head Start: First year curriculum evaluation results.* Paper presented at the meeting of the Society for Research in Child Development, Tampa, FL.

Goal One Technical Planning Group. (1991). The Goal One Technical Planning Subgroup report on school readiness. In National Education Goals Panel (Ed.), *Potential strategies for long-term indicator development: Reports of the technical planning subgroups* (Report No. 91–0, pp. 1–18). Washington, DC: National Education Goals Panel.

Harms, T., Clifford, R. M., & Cryer, D. (1998). *Early childhood environment rating scale—Revised edition.* New York: Teachers College Press.

Hart, B., & Risley, T. R. (1995). *Meaningful differences in the everyday experience of young American children.* Baltimore: Brookes.

Haskins, R. (1989). Beyond metaphor: The efficacy of early childhood education. *American Psychologist, 44*(2), 274–282.

Horn, W. F., & Packard, T. (1985). Early identification of learning problems: A meta-analysis. *Journal of Educational Psychology, 77,* 597–607.

Mason, J. M., & Stewart, J. (1989). *The CAP Early Childhood Diagnostic Instrument* (preprint). American Testronics.

McCarthy, D. (1972). *Manual for the McCarthy Scales of Children's Abilities.* San Antonio, TX: Psychological Corporation.

McKey, R. H., Condelli, L., Ganson, H., Barrett, B. J., McConkey, C., & Plantz, M. C. (1985). *The impact of Head Start on children, families, and communities* (DHHS Publication No. OHDS 85-31193). Washington, DC: U.S. Government Printing Office.

Nord, C. W., Lennon, J., Liu, B., & Chandler, K. (1999, November). *Home literacy activities and signs of children's emerging literacy: 1993 and 1999.* Washington, DC: U.S. Department of Education, Office of Educational Research and Improvement, National Center for Education Statistics. Retrieved from nces.ed.gov/pubs2000/2000026.pdf

Peisner-Feinberg, E. S., & Burchinal, M. R. (1997). Relations between preschool children's child-care experiences and concurrent development: The Cost, Quality and Outcomes Study. *Merrill-Palmer Quarterly, 43*(3), 451–477.

Pianta, R. C., & McCoy, S. J. (1997). The first day of school: The predictive validity of early school screening. *Journal of Applied Developmental Psychology, 18,* 1–22.

Ramey, C. T., Bryant, D. M., & Suarez, T. M. (1985). Preschool compensatory education and the modifiability of intelligence: A critical review. In D. Detterman (Ed.), *Current topics in human intelligence* (pp. 247–296). Norwood, NJ: Ablex.

Resnick, G., & Zill, N. (2003, April). *Understanding quality in Head Start classrooms: The role of teacher and program-level factors.* Paper presented at the meeting of the Society for Research in Child Development, Tampa, FL.

Reynolds, A. T. (1995). One year of preschool or two: Does it matter? *Early Childhood Research Quarterly, 10,* 1–31.

Rosenthal, R., & Rosnow, R. L. (1984). *Essentials of behavioral analysis: Methods and data analysis.* New York: McGraw-Hill.

Singer, J. (1998). Using SAS PROC MIXED to fit multilevel models, hierarchical models, and individual growth models. *Journal of Educational and Behavioral Statistics, 24*(4), 323–355.

Snow, C. E., Barnes, W., Chandler, J., Goodman, L., & Hemphill, L. (1991). *Unfulfilled expectations: Home and school influences on literacy.* Cambridge, MA: Harvard University Press.

Snow, C. E., Burns, M. S., & Griffin, P. (Eds.). (1998). *Preventing reading difficulties in young children.* Washington, DC: National Academy Press.

Snow, C. E., Tabors, P. O., Nicholson, P. A., & Kurland, B. F. (1995). SHELL: Oral language and early literacy skills in kindergarten and first-grade children. *Journal of Research in Early Childhood Education, 10*(1), 37–48.

Sorongon, A. (2004, June). *Predicting which Head Start graduates will have to repeat kindergarten.* Paper presented at the annual National Head Start Research Conference, Washington, DC.

Sprigle, J. E., & Schaefer, L. (1985). Longitudinal evaluation of the effects of two compensatory preschool programs on fourth- through sixth-grade students. *Developmental Psychology, 21,* 702–708.

Weiss, H. B., Resnick, G., & Hausman, B. (1987). *The place of family support and education programs on the social policy agenda.* Harvard Occasional Papers Series. Cambridge, MA: Harvard University, Harvard Family Research Project.

White, K. R. (1986). Efficacy of early intervention. *Journal of Special Education, 19,* 401–416.

White, K., & Casto, G. (1985). An integrative review of early-intervention efficacy studies with at-risk children: Implications for the handicapped. *Analysis and intervention in developmental disabilities, 5,* 7–31.

Whitehurst, G. J., & Lonigan, C. J. (1989). Child development and emergent literacy. *Child Development, 69*(3), 848–872.

Willet, J. B. (1988). Questions and answers in the measurement of change. In E. Rothkepf (Ed.), *Review of research in education (1988–1989)* (pp. 345–422). Washington, DC: American Educational Research Association.

Woodcock, R. W., & Mather, N. (1989). *WJ-R Tests of Achievement: Examiner's manual.* Chicago: Riverside.

Zill, N. (1999). The role of kindergarten in promoting educational quality and excellence. In R. Pianta & M. Cox (Eds.), *The transition to kindergarten.* Baltimore: Brookes.

Zill, N., Collins, M., West, J., & Hausken, E. G. (1995). *Approaching kindergarten: A look at preschoolers in the United States.* Washington, DC: U.S. Department of Education, Office of Educational Research and Improvement, National Center for Education Statistics, National Household Education Survey.

Zill, N., Moore, K. A., Smith, E. W., Stief, T., & Coiro, M. J. (1995). The life circumstances and development of children in welfare families: A profile based on national survey data. In P.L. Chase-Lansdale & J. Brooks-Gunn (Eds.), *Escape from poverty: What makes a difference for children?* (pp. 38–59). New York: Cambridge University Press.

Zill, N., & Sorongon, A. (2004, June). *Children's cognitive gains during Head Start and kindergarten.* Paper presented at the annual National Head Start Research Conference, Washington, DC.

Zill, N., & Resnick, G. (1998a). *Story and print concepts task.* Rockville, MD: Westat.

Zill, N., & Resnick, G. (1998b). *Color names and counting task.* Rockville, MD: Westat.

Zill, N., & West, J. (2001). *Entering kindergarten: A portrait of American children when they begin school.* Washington, DC: U.S. Department of Education National Center for Education Statistics.

VII

TOWARD EFFECTIVE
PRIMARY-GRADE INSTRUCTION

26

The Transition to School

FREDERICK J. MORRISON
CAROL McDONALD CONNOR
HEATHER J. BACHMAN

In the ongoing effort to understand and improve the literacy skills of American children, several important insights have emerged in recent years that have begun to focus and shape theoretical and empirical work. First, it is becoming increasingly evident that meaningful individual differences in important language, cognitive, literacy, and social skills emerge before children begin formal schooling in kindergarten or first grade (Morrison, Bachman, & Connor, 2005; Shonkoff & Phillips, 2000). Second, this early variability is influenced by a number of factors in the child, family, preschool, and larger sociocultural contexts (NICHD–Early Child Care Research Network, 2004). Third, these contributing influences do not operate in isolation but interact with each other in complex ways to shape children's variable trajectories (Storch & Whitehurst, 2002). Finally, recent work has discovered that the early schooling experiences of American children are highly variable, in some cases exacerbating the degree of difference found among children prior to school entry (NICHD–Early Child Care Research Network, 2002, 2004; Pianta, Paro, Payne, Cox, & Bradley, 2002). The cumulative impact of these ongoing trends has been to focus attention on the process of school transition as a unique and important milestone in the academic development of children and as a foundational experience for early school success.

In this chapter we first present a working conceptualization (or model) of the nature and sources of children's literacy development across the school transition period, from roughly 3 years of age to third grade. We then review the empirical literature on the major factors contributing to school readiness and early reading skill growth. Finally we will consider the implications for research and for improving literacy in the United States.

A Working Model of School Transition

Working from an ecological perspective (Bronfenbrenner, 1986) and utilizing a structural modeling framework, scientists have attempted to develop a coherent conceptualization of the process of school transition. Figure 26.1 depicts a working model of the major factors impinging on children's literacy development and their independent and combined influences over the school transition period. Four features should be noted. First, the model includes and distinguishes those processes that occur prior to school entry from those operative once school begins. At the same time the model depicts the continuity of influences (e.g., from parenting) across the two periods.

Second, the model attempts to capture the interplay of distal and proximal factors

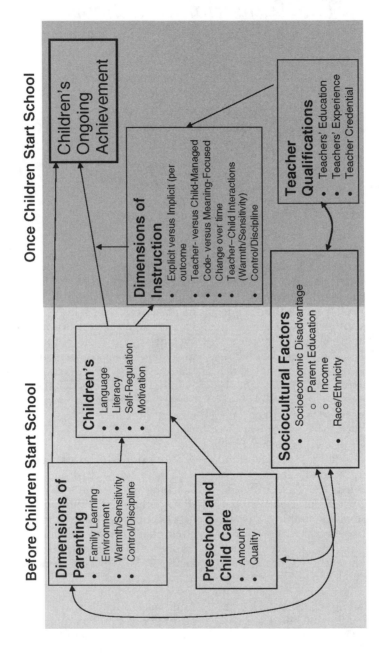

FIGURE 26.1. A working model of important sources of influence on children's literacy growth over the school transition period.

in shaping children's literacy trajectories. In particular, the mediational role of proximal factors linking distal factors to literacy outcomes is depicted. Hence, in the preschool period, the contribution of sociocultural factors, such as parental education or income, is shown as operating through their effect on more proximal parenting or preschool influences. Likewise, during early schooling the impact of teacher education or experience is seen in the model as manifesting itself primarily through the ongoing instructional activities of the teacher in the classroom.

Third, the model includes some of the important components of influence within each of the larger factors. For parenting, research has highlighted the unique influence of the learning environment, parental warmth/responsivity, and control/discipline. Fourth, the model attempts to depict some of the important interactions among these factors, recognizing the emerging consensus that these factors do not operate in isolation. For example, the home learning environment contributes directly to children's literacy growth but not to their self-regulation skills (Morrison & Cooney, 2002). Yet self-regulation and related social skills are shaped by parental control/discipline strategies and, in turn, contribute to literacy growth. On a broader plane, accumulating evidence increasingly highlights the need to capture the complex interplay of forces that shape children's literacy trajectories across the school transition period.

Before Children Get to School

Sociocultural Factors

Several decades of research have documented strong connections between socioeconomic status (SES) and academic achievement. Likewise, accumulating evidence has established links between race/ethnicity and school success, particularly the persistently lower performance of African American students compared with their European American peers. These factors are obviously linked, because the poverty rate among black families in the United States continues to be higher than it is for white families. Recently, scientists have attempted to disentangle the independent and combined influences of so-

cial, economic, and racial/ethnic influences on academic development.

SOCIOECONOMIC DISADVANTAGE
AND ACADEMIC ACHIEVEMENT

Whether measured by income, education, or occupational status, socioeconomic factors are substantially linked to a child's school success. The National Assessment of Educational Progress (National Assessment of Educational Progress, 2003; National Center for Educational Statistics, 1999) reports that 9-, 13-, and 17-year-old students with parents who have less than a high school education scored lower on tests of reading, math, and science than did children whose parents completed some education after high school. More significant for our discussion is the realization that children from low-SES families start school behind their more affluent peers and progress more slowly through the early years of elementary school (Alexander & Entwisle, 1988; Stipek & Ryan, 1997). More recent work has unearthed that children from lower SES families demonstrate delays in language and emergent literacy skills (Raviv, Kessenich, & Morrison, 2004). In a pioneering study, Hart and Risley (1995) found that preschool children from welfare families had smaller vocabularies compared with children from working-class and professional families as early as 3 years of age. Moreover, their rates of vocabulary acquisition were much slower.

How does SES affect academic achievement? Despite the strong association of socioeconomic disadvantage and poor school performance, it is not obvious how SES factors operate to shape children's academic trajectories, especially in the preschool years. In their efforts to probe more deeply into the mechanisms underlying the SES—performance connection, scientists have distinguished between direct and mediated pathways of influence.

Direct pathways reflect influences that operate directly on the child to affect academic performance. For example, poor children are more likely to have experienced negative perinatal events, such as prematurity (Saigal, Szatmari, Rosenbaum, Campbell, & King, 1991) or low birth weight, in addition to poorer nutrition and health care in early childhood (Korenman & Miller, 1997), all of which can directly limit a child's cognitive growth and potential. Yet, increasingly, scientists are describing the impact of SES as operating through more immediate influences in the child's environment. For instance, mothers living in poverty are less likely to receive adequate prenatal care, which could contribute, in part, to the connection between SES and prematurity (see Neuman, Chapter 2, this volume). Researchers describe these as *mediated pathways*, that is, SES is viewed as a distal variable that exerts its influence through a more immediate or proximal variable. The whole process is described as a *mediated relation*. Scientists are increasingly seeing the effects of SES as mediated through more proximal factors, one of which is parenting. Parents living in poverty are less likely to talk to their preschool children; they communicate with a more limited vocabulary, offer fewer questions or descriptive statements to them, and are more repetitive (Hart & Risley, 1995; Hoff-Ginsberg, 1991). In general, parents with fewer economic and/or educational resources are less likely to provide the stimulating home environments children seem to require if they are to be maximally ready for school. The important insight gained from seeing SES in this mediated fashion is that improving a family's economic circumstances alone may not translate into improved parenting, the more immediate causal agent shaping the child's development.

RACE, ETHNICITY, AND ACADEMIC ACHIEVEMENT

Similar issues have surfaced in trying to explain the disparities across racial and ethnic groups in academic attainment. Clearly, race and ethnicity, in and of themselves, are distal variables that do not directly affect academic performance. Their influence must be mediated by more proximal sources. Because most progress in understanding these complex relations comes from the study of differences between African American and European American students, we will focus on this issue here (for discussion of other ethnic groups, see Morrison, Bachman, & Connor, in 2005).

The Black–White Test Score Gap. In general, African American children do not perform as well academically as their European American counterparts (National Assessment of Educational Progress, 2000). Although some variation has been noted over the past three decades, sizable differences have persisted throughout the period in which scientists have been tracking children's performance.

The most common explanations for the "gap" have leaned on socioeconomic and sociocultural factors. In particular, the higher rate of poverty among African American families has been offered as an obvious cause for lower performance of black children. Likewise, the legacy of racial discrimination, which limits opportunities for black children, has been put forth as a contributor to lower academic attainment.

Although these factors are reasonable and, no doubt, play some role in the gap, two findings have caused scientists to reassess the nature and sources of the black–white discrepancies. First, it has become clear that the test-score gap is not limited to lower-SES groups (Phillips, Crouse, & Ralph, 1998). Black middle-SES children are performing more poorly than their white peers. Second, the gap in academic performance emerges before children begin school (Phillips et al., 1998). These two findings have caused researchers to look more deeply into the proximal environments of black families for a more comprehensive understanding of the roots of academic problems. For example, studies have found that infant mortality rates are higher in black families (Centers for Disease Control and Prevention, 2000) and, more significantly, that this difference occurs independently of SES (Schoendorf, Hogue, Kleinman, & Rowley, 1992).

Perhaps the most salient and controversial proximal factor implicated in the black–white test score gap is parenting. Mounting evidence has pointed to differences across racial groups in the types of learning experiences provided to children (Phillips et al., 1998) and other aspects of the literacy environment (see Morrison et al., 2005, for an overview). These differences also seem to extend to middle-class parenting practices (Bachman, 1999). Although the reasons for these differences in parenting are not clearly understood and many distal factors are implicated (Morrison et al., 2005), the focus on parenting and related proximal causes is yielding a clearer, more comprehensive picture of the complex forces that contribute to the continued underperformance of African American children.

Early Child Care and Preschool

Over 60% of the almost 20 million preschoolers in this country will spend some amount of time in alternate care (Smith, 2002). Hence, researchers have become increasingly interested in the psychological consequences of child care for children under 5 years of age, as well as its impact on school transition and later school functioning. In addition, for children most at risk for school failure, intensive interventions during the preschool years have attempted to help children at risk for academic failure (e.g., children living in poverty) catch up to their peers and be equally ready for school. In this section we first review the evidence on the impact of child care on children's cognitive and social development. Then we summarize the evidence on the outcome of early interventions for children at risk of academic underachievement.

IS DAY CARE GOOD OR BAD FOR CHILDREN?

Although stated rather simplistically, this question accurately captures the essence of the debate on the impact of early child care for preschool children. The importance of this question can be appreciated by realizing that the federal government undertook to fund a major national study of the nature and consequences of early child care in the late 1980s. That study, the NICHD Study of Early Child Care, as well as others, have yielded valuable insights on the role of child-care experiences in children's development and school performance.

As we stated before, the question of whether child care is good or bad oversimplifies the issue. Closer examination reveals that two variables—quality and quantity of care—are crucial to understanding the role of child care in children's lives. In broad terms, higher quality child care produces positive effects on children's cognitive, language, and literacy skills (NICHD-Early Child Care Research Network, 2002), whereas high quantities of care (defined as more than 30 hours per week) have been associated with poorer

social outcomes (Brooks-Gunn, Han, & Waldfogel, 2002). Even these conclusions do not capture the complexity of the role of child care. Parents are active agents in choosing alternate care for their children, and more educated mothers have been shown to be more sensitive and responsive to their children than mothers with less education (NICHD-Early Child Care Research Network, 2002). The more educated and responsive mothers likely chose higher quality child care, monitored it more closely, and could afford to pay for it. In fact, when direct comparisons have been made between parenting and child care environments, the impact of the quality of parenting was three to four times greater than that of child care on children's language and social skills (NICHD-Early Child Care Research Network, 2004). Nevertheless, there is early evidence that, independent of quality, children who spend more than 30 hours per week in center-based care may be less socially competent and somewhat more disruptive to other children and teachers (NICHD-Early Child Care Research Network, 2003).

In summary, in answer to our original question, research over the past two decades permits us to conclude that, in and of itself, day care is neither good nor bad for preschool children. High-quality child care enhances children's cognitive growth, whereas high amounts of child care per week may put children at risk for slightly poorer social outcomes.

ARE EARLY INTERVENTION PROGRAMS FOR AT-RISK STUDENTS EFFECTIVE?

Here, too, the question of program quality is central to answering this question. High-quality interventions can significantly enhance development. But poor-quality programs can impede children's progress (Barnett, 1995). High-quality preschool interventions have been shown to significantly improve children's prospects for academic success (Barnett, 1995), to promote stronger language and literacy development (Dickinson & Tabors, 2001), and to demonstrate significant return on investment over children's lifetimes (Reynolds, Temple, Robertson, & Mann, 2003).

A number of interventions have been implemented for at-risk children. The most visible (and controversial) is Head Start, the mixed outcomes of which illustrate the crucial importance of ensuring high-quality programs for producing consistently positive effects (see Morrison et al., 2005, for more in-depth review). Some of the more prominent and successful model programs include the Perry Preschool Project (Barnett, 1995), the Abecedarian Project (Campbell & Ramey, 1994), the School Development Program (Haynes, Comer, & Hamilton-Lee, 1988) and the Chicago Title I Child–Parent Centers (Reynolds et al., 2003). In virtually every instance, children receiving these interventions showed significantly stronger academic and social skill development compared with equally at-risk children not enrolled in the programs.

On balance, then, the mounting weight of evidence demonstrates that high-quality child care and high-quality interventions for at-risk children can and do improve the psychological well-being of preschool children, clearly enhance their school readiness, and improve their chances for successful school transition.

But what defines high-quality care? Examining the characteristics of programs that work, such as those listed previously and others (e.g., Home–School Study; Dickinson & Tabors, 2001), there are at least five crucial elements of high-quality early care programs:

1. *Strong support for parents.* Successful programs coupled intensive intervention with home visits, parent education, and parent involvement.
2. *Intensity.* Programs that were more available to children all day, 5 days a week, such as the Abecedarian Project, tended to produce stronger, more durable outcomes for children.
3. *Starting earlier.* Programs that yielded greater cost–benefit ratios (e.g., Abecedarian and Chicago Title I) began their interventions when participants were infants.
4. *Well-qualified teachers.* Programs with more teachers who were certified produced more consistently positive effects than those with fewer teachers who were certified.
5. *Rich linguistic and literacy environment.* Perhaps most fundamental to success was

an explicit focus on improving the language and literacy skills needed for early school success. Included were emphases on vocabulary, syntax, world knowledge, phonology, alphabet knowledge, and elementary word decoding.

In summary, the nature of a child's experience in alternate forms of care outside the home can have a measurable effect on subsequent psychological development and preparation for school. Although perhaps not as crucial as parenting (to which we turn next), high-quality experiences in a child-care environment can improve cognitive functioning in children at risk. Alternatively, for some children, more than 30 hours per week in child care, particularly prior to 1 year of age (Brooks-Gunn et al., 2002), may pose some short-term risks. On this latter point, it would, therefore, seem prudent to examine current parental leave policies to see whether giving parents more leave time with young infants might reduce the number of hours infants spend in child care and forestall some of the problems that may arise.

Parenting

Throughout the previous sections we have referred to parenting as a critical mediator of the effects of SES, as well as being inextricably linked to the influences of child care. Although it would seem obvious that parenting is an important, perhaps the most important, factor shaping a child's development, again the picture is not so simple. Recent work on the genetic bases of development has challenged the once-dominant position of parental socialization as the shaper of human nature. Further, efforts to improve parenting in at-risk families have proven surprisingly unsuccessful. In this section we review these issues and, although we conclude that parenting is a critical source of children's development, we need to broaden our conceptualization of parenting in order to appreciate its full sweep and power.

DOES PARENTING MATTER?

Until about 20 years ago, parenting was tacitly assumed to be the preeminent force shaping children's development (Collins,

Maccoby, Steinberg, Hetherington, & Bornstein, 2000; Cowan & Cowan, 2002). Most developmental theories accorded parents primacy over genetics, peers, and other contextual influences. Nevertheless, in the past two decades behavioral geneticists and others have challenged this simple view (Plomin, 1990; Rowe, Vazsonyi, & Flannery, 1994). Utilizing twin and related research methods designed to separate genetic from environmental influences, researchers have found that: (1) children's development can withstand substantial variability in parenting practices and emerge intact; and (2) other socializing forces, particularly peers, can exert long-term influence on selected personality traits (Harris, 1995; Rowe et al., 1994).

This work has had the salutary effect of yielding a more balanced view of the complex forces shaping human development. More recent work has attempted to gauge the complex interplay across children's development as affected by parenting, along with genetic and other factors (Collins et al., 2000). As an example, in a French study of late-adopted children (3–5 years old) with below-average IQs, those children who were adopted in higher SES families exhibited substantially greater IQ gains (19 points) by 11–18 years of age than did children adopted into lower SES households (8 points). This finding neatly demonstrates that children with similar genetic characteristics make differential progress depending on the SES of the family in which they are reared; this difference is, presumably, mediated in part by differing parenting practices.

CAN PARENTING BE MODIFIED?

One way to examine the power of parenting is to conduct intervention studies to examine whether programs actually improve parenting skills and, subsequently, whether there are corresponding increases in children's literacy skills. Two strategies have been adopted: (1) family-focused early childhood education (ECE) coupled with home-based services; and (2) exclusively parent-focused home-visiting programs. Recent reviews (Brooks-Gunn, 2004) have concluded that home-based interventions alone, without a center-based child-intervention component, were surprisingly ineffective in improving children's cognitive skills. Many of these adult-

based efforts did not substantially increase parental outcomes (e.g., educational attainment), which, in part, may explain why their children's cognitive performance did not improve (Magnusson & Duncan, 2004).

If parenting is so important to a child's development, then why haven't the interventions been more powerful? Actually, there are several reasons why these efforts may have fallen short. First, as the authors themselves noted, case managers in these studies quickly found that they needed to deal with a number of family crises and chronic adversities, such as inadequate housing, lack of food and heat, and legal problems, and that it was difficult to move beyond crisis intervention to work on parenting-for-literacy (St. Pierre & Layzer, 1999). In addition, there were sizable differences across families in the uptake of services, or the "dosage" effect. Specifically, because participation in these interventions was, ultimately, voluntary, parental participation varied widely, with about half the scheduled visits actually taking place (Gomby, Culross, & Behrman, 1999). Significantly, when eligible families were split by their participation level, children in families with greater involvement made greater gains than did their peers whose families participated less (Brooks-Gunn, Burchinal, & Lopez, 2001). Finally, it should be noted that smaller, more focused interventions (e.g., with book reading) have yielded measurable gains in children's oral language skills (Lonigan & Whitehurst, 1998; Payne, Whitehurst, & Angell, 1994; Reese & Cox, 1999; Sénéchal & LeFevre, 2001).

WHAT IS PARENTING, ANYWAY?

Most of the intervention efforts to improve parenting have been relatively limited in time and scope. For example, in the Comprehensive Child Development Program (St. Pierre & Layzer, 1999), parents received training from a home visitor for a maximum of 13 hours (½ hour biweekly), which may be insufficient to promote and maintain lasting change over time in parental habits. Further, interventions that focus primarily on one aspect of parenting may necessarily be limiting their impact. Research over the past 20 years has clearly demonstrated that parenting for literacy involves more than reading to children, and even more than providing a rich literacy environment (Christian, Bachman, & Morrison, 2001; Morrison & Cooney, 2002).

It has become useful to think of parenting as varying along a number of dimensions (Christian et al., 2001; Morrison et al., 2005; Morrison & Cooney, 2002), with three proximal dimensions being most salient for shaping literacy skills. These are (1) the family learning environment, (2) parental warmth/responsivity, and (3) parental control/discipline. A separate distal dimension posited, parental knowledge and beliefs, operates primarily through the other three proximal sources. These dimensions are conceived to exert independent influences on different aspects of a child's behavior and to be potentially independent of one another (although correlated in most instances). So, for example, parents who provide a rich learning environment for their child might not necessarily also give the child the high degree of emotional warmth needed for emotional security, nor the rules, standards, and limits needed to develop cognitive or moral self-regulation.

Family Learning Environment. In large national data sets, measures of "cognitive stimulation" or "home learning" have predicted preschoolers' IQ and receptive vocabulary (Berlin, Brooks-Gunn, Spiker, & Zaslow, 1995; Bradley et al., 1994; Johnson et al., 1993; Sugland et al., 1995), as well as reading, math, and vocabulary skills in elementary school (Smith, Brooks-Gunn, & Klebanov, 1997). Recent efforts have focused on identifying more precisely the connections between specific parental behaviors and child outcomes. This work has revealed a high degree of specificity in the impact of the learning environment; namely, parental behaviors, such as book reading, promote language development but do little for specific literacy skills such as letter knowledge and word decoding. In contrast, deliberate efforts by parents to teach these emergent literacy skills to their children help to promote their alphabet and word-decoding skills but do little to enrich vocabulary (Sénéchal & LeFevre, 2001).

Language-promoting behaviors include frequent labeling and describing objects in the environment (Hart & Risley, 1995; Hoff-Ginsburg, 1991). The overall amount and complexity of parental speech to children predicts their vocabulary and complex grammar acquisition (Huttenlocher, Haight, Bryk, Seltzer, & Lyons, 1991; Huttenlocher, Vasilyeva, Cymerman, & Levine, 2002). Beyond size and content, the manner of speaking and interacting with children contributes to oral language growth. In the Hart and Risley (1995) study, children with relatively limited vocabularies received a greater proportion of commands and prohibitions from their parents. In other work (Tomasello & Todd, 1983), parents who maintained longer periods of joint attention on an object had children with larger vocabularies.

Shared book reading has been demonstrated to be a powerful tool, for some children, to enhance vocabulary development (Haden, Reese, & Fivush, 1996; Lonigan & Whitehurst, 1998; Reese & Cox, 1999; but see Scarborough & Dobrich, 1994). In randomized experiments, book-reading styles that involve active labeling and describing illustrations or encouraging and assisting children's storytelling significantly enhances vocabulary development (Lonigan & Whitehurst, 1998; Whitehurst et al., 1988).

Literacy-promoting activities by parents may require more explicit instruction than do those that nurture oral language growth. When parents explicitly teach their children how to name and print letters and words, children's print knowledge improves (Sénéchal, LeFevre, Thomas, & Daley, 1998) as do later word-decoding and comprehension skills in school (Sénéchal & LeFevre, 2002).

In summary, parents' efforts to promote language and literacy in their children can substantially improve their development and school readiness. An important insight has been gained in recognizing the high degree of specificity in what parents do and what children learn.

Parental Warmth/Responsivity. The degree to which parents display open affection to their children, offer physical or verbal reinforcement, and show sensitivity to their feelings and wishes is predictive of preschoolers' literacy and language skills, as well as their later school achievement (Berlin et al., 1995). Mothers' sensitivity to children's developmental progress during the first 2 years of life has been shown to predict cognitive and language skills later in preschool (NICHD-ECCRN, 1998; Tamis-Lemonda, Bornstein, & Baumwell, 2001), kindergarten, and first grade (Coates & Lewis, 1984; Kelly, Morisset, Barnartd, Hammond, & Booth, 1996). More responsive mothers are more likely to reduce the length of their utterances to their infants so that the child can better comprehend them (Murray, Johnson, & Peters, 1990). Other research has shown that at-risk groups of children can make substantial progress when mothers interact with them in a highly responsive manner. A classic situation that combines elements of the learning environment with warmth and responsivity is shared book reading, especially at bedtime. In addition to the benefits to cognitive and language skills, shared book reading promotes emotional closeness and affection and provides the child with the undivided attention of a loving parent. Such interchanges may nurture self-regulation and emotional well-being.

Parental Control/Discipline. Though less well researched, the degree to which parents establish rules, standards, and limits on a child's behavior creates a structured and supportive context for literacy development (Chase-Lansdale & Pittman, 2002; Hartup, 1989). In book reading, for example, this interaction affords parents the opportunity to resist children's fidgeting and squirming and to sustain their attention until the story is finished. In one study, Cooney (1998) found that parents' use of disciplinary practices did not directly predict literacy outcomes but did reliably predict self-regulation measures (e.g., cooperation, independence, and responsibility), which in turn contributed positively to literacy skill levels at kindergarten entry.

In summary, the weight of evidence at this point supports a strong role for parenting in shaping children's literacy development, albeit in complex ways. Future research will evaluate whether and to what extent more intensive and comprehensive interventions (encompassing more dimensions of parenting) will yield measurable improvements in the literacy attainment of at-risk children.

Child Factors

Full assessment of the factors contributing to school transition would be incomplete without consideration of what the child brings to the process of development. Whether through inherited genetic differences or acquired differences, child characteristics by themselves and in interaction with environmental factors shape the course of children's early development. In reality, these child qualities are what we mean when we typically refer to "school readiness." Although most scientists now view readiness as a two-way street (with schools needing to be ready for children, as well as vice versa), there is still intense interest in the factors within the child that are most crucial for school readiness and successful school transition. In this section, we highlight recent discoveries about three domains of early functioning—language/literacy skills, self-regulation, and motivation (for a more complete overview, see Morrison et al., 2005).

LANGUAGE/LITERACY SKILLS

One of the most important discoveries of the past two decades has been the critical role that language plays in early reading and literacy development (see Dickinson, McCabe, & Essex, Chapter 1, this volume). Several language skills independently contribute to reading acquisition (Morrison et al., 2005). More important recent research points to possible interactions among these components over the course of learning to read.

Perhaps the biggest discovery of the past two decades has been the role of phonological skills (particularly phonemic awareness) in learning to read (Bradley & Bryant, 1983; Catts, Fey, Zhang, & Tomblin, 1999; Rayner, Foorman, Perfetti, Pesetsky, & Seidenberg, 2001). Increasing skill at consciously manipulating the component sounds in the speech stream facilitates the child's task of "cracking the code," that is, learning the symbol–sound correspondence rules and utilizing them in increasingly sophisticated ways to derive accurate word pronunciations. Locating the smallest units, phonemes, in a word seems to be the most critical level of segmentation for early word decoding. Children who have difficulty at this level, for whatever reason, experience significant problems progressing in word decoding (Rayner et al., 2001).

Vocabulary, both receptive and expressive, has been shown to predict early reading skill

(NICHD-ECCRN, 2004; Storch & Whitehurst, 2002). The number of different words a child understands, as well as the number he or she speaks, helps with word-decoding efforts and may facilitate growth of phonological awareness (Dickinson & Tabors, 2001).

Finally, children's knowledge of the alphabet when they enter kindergarten is one of the best predictors of learning to read (Snow, Burns, & Griffin, 1998). Letter knowledge predicts more advanced phonological awareness (Wagner et al., 1997) and better word-decoding skills throughout elementary school (Lonigan, Burgess, & Anthony, 2000).

There is some uncertainty at present about how and when each of these component skills exerts its influence. Some studies (Schatschneider, Fletcher, Francis, Carlson, & Foorman, 2004; Storch & Whitehurst, 2002) have demonstrated that vocabulary uniquely predicts early reading skills only through kindergarten, after which it contributes indirectly via its association with phonological processes, which continue to predict reading well into early elementary school. Other recent studies appear to find an independent contribution for vocabulary and other oral language skills through third grade (NICHD-ECCRN, 2004; Connor, Morrison, & Petrella, 2004). There is agreement, though, that development of early oral language facility, including vocabulary, is essential to later comprehension skills (Storch & Whitehurst, 2002).

SELF-REGULATION

Increasing attention in recent years has been paid to a class of skills that has been variously called executive functioning, learning-related social skills, social competence, and self-regulation. They refer to the coordination of processes involved in response inhibition, sustaining attention over time, and planning and organization in working memory. They contribute, among other things, to a child's ability to work independently, to control impulses, and to complete tasks on time. There is a growing sense that problems in self-regulation among U.S. children are contributing in major ways to the literacy problems in the nation (Morrison et al., 2005).

Children with poor learning-related social skills at the beginning of kindergarten have been shown to perform more poorly academically at school entry and at the end of second grade (McClelland, Morrison, & Holmes, 2000). Likewise, a child's skill at sustaining attention and restraining restlessness predicts academic functioning in first grade (Alexander, Entwisle, & Dauber, 1993). The close connection between social and academic skills persists throughout school. Adolescents who were rated more highly by teachers and peers on complying with rules and expectations outperformed their lower scoring peers on measures of academic achievement (Wentzel, 1991a, 1991b). Clearly, development of self-regulation is an important task for preschool children over the school transition period and one that has sustained influence throughout a child's life.

MOTIVATION

Motivational skills refer to students' values and beliefs when approaching school tasks, including their engagement with the material, interest in the topic, and beliefs about self-efficacy, as well as their attributions of success or failure and their goal orientations (for a review, see Eccles & Wigfield, 2002; Linnenbrink, 2002). The study of motivational processes in education has a long history, yet surprisingly little research has been conducted on young children (Morrison et al., 2005). This is unfortunate, because in practically every other area of academic functioning, it has become clear that the seeds of later success are sown during the preschool years. Hence laying a foundation of academic engagement, coupled with a strong sense of mastery and self-efficacy prior to school entry, could be expected to reap long-term benefits throughout a child's academic career. Clearly, more systematic empirical inquiry is needed on the early roots of motivational processes in children and their influence on academic functioning.

In summary, research over the past two decades has clearly revealed that a number of potent forces, independently and in combination, shape the literacy development of preschool children. Factors in the child, family, preschool, and broader sociocultural contexts all contribute to create the significant variability that U.S. children present when they walk in the school door. What happens to these children once they start school?

Once Children Begin School

This significant variability in children's language, literacy, self-regulation, and motivation is important to consider if we are to understand how classroom instruction affects students' literacy development. First, children's language and literacy skills appear to be highly stable once they reach kindergarten. Further, the effect of instruction appears to be specific, and, thus, how explicitly instruction targets particular domains, as well as the multiple dimension of instruction, are important to consider. Moreover, there appear to be child-by-instruction interactions. Although effective teachers provide instruction that yields strong student outcomes, there are too few effective teachers in today's classrooms. Finally, examining the system of education, including home and family, schools and teachers, and children themselves, we find there are multiple pathways that children may follow on their road to becoming literate members of society, with multiple opportunities to positively affect children's learning. The next section examines each of these.

Stability of Language and Literacy Skills

Children who begin school with strong language skills tend to be more successful academically throughout their school careers than are those with weaker language skills (Entwisle, Alexander, & Olson, 1997; Hart & Risley, 1995; Loban, 1976). Students who start first grade knowing the letters of the alphabet and with a firm grasp of other emergent literacy skills achieve stronger reading skills by the end of first grade than do students with weaker skills (NICHD-ECCRN, 2004; Storch & Whitehurst, 2002). Indeed, Entwisle, Alexander, and Olson (1997) have proposed a critical period for reading development encompassing the first three elementary school grades. Their research reveals that students who fail to reach grade expectations by third grade are unlikely to experience success in school later on. The stability of students' language and literacy development may be one reason that the achievement gap between children from low-SES and high-SES families is both pervasive and persistent (Entwisle et al., 1997; Ferguson, 1990; Jencks & Phillips, 1998; NAEP,

2003). As we discussed in the beginning of this chapter, children from low-SES families begin school with language and early reading skills that fall well behind their more affluent peers (Snow et al., 1998), with multiple sources of influence on this development—home, parenting, preschool, and child characteristics.

The Effect of Schooling and the Specificity of Learning

In the face of this stability, some have questioned whether schooling has any appreciable direct effect on children's cognitive development (Coleman et al., 1966; Rutter & Maughan, 2002). However, there are studies that demonstrate causal effects of schooling on children's literacy skill growth (Morrison & Connor, 2002). Some of these studies utilize a natural experiment employing the rather arbitrary birthdate cutoff that school districts mandate for school entry. Children who just make or just miss this cutoff birthdate are essentially the same age chronologically, but those whose birthdays fall before the cutoff date start first grade, while those whose birthdays fall just after go to kindergarten. In this way the schooling and maturational effects on children's development can be examined separately. If both groups demonstrate similar rates of growth in a particular skill, then that skill is most likely a product of maturation—there is *not* a *schooling effect*. On the other hand, if children who are the same age but a grade ahead demonstrate rates of skill growth that are greater than their age-peers who are a grade behind them, then there *is* a *schooling effect*.

First-grade schooling effects are evident for alphabet recognition, word decoding, phonemic (individual sounds within words) awareness, general knowledge, addition, short-term memory, sentence memory, and visuospatial memory. Yet there are no kindergarten or schooling effects for receptive vocabulary, rhyming, conservation of number and quantity, addition strategies, and narrative coherence (Morrison et al., 2005; Morrison, Smith, & Dow-Ehrensberger, 1995). Children demonstrate similar rates of growth in these skills regardless of whether they are in kindergarten or first grade. For example, for 89 children who attended the same school district, taking into account cognitive abilities and parents' education, there were kindergarten but not first-grade effects for letter naming (Christian, Morrison, Frazier, & Masseti, 2000). There were kindergarten and first-grade effects for basic reading skills, including word decoding. There were only first-grade effects for general information, mathematics, and phonemic segmentation (identifying the individual sounds in words).

These results are particularly revealing if we consider the three phonological-awareness tasks. These tasks differed only in the level of segmentation the child was asked to complete—syllabic, subsyllabic, and phonemic. For the syllabic-segmentation task, children were asked to identify the number of syllables in a word. For example, *cucumber* has three syllables, *cu-cum-ber*. In the subsyllabic task, children were asked to say the first sound in each word. For example, /t/ is the first sound in the word *toy*. For the phonemic task, children were asked to count the number of sounds in a word. For example, *rest* has four sounds, /r-e-s-t/. The study revealed that there were schooling effects, but only for specific skills. For syllabic segmentation, neither first grade nor kindergarten had an effect on growth in these skills. For subsyllabic segmentation, both first grade and kindergarten affected growth. In contrast, first grade, but *not* kindergarten, had an effect on phonemic segmentation. Additionally, emerging research (Morrison & Connor, in preparation) reveals that once the amount and type of instruction students receive is taken into account, the schooling effect disappears. Thus the schooling effect is most likely the result of instructional differences in kindergarten and first grade. In other words, learning is highly specific and related to the explicit focus of the instruction students receive. In first grade, children are provided more time in activities that supported their decoding skill growth, which result in first graders' demonstrating stronger decoding skills when compared with their age peers who are in kindergarten.

Dimensions of Instruction

By employing a more complex view of instruction across multiple dimensions of instruction, researchers can take this specificity

of learning into account. Recent research points to four salient dimensions of instruction (Connor, Morrison, & Katch, 2004). These include (1) explicit focus of instruction (explicit vs. implicit), (2) responsibility for focusing the students' attention (teacher vs. child), (3) whether instruction is code based or meaning based (word level vs. higher order), and (4) change in amount of instruction over the school year.

The first dimension, explicit versus implicit, is outcome specific. For example, if the student outcome of interest is reading comprehension, then instructional strategies that explicitly target comprehension, such as teaching children to predict, summarize, and infer information from text, would be considered explicit (National Reading Panel, 2000). Instructional activities that explicitly support children's decoding skill growth, such as phonological decoding or alphabet recognition (Rayner et al., 2001; Torgesen et al., 2001), might be expected to support children's reading comprehension, but in an implicit or indirect way. On the other hand, phonological decoding or phonics would be considered explicit instructional activities if the student outcome was decoding skill.

The second dimension, teacher versus child managed, considers the degree to which an instructional activity, and the child's attention to it, are primarily under the direction of the teacher (e.g., teachers demonstrating the alphabetic principle) or the child (e.g., sustained independent silent reading). A number of studies have described this dimension. For example, prescriptive instruction (Rayner et al., 2001) would be considered teacher managed; responsive instruction (Pearson & Gallagher, 1983) starts with teacher-managed and moves to child-managed instruction as students gain key skills. This dimension should not be confused with the teacher-directed versus child-centered styles of instruction (Bredekemp & Copple, 1997). Child-centered activities, such as discussions about books, would be teacher managed within this framework, whereas teacher-directed activities, such as children's completing worksheets, would be considered child managed.

The third dimension, code- versus meaning-focused, underscores a broader curriculum debate regarding code-based versus meaning-based instruction (Dahl & Freppon, 1995; Rayner et al., 2001) and which one is the more effective strategy for young readers. Code-focused instruction includes such code-based activities as spelling and teaching phonological decoding. Meaning-focused activities include instruction that focuses on meaning, such as vocabulary and comprehension, and that includes strategies that would be described as whole language. However, as Chall observed in her seminal work, *Beyond the Great Debate* (Chall, 1967), and as has been observed more recently (Connor, Morrison, & Katch, 2004; Juel & Minden-Cupp, 2000), throughout the school day, teachers provide both word-level and higher order instructional activities, but in varying amounts.

A key element of this more complex view of instruction is that these dimensions operate simultaneously. Thus, for reading comprehension, a whole-class activity in which the teacher is explicitly showing children how to summarize what they have read and how to predict what will happen next would be considered a teacher-managed meaning-focused explicit reading comprehension activity. In contrast, children reading quietly at their desks would be considered a child-managed meaning-focused implicit reading comprehension activity; sustained silent reading might be expected to implicitly support reading comprehension while explicitly supporting fluency. Students completing spelling worksheets would be an example of a code-focused implicit reading comprehension activity (or a code-focused explicit decoding activity).

The fourth dimension, change in amount of instruction over the school year, speaks to the timing of this instruction (Connor, Morrison, & Katch, 2004; Juel & Minden-Cupp, 2000). In our study we observed that first graders who began the year with low vocabulary skills exhibited greater decoding skill growth in classrooms in which teachers began the year providing smaller amounts of child-managed implicit decoding instruction (e.g., sustained silent reading) that sharply increased in amount by the spring. In contrast, students who began the school year with strong vocabulary skills demonstrated stronger decoding skill growth in classrooms with steady amounts of child-managed implicit decoding instruction all year long.

Child-by-Instruction Interactions

Given the specificity of instruction, as well as its complexity, it is important to consider the type and amount of instruction children receive *and* child-by-instruction interactions. The effect of instruction appears to depend on children's language and literacy skill levels (Connor, Morrison, & Katch, 2004; Connor, Morrison, & Petrella, 2004; Juel & Minden-Cupp, 2000). Child-by-instruction interactions are evident in preschool (Connor, 2002), first grade (Connor, Morrison, & Katch, 2004; Foorman, Francis, Fletcher, Schatschneider, & Mehta, 1998; Juel & Minden-Cupp, 2000), second grade (Foorman et al., 1998) and third grade (Connor, Morrison, & Petrella, 2004). In general, children who begin the school year with weaker language and literacy skills demonstrate greater skill growth in classrooms in which more time is spent in teacher-managed explicit instruction, whereas children with stronger language and literacy skills demonstrate substantial skill growth in classrooms with more child-managed learning opportunities. As might be expected, children with stronger language and literacy skills appear to demonstrate literacy skill growth almost regardless of the pattern of instruction they receive. It is the students most at risk, with weaker skills overall, who are most affected by the instruction they receive. They have the potential to make substantial gains in early literacy, decoding, and comprehension, but only if they receive the patterns of instruction that, research suggests, are most effective for them. They may demonstrate little or no growth at all in the face of less effective instruction (Connor, Morrison, & Katch, 2004; Connor, Morrison, & Petrella, 2004; Torgesen, 2000; Torgesen et al., 1999).

For example, in a recent study, we examined the effect of first-grade language arts instruction on children's decoding skill growth (Connor, Morrison, & Katch, 2004). We observed over 100 students in 43 first-grade classrooms in the fall, winter, and spring. Using the dimensions of instruction yielded four decoding instruction variables—teacher-managed explicit, child-managed explicit, teacher-managed implicit, and child-managed implicit decoding. Using multilevel modeling, we controlled for the effect of children's fall letter–word recognition (decoding) and vocabulary skills, as well as their home literacy environment and parent's educational level. Results revealed that children's fall decoding and vocabulary skills did positively predict their spring decoding scores (which would be expected based on the research demonstrating the stability of these skills). The pattern of instruction, amount, and type also predicted decoding skill growth, but the effect of this instruction depended on students' fall decoding and vocabulary scores. Children who demonstrated weaker decoding skills in the fall demonstrated greater decoding growth in classrooms in which teachers provided more time in teacher-managed explicit decoding instructional activities (e.g., instruction in the alphabetic principle, phonological awareness, etc.). They demonstrated less growth when teachers provided less time in such activities. In contrast, there was very little effect of teacher-managed explicit decoding instruction for children who began the year with strong decoding skills.

Additionally, there was an interaction between children's fall vocabulary scores and the amount and slope (i.e., change over the school year) of child-managed implicit decoding instruction provided. Children who began the year with weaker vocabulary skills exhibited greater decoding growth in classrooms with less time spent in child-managed implicit decoding activities (e.g., sustained silent reading) in the fall, with sharply increasing amounts over the school year (i.e., steep slope), than they did in classrooms with substantial amounts of child-managed implicit decoding instruction all year long (i.e., no slope). In contrast, children with strong vocabulary skills in the fall demonstrated greater decoding growth in classrooms that provided substantial amounts of child-managed implicit decoding activities all year long (no change in amount) than they did in classrooms with the opposite pattern of instruction.

Following the students into second grade revealed an interaction between their fall decoding scores and the amount of teacher-managed explicit decoding instruction provided (Morrison et al., 2005). Children with weaker decoding skills in the fall demonstrated greater decoding skill growth in classrooms in which teachers spent more time in teacher-managed explicit decoding instruction. The reverse was the case for children with strong decoding skills in the fall. Considering third-grade reading comprehension skills revealed interactions between students' fall reading comprehension scores and amount of teacher-managed explicit reading comprehension instruction (positive) and child-managed explicit reading comprehension instruction (negative) (Connor, Morrison, & Petrella, 2004). Children who began the school year with low to average (up to the 75th percentile) reading comprehension skills demonstrated greater growth in reading comprehension in classrooms with greater amounts of teacher-managed explicit reading comprehension instruction and less child-managed explicit instruction than they did in classrooms that provided the opposite pattern of instruction. Modeled results suggest that these differences were substantial and represented more than a two-grade-level difference in achievement for children with weaker language and literacy skills.

Implementing Effective Instruction

The implication of these results is that effective instruction in the early grades, designed and implemented based on children's skill strengths and weaknesses and mapped to the dimension of instruction, can have an important effect on children's learning. The hurdle is that designing instruction for each child individually (i.e., individualizing instruction) and then implementing it for every child in a classroom will be difficult, especially if students vary widely in their abilities. Nevertheless, studies of effective teachers and schools suggest a number of strategies that might facilitate individualized instruction (Morrison et al., 2005; Taylor & Pearson, 2002; Westat, 2001; Wharton-McDonald, Pressley, & Hampston, 1998). These include early and ongoing assessment of children's skills and using these results to design instruction and monitor students' progress; making sure that children receive enough time overall in instructional activities that, research indicates, will be effective for them (i.e., time on task and individualized instruction); use of flexible small groups based on learning goals; and putting effective teachers into the classroom.

TEACHER QUALIFICATIONS

Teachers who consistently obtain strong student outcomes have been described as masterful classroom managers (Brophy & Good, 1986; Wharton-McDonald et al., 1998). They effectively manage student behavior, time, instructional activities, student interactions, and outside resources. They follow a predictable classroom routine but at the same time are flexible and take advantage of opportunities to provide "mini-lessons" (Taylor & Pearson, 2002). They provide extra help to the students who need it. The most effective teachers "engage[d] virtually all of their students in the work of the classroom" (Taylor, Pearson, Clark, & Walpole, 2000, p. 158). However, there was clear variability in the effectiveness of teachers. In the studies reviewed, only about one third to one half of teachers were effective in promoting student reading skill growth. The rest were judged to be ineffective. They "struggled to complete morning routines and begin instruction" (Wharton-McDonald et al., 1998, p. 120) and their students failed to demonstrate substantial growth on important early literacy skills.

How do we train, find, and keep effective teachers in the classroom? There is evidence that, currently, the teaching profession may not attract the most qualified students. Education majors are more likely to be in the bottom quartile of their class than any other major (Henke, Knepper, Geis, & Giambattista, 1996). Additionally, young adults who do pursue education credentials often receive training that inadequately prepares them for teaching, which is a complex and demanding career. Nor are they adequately supported once they reach the classroom (Kauffman, Johnson, Kardos, Liu, & Peske, 2002). For example, 54% of teachers have students with limited English proficiency or who belong to a cultural minority, and 71% of teachers have students with disabilities. Yet only 20% of these teachers feel well prepared to meet the needs of these children. Only 28% feel well prepared to use student assessment to guide instruction (Lewis et al., 1999). However, almost all teachers have bachelor's degrees; half have master's-level degrees; over 90% hold regular or advanced teaching credentials (Department of Education, 2002).

Current policy calls for qualified teachers in every classroom. There is some evidence that students of more highly qualified teachers (i.e., credentials, education, and experience) tend to make greater gains in achievement. However, this body of research has failed to examine teacher qualifications within a system of instruction (Cohen, Raudenbush, & Ball, 2003), nor have they taken into account the effect of sociocultural factors, parents and home, preschool and child care, child characteristics, and instruction (Morrison et al., 2005). Using a systemic approach (Connor, Son, Morrison, & Hindman, in press), including the influence of socioeconomic status and home learning environment, reveals that teachers' years of education positively influences classroom practices, which, in turn, affect student achievement. In contrast, years of experience and class size did not relate to either classroom practices or student outcomes.

Thus, improving educational opportunities before and after teachers reach the classroom may support more effective teaching. This might include encouraging teachers to use research, rather than just personal childhood and classroom experience, to guide their practice (Boerst, 2003; Kaestle, 1993; Littlewood, 2001). This also means that the crucial reciprocal interactions between teachers and researchers must be strengthened (Martella, Nelson, & Marchand-Martella, 1999; Morrison et al., 2005). Research in education is accumulating critical amounts of information about children's learning (Shavelson & Towne, 2002). Recent policy has called for scientifically rigorous research and may put in place adequate funding for this endeavor. Without true dialogue, teachers will not learn and use the most effective practices as they are discovered, and critical research issues may be overlooked.

Developing a Coherent Model of Children's Early Literacy Development

Returning to the model we presented at the beginning of the chapter (Figure 26.1), we reviewed research that examines the effect of multiple factors both before and after children begin school. As we discussed in this chapter, there is substantial research evidence for each pathway, although arguably fewer studies examine these effects simultaneously. The model includes distal variables, such as socioeconomic status and teachers' qualifications, as well as more proximal sources of influence, such as parenting, classroom instruction, and child characteristics. Moreover, the model indicates child-by-instruction interactions; the effect of instruction depends on the language and literacy skills children bring to the classroom. Note also that the distal variables, such as teacher qualification, act through more proximal variables, such as instruction. Additionally, distal variables may operate through a number of other, more proximal variables. For example, family SES affects the home literacy environment (in general, higher SES families provide stronger home literacy environments), but it also affects teacher qualifications (children from higher SES families tend to have more qualified teachers). Further, the model displays that parenting has an immediate effect on children's language and literacy skills prior to school entry *and* has an ongoing effect on children's achievement once they begin school. The model presents multiple pathways to children's academic success and suggests points of influence—in the home, in the classroom, and in the community—that can contribute to students' success.

References

Alexander, K., & Entwisle, D. (1988). Achievement in the first 2 years of school: Patterns and processes. *Monographs of the Society for Research in Child Development, 53*(2).

Alexander, K., Entwisle, D., & Dauber, S. (1993). First-grade classroom behavior: Its short- and long-term consequences for school performance. *Child Development, 64*, 801–814.

Bachman, H. (1999, April). How did we get here? Examining the sources of White-Black differences in academic achievement. In F. Morrison (Chair), *Racial differences in academic achievement: When and why?* Symposium conducted at the biennial meeting of the Society for Research in Child Development, Albuquerque, NM.

Barnett, S. (1995). Long-term effects of early childhood programs on cognitive and school outcomes. *The Future of Children, 5*(3), 25–50.

Berlin, L. J., Brooks-Gunn, J., Spiker, D., & Zaslow, M. J. (1995). Examining observational measures of emotional support and cognitive stimulation in Black and White mothers of preschoolers. *Journal of Family Issues, 16*, 664–686.

Boerst, T. (2003). *Deliberative professional development communities as sites for teacher learning.* Unpublished doctoral dissertation, University of Michigan, Ann Arbor.

Bradley, L., & Bryant, P. E. (1983). Categorizing sounds and learning to read: A causal connection. *Nature, 301*(3), 419–421.

Bradley, R., Whiteside, L., Mundform, D., Casey, P., Kelleher, K., & Pope, S. (1994). Early indications of resilience and their relation to experiences in the home environments of low birthweight, premature children in poverty. *Child Development, 65*, 346–360.

Bredekemp, S., & Copple, C. (Eds.). (1997). *Developmentally appropriate practice in early childhood programs.* Washington, DC: National Association for the Education of Young Children.

Bronfenbrenner, U. (1986). Ecology of the family as a context for human development: Research perspectives. *Developmental Psychology, 22*, 723–742.

Brooks-Gunn, J. (2004). Intervention and policy as a change agent for young children. In P. L. Chase-Lansdale, K. E. Kiernan, & R. J. Friedman (Eds.), *Human development across lives and generations: The potential for change* (pp. 293–341). New York: Cambridge University Press.

Brooks-Gunn, J., Burchinal, M., & Lopez, M. (2004). *Enhancing the cognitive and social development of young children via parent education in the Comprehensive Child Development Program.* Unpublished manuscript.

Brooks-Gunn, J., Han, W., & Waldfogel, J. (2002). Maternal employment and child cognitive outcomes in the first three years of life: NICHD study of early child care. *Child Development, 73*(4), 1052–1072.

Brophy, J. E., & Good, T. L. (1986). Teacher behavior and student achievement. In M. C. Wittrock (Ed.), *Handbook of research on teaching* (3rd ed., pp. 328–375). New York: Macmillan.

Campbell, F., & Ramey, C. (1994). Effects of early intervention on intellectual and academic achievement: A follow-up study of children from low income families. *Child Development, 65*, 684–698.

Catts, H., Fey, M., Zhang, X., & Tomblin, B. (1999). Language basis of reading and reading disabilities: Evidence from a longitudinal investigation. *Scientific Studies of Reading, 3*(4), 331–361.

Centers for Disease Control and Prevention. (2000). *CDC Fact Book 2000/2001.* Washington, DC: U.S. Department of Health and Human Services.

Chall, J. (1967). *Learning to read: The great debate.* New York: McGraw-Hill.

Chase-Lansdale, P., & Pittman, L. (2002). Welfare reform and parenting: Reasonable expectations. In M. K. Shields (Ed.), *Children and welfare re-*

form (Vol. 12, pp. 167–183). Los Altos, CA: The David and Lucile Packard Foundation.

Christian, K., Bachman, H. J., & Morrison, F. J. (2001). Schooling and cognitive development. In R. Sternberg & R. L. Grigorenko (Eds.), *Environmental effects on cognitive abilities* (pp. 287–335). Mahwah, NJ: Erlbaum.

Christian, K., Morrison, F., Frazier, J., & Masseti, G. (2000). Specificity in the nature and timing of cognitive growth in kindergarten and first grade. *Journal of Cognition and Development, 1*(4), 429–449.

Coates, D., & Lewis, M. (1984). Early mother–infant interaction and infant cognitive status as predictors of school performance and cognitive behavior in six-year-olds. *Child Development, 55,* 1219–1230.

Cohen, D., Raudenbush, S., & Ball, D. (2003). Resources, instruction, and research. *Educational Evaluation and Policy Analysis, 25*(2), 119–142.

Coleman, J., Campbell, E., Hobson, C., McPartland, J., Mood, A., Weinfeld, F., et al. (1966). *Equality of educational opportunity.* Washington, DC: U.S. Government Printing Office.

Collins, W. A., Maccoby, E., Steinberg, L., Hetherington, E. M., & Bornstein, M. H. (2000). Contemporary research on parenting: The case for nature and nurture. *American Psychologist, 55,* 218–232.

Connor, C. (2002). *Preschool children and teachers talking together: The influence of child, family, teacher, and classroom characteristics on children's developing literacy.* Unpublished doctoral dissertation, University of Michigan, Ann Arbor.

Connor, C. M., Morrison, F. J., & Katch, L. (2004). Beyond the reading wars: Exploring the effect of child-instruction interaction on growth in early reading. *Scientific Studies of Reading, 8*(4), 305–336.

Connor, C. M., Morrison, F. J., & Petrella, J. (2004). Effective reading comprehension instruction: Understanding child by instruction interactions. *Journal of Educational Psychology, 96*(4), 682–698.

Connor, C. M., Son, S., Hindman, A., & Morrison, F. J. (in press). Teacher qualifications, classroom practices, family characteristics, and preschool experience: Complex effects on first graders' vocabulary and early reading outcomes. *Journal of School Psychology.*

Cooney, R. (1998, April). *Relations among aspects of parental control, children's work-related skills and academic achievement.* Paper presented at the Conference on Human Development, Mobile, AL.

Cowan, P. A., & Cowan, C. P. (2002). What an intervention design reveals about how parents affect their children's academic achievement and behavior problems. In J. G. Borkowski, S. L. Ramey, & M. Bristol-Power (Eds.), *Parenting and the child's*

world: Influences on academic, intellectual, and social-emotional development (pp. 75–97). Mahwah, NJ: Erlbaum.

Dahl, K. L., & Freppon, P. A. (1995). A comparison of inner-city children's interpretations of reading and writing instruction in the early grades in skills-based and whole language classrooms. *Reading Research Quarterly, 30*(1), 50–74.

Department of Education. (2002). *Meeting the highly qualified teachers challenge.* Washington DC: U.S. Department of Education, Office of Postsecondary Education, Office of Policy Planning and Innovation.

Dickinson, D. K., & Tabors, P. O. (2001). *Beginning literacy with language.* Baltimore: Brookes.

Eccles, J. S., & Wigfield, A. (2002). Motivational beliefs, values, and goals. *Annual Review of Psychology, 53,* 109–132.

Entwisle, D. R., Alexander, K. L., & Olson, L. S. (1997). *Children, schools, and inequality.* Boulder, CO: Westview Press.

Ferguson, R. F. (1990). *Racial patterns in how school and teacher quality affect achievement and earnings.* Dallas, TX: Meadows Foundation.

Foorman, B. R., Francis, D. J., Fletcher, J. M., Schatschneider, C., & Mehta, P. (1998). The role of instruction in learning to read: Preventing reading failure in at-risk children. *Journal of Educational Psychology, 90,* 37–55.

Gomby, D. S., Culross, P. L., & Behrman, R. E. (1999). Home visiting: Recent program evaluations—analysis and recommendations. *The Future of Children, 9,* 4–26.

Haden, C. A., Reese, E., & Fivush, R. (1996). Mothers' extratextual comments during storybook reading: Stylistic differences over time and across text. *Discourse Processes, 21,* 135–169.

Harris, J. R. (1995). Where is the child's environment? A group socialization theory of development. *Psychological Review, 102,* 458–489.

Hart, B., & Risley, T. R. (1995). *Meaningful differences in the everyday experience of young American children.* Baltimore: Brookes.

Hartup, W. (1989). Social relationships and their developmental significance. *American Psychologist, 44,* 120–126.

Haynes, N. M., Comer, J., & Hamilton-Lee, M. (1988). The School Development Program: A model for school improvement. *Journal of Negro Education, 57*(1), 11–21.

Henke, R. R., Knepper, P., Geis, S., & Giambattista, J. (1996). *Out of the lecture hall and into the classroom: 1992–1993 college graduates and elementary/secondary school teaching.* Washington, DC: U.S. Department of Education.

Hoff-Ginsberg, E. (1991). Mother–child conversation in different social classes and communicative settings. *Child Development, 62,* 782–796.

Huttenlocher, J., Haight, W., Bryk, A., Seltzer, M., & Lyons, T. (1991). Early vocabulary growth: Relation to language input and gender. *Developmental Psychology, 27*(2), 236–248.

Huttenlocher, J., Vasilyeva, M., Cymerman, E., & Levine, S. (2002). Language input and syntax. *Cognitive Psychology, 45,* 337–374.

Jencks, C., & Phillips, M. (1998). *The Black–White test score gap.* Washington, DC: Brookings Institute.

Johnson, D. L., Swank, P., Howie, V. M., Baldwin, C. D., Owen, M., & Luttman, D. (1993). Does HOME add to prediction of child intelligence over and above SES? *Journal of Genetic Psychology, 154,* 33–40.

Juel, C., & Minden-Cupp, C. (2000). Learning to read words: Linguistic units and instructional strategies. *Reading Research Quarterly, 35*(4), 498–492.

Kaestle, C. F. (1993). The awful reputation of education research. *Educational Researcher, 22*(1), 23–31.

Kauffman, D., Johnson, S. M., Kardos, S. M., Liu, E., & Peske, H. G. (2002). "Lost at sea": New teachers' experiences with curriculum and assessment. *Teachers College Record, 104*(2), 273–300.

Kelly, J., Morisset, C., Barnartd, K., Hammond, M., & Booth, C. (1996). The influence of early mother–child interaction on preschool cognitive/linguistic outcomes in a high-social-risk group. *Infant Mental Health Journal, 17,* 310–321.

Korenman, S., & Miller, J. (1997). Effects of long-term poverty on physical health of children in the national longitudinal survey of youth. In G. Duncan & J. Brooks-Gunn (Eds.), *Consequences of growing up poor* (pp. 70–99). New York: Russell Sage.

Lewis, L., Parsad, B., Carey, N., Bartfai, N., Farris, E., Smerdon, B., et al. (1999). *Teacher quality: A report on the preparation and qualifications of public school teachers* (No. 1999-080). Washington, DC: U.S. Department of Education, Office of Educational Research and Improvement, National Center for Educational Statistics.

Linnenbrink, E. A., & Pintrich, P. R. (2002). Motivation as an enabler for academic success. *School Psychology Review, 31*(3), 313–327.

Littlewood, E. M. J. (2001). Teaching perspectives of exemplary teachers. In M. C. Wang & H. J. Walberg (Eds.), *Tomorrow's teachers* (pp. 79–114). Richmond, CA: McCutchan.

Loban, W. (1976). *Language development: Kindergarten through grade twelve.* Urbana, IL: National Council of Teachers of English.

Lonigan, C., Burgess, S., & Anthony, J. (2000). Development of emergent literacy and early reading skills in preschool: Evidence from a latent-variable longitudinal study. *Developmental Psychology, 36,* 596–613.

Lonigan, C. J., & Whitehurst, G. J. (1998). Relative efficacy of parent and teacher involvement in a shared book-reading intervention for preschool children from low income backgrounds. *Early Childhood Research Quarterly, 13*(2), 263–290.

Magnusson, K., & Duncan, G. (2004). Parent versus child-based intervention strategies for promoting children's well-being. In A. Kalil & T. DeLeire (Eds.), *Family investments in children's potential* (pp. 209–236). Mahwah, NJ: Erlbaum.

Martella, R. C., Nelson, R., & Marchand-Martella, N. E. (1999). *Research methods: Learning to become a critical research consumer.* Boston: Allyn & Bacon.

McClelland, M., Morrison, F., & Holmes, D. (2000). Children at risk for early academic problems: The role of learning-related social skills. *Early Childhood Research Quarterly, 15*(3), 307–329.

Morrison, F. J., Bachman, H., & Connor, C. M. (2005). *Improving literacy in America: Lessons from research,* New Haven, CT: Yale University Press.

Morrison, F. J., & Connor, C. M. (2002). Understanding schooling effects on early literacy. *Journal of School Psychology, 40*(6), 493–500.

Morrison, F. J., & Connor, C. M. (in preparation). The causal nature of schooling effects and the impact of instruction.

Morrison, F. J., & Cooney, R. (2002). Parenting and academic achievement: Multiple paths to early literacy. In J. G. Borkowski, S. L. Ramey, & M. Bristol-Power (Eds.), *Parenting and the child's world: Influences on academic, intellectual, and social-emotional development* (pp. 141–160). Mahwah, NJ: Erlbaum.

Morrison, F. J., Smith, L., & Dow-Ehrensberger, M. (1995). Education and cognitive development: A natural experiment. *Developmental Psychology, 31*(5), 789–799.

Murray, A., Johnson, J., & Peters, J. (1990). Fine-tuning of utterance length to preverbal infants: Effects on later language development. *Journal of Child Language, 17,* 511–525.

National Assessment of Educational Progress. (2000). *U.S. Department of Education.* Washington, DC: National Center for Educational Statistics.

National Assessment of Educational Progress. (2003). *The nation's report card: Reading highlights* (No. NCES 2004-452). Washington, DC: National Center for Educational Statistics.

National Center for Educational Statistics. (1999). *NAEP 1999 trends in academic progress: Three decades of student performance* (NCES Statistical Analysis Report No. 2000-469). Jessup, MD: U. S. Department of Education.

NICHD-Early Child Care Research Network. (1998). Relations between family predictors and child outcomes: Are they weaker for children in child care? *Developmental Psychology, 34,* 1119–1128.

NICHD-Early Child Care Research Network. (2002). The relation of global first grade classroom environment to structural classroom features and teacher and student behaviors. *Elementary School Journal, 102*(5), 367–387.

NICHD-Early Child Care Research Network. (2003). Does amount of time spent in child care predict socioemotional adjustment during the transition to kindergarten? *Child Development, 74*(4), 969–1226.

NICHD-Early Child Care Research Network. (2004). Multiple pathways to early academic achievement. *Harvard Educational Review, 74*(1), 1–29.

NICHD-Early Child Care Research Network. (2004). Multiple pathways to early academic achievement. *Harvard Educational Review, 74*(1), 1–29.

National Reading Panel. (2000). *Teaching children to read: An evidence-based assessment of the scientific literature on reading and its implications for reading instruction* [Summary]. Washington DC: National Reading Panel.

Payne, A. C., Whitehurst, G. J., & Angell, A. L. (1994). The role of home literacy environment in the development of language ability in preschool children from low-income families. *Early Childhood Research Quarterly, 9*, 427–440.

Pearson, B. D., & Gallagher, M. C. (1983). The instruction of reading comprehension. *Contemporary Educational Psychology, 8*, 317–344.

Phillips, M., Crouse, J., & Ralph, J. (1998). Does the black–white test score gap widen after children enter school? In C. Jencks & M. Phillips (Eds.), *The Black–White test score gap* (pp. 229–272). Washington, DC: Brookings Institution Press.

Pianta, R., Paro, L., Payne, K., Cox, C., & Bradley, R. H. (2002). The relation of kindergarten classroom environment to teacher, family and school characteristics and child outcomes. *Elementary School Journal, 102*(3), 225–238.

Plomin, R. (1990). *Nature and nurture: An introduction to human behavioral genetics.* Pacific Grove, CA: Brooks/Cole.

Raviv, T., Kessenich, M., & Morrison, F. (2004). A mediational model of the association between socioeconomic status and preschool language abilities: The role of parenting factor. *Early Childhood Research Quarterly, 19*, 528–547.

Rayner, K., Foorman, B. R., Perfetti, C. A., Pesetsky, D., & Seidenberg, M. S. (2001). How psychological science informs the teaching of reading. *Psychological Science in the Public Interest, 2*(2), 31–74.

Reese, E., & Cox, A. (1999). Quality of adult book reading affects children's emergent literacy. *Developmental Psychology, 35*, 20–28.

Reynolds, A. J., Temple, J. A., Robertson, D. L., & Mann, E. A. (2003). Age 21 cost–benefit analysis of the Title I Chicago child–parent centers. *Educational Evaluation and Policy Analysis, 24*(4), 267–303.

Rowe, D., Vazsonyi, A., & Flannery, D. (1994). No more than skin deep: Ethnic and racial similarity in developmental process. *Psychological Review, 101*, 396–413.

Rutter, M., & Maughan, B. (2002). School effectiveness findings 1979–2002. *Journal of School Psychology, 40*(6), 451–475.

Saigal, S., Szatmari, P., Rosenbaum, P., Campbell, D., & King, S. (1991). Cognitive abilities and school performance of extremely low birth weight children and matched term control children at age 8 years: A regional study. *Journal of Pediatrics, 118*, 751–760.

Scarborough, H. S., & Dobrich, W. (1994). On the efficacy of reading to preschoolers. *Developmental Review, 14*, 245–302.

Schatschneider, C., Fletcher, J. M., Francis, D. J., Carlson, C. D., & Foorman, B. R. (2004). Kindergarten prediction of reading skills: A longitudinal comparative analysis. *Journal of Educational Psychology, 96*(2), 265–282.

Schoendorf, K., Hogue, C., Kleinman, J., & Rowley, D. (1992). Mortality among infants of black as compared with white college-educated parents. *New England Journal of Medicine, 326*(23), 1522–1526.

Sénéchal, M., & LeFevre, J. (2001). Storybook reading and parent teaching: Links to language and literacy development. In P. R. Britto & J. Brooks-Gunn (Eds.), *New directions in child development: Vol. 92. The role of family literacy environments in promoting young children's emerging literacy* (pp. 39–52). San Francisco: Jossey-Bass.

Sénéchal, M., LeFevre, J.-A., Thomas, E. M., & Daley, K. E. (1998). Differential effects of home literacy experiences on the development of oral and written language. *Reading Research Quarterly, 33*(1), 96–116.

Shavelson, R. J., & Towne, L. (Eds.). (2002). *Scientific research in education.* Washington DC: National Academy Press.

Shonkoff, J. P., & Phillips, D. A. (Eds.). (2000). *From neurons to neighborhoods: The science of early childhood development.* Washington DC: National Academy Press.

Smith, J., Brooks-Gunn, J., & Klebanov, P. (1997). Consequences of living in poverty for young children's cognitive and verbal ability and early school achievement. In G. J. Duncan & J. Brooks-Gunn (Eds.), *Consequences of growing up poor* (pp. 132–189). New York: Russell Sage.

Smith, K. (2002). *Who's minding the kids? Child care arrangements: Spring 1997.* Washington DC: U.S. Census Bureau.

Snow, C., Burns, M., & Griffin, P. (Eds.). (1998). *Preventing reading difficulties in young children.* Washington, DC: National Academy Press.

St. Pierre, R. G., & Layzer, J. I. (1999). Using home visits for multiple purposes: The Comprehensive Child Development Program. *The Future of Children, 9*, 134–151.

Stipek, D., & Ryan, R. (1997). Economically disadvantaged preschoolers: Ready to learn but further to go. *Developmental Psychology, 33*(4), 711–723.

Storch, S. A., & Whitehurst, G. J. (2002). Oral language and code-related precursors to reading: Evidence from a longitudinal structural model. *Developmental Psychology, 38*(6), 934–947.

Sugland, B., Zaslow, M., Smith, J., Brooks-Gunn, J., Moore, K., Blumenthal, C., et al. (1995). The early childhood HOME Inventory and HOME-Short Form in differing sociocultural groups: Are there differences in underlying structure, internal consistency of subscales, and patterns of prediction? *Journal of Family Issues, 16*, 632–663.

Tamis-Lemonda, C., Bornstein, M., & Baumwell, L. (2001). Maternal responsiveness and children's achievement of language milestones. *Child Development, 72*, 748–767.

Taylor, B. M., & Pearson, D. P. (Eds.). (2002). *Teaching reading: Effective schools, accomplished teachers.* Mahwah, NJ: Erlbaum.

Tomasello, M., & Todd, J. (1983). Joint attention and lexical acquisition style. *First Language, 4*, 197–212.

Torgesen, J. K. (2000). Individual differences in response to early intervention in reading: The lingering problem of treatment resisters. *Learning Disabilities Research and Practice, 15*, 55–64.

Torgesen, J. K., Alexander, A. W., Wagner, R. K., Rashotte, C. A., Voelier, K. K. S., & Conway, T. (2001). Intensive remedial instruction for children with severe reading disabilities: Immediate and long-term outcomes from two instructional approaches. *Journal of Learning Disabilities, 34*(1), 33–58.

Torgesen, J. K., Wagner, R. K., Rashotte, C. A., Rose, E., Lindamood, P., Conway, T., et al. (1999). Preventing reading failure in young children with phonological processing disabilities: Group and individual responses to instruction. *Journal of Educational Psychology, 91*, 579–593.

Wagner, R., Rashotte, C., Hecht, S., Barker, T., Burgess, S., & Donohue, J. (1997). Changing relations between phonological processing abilities and word level reading as children develop from beginning to skilled readers: A 5-year longitudinal study. *Developmental Psychology, 33*, 468–479.

Wentzel, K. (1991a). Relations between social competence and academic achievement in early adolescence. *Child Development, 62*, 1066–1078.

Wentzel, K. (1991b). Social competence at school: Relation between social responsibility and academic achievement. *Review of Educational Research, 61*(1), 1–24.

Westat. (2001). *The longitudinal evaluation of school change and performance in Title 1 schools: Final report* (No. 2001-20). Washington, DC: U.S. Department of Education.

Wharton-McDonald, R., Pressley, M., & Hampston, J. M. (1998). Literacy instruction in nine first-grade classrooms: Teacher characteristics and student achievement. *Elementary School Journal, 99*(2), 101–128.

Whitehurst, G. J., Falco, F. L., Lonigan, C. J., Fischel, J. E., DeBaryshe, B. D., Valdez-Menchaca, M. C., et al. (1988). Accelerating language development through picture book reading. *Developmental Psychology, 24*(4), 552–559.

27

Perspectives on the Difficulty of Beginning Reading Texts

ELFRIEDA H. HIEBERT
HEIDI ANNE E. MESMER

Features of the text influence the quality of the interaction that can occur between a reader and a text. For beginning readers who know only a handful of words (and likely idiosyncratic ones such as their names), most texts will require scaffolding by a proficient reader for an interaction with text to occur. Choosing texts for instruction that support beginning readers in moving from scaffolded to independent reading has been one of the most persistent challenges facing teachers and teacher educators.

The critical role of success in beginning reading has meant that considerable attention has focused on selecting texts. Over the past two decades, agencies in numerous American states have taken on the task of selecting appropriate texts for beginning readers in their jurisdiction. Of the four largest American states, three (California, Texas, and Florida) identify basal reading programs that are acceptable for use with state funds. The inclusion of programs on these state lists is often predicated on compliance with guidelines on the features of beginning-level texts. The systems for sorting first-grade texts would seem to be a first point for examining the scientific foundation that is the byword of current federal policies. The practices are critical, and the investments in state and federal dollars and of teacher and student time are high.

In this chapter, we review theory and research on schemes that are used currently to determine the difficulty of texts at the beginning levels of reading. In doing so, this chapter builds on and extends the work of Hiebert and Martin (2001), which reviewed the features of words and how they are learned. The three primary text-difficulty methods—readability, guided reading levels, and task-based systems—apply particular assumptions about what is critical in beginning reading acquisition. As a result, each yields a different index on beginning reading texts. To illustrate the data that the text difficulty systems produce, we have chosen a prototypical text that exemplifies a second-trimester, first-grade text from a program based on the text-difficulty system. For one of the text difficulty schemes—readability formulas—we have selected two prototypical texts: one for conventional readability formulas (e.g., Spache, 1981) and the other for lexiles, a current manifestation of readability formulas (Smith, Stenner, Horabin, & Smith, 1989). Excerpts from these four texts and a fifth, *The Cat in the Hat* (Geisel, 1957)—described by Anderson, Hiebert, Scott, and Wilkinson (1985) as an ideal first-grade text—appear in Table 27.1.

Following the scheme's ratings of the five texts, three aspects of a text-difficulty method are described: (1) its rationale and a

TABLE 27.1. Ratings According to Six Text-Difficulty Systems of Five First-Grade Texts

Text difficulty scheme	Excerpt from a prototypical text	Readability		Guided reading	STAS-1 (predictability, decodability ratings)	Task-based		Total words
		Spache	Lexile			Decodability	CWF	
Readability	Dad looked at Molly's red nose. "You will have to go to bed," said Dad. "You have a cold." "I don't have a cold!" said Molly, blowing her nose. But she went up to bed and went to sleep with her big red cat at her side. "I put Molly to bed," said Dad. (Cummings, 1983)	1.8	310	H	3.5 (4, 3)	1.7	2.6	426
Lexile	"Do you have a bed just right for a pig?" he asked the saleslady. "Hmmmm," she said, looking Poppleton over. "Right this way." Poppleton followed the saleslady to the biggest bed in the store. It was vast. It was enormous. "It's just my size," said Poppleton. (Rylant, 1998)	2.0	250	J	4.5 (5, 4)	2.0	8.4	665
Guided reading levels	She flew the hang-glider at the school picnic. We drew pictures of her. The next day, Mrs. Bold came to school with a broken arm. Look at Mrs. Bold! How did you break your arm? Were you driving the rally car? What happened? Did your hang-glider crash? (Beck, 1993)	2.2	290	F	3.5 (3, 4)	1.9	18	93
Task-based	"You must have a fever and a cold." "Dragons don't get colds," creaked Dee. "Dragons breathe hot flames." "Can you breathe flames?" asked Dad. "No," creaked Dee. Dad made a pot of tea. "This tea's heat will help you breathe," he said. "Dragons don't like tea," creaked Dee. (Raymer, 1993)	2.9	270	G	3.5 (4, 3)	1.6	.8	127
Prototype primer text (Anderson et al., 1985)	Then he got up on top with a tip of his hat. "I call this game FUN-IN-A-BOX," said the cat. "In this box are two things I will show to you now. You will like these two things," said the cat with a bow. "I will pick up the hook." (Geisel, 1957)	2.4	270	J	3 (4, 2)	1.6	1.4	1,625

brief history, (2) a review of empirical investigations on the reliability and validity of the system, and (3) conclusions about its strengths and weaknesses. The principle that drives the latter discussion is the usability of the information that a system supplies for teachers' use in knowing what to teach their students. We begin with the system that has the longest history—readability formulas—and then move to the two systems that have replaced readability formulas in many published programs—guided reading levels and systems that are based on tasks such as decodability.

Readability Formulas

The prototypical text from the era when readability formulas were used to vet texts, *Molly's Surprise* (Cummings, 1983), had a readability of 1.8 (Spache, 1981), a level very close to the 1.75 associated with the second trimester of grade 1. The other four texts had readabilities of between 2.0 and 2.9. From the readability perspective, *Dragons Don't Get Colds* (Raymer, 1993) was one grade level more difficult than *Molly's Surprise*.

The text at the 250 lexile level that corresponds with the second trimester of grade 1 (*Scholastic Reading Inventory*, 2002) is *Poppleton Everyday* (Rylant, 1998). In that grade levels are typically evaluated in terms of units of 200 on the lexile scale (Smith et al., 1989), the lexiles of the other four texts are within a narrow and comparable range to the prototypical second-trimester text of 250 lexile: 270–310.

Description of and Rationale for Readability Formulas

Although Lively and Pressey's (1923) proposal for the measurement of vocabulary burden in school textbooks is typically identified as the first readability formula, it was Gray and Leary's (1935) formula that provided the paradigm for readability formulas for the subsequent 60 years. From 289 factors that 100 experts and 100 library patrons identified as possible contributors to readability, Gray and Leary selected 44 that could be counted reliably and that occurred

with sufficient frequency in their criterion passages (the Adult Reading Test). Using the scores of poor adult readers on these passages, Gray and Leary identified five variables that accounted for a sufficient amount of variance on a multiple regression analysis ($R = .65$): (1) number of "hard words" not on a list of 769 words; (2) number of personal pronouns; (3) average number of words per sentence; (4) percentage of different words; and (5) number of prepositional phrases. Over the next five decades, researchers reduced the number of variables to two or three, but Gray and Leary's basic procedure became the model for numerous readability formulas.

As Klare noted in his review in 1984, formulas vary in the data that they provide on the same text as a function of developmental criteria and the range of readers' ability on the criterion task. The formula that has been described as most valid for primary-level texts, both currently (Good & Kaminiski, 2002) and historically (Klare, 1984), is the one developed by Spache (1953, 1981). Spache's formula used two dimensions of texts: sentence length and the percentage of total words that were difficult words (i.e., not on a list of 1,040 words that Spache identified from analyses of textbooks). The underlying perspective on text difficulty can be illustrated by slight alterations to the primer-level text, *Molly's Surprise* (Cummings, 1983): (1) breaking several sentences into shorter ones and (2) changing Molly's name to Penny. When *Molly's Surprise* becomes *Penny's Surprise*, the readability of the text changes from 1.8 to 1.5. Passages with fewer words per sentence are deemed easier for beginning readers than those with longer sentences. *Penny* is on Spache's list of 1,040 words that primary-level students are to know; *Molly* is not. According to Davison and Kantor (1982), readability formulas were used to create school texts, not simply to adjust texts to comply with formulas. For example, because words such as *ice cream, picket fence, milkman,* and *castle* were on the Spache or a similar list, writers for textbook programs developed stories with these words.

As a result of research from a cognitive science perspective in the 1980s (see, e.g., Davison & Kantor, 1982) that identified problems with texts that had been manipulated or written to satisfy readability constraints, the field's two primary professional associations, the International Reading Association and the National Council of Teachers of English, called for cautious use of readability formulas (Michelson, 1985). This call was echoed in *Becoming a Nation of Readers* (Anderson et al., 1985), in which a moratorium on the use of readability formulas was advocated. Such initiatives led to a decrease in the use of readability formulas and an increase in alternative text-difficulty schemes such as guided reading levels and decodability.

Although widely used textbook programs still appear to use readability formulas sparingly, if at all (see, e.g., Pikulski, 2002), two activities are drawing attention back to readability formulas. One is the use of readability formulas within prominent assessments such as the Dynamic Indicators of Basic Early Literacy Skills (DIBELS; Good & Kaminski, 2002) which was reported to be used in over 1 million kindergarten through third-grade classes during the 2003–2004 school year (see the DIBELS website, http://dibels.uoregon.edu/). According to Good and Kaminski, the difficulty of texts on the DIBELS was validated by Spache's readability formula.

A second source for renewed interest in readability formulas is the presence of several computer-based readability programs, such as lexiles (Smith et al., 1989) and ATOS (School Renaissance Institute, 2000). The lexile framework, for example, orders texts according to a scale from 0 to 2000, with beginning texts at the lower end and graduate school and technical texts at the upper end. Although the reporting units of lexiles or ATOS are different from the grade levels of conventional readability formulae, their criteria are syntactic complexity, as measured by sentence length, and semantic complexity, as measured by the number of words that fall within anticipated bands of words (Smith et al., 1989; School Renaissance Institute, 2000).

The digital technology that underlies this new generation of readability systems makes it possible to base text levels on large corpora of words. Further, words that have become archaic, such as *milkman*, are relegated to rare-word status. At the same time, educators who use these digital readability systems do not have access to the corpora that are associated with particular text levels, as was the case with the Spache. Whereas the words that designate *Poppleton Everyday* (Rylant, 1998) as a second-grade text according to the Spache can be identified (e.g., *enormous, saleslady, crackers, bluebirds, pillows)*, teachers, students, and parents are given no guidelines as to the vocabulary that underlies the designated lexile. Presumably the words that account for the lexile rating and the Spache level are similar. However, without data from the readability developers, this conclusion can only be inferred.

Empirical Evidence for Readability Formulas and Beginning Readers

According to Chall (1988), readability formulas at the primary level originated with studies of vocabulary control in the 1920s and 1930s that examined the number of new words per book, their repetitions, and their frequency. Researchers assumed that texts with high numbers of new words with few repetitions and/or low frequencies in written English created obstacles for reading acquisition. However, as Chall (1988) has observed, only one experiment had been conducted before these assumptions were used to create textbooks. This single study—that of Gates (1930)—considered the optimal number of repetitions for first graders of different ability levels. Based on a rather limited sample of text, Gates concluded that average-ability students (as defined by IQ) required 35 repetitions of high-frequency words and, from these data, extrapolated the number of repetitions required by high-achieving and low-achieving students.

Whereas experimental studies were infrequent, studies pertaining to the validity of different readability formulas were numerous. In 1984, Klare stated that over 1,000 studies had been conducted on readability. Many of these studies examined the variables that accounted for readers' performances on a set of passages, often the McCall–Crabbs Standard Test Lessons in Reading (McCall & Crabbs Schroeder, 1926/1979). Numerous other studies reported on the concurrent validity of a new set of variables relative to existing formulas. Syllable counts were proven to be valid by showing strong correlations with earlier formulas that used other measures of semantic complexity (Klare, 1984). Or lexiles were described as valid on the basis of strong correlations between lexile levels and graded texts within textbook programs that complied with conventional readability formulas (Smith et al., 1989).

The circuitous process whereby formulas were based on a set of passages that had been developed according to the same criteria as the formulas meant that texts could be ordered across a set of grades with consistency. However, the narrower the band of performance, the more difficult it was to make differentiations. Even more challenging was the task of applying the criteria of semantic complexity at the very earliest grades. The 10 readability formulas that are part of the Micro Power and Light (1999) software produced readabilities for *Molly's Surprise* that ranged from .6 to 5.7 grade levels and, for *Penny's Surprise*, from 0 to 4.6. The only formula to make a fine-tuned distinction across these two passages was the Spache (1981). In that the original and revised texts had been written to comply with the Spache formula, this finding should not be surprising.

In the 1980s, perspectives from cognitive science and linguistics were applied to the texts that resulted from this circular process of developing and validating readability formulas. These analyses showed that, when high-frequency words were substituted for less frequent but more descriptive words, meanings of texts were changed and even made more obscure (Davison & Kantor, 1982). By shortening sentences to comply with readability formulas, conjunctions were often eliminated, and causal connections between ideas were obscured. When comprehension of unmanipulated texts was compared with that of manipulated texts, students' superior performance on the former was taken as evidence that readability formulas were detrimental to effective comprehension (e.g., Beck, McKeown, Omanson, & Pople, 1984). In none of these studies of restructured texts, however, was the focus on beginning readers. No studies compared, for example, beginning readers' proficiency with texts with no vocabulary restrictions relative to texts with a modicum of vocabulary control.

Conclusions: Readability Systems

Even with extensive computerized databases (Smith et al., 1989), readability systems continue to be limited in their support of instruction. A grade level of 1.8 on the Spache (1981) does not indicate the proficiencies with which readers must be facile to read this level text. Neither does a lexile level of 250 indicate what beginning readers need to know to move to a higher level. However, when the new readability systems are evaluated relative to the old readability systems, the latter are more useful for instruction and assessment than the former. At least with a formula such as Spache's (1981), the words that are associated with the primary grades are known. This information is valuable for educators as they respond to policy mandates that are based on tests that use the Spache. The five texts in Table 27.1 differ in the distribution of high-frequency words and multisyllabic words, among other features. However, the lexile system does not distinguish between these texts in any discernible way, and little information is forthcoming from the system as to the underlying curriculum.

Text Leveling Systems

From the vantage point of current U.S. classrooms, the most widely used text-difficulty scheme consists of Fountas and Pinnell's (1996, 1999, 2001) guided reading levels. A text at the third of the four levels associated exclusively with grade 1—level F—was selected from available lists: *Mrs. Bold* (Beck, 1993). Fountas and Pinnell (1996, 1999) also provide levels for *The Cat in the Hat* and *Poppleton Everyday*. A reading specialist with a decade of experience in text leveling established the levels for the two remaining texts. As Table 27.1 shows, three were within the exclusive first-grade range, and two had second-grade levels. *The Cat in the Hat* was among the latter, with a level of mid- to late second grade.

Hoffman, Roser, Patterson, Salas, and Pennington (2001) have also developed a text-leveling system, the Scale for Text Accessibility and Support (STAS-1). Ratings of the texts according to the STAS-1 are included in Table 27.1. These ratings indicate that differentiation across the texts is not substantial with this 5-point scale. Three of the texts had the same rating (although they had somewhat different distributions, according to predictability and decodability scales).

Description of and Rationale for Text-Leveling Systems

The leveling of texts by experts or judges is not a recent phenomenon (see, e.g., Carver, 1976; Singer, 1975). However, this procedure was not prominent until readability formulas were eliminated as a criterion for textbook selection in America's largest states (California English/Language Arts Committee, 1987; Texas Education Agency, 1990). The theory underlying the use of literature and little books in textbook programs posited that readers employ multiple sources of information in understanding unknown words, including the structures of syntax and texts (Goodman, 1968). The Reading Recovery levels that have evolved into the guided reading levels were a response to this need. Like the guided reading levels, the STAS-1 (Hoffman et al., 1994) uses experts' judgments or ratings. Unlike guided reading levels, which are presented as a holistic score, the STAS-1 gives ratings on individual categories. Consequently, the uniquenesses of the two schemes will be developed.

READING RECOVERY/ GUIDED READING LEVELS

As little books became prominent in school reading programs, particularly as Reading Recovery programs were initiated in U.S. schools during the mid- to late 1980s, Peterson (1991) developed a scheme for establishing text difficulty of the little books. Similar to the primary trait model of holistic scoring that has a long history in writing assessment (Cooper & Odell, 1977), four dimensions were identified as the basis for a text level: (1) book and print features; (2) content, themes, and ideas; (3) text structure; and (4) language and literary elements. Unlike primary trait schemes in writing, however, the four separate dimensions of the guided reading levels were not analyzed individually. A single score was provided with no indication of the weight or scoring of individual dimensions.

Within guided reading levels, Fountas and Pinnell (2001) have extended the original four criteria (book and print features, content, text structure, and language and literary elements) to two additional criteria—vocabulary (e.g., multisyllabic words) and sentence complexity (length, embedded clauses, punctuation). Although Fountas and Pinnell (1999) mention the regularity of letter-sound spellings as a factor in determining sophistication of vocabulary, this feature is not highlighted in reports of leveled texts (e.g., Fountas & Pinnell, 1999, 2001).

SCALE FOR TEXT ACCESSIBILITY AND SUPPORT

The Scale for Text Accessibility and Support (STAS-1), developed by Hoffman and his associates (Hoffman et al., 2001), used a similar methodology as those used in Carver's (1976) Rauding Scale and Singer's Eyeball Estimate of Readability (SEER; Singer, 1975), in which experts use anchor passages that had been ordered according to specific criteria in leveling texts. Hoffman et al.'s system uses 5-point scales for two primary traits: decodability and predictability. *Highly decodable texts* (rated as 1) contain words with consonant–vowel–consonant (CVC) patterns, single syllables, and short high-frequency words, whereas *minimally decodable texts* (rated as 5) contain irregularly spelled words and a variety of patterns and offer little word-recognition support to the emerging reader, with three interim points of very decodable (2), decodable (3), and somewhat decodable (4). The predictability scale has a similar 5-point range, with highly predictable texts awarded a score of 1 and minimally predictable, a score of 5. The scale used four predictable features (picture support, repetition, rhyming elements, and familiar events/concepts) that texts contained to different degrees.

Empirical Evidence for Text-Leveling Systems

GUIDED READING LEVELS

Publishers and educators have applied the text leveling of Reading Recovery and guided reading to literally thousands of texts. Despite its widespread use, we were unable to find any reports of reliability across coders in leveling texts for either scheme. Further, although proponents of this form of leveling present it as an alternative to readability formulas, one of the only studies of its validity has reported a strong correlation between text levels and the principal factors that make up traditional readability formulas (Hatcher, 2000). Hatcher (2000) considered how five variables predicted Reading Recovery levels of 200 texts (10 at each of 20 levels) on numbers of (1) words; (2) words in the longest sentence; (3) words with six or more letters; (4) contractions, negatives, auxiliary verb plus a main verb, and auxiliary verb that changes tense; and (5) pages. Two variables—length of words and of the longest sentences—predicted Reading Recovery levels best ($R = .82$).

We could find no studies that examined how instruction with texts ordered according to either Reading Recovery or guided reading levels influenced reading acquisition. We located a single study that examined students' reading of texts of different levels. This examination was part of Hoffman et al.'s (2001) validation of their STAS-1 ratings with Reading Recovery levels and is described shortly. We should note that studies on several of the features that figure prominently in the text-leveling scheme, particularly text predictability and illustrations, exist and have been reviewed elsewhere (Hiebert & Martin, 2001). To briefly summarize, the existing evidence suggests that overreliance on these scaffolds appears to detract from independent word recognition.

STAS-1

Hoffman, Sailors, and Patterson (2002) have applied the two indices that make up the STAS-1—decodability and predictability—to the first-grade texts that have been approved by the Texas Education Agency for purchase with state funds over three adoption periods: 1987, 1993, and 2000. After applying the scale to the first 1,000 words of text that beginning readers encounter in the Texas-approved programs over this time period, Hoffman et al. (2002) report that the 1987 texts were the most decodable ($\overline{X} = 1.2$), the

2000 texts were next ($\overline{X} = 1.7$), and the 1993 texts were least decodable ($\overline{X} = 2.5$). On the predictability scale, the 1993 texts had the highest ratings of predictability ($\overline{X} = 2.5$), the 2000 texts were next ($\overline{X} = 3.5$), and the 1987 texts had the lowest ratings ($\overline{X} = 4.5$). Analyses of cohorts of students in the state of Texas for the effects of these changes in features of predictability and decodability of their beginning reading textbooks have yet to be conducted.

However, Hoffman et al. (2001) have considered the concurrent and predictive validity of the STAS-1 in experimental contexts. With three books from each of seven levels that reflected the guided reading and Reading Recovery levels, the scale as a whole correlated at .78. Next, Hoffman et al. examined the ability of the STAS-1 and the guided reading levels to predict student accuracy and rate across three instructional conditions (preview and read, no preview, and adult modeled). Significant effects were found for condition and reader ability in the expected directions. High-ability students and those who received adult modeling had the highest performances. Because two thirds of the Hoffman et al. (2001) students were unable to read any of the texts above the criterion for accuracy (92%), it is difficult to know how well these two systems discriminate among readers of differing abilities.

Conclusion: Text-Leveling Systems

The need for using expert judgment in the evaluation of text difficulty has been recognized from the initiation of work on text difficulty. As Gray and Leary's (1935) analysis showed, numerous variables cannot be evaluated quantitatively. There are many contexts in which experts' ratings according to particular criteria have been found to be highly reliable in sorting, evaluating, or judging, such as writing samples (Cooper & Odell, 1977). Hoffman et al.'s (2001) system, building on a tradition initiated by Singer (1975) and Carver (1976), illustrates how traits can be operationalized into rating schemes. Anchors can be identified and raters can be trained to code the categories with high levels of reliability. The two domains that form Hoffman et al.'s (2001) scale appear to be highly correlated, at least in the texts that they have analyzed to date. Further, their students were either reading at the same level of accuracy across texts of all difficulty levels (96–98%) or below the specified level of accuracy on all texts (i.e., 91% or lower), making interpretations of predictive validity difficult. Further, this scale does not discriminate across texts that, at least according to other schemes, have differences in their word-recognition demands.

However, the effort of Hoffman et al. (2001) does illustrate that particular dimensions can be defined and that raters, when given clear parameters, can sort a group of texts reliably on a recognized trait of beginning reading such as decodability. The STAS-1 demonstrates that reliable teacher-based rating schemes of text difficulty can be developed. Further, classroom teachers can use the information that a particular text is highly decodable or somewhat predictable when teaching students. By contrast, the implications for teaching *Danny and the Dinosaur* and *The Cat in the Hat*—texts that differ by five guided reading levels—are not clear.

The guided reading levels fail to convey a sufficient amount of information for teachers to use in designing lessons or selecting materials that will support their students in developing proficiency in the skills that they require to read harder material. The developers of this system have failed to demonstrate the manner in which different dimensions figure into the evaluation of difficulty of text at different levels. When the scheme was limited to the very earliest stages of reading, as it was in Peterson's (1991) work, distinctions across levels may have been apparent as teachers examined books. With the extension of the system to the entire elementary period (Fountas & Pinnell, 2001), the designations of a text as level F or level J, as was illustrated in the evaluations in Table 27.1 provide little indication as to the underlying proficiencies that students require to read particular texts.

The construct of text leveling holds promise for addressing text features such as usefulness of illustrations in beginning readers' recognition of unknown words. To date, however, developers of text-leveling schemes have not followed through on this promise by providing research on how particular text features in these systems influence young children's reading at different developmental points.

Task-Based Text Difficulty Systems

The prototypical second-trimester decodable text, *Dragons Don't Get Colds* (Raymer, 1993), is the 50th of the 75 decodable readers that make up a first-grade reading program (Adams et al., 2000). Two text-difficulty systems that illustrate task-based text-difficulty systems are applied to this book and the other four prototypes: Juel and Roper/Schneider's (1985) decodability system and Hiebert and Fisher's (2002) Critical Word Factor (CWF).

In Juel and Roper/Schneider's (1985) decodability system, an individual score from 1 to 3 is given to each word in a text. A word receives a score of 1 if it is a *transfer* word (words with regular vowel patterns such as *bag or seat*); of 2 if it is an *association* word (words with *l-*, *r-*, and *w*-controlled vowels; diphthongs; digraphs such as *law, car, boy*); and of 3 if it has irregular or unpredictable vowel patterns (words such as *come* and *pear*). The scores in Table 27.1 indicate that the decodability rating is within a narrow range, from the 1.6 of *Dragons Don't Get Colds* and *The Cat in the Hat* to the 1.9 of *Mrs. Bold*. These data indicate that the typical words in the first set of texts will be fairly evenly distributed between transfer and association words, whereas the typical word in *Mrs. Bold* will be an association word.

The second task-based text-difficulty scheme, the Critical Word Factor (CWF; Hiebert & Fisher, 2002), indicates the number of unique words per 100 running words of text that fall outside a particular curriculum. The primer curriculum, based on evaluations of tests (Menon & Hiebert, 2005), is proficiency with the 300 most frequent words and monosyllabic words with short and long vowels. As can be seen in Table 27.1, three of the texts have 5 or fewer words per 100 running words of text that fall beyond this curriculum. The fifth text—*Mrs. Bold*—has 18 unique words per 100 running words beyond this primer curriculum. If the curriculum is designated as the 100 most frequent words and monosyllabic words with CVC patterns, then the CWF would likely be higher for all of the texts. Or if the curriculum were the 500 most frequent words and all monosyllabic words, the CWF would likely be lower for the texts.

Rationale for and Description of Task-Based Text-Difficulty Schemes

As these examples show, task-based text-difficulty systems evaluate texts on their match to a curriculum, their instructional scope and sequence, or their developmental progression. The focus in this chapter is on the decodability schemes that are currently used and on alternative task-based systems such as the CWF. In that these two types of schemes have different histories, they are described separately.

Decodability text-difficulty schemes are of two types: a priori schemes, such as that of Juel and Roper/Schneider (1985), and instructional consistency schemes (Hoffman et al., 2002). In the former, letter–sound relationships are presented in a hierarchy of difficulty. Schemes can be more extensive than that of the three categories of Juel and Roper/Schneider, such as the eight categories of Menon and Hiebert (2005) that distinguish between words with complex consonant patterns, not simply vowel patterns. What all of these schemes have in common, however, is that any text can be reviewed against the same curriculum.

Instructional consistency schemes (Hoffman et al., 2002) evaluate the letter–sound relationships of a text in relation to the instructional scope and sequence of the program of which it is part. For example, if a child has been taught the /æ/ sound as in "cab," and then reads a number of /æ/ words in text (e.g. flag, rat, can), then the instructional consistency is high. In contrast, if a child encounters few /æ/ words in text, then the instructional consistency is low. Instructional consistency is usually expressed as a percentage of words that match phonics lessons. Instructional consistency formed the cornerstone of recent mandates regarding textbook purchases in the nation's two largest states (California English/Language Arts Committee, 1999; Texas Education Agency, 1997), in which particular percentages of decodable words in at least some components of first-grade programs and in first- and second-grade programs were specified: Texas, 80%; California, 90%.

The CWF is an index of two aspects of a text: (1) the match of linguistic content in the text with the phonetically regular and high-frequency words that are associated with particular stages of reading development and (2) the demands on cognitive processing as represented by the number of different words that cannot be figured out with a stage's target linguistic knowledge (Hiebert & Fisher, 2002). Because the Text Elements by Task (TExT) software program (Hiebert & Martin, 2002) is used to identify groups of words within a text, the curriculum can be tailored for different developmental levels. Whatever the targeted curriculum of phonetically regular and high-frequency words, the CWF is an indicator of the number of words that fall outside the specified curriculum in 100 running words of text.

Research Validating Task-Based Text Difficulty Systems

VALIDATION OF DECODABILITY SCHEMES

The most prominent of the a priori schemes has been Juel and Roper/Schneider's (1985). In the Juel and Roper/Schneider study, overall regularity ratings for basal reading texts differed only at the preprimer levels, not at the primer and first-reader levels. Descriptions of beginning reading programs from the perspective of instructional consistency have been compiled for the textbooks of most eras. The most widely publicized of these instructional consistency studies was Chall's (1967/1983) analysis of the match in the words in the texts of four basal programs relative to the instructional guidance in the accompanying teachers' editions. This paradigm was extended by Beck and McCaslin's (1978) study to include the *potential for accuracy* criterion. Beck and McCaslin's paradigm has been applied in a number of studies (e.g., Reutzel & Daines, 1987). A recent study of this type was conducted by Stein, Johnson, and Gutlohn (1999) of the texts intended for the first half of first grade from seven basal reading programs. A word had the potential for accuracy if all constituent parts could be decoded based on instruction to that point, as described in the teacher's guide for the program, or if recognition of a word by sight had been part of a lesson. Across the seven programs, Stein et al.

(1999) identified 14 components that provided three types of texts: student readers, phonics readers, or phonics support materials. One program (Scholastic's Literacy Place) had all three of the components; another program (Open Court) had only one component. Across the 14 components, the average potential-for-accuracy percentage was 59%. Two components attained Stein et al.'s criterion of 90% potential for accuracy: Open Court's student readers and Scholastic's phonics readers. Without these two components, the average percentage for potential for accuracy across texts was 53%.

Similarly, Foorman, Francis, Davidson, Harm, and Griffin (2004) examined all words in all text components (including phonics minibooks, big books, and anthologies) of six first-grade basal readers published from 1995 to 2002 using a scheme of: (1) decodable now, (2) decodable later (later instruction will make it readable), (3) holistically taught (word taught as a sight word), or (4) never decodable (neither letter–sound nor holistic information was given). When the decodable-now and holistically taught classifications were collapsed, the words in the most decodable basals were within a range of 51–85% decodable. The words in the least decodable basals ranged from approximately 25–50%.

In an earlier study, Foorman, Francis, Fletcher, Schatschneider, and Mehta (1998) considered the progress of Title I first and second graders with one of the less decodable basals and one of the most decodable basals when the first half of grade 1 relied on highly decodable texts. The instruction included differences other than the texts that students read, including different emphasis on opportunities for independent writing and spelling. Foorman et al. (1998) reported significant effects for word recognition and comprehension with the decodable texts relative to the texts of the other programs.

Precisely how the text features that Foorman et al. (1998) and Stein et al. (1999) have described influence students' reading over the long run requires substantial classroom investigations to understand. Such studies are hampered by the frequent changes that characterize programs from one copyright period to the next. For example, the Open Court program that Stein et al.

(1999) and Foorman et al. (2004) identified as high in potential for accuracy has been replaced by 2000 and 2002 copyright versions. When state mandates vary in requirements from one textbook adoption to the next, the results of analyses of a publisher's program from one decade to the next can similarly vary (see, e.g., Hoffman et al., 2002).

Further, the application of instructional consistency and a priori schemes can produce quite different perspectives on the same texts. Hoffman et al. (2002) compared the results of an instructional consistency and an a priori scheme that were applied to the same texts. For instructional consistency, they used the potential-for-accuracy scores reported by the Texas Education Agency (1997) in their review. This measure is the sum of decodable words plus words taught as sight words divided by the total number of words. For the a priori scheme, they used Menon and Hiebert's (2005) eight categories to analyze each word in the same texts. The correlation between the two measures was low: $r = -.07$.

To this point, data are not available on the number of lessons that teachers need to teach for assessments of instructional consistency to be robust. However, several studies have linked a priori decodability schemes with students' success in reading in particular programs, the most widely cited of which was conducted by Juel and Roper/Schneider (1985). In this quasi-experimental study, the treatment group read from a decodable basal, and the other group from a high-frequency basal, but both groups received the same scripted phonics instruction. At the study's conclusion, groups did not differ in reading words in lists or texts from their own basals, but they did differ in decoding ability and in reading the unknown words from the other basal. The decodable group performed better on the decoding measure at interim and end-of-year assessments but not on reading words from their basal reader or a norm-referenced reading test. Juel and Roper/Schneider (1985) also examined word-level features of the two textbook programs in relation to students' performances. The decodable group was most influenced by the degree to which words were decodable, whereas the high-frequency group was most influenced by the number of times words were repeated. The conclusion of this study was that text difficulty, as measured by decodability, was most influential during the first two trimesters of first grade.

More recently, Compton, Appleton, and Hosp (2004) have used an a priori analysis of decodability to predict students' reading performances. They found that second graders' accuracy and fluency across a 15-week period were related to the percent of high-frequency words; fluency was influenced by decodability of texts. Whereas performances of average-achieving students were influenced by the percentage of decodable words, the performances of low-achieving students were not. Compton et al. suggest that the decoding skills of low achievers may have been so poor that few words were decodable for them.

In another recent experiment, Jenkins, Peyton, Sanders, and Vadasy (2004) randomly assigned struggling readers to a tutorial with either decodable or nondecodable text. The treatments of both groups involved the same scripted tutorial lessons, only differing in the texts used for practice. Jenkins et al. used an instructional consistency criterion for decodability, with 71–84% of the words in decodable texts and 11–68% of words in the nondecodable texts consistent with their curriculum. Students in the two groups and those in a nonrandom control group performed similarly on the pretests. Although both treatment groups performed significantly higher on the posttest than the control group, the two treatment groups did not differ on any posttest measure. Jenkins et al. (2004) give two possible explanations for these patterns. First, the phonics instruction of the scripted lessons may have been sufficient for reading improvement. Second, tutors may have made texts "decodable" by directing tutees to use decoding strategies. Analyses of the books used in the nondecodable treatment (Mesmer, 2001) suggest another explanation. Many more words may have been identified as decodable in the nondecodable texts if an a priori analysis of decodability rather than an instructional consistency criterion had been applied.

VALIDATION OF THE CWF

Hiebert (2005) examined the first-grade anthologies for the five reading programs approved by the Texas Education Agency

(1997) and another mainstream textbook program not submitted to Texas. For comparative purposes, Hiebert included three historical copyrights (starting with 1962) for one of the Texas-approved programs and end-of-grade-two anthologies for all programs. Analyses showed that 41% of the unique words in current textbooks appeared once in 10 consecutive texts. Further, between 1962 and 2000, the number of unique words increased substantially, whereas word repetition was curtailed.

Another line of inquiry (Hiebert & Fisher, 2002) has considered the ability of the CWF model to predict the words that children will pause over or be unable to identify. In one study, first graders read four texts in a randomized order—two with high CWFs (a substantial number of unique words fell beyond the curriculum of the 100 most frequent words and words with CVC and long-vowel patterns) and two with low CWFs (most unique words fell within the designated curriculum). Analyses showed strong main effects for CWF on reading speed, accuracy, and comprehension, with all three variables in the direction predicted by the model.

A second set of studies has considered the effects of reading texts with different CWFs on children's reading development. In Menon and Hiebert's (2005) study, children in two classes in an inner-city school read from books that had been leveled according to a graduated CWF curriculum (i.e., the number of difficult or hard words remained consistent, but the underlying curriculum got progressively more difficult), whereas two other classes read from basal literature texts that had a consistently high CWF. Pretest scores were similar but, on the posttest, children in the low-CWF classes performed at significantly higher levels on word-list and text reading tasks than students who read from the high-CWF texts.

In a subsequent study, Hiebert and Fisher (2004) compared the performances of two groups of first-grade English-language learners who received the same scripted small-group instruction over 12 hours with those of a passive control group. One group received texts for which the CWF was 1 and the second group of texts had a CWF of 3, relative to a curriculum of the 100 most frequent words and CVC vowel patterns. Students who read from the texts with the lower

CWFs had higher fluency and accuracy levels than students who read texts with somewhat higher CWFs, and both groups had significantly higher fluency and accuracy levels than students in the passive control group.

Conclusion: Task-Based Schemes

Relative to phonics schemes based on instructional consistency, a priori schemes have an advantage in representing difficulty on a clearly defined scale. Instructional-consistency schemes can be manipulated to ensure high percentages of potential for accuracy. For example, if lessons on *r*-controlled and vowel diphthongs had preceded the introduction of *Mrs. Bold* (Beck, 1993), the publishers could argue that words such as *flew, drew,* and *school* have the potential for accuracy even though the program had only a handful of phonics lessons. Unless a priori schemes are comprehensive, however, they provide little guidance for instruction. For example, the rating of 1.6 for *Dragons Don't Get Colds* (Raymer, 1993) on Juel and Roper/Schneider's (1985) scale leaves teachers with little information on which word-vowel patterns should be emphasized in lessons with struggling students.

By providing an index that is derived from a curriculum, the CWF provides teachers with an indication of what knowledge is required for students to independently read a text. This information is particularly useful in that it allows teachers to measure texts against bodies of knowledge that are viewed to be acquired developmentally. Recognition of the 100 words that appear 1,000 or more times per 1 million words of text (Zeno, Ivens, Millard, & Duvvuri, 1995) would be expected to be acquired before recognition of words that have a likelihood of appearing 100 times in a similar-sized sample or those that appear 10 times or fewer. If the curriculum is emphasizing CVC words, the word *cap* should have a higher likelihood of being recognized by children who are being taught CVC words than should words such as *cape* or *capture*.

Similar to all text-leveling systems at the current point, the CWF does not take into account the presence of highly concrete words in texts and the usefulness of background knowledge and even accompanying illustrations in children's recognition of words. Research has confirmed that children learn highly concrete words with greater ease than less concrete words (Hargis, Terhaar-Yonkers, Williams, & Reed, 1988). The inclusion of picture–text match in the guided reading levels (Fountas & Pinnell, 1996) recognizes this aspect of word learning. However, pictures can provide different levels of information, and asking children to focus on the pictures rather than on applying context strategies that integrate the use of illustrations can create problems for subsequent independent reading. One possible technique for future use that quantifies the quick usability of illustrations as a context clue has been suggested by Menon and Hiebert (2005), who evaluated the match between words that adults associated with the illustrations from pages in children's texts and the words that appeared on those pages. Additional efforts such as that of Menon and Hiebert are needed to establish how particular elements influence the difficulty of texts for beginning readers in the immediate reading task and the manner in which such elements influence proficient reading in the long run.

Discussion: Next Steps

The most fundamental conclusion of this review is how little scholarship there has been on any of the text-difficulty schemes. We use the word *scholarship* rather than *research* because theoretical frameworks on the role of text in beginning reading, not just empirical investigations of text difficulty, are conspicuously absent. Regardless of the text-difficulty scheme, we could locate few theoretical frameworks on the role of text in beginning reading acquisition.

Gray and Leary's (1935) analysis remains the most extensive effort to identify features that may influence text difficulty. As behaviorists, they focused on readily quantifiable variables that accounted for the most variance in analyses of adult readers' performances on particular texts. Once sentence length and semantic difficulty had been identified as accounting for much of the variance, efforts to understand what these variables represented ceased for approximately four decades. When cognitive scientists addressed the complexity of text four decades later, they offered ideas for theoretical frameworks but did not directly address texts for beginning readers.

In the current emphasis on empirical investigations, we cannot forget that empirical investigations need to build on underlying theoretical frameworks if they are to address critical questions. Regardless of the perspective on text difficulty, underlying theoretical frameworks on appropriate texts for beginning readers have either been lacking or inadequately developed. Readability formulas have emphasized two variables that can be easily quantified and that discriminate across texts. Leveling systems have included a range of variables, but the most popular of these systems has not indicated how these different variables contribute to evaluations of difficulty. Task systems have focused, at most, on a handful of word-level variables. To date, none of the systems has a comprehensive conceptual framework that differentiates the influence of variables at both the word and text levels at different developmental periods of reading. For example, the manner in which figurative and idiomatic language influences text difficulty needs consideration, even at the early levels, where many such devices can be found in children's literature. Another aspect of text for which a strong theoretical and empirical scholarship exists is the influence on reading and memory of imagery and concreteness of language (Sadoski & Paivio, 2001). At a time when children are exposed to highly visible electronic media for thousands of hours, text difficulty schemes cannot ignore the role of illustrations in texts.

Perspectives on text difficulty have been particularly lacking with respect to the kinds of texts beginning readers need *over time*. In focusing on the individual text—even when "ordered or graduated"—the readability and text-leveling schemes draw attention away from the need to consider a group of texts as the critical unit for beginning readers. More comprehensive text-difficulty schemes are needed, and these schemes need to consider progression over the entire period of reading acquisition, if students are to receive the supportive texts many require to become proficient readers.

References

Adams, M. J., Bereiter, C., McKeough, A., Case, R., Roit, M., Hirschberg, J., et al. (2000). *Open court reading*. Columbus, OH: SRA/McGraw-Hill.

Anderson, R. C., Hiebert, E. H., Scott, J. A., & Wilkinson, I. A. G. (1985). *Becoming a nation of readers: The report of the Commission on Reading*. Champaign, IL: Center for the Study of Reading.

Beck, I. L., & McCaslin, E. S. (1978). *An analysis of dimensions that affect the development of code-breaking ability in eight beginning reading programs* (Report No. 6). Pittsburgh, PA: Learning Research and Development Center.

Beck, I. L., McKeown, M., Omanson, R., & Pople, M. (1984). Improving the comprehensibility of stories: The effects of revisions that improve coherence. *Reading Research Quarterly, 19,* 263–277.

Beck, J. (1993). *Mrs. Bold*. Auckland, New Zealand: Shortland.

California English/Language Arts Committee. (1987). *English-language arts framework for California public schools (kindergarten through grade twelve)*. Sacramento: California Department of Education.

California English/Language Arts Committee. (1999). *English-language arts content standards for California public schools (kindergarten through grade twelve)*. Sacramento: California Department of Education.

Carver, R. P. (1976). Measuring prose difficulty using the Rauding scale. *Reading Research Quarterly, 11,* 660–685.

Chall, J. S. (1983). *Learning to read: The great debate*. New York: McGraw-Hill. (Original work published 1967)

Chall, J. S. (1988). The beginning years. In B. L. Zakaluk & S.J. Samuels (Eds.), *Readability: Its past, present, and future* (pp. 2–13). Newark, DE: IRA.

Compton, D. L., Appleton, A. C., & Hosp, M. K. (2004). Exploring the relationship between text-leveling systems and reading accuracy and fluency in second grade students who are average and poor decoders. *Learning Disabilities Research and Practice, 19,* 176–184.

Cooper, C. R., & Odell, L. (Eds.). (1977). *Evaluating Writing: Describing, measuring, judging*. Buffalo: State University of New York at Buffalo.

Cummings, P. (1983). *Molly's surprise*. In I. E. Aaron, D. Jackson, C. Riggs, R. G. Smith, R. J. Tierney, R. E. & Jennings (Eds.), *Scott, Foresman Reading* [Primer] (pp. 14–23). Glenview, IL: Scott, Foresman.

Davison, A., & Kantor, R. N. (1982). On the failure of readability formulas to define readable texts: A case study from adaptations. *Reading Research Quarterly, 17*(2), 187–208.

Foorman, B. R., Francis, D. J., Davidson, K. C., Harm, M. W., & Griffin, J. (2004). Variability in text features in six grade 1 basal reading programs. *Scientific Studies of Reading, 8,* 167–197.

Foorman, B. R., Francis, D. J., Fletcher, J. M., Schatschneider, C., & Mehta, P. (1998). The role of instruction in learning to read: Preventing reading failure in at-risk children. *Journal of Educational Psychology, 90,* 37–55.

Fountas, I., & Pinnell, G. S. (1996). *Guided reading: Good first teaching for all children.* Portsmouth, NH: Heinemann.

Fountas, I., & Pinnell, G. S. (1999). *Matching books to readers: Using leveled books in guided reading, K–3.* New York: Heinemann.

Fountas, I. C., & Pinnell, G. S. (2001). *Guiding readers and writers: Grades 3–6.* Portsmouth, NH: Heinemann.

Gates, A. I. (1930). *Interest and ability in reading.* New York: Macmillan.

Geisel, T. S. [Dr. Seuss]. (1957). *The cat in the hat.* New York: Random House Books for Young Readers.

Good, R. H., & Kaminski, R. A. (2002). *DIBELS oral reading fluency passages for first through third grade* (Tech. Rep. No. 10). Eugene, OR: University of Oregon.

Goodman, K. S. (1968). The psycholinguistic nature of the reading process. In K.S. Goodman (Ed.), *The psycholinguistic nature of the reading process* (pp. 13–26). Detroit, MI: Wayne State University.

Gray, W. S., & Leary, B. W. (1935). *What makes a book readable.* Chicago: University of Chicago Press.

Hargis, C. H., Terhaar-Yonkers, M., Williams, P. C., & Reed, M. T. (1988). Repetition requirements for word recognition. *Journal of Reading, 31,* 320–327.

Hatcher, P. J. (2000). Predictors of Reading Recovery book levels. *Journal of Research in Reading, 23,* 67–77.

Hiebert, E.H. (2005). State reform policies and the task for first-grade readers. *Elementary School Journal, 105,* 245–266.

Hiebert, E. H., & Fisher, C. W. (2002, April). *The critical word factor in texts for beginning readers: Effects on reading speed, accuracy, and comprehension.* Paper presented at the annual meeting of the American Educational Research Association, New Orleans, LA.

Hiebert, E. H., & Fisher, C. W. (2004, April). *Effects of text type on the reading acquisition of English Language learners.* Paper presented at the annual meeting of the American Educational Research Association, San Diego, CA.

Hiebert, E. H., & Martin, L. A. (2001). The texts of beginning reading instruction. In S. B. Neuman & D. K. Dickinson (Eds.), *Handbook of early literacy research* (pp. 361–376). New York: Guilford Press.

Hiebert, E. H., & Martin, L. A. (2002). TExT (Task Elements by Task) (3rd ed.) [Computer software]. Santa Cruz, CA: TextProject.

Hoffman, J., Roser, N., Patterson, E., Salas, R., & Pennington, J. (2001). Text leveling and little books in first-grade reading. *Journal of Literacy Research, 33,* 507–528.

Hoffman, J. V. (2002). The words in basal readers: A historical perspective from the United States. In R. Fisher, G. Brooks, & M. Lewis (Eds.), *Raising standards in literacy* (pp. 82–97). London: Routledge Falmer.

Hoffman, J. V., McCarthey, S. J., Abbott, J., Christian, C., Corman, L., Dressman, M., et al. (1994). So what's new in the "new" basals? A focus on first grade. *Journal of Reading Behavior, 26,* 47–73.

Hoffman, J. V., Sailors, M., & Patterson, E. U. (2002). Decodable texts for beginning reading instruction: The year 2000 basals. *Journal of Literacy Research, 34,* 269–298.

Jenkins, J. R., Peyton, J. A., Sanders, E. A., & Vadasy, P. F. (2004). Effects of reading decodable texts in supplementary first-grade tutoring. *Scientific Studies of Reading, 8,* 53–86.

Juel, C., & Roper/Schneider, D. (1985). The influence of basal readers on first-grade reading. *Reading Research Quarterly, 20*(2), 134–152.

Klare, G. (1984). Readability. In P. D. Pearson, R. Barr, M. L. Kamil, & P. Mosenthal (Eds.), *Handbook of reading research* (pp. 681–744). New York: Longman.

Lively, B., & Pressey, S. (1923). A method for measuring the "vocabulary burden" of textbooks. *Educational Administration and Supervision, 9,* 389–398.

McCall, W. A., & Crabbs Schroeder, L. (1979). *McCall–Crabbs Standard Test Lessons in Reading.* New York: Teachers College, Columbia University. (Original work published 1926)

Menon, S., & Hiebert, E. H. (2005). A comparison of first-graders' reading with little books or literature-based basal anthologies. *Reading Research Quarterly, 40*(1), 12–38.

Mesmer, H. A. (2001). Decodable text: A review of what we know. *Reading Research and Instruction, 40*(2), 121–141.

Michelson, J. (1985). IRA, NCTE take stand on readability formulae. *Reading Today, 2*(3), 1.

Micro Power & Light. (1999). *Readability calculations* [Computer software]. Dallas, TX: Author.

Peterson, B. (1991). Selecting books for beginning readers: Children's literature suitable for young readers. In D. E. DeFord, C. A. Lyons, & G. S. Pinnell (Eds.), *Bridges to literacy: Learning from*

Reading Recovery (pp. 119–147). Portsmouth, NH: Heinemann.

Pikulski, J. J. (2002). *Readability*. Boston: Houghton Mifflin.

Raymer, D. (1993). *Dragons don't get colds*. Columbus, OH: Open Court SRA.

Reutzel, R., & Daines, D. (1987). The text-relatedness of seven basal reading series. *Reading Research and Instruction, 27*(3), 26–35.

Rylant, C. (1998). *Poppleton everyday*. New York: Scholastic.

Sadoski, S. M., & Paivio, A. (2001). *Imagery and text: A dual coding theory of reading and writing*. Mahwah, NJ: Erlbaum.

Scholastic Reading Inventory: Lexile levels/performance standards. (2002). New York: Scholastic.

School Renaissance Institute. (2000). *The ATOS readability formula for books and how it compares to other formulas*. Madison, WI: Author.

Singer, H. (1975). The SEER technique: A noncomputational procedure for quickly estimating readability level. *Journal of Reading Behavior, 7*, 255–267.

Smith, D., Stenner, A. J., Horabin, I., & Smith, M. (1989). *The Lexile scale in theory and practice: Final report*. Washington, DC: MetaMetrics. (ERIC Document Reproduction Service No. ED307577).

Spache, G. (1953). A new readability formula for primary-grade reading materials. *Elementary School Journal, 55*, 410–413.

Spache, G. D. (1981). *Diagnosing and correcting reading disabilities*. Boston: Allyn & Bacon.

Stein, M. L., Johnson, B. J., & Gutlohn, L. (1999). Analyzing beginning reading programs: The relationship between decoding instruction and text. *Remedial and Special Education, 20*(5), 275–287.

Texas Education Agency. (1990). *Proclamation of the State Board of Education advertising for bids on textbooks*. Austin, TX: Author.

Texas Education Agency. (1997). *Proclamation of the State Board of Education advertising for bids on textbooks*. Austin, TX: Author.

Zeno, S. M., Ivens, S. H., Millard, R. T., & Duvvuri, R. (1995). *The educator's word frequency guide*. Brewster, NY: Touchstone Applied Science Associates, Inc.

28

The Impact of Early School Experiences on Initial Reading

CONNIE JUEL

The true nightmare of every educator is that what we do in school has relatively little impact on children. In this nightmare, the impact of social and economic forces far outweighs that of education in the lives of children.

Results of the 2003 National Assessment of Educational Progress (NAEP), mirroring a couple of decades of similar findings, indicate that 37% of fourth-grade children nationwide score below a basic level in reading. For children from low-income families, the scores are even more disturbing: Fifty-six percent of children who qualify for a free or reduced-price lunch in the United States scored below the basic level in reading compared with 25% of noneligible children (NAEP; nces.ed.gov/nationsreportcard/reading/results2003/). The percentages of different ethnic groups scoring below the basic level on the NAEP were: white, 26%; black, 61%; and Hispanic, 57%. From the nightmare view, we look at these statistics and see education as, perhaps, not that successful overall and certainly not that successful in altering the effects of years of racism and poverty. When we are feeling particularly glum, we even consider how schools may help institutionalize the status quo.

How much can schools do? In a documentary aired almost 20 years ago, the late senator from New York, Daniel Moynihan, remarked on the plight of inner-city youths trapped in poverty:

You could say as a matter of established research that a sample of children who have grown up poor, in a single parent family, will enter the first grade hopelessly behind their peers. They do not catch up. The individual does, but the group won't. (Moynihan, 1986)

At the time I heard Moynihan's remarks, I was following the literacy development of children from a low-SES, multiethnic neighborhood school. His words hit too close to home. In my study, I found that if a child was a poor reader at the end of first grade, there was a .88 probability that that child would still be a poor reader at the end of fourth grade (Juel, 1988). Children who were poor readers at the end of the first grade were ones who had not developed adequate word recognition during the school year. The best predictor of first-grade reading achievement was phonemic awareness: Children who struggled with learning to read words had entered the first grade with little phonemic awareness and were slow to acquire it. Poor readers had, as a group, less phonemic awareness at the *end* of the first grade than average and good readers had at the *beginning* of first grade. Without phonemic awareness, phonics instruction is meaningless. More recent studies continue to find that children who are poor readers at the end of first grade generally remain behind their peers in subsequent grades (Francis, Shaywitz,

Stuebing, Shaywitz, & Fletcher, 1996; Torgesen & Burgess, 1998).

It is sobering how early predictive trends emerge and how early poor SES and minority group children appear behind. A quote from a policy brief on a just-completed large-scale study of the effects of preschool attendance on 2,314 children in California reads:

> English-proficient Latino children are about three months behind White children, at age five, in their *pre-reading skills* [vocabulary, letter recognition, storybook understanding]. This early gap—already wide at entry to kindergarten—is equivalent to over 80 percent of the gap observed in reading skills among Latino children at fourth grade. (Bridges, Fuller, Rumberger, & Tran, 2004, p. 2)

Yet the study offers hope that schooling, in particular preschool, can narrow these gaps:

> Our findings suggest that participation in preschool may close as much as half of the gap in children's developmental proficiencies among socio-economic and ethnic groups, a disparity that is firmly established at entry to kindergarten. (Bridges et al., 2004, p. 2)

While researchers tend to focus on the predictive power of letter sounds, vocabulary, and storybooks, we need to keep our minds solidly on the fact that this is the knowledge that the primary grades can affect. Schools must assume the blame when children fail to learn to read words because we know how to teach this: We know how to build phonemic awareness and decoding skills even though, as the second half of this chapter outlines, we have some real misunderstandings about phonemic awareness and have allowed phonics instruction too ponderous a place in instructional school time. Growth in word recognition is also hampered, though, when the printed words a child is trying to sound out are not in the child's oral vocabulary. The predictive power of vocabulary goes beyond that, however, into every facet of reading. Being able to describe the world through language advances both thinking about the world and growth in knowledge. If a child can label animals as "crabs" or "lobsters," and both as "crustaceans," the child can more easily focus on their similarities and what makes them distinctive from non-crustaceans. Vocabulary and knowledge are

eventually most responsible for reading comprehension. Growth in these areas occurs throughout life, in everyday interactions with the world; certainly, children who grow up with richer language experiences start out with, and continue to experience throughout their schooling, more opportunities for growth. Word recognition skill is circumscribed; accumulation of vocabulary and world knowledge is omnipresent. Nevertheless, we must ask if we have done all we can in schools. Have schools done their best to ensure that children can read well enough and have a wide enough vocabulary and knowledge of the world to comprehend texts on the fourth-grade NAEP?

What are children who score below basic level on the fourth-grade NAEP not able to do? What isn't school preparing them to do? We know they don't do well in demonstrating basic understanding of a fairly long text. The fourth-grade demonstration booklet contains an illustrative text. Here are two paragraphs from the 14-paragraph text about blue crabs:

> Crabs are arthropods, a very large group of animals that have an external skeleton and jointed legs. Other kinds of arthropods are insects, spiders, and centipedes. Blue crabs belong to a particular arthropod group called crustaceans. Crustaceans are abundant in the ocean, just as insects are on land.
>
> The blue crab's shell is a strong armor. But the armor must be cast off from time to time so the crab can grow bigger. Getting rid of its shell is called molting. (nces.ed.gov/nationsreportcard.pdf/demo-booklet/gr4demobookpdf)

To understand this text the child needs pretty sophisticated word recognition, vocabulary, and world knowledge. If a child has eaten a lobster or seen a crab crawling along the beach, heor she may be able to put the information in the text together to understand what the text is saying about those external skeletons being molted. The NAEP assessment is attempting to measure learning through reading, that is, comprehension and new knowledge created from reading the text, not just the knowledge a child brought in to the testing room. It is hard, however, to get around world knowledge. It is very hard to get around vocabulary. Carver and Leibert (1995) found that reading a text with a vocabulary containing more than 2% unknown words halts reading comprehension. The vocabulary load in this text is heavy for fourth-grade students (using Biemiller, 1999, as a guide). It is especially likely to be hard for English-language learners. The NAEP sets a high bar.

The Essentials: Two Areas We Have to Get Right in School

In this chapter I concentrate on two areas we have to get right in school instruction in the early school years for children to even have a chance with texts such as the one just quoted. These areas will not come as a surprise. They are vocabulary and word recognition. Of the two, vocabulary is the one that requires *intense* investment in instructional activities to foster it, and this investment has to extend from preschool on. I discuss why that is, and what some of the issues are in doing it. The second area, word recognition, usually is a more focused, time-specific undertaking in instruction. It needs to be done well early on because learning to read is the vehicle to wide reading. Wide reading is related to growth in vocabulary, world knowledge, and thinking. How else are you as likely to learn about the molting of crabs and reflect on the roles of external and internal skeletons? A further point that needs to be considered is that gaining skill over word recognition is the first big hurdle in school. Too protracted a struggle with it can deliver a major blow to self-esteem.

Vocabulary

Vocabulary plays a powerful role in reading comprehension (Baker, Simmons, & Kame'enui, 1998; Dickinson & Tabors, 2001; Hoover & Gough, 1990). The vocabulary of entering first graders predicts not only their word reading ability at the end of first grade (Sénéchal & Cornell, 1993) but also their 11th-grade reading comprehension (Cunningham & Stanovich, 1998). We have become increasingly aware of the wide range in oral vocabulary that children possess at each grade level and of how early differences in knowledge tend to linger (Cunningham & Stanovich, 1998; Stanovich, 1986). Considerable vocabulary gaps are apparent very

early on, and these tend to widen year by year (Hart & Risley, 1995; Snow, Barnes, Chandler, Goodman, & Hemphill, 1991; Stanovich, 1986).

VOCABULARY AND SOCIOECONOMIC STATUS

We know that children who grow up in low-income neighborhoods are likely to have smaller vocabularies than children who grow up in affluent neighborhoods (Duncan, Brooks-Gunn, & Klebanov, 1994; Hart & Risley, 1995; Lonigan & Whitehurst, 1998; McLloyd, 1998; Whitehurst & Lonigan, 2001). Parents with lower socioeconomic status (SES) are often less well educated than affluent parents and generally expose their children both to a smaller number of words overall and to less analytic interchange about the meanings of those words (Heath, 1983; Hart & Risley, 1995; Wells, 1985; White & Watts, 1973). Moats (2001) labels this language gap *word poverty* and estimates the difference at entry into first grade to be 15,000 words.

There Are Differences in Quantity and Quality of Language Exposure That Affect Vocabulary Development, and These Are Linked to SES. Hart and Risley (1995) examined the language development of children in 42 families, from the time the child was 10 months old to 3 years of age. The families varied in SES and were observed for 1 hour each month. On average, children in professional families heard 2,153 words per hour, whereas children in working-class families heard 1,251 words, and children in welfare families heard 616. By extrapolation, that suggests that by kindergarten age, a child in a professional family would have heard 32 million more words than a child growing up in a welfare family. And quantity of language exposure seems to be directly related to language growth. By age 3, the observed cumulative vocabulary for children in professional families was about 1,100 words, compared with 750 for children from working-class families and about 500 words for children from welfare families.

Hart and Risley (1995) describe how it is not just exposure that affects language development in the affluent families:

In professional families the extraordinary amount of talk, the many different words, and the greater richness of nouns, modifiers, and past-tense verbs suggest a culture concerned with symbols and analytic problem solving. To ensure their children access to advanced education, parents spent time and effort developing their children's potential, asking questions, and using affirmatives to encourage their children to listen, to notice how words refer and relate, and to practice the distinctions to be made among them. (p. 132)

English Language Learners in Communities with Limited Exposure to Rich English. One in 12 kindergarten children in the United States comes from a home in which English is not the primary language (August & Hakuta, 1997). Many are concentrated in low-SES urban areas. In Los Angeles Unified School District, for example, 74% of children are Hispanic, and 83% of school-age children qualify for free or reduced-cost lunch. If a child's exposure to a wide swath of English vocabulary is limited by characteristics of living in low-SES and/or limited-English communities, language growth in English is likely to lag (Wong Fillmore, 1982, 1985, 1991, 1992; Valdés, 1998). Children who grow up interacting with peers and community members who themselves speak limited English are not hearing lots of rich vocabulary. And, as shown in the Hart & Risley (1995) study, exposure matters.

Reading to Children Makes a Difference in Vocabulary, but There Are Fewer Books in Low-SES Homes and Communities. Besides conversational interactions, reading books to children can be a major source for vocabulary development. Books contain a wider vocabulary than occurs in ordinary conversations. Books provide a stimulus for adult–child conversations that can stimulate knowledge and thinking. Bus, Van IJzendoorn, and Pellegrini (1995) found the average effect size of studies that have examined the outcomes of reading to children on vocabulary growth and comprehension to be .67, or about two thirds of a standard deviation, a major effect. The effect size on vocabulary growth was notably larger for children ages 5 and 6 (mean effect size: 0.86) than for children under 4½ years old (mean effect size: 0.34). The effect on older children obviously

has importance for schooling. However, to get that vocabulary boost, reading had to include verbal clarification of the book words that children did not know.

Poor economic conditions mean there are not as likely to be as many resources in the home to buy storybooks or other reading materials (see Neuman, this volume). On average, the number of books in homes of families with different incomes in Los Angeles varies dramatically (Smith, Constantino, & Krashen, 1997). Whereas homes in very low-income households in Watts frequently were found to have no children's books (on average, 0.4), low- to middle-income homes in Compton had an average of 2.6 children's books, and children from wealthy Beverly Hills were likely to live in homes with 199 children's books. These differences are only magnified by similar disparities in the children's books available in both the public libraries of the respective neighborhoods and in the classrooms in the neighborhood schools. The opportunity to hear the rich vocabulary in, and participate in the discussion of, children's books is sorely curtailed in low-SES areas (Neuman & Celano, 2001).

HOW MANY WORDS DO CHILDREN NEED TO LEARN?

You might recall the last time you brought up *arthropods* or *crustaceans* or *molting* in a conversation. Perhaps you can't; or perhaps you can, precisely because it was so rare to hear those words. Books include vocabulary that is not typical of ordinary conversations. It is true for narrative text, as well. Authors are likely to substitute *thump* for *tap* or *quarrel* for *fight*; that is what makes it interesting to read (Snow, 1983).

There are a lot of different words from which authors can choose. Carroll, Davies, and Richman (1971) sampled over 5 million words from school texts used in grades 3–8 and counted the number of times different words occurred. They found 86,741 different words in books up to 8th grade, though they counted as distinct variations words that differed only by an affix (e.g., -*ing*). Nagy and Anderson (1984) estimated that 88,700 word families are used in books through 12th grade (*not* counting variations such as -*ing* as distinct). In either case, a lot of different words can appear in the universe of printed words. In either count, about 5,000 words account for about 90% of the words in books. But it is the remaining 10% that blow out the distribution. And these are the words that make reading most informative.

Nagy and Anderson (1984) estimate that the average student actually learns about 45,000 of these 80,000-plus different words by the end of high school. Some students learn a lot more words, and some learn a lot less. Estimates of how many words an average student knows vary rather considerably, as it is fairly impossible to ask anyone the meaning of, say, 80,000 different words. Moats (2001) estimates that *linguistically advantaged* children know about 20,000 words on entering first grade, whereas *linguistically disadvantaged children* know about 5,000.

Anglin (1993) found that *root* words (e.g., not counting *smile* and *smiling* as different) grow from 3,200 in first grade to 5,200 in third grade and to 10,000 in fifth grade. Dale and O'Rourke (1981) list words used in school texts and specify the grade levels at which 67–80% of students know them. Biemiller (1999) adjusted their counts so that they would be based on the same criteria as those of Anglin and reports that most fourth-grade students would know about 5,000 *root* words. These 5,000 words include the following: *agree, bad, car, chicken, detergent, grape, hawk, hen, monster, ordinary, peep, pillow, rough, second, switch, terrible, umbrella, vegetable, wander, yawn,* and *zoo* (Biemiller, 1999).

Although not in perfect ranked accord, there is certainly considerable overlap between the 5,000 most common root words used in schoolbooks and the 5,000 words known by most fourth-grade children. Children encounter some of those 80,000 words, too, in stories that are read to them or in texts they read in school. They just don't encounter most words (or either type) very often, with this being particularly the case for the lower frequency ones. A child may hear about Rosie the *hen,* as her kindergarten teacher reads *Rosie's Walk* (Hutchins, 1968). But that child is not likely to encounter *hen* (a top-5,000 word) in a text again very soon, nor to meet a word such as *haystack* (toward the rare end of the 80,000 less-frequent words category) for an even longer time. To be precise, in 5 million words of running text, *hen* occurs only 77 times, and *haystack* occurs 11 times (Carroll, Davies, & Richman, 1971). One encounter with Rosie the hen does not mean a child knows all about hens. Maybe all that was gleaned from the text came from the illustration, and what is remembered is the peculiar shape of hens. It is easy to see why storybook reading was shown to effect vocabulary knowledge only when it was combined with some clarification about the meanings of words (Biemiller, 1999; Bus et al., 1995).

It's hard to predict which particular words a child might meet in a book on any given day. Assessment day in fourth grade might be the one and only day in years that the child sees *crustacean.* An important point to understand, though, about most of these 80,000 words is that they are not that strange. Words in this group include *beneficial, warn, fiction, pebble, remark, disappointment, astronomer, suggestion, iceberg,* and *horrible* (Adams, 1990; Stahl, 1999).

LEARNING WORDS THROUGH READING: TOUGH, POSSIBLE, AND NECESSARY

The more words known, the easier and more likely is text comprehension. But all children are going to encounter unknown words in their reading. Recall that by the 12th grade students, on average, know about half of the 80,000 words they are likely to encounter in their texts. Stahl (1999) wonderfully describes the situation:

> We live in a sea of words. Most of these words are known to us, either as very familiar or at least as somewhat familiar. Ordinarily, when we encounter a word we don't know, we skip it, especially if the word is not needed to make sense of what we are reading (Stahl, 1991). But we remember something about the words we skip. This something could be where we saw it, something about the context where it appeared, or some other aspect. This information is in memory, but the memory is not strong enough to be accessible to our conscious mind. As we encounter a word repeatedly, more and more information accumulates about that word, until we have a vague notion of what it *means.* (p. 14)

If children know enough of the concepts behind enough of the words, new knowledge is constantly added to words in reading—as tentative as that knowledge may be at first. Nagy and Anderson (1984) postulate that "beginning in about third grade, the major determinant of vocabulary growth is amount of free reading" (p. 327).

Children who read more have more chances to learn words. Learning vocabulary from context is not that easy, however. Context itself is frequently not very helpful. Outside of textbook usage, words are usually not defined. Researchers estimate that of 100 unknown words encountered in texts, only 5–15% will be learned (Nagy, Herman, & Anderson, 1985; Swanborn & de Glopper, 1999). Attempts to help children be more strategic at learning from context have generally not succeeded (Kuhn & Stahl, 1998). Wide reading seems the most logical candidate to promote vocabulary growth. But there is evidence that if it is not often supported by enriched discussion of new vocabulary, it alone does not suffice. This is a similar circumstance to the findings on storybook reading that were discussed earlier.

One of the saddest findings in my own longitudinal work has been that children from lower SES and limited English backgrounds come into first grade with lower language skills, work hard and learn to decode, begin to like reading, bring books home and read them for enjoyment starting about second grade, see considerable increases in their listening comprehension and vocabulary in second and third grade, but then find a tapering in language development toward the end of fourth grade (Juel, 1988; Juel, 1994a). At this point their reading comprehension begins to suffer because of limited world knowledge and the vocabulary for that knowledge (e.g., knowledge of geography). It is as if their early gaps in language come back to haunt them as they are thrown into upper-grade texts—ones that demand considerably more knowledge from them. It is also probably the case that wide reading (and they may not be doing enough) can get them only so far. Whatever circumstances caused their lower language skills on entry to school are also probably still in effect throughout their school careers. It is indeed, as Moynihan (1986) suggested, hard even for the individual to rise out of his or her group circumstances.

A CLEAR ROLE FOR DIRECT INSTRUCTION IN VOCABULARY

What is promising in helping to avert situations such as this, from preschool on, is not just to focus on activities such as storybook reading and fostering wide reading in children but also to include calculated instruction about some of the words in those books. Beck, McKeown, and Kucan (2002), in their wonderful book on vocabulary instruction, write:

> Finally, the major argument for emphasizing learning from context comes from those who have examined the number of words that students will encounter during their school years and pronounced the task of directly teaching vocabulary simply too large. The logic that follows is that there is virtually no choice but to emphasize learning from context. A major point that we will emphasize, however, is that not all words call for attention. It is this situation that makes direct instruction in word meaning feasible, for if all words in the language required instruction equally, clearly there would be too many words to cover in school. (p. 7)

In their book, Beck, McKeown, and Kucan (2002) provide teachers with guidelines to use to select the words from texts that are useful to spend time with in vocabulary instruction; they also discuss how to do this instruction. I suspect that if the text children were going to read was the NAEP passage, they might give the following advice. First, identify the words on which to spend instructional time. They divide words into Tiers 1, 2, and 3 and suggest that time be spent with Tier 2 words. Tier 1 words are those basic vocabulary words that most children already know. In fourth grade, these might be the 5,000 words described earlier. Instructional time is not needed here (though be cautious about making that decision). Tier 3 words are ones that are quite rare or are limited to specific domains, and they need not be taught unless they are in the domain of the class, say science. Hence a decision could be made on *crustacean* and *arthropod*. So what words might a teacher focus on? Here we are basically deciding from the 80,000-word category. My choices would be *crab, crustacean, external*, and *skeleton* because they lend themselves to a discussion of adaptation and evolution. But whichever words they are, it will be important to spend a little time with them, to relate them to other words, as too brief an explanation is unlikely to either stick or be meaningful. Beck et al. (2002) hope it is in the spirit of fostering knowledge and engagement with words that children are also likely to go on and pay increased attention to them in both conversations and their own reading.

Currently, teachers of young children are observed to be spending little time carefully analyzing word meanings in texts with their classes (Biemiller, 2001a, 2001b; Juel, Biancarosa, Coker, & Deffes, 2003). It may be difficult for a kindergarten teacher to see the advantage in analyzing the terms *quarrel* or *quibble* from Leo Lionni's (1986) *It's Mine*. *Fight*, these teachers may reflexively think, will do in conversation, and children this age are unlikely to be reading these words on their own. In a sense, what teachers of young children need to do, though, is prepare children for what lies down the road. This is exactly what is needed to offset the early gaps in vocabulary that have been described previously in this chapter and to keep new ones at bay. We have gained an understanding of the enormity of the language gap. We have yet to mount serious efforts to decrease it.

Word Recognition

Reading improves overall intellectual growth (Cunningham & Stanovich, 1998)—whether it comes from understanding the emotional nuances of different words for fighting or learning the advantages and disadvantages of external skeletons. As discussed earlier, wide reading is part of the way new vocabulary is learned. Word recognition is important because it is the access card to reading. It is also the prime learning task in the early grades, becoming a kind of initiation rite to schooling. As such, we should recognize the risk of failure.

SELF-ESTEEM AND LEARNING TO READ

Johnston (1985) poignantly reports several adult males recalling their frustration in learning to read:

> I had learned symbols . . . 1 and 2 and 3 . . . so I wanted that for five-letter words. . . . I had

this idea that I was going to know just by looking. . . . But there's no way you could possibly take all the words in the dictionary and just learn them by sight. . . . Of course the teacher would hold these flash cards out and everybody would be hollering the words, and I don't know what the heck is going on . . . what's she doing . . . how do they know the word? (Johnston, 1985, p. 157).

Juel (1994b) describes her difficulty in learning to read:

> When I was in first grade I had a terrible time learning to read. I couldn't figure out how the other kids could look at the print and know what it said. I kept wondering how they knew what the cards the teacher held up said and how they could tell what was on the pages in our books. I just couldn't figure out how they did it. I also remember thinking I was glad my dog at home wasn't named *Spot*, like the dog in the book at school, because I'd never be able to read her name. And I very distinctly remember looking up at a chart in my class that had gold stars on it. The chart stood for how well we read the words in our books. I never had any gold stars by my name and I felt very ashamed. (Juel, 1994b, p. 133)

Or consider the words of a man who was committed to helping the young child he was tutoring learn to read:

> I was the little kid that had trouble reading, the one that use to do anything to get out of reading. I use to tell the teacher that I did not feel well, lost my voice, and use to try to get in trouble just so I wouldn't have to read and instead would be sent to the office or to the corner. Because of these experiences as a child I understand how some of these children are feeling. I have been there. The worse thing that happened to me when I was a child was to be embarrassed. Not knowing how to read can be embarrassing to a child. The other kids in the class laugh at you and make fun. (Juel, 1996, pp. 282–283)

First-grade children are, in general, more likely than slightly older children to attribute their literacy problems to effort rather than ingrained ability (see Pressley, 2002, chapter on motivation and literacy, for a review of this literature). This is good in that they have a higher tolerance for trial and error than they may have as they age. That is, we have a window in school to help children succeed at learning to read before their self-esteem is seriously eroded or they stop even trying to learn, feeling they simply can't do it. There are two elements of word recognition that present predictable sticking points for learners: phonemic understanding and orthography.

THE PHONEME LEVEL IN THE ENGLISH WRITING SYSTEM

In learning to read, as John Downing (1979) so eloquently put it some years ago, the child has to rediscover the coding rules of the writing system: "their rediscovery depends on the learner's linguistic awareness of the same features of communication and language as were accessible to the creators of the writing system" (p. 37). The linguistic insight the child will need to acquire is a difficult one: It is to perceive the dimension of speech that is represented in alphabetic writing systems, and that is the phoneme level. What makes this level so difficult to perceive lies in the nature of phonetic representation.

I am well aware that *phonemic awareness* has become a buzz word in early instruction. This does not diminish its importance. But there is an unfortunate tendency in education to reify what is good until it no longer is. Mae West is reported to have said, "Too much of a good thing is . . . wonderful." But it is doubtful she had in mind either phonemic awareness or phonics instruction. We have learned a lot about phonemic awareness in the past three decades. One thing we have learned is that doing a lot of oral phonemic awareness training prior to reading instruction is neither necessary nor desirable. We have learned that the critical discoveries that Downing alluded to are that words have an internal phonological structure and that letters represent it. Blachman (1997) summarizes this research: "There is no evidence that it is advantageous to continue to develop phonemic awareness *outside* of learning to read and spell words, once those discoveries have been made" (Blachman, 1997, p. 417).

At the risk of erring on the *too much* side, I think it is very important for both teachers and researchers not to pass over this topic lightly. It is important to see how critical this level is for children, how children think of the phonological structure of words *differently* than adults do, and how this informs

what we do with children, as well as to realize what we do and don't know about phonemic awareness. So be prepared for, perhaps, more than you wanted to read on this topic.

Where Phonemes Start: With Speech. Human evolution has put a premium on speech (Lenneberg, 1967). There are, for example, seemingly small but vital differences in the muscles of the lips and tongues of humans, making them more agile than those in corresponding muscles in other animals. This added agility is in part what allows humans to emit a more varied palette of speech sounds than other primates. Beyond better motor control, though, biological specialization also evolved in humans' brains, with dominant hemispheres and the unique abilities of the species to perceive and produce speech (Liberman, 1997; Rayner & Pollatsek, 1989). Although we don't know the exact mechanisms involved, we know that humans can do two rather amazing things for primates. They can (1) create an articulatory gesture (I'm borrowing Liberman's [1997] term, and probably using it more broadly than he would have liked) with the vocal tract (e.g., the consonant /b/ is a closure of the vocal tract at the lips), and (2) overlap these gestures (e.g., the /b/ and /a/ in *bat*). It is the overlapping, or coarticulation, that allows for rapid speech. For the speaker and listener, the process of either executing or extracting the particular combination of overlapped gestures that form a specific word is automatic: There is no *conscious* manipulation of phonetic elements. Cognitive inspection of the phonetic elements is required only when reading and writing are involved.

An articulatory gesture, or in conventional terminology, a speech sound or phoneme, begins as air is expelled from the lungs. Vowels are formed when the vocal cords are vibrated with varied degrees of tautness and the air passes relatively unimpeded out of the mouth. As the air exits, different frequencies can be emphasized by the position of the tongue and lips, creating different vowels (e.g., the fairly open mouth on the vowel in *pond*). Consonants occur when exiting air is either completely or almost completely closed off, as with the burst that happens on /p/ in *pond* or with less drama in the final consonants.

From the seemingly unlimited way humans can form vowels and consonants, every oral language has settled on a small subset of each to use to represent meaningful units of thought. These meaningful units are called *morphemes*, which often correspond to words (e.g., *pond*). Across languages, morphemes are represented by a specific combination of *vowels* and *consonants* that wrap around each other to form syllables. Most syllables are composed of initial consonants or consonant clusters called *onsets* (e.g., the /p/ in *pond* the /sk/ in *scum*) and the vowel and what follow it, called *rimes* (e.g., the *änd* in *pond* and the *um* in *scum*; Pinker, 1994). Onsets and rimes are each composed of phonemes (e.g., there are four phonemes in both *pond* and *scum*). But to say there are four phonemes in a word is to create them, to conjure them, because, due to coarticulation, they do not exist in the mouth nor in speech as four distinct entities.

The particular vowels and consonants that a particular language has settled on as important—because in that language a minimal pair of morphemes exists that differ only in having that speech sound—are called *phonemes* (e.g., /k/ and /t/ are classified as phonemes in English because of such pairs as *key* and *tea*). Depending on what distinctions are counted, there are between 36 and 44 phonemes in English, which is about average for languages. A phoneme is actually a class of speech sounds that a language has come to treat as equivalent (e.g., the three /k/'s in *ski, key, caw*). These different versions of /k/ are the allophones of /k/, and they differ in both aspiration and tongue position. Because they each occur in specific contexts (e.g., the unaspirated /k/ after /s/) in English, however, there can be no minimal pairs of words that differ only in having different versions of /k/.

English-speaking adults tend to clump allophones together in perception and classification. In effect, they have learned not to attend to what actually could be counted as distinctive. If you are a native English speaker and are asked whether there is a /k/ in both *ski* and *key*, you will say "yes." If you are a native speaker of Hindi, you will likely be puzzled, as the puff of air on the release of /k/ in *key*, the aspiration, is a difference you have learned to attend to because Hindi contains minimal pairs of words (words that differ in meaning) in which the only differ-ence is aspiration (Dale, 1972, p. 167). (Of course, if you have learned to read English, you will be biased by your knowledge of orthography of the letter *k* to say yes.) But the point here is that learning to speak a language actually changes your categorization or perception of phonemes. Children learning to read or speak English and who already speak another language, or even a variant vernacular dialect, are likely to have difficulties perceiving and categorizing phonemes that are not privileged in their first language, for they have learned to ignore them.

For all learners, it appears that the more spoken words a child learns, the finer is the level of phonological information that needs to be stored so that these words can be differentiated. In the course of that finer analysis, increased segmentation occurs that leads to restructuring the way the words are represented in memory (Scarborough, 2001; Metsala & Walley, 1998). In other words, a rich vocabulary probably fosters phonemic awareness. Yet another reason to develop rich vocabularies!

Phonemic Awareness Instruction: What Is Relevant for Children? We are not certain how the brain captures phonemes in running speech (Lyon, 1995). We are not certain, for example, how, or even whether, the articulatory gesture is actually retrieved. In this respect our understanding of being "aware" of phonemes is still uncharted. We do have considerable longitudinal and experimental research to confirm that phonemic awareness is highly predictive of learning to read, that it can be promoted by instruction, and that this instruction seems to help children learn to read. (For an excellent review of these studies, see Rayner, Foorman, Perfetti, Pesetsky, and Seidenberg, 2001). Yet, perhaps reflecting our incomplete knowledge of how phonemes are perceived, there is considerable variation both in the instructional procedures and in the assessments that are used in these studies.

Though we lack precise knowledge, we have in the past few decades learned a fair amount of what is most effective in bringing children's attention to the parts of speech (phonemes) that map to letters. We have learned a lot about what to do instructionally and why that is effective. There are two particular aspects of phonemic awareness instruction that seem most pertinent. First, we are now aware that the act of reading itself fosters phonemic awareness. Second, the act of writing facilitates phonemic awareness.

First, there is a reciprocal relation between reading and phonemic awareness (see chapter by Ehri and Robbins, this volume). Seeing letters in printed words probably helps children by providing a concrete, even if imperfect, referent for what is abstract (Hohn & Ehri, 1983; Murray, Stahl, & Ivey, 199;, Stahl, 2001; Rayner, et al., 2001). In the preceding section I noted that learning to speak changes our perception of phonemes. It is also likely that learning to read changes our perception of elements of language. Olson (1994) suggests that print *fixes* the word as a representation of language that allows reflection and interpretation. If you ask a young child for the first sound in *cat*, they may well tell you, quite naturally and reasonably, that it is *meow* (Adams, 1990). It is the *fix* of letters that can be used to offer another way to think about a word. Letters are the anchors to which articulatory gestures and approximations of phonemes can be attached (e.g., in *cat*, the click of the /k/, the vowel—which is usually the easiest to artificially elongate as the outflow of air on producing it is not obstructed—and the feel of the tongue moving to the ridge just behind the upper front teeth on /t/). Eventually, the printed rendition comes to rule the phonology, as in the previous example of the response to whether there is a /k/ in *ski* and *key*.

Both the concreteness of letters and the reciprocity of learning to read with growth in phonemic awareness suggest that children not be held back from reading instruction because an assessment indicates they lack phonemic awareness. Assessments are far from ideal in this area because we are not yet certain what it is about phonemes in speech that is being captured by the listener. Further, due to coarticulation, phonemes are so mixed together that it is probably less than accurate to think about such things as "first sounds." Directions to children on these assessments that ask them, say, to circle the word that has the same first sound as *cat* and gives choices of pictures of a *key*, an *apple*, or a *boy* are somewhat misleading. A child may start to say *key*, feeling how that sits in the mouth, and compare it to how *cat* feels. Straightaway, the vowel influences the for-

mation of /k/, and the child feels a difference between words. The task becomes to decide which is more alike among the words, and this is tricky. To make the correct choice requires a fair amount of sophistication, and although such reflection would surely influence gains in skill in reading, that kind of reflection, as discussed, is more likely to flourish in the presence of the printed word. Hence, it makes sense to emphasize gestures and speech sounds in the act of attaching them to letters while learning to read and write, rather than just as oral discriminations.

Second, the rich literature on children's early attempts to write words through invented spellings indicates both that the act of writing is a way into phonological understandings and that the connection of writing to phonology occurs early in the process. Spend any time watching young children write, and you see, in exaggerated form, articulatory gestures. Children visibly exaggerate the pronunciations of words in order to feel the word they are attempting to write in their mouths. The easiest sounds to feel in the mouth are those in which the air is stopped, diverted by closed lips or by the tongue, or sent through the nose. Consonants, then, make a frequent early appearance in children's beginning writings. *Cat* might initially be represented as *K*, then *KT*, and then *KAT*, and seeing *cat* in print a few times helps straighten out the use of the letter *c*.

Invented spellings reflect a *point of articulation* reference. At certain times in development, for instance, children predictably substitute a *j* for *dr*, spelling *drip* as *JP* or *drive* as *JRIV*, because of the affrication of *dr*. *Letter-name* spellers carefully feel the beginning sound unit of these words in the mouth as an initial block of air and then a relatively slow release of it with the tip of the tongue against the palate. That gesture bears more similarity to the letter name for *j* than to the letter name for *d* (Henderson, 1981; Read, 1971). *Phonemic awareness may, especially initially, not mean the ability to hear or perceive phonemes as much as to feel them.*

Letter-name knowledge plays a pivotal *phonological* role in literacy learning (Ehri, 1987, 1988; Ehri & Wilce, 1985; Treiman & Rodriguez, 1999; Roberts, 2003; Stuart & Coltheart, 1988). Note, too, that the child who approaches learning the correct spelling, or for that matter the correct reading response to a printed word, has a real advantage if she already has the backdrop of the word's phonological structure. A child, for example, whose invented spelling of cat is KT or KAT has a frame or scaffold for the letters with which to support learning the correct ones.

Awareness of the phonological structure of words seems to be fostered by invented spelling (Clarke, 1988; Torgeson & Davis, 1996). Teachers can even direct this activity, exaggerating gestures and sounds and helping children attach letters to them. Here we are verging into reading instruction, and that makes sense, as I outlined earlier.

ORTHOGRAPHY

Speech may have evolved roughly 125,000 years ago, symbolic art such as the cave paintings appeared about 20,000 years ago, but writing systems are relatively recent inventions, emerging in full force only about 4,000 years ago. Writing systems were probably so late in emerging in human history for two reasons: (1) There needed to be a reason to make a written record (e.g., the development of commerce and exchanges required a written record to communicate across distance or time); and (2) unlike spoken language, there is no biological specialization for writing systems. As Downing stated in the quotation presented earlier (1979), the creators of writing systems, particularly alphabetic ones, had to have some sophisticated linguistic insight and truly inventive minds.

Writing Systems Have Moved toward Direct Sound Representations. Given that writing systems are derived from spoken language, there are three likely candidates for representation: the morpheme, the syllable, or the phoneme. During the bumpy evolution of written languages, these various levels have been intermixed (Rayner & Pollatsek, 1989). Through time, though, writing systems have moved away from trying to directly depict the morpheme (meaning) toward direct sound (phoneme level) representations (DeFrancis, 1989; Gelb, 1952; Hung & Tzeng, 1981; Rayner et al., 2001). The reason for this is that it is far too cumbersome to try to directly represent, or recall, the sheer number of morphemes in a language in a symbolic form. When universal literacy became a goal in China back in the 1940s, for example, the Roman alphabet was adopted and used as a transitional alphabet to represent speech sounds symbolized in the characters. This transitional alphabet, *pinyin*, is taught during the first 7 weeks of first grade. When the characters are then introduced, pinyin is written across the top of them. Gradually, through the school years, the pinyin is removed.

Learning to Read: Some Orthographies, Such as That of Printed English, Are Harder Than Others. There are features of different spoken languages, such as the number of syllables used in speech and the number of phonemes, that influenced the form of the writing system. Spoken Japanese, for example, uses a far smaller number of different syllables than does spoken English. In Japanese a syllabic-based writing system—that is, one in which a grapheme represents a syllable rather than a phoneme—made sense. Theoretically, all the 100 different syllables that make up spoken Japanese could be, and are, represented in the *kana* writing system of Japan. (However, for historical reasons, other symbol systems are used.) Children begin to read, both at home and school, with the syllabic *kana*. The syllable is a much more transparent, separable, and accessible unit in running speech than is the phoneme. It is not surprising that a writing system that employs this base for speech representation is easier to learn than one that works on the phoneme level. Acquisition of literacy is not a particular concern in Japan. The initial *kana* system, as well as the cultural insistence on learning to read, most likely facilitates the process of learning to read (Snow & Juel, in press).

Most oral languages, including English, contain too many distinct syllables to offer syllabic writing systems as a viable option. Alphabetic writing systems are tremendous inventions, but, by their very dependence on the elusive phoneme, they are not going to be readily grasped by the learner. A further complication, however, is that there are degrees to which writing systems preserve morphemic, as well as phonemic, information. That is, morphemes can be purely phonological representations or can also be related to meaning. Consider the sacrifice of phonology to morphemic meaning in English in the spellings of *courage* and *courageous* or the preservation of the *-ed* spelling for expressing the past tense, regardless of whether the pronunciation is /ed/ *(roasted)*, /t/ *(baked)*, or /d/ *(fried)*. Although the more phonologically transparent the representation of a morpheme is, the easier it may be to initially learn to read it, the preservation of some meaning-related characteristics facilitates comprehension. Morphemic elements in written English can also serve readers of languages that share similar roots, such as Spanish (Carlo et al., 2004).

A purely alphabetic writing system would be one in which a grapheme (i.e., letter) represents one and only one phoneme. Clearly, the printed English writing system lacks this one-to-one correspondence, as 26 letters are used to represent 40 or so phonemes. As noted before, it also sacrifices some phonological transparency, because spelling patterns sometimes preserve meaning. It is hard to find a writing system with perfect one-to-one correspondences. Finnish is deemed pretty close.

Learning to read in a perfect alphabetic writing system would still depend on having the oral language with which to understand the morphemes. It would still depend on being able to connect letter sequences to their pronunciations. Encountering more reliable letter–sound correspondences in texts, though, appears to foster a mindset for using them and figuring out how they work (Juel & Roper/Schneider, 1985). And, in general, the more transparent or regular the orthography, the easier it is to learn to read. English is neither transparent nor easy.

Not only is learning to read in a writing system with more regular orthographies easier, but also the differences in reading performance among dyslexics of different countries appear to be due to differences attributed to orthography. Recent brain scan and neurocognitive processing data suggest that dyslexia is a disorder with a universal neuroanatomical basis and a phonological processing deficit at its core. Deep orthographies such as those encountered in English and French can aggravate the reading problem, whereas the dyslexic reader of Italian, with its comparatively transparent orthography, will find it easier (Paulesu et al., 2001).

Some Words about Phonics. Earlier in this chapter, the likely positive relation of vocabulary size to acquiring phonemic awareness was discussed (Metsala & Walley, 1998). It should also be recognized that *phonics instruction is based on the assumption that, in sounding out a word, the child will hit upon something that is recognizable in his or her oral vocabulary.* Sounding out a word using the rules and letter–sound associations taught in phonics yields the child a shaky-sounding representation, not an exact match, to the spoken version of the word (e.g., *hog* as *huh, huhaaawwwguh*). Getting to a meaningful representation of *hog* depends upon the animal being one the reader knows. When there is no match, the reader may attach the spoken or written word to one that shares some of its sounds (Juel & Deffes, 2004). This is particularly likely to happen if there is little context around the word, such as can happen in phonics instruction. We have encountered children who, sometimes due to vernacular dialect and sometimes because they do not attach meaning to the word, say that a *hog* is a *hawk* or a *log*. *Thorn* means *Like if you rip somebody's paper. Troop* means *don't tell lies.* As with every other aspect of reading, oral vocabulary underlies the success of the venture.

Some reading researchers have claimed that when a child is sufficiently armed with phonemic awareness and some basic letter–sound correspondences and has a rich exposure to print (including pairings of spoken and written words), the child can then teach him- or herself to read. This has been called the "self-teaching" hypothesis of learning to read (Share, 1995; Share & Stanovich, 1995; Torgesen & Hecht, 1996). Key to this hypothesis is that a child carefully scrutinizes the letter sequences within a word, probably explicitly sounding out these patterns, and that after a few repetitions of this process the complete orthography of a specific word is fixed in memory so that it no longer requires such laborious processing for identification.

Word-specific representations are what adults eventually use to read and spell. The phoneme /u/, for example, normally maps to 17 different spellings in printed English (*ruby, rule, do, move, fruit, bruise, group, through, moon, wooed, loose, rheumatism, flue, maneuver, grew, canoe,* and *two*; Dale, 1972, p. 190). An adult may have to think for a second with some of these, "Is it *eu* or *ue*?" Word-specific information may be incomplete for some words because they fall in that rare end of the 80,000-word distribution that was previously discussed. These words are not seen very often, which means there is less opportunity to form a complete orthographic representation of them. So a common word such as *move* or *do* is easily recalled, whereas *maneuver* gives one pause. For either the child or adult, the most predicable spelling problem in English comes with the vowels, because there are so many spelling patterns for them.

Phonics is, of course, the method that is supposed to foster full alphabetic processing to enable children to handle the orthography. Phonics instruction, I fear, became reified in the manner I discussed for phonemic awareness. Somehow the transparency of showing a child how to approach an unknown word, how to attach sounds to letters and to blend them into something that could be recognized and attached to meaning, became confused with thinking that the exact letter–sound correspondences taught are isomorphic to those used in reading. Sometimes phonics programs teach letter–sound correspondences past the point at which children need them. That is, once a child is able to read enough to negotiate easy texts, that child is most likely at the point at which he or she can learn word-specific spellings. The contribution of the child, as one who can and must generalize, is sometimes lost.

Even the most explicit of phonics programs rarely teach more than 100 specific spelling patterns, whereas at least 500 "rules" would be needed for skilled reading (Honeycutt, n.d.; Venezky, 1967). Of course, it is not rules that ultimately account for skilled reading, as connectionist models have illustrated (Rayner et al., 2001). The self-teaching hypothesis has to be true to a large extent because the reader is going to have to identify many words that are never taught.

Through history, and without benefit of phonics, children did learn to read. Most were eventually capable of reasoning and generalizing from taught orthographic elements to untaught ones, even if the original orthographic elements were whole words (Byrne & Fielding-Barnsley, 1990; Roberts, 2003). If a child in the 1940s saw "See, see. See Sally," enough times, it could lead to induction of /s/ and *ee*. But there seems no doubt that such induction was a slow-going process that put more children at risk for serious frustration, and even failure, than methods that explicitly taught some basic letter–sound correspondences to get them looking in the right direction.

Phonics is an umbrella term that stands for many forms of instruction that help children realize the alphabetic principle through instruction that links letters and sounds. There is now ample evidence that letter–sound instruction facilitates learning to read compared with methods with little or no phonics instruction (Adams, 1990; Chall, 1996; Rayner, Foorman, Perfetti, Pesetsky, & Seidenberg 2001; National Reading Panel, 2000).

There are multiple problems with horserace models of research, however, that pit one method against another (see Snow & Juel, in press, for a review of these problems). Two basic problems are: (1) They tend to be based on mean comparisons that hide the effect of how a curriculum or method actually affects children with differential profiles of skills; and (2) although these studies overall have shown an advantage for phonics, the curricular method actually accounts for only a small portion of variance in reading outcomes compared with the factor of the teacher.

Tivnan and Hemphill's (in press) recent study is particularly compelling, as its major finding echoes that often cited from the original first-grade studies (Bond & Dykstra, 1967)—that the individual classroom teacher makes a difference in learning outcomes, no matter what the program or curriculum. Tivnan and Hemphill (in press) evaluated the effects of four programs (which differed in amount of phonics)—Balanced Early Literacy, Literacy Collaborative, Developing Literacy First, and Success for All—used in a large urban school district. At the end of first grade, no differences were found in student performance in word reading, pseudoword reading, spelling, or vocabulary.

The most notable findings of the study, however, were that, in this urban district filled with many high-risk children, (1) the majority of children in all four programs scored below grade level at the end of the year, and this was most noticeable on comprehension measures; and (2) differences in the classroom performance of individual teachers were large, and high-performing teachers were not clustered within any of the programs. Similar to other "beat the odds" studies, effective teachers tailored explicit instruction to fit the needs of the children, engaged children in high-level discussions about text, and held high expectations overall for the children in their class (Barone, 2003/04; Bogner, Raphael, & Pressley, 2002; Pressley et al., 2001; Taylor, Pearson, Clark, & Walpole, 2000).

Juel and Minden-Cupp (2000), in a year-long detailed classroom analysis of four first-grade classrooms, found that differentiated instruction had the most payoffs for students: Students who most needed letter–sound instruction got more of it than students who did not. Further, the students received this instruction in small groups, and the teacher was responsive to their individual understandings of letters and sounds in her feedback. The most successful teacher for the children who entered first grade with the fewest literacy skills was the one who included successive letter-by-letter sounding out of words *in writing*, while word-reading instruction included work with word families and word chunks (onsets and rimes).

I suspect we do not yet know the best way to help children into words, as the self-teaching model describes. Given the currently available instructional tools, phonics is clearly the best option. But it is imperfect and a temporary stand-in until the child is launched enough into print to take over.

Some Final Words

Learning to read includes learning about letter sounds. Part of what makes that difficult is indeed the difficulty with phonemic awareness—with gaining a phonological frame for letters. But that does not mean that phonemic awareness curricula are needed. A central point of this chapter is that it is through actual reading, and especially writing, that frames are developed. Word recognition skill is critical. But when phonics takes over the curriculum, when teachers focus primarily on developing phonological awareness and decoding without attention to the meanings of words and texts, then there is a serious problem.

In observing classroom instruction in 13 kindergarten and 13 first-grade classrooms, we found some classrooms in which over 60% of language arts activities focused exclusively on letter sounds, with little, if any, reference to the meaning of the words being decoded (Juel et al., 2003). That is a serious concern for at least two reasons discussed in the chapter. First, phonics, or sounding out words, is based on the assumption that children know the meanings of the words they are decoding. Phonics works only if the string of produced letter sounds approximates a recognizable word. In too many cases, that assumption is being violated. Second, spending such large amounts of time on letter sounds means spending less time on developing oral vocabulary and knowledge. Development of oral vocabulary is a serious problem.

Reading improves overall intellectual growth (Cunningham & Stanovich, 1998)—whether it is in understanding the nuances in meaning of different words for *fight*, such as *squabble* or *quibble*, and, in so doing, clarifying emotional responses, or in learning the advantages and disadvantages of external skeletons and something about adaptation and evolution. Although the nightmare may be that Moynihan was right, most educators will not accept differences at school entry as creating children who are *hopelessly* behind. It seems likely that it will be the combined influence of robust preschools, enriching summer and after-school programs, the revitalization and valuing of community resources for young and very young children and their families, *and* the best of classroom instruction that jointly move us closer to "no child left behind." Moving individuals forward has to have promise for moving groups.

References

Adams, M. J. (1990). *Beginning to read: Thinking and learning about print.* Cambridge, MA: MIT Press.

Anglin, J. M. (1993). Vocabulary development: A morphological analysis. *Monographs of the Society for Research in Child Development, 58* (10, Serial No. 238).

August, D., & Hakuta, K. (Eds.). (1997). *Improving schooling for language-minority children: A research agenda.* Washington, DC: National Academy Press.

Baker, S. K., Simmons, D. C., & Kame'enui, E. J. (1998). Vocabulary acquisition: Research bases. In D. C. Simmons & E. J. Kame'enui (Eds.), *What reading research tells us about children with diverse learning needs* (pp. 183–218). Mahwah, NJ: Erlbaum.

Beck, I., McKeown, M., & Kucan, L. (2002). *Bringing words to life: Robust vocabulary instruction.* New York: Guilford Press.

Biemiller, A. (1999). *Language and reading success.* Newton Upper Falls, MA: Brookline Books.

Biemiller, A. (2001a, January). *Building vocabulary: A key to reading success.* Paper presented at the Norma Broussard Memorial Reading Conference, Miami, FL.

Biemiller, A. (2001b). Teaching vocabulary. *American Educator, 26*(4), 24–28, 47.

Blachman, B. A. (1997). Early intervention and phonological awareness: A cautionary tale. In B. A. Blachman (Ed.), *Foundations of reading acquisition and dyslexia* (pp. 409–430). Mahwah, NJ: Erlbaum.

Bogner, K., Raphael, L. M., & Pressley, M. (2002). How grade-1 teachers motivate literate activity by their students. *Scientific Studies in Reading, 6,* 135–165.

Bond, G., & Dykstra, R. (1967). The cooperative research program in first grade reading. *Reading Research Quarterly, 2,* 5–142.

Bridges, M., Fuller, B., Rumberger, R., & Tran, L. (2004) Preschool for California's children [Policy Brief 04-3]. Retrieved September 2004 from http://pace.berkeley.edu

Bus, A. G., Van IJzendoorn, M. H., & Pellefrini, A. D. (1995). Joint book reading makes for success in learning to read: A meta-analysis on intergenerational transmission of literacy. *Review of Educational Research, 65,* 1–21.

Byrne, B., & Fielding-Barnsley, R. (1990). Acquiring the alphabetic principle: A case for teaching recognition of phoneme identity. *Journal of Educational Psychology, 82,* 805–812.

Carlo, M., August, D., McLaughlin, B., Snow, C. E., Dressler, C., Lippman, D. N., et al. (2004). Closing the gap: Addressing the vocabulary needs of English-language learners in bilingual and mainstream classrooms. *Reading Research Quarterly, 39*(2), 188–215.

Carroll, J. B., Davies, P., & Richman, B. (1971). *Word frequency book.* New York: American Heritage.

Carver, R. P., & Leibert, R. E. (1995). The effect of reading library books at different levels of difficulty upon gain in reading ability. *Reading Research Quarterly, 30*(1), 26–48.

Chall, J. S. (1996). *Learning to read: The great debate.* New York: Harcourt Brace. (Original work published 1967)

Clarke, L. K. (1988). Invented spelling in the open classroom. *Word, 22,* 281–309.

Cunningham, A. E., & Stanovich, K. E. (1998). What reading does for the mind. *American Educator, 22*(1–2), 8–15.

Dale, E., & O'Rourke, J. (1981). *The living word vocabulary.* Chicago: World Book/Childcraft International.

Dale, P. S. (1972) *Language development.* Hinsdale, IL: Dryden.

DeFrancis, J. (1989). *Visible speech: The diverse oneness of writing systems.* Honolulu: University of Hawaii.

Dickinson, D. K., & Tabors, P. (Eds.) (2001). *Building literacy with language: Young children learning at home and school.* Baltimore: Brookes.

Downing, J. (1979). *Reading and reasoning.* New York: Springer-Verlag.

Duncan, G., Brooks–Gunn, J., & Klebanov, P. (1994). Economic deprivation and early childhood development. *Child Development, 65,* 296–318.

Ehri, L. C. (1987). Learning to read and spell words. *Journal of Reading Behavior, 19,* 5–31.

Ehri, L. C., & Wilce, L. S. (1985). Movement into reading: Is the first stage of printed word learning visual or phonetic? *Reading Research Quarterly, 20,* 163–179.

Francis, D. J., Shaywitz, S. E., Stuebing, K. K., Shaywitz, B. A., & Fletcher, J. M. (1996). Developmental lag versus deficit models of reading disability: A longitudinal, individual growth curves analysis. *Journal of Educational Psychology, 88*(1), 3–17.

Gelb, I. J. (1952). *A study of writing.* Chicago: University of Chicago Press.

Hart, B., & Risley, R. T. (1995). *Meaningful differences in the everyday experiences of young American children.* Baltimore: Brookes.

Heath, S. B. (1983). *Ways with words.* Cambridge, UK: Cambridge University Press.

Henderson, E. (1981). *Learning to read and spell: The child's knowledge of words.* DeKalb: Northern Illinois Press.

Hohn, W. E., & Ehri, L. C. (1983). Do alphabet letters help prereaders acquire phonemic segmentation skill? *Journal of Educational Psychology, 75,* 752–762.

Honeycutt, S. (n.d.). Phonological rules for a text-to-speech system. Natural Language Processing Group. MIT. Undated manuscript.

Hoover, W., & Gough, P. B. (1990). The simple view of reading. *Reading and Writing: An Interdisciplinary Journal, 2,* 127–160.

Hung, D. L., & Tzeng, O. J. L. (1981). Orthographic variations and visual information processing. *Psychological Bulletin, 90,* 377–414.

Hutchins, P. (1968). *Rosie's walk.* New York: Macmillan.

Johnston, P. H. (1985). Understanding reading disability: A case study approach. *Harvard Educational Review, 55,* 153–177.

Juel, C. (1988). Learning to read and write: A longitudinal study of fifty-four children from first through fourth grade. *Journal of Educational Psychology, 80*(4), 437–447.

Juel, C. (1994a). *Learning to read and write in one elementary school.* New York: Springer-Verlag.

Juel, C. (1994b). Teaching phonics in the context of the integrated language arts. In L. M. Morrow, J. K., Smith, L. C. & Wilkinson (Eds.), *Integrated language arts* (pp. 133–154). Needham Heights, MA: Allyn & Bacon.

Juel, C. (1996). What makes literacy tutoring effective? *Reading Research Quarterly, 31*(3), 268–289.

Juel, C., Biancarosa, G., Coker, D., & Deffes, R. (2003). Walking with Rosie: A cautionary tale of literacy instruction. *Educational Leadership, 60*(7), 12–18.

Juel, C., & Deffes, R. (2004). Making words stick. *Educational Leadership, 61*(6), 30–34.

Juel, C., & Minden-Cupp, C. (2000). Learning to read words: Linguistic units and instructional strategies. *Reading Research Quarterly, 35*, 458–492.

Juel, C., & Roper/Schneider, D. (1985). The influence of basal readers on first-grade reading. *Reading Research Quarterly, 18*, 306–327.

Kuhn, M. R., & Stahl, S. A. (1998). Teaching children to learn word meanings from context: A synthesis and some questions. *Journal of Literacy Research, 30*(1), 19–38.

Lenneberg, E. H. (1967). *Biological foundations of language.* New York: Wiley.

Liberman, A. M. (1997). How theories of speech affect research in reading and writing. In B. A. Blachman (Ed.), *Foundations of reading acquisition and dyslexia* (pp. 3–19). Mahwah, NJ: Erlbaum.

Lionni, L. (1986). *It's mine.* New York: Dragonfly.

Lonigan, C. J., & Whitehurst, G. J. (1998). Examination of the relative efficacy of parent and teacher involvement in a shared-reading intervention for preschool children from low-income backgrounds. *Early Childhood Research Quarterly, 13*, 263–290.

Lyon, R. (1995). Toward a definition of dyslexia. *Annals of Dyslexia, 45*, 3–27.

McLloyd, V. C. (1998). Socioeconomic disadvantage and child development. *American Psychologist, 53*, 185–204.

Metsala, J., & Walley, A. (1998). Spoken vocabulary growth and the segmental restructuring of lexical representations: Precursors to phonemic awareness and early reading ability. In J. L. Metsala & L. C. Ehri (Eds.), *Word recognition in beginning reading* (pp. 89–120). Mahwah, NJ: Erlbaum.

Moats, L. (2001, Summer). Overcoming the language gap. *American Educator,* 5–9.

Moynihan, D. (1986). *At a loss for words: Illiterate in America.* [Television broadcast, interviewed by Peter Jennings]. New York: American Broadcasting Company.

Murray, B. A., Stahl, S. A., & Ivey, M. G. (1996). Developing phoneme awareness through alphabet books. *Reading and Writing: An Interdisciplinary Journal, 8*, 307–322.

Nagy, W. E., & Anderson, R. C. (1984). How many words are there in printed school English? *Reading Research Quarterly, 19*, 304–330.

Nagy, W. E., Herman, P. A., & Anderson, R. C. (1985). Learning words from context. *Reading Research Quarterly, 20*, 233–253.

National Reading Panel. (2000). *Teaching children to read: An evidence-based assessment of the scientific research literature on reading and its implications for reading instruction.* Washington, DC: National Institute for Child Health and Human Development.

Neuman, S. B., & Celano, D. (2001). Access to print for middle- and low-income neighborhoods: An ecological study of four neighborhoods. *Reading Research Quarterly, 36*, 6–26.

Olson, D. R. (1994). *The world on paper.* Cambridge, UK: Cambridge University Press.

Paulesu, E., Démonet, J. F., Fazio, F., McCrory, E., Chanoline, V., Brunswick, N., et al. (2001). Dyslexia: Cultural diversity and biological unity. *Science, 291*, 2165–2167.

Pinker, S. (1994). *The language instinct.* New York: HarperPerennial.

Pressley, M. (2002). *Reading instruction that works: The case for balanced reading* (2nd ed.). New York: Guilford Press.

Pressley, M., Wharton-McDonald, R., Allington, R., Block, C., Morrow, L., Tracey, D., et al. (2001). A study of the effective first-grade literacy instruction. *Scientific Studies in Reading, 5*, 35–58.

Rayner, K., Foorman, B. R., Perfetti, C. A., Pesetsky, D., & Seidenberg, M. S. (2001). How psychological science informs the teaching of reading. *Psychological Science in the Public Interest, 2*(2), 31–74.

Rayner, K., & Pollatsek, A. (1989). *The psychology of reading.* Englewood Cliffs, NJ: Prentice-Hall.

Read, C. (1971). Pre-school children's knowledge of English phonology. *Harvard Educational Review, 41*, 1–34.

Roberts, T. A. (2003). Effects of alphabet-letter instruction on young children's word recognition. *Journal of Educational Psychology, 95*(1), 41–51.

Scarborough, H. S. (2001). Connecting early language and literacy to later reading (dis)abilities: Evidence, theory, and practice. In S. B. Neuman & D. K. Dickinson (Eds.) *Handbook of early literacy research* (pp. 97–110). New York: Guilford Press.

Sénéchal, M., & Cornell, E. H. (1993). Vocabulary acquisition through shared reading experiences. *Reading Research Quarterly, 28*, 360–374.

Share, D. L. (1995). Phonological recoding and self-teaching: Sine qua non of reading acquisition. *Cognition, 55*, 151–218.

Share, D. L., & Stanovich, K. E. (1995). Cognitive

processes in early reading development: Accommodating individual differences into a model of acquisition. *Issues in Education, 1,* 1–57.

Smith, C., Constantino, R., & Krashen, S. (1997). Differences in print environment for children in Beverly Hills, Compton, and Watts. *Emergency Librarian, 24(4),* 4–5.

Snow, C. E. (1983). Literacy and language: Relationships during the preschool years. *Harvard Educational Review, 53,* 165–189.

Snow, C. E., Barnes, W., Chandler, J., Goodman, I., & Hemphill, L. (1991). *Unfulfilled expectations: Home and school influences on literacy.* Cambridge, MA: Harvard University Press.

Snow, C. E., Burns, M. S., & Griffin, P. (Eds.). (1998). *Preventing reading difficulties in young children.* Washington, DC: National Academy Press.

Snow, C. E., & Juel, C. (in press). Teaching children to read: What do we know about how to do it? In M. J. Snowling & C. Hulme (Eds.), *The science of reading: A handbook.* Oxford, UK: Blackwell.

Stahl, S. A. (1991). Beyond the instrumentalist hypothesis: Some relationships between word meanings and comprehension. In P. Schwanenfluegel (Ed.), *The psychology of word meanings* (pp. 157–178). Hillsdale, NJ: Erlbaum.

Stahl, S. A. (1999). *Vocabulary development.* Newton Upper Falls, MA: Brookline Books.

Stahl, S. A. (2001). Teaching phonics and phonological awareness. In S. B. Neuman & D. K. Dickinson (Eds.), *Handbook of early literacy research* (pp. 333–347). New York: Guilford Press.

Stanovich, K. E. (1986). Matthew effects in reading: Some consequences of individual differences in the acquisition of literacy. *Reading Research Quarterly, 21,* 360–406.

Stuart, M., & Coltheart, M. (1988). Does reading develop in a sequence of stages? *Cognition, 30,* 139–181.

Swanborn, M. S. L., & de Glopper, K. (1999). Incidental word learning while reading: A meta-analysis. *Review of Educational Research, 69(3),* 261–285.

Taylor, B. M., Pearson, P. D., Clark, K., & Walpole, S. (2000). Effective schools and accomplished teachers: Lessons about primary-grade reading instruction in low-income schools. *Elementary School Journal, 101,* 121–166.

Tivnan, T., & Hemphill, L. (in press). *Comparing four literacy reform models in high-poverty schools: Patterns of first grade achievement.* Elementary School Journal, *105,* 5.

Torgesen, J. K., & Burgess, S. R. (1998). Consistency of reading-related phonological processes throughout early childhood: Evidence from longitudinal-correlational and instructional studies. In J. L. Metsala & L. C. Ehri (Eds.), *Word recognition in beginning literacy* (pp. 161–188). Hillsdale, NJ: Erlbaum.

Torgeson, J. K., & Davis, C. (1996). Individual difference variables that predict response to training in phonological awareness. *Journal of Experimental Child Psychology, 63,* 1–21.

Torgeson, J. K., & Hecht, S. A. (1996). Preventing and remediating reading disabilities: Instructional variables that make a difference for special students. In M. F. Graves, P. van den Broek, & B. M. Taylor (Eds.), *The first R: Every child's right to read* (pp. 133–159). New York: Teachers College Press.

Treiman, R., & Rodriguez, R. (1999). Young children use letter names to read words. *Psychological Science, 10,* 334–339.

Valdés, G. (1998). The world outside and inside schools: Language and immigrant children. *Educational Researcher, 27,* 4–18.

Venezky, R. L. (1967). English orthography: Its graphical nature and its relation to sound. *Reading Research Quarterly, 2,* 75–106.

Wells, G. G. (1985). *Language development in the preschool years.* New York: Cambridge University Press.

White, B. L., & Watts, J. C. (1973). *Experience and environment.* Englewood, Cliffs, NJ: Prentice-Hall.

Whitehurst, G. J., & Lonigan, C. J. (2001). Emergent literacy: Development from prereaders to readers. In S. B. Neuman & D. K. Dickinson (Eds.), *Handbook of early literacy research* (pp. 11–29. New York: Guilford Press.

Wong Fillmore, L. (1982). Language minority students and school participation: What kind of English is needed? *Journal of Education, 164(2),* 143–156.

Wong Fillmore, L. (1985). When does teacher talk work as input? In S. Gass & C. Madden (Eds.), *Input in second language acquisition* (pp. 17–50). Rowley, MA: Newbury.

Wong Fillmore, L. (1991). Second language learning in children: A model of language learning in social context. In E. Bialystok (Ed.), *Language processing in bilingual children* (pp. 49–69). Cambridge, UK: Cambridge University Press.

Wong Fillmore, L. (1992). Learning a language from learners. In C. Kramsch & S. McConnell-Ginet (Eds.), *Text and context: Cross-disciplinary perspectives on language study* (pp. 46–66). Lexington MA: Heath.

29

Policy Decisions in Early Literacy Assessment

TERRY SALINGER

Assessment of reading skills—especially those of young learners—has long been a controversial topic (National Association for the Education of Young Children [NAEYC], 1988; Shepard, 1991, 1994, 1997, 2000; Shepard et al., 1996). Debate among researchers, teachers, and parents has centered on what are and are not appropriate means for gathering information about literacy acquisition and growth. Debate is continuing, often with strong political overtones, especially in light of the No Child Left Behind legislation and its ambitious reading program, Reading First.[1]

This chapter discusses issues concerning early literacy assessment, focusing especially on the policy decisions surrounding the topic and the consequences of the ways in which some of these decisions are being implemented. Readers are asked to remember the metaphor of "games" that Constance Kamii put forth in her still-relevant 1990 book for NAEYC, *Achievement Testing in the Early Grades: The Games Grown-ups Play.* The debate has acquired a wider scope than achievement testing, but the metaphor applies as much as ever. In fact, the current situation regarding early reading testing is a good example of what Kamii referred to as "the vote-getting game" (p. ii). Support for the early development of strong reading and academic skills has been shown to be an attractive political platform. Inherent in support for this platform is support for assessment techniques to measure whether the political goal is being accomplished.

The chapter is not an attack on Reading First, but rather a discussion of the consequences of the national attention currently being paid to early reading and its assessment. To contextualize the current situation, the chapter begins with some background and then discusses the potential impact of the requirements of the Reading First legislation on early literacy assessment in general. Illustrative examples from one state's efforts to develop a standards-based early literacy assessment are used to highlight critical issues, as are observations gathered from analysis of state and local Reading First funding proposals.

Some Background

Testing of young learners was relatively uncommon before 1965, but it has increased constantly since then. Reasons include the alarms raised by the publication of *A Nation at Risk* (National Commission on Excellence in Education, 1983), the influx of federal and state money to schools, requirements for subsequent accountability measures, and the need to measure students' "readiness" to see whether they have met the National Education Goals Panel's first goal of "all children ready to learn" by the age of 5. In 1988, NAECY cataloged the uses of tests: as screens for entry into and exit from kindergarten, for placement, and for early tracking within schools. Screening tests seemed to cause the most concern among researchers (Meisels, 1996, 1998), yet many parents adopted the concept enthusiastically, wanting to give their children "the gift of time" provided by delayed school entry or by an extra preparatory year of prekindergarten. The darker side of screening test use included the misclassification of many children as "not ready" for kindergarten; most of these children were poor, male, black, and young in relation to the required age for formal school entry (Ellwein, Walsh, Eads, & Miller, 1991). Misclassification should have been anticipated when one realizes that most of the screening tests focus on vocabulary. Indeed, it is not too much to infer that such tests were measuring home language patterns. Hart and Risley (1995), for example, found correlations between the size of preschoolers' vocabularies and variables in their parents' verbal interactions with them. There were striking differences in the quantity and type of speech directed toward preschoolers by high- and low-income parents, with children from higher income backgrounds better prepared for the language challenges that school entry presents. These differences are reflected in results of tests of young children's language.

In 1998—10 years after NAEYC issued its catalog of tests and 9 years after the Governors' Education Summit announced its "ready to learn" goal—the National Education Goals Panel (NEGP) published a short document proposing four purposes for assessment from birth to grade 3. This was a highly political document, rejected by some, embraced by others, and now relegated to obscurity. The publication begins with strong statements:

> an increase in formal assessments and testing, the results of which are used to make 'high-stakes' decisions such as tracking youngsters into high- and low-ability groups, (mis)labeling or retaining them, or using test results to sort children into or out of kindergarten and preschools. . . . As a result, schools have often identified . . . large proportions of youngsters . . . who would benefit enormously from the learning opportunities provided in those [school] settings. In particular, because the alternative treatment is often inadequate, screening out has fostered inequalities, widening—and perpetuating—the gap between youngsters deemed ready and unready. (p. 4)

The Goals Panel's (1998) purposes for assessment are immanently practical: (1) to promote learning and development, (2) to identify children for health and special services, (3) to monitor trends and evaluate programs and services, and (4) to assess academic achievement to hold individual students, teachers, and schools accountable. According to the recommendations, program monitoring can best be accomplished through matrix sampling—that is, generalizing results after testing only the smaller statistical sample of students, rather than depending on test data from all students within a target population. Further, informed observation, not standardized testing, should suffice for gathering data for program accountability until grade 3 or grade 4. The Goals Panel's recommendations asserted that standardized tests were not sufficiently accurate measures of achievement if used prior to grade 3 or ideally, grade 4.

The primary authors of the Goals Panel (1998) publication, Lorrie Shepard and Sharon Lynn Kagan, did not dispute the need to collect information about young children, especially information that could secure special services in advance of children's falling into risk categories. But they sought to balance the hunger for data with the reality of how difficult it is to collect valid information about young children. They also sought to end the frenzy of overtesting of young children. Unfortunately, the frenzy continues and is getting worse. A recent article from the *New York Times* special section on education (Brenna, 2003), titled "The Littlest Test Takers," carried the subheading "Preschoolers can be thrown off their games by a stomachache or an itchy shirt. Assessment can be highly unreliable. And yet there it is." The note of resignation in this statement is hard to miss.

Where We Are Now

Until recently, the main questions seemed to be *why* and *when* to assess young learners; the passage of the No Child Left Behind Act of 2001 (NCLB) has broadened the questions, adding considerable emphasis on *how* and *how much*. Among the many features of NCLB, three are particularly relevant to this discussion at this point:

- Reading First, the federal program for kindergarten to grade 3 students, mandates specific kinds of data collection and a three-tiered assessment system.
- NCLB mandates that all students be tested in reading and mathematics in grades 3 to 8 and that states administer the National Assessment of Educational Progress if they want to continue to receive Title I funding.
- States must develop and implement broad accountability plans that will allow them to track their movement toward improved academic achievement and report each school's adequate yearly progress (AYP) toward meeting achievement goals.

Several points bear emphasizing here, especially regarding students' reading achievement. First, the No Child Left Behind legislation means that fresh attention is being paid to the reality that many children, especially those who are least advantaged, reach grade 4 unable to read successfully enough to progress academically. Reading First has real money behind it—$6 billion—and 80% of the funds will go directly to local education agencies and from there to schools. Second, there is recognition that too many children have been off-loaded into special education as a way to get them out of mainstream education and mainstream testing; in theory, this isn't going to happen, because children will be screened, diagnosed, and given intervention early and systematically before initial reading difficulties become major academic obstacles. Third, the Reading First statute and guidance place a strong emphasis on professional development, family literacy, teacher training, and libraries. These em-

phases suggest that the program is envisioned as comprehensive and reaching into the communities that can and should support children's literacy growth. Finally, NCLB has put some teeth into Reading First; one may disagree with the program's regulations and mandates, but vague guidance and lack of monitoring and technical assistance doomed the Reading Excellence Act to failure long before the 2000 election.

NCLB and the enabling legislation for Reading First lay out a model assessment program that has considerable potential value, along with the possibility of severe negative consequences. Table 29.1 shows the intersection of the testing that will be required because of NCLB, Reading First, and other legislative mandates.

This model could be an excellent approach for all districts and states, with or without Reading First funding. It enables teachers to collect multiple forms of evidence, ideally as students engage in different kinds of reading tasks, primarily within their familiar classroom environment. Essentially there would be safety nets for young learners in advance of the supposedly high-stakes testing at grade 3. More specifically, the model for early literacy assessment seems to be predicated on the assumption that the best forms of assessment for young learners are classroom based and are not necessarily standardized, fill-in-the-answer-bubble tests before grade 3. It would appear that there is federal support for the concept of teachers as capable of collecting assessment data about young learners and acting upon the data to tailor their own instruction or to seek intervention for learners who are at risk for problems as they move through school.

TABLE 29.1. Testing Requirements of NCLB Legislation.

Grade	Kindergarten	Grades 1 and 2	Grade 3	Grade 4
Reading First	Screening Diagnostic Progress monitoring	Screening Diagnostic Progress monitoring	Screening Diagnostic Progress monitoring	State NCL reading achievement test NAEP national testing NAEP state or urban district testing
All classes	State/district screening tests	Any state/district tests	State NCLB reading achievement test	

Legislative action in one state illustrates the potential value of this model. The state had a long history of attention to early literacy and of testing. Shepard, Taylor, and Kagan (1996) reported that the state screened all children at entry to kindergarten or first grade; screens included testing for vision, physical well-being, and health, along with communication, language, and potential developmental delays. A year prior to the passage of NCLB legislation, the state senate passed a statutory requirement for a standards-based screening, diagnostic, and progress monitoring triad in all kindergarten to grade 2 classrooms in reading, writing, and mathematics, along with grade 3 achievement tests in the same subjects. Districts in good academic standing could use a test of their own choosing, and many were already using the Dynamic Indicators of Basic Early Literacy Skills (DIBELS) or the Texas Primary Reading Inventory (TPRI). Other districts would be required to use the state assessments, whose introduction would be accompanied by extensive training. The development and implementation of this state's early literacy testing program will be used illustratively throughout this chapter.

Advantages of Classroom-Based Assessments

In the best of situations, the screening, diagnostic, and progress monitoring assessment triad could capture all aspects of early reading, while also being sensitive to children's development and to differences in instruction. This sensitivity is needed to accommodate the dynamic nature of young learners' progression from preliteracy to literacy. The tests would be quick and easy to administer, score, and interpret; and data would have immediate utility to teachers. Because the testing situations would not necessarily be standardized, data would not be used for high-stakes decisions, thereby removing some of the pressure that surrounds testing events for both teachers and students. And, of course, teachers would be well trained to give the tests and understand their results.

In countless places, similar classroom-based assessment models have been in place for many years. In New York, the variation of the Primary Language Record developed at the National Center for Restructuring Edu-

cation, Schools, and Teaching (NCREST) at Columbia Teachers College has been widely used (Falk, 1998); the Early Literacy Portfolio developed in South Brunswick, New Jersey (Salinger, 1998) evolved successfully over many years and ultimately became the model for CBT-McGraw-Hill's *Fox in a Box;* New York State (New York State Department of Education, 1999) and Michigan (Michigan Department of Education, 1998) have had state-level models of early literacy dependent on the collection of multiple forms of evidence; and the School District of Philadelphia developed a kindergarten to grade 3 literacy assessment aligned to their Balanced Literacy Framework (Chester, Maraschiello, & Salinger, 2000). The initial plan of the chapter's illustrative state follows in this model.

In theory, classroom-based assessments should provide a comprehensive picture of achievement and should profile students' strengths as they progress (Salinger, 2002). Standardized tests suffer in comparison because they measure students' learning at one particular time, are rarely reflective of classroom situations, and may limit the "construct" or definition of reading that is being assessed. They are prone to unexpected obstacles to good measurement, such as the "stomachache" or "itchy shirt" mentioned already, "errors" resulting from students' lack of familiarity with the fill-in-bubbles process, or even students' sensitivity to teachers' attitudes toward tests (Perrone, 1990), as illustrated in the poignant book *Miss Milarky Takes a Test* (Finchler, 2000). The measurement that results may be seriously flawed or at least questionable. Reeves and Hunt (1987) summarized the situation as follows: "The marked fluctuations in attention and mood from hour to hour, the lack of experience with the assessment situation, and the spurts and plateaus of development typical of young children combine to compromise the reliability and validity of test results" (p. 503).

However, standardized tests do carry extensive evidence about their psychometric characteristics and come with a tacit "guarantee" that they have been developed according to rigorous professional standards (American Educational Research Association, American Psychological Association, & National Council on Measurement in Education 1999), so their reports can be "trusted" to be valid and reliable measures of the constructs being measured (Shepard et. al., 1996). This "guarantee" has considerable power over many end users of the test development process. On the other hand, there are few studies that establish the psychometric and predictive properties of classroom-based assessments in the most rigorous ways. To a certain extent, the reason is that these tests are often used primarily to fine-tune instruction. Their "validation" is the effectiveness of teachers' ongoing translation of assessment data to instruction and resulting changes in student understanding; their "reliability" is shown when teachers learn to generalize about patterns of performance from child to child and can make large-scale instructional changes to suit the needs of groups of children.

Some of the few existing studies show careful attention to the psychometric characteristics of tests, including work by researchers at the Educational Testing Service (ETS) to establish the interrater reliability of scores of the South Brunswick Early Literacy Portfolio and to validate the predictive validity of its ratings of students' progress against a standardized test (Bridgeman, Chittenden, & Cline, 1995). In Texas, Hoffman and colleagues (Hoffman, Roser, & Worthy, 1998) found an R value of .86 between a theory-grounded early-grades performance assessment system, the Primary Assessment of Language Arts and Mathematics (PALM), and the Iowa Test of Basic Skills (ITBS) and further found strong teacher support for the approach.

Other studies (see Harrison & Salinger, 1998; Valencia, Hiebert, & Afflerbach, 1994) suggest that even lacking thick technical manuals about their psychometric properties, classroom-based assessments usually possess high levels of *face* validity. And this is good because it means that teachers can see the inherent benefits of the approach and value the data that result. When teachers and administrators say that standardized tests do not test what is being taught, they are saying that the tests lack face validity.

Implementing the Assessment Plan

What It Could Actually Be

Reading First has brought to the fore the possibility of nationwide use of an assessment approach that is close to what teachers seem to value for classroom use. Even though lack of proven psychometric properties disqualifies many classroom-based assessment systems for use in Reading First classrooms, many commercial assessments are classroom based and seek multiple examples of student performance as evidence of achievement. Among the most widely used are assessments that have been meticulously developed at universities and are now available through commercial vendors. These include systems such as Work Sampling, the Primary Language Record, and more recent assessments such as the Texas Primary Reading Inventory, the DIBELS, or the PALS (the Phonological Awareness Literacy Screening). Additionally, Harcourt Educational Measurement has recently began to market a new test called the Stanford Reading First, created by combining items from the SAT-9 and the SAT-10 and including an oral fluency measure. Surprisingly, the description on the Harcourt website maintains that it is somehow aligned to NAEP and the IRA/NCTE standards, neither of which addresses early-grade literacy learning.

Even commercial classroom-based assessments that collect multiple forms of evidence have higher face validity and stronger construct validity than many one-shot, paper-and-pencil tests. Their data can have immediate utility for teachers and more meaning for parents than standardized test scores. But good as the ideal of classroom-based assessment might be, there are potential problems, and the problems are exacerbated as we contemplate use of classroom-based assessments in what might be called the "pre-high-stakes" environment of early childhood grades.

Consequences at the Policy Level

The devil is in the details in planning and implementing assessments as much as anything else—and in funding them. Test development, administration, scoring, and reporting are time- and labor-intensive endeavors. The preponderance of multiple-choice tests speaks to issues of expense, not because it is necessarily cheaper to develop multiple-choice items but because they can be administered easily and scored quickly, accurately, and relatively inexpensively by machine. Results can also be returned to users and stakeholders far more rapidly than human scoring allows. In theory, getting test data quickly and knowing that it is valid mean that data can be put to immediate use to improve instruction. Classroom-based assessments are labor intensive and costly.

Building on concerns about cost, states and local education agencies must balance their receipt of Reading First funding with the accountability demands of No Child Left Behind and the testing/accountability mechanisms in non-Reading First schools. This can be a complex relationship. Test data carry considerable import in Reading First schools, more so than has been customary in many states.[2] At the classroom level, data from the assessment triad are supposed to guide instructional decisions. On a higher level, the program is supposed to run for 6 years, but if achievement does not improve by year 3, funding can be cut. As states plan for Reading First implementation and for the NCLB grade 3 reading achievement test, they can choose to run a two-pronged assessment and data-gathering system that consists of a Reading First model and a business-as-usual model in other schools. Business as usual may or may not include collecting and reporting data on literacy learning in the early grades. State administrators concerned about grade 3 reading achievement may well reason that without accountability measures in previous grades, they will have no way to anticipate what the grade 3 results will be. Requiring that data be collected and reported on all K–2 students, not just on Reading First students, would provide assurance that students are making progress toward the grade 3 achievement test, and that assurance could easily offset any changes needed to existing data-gathering mechanisms.

The ultimate policy question is whether there would be any benefit to gathering data on reading progress in all kindergarten to grade 2 classrooms, rather than assuming that local education agencies are offering sound professional development to ensure good teaching, are providing appropriate, ideally scientifically based instructional materials, and are monitoring students' progress at their level. One benefit for states, to recall Kamii (1990), is the ability to play the "looking good" game at grade 3 by ensuring that students are indeed progressing toward the achievement test that will mark the first data collection point for "adequate yearly progress."

Alignment of Reading First and other classrooms became the goal in the case-study state when Department of Education officials realized the impact that NCLB and Reading First would have on their proposed system. Its planned three-part early-grade assessment system would have been perfect for Reading First, except that the assessment system had not been completed, let alone validated psychometrically. Plans were made to validate the system through a "bridge study" using validated tests. In the meantime, the assessment system was redesigned to include an optional screening test spanning all three grades and a diagnostic measure for use once a year and to embed progress monitoring deeply into state-developed, standards-based optional instructional units. For many reasons, the pilot implementation year was not as successful as anticipated, thereby scuttling possibilities for the validation study. As local districts wrote Reading First proposals, they included tests such as DIBELS, TPRI, and Diagnostic Reading Assessment. Districts that were already using a diagnostic test of some sort asserted that they liked the commercial tests they were already using. It became clear that the state-developed test might be in jeopardy.

Consequences at the Classroom Level

The three forms of assessment to be used in Reading First classrooms will result in considerable data on student learning. In theory, this is positive, because data can inform teachers' instructional decisions. Venezky and Winfield (1979) found that consistent use of data on student performance is a hallmark of effective schools as they investigated high-poverty schools that demonstrated strong achievement. More recently, the Beat the Odds study of the Center for the Improvement of Early Reading Achievement (CIERA; Taylor, Pearson, Clark, & Walpole, 1999) reported that student achievement improved as teachers began to understand test data and its appropriate use.

However, the assessment triad introduces more than data into the classroom mix; it can also introduce negative, or at least challenging, consequences with the potential to alter the way in which teachers and students carry out their lives together. These consequences include: (1) the impact of the assessments on the role of teachers; (2) changes in the instruction offered to young students; (3) the expectations placed on students' learning; and (4) the burden imposed by the testing system. It is toward these issues that our discussion now moves, but not without noting that these are the same criticisms that have most frequently been leveled against commercial, norm-referenced tests (Johnston & Rogers, 2001; Salinger, 2001).

Impact on the Role of Teachers

The success of the assessment triad depends to a large extent on teachers. Johnston (1987) encouraged teachers to become "assessment experts," but his urging was for them to assume a different role than the one required by Reading First. Along with many other researchers, Johnston saw teachers growing in their ability to observe students and use student work as real assessment data (Engel, 1990; Salinger, 2001; South Brunswick Township Public Schools, 1992; Valencia & Place, 1994). Reading First introduces a more formal structure, which may or may not foster the kind of expertise Johnston envisioned. In Reading First classrooms, teachers will be asked to administer and score specific instruments. Many teachers will be able to accomplish these tasks successfully, but certain prerequisites must be in place:

1. Teachers must see the value of what they are doing and of the instruments they are using to assess their students.
2. The logistics of administration, scoring, and interpreting results must be clear and well articulated.
3. Teachers must have good classroom management skills or maybe small classes or both.

These requirements are by no means inconsequential.

Value

Value is more than an affective dimension. It relates directly to the face validity of the instruments teachers must use; and use of the instruments and their data have the potential to influence consequential validity, that is, what happens in the classroom as a result of the assessment system. In actuality, teachers may simply not see the value in what they are being asked to do. A study conducted in South Brunswick (Salinger & Chittenden, 1994) found that teachers eventually accepted the Early Literacy Assessment as a routine part of teaching but did not see it as directly affecting their teaching; consequential validity was low. More recently, Block, Oakas, and Hurt (2002) compared the aspects of literacy instruction, from kindergarten through grade 5, that classroom teachers and researchers said they valued most. The study reported no mention of knowledge about assessment, skill in actually conducting effective assessments, nor the importance of using assessment data, even classroom-generated, as valuable professional goals.

In the case-study state, as in many other test development projects, committees of teachers were involved in crafting the assessment, with the ostensible goal of transferring "ownership" from the small number of participants to the teaching force as a whole. As the assessment design changed, however, administrators at the state Department of Education made many of the decisions, overriding some of the beliefs that teachers had brought to the development process. For example, teachers studied their detailed early literacy standards to categorize benchmarks and indicators as appropriate for formal one-on-one testing versus curriculum-embedded observational assessment strategies. Doing so gave them insight into the state's intended curriculum. However, state department officials determined that teachers would take the standards, benchmarks, and indicators seriously only if each one was tested with at least one discrete item, even if the indicator addressed developmental milestones such as writing one's name. This extreme interpretation of "what gets tested gets taught" atomized the early literacy curriculum.

Logistics

Valuing them or not, teachers will be required to work these assessments into the fabric of their classrooms. Intense training and professional development are essential (Shepard, Taylor, & Kagan 1996). Salinger and Chittenden (1994) found that teachers in South Brunswick stated that ongoing professional development was missing after the first few years of implementation of the Early Literacy Portfolio. "Novice" teachers depended on "veterans" to teach them how to use the system appropriately, but the "training" was often incidental and insufficient.

If teachers are not well trained and if manuals are not detailed, assessment results will likely be suspect. If the direct implications of assessment data are not clear, teachers will not be able to use them effectively. Faced with data they do not understand or that do not confirm their sense of their students' achievement, teachers often default to their own observations and intuitive assessment devices so that they can maintain an even instructional direction. Research has affirmed that teachers' observations and ratings (Hecht & Greenfield, 2001; Price, Schwabacher, & Chittenden, 1994) often have strong correlations with test data and may even provide more accurate information about students' actual achievement. Defaulting to more intuitive approaches to assessment will not be possible in Reading First classrooms, as the comprehensive reading program and assessment requirements will undoubtedly put tight limits on what teachers can do.

Consider another example from the illustrative state. Train-the-trainer workshops were conducted throughout the state on how to administer and score the assessments; trainers went away with their mandate to train others. Teachers complained that the training was not sufficient. Further, in some pilot sites, teachers were supposed to collect data on handheld electronic devices, but the training had not fully covered the technology aspects of data collection. In such situations, resulting test data include a measure of teachers' frustration, along with evidence of student achievement.

Classroom Management

Teachers' classroom management skills or the availability of teacher aides will contribute to the assessment system in Reading First classrooms. Peter Johnston (1987) wrote that "simple classroom management skills are part of evaluation expertise. Without a well managed classroom in which children have learned to work independently, a teacher cannot step back from instruction and watch the class as a whole, or work uninterrupted with particular individuals" (p. 745).

More recently, a member of the Bias and Fairness Committee reviewing test material in that illustrative state commented that it wouldn't matter how fair, unbiased, or sensitive material on the test was; the basic unfairness in the system would be the disparate quality of classroom management skills among the state's early-grade teachers.

Impact on Instruction

Perrone (1990) suggested that "used as they are in many settings for major educational decisions, the various tests clearly limit the educational possibilities of children" (p. 3). His statement is no less true for classroom-based assessments than for commercial standardized tests. When districts or states develop their own early literacy assessments, they shape them to their state standards or, more often, to their collective vision of what literacy learning is all about. This effort produces what is often called "curriculum alignment" and can lead to seamlessness between instruction and testing. This seamlessness does not come easily, though, as it results not merely from handing teachers explanatory documentation but from extensive, congruent, and participatory professional development that helps teachers understand the theoretical and practical underpinnings of what is usually called the "intended curriculum." Creating such a seamless assessment system was the initial intent of the midwestern state: Assessments were to be aligned to the very detailed state standards and would be introduced accompanied by extensive professional development.

The same seamlessness of curriculum and instruction is a goal for Reading First classrooms—and is probably the federal goal for all early instruction built on findings of scientific research on reading acquisition (National Reading Panel, 2000). There are definite guidelines to help state and local education agencies (LEAs) achieve congruency with scientifically based reading research across core reading programs, supplemental material, and assessments. For example, *A Consumer's Guide to Evaluating a Core Reading Program, Grades K–3: A Critical Elements Analysis* (Simmons & Kame'enui, 2000) directs users through the process of selecting a reading series to use as the "core" or "base" instructional material for beginning reading. These programs must emphasize the five essential components of reading (phonemic awareness, phonics, fluency, vocabulary, and comprehension) and must be supported with ample scientific research.

Finding congruent assessments is not always an easy task, and very often a system must be cobbled together to accomplish the goal of three levels of assessment that can validly assess the five essential components of reading. Common instruments such as the TPRI, DIBELS, or PALS, which have been specifically designed for classroom use, cannot offer the full range of constructs and purposes required, leading to the need for specialized tests or batteries of tests. For example, *A Practical Guide to Reading Assessments* (Kame'enui, Simmons, & Cornachione, 2000) states that the DIBELS is appropriate for screening, progress monitoring, and skill grouping but should be used for diagnosis *only* of alphabetic understanding through its nonsense word-fluency measure. The Florida Center for Reading Research (2003) deems the TPRI acceptable for diagnosing problems in phonemic awareness, phonics, listening vocabulary at kindergarten only, and comprehension. Some of the assessments considered appropriate for diagnosis, such as the Peabody Picture Vocabulary Test, ought to be conducted in a clinical interview and require considerable technical expertise to administer and score.

A Practical Guide to Reading Assessments lists many more tests as appropriate for screening and progress monitoring, rather than for diagnosis. For its purposes, screening tests are used as an initial measure, and progress monitoring is defined as "repeated assessments of a skill area or areas, over time, to evaluate individual progress. Assessment results are sensitive to small changes in student performance, quick and easy to administer, and include alternate forms for repeated measurement" (Kame'enui, Simmons, & Cornachione, 2000, p. 3). Progress monitoring, as defined in this way, becomes an external measure, distinct from classroom teachers' frequent observations and from assessments included in the core reading program. Indeed, Reading First guidance requires that progress monitoring instruments be used three times per year, hardly the sort of curriculum-embedded assessment frequently used to monitor growth.

Cumulatively, the assessments will shape the curriculum, even more so than the selected reading program. The major reading programs warranted to be based on SBRR are remarkably similar, varying primarily in the level of scriptedness or direction to teachers on what to say in each lesson.[3] Many of the assessments currently available are quite specialized: They assess what they purport to assess, and most often it is phonemic awareness and phonics. If they try to assess vocabulary, it is often done in isolation from real text. The emphasis on phonemic awareness and other basic skill elements of reading may overshadow the implied "balance" of instructional emphases in the five components of reading, especially for students who continue to struggle even when given a heavy diet of phonemic awareness and phonics.

Teaching to the test, which Popham (2000) has recently called the "score-boosting game," is highly likely. Thus classroom-based assessments, supposedly sensitive to students' learning trajectories, may become as static as external norm-referenced instruments—and just as powerful in determining what gets taught. They have the potential to limit teachers' view of early literacy curriculum to a focus on the enabling skills that are only part of what young students should be learning and practicing as they move toward literacy.

Such a focus has been found to be shortsighted. For example, Knapp (1995) found that effective teachers of low-income students balance instruction in high levels of thinking skills with instruction in more foundational skills. Doing so helps students understand from their earliest experiences that the goal of reading is to obtain meaning from print. Teaching to the atomized units of many early literacy tests may produce good test scores, but later comprehension tests will show this initial achievement to be hollow.

Expectations for Student Learning

Focusing on enabling skills because they constitute the major target of Reading First assessment can also shape expectations for students' learning, obscuring the fact that what will ultimately be measured is application of a unified body of strategies and skills orchestrated to make sense out of continuous text. The timetable for deemphasizing enabling skills and focusing on comprehension varies in Reading First state plans and in their choice of assessments. This timetable is important because it helps define expectations for students' achievement at the individual level and also at the level of aggregate data for accountability purposes. NCLB and Reading First have placed beginning and end points on the timetable, aligning them with state standards, along with screening tests at entry to kindergarten and grade 3 reading achievement tests. Administration of the NAEP in reading at grade 4 might well be considered as part of this timetable as well.

State standards cannot necessarily offset an emphasis on enabling skills in Reading First assessments. Wixson and Dutro (1988) examined 14 sets of state standards and found considerable variability in how standards statements were arranged (distinguished grade by grade or arranged in clusters of grades) and in the specificity with which learning goals are stated. They cautioned that "the way reading is parsed is likely to have a significant impact on how local curriculum is organized, how instructional time is spent, how assessments are developed and configured, and how student achievement is communicated to external audiences" (p. 10).

Wixson and Dutro (1988) found much more specificity in statements describing learning goals for enabling skills than for comprehension, stating, however, that too great a level of detail could decrease the coherence of the vision for learning that the documents sought to present. This is an interesting conundrum, which has more relevance than ever in light of the specificity of assessment and instructional practices required by Reading First. Teachers in Reading First classrooms must employ specific reading programs and use specific assessments within a state or local context that may "parse" kindergarten to grade 3 reading learning in vague or contradictory ways. If the state standards are not strong—if they exclude important content or place disproportionate emphasis on enabling skills— teachers may actually benefit from a clear-cut set of instructional guidelines and expectations for students' progress. However, if state standards lay out a clear, well-grounded trajectory of early learning that culminates in strong skills for independent reading, the ne-

cessity of teaching to tests that emphasize enabling skills over comprehension may violate what Wixson and Dutro (1988) refer to as a state's "clarity of the curriculum path."

To be in accordance with NCLB, the curriculum path for all students—Reading First and others—ought to be toward achievement on the grade 3 reading achievement test. This test will evaluate achievement over the previous years of school and will provide important data for states' measure of "adequate yearly progress." Cut scores and standards set for this test (and for subsequent reading tests in grades 4 to 8) will express states' expectations for student learning. Although state standards will dictate the balance of enabling skills and comprehension on this test, it will do no child good to avoid the need for a solid measure of how the enabling skills can be orchestrated in real reading.

Many of the common classroom-based early literacy assessments do not do a thorough job of testing comprehension. Of the tests reviewed, Kame'enui (1999) singles out only three as based. Table 29.2 compares some of the characteristics of these tests to illustrate that although these are primarily individually administered, they do not fall under the general rubric of "classroom-based assessments" that can provide teachers the information they need to monitor progress. Only the Qualitative Reading Inventory, 2nd edition (Leslie & Caldwell, 1995) is an informal measure that can readily be administered by teachers. It includes graded reading passages for comprehension assessment. *The Guide* (Kame'enui et al., 2000), however, cautions that it may be "time-consuming" to administer, an important consideration in an individually administered test.

These tests described in Table 29.2 cannot be used for progress monitoring, so even if they are chosen for use as screening or diagnostic instruments, their impact on expectations for comprehension growth would probably be limited. It will be the progressing monitoring instruments, with limited emphasis on comprehension that will most substantially influence the day-to-day parsing of reading and the interim expectations for students' achievement. These interim expectations may well be discongruent with grade 3 expectations, and students in Reading First classes may appear to be doing well as they

TABLE 29.2. Comparison of Commonly Used Early Reading Tests.

Test	Comprehensive	Informal measure	Diagnostic	Screening	Progress monitoring	Group or individual	Timed	Training
Reading Ready: Woodcock Mastery Test, Revised	Yes	No	Yes	Yes	No	I	No	Yes
Diagnostic Reading Scales	Yes	No	Yes	Yes	No	I	No	Yes
Qualitative Reading Inventory II	Yes	Yes	Yes	Yes	No	I	No	No
Peabody Individual Achievement Test—Revised	Yes	No	Yes	Yes	No	I	Yes	Yes
Stanford Diagnostic Reading Test–4	No	No	Yes	Yes	No	G	No	Yes
Test of Reading Comprehension 3 (TORC-3)	No	No	Yes	Yes	No	I	No	Yes
Gates–MacGinite Reading Tests, third edition	No	No	Yes	Yes	No	G	Yes	Yes

move forward, whereas, in fact, the "big picture" goal of putting enabling skills to work in real reading situations is sidelined. Interim results may show that students are meeting interim expectations—perhaps even doing very well—but the data will be deceptive. This focus on interim expectations—and applause at their being met—is a good example of testing to accomplish what Kamii (1990, p. ii) referred to as the "looking good game." It can lead, unfortunately, to another game, the "pass the buck game," which is played out when more comprehensive expectations are not met. Upper-grade teachers, administrators, parents, the press, and others pass responsibility on to teachers in earlier grades, wondering "what were they teaching?" that produced poor test results. Playing this game has some interesting twists if grade 3 achievement data from Reading First schools do not show improvement and if grade 4 NAEP reading scores do not begin to ascend nationally, in state-by-state comparisons, and in the large urban districts participating in the Trial Urban Assessment component of NAEP.

One perhaps sanguine view of this situation is that the K–2 assessments should "pre-dict" performance at grade 3, but this view is shortsighted both conceptually and instructionally. Predictive validity is a slippery concept, as illustrated by the following segment of an e-mail exchange on the topic, which Kame'enui cited in his 2002 report on early-grade reading assessments. That the comment refers to screening instruments does not mean that it cannot be generalized to progress monitoring tests or other instruments used to assess early reading. "The most fundamental criterion for a good screening instrument is to have good predictive validity. Of course, the instrument must have reasonable reliability in order to achieve good predictive validity. However, good reliability does not guarantee that the test is a valid predictor. One problem is that the standard for exactly what good predictive validly is not as well worked out as the standards for reliability" (p. 70). The psychometric constructs of reliability and validity are difficult enough to achieve in standardized measures of early reading; they are elusive indeed in tests administered by classroom teachers to their familiar, trusting young students.

It is not just Donald Graves (2002) who is saying that testing is not teaching. Bob Linn (Linn, Baker, Betebenner, 2002) has questioned whether gains on state- or district-mandated tests generalize to other measures of achievement, such as NAEP. The question stems from "concerns that the narrow focus on teaching to a state test may produce inflated gains in scores. ... The fundamental concern [ought to be] with improved achievement, not just higher test scores" (p. 6). For several reasons, the real target might best be the grade 4 NAEP reading assessment. First, NAEP is a reading comprehension test, a curriculum-free measure whose achievement level statements are serious statements of competence. NAEP assumes that even grade 4 students have learned to orchestrate reading strategies and skills very well. Second, NAEP will play a role in determining how states are progressing toward the 12-year goal of improved student achievement. States and large urban districts that want to continue to receive Title I funding must participate in the NAEP reading assessment.

Intrusion into Classroom Time

Finally, it is important to consider the intrusion that the Reading First assessment triad can have on teachers and students' lives. This intrusion is often referred to as a burden. Herein lies a major dilemma in classroom-based assessment and a subtle irony. Standardized tests are quick to administer; classroom-based assessments are not, especially if their use for accountability requires some standardized administration procedures. They should be administered at numerous times during the year in systematic, standard ways; and they must produce credible, unambiguous evidence. That's a tall order. Educators, parents, and unions complain about the ways in which standardized tests rob students of teaching time, but classroom-based assessments can do the same thing, especially if the assessment requires teachers to administer tasks individually. No one will dispute the value of one-on-one interaction with students over varied aspects of literacy learning, and, indeed, Reading First is to be lauded for supporting this model. But this interaction can be costly in terms of time and energy.

The case-study state has only recently conducted its initial round of competitions for Reading First district grants; districts seem to be selecting the DIBELS, TPRI, and Terra Nova as their tests. The Department of Education had been conducting a validation study of the new assessment system so that it could be ready for use in Reading First classrooms, but as previously suggested, this plan has encountered problems. The initial design of the assessment system would have required kindergarten teachers to spend approximately 165 minutes of testing time per student. With a class of 25 students, that's almost 69 hours per year; double that if a district has half-day kindergarten programs. The plan was winnowed down somewhat, but during its first year of implementation, teachers found the assessment still so burdensome that they started to complain. Their complaints reached not just principals but also their unions and ultimately their legislators. The core screening test took approximately 50 minutes per child to administer and was supposed to be administered multiple times per year. Reacting to the situation, the legislature has suspended its mandated testing program and given the department a year to streamline the instruments and find better ways to manage the administration process. Many districts are already using DIBELS or TPRI, and within the year set aside to solve the problem, more and more districts will be rolling out Reading First plans. It is anyone's guess whether the state-developed test will survive.

Other states are struggling with the assessment issue as well. District plans from several states reveal a wide range of tests proposed for use. For example, the plan for the largest district in one recently funded state listed 13 distinct tests, ranging from the Brigance to the DIBELS to Jerry Johns's Informal Reading Inventory (Johns, 2001). Two other districts in the state whose plans were studied listed a total of 19 completely different tests, including one district that included the generic category of "teacher-made tests." Many of the suggested tests would probably not pass muster according to most criteria for Reading First use; however, they have inherent value because they test students in their home languages. In this particular state, home languages include Spanish, as well as several Native American languages.

Many other district plans suggest continued use of familiar assessments. Mention of Clay's assessments, Gentry's spelling test, and letter-identification and sight-word tests show recognition of some of the foundational approaches to classroom-based assessment (Salinger, 2002). These instruments, not grounded in scientific research (Kame'enui, 2002), will have to be replaced, and teachers will have to be retrained. Many replacements, such as the Gates–McGinite or the Woodcock–Johnson, are most frequently used for clinical diagnosis by reading specialists; they require specialized training for smooth administration and accurate analysis of results. An analysis of Reading First plans indicates that, even if trained teams of test administrators conduct initial rounds of testing, the task most often will devolve to teachers. The analysis further indicates that the test administrators are often district reading coaches whose real focus within Reading First schools is to mentor and support teachers, not to pull students from classes for testing.

As previously stated, the Reading First triad of assessments will give teachers copious amounts of data about students. But that is positive only so long as the data can be interpreted correctly. The CIERA study (Taylor, Pearson, Clark, & Walpole, 1999) used data interpretation and use as the core of professional development—a highly time-intensive undertaking. Participating teachers learned to value assessment data because they could understand it, and they also learned that assessment data should be used in conjunction with their own less formal "data" about students. Reading First cannot mandate that this kind of professional development be brought to scale, especially as teachers work to master SBRR instructional strategies and comprehensive reading programs that may be new to them. States and districts, hard pressed to live up to their Reading First proposals, may let understanding of assessments fall lower and lower on their list of goals.

If teachers do not understand test data and if they are not empowered to use their own knowledge base to offset data that seem inappropriate, assessments will result in numerous false positives and false negatives, leading to wrong instructional decisions. The technical report for the TPRI (Foorman et al., 1998; Center for Academic and Reading Skills & Texas Institute for Measurement, Evaluation, and Statistics, 1998–1999) acknowledge that the link between test constructs and actual reading skills is not a simple one and that "false positive errors may reflect the assessment of children from communities where many families have limited resources and are from diverse cultural and linguistic backgrounds with less exposure to English literacy-related activities" (p. 12). Similarly Hintze, Ryan, and Stoner (2001), studying the concurrent validity and diagnostic accuracy of the DIBELS, found that the DIBELS recommended cut scores that were so sensitive that "use of these cut-scores led to a very high percentage of true positives; however, this came at the expense of an exceeding number of false-positives" (Hintze, Ryan, & Stoner, p. 16). Thus students were undoubtedly kept from instruction that could help them progress.

It is easy to see that Reading First will place a huge assessment burden on teachers and their students, one that may not even result in accurate data. Causes of faulty data will be many, including contextual factors inherent in students and in classrooms, teachers' lack of understanding and skills, and mismatch of tests and the purposes for which they are used. As in the illustrative state, one can easily see the proposed Reading First assessment system imploding.

Revisiting Where We Are

Given the influence that tests can have on instruction and expectations for learning, the burden they place on teachers and students, and the likelihood of misunderstanding data, one has to question what this kind of testing will do to the fabric of classroom life and when the testing reaches a point of diminishing returns for all concerned. Such questioning becomes even more acute when one thinks about the individual teachers and young learners behind the debates. These are individuals who have their own strengths, weaknesses, and expectations and who differ along social, cultural, linguistic, and motivational dimensions.

First there are the children, who usually come to school full of motivation to learn to read. Sometimes, however, they move through school with labels and accompanying expectations that are hard to shake. These labels often reflect the neighborhoods the kids live in, the languages spoken in their homes, or their home environments in general: crack baby, homeless, non-English speaker. Labels may also be derived from early childhood testing. Writing about state-mandated screening tests administered prior to kindergarten entry, Ellwein and her colleagues (1990) suggested that this practice led to "preflunking" (p. 160) students with tests administered in the spring or summer prior to anticipated kindergarten entry and to relegating them to the "ghetto" of junior kindergartens that were supposed to get kids "ready" for entry into "real" school (p. 170). The amount of testing that is currently being advocated can have the same result: assigning children to specific categories early in their school careers, limiting expectations for their progress, and routing students into steady diets of instruction that may limit rather than expand their chances for success.

In an entirely different way, Valencia and Buly (2004) categorized and labeled students who had failed a state reading test. They studied the performance of these students on a battery of diagnostic tests and found 10 specific clusters among these low-performing children. Only two of the clusters were truly disabled readers. It is interesting to contrast these clusters with the clusters of behaviors of beginning readers identified in the ETS early-reading study that was originally published in the mid-1980s and recently reanalyzed (Chittenden & Salinger, 2001). *Inquiry into Meaning*, along with other studies, makes the strong case that students differ in the patterns they adopt as they learn to read and that the best way to assess students is for teachers to look at and think carefully about what students are demonstrating in a comprehensive way. Comparing these two patterns of children's interactions with reading suggest that if teachers were able to take the time to look closely at how kids orchestrate the learning-to-read process, they might be able to identify some of the subtle behavior patterns that may lead to poor test performance. Table 29.3 presents such a comparison.

What is significant about the ETS study is that teachers identified these clusters by close observation of students and thoughtful anal-

ysis of work products, not through administration of series of assessment instruments. True, teachers were working together under the guidance of skilled leaders, but they were not dependent on external measures. In a similar vein, Meisels and Piker (2001) found that students in classes using the Work Sampling System, which scaffolds teachers' close analysis of student work, actually did better on a standardized reading test at grade 3 than students in a demographically matched class without the Work Sampling System. This suggests that teachers who are trained to depend on their own skilled (or scaffolded) analytic skills can gather and use significant data about their students.

Further, Hecht and Greenfield (2001) investigated first-grade teachers' ratings of students' potential predictors of reading success or difficulty at grade 3. They found that teachers were able to classify students into grade 3 reading groups with a relatively high level of accuracy (73% of the time) and that the accuracy of teachers' predictions was similar to that of predictions made by using a letter–word identification test, a comprehension test, and the Peabody Picture Vocabulary Test standard score. One wonders what teachers making these predictions thought about their own powers to teach successfully, but the point of their ability to put aside their egos and make accurate predictions is a good one.

Finally, one more study bears on the test-then-intervene-then-test again model that undergirds Reading First and other programs. Four Canadian researchers (Phillips, Norris, Osmond, & Maynard, 2002) conducted a longitudinal study of the relative reading achievement of 187 students in a rural district of Newfoundland. They wanted to test the long-accepted tenet that reading achievement is largely immutable from early to later grades in school, that is, to see if children whom tests classified as poor readers remained poor readers. The immutability perspective is a cornerstone of belief in early, intense phonemic awareness and phonics instruction. The researchers tested students at different points in the grade 1 to grade 6 span and classified them into below-average, average, and above-average bands. Per district policy, teachers focused on teaching and did not offer intervention programs. The researchers looked at students' trajectory from grade 1 to grade 6 under "business as usual"

TABLE 29.3. Comparison of Clusters of Student Reading Behaviors.

Chittenden and Salinger (2001) clusters of behaviors of beginning readers

Style	Cluster A	Cluster B
Preferred expression of meaning	Imaginative and divergent	Realistic and convergent
Manner of work	Mobile and fluid	Contained and methodical
Attentional scope and emphasis	Broad and integrative	Narrowed and analytical
Sequencing of thought processes	Parallel sequencing	Linear sequencing
Manifestation of styles in reading behavior	*Upholding momentum* • After-the-fact corrections • Skipping over words • Inventing/omitting portions of text • Reading broad spans of text • Substitutions based on memory, picture cues, etc. • Erring with confidence/fixing up—"oops!" corrections	*Striving for accuracy* • Before-the-fact corrections by attending to every word • Asking for help, applying word attack painstakingly • Considerable wait time for help, inspiration (30–60 seconds of quiet) • No guessing • Determination to get each word RIGHT

Buly and Valencia (2002) clusters of reading behaviors of students who failed their state reading test

Clusters 1 and 2:
Automatic word callers (18%):

• Fail to read for meaning
• May be reading too fast
• Can write—except in response to reading
• May have limited vocabulary or know surface language

Cluster 3:
Struggling word callers (15%)

• Relatively good fluency
• Some difficulty in word ID
• Word attack and word ID may be uneven
• May have vocabulary problems
• Belief that good reading is fast reading
• May read too fast

Cluster 4: Word stumblers (18%)

• Meaning as a relative strength
• Word ID as problem
• Slow reader
• Knows meanings
• Can get overall meaning of text
• Understands that reading should make sense
• Needs phonics as word attack strategy, overreliance on context

Clusters 5 and 6:
Slow and steady comprehenders (24%)

• Proficient writers
• Slow readers—very low rate
• Word ID and comprehension abilities are relatively strong
• Do not need phonics—difficulty with multisyllabic words
• Tendency to self-correct
• Extremely slow reading rate coupled with strong comprehension
• Lack of automatic word ID
• Probably limited enjoyment of reading

Clusters 7 and 8:
Slow word callers (17%)

• Like clusters 1 and 2 but lack fluency
• "Accurate readers who are both slow and struggle with meaning"
• Lack of prerequisite skills in fluency and meaning, not necessarily in word ID
• Slowing down to attend to comprehension but slowing down so much they have difficulty remembering

Clusters 9 and 10:
Disabled readers (9%)

• Low in all three areas

conditions and found that early labeling as good or poor readers did not necessarily hold up over time. In fact, "for children who were below average in first grade, there was an approximately equal probability that they would be below average *or* average in sixth grade, with a greater probability of improvement found among girls than among boys" (2002, p. 5; emphasis added). For other children, there seemed to be an overwhelming probability that young "average" readers would stay average, but only a 48 to 52% chance that young "above average" readers will continue in that category. This study strongly suggests that students' early reading performance is not the only indicator of their reading level at later grades. That's a provocative idea to consider when one thinks about translating scientifically based research into practice.

Teachers differ in their skill levels, understanding of literacy and of instruction, and ability to do a good job in a high-stakes environment. Teachers are being asked to teach in accord with practices supported by scientifically based reading research (the SBRR of NCLB). Yet they are not necessarily being asked to look at students and understand what they are seeing. The currently accepted model of a three-part assessment system has the capacity to hone teachers' skills in looking at students and understanding their behaviors, but it may not accomplish this goal. Instead, it has the capacity to regiment teachers and their teaching in unprecedented ways and result simply in more testing.

Notes

1. Although not the focus of this chapter, the Head Start National Reporting System, which will instantiate academic testing in all Head Start programs, is another example of the proliferation of testing of young children.
2. The *Guide* was developed with funding from the U.S. Department of Education Office of Planning and Evaluation and distributed jointly with the International Reading Association.
3. Analysis of Reading First plans suggests that Reading Mastery, Open Court, Harcourt Trophies, Houghton Mifflin Reading: The Nation's Choice, and McGraw-Hill Reading 2003 are the most widely proposed series; of these, Reading Mastery is the most distinct, demarked by its high level of scriptedness.

References

American Educational Research Association, American Psychological Association, & National Council on Measurement in Education. (1999). *Standards for educational and psychological testing.* Washington, DC. American Educational Research Association.

Block, C. C., Oakas, M., & Hurt, N. (2002). The expertise of literacy teachers: A continuum from preschool to grade 5. *Reading Research Quarterly, 37,* 178–206.

Brenna, S. (2003, November 9). The littlest test takers. *New York Times Education Life,* [Supplement], pp. 32–33.

Bridgeman, B., Chittenden, E., & Cline, F. (1995). *Characteristics of a portfolio scale for rating early literacy.* Princeton, NJ: Educational Testing Center.

Center for Academic and Reading Skills & Texas Institute for Measurement, Evaluation, and Statistics. (1998–1999). *Technical Report: Texas Primary Reading Inventory.* Houston: University of Texas–Houston Health Science Center & University of Houston.

Chester, M., Maraschiello, R., & Salinger, T. (2000, April). *K–3 assessments in Philadelphia: Innovation and reality.* Paper presented at the conference of the American Educational Research Association, New Orleans, LA.

Chittenden, E., & Salinger, T. (2001). *Inquiry into meaning: An investigation of learning to read.* New York: Teachers College Press.

Ellwein, M. C., Walsh, D. J., Eads, G. M., & Miller, A. (1990). Using readiness tests to route kindergarten students: The snarled intersection of psychometrics, policy, and practice. *Educational Evaluation and Policy Analysis, 13,* 159–175.

Engel, B. (1990). An approach to assessment in early literacy. In C. Kamii (Ed.), *Achievement testing in the early grades: The games grown-ups play* (pp. 119–134). Washington, DC: National Association for the Education of Young Children.

Falk, B. (1998). Using direct evidence to assess student progress: How the Primary Language Record supports teaching and learning. In C. Harrison & T. Salinger (Eds.) *Assessing reading: 1. Theory and practice* (pp. 152–165). London: Routledge.

Finchler, J. (2000). *Testing Miss Malarkey.* New York: Walker.

Florida Center for Reading Research. (2003). Diagnostic tools appropriate for primary and secondary grades. Retrieved November 11, 2003, from http://www.fcrr.org/assessment/diagnostictools.htm

Foorman, B. R., Fletcher, J. M., Francis, D. J., Carlson, C. D., Chen, D, Mouziaki, A., et al. (1998). Technical Report: *Texas Primary Reading Inventory* [Tech. Rep.]. Austin: Texas Education Agency.

Graves, D. H. (2001). *Testing is not teaching: What*

should count in education. Portsmouth, NH: Heinemann.

Hart, B., & Risley, T. R. (1995). *Meaningful differences in the everyday experiences of young American children.* Baltimore: Brookes.

Hecht, S. A., & Greenfield, D. B. (2001). Comparing the predictive validity of first grade teacher ratings and reading-related tests on third grade levels of reading skills in young children exposed to poverty. *School Psychology Review, 30,* 50–69.

Hintze, J. M., Ryan, A. L., & Stoner, G. (2001). *Concurrent validity and diagnostic accuracy of the Dynamic Indicators of Basic Early Literacy Skills and the Comprehensive Test of Phonological Processing* (Technical Report). Amherst, MA: University of Massachusetts.

Hoffman, J., Roser, N., & Worthy, J. (1998). Challenging the assessment context for literacy instruction in first grade: A collaborative study. In C. Harrison & T. Salinger (Eds.) *Assessing reading: 1. Theory and practice* (pp. 166–181). London: Routledge.

Johns, J. (2001). *Basic reading inventory.* Dubuque, IO: Kendall/Hunt.

Johnston, P. (1987). Teachers as evaluation experts. *The Reading Teacher, 40,* 744–748.

Johnston, P. H., & Rogers, R. (2001). Early literacy development: The case for "informed assessment." In S. B. Neuman & D. K. Dickinson (Eds.) *Handbook of early literacy research* (pp. 377–389). New York: Guilford Press.

Kame'enui, E. J. (2002). *An analysis of reading assessment instruments for K–3.* Eugene, OR: University of Oregon Institute for the Development of Educational Achievement.

Kame'enui, E. J., Simmons, D., & Cornachione, C. (2000). *A practical guide to reading assessments.* Washington, DC: U.S. Department of Education & Newark, DE: International Reading Association.

Kamii, C. (Ed.). (1990). *Achievement testing in the early grades: The games grown-ups play.* Washington, DC: National Association for the Education of Young Children.

Knapp, M. S. (1995). *Teaching for meaning in high-poverty classrooms.* New York: Teachers College Press.

Linn, R. L., Baker, E. L., & Betebenner, D. W. (2002). Accountability systems: Implications of requirements of the "No Child Left Behind Act of 2001." *Educational Researcher, 31*(6), 3–26.

Meisels, S. J. (1996). Performance in context: Assessing children's achievement at the outset of school In A. J. Sameroff & M. M. Haith (Eds.) *The five-to-seven year shift: The age of reason and responsibility* (pp. 410–431). Chicago: University of Chicago Press.

Meisels, S. J. (1998). *Assessing readiness.* [CIERA Report No. 3-002]. Ann Arbor, MI: University of Michigan Center for the Improvement of Early Reading Achievement.

Meisels, S. J., & Piker, R. (2001). *An analysis of early literacy assessments used for instruction.* Ann Arbor, MI: Center for the Improvement of Early Reading Achievement.

Michigan Department of Education. (1998). *Michigan in literacy progress portfolio.* East Lansing, MI: Author.

National Association for the Education of Young Children. (1988). NAEYC position statement on standardized testing of young children 3–8 years of age. *Young Children, 43*(3), 42–47.

National Commission on Excellence in Education. (1983). *A nation at risk: The imperative for educational reform.* Washington, DC: Author.

National Education Goals Panel. (1989). *Principles and recommendations for early childhood assessment.* Washington, DC: Author.

National Reading Panel. (2002). *Report of the National Reading Panel: Teaching children to read.* Washington, DC: Author.

New York State Department of Education. (1999). *Early literacy profile.* Albany: Author.

Perrone, V. (1990). How did we get here? In C. Kamii (Ed.), *Achievement testing in the early grades: The games grown-ups play* (pp. 1–14). Washington, DC: National Association for the Education of Young Children.

Phillips, L. M., Norris, S. P., Osmond, W. C., & Maynard, A. G. (2002). Relative reading achievement: A longitudinal study of 187 children from first through sixth grade. *Journal of Educational Psychology, 94,* 3–13.

Popham, W. J. (2000). *Testing! Testing! What every parent should know about school tests.* Boston: Allyn & Bacon.

Price, J., Schwabacher, S., & Chittenden, T. (1994). *The multiple forms of evidence study: Assessing reading through student work samples, teacher observation, and tests.* New York: National Center for Restructuring Education, Schools, and Teaching.

Reeves, R. E., & Holt, I. S. (1987). Children and school entry decisions. In A. Thomas & J. Grimes (Eds.) *Children's needs: Psychological perspectives* (pp. 499–505). Kent, OH: National Association at School Psychologists.

Riddle Buly, M., & Valencia, S. W. (2002). Below the bar: Profiles of students who fail state reading assessments. *Educational Evaluation and Policy Analysis, 24,* 219–239.

Salinger, T. (1998). Consequential validity of an early literacy portfolio: The "backwash" of reform. In C. Harrison & T. Salinger (Eds.) *Assessing reading: 1. Theory and practice* (pp. 182–204). London: Routledge.

Salinger, T. (2001). Assessing the literacy of young children: The case for multiple forms of evidence. In S. B. Neuman & D. K. Dickinson (Eds.), *Handbook of early literacy research* (pp. 390–418). New York: Guilford Press.

Salinger, T., & Chittenden, E. (1994). Analysis of an early literacy portfolio: Consequence for instruction. *Language Arts, 71,* 446–452.

Shepard, L. A. (1991). The influence of standardized tests on early childhood curriculum, teachers, and children. In B. Spodek & O. N. Saracho (Eds.), *Yearbook in early childhood education* (Vol. 2). New York: Teachers College Press.

Shepard, L. A. (1994). The challenges of assessing young children appropriately. *Phi Delta Kappan, 76*(3), 206–213.

Shepard, L. A. (1997). Children not ready to learn? The invalidity of school readiness testing. *Psychology in the Schools, 34*(2), 85–97.

Shepard, L. A. (2000). The role of assessment in a learning culture. *Educational Researcher, 29,* 4–14.

Shepard, L. A., Flexer, R. J., Hiebert, E. H., Marion, S. F., Mayfield, V., & Weston, J. T. (1996). Effects of introducing classroom performance assessments on student learning. *Educational Measurement: Issues and Practice, 15*(3), 7–18.

Shepard, L. A., Taylor, G. A., & Kagan, S. L. (1996). *Trends in early childhood assessment and policies.* Boulder, CO: Center for Research on Evaluation, Standards, and Student Testing.

Simmons, D. C., & Kame'enui, E. J. (2000). *A consumer's guide to evaluating a core reading program, grades K–3: A critical elements analysis.* Eugene, OR: University of Oregon National Center to Improve the Tools of Educators.

South Brunswick Township Public Schools. (1992). *Early childhood education in South Brunswick schools: A guide for parents and children.* South Brunswick NJ: Author.

Taylor, B. M., Pearson, P. D., Clark, K. F., & Walpole, S. (1999). *Beating the odds in teaching all children to read.* CLERA Report #2-006. Ann Arbor, MI: University of Michigan Center for the Improvement of Early Reading.

Valencia, S. W., & Buly, M. R. (2004). Behind test scores: What struggling readers really need. *The Reading Teacher, 57,* 520–531.

Valencia, S. W., Hiebert, E. H., & Afflerbach, P. P. (Eds.). (1994). *Authentic reading assessment: Practices and possibilities.* Newark, DE: International Reading Association.

Valencia, S. W., & Place, N. A. (1994). Literacy portfolios for teaching, learning, and accountability: The Bellevue Literacy Assessment Project. In S. W. Valencia, E. H. Hiebert, & P. P. Afflerbach (Eds.), *Authentic reading assessment: Practices and possibilities.* (pp. 134–156). Newark, DE: International Reading Association.

Valencia, S. W., & Wixson, K. K. (1999). *Policy-oriented research on literacy standards and assessments* (CIERA Report #3-004). Ann Arbor: University of Michigan Center for the Improvement of Early Reading Achievement.

Venezky, R. L., & Winfield, L. F. (1979). *Schools that succeed beyond expectations in teaching reading* (Technical Report No. 1). Newark, DE: University of Delaware, Studies in Education.

Wixson, K. K., & Dutro, E. (1998). *Standards for primary-grade reading: An analysis of state frameworks* [CIERA Report #3-001]. Ann Arbor, MI: University of Michigan Center for the Improvement of Early Reading Achievement.

30

Early Educational Interventions: Principles of Effective and Sustained Benefits from Targeted Early Education Programs

SHARON LANDESMAN RAMEY
CRAIG T. RAMEY

Our nation is deeply concerned about preparing young children for success in school and life. This concern is shared by parents from all walks of life and has had strong national support for decades. A child's entry into "big school" and those first few years in elementary school establish a course that predicts who stays in school or drops out, who achieves robust literacy and language competency or lags behind age peers, and who maintains the eagerness to learn from teachers and parents or withdraws and seeks fulfillment in a world outside the realm of school and family (Ramey & Ramey, 2000; Ramey, Ramey, & Lanzi, 2004). Although the descriptive statistics about who is at risk for low achievement in reading and math, grade retention, special education placement, and school dropout continue to identify markedly elevated rates for children from poverty (e.g., Montgomery & Rossi, 1994), the alarming fact is that many children from middle- and upper-class homes also encounter serious difficulties in school. Similarly, there are academically talented children from low-income and poor families (e.g., Robinson, Lanzi, Weinberg, Ramey, & Ramey, 2002), and their educational supports may be overlooked or be less than those of comparably talented children from high-resource families. *No matter how much public schools improve their kindergarten through high school curricula and instruction, the irrefutable evidence indicates that a child's entry level skills, and the family's ability to support a child's literacy development, are paramount in early school success.* Literally hundreds of studies affirm that academic success in school is determined by a combination of child, family, and school factors (cf. Zigler & Styfco, 2004; Shonkoff & Phillips, 2000). In this chapter, we focus particularly on the issue of early educational interventions—interventions that are designed to improve children's academic and social preparation for the transition to school.

A robust body of knowledge exists about the first 5 years of life and the extent to which children's early experiences correlate with their emerging competencies in language and literacy. From these carefully conducted scientific studies, a set of well-established principles has been derived (Ramey & Ramey, 1998; Ramey & Ramey, 1999, 2000). The research base derives from a wide array of studies, including randomized controlled trials and their replication studies, longitudinal studies that span from birth through adolescence or adulthood, comparisons of alternative modes of delivering the intervention, and analyses that address a key question: Who benefits the most from early educational interventions? In this chapter, we summarize the major findings from the past 40 years of scientific inquiry about early experience and educational interventions for children in the first 5 years of life. The principles of effective early intervention have continued to be affirmed, with recent findings from longitudinal follow-ups from randomized controlled trials (RCTs) and from application of more sophisticated data analytic techniques to existing data sets (e.g., Blair, Ramey, & Hardin, 1995; Hill, Brooks-Gunn, & Waldfogel, 2003).

What Is Early Educational Intervention?

"Early educational intervention" refers generally to systematic and intentional endeavors to provide supplemental educational experiences to children before they enter into the formal educational system in kindergarten. Early educational interventions are designed to offer additional learning opportunities that are theoretically linked to later academic achievement. Because success in school involves more than just academic skills and depends upon a combination of intertwined social-emotional, health, language, and other cognitive factors, early educational interventions typically seek to address the "whole child." Accordingly, many early educational interventions also include some social and health services and parent educational components.

Early educational intervention does not refer to all forms of nonparental child care that occur prior to school entry, although high-quality child care does include strong supports for children's learning and school preparation; conversely, poor-quality child-care and preschool programs have been harmful to children's educational progress (Ramey, 2005). In the public policy arena, however, child care is often considered a single entity, regardless of quality or instructional content. Similarly, "early intervention" (that does specify "educational") is a broad catchall phrase that includes programs to prevent child neglect and abuse, programs to serve infants and toddlers with diagnosed disabilities and documented developmental delay,

treatment programs for children with serious emotional and behavioral disorders, and home-visiting programs to improve parenting skills and health monitoring, as well as educational interventions. Early educational intervention thus represents one form of early intervention, distinguished by its central focus on improving children's language and cognitive outcomes and increasing children's later educational achievement. Understandably, the efforts to improve children's short- and long-term educational outcomes have been targeted for "at risk" children.

The "At-Risk" Designation and Who Participates in Early Educational Interventions

"At-risk" children are the primary participants in early educational interventions. How is "at risk" defined? From a historical perspective, the concerted effort to provide early educational interventions is closely linked to the landmark U.S. Supreme Court decision of *Brown v. Board of Education* in 1954, the War on Poverty launched in the 1960s, and the accumulated scientific and clinical evidence from around the world that early and sustained deprivation results in impaired behavioral and brain development (cf. Ramey & Ramey, 1998; Ramey & Sackett, 2000). The 1954 Supreme Court decision affirmed that separate education for black children was inherently not equal and thus placed many children at high risk for poor school achievement. Implicit in this decision was the recognition that educational attainment was influenced by a combination of social and cultural experiences embedded within and surrounding an educational institution. Although this decision did not address preschool experiences per se, educators and psychologists used this decision to fuel their own thinking and action to prevent educational inequality that originates prior to entering the formal educational system. Specifically, being born into a family earning poverty-level wages often equated to living in a segregated neighborhood with impoverished educational opportunities during the first 5 years of life. The legacy of slavery and racism placed many black children at risk for both poverty and segregation. Within the next decade, U.S. politicians and the media brought to light the devastating reality of poverty, as exemplified in John F. Kennedy's promise to West Virginians that he would not forget their plight and their children's needs if he became president. After Kennedy's assassination, when Vice President Lyndon B. Johnson became president, he declared a national War on Poverty, which placed the well-being of poor children—from all ethnic groups—in a center-stage position. The launching of the national Head Start program in the mid-1960s demonstrated a strong national commitment to preparing young at-risk children for school. Initially, Head Start was a brief summer program, just prior to entering kindergarten. Head Start programs engaged local groups and many volunteers and offered poor children a chance to experience a school-like group setting, with teacher-like adults who would help children become comfortable with school-like activities and academic demands, including increased exposure to books and to a wider experience with language (Zigler & Styfco, 2004). Finally, the scientific literature regarding early deprivation in children living in orphanages and the nonhuman primate experiments about "mother love" and sensory and social isolation presented a unified conclusion: Early experiences lay the foundation for subsequent learning and normal social and cognitive development (Ramey, Ramey, & Lanzi, 2001; Ramey & Sackett, 2000). This awareness of the cumulative and lifelong consequences of early deprivation coincided with the flourishing of a new era of research on infancy, with the primary early thrust concentrated on delineating how, when, and what types of early learning occur and the course of early communication and language acquisition (cf. Slater & Lewis, 2002). Collectively, this multidecade movement to correct the social and educational inequities associated with racism and the negative consequences associated with poverty environments has framed much of the scientific inquiry about early educational interventions.

There is no single definition of "at risk," although the majority of studies concerning the effects of participation in early educational interventions enrolled children based primarily on family income, usually below the federal poverty level. Some programs have had more specific risk enrollment criteria based on (1) a composite family risk index that includes variables such as maternal education or tested intelligence (IQ score), maternal education less than a high school degree, a single-mother household, and family household income; (2) child characteristics, such as tested developmental or cognitive delay and biological risks such as prematurity, low birth weight, or medical conditions; or (3) a combination of both family and child characteristics (e.g., Coie et al., 1991; Ramey, MacPhee, & Yeates, 1982; Reynolds, Wang, & Walberg, 2003; Sameroff, Seifer, Barocas, Zax, & Greenspan, 1987). The community context is sometimes considered as well, such as in geographical areas known to have inadequate services for young children and their families (Birch, Richardson, Baird, Horobin, & Illsley, 1970).

The term *at risk* typically is used interchangeably with *high risk* and *disadvantaged*, all indicating an increased probability that a child will not meet minimal or normative achievement levels in school. Stated otherwise, the child is at risk for progressing poorly in school, with concomitant risks related to grade failure or grade retention, special education placement, school dropout, and adult unemployment and inability to be self-sufficient.

The primary criterion for family disadvantage or high risk has been family income. In the 1970s, a group of 13 experimental programs of early educational intervention were conducted and later analyzed as part the Consortium for Longitudinal Studies (Lazar, Darlington, Murray, Royce, & Snipper, 1982). All of these now-classic studies served children from economically impoverished families, although additional child variables were used in several of these programs. Although very low family income generally has been associated with other negative life circumstances (e.g. unemployment, inadequate health care, poor housing, limited parental education, violent neighborhoods), many children from poor homes do show positive adaptation to school and average to superior intellectual performance. What differentiates these successful children from their less successful peers has been the topic of much study since the 1970s (e.g., Garmezy, 1983; Grotberg, 2003; Rutter, 1985; Werner, Bierman, & French, 1971). Many of these children probably have a combination of environmental protective factors, such as exceptionally positive, stable relationships with one or more responsible adults, and individual characteristics, such as higher than average inquisitiveness, positive self-appraisal, and good social interaction skills that contribute to their success (Coie et al., 1991; Grotberg, 2003).

At the clinical and practical levels, most educators recognize that children with externally similar family circumstances or biological conditions do not necessarily *experience* identical levels of disadvantage. Accordingly, more functionally oriented and child-specific assessments of disadvantage are useful in planning individualized early intervention programs. At the program administrative level (e.g., to determine eligibility), however, categorical definitions of disadvantage are likely to continue, based on their perceived fairness or minimal stigmatization and their ease of use administratively.

Evidence for Efficacy of Early Educational Interventions: Principles of Effective Intervention

For many decades, the single most pressing question was simply, Do these interventions work? There was robust skepticism that early educational interventions could alter the cumulative negative toll that poverty and other risk circumstances take on the development of young children. But by the mid-1980s, a professional consensus was reached (cf. Guralnick & Bennett, 1987) that early educational interventions could—under certain conditions—produce meaningful benefits as reflected in the academic achievement of young children. Just as important, in the absence of these conditions, early educational interventions did not yield their intended benefits, or the benefits were smaller and not sustainable. Given the cross-study consistencies in findings, we summarize in this chapter the evidence regarding early educational interventions in terms of five major scientific principles: (1) the dosage principle, (2) the timing principle, (3) the academic instruction and language principle, (4) the differential benefits principle, and (5) the educational continuity of supports principle.

The Principle of Dosage

Programs that provide higher amounts of educational intervention (dosage) produce larger gains in children's academic performance. This principle of dosage or intervention intensity has considerable scientific support, derived from cross-study comparisons of the magnitude of benefits from programs that differed in their dosage, from experimental studies that directly tested different dosage levels within the same study, and from post hoc analyses that analyzed rates of participation using sophisticated analytical techniques.

Dosage is indexed by the number of hours per day, the number of days per week, and the number of weeks per year that children receive the educational intervention. An ideal measure—one that has not ever been calculated and analyzed in relationship to children's outcome—would be the actual amount of instructional and learning time that children have when they attend, multiplied by the amount of children's attendance. Theoretically, the reason that more intensive programs produce significantly larger positive effects than do interventions that are less intensive is straightforward: Children are engaged in more learning, which in turn supports their continued growth and development in the domains in which the learning occurs.

There are numerous examples of early interventions that did not significantly improve children's intellectual or academic performance. A characteristic of many of these unsuccessful interventions is that they were not very intensive. For instance, none of the 16 randomized trials of early interventions for young children with disabilities or delays evaluated by the Utah State Early Intervention Research Institute (White, 1991) provided full-day 5-days-per-week programs, and none of these programs produced any measurable benefits for children in terms of their competencies. Similarly, Scarr and McCartney (1988) provided intervention only once per week to economically impoverished families in Bermuda in an effort to replicate the findings of Levenstein's Verbal Interaction Project (1970). They also failed to detect any positive cognitive effects.

In marked contrast, two RCTs conducted in North Carolina using the same educational curriculum—the Abecedarian Project and Project CARE—produced multiple significant benefits to participants in this high-dosage educational intervention. The Abecedarian Project and Project CARE both provided educational supports to children within a full-day, 5-days-per-week, 50-weeks-per-year program for 5 consecutive years using a structured and individualized curriculum delivered in a high-quality, university-based child development center that was continuously monitored and supported for quality of curriculum implementation (Ramey & Ramey, 2004b). To our knowledge, these two programs are among the most intensive (high dosage) that have been subjected to rigorous experimental study, and the principle of dosage may account for a large portion of the increased magnitude of benefit detected at ages 8, 12, 15, and 21 years of age. We particularly note the benefits for language and literacy, as demonstrated in significant gains at every age on every language measure and all reading assessments (Ramey et al, 2001; Ramey & Ramey, 2004b). Other educationally important outcomes include markedly lower rates of placement in special education, reduced from 48% in the comparison group to 12% in the educational intervention group (close to the national average of 11%), and reduced rates of grade repetition, from 56% in the control group to 30% in the educational group.

Another RCT that produced large immediate benefits in intelligence and language was the Milwaukee Project (Garber, 1988), which also was a high-dosage early educational intervention that began at birth and continued through the transition to school, with a university child development program offered daily (see review by Ramey & Ramey, 2000). However, long-term benefits were not sustained to the same degree as in the North Carolina projects, perhaps because of the influence of the principle of educational continuity of supports (discussed later) and the differences in the enrollment criteria across these projects (the North Carolina projects enrolled on a combination of family risk variables; the Milwaukee Project enrolled only children born to mothers with mental retardation).

Two studies provide experimental evidence that program intensity matters: (1) an early intervention home-visit program (Powell & Grantham-McGregor, 1989) that systematically tested different levels of intensity discovered significant cognitive benefits at a dosage level of three visits per week, whereas fewer visits per week did not produce any significant gains; and (2) the Brookline Early Education Project (Hauser-Cram, Pierson, Walker, & Tivnan, 1991) reported that only the most intensive services were sufficient to benefit children from less-well-educated families, whereas the lowest and intermediate intensities had no measurable consequences.

The eight-site RCT Infant Health and Development Program has systematically investigated the topic of program intensity at the level of the individual child's participation, and these analyses have been conducted using diverse data analytic procedures and different methodologies to calculate intensity or dosage. Originally, Ramey et al. (1992) reported that the amount (i.e., intensity) of educational intervention each child and family received related significantly to the children's cognitive outcomes at age 3. The dosage was based on a simple sum of three program components: (1) the total days' attendance at the child development center between the ages of 12 and 36 months (corrected age for premature children), (2) the number of completed home visits from birth to age 3, and (3) the number of monthly educational meetings that the child's parents attended. This "participation index" demonstrated a strong linear relationship to the child's intellectual and behavioral development at 36 months, even after controlling for variables that might have influenced individual rates of participation (such as maternal education, maternal verbal competence, family income, child health status, and ethnicity). When considering the efficacy of this 3-year, multipronged educational intervention to prevent mental retardation (IQ less than 70 points) at age 3, the results showed that the highest participation group had nearly a ninefold reduction in the percent of low-birth-weight children who were mentally retarded (under 2%) compared with control-group children, who received only high-quality pediatric follow-up services (about

18%). For children who were in the intermediate-participation group, incidence of retardation was reduced by a 4.9-fold factor, whereas for those in the low-participation group, the reduction was only 1.3-fold.

Two alternative data analyses from this same study provide important findings about the principle of dosage. Blair et al. (1995) pursued an analytic framework that addressed the question of year-by-year participation rates and whether the course of development diverged systematically as a result of varying annual levels of participation. Their analyses showed that each year's participation in the Infant Health and Development Program produced significant and independent effects on the course of the child's measured cognitive competence at 12, 24, and 36 months of age.

Hill, Brooks-Gunn, and Waldfogel (2003) extended these earlier analyses to address two additional questions. One question concerned whether longer term effects after the educational intervention ended at 3 years of age were related to dosage. Another question addressed methodology and how to pursue post hoc analyses when different rates of participation are not random; in other words, higher rates of participation are likely to be correlated with other variables that also influence children's educational outcomes. When the children were 3, 5, and 8 years of age, multiple assessments of language and cognition were completed, with the 8-year-old battery including the full Weschler Intelligence Scale for Children (WISC; Verbal, Performance, and Full Scale IQ scores), the Woodcock–Johnson Reading and Math assessments, and the Peabody Picture Vocabulary Test—Revised (PPVT-R). On 12 major outcome measures across 3 age periods, all measures showed higher performance for children in two higher participation groups (attending more than 350 days and more than 400 days in the child development center, respectively) relative to the randomly assigned follow-up group, which received pediatric and social services but not the educational component of this multipronged early intervention. The first set of analyses confirmed, however, that children who participated at higher rates differed significantly from the comparison group, with site-specific differences in which variables (e.g., maternal ethnicity, maternal education,

maternal use of drugs, and prenatal care) correlated with amounts of participation. Accordingly, this team applied a sophisticated set of data-analytic techniques that are well known in medical RCTs, involving an adaptation of a propensity score matching procedure coupled with logistic regression to reduce the influence of the natural selection bias when evaluating treatment effects. The results yielded compelling support for the dosage principle, demonstrating differences between matched high dosage and control children and between higher and lower dosage children within the treatment group. The magnitude of these differences is impressive at all three ages analyzed and extends to the reading and math scores at age 8, with sustained benefits of the early educational intervention corresponding to gains of 6.1 to 11.1 points higher (depending on the definition used for high dosage) on the Woodcock–Johnson, as well as sustained (although slightly reduced) benefits at ages 5 and 8 for PPVT (4.1–6.6 points at age 8) and WISC IQ scores (6.5 to 8.4 points at age 8).

The Principle of Timing

Generally, the early educational interventions that begin earlier and continue longer produce larger and longer lasting benefits to the participants than do those that begin much later and do not last as long.

The age at which children enter early educational interventions ranges from birth through 5 years of age. Typically, children from economically disadvantaged families become eligible for early educational interventions (e.g., Head Start, public school pre-K for "at-risk" children) in their home communities beginning at 4 years of age, and sometimes at 3 years of age. Many of the well-cited early educational interventions, however, began when children were young infants, such as the Abecedarian Project (Ramey, Bryant, Campbell, Sparling, & Wasik, 1988), the Brookline Early Education Project (Hauser-Kram et al., 1991), the Milwaukee Project (Garber, 1988), Project CARE (Wasik, Ramey, Bryant, & Sparling, 1990), and the Infant Health and Development Program (1990). Two noteworthy exceptions, however, are the Perry Preschool Project, conducted in Ypsilanti, Michigan (Schweinhart & Weikart, 1983), and the

Early Training Project (Gray, Ramsey, & Klaus, 1982), which began when children were 3 years of age. An important difference in these two interventions that began later in life and did produce significant benefits is that the children were documented to be significantly delayed in their cognitive development at age 3—whereas the other studies that enrolled children earlier sought to prevent intellectual decline linked to early and continued impoverished language and learning environments.

The principle of timing has always been one of high interest, vigorous debate, and remarkably little direct research with children. The surgency of interest in early brain development and how experiences contribute to the structure and functioning of the brain lends support to the proposition that earlier and sustained educational interventions are the most promising for maximizing benefits to children. Even the carefully controlled animal experiments on early experience, which support the general principle of timing, do not refute the possibility that educational interventions begun at later ages can produce measurable gains. Rather, findings concerning normal development of speech and linguistic capacity, such as those generated by Kuhl (2004) concerning acquisition of first-language discrimination skills, lend further support by demonstrating that when infants are not exposed to certain sensory–perceptual experiences very early in life, they may lose initial capacity (such as the universal ability of young babies to recognize phonemes in all languages, later narrowing to recognizing primarily their own native language). Remarkably, there are no published studies that directly test the differential benefits of starting the same educational intervention at different ages. This type of research is understandably challenging to conduct, in part because of the need to adapt the educational intervention to the age and stage of the children when they enter and because of increasing concerns about the ethical issues of delaying an educational intervention for children with documented risk conditions. Because Head Start nationally has expanded to permit serving both 3- and 4-year-olds, and because many public education pre-K initiatives are deliberating about the value of serving at-risk 3-year-olds, there may be naturally occurring opportunities to conduct this vitally needed research to determine, with greater conclusiveness, the magnitude of benefits associated with educational interventions that begin at earlier ages.

The Abecedarian Project involved a two-phase educational intervention in which 50% of the children who received 5 consecutive years of early educational intervention and 50% of those in the comparison group (receiving nutritional, pediatric, and social services only) were randomly selected to participated in an elementary school home-school resource program that lasted for 3 consecutive years. This partially tested the issue of timing by asking the question of whether extra educational supports during the school year (provided by individualized assistance to children and their families with schoolwork and school–family communication) and a summer educational camp that sought to increase children's learning opportunities from kindergarten through entry into third grade could improve children's school achievement. The results demonstrate two clear sets of findings. First, the elementary school support program (that is, the later onset of intervention) did yield measurable benefits to participants, as indexed by higher scores on standardized assessments of reading and math achievement at age 8. However, there were no comparable gains on general tests of intelligence or language to those of children who received the preschool early educational intervention. Second, the magnitude of benefits, even for the reading and math achievement scores, was smaller than for children who received the earlier onset educational intervention (see Ramey et al., 2000). This study is not germane, however, to helping to resolve the vital question about differential timing benefits during the preschool years. Further, this study tested a reasonably well-designed and replicable public school enhancement program, but it did not seek to directly control the overall classroom curriculum and instruction and thus is not a simple and pure test of timing effects alone.

In summary, the principle of timing has received modest support from human studies, but further research is needed for conclusive evidence about its importance for different aspects of language, literacy, and other academic competencies. There are no compelling data, at this time, to support the notion of an absolute critical period, such that educational intervention provided after a certain age cannot be beneficial; rather, this is a principle of *relative* timing effects.

The Principle of Academic and Language Instruction

This principle affirms that children who receive early educational interventions that directly alter their daily learning experiences produce larger positive and longer lasting results than do those interventions that rely primarily on indirect routes to change competencies, most notably the large number of home-based visiting programs and the parent-training programs.

Early education interventions have been presented in many different forms, including those that are based in a child development center with trained teaching staff, those that are home based and seek to change parents' behavior and provide environmental enrichments (books, learning games, educational videos), and those that combine center and home-based components. These different types of early educational interventions may be divided into two major categories: (1) those that rely primarily on direct provision of academic and language instruction to children and (2) those that seek indirect means of enhancing child learning, such as seeking to change the parent, or increasing environmental supports for learning or that focus mostly on social-emotional and play interventions that do not explicitly provide language and academic instruction.

The empirical findings regarding the differential effects of these two quite different strategies are clear: The indirect interventions that seek to change intermediary factors are not as powerful in changing children's language, reading, or intellectual performance (Castro & Lewis, 1984; Madden, Levenstein, & Levenstein, 1976; Ramey, Ramey, Gaines, & Blair, 1995; Scarr & McCartney, 1988; Wasik et al., 1990). This generalization holds true for economically disadvantaged children, seriously biologically disadvantaged children, and high-risk children with both environmental and individual risk conditions.

Wasik et al. (1990) conducted the first systematic and experimental study of direct provision of instruction versus intermediary

forms of early educational intervention. Using a RCT, high-risk children were randomly assigned just after birth to receive one of three interventions: (1) the daily, highly intense child development center program, identical to that provided to children in the Abecedarian Project, coupled with a home-visiting program; (2) a home-visiting (intermediary) program that lasted for 5 years, used the same educational curriculum as the center-based intervention, and sought to have parents deliver the intervention; and (3) a comparison group that received enhanced nutritional, pediatric, and social services only (note: both intervention groups also received these health and social support services). An important achievement in this study—the longest lasting home-visiting program we know of—is that participants in all three groups remained highly engaged in the program and the assessments. The home visiting was planned to be weekly during the first 2 years of life and then every other week for the next 3 years. Further, the home visitors received ongoing supervision and continuing support throughout the 5 years and used a structured but adaptable curriculum. Both the home visitors and the families reported that they perceived the home-visiting program to very positive. Despite the enthusiasm for the effort to change the behaviors of parents, who in turn could transmit increased learning opportunities to their children, the outcome data demonstrated no measurable gains for the children in the home-visiting program compared with the control children, and both of these groups fared significantly worse than the group that received the daily, year-round center-based educational curriculum plus home visiting. Post hoc analyses indicated that magnitude of benefits associated with the children who received direct language and academic instruction (in the center) plus the 5 years of home visiting was almost identical to that reported for the Abecedarian Project participants, who did not receive the same intensive home-visiting educational component. On a promising note, from another home-visiting program, Powell and Grantham-McGregor (1989) indicated that three home visits per week—but not fewer—can produce significant child improvement through the intermediary or indirect intervention approach.

Overall, these findings are particularly discouraging, because the vast majority of federal, state, and private money spent to improve the lives of vulnerable young children and to increase school readiness has been spent on programs designed to change parental behaviors and home environments (Roberts, Wasik, Casto, & Ramey, 1990). There clearly is a popular appeal to the idea that increasing the skills and knowledge of young children's "first teachers"—their parents—will be beneficial, because parents are children's natural support system, and they care deeply about their children's well-being. Also, most programs hope that changing parent behaviors and improving the home environment will have spillover effects to the next children born into these families and will help to increase the local community's competence in providing the right types of learning and language experiences, at the right times, for many other young children. Increasingly, many of these parent-focused educational interventions consider that some parents themselves lacked good educational opportunities when they were growing up and that some parents lacked positive parenting models in their own lives. Accordingly, the curricula used for the parenting and home-visiting programs often addresses the parent's own developmental needs and crucial aspects of culture and local community, along with "how to parent" issues.

What are the likely reasons that center-based programs with more traditional types of language enrichment and teacher-provided instruction relating to academic skills yield positive results in terms of academic achievement and cognition, whereas the indirect or intermediary programs do not? We hypothesize that at least four factors may be contributing to this pattern of results. One is that most home-visiting programs are not equated for intensity or dosage with the center-based programs—and certainly daily home visiting for the full year and 5 consecutive years of life would be cost-prohibitive, highly intrusive, and probably impossible to deliver given the rates of maternal employment across all income groups. Another is that the natural language and academic skills of some parents in at-risk families may not be equal to those of teachers or caregivers in the center-based programs, even when parents are encouraged to provide more language and academic learning experiences to their preschool children. Thus the children in the two groups would not receive similar levels of exposure to a rich language environment on an everyday basis (cf. Hart & Risley, 1995; Huttenlocher, 1990). A third reason is that parents who respond positively to the home visiting still may not spend enough time with their children to give them the full benefit of their increased skills. For many parents, their children may be in the care of others for extended periods during the day or night, and these other caregivers may not meet the needs of these at-risk children (Ramey, 2005). Fourth and finally, the rate at which participating parents acquire and then implement their enhanced parenting and instructional skills may not be rapid enough to achieve the intended benefits for their children. This harkens back to the principles of both dosage and timing (see previous sections). We also note that home-visiting programs may serve other valuable purposes, such as preventing child neglect and abuse and increasing children's health and safety, as demonstrated in research projects such as that of Olds and colleagues (2004).

For reasons that we do not fully understand, the early childhood community has become polarized over issues that concern direct or explicit teaching of certain skills to young children. It appears to be common knowledge that babies are born without knowing any specific words or ideas, and that skills related to reading, writing, and math require direct exposure—that is, their advancement cannot occur without some introduction, scaffolding, modeling or demonstration, and practice and feedback. What we think has happened is that some practitioners in early childhood programs mistakenly tried to enact kindergarten or first-grade-level instruction with much younger children and adopted ineffective methods of repetitive drill, restricted young children's spontaneous play and exploration, and tried to force very young children to attend and behave in ways that were counterproductive. Accordingly, the anti-instruction movement could be viewed as a backlash to such inappropriate applications of early educational interventions. An alternative explanation is that some of the competent caregivers for young children, particularly low-income and minority children, in the United States have low levels of formal education and lack formal teaching credentials. There may be a fear that all of these individuals will be excluded from the future of child care and early education and judged to be incompetent simply because they cannot articulate precisely how they "instruct" children to prepare them for school. Although there are many published studies documenting a general relationship between an adult's level of education, language skills, and intelligence and his or her skills in promoting children's cognitive and language development (cf. Ramey, 2005), there are notable exceptions to the generalization. From our own professional experiences, we have observed highly competent teachers of young children who come from all types of educational, linguistic, and cultural backgrounds. Advanced degrees in early childhood education are not a guarantee of high-quality instruction occurring on a responsive and regular basis; neither does the lack of a college degree or sophisticated language skills prohibit an adult from providing high-quality language and academic learning opportunities.

Currently, the Institute of Educational Sciences is coordinating an effort to evaluate RCTs that test the benefits of different published preschool curricula, mostly for 4-year-olds. This effort is designed to yield much-needed information about "what works" in pre-K settings. There are, however, already recognized limits that have surfaced in this new research endeavor, such as differences across sites regarding the dosage of the intervention (hours per day, weeks per year), the degree of risk in the children participating, the quality and control over curriculum implementation, and the levels of participation from the children and families. What is admirable about this research initiative is that both educational science and curriculum development are being advanced, and the practical importance of this type of scientific inquiry has become paramount by creating a national network of projects concerned with children's language and literacy outcomes. Content analysis of existing early educational interventions that have already produced large and lasting benefits through RCTs would be a worthwhile endeavor, as would efforts to measure the actual classroom instruction at levels that correspond to the particular types of learning and language

experiences hypothesized to be most essential for young children's learning (e.g., C. Ramey & Ramey, 1999; S. Ramey & Ramey, 1999).

The Principle of Differential Benefits

This principle asserts that some children show greater benefits from participation in early educational interventions than do other children. These individual differences appear to relate to aspects of the children's initial risk condition and the degree to which the program meets the child's needs or services to prevent the harmful consequences of those risk conditions over time (for example, by providing sufficient amounts of direct positive learning experiences that otherwise would not have been present).

A fundamental assumption in the fields of education and social ecology is person × environment or person × treatment effects. This assumption is that different individuals respond differently to the same program and that, correspondingly, different programs may be needed to produce the same outcome for different participants. These ideas have long prevailed in the clinical and educational literature, but only recently have they been explored systematically in the early educational intervention field.

In providing broad-based early educational intervention for premature, low-birth-weight infants, the Infant Health and Development Program (1990) reported that children at greater biological risk, as indexed by their lower birth weights (less than 2,000 gm), did not initially benefit at age 3 as much from the program as did children at lesser risk (with birth weights between 2,000 and 2,499 gm), even though both groups showed significant gains. In a longer term follow-up of these children at 5 and 8 years of age, Hill, Brooks-Gunn, and Waldfogel (2003) reported large and significant risk × intervention effects, such that the heavier low-birth-weight children showed IQ point benefits of about 14 points, whereas lighter babies had effects of about 8 points, compared with their appropriate birth-weight-matched controls, who did not receive the educational component of the intervention.

Another study focused on early educational intervention for children with disabilities and considered two influences simultaneously: the degree of the child's impairment and the form of educational intervention provided. Cole, Dale, Mills, and Jenkins (1991) found an aptitude × treatment effect in a randomized design comparing Feuerstein's (1979) "mediated learning" techniques and more traditional "direct instruction." Contrary to conventional wisdom, students who performed relatively higher (as measured on the pretest battery of cognitive, language, and motor test) gained more from direct instruction, whereas students who performed lower showed greater benefits from the mediated learning treatment.

From the Abecedarian Project, Martin, Ramey, and Ramey (1990) revealed that the children who showed the greatest relative gains (i.e., compared with controls) were those whose mothers were the most intellectually limited (i.e., maternal IQ scores below 70). In fact, all experimental-group children whose mothers were mentally retarded performed at least 20 points higher and averaged 32 points higher than did their own mothers (Landesman & Ramey, 1989). These dramatic findings are comparable to the large benefits reported in the Milwaukee Project, which enrolled only economically disadvantaged mothers with IQs below 75 (Garber, 1988).

Some of the programs that have failed to detect any significant overall benefits may have enrolled a highly heterogeneous group of children, some of whom were at very low or no risk for poor educational outcomes. This could serve to lessen the power to detect real intervention effects if, in fact, only the high-risk children showed benefits. As an example, analyses conducted on children participating in the Infant Health and Development Program showed significantly different levels of benefit based on the educational level of the children's mothers. The degree of benefits—as indexed by children's IQ scores on the Stanford–Binet at age 3—displayed a highly orderly relationship to mother's education. If the child's mother had less than a high school education, the gains were the greatest (comparing treated and control children), followed by those whose mothers earned a high school degree or general equivalency diploma, and then those with some college. Interestingly, neither any benefits nor any harm were related to participating in this educational intervention for children

whose mothers had earned a 4-year college degree or higher (see Ramey & Ramey, 2000). These findings of differential benefits are consistent with an interpretation that these educational interventions supplement children's experiences at homes in ways that are essential for the development of average (or above average) intelligence; accordingly, for children whose cognitive and linguistic development is strongly supported by their families and other natural environments, additional educational interventions are not needed to prevent sub-average performance. We also note that in this study, the control children—like those in all of the RCTs we have reviewed—were never prevented from participating in other programs, and many of the college-educated parents in the Infant Health and Development Program sought, on their own, additional help and information to support the early development of their premature and low-birth-weight infants.

The Principle of Educational Continuity of Supports

This principle states that over time, the initial positive effects of early interventions will diminish if there are inadequate educational supports to maintain children's positive attitudes and behavior and to encourage continued learning relevant to the children's lives. The reason that postintervention programs continue to matter is that children continue to learn at high rates, with educational progress that depends not only upon a child's entry-level skills but also on his or her continued acquisition of the cognitive, language, and academic skills—complemented by appropriate social and emotional skills—to have a positive transition to school (Ramey, Ramey, & Lanzi, 2004).

For many programs, long-lasting and substantial effects on school achievement, grade retention, and special education placement have been detected. In some but not all studies (e.g., Garber, 1988), the long-term effects of early educational intervention on IQ scores lessen over time. Two important issues are relevant. First, it is not sufficient for disadvantaged children merely to maintain the advantages from effective early educational intervention. Rather, children must continue to develop at normative rates in multiple domains if they are to succeed in school settings. Second, no developmental theory is premised on the assumptions that positive early learning experiences are sufficient by themselves to ensure that children will perform well throughout their lives. Poor school environments, suboptimal health, seriously disrupted home environment, and many other conditions influence the behavior of children at all ages. Thus longitudinal inquiry about the long-term effects of early intervention must take into consideration children's subsequent environments and experiences (i.e., after early intervention).

As described herein, only one experimental study has extended early intervention into the elementary school years to evaluate the importance of environmental supports during the transitions to school. At 8 years of age, children who had received continuous educational intervention for the first 8 years performed the best of any group in reading and mathematics, followed next by those who received early intervention for 5 years, followed next by those who received the elementary school treatment only (Horacek, Ramey, Campbell, Hoffman, & Fletcher, 1987). Further analysis of IQ scores revealed effects only for the early intervention groups—that is, the supplemental program from kindergarten through age 8 did not result in higher IQ scores (Ramey & Campbell, 1994). Later, at age 12, children who had received the early educational intervention continued to show benefits in terms of both academic achievement and IQ scores and a reduction of nearly 50% in the rate of repetition of at least one grade in the elementary school year. Overall, however, the group of children who performed best across all measures were those who had *both* the preschool and school-age educational interventions.

Currie and Thomas (1995) have conducted important analyses of the long-term educational progress of former Head Start children that demonstrates that those who go to average or above-average schools continue to keep up with their age or grade peers, whereas those who show a decline (relative to their school entry level) are those in the very lowest performing schools. Tragically, 50 years after *Brown v. Board of Education*, it remains true that low-income African American children disproportion-

ately attend very poor quality schools at rates far higher than for other ethnic groups, even when family income is below the poverty line. Recently, Barnett (2004) has written an excellent and integrative review that confronts the "myth of fade-out." Although it is true that IQ scores per se show diminished group difference over time, achievements in reading, language, math, and overall school adjustment as indexed by grade retention and special education placement show long-lasting benefits. When these sustained effects do not appear, one of the contributing factors—in addition to the principles already detailed in this chapter—may well be the quality and intensity of the educational programs that follow the early educational intervention. The opportunity to conduct more rigorous post hoc analyses of the schools that children attended across the well-conducted RCTs that have longitudinal data would be valuable, as well as more description of the natural variation in the alignment and educational supports for children transitioning from early educational interventions into public school programs (Kagan, 1994).

Conclusion: Putting Results into Action and Advancing Educational Science

Early educational intervention began in an era of social conscience, amid optimism and with strong scientific evidence that early experiences affect both brain and behavioral development. Over the past 40 years, a robust set of findings affirms that early educational interventions can produce significant and often lasting benefits. However, these benefits are strongly linked to the intensity or the dosage of the intervention that was provided, to the timing of the intervention, and to the degree to which the children receive direct learning experiences and enhanced language interactions conducive to continued advancement in domains related to school academic success. Other important factors related to the magnitude of benefits include the degree of initial risk, such that certain children are likely to benefit more or less than others do, and the extent to which children's learning is supported in their postintervention environments. Much remains to be learned about the content of the curricula used in pre-K programs and programs for infants and toddlers, as well as the importance of different instructional and classroom variables, in contributing to the observed benefits associated with intensive, high-quality programs for children truly at risk.

References

Barnett, W. S. (2004). Does Head Start have lasting cognitive effects? The myth of fade out. In E. Zigler & S. J. Styfco (Eds.) The Head Start debates (pp. 221–249). Baltimore: Brookes.

Birch, H. G., Richardson, S. A., Baird, D., Horobin, G., & Illsley, R. (1970). *Mental subnormality in the community: A clinical and epidemiological study*. Baltimore: Williams & Wilkins.

Blair, C., Ramey, C. T., & Hardin, M. (1995). Early intervention for low birth weight premature infants: Participation and intellectual development. *American Journal on Mental Retardation, 99*, 542–554.

Castro, G., & Lewis, A. (1984). Parent involvement in infant and preschool programs. *Division of Early Childhood, 9*, 49–56.

Coie, J. D., Watt, N., Markman, H., West, S., Hawkins, D., Asarnow, J., et al. (1991). *The science of prevention: A conceptual framework and some directions for a national research program*. Bethesda, MD: National Institute of Mental Health.

Cole, K. N., Dale, P. S., Mills, P. E., & Jenkins, J. R. (1991). Effects of preschool integration for children with disabilities. *Exceptional Children, 58*, 36–45.

Currie, J., & Thomas, D. (1995). Does Head Start make a difference? *American Economic Review, 83*, 241–364.

Feuerstein, R. (1979). Redevelopment cognitive functions of retarded performers. Baltimore: University Park Press.

Garber, H. L. (1988). *The Milwaukee Project: Preventing mental retardation in children at risk*. Washington, DC: American Association on Mental Retardation.

Garmezy, N. (1983). Stressors of childhood. In N. Garmezy & M. Rutter (Eds.), *Stress, coping and development in children* (pp. 43–84). New York: McGraw-Hill.

Gray, S. W., Ramsey, B. K., & Klaus, R. A. (1982). *From 3 to 20: The Early Training Project*. Baltimore: University Park Press.

Grotberg, E. H. (Ed.). (2003). *Resilience for today*. Westport, CT: Praeger.

Guralnick, M. J., & Bennett, F. C. (Eds.). (1987). *The effectiveness of early intervention for at risk and handicapped children*. San Diego: Academic Press.

Hart, B., & Risley, T. R. (1995) *Meaningful differences in the everyday experience of young American children*. Baltimore: Brookes.

Hauser-Cram, P., Pierson, D. E., Walker, D. K., & Tivnan, T. (1991). *Early education in the public schools*. San Francisco: Jossey-Bass.

Hill, J. L., Brooks-Gunn, J., & Waldfogel, J. (2003). Sustained effects of high participation in an early intervention for low birth-weight premature infants. *Developmental Psychology, 39*, 730–744.

Horacek, H. J., Ramey, C. T., Campbell, F. A., Hoffman, K. P., & Fletcher, R. H. (1987). Predicting school failure and assessing early interventions with high-risk children. *Journal of the American Academy of Child Psychiatry, 26(5)*, 758–763.

Huttenlocher, J., Harght, W., Bruk, A., Seltzer, M., & Lyons, T. (1991). Early vocabulary growth: Relation to language input and gender. *Developmental Psychology, 27*, 236–248.

Infant Health and Development Program. (1990). Enhancing the outcomes of low birth weight, premature infants: A multisite randomized trial. *Journal of the American Medical Association, 263*, 3035–3042.

Kagan, S. L. (1994). Defining and achieving quality in family support. In B. Weissbourd & S. L. Kagan (Eds.), *Putting families first: America's family support movement and the challenge of change* (pp. 375–400). San Francisco: Jossey-Bass.

Kuhl, P. K. (2004). Early language acquisition: Cracking the speech code. *Nature Reviews Neuroscience, 5*, 831–843.

Landesman, S., & Ramey, C. T. (1989). Developmental psychology and mental retardation: Integrating scientific principles with treatment practices. *American Psychologist, 44*, 409–415.

Lazar, I., Darlington, R. B., Murray, H., Royce, J., & Snipper, A. (1982). Lasting effects of early education: A report from the Consortium for Longitudinal Studies. *Monographs of the Society for Research in Child Development, 47(2–3*, Serial No. 195).

Levenstein, P. (1970). Cognitive growth in preschoolers through verbal interaction with mothers. *American Journal of Diseases of Children, 136*, 303–309.

Madden, J., Levenstein, P., & Levenstein, S. (1976). Longitudinal IQ outcomes of the Mother–Child Home Program. *Child Development, 76*, 1015–1025.

Martin, S. L., Ramey, C. T., & Ramey, S. L. (1990). The prevention of intellectual impairment in children of impoverished families: Findings of a randomized trial of educational day care. *American Journal of Public Health, 80*, 844–847.

Olds, D. L., Kitzman, H., Cole, R., Robinson, J., Sidora, K., Luckey, D. W., et al. (2004). Effects of nurse home visiting on maternal life-course and child development: Age-six follow-up of a randomized trial. *Pediatrics, 114,* 1550–1559.

Powell, C., & Grantham-McGregor, S. (1989). Home visiting of varying frequency and child development. *Pediatrics, 84,* 157–164.

Ramey, C. T., Bryant, D. M., Wasik, B. H., Sparling, J. J., Fendt, K. H., & LaVange, L. M. (1992). Infant health and development program for low birth weight, premature infants: Program elements, family participation, and child intelligence. *Pediatrics, 89,* 454–465.

Ramey, C. T., & Campbell, F. A. (1994). Poverty, early childhood education, and academic competence: The Abecedarian experiment. In A. C. Huston (Ed.), *Children in poverty: Child development and public policy* (pp. 190–221). New York: Cambridge University Press.

Ramey, C. T., Campbell, F. A., Burchinal, M., Skinner, M. L., Gardner, D. M., & Ramey, S. L. (2000). Persistent effects of early childhood education on high-risk children and their mothers. *Applied Developmental Science, 4,* 2–14.

Ramey, C. T., & Ramey, S. L. (1998). Early intervention and early experience. *American Psychologist, 53,* 109–120.

Ramey, C. T., & Ramey, S. L. (1999). Beginning school for children at risk. In R.C. Pianta & M.J. Cox (Eds.), *The transition to kindergarten* (pp. 217–251). Baltimore: Brookes.

Ramey, C. T., & Ramey, S. L. (2004a). Early educational interventions and intelligence: Implications for Head Start. In E. Zigler & S. Styfco (Eds.), *The Head Start debates* (pp. 3–17). Baltimore: Brookes.

Ramey, C. T., & Ramey, S. L. (2004b). Early learning and school readiness: Can early intervention make a difference? *Merrill-Palmer Quarterly, 50,* 471–491.

Ramey, C. T., Ramey, S. L., Gaines, R., & Blair, C. (1995). Two-generation early intervention programs: A child development perspective. In I. Sigel (Series Ed.) and S. Smith (Vol. Ed.), *Two-generation programs for families in poverty: A new intervention strategy, Vol. 9 Advances in applied developmental psychology* (pp. 199–228). Norwood, NJ: Ablex.

Ramey, C. T., Ramey, S. L., & Lanzi, R. G. (2001). Intelligence and experience. In R. J. Sternberg (Ed.), *Environmental effects on cognitive abilities.* (pp. 83–115). Los Angeles: Erlbaum.

Ramey, S. L. Ramey, C. T., & Lanzi, R. G. (2004). The transition to school: Building on preschool foundations and preparing for lifelong learning. In E. Zigler & S. J. Styfco (Eds.), *The Head Start debates* (pp. 397–413). Baltimore: Brookes.

Ramey, C. T., Ramey, S. L., & Lanzi, R. G. (2005). The health and education of young children: Theory, intervention research, and public policy. In I. Sigel & A. Renninger (Eds.), *The handbook of child psychology.* New York: Wiley.

Ramey, S. L. (2005). Human developmental science serving children and families: Contributions of the NICHD Study of Early Child Care. In NICHD Early Child Care Research Network (Ed.), *Child care and child development: Results from the NICHD Study of Early Child Care and Youth Development* (pp. 427–436). New York: Plenum Press.

Ramey, S. L., Dossett, E., & Echols, K. (1996). The social ecology of mental retardation. In J. Jacobson & J. Mulick (Eds.), *Manual of diagnosis and professional practice in mental retardation* (pp. 55–65). Washington, DC: American Psychological Association.

Ramey, S. L., & Ramey, C. T. (1999). Early experience and early intervention for children "at risk" for developmental delay and mental retardation. *Mental Retardation and Developmental Disabilities Research Reviews, 5,* 1–10.

Ramey, S. L., & Ramey, C. T. (2000). Early childhood experiences and developmental competence. In J. Waldfogel & S. Danziger (Eds.), *Securing the future: Investing in children from birth to college* (pp. 122–150). New York: Russell Sage.

Ramey, S. L., & Sackett, G. P. (2000). The early caregiving environment: Expanding views on nonparental care and cumulative life experiences. In A. Sameroff, M. Lewis, & S. Miller (Eds.), *Handbook of developmental psychopathology* (2nd ed., pp. 365–380). New York: Plenum.

Reynolds, A. J., Wand, M. C., & Walberg, H. J. (Eds.). (2003). *Early childhood programs for a new century.* Washington, DC: Child Welfare League of America, Inc.

Roberts, R., Wasik, B., Casto, G., & Ramey, C. T. (1991). Family support in the home: Programs, policy, and social change. *American Psychologist, 46,* 131–137.

Robinson, N. M., Lanzi, R. G., Weinberg, R. A., Ramey, S. L., & Ramey, C. T. (2002). Family factors associated with high academic competence in former Head Start children at third grade. *Gifted Child Quarterly, 46,* 281–294.

Rutter, M. (1985) Resilient in the face of adversity: Protective factors and resistance to psychiatric disorder. *British Journal of Psychiatry, 147,* 598–611.

Sameroff, A. J., Seifer, R., Barocas, B., Zax, M., & Greenspan, S. (1987). Intelligence scores of 4-year-old children: Social-environmental risk factors. *Pediatrics, 79,* 343–350.

Scarr, S., & McCartney, K. (1988). Far from home: An experimental evaluation of the mother–child home program in Bermuda. *Child Development, 59,* 531–543.

Schweinhart, L. J., & Weikart, D. P. (1983). The effects of the Perry Preschool Program on youths through age 15. In Consortium for Longitudinal Studies (Ed.), *As the twig is bent . . . Lasting effects of preschool programs* (pp. 71–101). Hillsdale, NJ: Erlbaum.

Slater, A., & Lewis, M. (Eds.). (2002). *Introduction to infant development.* Oxford, UK: Oxford University Press.

Wasik, B. H., Ramey, C. T., Bryant, D. M., & Sparling, J. J. (1990). A longitudinal study of two early intervention strategies: Project CARE. *Child Development, 61,* 1682–1696.

Werner, E. E., Bierman, J. M., & French, F. E. (1971). *The children of Kauai: A longitudinal study from the prenatal to age ten.* Honolulu: University Press of Hawaii.

White, K. R. (1991). Longitudinal studies of the effects of alternative types of early intervention for children with disabilities. *Annual report for project period October 1, 1990–September 30, 1991.* Logan: Utah State University Early Intervention Research Institute.

White, K. R., & Boyce, G. C. (Eds.). (1993). Comparative evaluations of early intervention alternatives [Special issue]. *Early Educational Development, 4.*

Zigler, E., & Styfco, S. (Eds.). (2004). *The Head Start debates.* Baltimore: Brookes.

Index

Development *(cont.)*
  of phonological awareness, 82–83
  of phonological memory, 107
  of phonological sensitivity, 94–97
  of school literacy, 217
  of sight word vocabulary, 107–108
  of written speech, 250–252
  See also Language development;
    Literacy development;
    Prereaders; Vocabulary
    development
Developmental approach to early
  literacy, 215
Developmental history of parent, 141
Developmental systems theory
  adult–child relationship role and,
    150–151
  interactions of literacy systems and
    subsystems, 151
  interactions within contexts, 151–
    152
  teacher role and, 150
Development and poverty, 29–30
Dialect Density Measure, 203
Dialects, 199
Dialect shifting, 203–205, 206
Dialogic reading
  as approach to book reading, 138
  benefits of, 283
  description of, 46–47
  pediatric approach and, 336
DIBELS (Dynamic Indicators of Basic
  Early Literacy Skills), 398, 431,
  435, 439
Differential benefits principle, 454–455
Direct access, 53, 55, 58
Direct instruction in vocabulary, 415–
  416
Direct pathways of influence, 377–
  378
Direct versus indirect intervention,
  452–454
Disadvantage
  definition of, 447–448
  sociocultural, pattern on, 211
Discipline, 383
Distributional properties of child
  African American English, 203
Dosage effects, 324, 448–450
Double deficit, 78
Drawing, 250–252, 253
Dyslexia, 421

Eager to Learn (National Research
  Council), 297
Early childhood education system,
  failings of, 12, 23
Early educational interventions
  academic and language instruction
    principle, 452–454
  "at-risk" children and participants
    in, 446–448
  description of, 445–446
  differential benefits principle and,
    454–455
  dosage principle and, 448–450
  educational continuity of supports
    principle and, 455–456
  evidence for efficacy of, 448–456
  putting results into action, 456–
    457
  timing principle and, 450–452

Early Head Start, 321, 322, 323–324
*Early Learning Standards: Creating
  the Conditions for Success*, 299
Early literacy
  child care and, 317–318
  content of, 301
  cultural diversity in, 216–217,
    225–226, 229–231, 238
  experiences with and language
    development, 137–138
  family support for, and SES, 313–
    317
  as field, 1
  measurement of, 312–313
  poverty, African American
    students, and, 205–206
  variables associated with, 269
  vocabulary development and, 41–
    42
*Early Literacy Assessment Systems:
  Essential Elements* (Educational
  Testing Service), 305
Early literacy research, biases in,
  212–214
Early Reading First, 269, 295, 299–
  300, 305–306
Early Training Project, 450–451
Education
  in early literacy development, 274
  of teachers, 21, 363, 453–454
  See also Professional development
Education, maternal. *See* Maternal
  education
Education system, early childhood,
  12, 23
Elkonin, Daniel, works of, 249–250,
  252
Elkonin boxes, 119, 244, 248, 252
Emergent literacy
  components of, 135
  definition of, 312
  development of skills in
    prereaders, 79–86
  measurement of, 351–352
  parenting and, 135–136
  recognition of, 297
Emotional support, cultural
  differences in, 221, 226
Enabling skills, 435–438
Engagement
  with literacy materials, 263–264
  measurement of, 164
  in play, 272–274, 276
  regulation of arousal and, 152–
    153
  vocabulary development and, 166
English-language learners (ELLs)
  English and Spanish interventions
    for, 190–192
  English interventions for, 186–188
  exposure to rich English and, 413
  future directions for, 194
  implications for at-risk readers,
    192–194
  interventions for, 185–192
  letter knowledge and, 126–127
  longitudinal research on, 191–192
  Spanish interventions for, 188–189
Environmental experiences
  brain development and, 135
  language acquisition and, 163–164
  oral language skills and, 168–170

  phonological sensitivity and, 95–96
  provision of, 170
  vocabulary usage and, 164–168
  See also Classroom environment;
    Home environment
Environmental print, 121–122, 205
Ethnicity and academic achievement,
  378–379
Evaluation-oriented research, 305–
  306
Explanations of words, narrative-
  based, 48
Explicit instruction
  African American students and,
    206
  debate over, 453–454
  emotional growth and, 12
  transition to school and, 386
  vocabulary development and, 193
Expository texts, 49
Exposure to language, 412–413
Exposure to print. *See* Print exposure
Extending play behavior, 274
Eye movements in reading, 55–58

FACES. *See* Family and Child
  Experiences Survey (FACES) of
  Head Start
Face validity, 431, 433
Failure, educational
  risk factors for, 257–258
  risk-taking behavior and, 334
Families
  cultural diversity and, 230
  interventions for, 324–325
  support for early literacy and
    socioeconomic status of, 313–
    317
  talk, building meaning through,
    283–284
  talk, genres of, 217–219
Family activities
  as basis for intervention, 234
  cultural identity and, 231–233
  modifying, as form of intervention,
    235
Family and Child Experiences Survey
  (FACES) of Head Start
  conceptual framework for, 349–
    372
  description of, 347, 349
  differences in gains and length of
    attendance, 356–357
  gains during program, 355–356
  limitations of, 368
  methods, 351–353
  predictors of outcomes, 363–365,
    366
  program and classroom factors
    associated with emergent
    literacy skills, 360, 362–363
  research questions, 372–351
  skills compared to national norms,
    354
  variation across programs and
    classes, 357–365
"Fast mapping" word acquisition,
  43–44
Fluency, in reading, definition of,
  104–105
Fluent reading and phonemic
  awareness, 104–109

Neighborhood and early literacy
development, 318–319
Neural functioning, 17–19, 334
Neuroimaging techniques, 1–2, 64–
65, 66
Neurons to Neighborhoods (Shonkoff
& Phillips), 12
New Zealand
immigrants in, 229
Samoan culture in, 234
Tongan language preschool in, 234
No Child Left Behind legislation
assessment and, 297, 428–430
curriculum path and, 436
early literacy pedagogy and, 295
limitations of, 442
preschool initiatives and, 269
See also Early Reading First;
Reading First initiative
North Carolina projects, 449
Number of words read per year, 77
Nurse–Family Partnership, 320, 322
Nursery rhymes, singing, 215

Occipitotemporal/visual word form
area, 66
Onlooker role in play, 274, 275
Onset–rime awareness, 215, 418
Oral language skills
decoding, comprehension, and, 80
English-language learners and, 193
environmental support for, 168–
170
intervention for, 170–171
orthography and, 420–421
phonological awareness and, 84–
85
phonological sensitivity and, 95,
96
Oral language use, exposure to
genres of, 217–219
Orthography of language, 105–106,
108–109, 192–193, 420–423
Outcomes, measurement of, 325
Outside-in processes, 79, 136–137,
312, 351

Parental expectations
about literacy activities, 233–234
for letter knowledge, 97, 98
See also Maternal education
Parenting
attachment relationship and, 153–
154, 216
black–white test score gap and,
378–379
book reading and, 138, 173, 317,
365
cognitive–linguistic experiences
and, 219–221
control and discipline, 383
conversations with children, 276–
277
conversations with infants, 137
developmental themes of
interaction, 152
emergent literacy and, 135–136
family talk, genres of, 217–219
frequency of reading aloud, 339–
340
interventions for, 142–143, 324,
381, 452–453

language development and, 136–
137, 138–140
for literacy, 143–144, 382
as predictor of functioning, 151–
152
reading aloud and, 336, 338–339
regulation of arousal and, 152–
153
responsiveness and, 140–141, 142–
143, 216, 382–383
scaffolding and, 141–142
school transition and, 380–383
socioeconomic status and, 31–32
vocabulary development and, 164–
168
See also Home environment
Parents as Teachers (PAT), 320, 322–
323, 324
Partial alphabetic phase of reading,
116
Participation index, 449
Pedagogy, early literacy
attempts to change for improved
learning outcomes, 301, 304–
305
overview of, 295
Pediatric approach
efficacy of, 336–343
implications for program
development, 343–344
program implementation, 335–336
rationale and program operation,
333–335
research on, 344
Peer collaboration, 246
Peer pairing, 194
Peer relationships, 16, 17
Perceptual span in reading, 56, 57–58
Perry Preschool Project, 450–451
Personal name learning, 122
Phoneme level in English writing
system, 417–420
Phoneme manipulation, 81
Phonemic awareness
definition of, 102
development of, 215–216
focusing too much on, 417
informal experiences for learning,
116–117
instruction in, 118–121, 418–420
as predictor of reading
achievement, 410–411
reading accuracy and, 102–104
Reading First initiative and, 101
reading fluency and, 104–109
reading in Spanish and, 189
writing system and, 113–114
Phonemic decoding, 102–103, 106–
107
Phonemic segmentation, 118, 120
Phonics, 421–423
Phonological access to lexical store.
See Lexical access
Phonological awareness
conceptualization of, 81–83
decoding, comprehension, and, 79–
81
definition of, 78, 90–91, 113
environmental support for, 168–
169
oral language and, 84–85
predictors of, 175–176

primitives underlying, 71
reading disability and, 65–66
reciprocal linkages between letter
knowledge, decoding, and, 83–
84
schooling effect and, 386
vocabulary development and, 173–
176
See also Phonemic awareness
Phonological Awareness Literacy
Screening (PALS), 431, 435
Phonological coding
importance of, 60
instruction and, 58–60, 61
lexical access and, 54–57
reading and, 53
reading disability and, 69
skilled readers and, 58
Phonological features of child African
American English, 202
Phonological memory
decoding, comprehension, and, 80
description of, 78–79
development of, 107
measurement of, 83
Phonological processing, 77–79
Phonological sensitivity
conceptualization of, 90–92
definition of, 90, 91
development of, 94–97
early print exposure and, 93–94
literacy development and, 13
reading ability and, 92–93
Phonological skills and developmental
perspective, 215
Piagetian view of play, 270
Plasticity of brain
age and, 71
neural development and, 18–19
Play
adult participation in, 270–271
conversations in, 276–277
effects of adult support of, 275–276
history of theories about, 270–271
as literacy behavior, 271–272
literacy development and, 278–279
literacy materials and, 260, 272–
274
make-believe, 249–250, 251
research on, 269–271
risk of loss of, 278–279
as supporting learning, 35–36
teacher participation in, 274–275
written speech and, 250–252
Play planning method, 254
Point of articulation, 419
Policy, early literacy
consequences of assessment and,
431–432
genesis of, 295–297
overview of, 295
quality of reading instruction,
304–305
quality of reading standards, 301–
302
quality of standards
implementation, 302–303
recent history of, 297–301
research related to, 2, 301–304,
305–306
See also Assessment; No Child Left
Behind legislation